American Foreign Policy

American Foreign Policy

A History / since 1900

Second Edition

Thomas G. Paterson
University of Connecticut

J. Garry Clifford
University of Connecticut

Kenneth J. Hagan
United States Naval Academy

D. C. HEATH AND COMPANY
Lexington, Massachusetts   Toronto

Cover: *ALLIES DAY, MAY 1917*, by Childe Hassam; National Gallery of Art, Washington; Gift of Ethelyn McKinney in memory of her brother, Glenn Ford McKinney.

The poem by Robert Underwood Johnson on p. 316 is © 1928 by The New York Times Company. Reprinted by permission.

For

HOLLY IZARD PATERSON

CAROL DAVIDGE

VERA LOW HAGAN

Preface to the Second Edition

In revising the first edition of *American Foreign Policy*, we have changed the format from one volume to two. Volume I ends with a chapter on events leading to the First World War, and Volume II begins with this same chapter. We have revised Chapters 1-14 to reflect recent scholarship, our own primary research, and readers' comments on the first edition. Thomas G. Paterson has substantially reworked Chapter 15 and has written a completely new Chapter 16. New illustrations, charts, and maps appear throughout, and the "further reading" sections following each chapter have been enlarged and updated. To the Appendix we have added a chart of the Assistants to the President for National Security Affairs, and a new General Bibliography provides lists of reference works, documents, bibliographies, and overviews of relations with specific countries and regions and diplomatic subjects.

Two years after the publication of our first edition, the People's Republic of China adopted a new system for rendering Chinese phonetic characters into the Roman alphabet. Called the Pinyin method, it replaced the Wade-Giles technique, which had long been used in English. The United Nations, United States Board of Geographic Names, *National Geographic*, *Foreign Affairs*, and many other newspapers and journals soon adopted the new Pinyin system, and, accordingly, we have used it in this new edition. Many changes are minor and pose no problem: *Mao Tse-tung*, for example, has become *Mao Zedong* and *Shantung* has become *Shandong*. But when we first use a possibly confusing Pinyin spelling in this second edition, we have put the Wade-Giles spelling in parenthesis, for example: *Jiang Jieshi* (*Chiang Kai-shek*) or *Beijing* (*Peking*). Some names deeply rooted in English usage, such as *Canton*, have not been changed in this edition. Although the transition from Wade-Giles to Pinyin may cause occasional confusion, we think students should be exposed to a practice that has become familiar in the world of diplomacy.

As before, many people have helped us. The footnotes and suggestions for further reading indicate the scholars whose works have informed this book. We benefited especially from the comments of several readers: Kinley J. Brauer of the University of Minnesota; Gregg Herken of Yale University; Michael Hunt of the University of North Carolina, Chapel Hill; Thomas Lairson of Rollins College; Lester D. Langley of the University of Georgia; J. Donald Miller of Virginia Polytechnic Institute and State University; Stephen Rabe of the University of Texas, Dallas; Thomas G. Smith of Nichols College; Mark Stoler of the University of Vermont; Ralph E. Weber of Marquette University; Dennis Merrill and Thomas Zoumaras, doctoral students at the University of Connecticut; and the following

Naval Academy midshipmen: Bradley Arnold, Steven Corley, William Dawson, George DuPont, Jr., Michael Fierro, Andrew Harper, Ronald Jackson, Randal Mayer, Dana Moss, Sharon Pfeiffer, Lang Reese, Laurent Reinhardt, Thomas Snyder, John Steckel, Keith Wixler, and James Yohe. We could never have mastered the Pinyin system without the generous help of Professor Herman Mast, Li Yan, and Mark DelVecchio of the University of Connecticut. Richard Dean Burns of California State University at Los Angeles sent us an invaluable late draft of the extensive bibliography he edited for the Society for Historians of American Foreign Relations, *A Guide to American Foreign Relations Since 1700* (1982). For various acts of assistance, we also thank Justus Doenecke of the New College, University of South Florida; William Stueck of Purdue University; Burton I. Kaufman of Kansas State University; and Xavier Franco, Eric Hafter, and Leith Johnson, graduate students at the University of Connecticut. Holly Izard Paterson once again steered this project to its conclusion; it is a better book because of her care.

We welcome comments on this second edition from both students and instructors.

Thomas G. Paterson
Storrs, Connecticut

J. Garry Clifford
Eastford, Connecticut

Kenneth J. Hagan
Annapolis, Maryland

Preface to the First Edition

Writing a survey book is necessarily a learning experience, for the authors must read and synthesize the prolific work of fellow scholars. We have brought our own research in primary sources and our own interpretations to this synthesis, but the scholarship of our friends and colleagues in diplomatic history has proven indispensable. We have cited their contributions in our extensive footnotes and in the bibliographic sections, and we heartily thank them.

We have designed this book to include the tools needed to study American diplomatic history. The illustrations, many of them rare and unusual prints selected from some seventy depositories in the United States and Great Britain, have been closely integrated with the text. The map program is unique, especially for its "perspective" maps. The book also includes charts and graphs to render the historical record precise and complete. Each chapter presents a listing of the Presidents and Secretaries of State, with their terms of office, and an appendix adds Chairmen of the Senate Foreign Relations Committee and the Secretaries of Defense. The footnotes and "further reading" sections, reflecting excellent recent scholarship, will assist the curious in further exploration. A thorough index, in itself an important study tool, is provided.

For continuity, thoroughness, and thematic unity, we have treated in each chapter such basic points as the comparative influence of ideology, economics, and strategy, the importance of personalities and styles, domestic politics, bureaucratic and executive-legislative competition, criticisms of and alternatives to American foreign policy, definitions of the national interest, historical "lessons," measurements of American power, and the impact of American interventions on other cultures. We emphasize the theme of expansionism. "People" are central to history as both victors and victims. Thus we have incorporated a good deal of biography in the diplomatic story and have liberally quoted participants (and scholars), letting them speak for themselves. Each chapter opens with a "diplomatic crossroad," a significant event that helps illustrate the chief characteristics and issues of the era. The opening episode is then placed in its large historical context and the main themes and characters of the period are discussed. Chronological and topical sections follow next. Each chapter closes with a discussion of the legacy of the period—the lessons each generation bequeathed to the next generation of Americans.

Thomas G. Paterson initiated this project and coordinated its development. With Holly Izard Paterson he researched print collections and wrote captions for the illustrations. He held primary writing responsibility for chapters 5, 6, 8, 9, 10, 12, 13, 14, and 15 and shared in writing chapters 4 and 11. J. Garry Clifford held primary writing responsibility for chapters 1, 2, and 3 and shared in writing chapter 11. Kenneth J. Hagan held primary writing responsibility for chapter 7 and shared in writing chapter 4. The authors criticized one another's work, interchanged suggestions and ideas frequently, and worked as a team to insure a unified book.

We acknowledge with sincere gratitude the help of many people. Professor Alan Henrikson suggested many of the maps and Norman Adams skillfully prepared them. Sol Woolman of the University of Connecticut Photo Lab assisted with the illustrations, always reaching for the highest standards. We thank Robert Beisner, R. Christian Berg, Paul Goodwin, Alan Henrikson, George Herring, Burton Kaufman, Jean-Donald Miller, Stephen Rabe, Thomas G. Smith, Edmund S. Wehrle, Joan Hoff Wilson, and Thomas Zoumaras for reading all or parts of the manuscript and for improving it. For other assistance, we thank Richard Baker, Carol Davidge, James Gormly, Edythe and Richard Izard, Robert McMahon, R. Kent Newmyer, Wayne Repeta, Anna Lou Smethurst, and George Turner. With her customary care and craftsmanship, Sondra Astor Stave prepared the index. We wish also to thank the many museums, libraries, picture agencies, archives, and individuals who helped us locate and obtain illustrations. Their contributions are acknowledged in the credit line for each print. Special thanks go to Max Ascoli of *The Reporter* for permission to reprint several striking caricatures.

To Holly Izard Paterson we particularly extend our gratitude. She too often put aside her quilting, reading, plants, swimming, travel, and piano to edit and type the manuscript, conduct research, manage the illustration program, and press us to write with spirit and clarity.

As scholars whose work is in a constant state of revision, we welcome comments and suggestions from readers of *American Foreign Policy: A History*.

Thomas G. Paterson
Storrs, Connecticut

J. Garry Clifford
Eastford, Connecticut

Kenneth J. Hagan
Annapolis, Maryland

Contents

7 Managing and Extending the American Empire, 1900–1914

8 World Reform Through World War, 1914–1920

9

Power Without Punch: Relations with Europe, 1920–1939

10

A Question of Power: Relations with Asia and Latin America, 1920–1939

11 World War II: The Ordeal of Allied Diplomacy, 1939–1945

12 The Origins of the Cold War, 1945–1950

13 Something Old, Something New: Global Confrontations, 1950–1961

14 Bearing the Burden: The Vietnam Years, 1961–1969

15 The Perils of a Grand Design, 1969–1977

16 Reviving America in a World of Diffused Power: Foreign Policy Since 1977

Appendix

General Bibliography

Index

Maps and Charts

American Foreign Policy

Teddy Roosevelt the Pirate. The Colombian minister called the United States a ''pirate'' that had ''mutilated'' his nation by severing Panama. Cartoonist Frank Nankivell's rendering of the strong-willed President captured the Colombian viewpoint. (Swann Collection of Caricature and Cartoon)

7 Managing and Extending the American Empire, 1900–1914

Diplomatic Crossroad: Taking Panama, 1903

"Revolution imminent," read the cable from the American consul at Colón, a normally sleepy Colombian seaport on the Atlantic side of the Isthmus of Panama. Acting Secretary of State Francis B. Loomis bridled his curiosity for an hour and five minutes. Then he fired off an inquiry to the United States consul at Panama City, on the Pacific slope: "Uprising on Isthmus reported. Keep Department promptly and fully informed." The response came back in four hours: "No uprising yet. Reported will be in the night. Situation is critical." Loomis' anxiety, already intense, increased sharply five minutes later when he learned that an "important message" intended for the U.S.S. *Nashville* anchored at Colón had miscarried, and troops of the Colombian government had landed in the city.

At the Department of State it was now 8:20 P.M., November 3, 1903. As far as Loomis knew, a revolution had not yet broken out on the isthmus. Nonetheless, he hurriedly drafted instructions for the consuls at Panama and Colón. "Act promptly," he directed in near desperation. Somehow convey to the commanding officer of the *Nashville* this order: "In the interests of peace make every effort to prevent [Colombian] Government troops at Colón from proceeding to Panama." Having ordered intervention against a friendly government during a revolution that to his knowledge had not yet begun, Loomis was left to agonize for another hour. Finally, a new cable arrived: "Uprising occurred to-night . . . no bloodshed. . . . Government will be organized to-night." Loomis no doubt sighed in relief. He had done his part to insure success in the reckless gamble for a canal controlled by the United States.

If November third was a busy day for Francis Loomis, it was far more hectic for José Augustín Arango and his fellow conspirators in Panama. The tiny mixed band of Panamanians and Americans living on the isthmus had been actively plotting revolution since August, when the Colombian Congress dashed their hopes for prosperity by defeating the treaty that would have permitted the United

States to construct an isthmian canal. By the end of October, they had become convinced that the North American colossus, frustrated in its overtures to Colombia, would lend them moral and physical support. Confident that American naval vessels would be at hand, they selected November fourth as the date of their coup d'état. To their dismay, however, the Colombian steamer *Cartagena* disembarked about 400 troops at Colón early in the morning of November 3. Because the "important message" directing him to prevent the "landing of any armed force . . . either Government or insurgent at Colón" had been delayed in transmission, Commander John Hubbard of the *Nashville* did not interfere with the landing.

Forced to rely on their own wits, the conspirators made good use of the transisthmian railroad. They deviously separated the Colombian commanding general from his troops, lured him aboard a train, and sped him ceremoniously across the isthmus to Panama City. At 6:00 P.M. on the third, the revolutionaries arrested their guest, formed a provisional government, and paraded before a cheering crowd at the Cathedral Plaza. But the revolution would remain perilously unfinished so long as armed Colombian soldiers occupied Colón. Too weak to expel the soldiers by force, the insurgents gave the colonel in charge $8000 in gold, whereupon he ordered his troops aboard a departing steamer. The American consul at Panama City cabled: "Quiet prevails." At noon the next day, Secretary of State John Hay recognized the sovereign Republic of Panama.

The frantic pace of American isthmian diplomacy continued. The new Panamanian government appointed as its minister plenipotentiary a Frenchman, Philippe Bunau-Varilla, who had long agitated for a Panama canal and who recently had conspired for Panamanian independence from Colombia. With Gallic flourish Bunau-Varilla descended upon Secretary Hay. He extolled the United States for rescuing Panama "from the barbarism of unnecessary and wasteful civil wars to consecrate it to the destiny assigned to it by Providence, the service of humanity, and the progress of civilization."[1] John Hay thoroughly understood the meaning of Bunau-Varilla's rhetoric and eagerly negotiated the treaty both men wanted. On November 18, 1903, less than two weeks after American recognition of Panama, they signed the Hay–Bunau-Varilla Treaty, by which the United States government would build, fortify, and operate a canal linking the Atlantic and Pacific oceans.

Hay had at last achieved a goal set by his chief, President Theodore Roosevelt, several years earlier. "I do not see why we should dig the canal if we are not to fortify it," Roosevelt had explained to navalist Alfred Thayer Mahan early in 1900. If an unfortified, neutral canal had existed in Central America during the recent war with Spain, Roosevelt argued in another letter, "we could have got the *Oregon* around in time," but the United States would have spent most of the war in "wild panic," fearful that the Spanish fleet would slip through the waterway and rush to the Philippines to attack Admiral Dewey. The lesson was manifest. Enemy fleets of the future must not be allowed to steam through an isthmian canal to strike the United States at exposed and vulnerable places. "Better to have no canal at all, than not give us the power to control it in time of war," Roosevelt expostulated.[2] What he really wanted, of course, was a canal run by Americans for the benefit of the United States.

The major barrier to that goal was the Clayton-Bulwer Treaty of 1850, stipulating joint Anglo-American construction and operation of any Central American canal. In December, 1898, flushed with victory over Spain, President William McKinley had directed Secretary Hay to discuss modification of that agreement

Theodore Roosevelt (1858–1919).
Graduate of Harvard, historian, Rough
Rider, and New York governor, Republican Roosevelt became President in
1901 after William McKinley was
assassinated. TR's famed impetuosity notwithstanding, biographer Frederick W.
Marks has written that the President
"stands in a class by himself for that
blend of statesmanlike qualities which
might best be described as velvet on
iron." (Library of Congress)

with the British Ambassador, Sir Julian Pauncefote. The Hay-Pauncefote Treaty of
February, 1900 permitted the United States to build a canal but forbade its
fortification, much to the chagrin of Theodore Roosevelt, then governor of New
York. He spearheaded an attack that defeated the treaty in the Senate, forcing
renegotiation. On November 18, 1901, with Roosevelt now President, Hay and
Pauncefote signed a pact satisfactory to the Rough Rider.

Then began the complex process of determining the route. In November, 1901,
after an investigation lasting two years, the Walker Isthmian Canal Commission
reported in favor of Nicaragua. The decisive criterion was cost, which in the case of
Panama was made incalculable by the obduracy of the New Panama Canal
Company, a French-chartered firm that held the Colombian concession for canal
rights. The company estimated its assets on the isthmus at $109 million—

machinery, property, and excavated soil left by the defunct de Lesseps organization after its failure to cut through Panama in 1888. When coupled with the engineering costs, purchase of the New Panama Canal Company's rights and holdings would make construction through Panama prohibitively expensive, even though technologically easier. For these reasons, the House of Representatives on January 8, 1902 passed the Hepburn Bill authorizing a canal through Nicaragua.

The New Panama Canal Company's American lawyer, William Nelson Cromwell, described by one irritated congressman as "the most dangerous man this country has produced since the days of Aaron Burr—a professional revolutionist," swung into action.[3] Cromwell was a partner in the prestigious New York law firm of Sullivan and Cromwell, and his fixed purpose in 1902–1903 was to sell the assets of his French client for the highest possible price. The Walker Commission had estimated the company's worth at $40 million, a figure Cromwell reluctantly accepted in face of the passage of the Hepburn Bill. The attorney began an intense

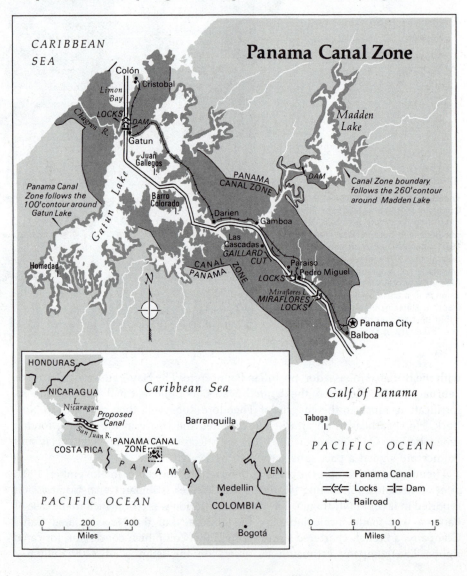

Panama Canal Zone

CARIBBEAN SEA

Colón
Cristobal
Limon Bay
Chagres R.
LOCKS
DAM
Gatun
Gatun Lake
Juan Gallegos I.
Madden Lake
DAM
Canal Zone boundary follows the 260' contour around Madden Lake

Panama Canal Zone follows the 100' contour around Gatun Lake

Barro Colorado I.

PANAMA CANAL ZONE

Darien
Gamboa
Las Cascadas
GAILLARD CUT
Paraiso
Pedro Miguel
LOCKS
CANAL ZONE
PANAMA
Homedad I.

Miraflores L.
MIRAFLORES LOCKS

Panama City
Balboa

HONDURAS
NICARAGUA
L. Nicaragua
Proposed Canal
San Juan R.
Caribbean Sea
Barranquilla
Gulf of Panama
Taboga I.
PACIFIC OCEAN
COSTA RICA
PANAMA CANAL ZONE
PANAMA
VEN.
Medellin
COLOMBIA
PACIFIC OCEAN
Bogotá

	Panama Canal
	Locks Dam
	Railroad

0 200 400
Miles

0 5 10 15
Miles

lobbying campaign directed principally at President Roosevelt, Republican senators Mark Hanna and John C. Spooner, and members of the Walker Commission. Cromwell was joined by Bunau-Varilla, formerly chief engineer for de Lesseps, in what has been described as one of the "masterpieces of the lobbyist's art."[4]

On January 18, 1902, the Walker Commission reversed itself and decided for the technologically preferable Panama passage, citing the company's willingness to sell out for the reduced sum of $40 million. Guided by Roosevelt, Spooner, and Cromwell, Congress five months later passed the Spooner Act, approving the Panama route. The State Department soon opened negotiations with Colombia. The price of the annual rental became a stumbling block, which Hay removed only by delivering an ultimatum to the Colombian chargé d'affaires, Tomás Herrán, in January, 1903. On January 22 he and Hay signed a treaty granting Colombia an initial payment of $10 million and $250,000 annually. The United States reaped control over the six-mile wide canal zone for 100 years, a privilege renewable at the "sole and absolute option" of the North American republic.[5]

The United States Senate approved the Hay-Herrán Treaty on March 17, 1903, but the Colombian government, although genuinely desiring American construction of a canal, moved slowly. Faced with a treasury drained by a long and costly civil war, Bogotá attempted to extract a $10 million payment from the New Panama Canal Company for permitting the transfer of its assets to the American government. At this juncture Hay succumbed to the blandishments of William Nelson Cromwell. After meeting with the lawyer in April, the secretary bluntly announced that any discussion of a payment by the new Panama Canal Company to Colombia "would be in violation of the Spooner law and not permissible."[6]

As a second stratagem, the Colombian government attempted to raise the initial American cash payment from $10 to $15 million. Roosevelt waxed indignant, snapping to Hay that "those contemptible little creatures in Bogotá ought to understand how much they are jeopardizing things and imperilling their own future."[7] The President came to believe that "you could no more make an agreement with the Colombian rulers than you could nail currant jelly to the wall."[8] TR's intransigence and Hay's extraordinary intercession on behalf of a privately owned foreign corporation increased the anxiety felt by many Colombian congressmen about the Hay-Herrán Treaty's severe infringement upon Colombia's sovereignty over Panama. They unanimously defeated the treaty on August 12, 1903.

Bogotá's rejection did not catch Roosevelt napping. As early as March 30, Minister Arthur N. Beaupré had cautioned Washington that "without question public opinion is strongly against its ratification," and Roosevelt had begun to ponder undiplomatic alternatives.[9] On June 13 the ubiquitous Cromwell had met with Roosevelt and then planted a story in the *New York World* reporting that, if Colombia rejected the treaty, Panama would secede and grant to the United States "the equivalent of absolute sovereignty over the Canal Zone." Moreover, alleged the *World*, "President Roosevelt is said to strongly favor this plan."[10] As it became increasingly likely that Colombia would repudiate the Hay-Herrán pact, Roosevelt's contempt for the Colombian people mounted. In private letters to Hay and others he denounced them as "jack rabbits," "foolish and homicidal corruptionists," and "cat-rabbits."[11] Hay, usually urbane and restrained, uttered a diatribe against "the government of folly and graft that now rules at Bogotá."[12]

Roosevelt and Hay now considered two options: seizure of Panama by force, or extension of instant recognition and support to any revolutionary regime in Panama. The President inclined sharply toward the latter course after a meeting with Bunau-Varilla on October 10, during which the Frenchman predicted an uprising. Although TR was guarded in his reply, he later admitted that Bunau-Varilla "would have been a very dull man" if unable to "guess" that the United States would respond favorably to a revolution.[13] One week later, on October 16, Secretary Hay informed Bunau-Varilla that American naval vessels were heading toward the isthmus. Bunau-Varilla shrewdly calculated the steaming time and cabled the revolutionaries waiting on the isthmus that American warships would arrive by November 2. Early that evening the U.S.S. *Nashville* dropped anchor at Colón as predicted.

In his annual message to Congress after the Panamanian revolution, Roosevelt urged swift ratification of the Hay-Bunau-Varilla Treaty, saying that the colossal canal project would benefit the United States and the rest of mankind as well. When Democrats in the Senate questioned the President's role in the insurrection, Roosevelt disingenuously replied: "No one connected with this Government had any part in preparing, inciting, or encouraging the late revolution."[14] Apparently mollified, on February 23, 1904, the Senate approved the treaty by a vote of 66 to 14. The treaty granted the United States "power and authority" within the zone as "if it were the sovereign of the territory. . . ."[15] Later, in 1911, TR was widely reported as boasting that "I took the Canal Zone and let Congress debate; and while the debate goes on the Canal does also."[16]

Construction began in mid-1904, and the fifty-mile-long canal opened to traffic on August 15, 1914. During the first year of operation alone, 1,058 merchant vessels slid through the locks, while the Atlantic and Pacific fleets of the United

"Just Where the Paper Tore." Roosevelt uses indelible ink to make his point across the Isthmus of Panama. Roosevelt defended himself at a Cabinet meeting and asked Secretary Elihu Root about his impressions of the spirited defense. Root replied: "You have shown that you were accused of seduction and you have conclusively proved that you were guilty of rape." (*Chicago Daily News,* 1903)

States Navy freely exchanged ships. In 1922 the United States paid "conscience money" or "canalimony" of $25 million to Colombia but did not formally apologize for having taken the canal zone. Although Roosevelt's handling of the Panama issue, according to historian William Harbaugh, constitutes "one of the ineradicable blots on his record," most Americans have applauded his bold meddling in the internal affairs of the sovereign nation of Colombia.[17] Roosevelt himself ranked his accomplishment alongside the Louisiana Purchase and the acquisition of Texas.

The Conservative Shapers of the American Empire

The taking of Panama symbolized the new activism characteristic of American foreign policy after the Spanish-American War, and construction of the canal placed the United States in a physical position of undisputed domination over Latin America. Great Britain, the only Old World power that might have contested America's new pre-eminence, faced a stiff political and naval challenge from Germany. In a series of remarkable retreats beginning with the first Hay-Pauncefote Treaty, London diplomatically recognized the shifting balance of power in Europe and the Americas and acquiesced in United States hegemony over Latin America. President Roosevelt perceived more clearly than most Americans an opportunity to capitalize on this historic transformation. The Panama Canal marked one result.

In the late nineteenth century, Roosevelt had associated closely with the most vocal pressure group agitating for an American canal, the uniformed "professors of war" at the Naval War College.[18] He corresponded regularly with one of those officers, Alfred Thayer Mahan, the navalist who tirelessly explained the strategic advantages of a canal in the idiom of the 1890s. "Wherever situated, whether at Panama or Nicaragua," Mahan preached, "the fundamental meaning of the canal will be that it advances by thousands of miles the frontiers . . . of the United States."[19] In the course of expanding those frontiers during the "splendid little war" of 1898, the cruiser *Oregon* dashed at full speed from San Francisco to the tip of South America and through the Strait of Magellan to Cuba in time to help destroy the Spanish fleet off Santiago. The race of over 14,000 miles fired American imaginations, but it also consumed sixty-eight days and dramatically underscored the need for an interoceanic canal across Central America.

Roosevelt's sense of isthmian strategic necessity reflected a broad world view he shared with many "progressives" in the reform era of the early twentieth century. A conservative patrician reformer motivated by noblesse oblige, he "feared that unrest caused by social and economic inequities would impair the nation's strength and efficiency."[20] He saw a similar danger to American interests in unrest abroad, and he sought to exert United States influence to create order on a global scale. "More and more," Roosevelt told Congress in 1902, "the increasing interdependence and complexity of international political and economic relations render it incumbent on all civilized and orderly powers to insist on the proper policing of the world."[21] A quintessential chauvinist, Roosevelt talked about doing the "rough work of the world" and about the need to "speak softly and carry a big stick."[22] Like his contemporaries, TR had imbibed the Social Darwinist doctrines of "natural selection" and the "survival of the fittest," and he articulated racist notions about Anglo-Saxon superiority and the "white man's burden" to tutor "backward" peoples. For Roosevelt in particular, that superiority was best ex-

Makers of American Foreign Policy from 1900 to 1914

Presidents	Secretaries of State
Theodore Roosevelt, 1901–1909	John Hay, 1898–1905
	Elihu Root, 1905–1909
	Robert Bacon, 1909
William Howard Taft, 1909–1913	Philander C. Knox, 1909–1913
Woodrow Wilson, 1913–1921	William Jennings Bryan, 1913–1915

pressed in war. "All the great masterful races have been fighting races," he lectured an audience at the Naval War College.[23] Progressive politicians, however, were decidedly split over foreign policy questions. Some joined Roosevelt in advocating a vigorous activism abroad. Others, like Wisconsin's Senator Robert M. LaFollette, were anti-imperialists and critics of war who believed that the corporate monopolies they were battling at home were dragging the United States into perpetual interventionism abroad.

Roosevelt always vigorously debated his critics and added his unique personal characteristics to American foreign policy. Often impatient and impetuous, having the instinct for the jugular, he centralized and personalized foreign policy decisionmaking, frequently bypassed Congress, and believed "the people" so ignorant about foreign affairs that they should not direct an informed president like himself. In the search for a stable world order and a balance of power, Roosevelt could assume the garb of the peacemaker trying to reconcile competing national interests. For example, he won the Nobel Peace Prize in 1906 for his mediating effort at the Portsmouth Conference (see p. 239). The candid President disliked the pomp and ceremony of traditional diplomacy and on occasion disrupted protocol with a memorable incident: he once broke up a luncheon by demonstrating jujitsu holds on the Swiss minister. He could be seen running into the Potomac for a swim, a trail of exhausted, less active diplomats stumbling along behind him. But Roosevelt usually preserved his dignity. He dealt with foreign leaders "friend to friend, with the directness of a North Dakotan cowboy sheathed under the grace of aristocratic manners."[24]

Roosevelt and other shapers of American foreign policy between the Spanish-American War and the First World War were members of an American quasi-aristocracy and sure-footed devotees of "order." Most had graduated from prestigious eastern colleges and distinguished themselves in high political office or in the professions. They moved comfortably in the affluent, cosmopolitan, upper-class society of the Atlantic seaboard. Roosevelt, a graduate of Harvard College, had been assistant secretary of the Navy and governor of New York and was a prolific author. His successor, Ohioan William Howard Taft, a graduate of Yale, had served as a federal circuit court judge, governor of the Philippines (1901–1904), and secretary of war (1904–1908). Woodrow Wilson earned a Ph.D. from Johns Hopkins, wrote books on history, presided over Princeton, and governed New Jersey before entering the White House.

Their secretaries of state, with one exception, were members of the same elite. John Hay, secretary for 1898–1905, was born in Indiana and educated at Brown

University. Wealthy and recognized as a poet, novelist, biographer, and editor of the *New York Tribune,* he had served as Lincoln's personal secretary during the Civil War and later as McKinley's ambassador to Great Britain. He thought the "indispensable feature of our foreign policy should be a firm understanding with England," and he was one of the chief architects of the Anglo-American rapprochement of the early twentieth century.[25] His successor Elihu Root (1905–1909), a cautious conservative who praised Theodore Roosevelt as "the greatest conservative force for the protection of property and capital," was born in upstate New York, graduated from Hamilton College, took a law degree at New York University, and became one of America's most successful corporation lawyers.[26] As secretary of war from 1899 to 1904, he created mechanisms, such as the Platt Amendment for Cuba, for managing the American empire. Like TR, he believed that the "main object of diplomacy is to keep the country out of trouble" and maintain order abroad.[27] Philander C. Knox (1909–1913) followed Root. A corporation lawyer born in Pennsylvania, he had helped form the giant United States Steel Corporation. He served as attorney general and United States senator before entering the State Department. Habitually seeking leisure, Knox liked to play golf at Chevy Chase, spend summers with his trotters at his Valley Forge Farms estate, vacation in Florida in the winter, and delegate departmental work to subordinates. He advocated "dollar diplomacy" as a means of creating order in revolution-prone areas—that is, the use of private financiers and businessmen to promote foreign policy, and vice versa. The second man to serve under President Wilson was New Yorker Robert Lansing (1915–1920), a graduate of Amherst College, son-in-law of a former secretary of state, and practitioner of international law. Reserved and conservative, Lansing also would not tolerate disorder in the United States sphere of Latin America.

William Jennings Bryan, Wilson's first appointment (1913–1915), did not conform to the conservative elite status of most makers of foreign policy. The "boy orator" of Nebraska could mesmerize crowds by decrying the "cross of gold" upon which eastern capitalists were crucifying western and southern farmers, but he could not win a presidential election (he ran in 1896, 1900, and 1908). The "Great Commoner" languished for years as the most prominent has-been of the Democratic party, until Wilson appointed him secretary of state out of deference to his long service to the partisan cause and as a reward for support at the convention of 1912. The President let Bryan appoint "deserving Democrats" to diplomatic posts and indulge his fascination with peace or "cooling off" treaties, but Wilson bypassed him in most important diplomatic decisions, even to the point of composing overseas cables on his own White House typewriter. In 1915, during World War I, Bryan resigned to protest Wilson's pro-British leanings.

These conservative managers of American foreign policy believed that a major component of national power was a prosperous, expanding economy invigorated by a healthy foreign trade. The principle of the "Open Door"—to keep open trade and investment opportunities—became a governing tenet voiced globally, although often tarnished in application. Mahan believed that commerce was the "energizer of material civilization," and Roosevelt declared to Congress in his annual message of 1901 that "America has only just begun to assume that commanding position in the international business world which we believe will more and more be hers."[28] In 1900 the United States exported goods valued at $1.5 billion. By 1914, at the start of World War I, that figure stood at $2.5 billion.

Elihu Root (1845–1937). Graduate of Hamilton College, corporate lawyer, Republican, Secretary of War (1899–1904), and Secretary of State (1905–1909), Root was a skilled administrator who helped devise methods for controlling the American empire. (*PBT,* Buenos Aires, 1906)

Exports to Latin America increased markedly from $132 million at the turn of the century to $309 million in 1914. Investments there in sugar, transportation, and banking shot up. By 1913 the United Fruit Company, the banana empire, had some 130,000 acres in cultivation in Central America, a fleet of freighters, and political influence as well. By 1914 the United States dominated nickel mining in Canada and sugar production in Cuba, and total American investments abroad equaled $3.5 billion.

But those statistics were not important solely as contributions to pocketbooks. Americans believed that economic expansion also meant that the best of "Americanism," the values of industriousness, honesty, morality, and private initiative, were carried abroad. Thus Yale University-in-China and the Young Men's Christian Association (YMCA) joined the Standard Oil Company and Singer Sewing in China as advance agents of civilization. And, as Secretary of War Taft said about the Chinese in 1908, "The more civilized they become the more active their industries, the wealthier they become, and the better market they will become for us."[29] President Wilson, who added a conspicuous tinge of missionary paternalism to the quest for order, said simply that he would "teach the South American Republics to elect good men."[30] As historian Jerry Israel has noted, "reforming cultures, making profits, and saving souls were not incompatible goals."[31] All were intertwined in the American compulsion to shape the lives of other people while denying any intention of dominating them.

The Cuban Protectorate

President William McKinley faced a dilemma in 1898. The Teller Amendment, which he had unsuccessfully opposed, forbade the annexation of Cuba. Yet, in negotiating the preliminary protocol of peace he had insisted that Spain relinquish sovereignty over the island. Cuba lay athwart the approaches to the Gulf of Mexico and Caribbean Sea. Unless brought firmly within the American orbit, it could threaten the security of the Gulf states and United States hegemony over Central America. The President understandably equivocated. In his annual message of December, 1898, he promised to help the Cubans build a "free and independent" government, but he also warned that American military rule would continue until "complete tranquillity" and a "stable government" existed on the island.[32]

Two months later the Philippine insurrection erupted, sending shock waves through America's policy-makers. Secretary of War Elihu Root, charged with the formulation of Cuban occupation policy, feared that in Cuba the United States was "on the verge daily of the same sort of thing that happened to us in the Philippines."[33] To accelerate the evolution of Cuban democracy and stability, Root appointed General Leonard Wood the military governor of the island. A Harvard graduate with a degree in medicine, Wood had entered the Army for excitement. A spiritual relative and a friend of the adventurous Roosevelt, Wood favored outright annexation of Cuba, but he loyally subordinated his own preferences to the Administration's policy of patrician tutelage in the ways of progress and freedom. During his tenure as military governor (1899–1902), he worked to eradicate yellow fever, Americanize education, construct highways, and formulate an electoral law guaranteeing order. The general defined his objectives in a conservative manner: "When money can be borrowed at a reasonable rate of interest and when capital is willing to invest in the Island, a condition of stability will have been reached."[34] Senator Joseph B. Foraker, an old Ohio rival of McKinley, viewed overseas investments in a less friendly light and sought to retard the annexationist tendencies that followed the flow of capital abroad. In February of 1899 he successfully attached an amendment to the Army Appropriation Bill that prohibited the American military government of Cuba from granting permanent economic concessions. However, Secretary of War Root outflanked the senator by granting revocable permits, beginning with a railroad franchise in 1901.

With the economic foundation of his policy safely laid, Root began construction of a Cuban-American political relationship designed to weather the storms of independence. Working closely with Senator Orville Platt, an Administration spokesman, Root fashioned the so-called Platt Amendment to the Army Appropriation Bill of 1901. By the Platt Amendment's terms, Cuba could not make a treaty with any nation that might impair its independence. Should Cuban independence ever be threatened, or should it fail to protect adequately "life, property, and individual liberty," the United States had the right to intervene. For these purposes, Cuba would cede to the United States "lands necessary for coaling or naval stations." The Platt Amendment also stipulated that "by way of further assurance" Cuba and the United States would "embody the foregoing provisions in a permanent treaty."[35]

Cubans howled. On Good Friday, 1901, the front page of Havana's *La Discusión* carried a cartoon of "The Cuban Calvary" depicting the Cuban people as Christ and Senator Platt as a Roman soldier. Many Americans agreed that the amendment

"If General Wood Is Unpopular with Cuba, We Can Guess the Reason." General Leonard Wood (1860–1927), before he served as military governor of Cuba (1899–1903), was a surgeon from Boston who entered the Army in 1886 and earned a promotion for his role in capturing Indian leader Geronimo. He also commanded the Rough Riders at San Juan Hill during the Spanish-American War. Later he helped govern the Philippines. (*Minneapolis Tribune* in *Literary Digest,* 1901)

relegated Cuba to the status of a protectorate. Theodore Roosevelt retorted that the critics were "unhung traitors . . . liars, slanderers and scandal mongers."[36] Root ingeniously informed Wood that intervention was not "synonymous with intermeddling or interference with the affairs of a Cuban government," but the more straightforward general privately conceded that there was, "of course, little or no independence left Cuba under the Platt Amendment."[37] Wood himself forced a resistant Cuban convention to adopt the measure as an amendment to the new constitution on June 12, 1901, and the two governments signed a treaty embodying the provisions of the Platt Amendment on May 22, 1903. In 1903 the United States Navy constructed a naval base at Guantánamo Bay; "Gitmo," as the Marines christened it, was leased to the United States in perpetuity. A Reciprocity Treaty of 1902 permitted Cuban products to enter the United States at specially reduced tariff rates, thereby interlocking the economies of the two countries.

The first President of the Republic of Cuba, Tomás Estrada Palma, has been described as "more plattish than Platt himself."[38] Following his rigged re-election and second inauguration, discontented Cuban nationalists revolted. In a cable of September 8, 1906, the American consul-general in Havana reported Estrada Palma's inability to quell the rebellion or "protect life and property."[39] He pleaded for warships. President Roosevelt immediately ordered the cruiser *Denver* to Havana, but his tardy instructions failed to leash the ship's commanding officer, who landed a battalion of sailors at Estrada Palma's request. Roosevelt summarily ordered the men back aboard ship, adding further to the political chaos. "Just at the moment I am so angry with that infernal little Cuban republic," exploded the Rough Rider, "that I would like to wipe its people off the face of the earth." All he wanted from the Cubans, he said, was that "they should behave themselves."[40]

Into this turmoil stepped the portly Secretary of War, William Howard Taft, whom Roosevelt ordered to Cuba on a peace mission. Groping for a solution that would "put an end to anarchy without necessitating a reoccupation of the island by our troops," Roosevelt instructed Taft to mediate between the warring factions.[41] The Teller Amendment weighed upon the President's mind, as did memory of the bloody crushing of insurgent Emilio Aguinaldo in the Philippines. Army officers predicted that American suppression of the Cuban revolution would necessitate drastic reconcentration of the Cuban population, making political annexation inevitable. Estrada Palma resigned, permitting Taft to establish a new provisional government. Taft, the American secretary of war, thus became the provisional governor of Cuba on September 29, 1906. He soon lectured students of the National University of Havana that Cubans needed a "mercantile spirit," a "desire to make money, to found great enterprises."[42] Taft returned home in mid-October, leaving behind a government headed by an American civilian, administered by United States Army officers, and supported by over 5,000 American soldiers. For twenty-eight months Governor Charles E. Magoon attempted to reinstate Leonard Wood's electoral and humanitarian reforms, while Roosevelt publicly scolded the Cubans that if their "insurrectionary habit" persisted it was "absolutely out of the question that the Island should continue independent."[43] Privately he mused, "it is not our fault if things go badly there."[44]

Under his successor Taft, and under Taft's successor Woodrow Wilson, American policy toward Cuba consisted of reflexive support for existing governments, by means of force if necessary. Taft and Wilson made no serious effort to reform

Cuba in the American image. In what has been called both "a preventive policy" and "Dollar Diplomacy," the United States sought order in Cuban politics and security for American investments and commerce, particularly in sugar.[45] The $50 million invested by Americans in 1896 jumped to $220 million in 1913. By 1920 American-owned mills produced about half of Cuba's sugar. Cuban exports to the United States in 1900 equaled $31 million, by 1914 $131 million, and by 1920 $722 million. When these interests were threatened by revolution, as in May of 1912 and February of 1917, the Marines went ashore. After Havana followed Washington's lead and declared war against Germany in April, 1917, some 2,500 American troops were sent to Cuba for the protection of the sugar plantations that helped feed the Allied armies. Cuba, under the yoke of the Platt Amendment, the American military, and American economic interests, remained a protectorate of the United States. The island's "independence" was a myth, but its frustrated nationalism was a reality with which Americans always had to contend.

Policing the Caribbean: Venezuela, the Dominican Republic, and the Roosevelt Corollary

President Theodore Roosevelt devoted a great deal of thought to Latin America in the winter of 1901–1902. He guided the second Hay-Pauncefote Treaty through the Senate, fretted over the route of his isthmian canal, and helped Elihu Root shape the terms of the occupation of Cuba. He also turned his mind toward the most hallowed of American doctrines, that propounded by James Monroe in 1823. In his first annual message, on December 3, 1901, Roosevelt emphasized the economic aspect of the doctrine: "It is really a guarantee of the commercial independence of the Americas." The United States, however, as protector of that independence, would "not guarantee any state against punishment if it misconducts itself, provided that punishment does not take the form of the acquisition of territory by any non-American power."[46] If a South American country misbehaved in its relations with a European nation, Roosevelt would "let the European country spank it."[47]

The President was thinking principally of Germany and Venezuela. Under the rule of Cipriano Castro, an unsavory dictator whom Roosevelt once characterized as an "unspeakable villainous monkey," Venezuela perpetually deferred payment on bonds worth more than $12.5 million and held by German investors.[48] Berlin became understandably impatient. Great Britain felt equally irritated by Venezuela's failure to meet its debts to British subjects. In December, 1902, after clearing the way with Washington, Germany and Britain delivered an ultimatum demanding immediate settlement of their claims, seized several Venezuelan vessels, bombarded two forts, and proclaimed a blockade closing Venezuela to commerce. To all of this Theodore Roosevelt acquiesced, but American congressional and editorial opinion reacted adversely. The *Literary Digest* of December 20 worried "that England and Germany will overstep the limits prescribed by the Monroe Doctrine" and concluded that many newspapers "think that the allies have already gone too far."[49]

In mid-January, 1903, the German Navy bombarded two more forts. Popular criticism of the intervention sharpened in the United States, while in Great Britain Rudyard Kipling denounced his government's cooperation with "the breed that have wronged us most."[50] Shaken by the American reaction, Kaiser Wilhelm II

Roosevelt at Work. TR was, according to biographer William Harbaugh, "a man of surpassing charm, extraordinary charisma, and broad intellectual interests . . . , a curious compound of realist and idealist, pragmatist and moral absolutist." A lover of power, he knew that one way to achieve it was through vigorous oratory. (*Kladderadatsch*, Berlin)

replaced his ill-informed ambassador with Hermann Speck von Sternburg, an old friend of Roosevelt. The President received Speck on the day of his arrival in Washington and urged a quick settlement to quell the clamor in Britain and the United States. Under this mounting criticism and pressure from Roosevelt, Britain and Germany in early February lifted the blockade and submitted the dispute to the Permanent Court at the Hague. Prime Minister Arthur Balfour calmed troubled Anglo-American waters by publicly denying any intention of acquiring additional territory in the western hemisphere and welcoming an "increase of the influence of the United States" in Latin America.[51] Even more, he accepted the Monroe Doctrine as international law. On February 22, 1904, the Hague Tribunal awarded preferential treatment to the claims of the two nations that had used force against Venezuela. A prominent State Department official complained that this decision put "a premium on violence" and made likely similar European interventions in the future.[52]

Theodore Roosevelt also worried increasingly about the chronic disorder and fiscal insolvency of the Dominican Republic, which had been torn continually by revolution since 1899. "I have about the same desire to annex it," Roosevelt said privately, "as a gorged boa constrictor might have to swallow a porcupine wrong-end to."[53] An American firm that formerly handled the country's tariff collections (customs) claimed damages of several million dollars, and European creditors demanded action by their governments. The President had been "hoping and praying . . . that the Santo Dominigans would behave so that I would not have to act in any way." By the spring of 1904 he thought he might have "to do nothing but what a policeman has to do."[54] He preferred to do it after the presidential election of 1904.

After the electorate resoundingly endorsed his presidency, he described to Congress his conception of the United States as policeman of the western hemisphere. "Chronic wrongdoing, or an impotence which results in a general loosening of the ties of civilized society," he proclaimed, "may in America, as elsewhere, ultimately require intervention by some civilized nation, and in the Western Hemisphere the adherence of the United States to the Monroe Doctrine may force the United States, however reluctantly, in flagrant cases of such wrongdoing or impotence, to the exercise of an international police power."[55] With this statement of December 6, 1904, the twenty-sixth President of the United States added to the Monroe Doctrine his corollary, which fundamentally transformed that prohibition upon European meddling into a brash promise of United States regulation of the Americas.

The Rough Rider acted accordingly. In December the State Department initiated discussions with the Dominican Republic aimed at American collection and distribution of the Latin republic's customs revenues. A protocol to this effect was signed on February 7, 1905, but it ran into determined Democratic opposition in the Senate. Roosevelt, however, would not be deterred. He arranged a modus vivendi, assigning an American collector of the Dominican customs, an arrangement finally sanctified in a treaty negotiated by Secretary of State Root and approved by the Senate on February 25, 1907. While easing the new Dominican customs treaty through the Senate, Root explained the interrelationship between Latin American political stability and the security of the Panama Canal. The "inevitable effect of our building the Canal," he wrote, "must be to require us to police the surrounding premises."[56] The United States would reap "trade and control, and the obligation to keep order" and would simultaneously draw Latin America "up out of the discord and turmoil of continual revolution into a general public sense of justice and determination to maintain order."[57]

Taft's Secretary of State, Philander C. Knox, applauded Root's customs receivership in the Dominican Republic because it denied to rebels the funds they so eagerly "collected" through the capture of customs houses. Knox credited the receivership with curing "century-old evils."[58] The assassination of the Dominican President the following November, 1911, demonstrated that Knox spoke somewhat prematurely. And in 1912 revolutionaries operating from the contiguous country of Haiti marauded throughout the Dominican Republic. Their forays forced the closure of several customs houses that the United States had protected under the Treaty of 1907. To restore order, Taft in September, 1912, sent a commission backed by 750 Marines. The commissioners redefined the Haiti–Dominican Republic border, forced the corrupt Dominican president to resign by stopping his revenues from the customs service, avoided direct interference in a new election, and returned to Washington in December.

President Wilson and Secretary Bryan eloquently disparaged the evils of "dollar diplomacy" and promised that the United States would "never again seek one additional foot of territory by conquest."[59] That sounded new, but Roosevelt and Taft had already repudiated further American territorial acquisitions. Moreover, Wilson's search for stability in Latin America retraced familiar steps. When, in September, 1913, revolution again threatened the Dominican government, Bryan warned "that this Government will employ every legitimate means to assist in the restoration of order and the prevention of further insurrections."[60] The Navy Department sent a cruiser to the island, and Wilson urged political and economic reforms. Discouraged by a new revolutionary outburst in May of 1916, the Administration sent two warships, landed men, and permitted the admiral in command to threaten bombardment of the city of Santo Domingo if the leading revolutionary did not surrender. The Dominican and American governments thereupon debated terms of a treaty giving the United States full control over Dominican finances, while the United States Navy tightened its grip on the island. In November, as American involvement in the European war became increasingly probable, President Wilson proclaimed the formal military occupation of the Dominican Republic, ostensibly to curtail the activities of revolutionaries suspected of a pro-German bias. The American Navy governed the Dominican Republic until 1922.

The Quest for Stability in Haiti and Nicaragua

The Dominican Republic shares the island of Hispaniola with Haiti, where revolution became an increasingly popular mode of changing governments after 1911. American investments in the country were limited to ownership of a small railroad and a one-third share in the Haitian National Bank. Nationals of France and Germany controlled the bank, and disorder thus could give either European nation a pretext for intervention. After the outbreak of World War I, the Wilson Administration worried about "the ever present danger of German control" of Haiti.[61] At stake was the security of the Panama Canal, along the approaches to which lay Haiti's deep water harbor of Môle Saint Nicolas. The Navy Department, content with bases in Cuba and Puerto Rico, no longer desired a station in Haiti, but

Wilson could not let Môle Saint Nicolas fall into the unfriendly hands of Germany. Moreover, the President realized that Haitian instability fueled the revolution in the Dominican Republic, which he was also combatting. He therefore pressed for an American customs receivership on the Dominican model.

The Haitians resisted successfully until July, 1915, when the regime of Guillaume Sam fell in an orgy of grisly political murders. Wilson could stomach no more, and he ordered the Navy to Haiti. While 2,000 Marines imposed martial law, Secretary of State Robert Lansing explained to the Haitians that his government expected "to be entrusted with the practical control of the customs, and such financial control over the affairs of the Republic of Haiti as the United States may deem necessary for an efficient administration."[62] Lansing drafted a treaty putting Americans in charge of all aspects of Haiti's finances, privately admitting to Wilson that "this method of negotiation, with our marines policing the Haytian Capital, is high handed."[63] The United States naval and diplomatic vise meant that Haiti would be ruled until 1934 by what historian David Healy has called "an American military regime which acted, when it pleased, through the [Haitian] president."[64]

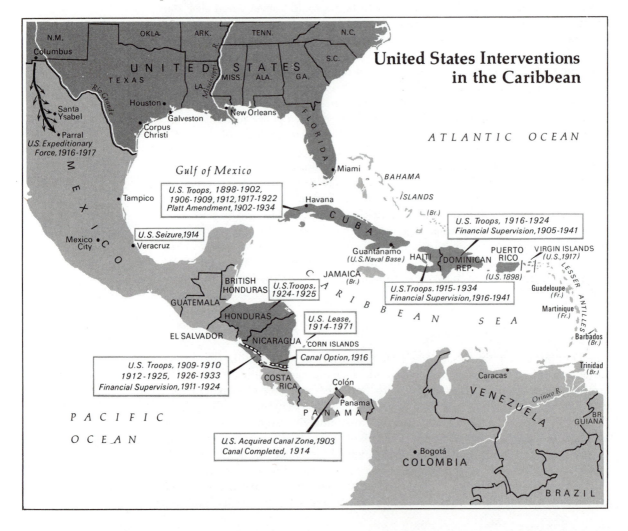

United States Interventions in the Caribbean

The United States also intervened, virtually at will, in hapless Nicaragua. For Theodore Roosevelt, Nicaragua had been important primarily as a potential canal route, a rivalry decided in Panama's favor in 1903. Subsequently, he manifested interest in Nicaragua only briefly, during 1907, when he and the President of Mexico jointly proposed a peace conference to end the incessant warfare among Central American states. Secretary Root explained that the conduct of those countries was "important to us," because the Panama Canal put them "in the front yard of the United States."[65] Philander C. Knox continued the search for stability in Central America, but an abiding antipathy "to all Spanish-American modes of thought" made him more ready to countenance the use of force.[66] Thus, when José Santo Zelaya's Nicaraguan government executed two Americans for joining a revolutionary army in 1909, Knox broke diplomatic relations, gave "the revolution strong moral support," and tolerated an American naval interposition favoring the rebels in a decisive battle.[67] He then negotiated a treaty with the victorious revolutionaries led by Adolfo Díaz, providing for American control of the customs service and an American loan. The United States Senate refused ratification, but Knox and a group of bankers simply acted ad interim without the authorization of a treaty. In September, 1912, the Administration ordered the Marines into battle alongside Díaz's troops. After tipping the scales against the newest revolutionary army, the leathernecks returned home, leaving one hundred behind as a legation guard in Managua.

The Marines could prevent a coup d'état, but they could not easily put Díaz's house in fiscal order. Although critical of Taft's "dollar diplomacy," Bryan in the spring of 1913 dusted off a shelved draft treaty granting the United States a canal option in Nicaragua in exchange for three million dollars. Bryan hoped that this monetary prospect would "give sufficient encouragement" to American bankers to lend Díaz more money.[68] The secretary also added a clause similar to the Platt Amendment before sending the Bryan-Chamorro Treaty to the Senate. The upper house balked at this extension of American commitments and, to gain approval, the Wilson Administration had to delete the right of intervention. Ratification in February, 1916, did help to shore up Nicaragua's finances. The treaty also insured that European powers could not gain naval bases in the Gulf of Fonseca, and to make that point stick, Wilson ordered United States warships to cruise offshore during the 1916 Nicaraguan presidential campaign. Although nominally independent, Nicaragua remained a United States protectorate until 1933.

Meddling in Mexico

Mexico changed governments with uncharacteristic frequency after the outbreak of revolution in 1910. In 1911 Francisco I. Madero toppled Porfirio Díaz, the aged dictator who had maintained order, personal power, and a healthy environment for American investments since the late 1870s. United States citizens owned over 40 percent of Mexico's property and thus the Mexican Revolution was tinged with an anti-American bias. President Taft grew angry with the chaos that threatened American lives and property, but he determined to "sit tight on the lid and it will take a good deal to pry me off."[69] In February, 1913, United States Ambassador Henry Lane Wilson encouraged one of Madero's trusted generals, Victoriano Huerta, to overthrow the revolutionary nationalist. Indeed, Huerta had Madero shot and then set about to consolidate his own power. The Taft Administration prepared to recognize Huerta's government in return for a settlement of claims against Mexico. But after Huerta requested formal oaths of allegiance from Mexican state governors, one of them, Venustiano Carranza, took up arms and led the "Constitutionalist" revolt on February 26. Americans and their property were caught in the crossfire. Just before leaving office, Taft recoiled from recognition of Huerta's government, insisting that it first punish the "murderers of American citizens" and "put an end to the discriminations against American interests."[70]

Woodrow Wilson seemed to worry less about the large private American investment of one billion dollars. He redefined American recognition policy, requiring governments to meet a test of morality. Referring to Mexico, he said he would not recognize a "government of butchers."[71] Despising Huerta's treachery, Wilson denounced the Mexican as a "diverting brute! . . . seldom sober and always impossible."[72] Unlike Ambassador Wilson, who advocated recognition of Huerta to protect American financial and commercial interests, the President remarked that he himself was "not the servant of those who wish to enhance the value of their Mexican investments."[73] In July, 1913, he had the ambassador recalled; a month later Henry Lane Wilson was dismissed from the diplomatic corps. Thereafter the President treated with Mexico through special emissaries, only one of whom spoke fluent Spanish. None was intimately familiar with Mexico and all were chosen because of earlier friendships with the President or Secretary Bryan.

On August 8, 1913, one of these representatives, John Lind, arrived in Mexico City, after landing on Mexican soil from an American warship. A rabid anti-Catholic and former governor of Minnesota without diplomatic experience, Lind delivered Wilson's plan of "counsel and assistance." The American President wanted an armistice between Huerta's federalist troops and all revolutionary groups, "an early and free election," and Huerta's promise not to run for president. In exchange, the United States pledged recognition and aid to "the administration chosen and set up . . . in the way and on the conditions suggested." With sublime arrogance, Woodrow Wilson wondered, "can Mexico give the civilized world a satisfactory reason for rejecting our good offices?"[74] The Mexican minister of foreign relations thought he could. Already annoyed that Lind had arrived on a warship and held no formal diplomatic rank, Federico Gamboa issued a scathing reply on August 26, excoriating Wilson's "counsels and advice (let us call them thus)." Adherence to American dictates would mean that "all the future elections for president would be submitted to the veto of any President of the United States of America," and no government of Mexico would ever perpetrate "such an enormity" upon its people.[75] After this snub, Woodrow Wilson announced a restrained policy of "watchful waiting," clamped an embargo on arms to Mexico, and advised Americans to leave that country.[76]

Undeterred, Huerta in October dissolved an unruly legislature, arrested its members, and held a special election, which returned an entirely submissive congress ready to extend his presidency indefinitely. Wilson then turned to Carranza. He sent a personal representative to the revolutionary chief's headquarters in northern Mexico with the same proposal Huerta's foreign minister had rejected in August. Carranza proved ardently nationalistic as well as revolutionary. He contemptuously rejected Wilsonian mediation in the civil war and refused any solution short of his own triumph. Thoroughly isolated himself, Wilson on November 24 issued a circular note to the other powers informing them of his

Woodrow Wilson (1856–1924). The twenty-eighth President was proud of his "missionary diplomacy" because he believed that "every nation needs to be drawn into the tutelage of America." Latin Americans, however, resisted his paternalism, just as they had resisted Roosevelt's "big stick" and Taft's "dollar diplomacy." (U.S. Signal Corps, National Archives)

policy "to isolate General Huerta entirely; to cut him off from foreign sympathy . . . and so to force him out." But if political and economic pressure failed to induce Huerta's retirement, "it will become the duty of the United States to use less peaceful means to put him out."[77]

Most European powers had recognized Huerta and disapproved of Wilson's indignant opposition to him. The nation most deeply affected was Great Britain, whose capital investments in Mexico were second only to those of the United States. Also, the Royal Navy relied on Mexican oil as a backup to Middle Eastern sources. It took the British Foreign Office several months to realize that Wilson was serious about deposing Huerta. One senior official concluded darkly, "the United States cherish very sinister designs toward Mexico and desire that a condition of complete anarchy should supervene."[78] For London, however, the growing menace of Germany made American goodwill absolutely essential. In the event of conflict, England would need American war materiel. The Foreign Office therefore notified Huerta that it could not support him against the United States, advised him to retire as president, and recalled the British minister because of American antipathy toward him—all the while believing American views were "most impractical and unreasonable."[79]

With British compliance assured, Wilson acted. On February 1, 1914, he lifted the arms embargo, permitting large quantities of arms to flow to both factions. As Carranza's resupplied forces pushed south, the President sent American naval vessels to the busy port of Veracruz and the oil-producing town of Tampico, both on the Gulf of Mexico. On April 9, at Tampico, Huerta's inexperienced federal troops arrested several American sailors loading gasoline aboard a whaleboat docked provocatively near their forward outpost. The Mexican colonel in charge quickly disavowed the arrest, freed the sailors, and apologized orally. This redress failed to appease the hotheaded commander of the American squadron at Tampico, Rear Admiral Henry T. Mayo. He demanded a formal written apology and a twenty-one-gun salute to the American flag, because "taking men from a boat flying the American flag is a hostile act, not to be excused."[80] Wilson immediately warned the Mexican government "that unless the guilty persons are promptly punished consequences of [the] gravest sort might ensue." To reporters he bluntly said, "the salute will be fired."[81] He soon decided to use Huerta's rejection of the Mayo ultimatum as justification for military intervention designed to humiliate the Mexican leader and drive him from power. In the early afternoon of April 20 Wilson requested congressional approval to use armed force "to obtain from General Huerta and his adherents the fullest recognition of the rights and dignity of the United States."[82] Meanwhile, Secretary of the Navy Josephus Daniels had learned of the imminent arrival at Veracruz of a German-owned steamer, the *Ypiranga,* carrying two hundred machine guns and over fifteen million cartridges. The United States could not allow these arms to reach Huerta on the eve of American military intervention. Thus Daniels ordered the Navy to interdict the shipment by seizing the customs house at Veracruz.

On April 21, 1914, eight hundred American sailors and Marines landed. Although most of Huerta's federal troops withdrew under orders from the Ministry of War, a local federalist liberated prisoners from city jails and armed them to resist the Americans. These desperadoes and other irregulars fought in the streets and sniped from hiding places so tenaciously that four Americans were killed and twenty were wounded on the first day alone. Nineteen Americans and several hundred Mexicans died before the fighting stopped. Wilson was stunned by the bloody turn of events. To one observer, the shaken President appeared "preternaturally pale, almost parchmenty," and to his personal physician Wilson moaned, "the thought haunts me that it was I who ordered those young men to their deaths."[83] Carranza added an angry rebuke, warning Wilson that the invasion could "drag us into an unequal war . . . which until today we have desired to avoid."[84] Newspaper editorials in the United States and abroad roundly denounced the aggression. Apparently chastened, Wilson accepted mediation when proposed by Argentina, Brazil, and Chile (the ABC powers) on April 25.

A month later, representatives of the United States, Huerta, and the ABC powers met on the Canadian side of Niagara Falls. From the outset, Wilson and Carranza doomed the mediation by their intransigence. The American President refused to allow his delegates to discuss the evacuation of Veracruz or Tampico, a major reason for convening the conference. He sought instead "the entire elimination of General Huerta" and creation of a provisional government under the Constitutionalists.[85] But Carranza indignantly refused to attend any foreign meeting dealing with Mexico's internal affairs. By early June the deadlock was complete, and one newspaper editor sarcastically proposed: "Why should not Abyssinia, Servia, and Senegabia—the A.S.S. powers—tender their good offices? Send out the SOS for the A.S.S."[86] On July 2 the hapless mediators adjourned; two weeks later Huerta fled to Europe, and on August 20 a triumphant Carranza paraded before enthusiastic throngs in Mexico City.

The Constitutionalist triumph was short-lived. One of Carranza's northern generals, Francisco (Pancho) Villa, soon broke from the ranks, marched south, and in December occupied Mexico City. Villa, a cunningly intelligent and dedicated revolutionary, initially showed restraint toward Americans and seemed to approve President Wilson's Mexican policies, including the intervention at Veracruz. Wilson persuaded himself that "General Villa certainly seems capable of some good things and often shows susceptibility of the best influences," and encouraged him by refusing to recognize Carranza's government.[87] To avoid danger of a military clash with any Mexican faction, Wilson withdrew all American troops from Veracruz on November 23, 1914. Once again, Wilson watched and waited, thereby stimulating continued disorder in Mexico with his refusal to recognize the legitimacy of its government.

Mexican-American relations remained tense during the first months of 1915. Carranza's forces gradually drove Villa north, but in the process Mexico City became a no-man's-land, with bread riots and starvation threatening its inhabitants, including 2,500 Americans and 23,000 other foreign residents. Wilson gave some thought to relieving the city by force, perhaps with Pan American cooperation, but deteriorating German-American relations preoccupied him, especially after a German U-boat torpedoed the *Lusitania* in May. Resigned to failure in Mexico, Wilson seemed to repudiate all further interference in Mexican affairs: "Carranza will somehow have to be digested."[88] Two months later the United States extended partial, or de facto, recognition to the Constitutionalist government and permitted munitions exports, while embargoing arms to the Constitutionalists' enemies.

Convinced that Wilson and Carranza planned to make Mexico a protectorate of the United States, Villa denounced *Carranzistas* as "vassals" and prepared to show Americans that "Mexico is a land for the free and a tomb for thrones, crowns, and

Pancho Villa (1878–1923). The colorful Mexican rebel bedeviled both Mexico and the United States. His daring raid on an American town was shrewdly calculated to outrage President Wilson, whom he mocked as "an evangelizing professor of philosophy who is destroying the independence of a friendly people." (Library of Congress)

Uncle Sam Shooting Dice with Carranza. The Mexican leader tells a grudging Uncle Sam in 1917 to put his dice (army) back in the box. (*Washington Evening Star,* Library of Congress)

traitors."[89] In the predawn hours of March 9, 1916, Villa led a band of *Villistas* across the border and tore into Columbus, New Mexico, initiating a bloody battle that left seventeen Americans and more than a hundred Mexicans dead. Within hours of the tragedy, Wilson unleashed the United States Army against Villa. General John J. "Black Jack" Pershing commanded a Punitive Expedition, eventually totaling almost 7,000 men, which reached 350 miles into Mexico in a vain search for Pancho Villa. A clash with Carranza's forces in August occurred instead.

Carranza kept up drumfire pressure for American withdrawal, but Wilson hesitated for fear of appearing weak during a presidential election year. When United States participation in the European war finally became inescapable, Wilson disengaged from Mexico. On January 28, 1917, three days before Ambassador Johann von Bernstorff notified Secretary of State Lansing of Germany's resumption of unrestricted submarine warfare, Secretary of War Newton D. Baker announced that Pershing's troops were marching home. The last American soldier left Mexico on February 5. In late February, the secret Zimmermann telegram proposing an anti-American alliance between Germany, Japan, and Mexico came into the hands of the State Department, courtesy of British intelligence. This dire German ploy accelerated Wilson's movement toward full diplomatic relations with Carranza's government. The United States extended de jure recognition on August 31, 1917, in order to insure Mexican neutrality during the fight against

Germany. Thus, after four futile years, Wilson had given up on his haughty attempt to tell the Mexicans how to run their own affairs.

The Open Door and Dollar Diplomacy in East Asia

Telling Asians how to run their affairs proved even more difficult. Secretary of State John Hay's endorsement of Chinese political and administrative integrity in the Open Door Note of July, 1900, did not prevent the further emasculation of China. During the Boxer Rebellion Russia stationed 175,000 troops in Manchuria and demanded exclusive rights from China, including a commercial monopoly. President Roosevelt and Hay could do little to stop this infringement of China's sovereignty. The United States, they said, had "always recognized the exceptional position of Russia" in Manchuria and had merely sought the commercial freedom "guaranteed to us by . . . the whole civilized world."[90] Washington retreated from the Open Door Circular of 1900 because Roosevelt realized that the American people would not fight for nebulous principles of Chinese integrity in Manchuria, an area considered strategically remote and economically inconsequential. He understood the futility of trying, in historian Akira Iriye's words, "to play the role of an Asian power without military power."[91]

Japan viewed the question quite differently. Russia blocked Japanese economic expansion into Manchuria, posed a potential naval menace, and endangered the Japanese position in Korea. Tokyo covered its flanks with an Anglo-Japanese Alliance in 1902, opened negotiations aimed at explicit Russian recognition of nominal Chinese governance over Manchuria, and prepared for war. On February 8, 1904, the Japanese Navy suddenly captured headlines when it destroyed Russia's Far Eastern Fleet in a surprise attack at Port Arthur. At first Roosevelt cheered privately, "for Japan is playing our game," but as the enormity of Japanese victories became apparent he began to hope for peace "on terms which will not mean the creation of either a yellow peril or a Slav peril."[92] By the spring of 1905 Japanese soldiers had triumphed at Mukden, where Russia lost 97,000 men, and the navy had sunk the Russian Baltic Fleet in the straits of Tsushima. Still, the imperial treasury was drained and the army stretched thin. On May 31, Minister Kogoro Takahira requested Roosevelt, "on his own motion and initiative," to invite Russia and Japan to negotiate a peace treaty.[93]

Seizing the opportunity to balance the powers in order to protect America's territorial and commercial interests in the Pacific and Asia, the President invited Japanese and Russian representatives to meet at Portsmouth, New Hampshire on August 9, 1905. The Japanese delegates demanded Russia's leasehold on the Liaodong Peninsula and the railroad running from Harbin to Port Arthur, evacuation of Russian troops from Manchuria, and complete freedom of action for Japan in Korea. The Russians quickly conceded these points, but rejected additional Japanese requests for a monetary indemnity and cession of the island of Sakhalin. With negotiations deadlocked, Roosevelt telegraphed Tsar Nicholas II proposing division of Sakhalin between the belligerents and agreement "in principle" upon an indemnity. The Tsar agreed to partition the island but refused any payment. Needing peace more than money, Japan yielded on August 29.

The Roosevelt Administration's search for equipoise in East Asia neither began nor ended at Portsmouth. As early as March, 1904, TR had conceded to Japan a relationship with Korea "just like we have with Cuba."[94] Secretary of War Taft reaffirmed the concession during a discussion with Prime Minister Taro Katsura on July 27, 1905. In the Taft-Katsura "agreed memorandum of conversation," the Prime Minister also emphatically denied any Japanese designs on the Philippine Islands.[95] A year later southern Manchuria was reopened to foreign and American trade, although the Japanese systematically discouraged foreign capital investments.

This artful balancing of interests augured well for a continuation of traditional Japanese-American cordiality, until a local dispute in California abruptly undercut Rooseveltian diplomacy. On October 11, 1906, the San Francisco School Board created a special "Oriental Public School" for all Japanese, Chinese and Korean children. Japan immediately protested this racial discrimination against its citizens, and Theodore Roosevelt denounced the "infernal fools in California" whose exclusion of Japanese from all other public schools constituted "a confession of inferiority in our civilization."[96] At one point he wrote that the "feeling on the Pacific slope . . . is as foolish as if conceived by the mind of a Hottentot."[97] Yet there was little he constitutionally could do, other than rail against the recalcitrant school board, apply political pressure to the California legislature to prevent statewide discriminatory measures, and propose congressional legislation to naturalize Japanese residing permanently in the United States. The public outburst against naturalization finally convinced Roosevelt that he had seriously underestimated the depth of "genuine race feeling" throughout the United States, especially in California.[98] Always the political realist, Roosevelt accepted what he personally disliked and sought accommodation with Japan. By March, 1907, he had contrived a "Gentlemen's Agreement" with Tokyo sharply restricting Japanese immigration.

Two months later anti-Japanese riots and yellow journalistic agitation by what Secretary Root called the "leprous vampires" of San Francisco confirmed Roosevelt's apprehensions that local disturbances in California would create further crises with Japan.[99] The President shrewdly pressed for more battleships and fortification of Hawaii and the vulnerable Philippines, now America's "heel of Achilles," so that the United States would "be ready for anything that comes."[100] He also dramatized the importance of a strong navy to Congress and Japan by ordering the battle fleet on a voyage to the Pacific and around the world. This "good will cruise" by the "sixteen messengers of peace" netted two goals for Roosevelt.[101] In the spring of 1908 Congress endorsed a policy of building two battleships per year, and Ambassador Takahira invited the "Great White Fleet" to Tokyo, where it received a rousing popular reception. On the day the ships sailed from Tokyo Bay, Takahira received instructions to seek an agreement with the United States recognizing the Pacific Ocean as an open avenue of trade, pledging the integrity of Japanese and American insular possessions in the Pacific, supporting the status quo, and promising equal opportunity in China. After extensive refinement of rhetoric, these concepts were promulgated as the Root-Takahira declaration of policy on November 30, 1908. Japanese-American relations appeared ready for a period of mature harmony premised on mutual understanding of one another's national interests.

The new epoch did not materialize. William Howard Taft and Philander C. Knox chose to champion the "Open Door" and Chinese nationalism, thereby threatening Japan. The first explosion of twentieth-century Chinese nationalism had occurred in 1900, when the Boxers challenged both the Manchus and the Western powers exploiting the old dynasty. Angry Chinese patriots thereafter decried American participation in the suppression of the uprising, the concurrent bloody extirpation of Aguinaldo's Filipino partisans, and a racist 1904 act of Congress permanently barring Chinese immigration into the United States and its territories. Chinese nationalists inspired a short-lived boycott of American goods in 1905 and official revocation of a railroad franchise held by financier J. P. Morgan. Roosevelt explained to the financial baron his interest in seeing American commercial interests prosper in the Orient, but he restricted his diplomatic initiatives in East Asia to matters directly touching Japan.

Not everyone shared Roosevelt's fixation on Japan. As early as 1905 Secretary of War Taft dreamed about the American share of "one of the greatest commercial prizes of the world," the China market.[102] During a trip to East Asia in 1905, Taft met the impressive, intensely anti-Japanese American Consul General in Mukden, Willard Straight. Two years later Straight proposed the creation of a Manchurian bank, to be financed by the American railroad magnate E. H. Harriman, only to have the economic panic of 1907 dash all hopes for subsidizing the Chinese administration of Manchuria. When Wall Street revived in 1908, Straight was

"**Jumping on Your Uncle Samuel.**" Chinese nationalists, angered over American immigration restrictions, retaliated with a boycott of American products, trampling Uncle Sam. (*Philadelphia Inquirer,* in *Literary Digest,* 1906)

recalled to advise New York financiers on the exploitation of Manchuria. He arrived in time to condemn the Root-Takahira agreement as "a terrible diplomatic blunder," because it seemed to recognize Japan's exploitative position in Manchuria.[103] Under Taft, Straight and the State Department quickly inspired several New York banks to form a combination, headed by J. P. Morgan, to serve as the official agency of American railroad investment in China. As acting chief of the department's new Far Eastern Division, Straight instructed Minister William W. Rockhill in Beijing to demand admission of the American bankers into a European banking consortium undertaking construction of the Huguang Railway running southwest from Hankou. Having thus set up an American financial challenge in both Manchuria and China proper, Straight resigned from the State Department to become the Morgan group's roving representative.

Secretary of State Knox continued Straight's policy of injecting American capital into China and Manchuria. In November, 1909, Knox proposed to Britain the neutralization of Manchurian railroads through a large international loan to China for the purchase of the lines. Britain, however, joined both Japan and Russia to reject the neutralization proposal in January, 1910. "Instead of dividing Russia and Japan, and opening the door to American financial exploitation of Manchuria," historian A. Whitney Griswold has observed of Knox, "he had, as it were, nailed that door closed with himself on the outside."[104]

Although international resistance had shattered their Manchurian policy, Knox and Taft continued to seek American entrée to the British, French, and German consortium negotiating the Huguang loan. They made persistent representations at the Court of St. James's, and Taft sent an extraordinary personal message to the Regent of China insisting upon "equal participation by American capital in the present railway loan."[105] At length, on November 10, 1910, a quadruple agreement expanded the consortium to include the American bankers, and the loan was floated the following June. But the Chinese Revolution of 1911, sparked in part by this new intrusion upon China's autonomy, delayed any actual railroad construction until 1913. "'Dollar' diplomacy," Willard Straight ruefully admitted, "made no friends in the Hukuang matter."[106]

This stringent assessment by one of dollar diplomacy's earliest advocates failed to dissuade Knox from coming to the financial aid of Yuan Shikai, the dominant leader of the 1911 revolution. Yüan asserted his power ruthlessly, but American missionaries overlooked his faults because he promised religious toleration. They saw in his new republic "the coming of the larger civilization of men which draws no national boundaries and which is controlled by good will. Jesus called it the Kingdom of God."[107] This "wishful thinking," as Akira Iriye describes it, reinforced the Taft Administration's pro-China orientation.[108] When Yüan sought dollars to bolster his nascent republic, Knox urged expansion of the four-power consortium to include Japan and Russia, whom he now thought might be restrained or co-opted by the others. Instead, Tokyo and St. Petersburg stipulated further erosion of Chinese sovereignty over Manchuria and Mongolia as the price for their participation. London and Paris backed them, but Beijing resisted. Britain, France, Germany, and the United States then attempted to extort concessions from stubborn China by withholding diplomatic recognition throughout 1912.

Within days of Woodrow Wilson's inauguration, Straight and other representatives of the American banking group called the new President's attention to the convoluted result of dollar diplomacy in China. Wilson and Secretary Bryan at

William Howard Taft (1857–1930).
Ohioan, Yale graduate, lawyer, and
judge, the good-natured and overweight
Taft became civil governor of the Philippines in 1901, served as secretary of
war (1904–1908), and succeeded
Roosevelt to the presidency. Taft characterized his own administration's policy
"as substituting dollars for bullets," a
pithy explanation of dollar diplomacy.
(Library of Congress)

once perceived the infringement on Chinese sovereignty inherent in the proposed
six-power loan, and the President repudiated American participation in the
international consortium on March 18, 1913. Failure to cancel the loan, Wilson
believed, would have cost the United States "the proud position . . . secured when
Secretary Hay stood for the open door in China after the Boxer Uprising." Because
he felt "so keenly the desire to help China," he extended diplomatic recognition to
the struggling republic on May 2.[109] After less than two months in office Wilson
had renewed America's commitment to the political integrity of China, a goal
pragmatically abandoned by Roosevelt, unsuccessfully resuscitated by Taft, and
consistently opposed by Japan.

Events in California shortly proved that, despite his moralistic disdain for dollar
diplomacy, Wilson's disregard for Japan's sensibilities made his Far Eastern policy
resemble Taft's more than Roosevelt's. In April, 1913, Democratic and Progressive
politicians placed before the California legislature a bill denying residents "ineligible to citizenship" the right to own land. The measure struck directly at the 50,000
Japanese living in California, whose exceptional agricultural productivity had
raised fears that they were, in the words of Governor Hiram Johnson, "driving the

root of their civilization deep into California soil."[110] Racist passion erupted in California. One farmer pointed out that his neighbors were actually a Japanese man and a white woman with an interracial baby: "What is that baby? It isn't a Japanese. It isn't white. It is a germ of the mightiest problem that ever faced this state; a problem that will make the black problem of the South look white."[111] Basically sharing the Californians' anti-Japanese prejudices, and philosophically sensitive to states' rights, Wilson reacted cautiously. He urged restraint upon the California government, sent Bryan to Sacramento to beg for a euphemistic statute, and publicly discounted the "criminal possibility" of war when jingoes in Japan and the United States beat the drums.[112] But the California legislature passed the offensive bill on May 3, 1913, and when Japan protested strongly against the "unfair and intentionally racially discriminatory" measure, Wilson and Bryan took refuge in the legalistic defense that one state's legislation did not constitute a "national discriminatory policy."[113]

Wilson's antipathy toward Japan reappeared during the First World War. In the fall of 1914 Japan declared war on Germany, seized the German Pacific islands north of the equator, and swept across China's Shandong Peninsula to capture the German leasehold of Jiaozhou. Tokyo immediately followed this grab with the Twenty-One Demands of January 18, 1915, by which it insisted upon a virtual protectorate over all of China. Stout resistance by Beijing resulted in amelioration of the harshest exactions, but Japan emerged with extensive new political and economic rights in Shandong, southern Manchuria, and Mongolia. Preoccupied with Mexico, the British blockade, and the *Lusitania* crisis, the Wilson Administration limited its reaction to Secretary Bryan's caveat of May 11, 1915, refusing to recognize "any agreement . . . impairing the treaty rights of the United States and its citizens in China, the political or territorial integrity of the Republic of China, or . . . the open door policy."[114]

Wilson's nonrecognition policy was undermined, however, by secret treaties in which the European Allies promised to support Japan's conquests at the peace conference. Diplomatically isolated, the United States sought recourse in ambiguity. In an agreement with Viscount Kikujiro Ishii, signed November 2, 1917, Secretary Lansing admitted that "territorial propinquity creates special relationships between countries, and consequently . . . Japan has special interests in China," while Ishii pledged his nation's dedication to the Open Door and integrity of China.[115] Simultaneously, the Wilson Administration revived the international banking consortium as a means of checking further unilateral Japanese economic penetration of China proper. Once again, however, as in 1912, Britain, France, and the United States ultimately had to exclude the consortium from Manchuria as the price of Japanese participation. The wheel had turned full circle for Wilson. Like Taft before him, his attempt to succor Chinese independence had been thwarted by Japan.

The Anglo-American Rapprochement

After the Venezuelan crisis of 1895, London and Washington sought closer relations, encouraging Theodore Roosevelt to conclude that "together . . . the two branches of the Anglo-Saxon race . . . can whip the world." Indeed, "I think the twentieth century will still be the century of the men who speak English."[116] But

TR's chauvinistic prediction first had to overcome serious strains in Anglo-American relations. Control of the isthmian canal ranked high as a point of contention. In December, 1898, President McKinley directed Secretary Hay to negotiate modification of the Clayton-Bulwer Treaty (1850), which forbade unilateral construction, operation, or fortification of a canal in Central America. For almost a year negotiations foundered on Ambassador Pauncefote's insistence that the United States make concessions along the ill-defined boundary of the Alaskan panhandle, in exchange for British compromises on the canal. At length, made painfully aware of their diplomatic isolation during the Boer War, and apprehensive of unilateral congressional abrogation of the Clayton-Bulwer Treaty, the British yielded and signed the first Hay-Pauncefote Treaty on February 5, 1900. The United States would now be permitted to construct and operate a canal, but one that was neutralized and not fortified.

Overcoming a self-proclaimed, if dubious, reluctance "to meddle in National Affairs," then New York Governor Theodore Roosevelt campaigned against the Hay-Pauncefote Treaty from the governor's mansion in Albany. Only a week after the agreement had been signed, Roosevelt argued publicly that complete American control of the canal was "vital, from the standpoint of our sea power, no less than from the standpoint of the Monroe Doctrine."[117] When the aggrieved Hay protested, Roosevelt praised him as "the greatest Secretary of State I have seen in my time," but advised him to "drop the treaty and push through a bill to build *and fortify* our own canal."[118] He then urged Senator Henry Cabot Lodge and other exponents of a "large policy" to amend the treaty so as to allow fortification and exclusive United States regulation of a canal.

Lodge and his allies succeeded in amending the Hay-Pauncefote Treaty as Roosevelt urged, but in March of 1901 Great Britain understandably rejected the butchered pact, forcing Pauncefote and Hay to reopen negotiations. This time the secretary of state worked closely with Lodge to forestall further embarrassing senatorial opposition, while Roosevelt, first as vice-president and then as president, lectured the British on the firm American resolve to build, fortify, and control the canal. Britain conceded every point in order to win American friendship, and a second Hay-Pauncefote Treaty was signed on November 18, 1901. President Roosevelt and his sympathizers in the Senate rushed it to ratification a month later. This British capitulation constituted a very significant element of what one historian has called the "great rapprochement" marking Anglo-American relations between 1895 and 1914.[119]

Another obstacle to entente was overcome almost simultaneously and for the same reasons. After the discovery of gold along the Klondike in 1896, Canadian politicians revived an old boundary dispute with the Americans. The Anglo-Russian Treaty of 1825, which the United States inherited with Alaska in 1867, had left vague the territorial demarcation between the Alaskan panhandle and British North America. Advancing a maximum claim, Canada sought to run the line along the mouths of the numerous inlets reaching inland from the Pacific Ocean. The United States stood for a more easterly isogram at the water's high tide. Ottawa's interpretation would figuratively drive Americans into the sea, and Washington's claim would literally set the United States astride the avenues of approach to a suddenly valuable part of Canada. London initially supported the extreme Canadian claim by linking this issue to abrogation of the Clayton-Bulwer Treaty, hoping that the United States would sacrifice Alaskan territory in exchange for enlarged rights in Central America. Shrill European denunciations of Britain's painful suppression of the Boers in South Africa, coupled with benevolent official American silence on the same topic, persuaded Sir Julian Pauncefote to advocate separation of the two disputes in early 1900. "America seems to be our only friend just now," he commented to Foreign Secretary Lansdowne, "and it would be unfortunate to quarrel with her."[120] Disentanglement followed, but the Alaskan boundary dispute remained unresolved when Theodore Roosevelt entered the White House.

Declining arbitration by a third party on the grounds that the "manifestly clear and unanswerable" claim of the United States constituted a case where the "nation had no business to arbitrate," the President sent 800 soldiers to Alaska to impress England.[121] London hesitated, but Washington's criticism of British collaboration

John Bull in Need of Friends. Battered by criticism over its war against the Boers in South Africa and challenged by a rising Germany, Great Britain could have used some friends in the early twentieth century. London turned to the United States for one. (*Des Moines Leader* in *Literary Digest,* 1901)

with Germany in chastising Venezuela soon impelled the Foreign Office to eliminate all Anglo-American irritants. On January 24, 1903, Britain agreed to an American proposal for a mixed boundary commission composed of six "impartial jurists of repute," three from each side.[122] Roosevelt took no chances. He appointed Senator Lodge and Secretary Root, hardly disinterested judges, to the commission. He informed them that the 1825 treaty "was undoubtedly intended to cut off England, which owned the Hinterland, from access to the sea," and informally warned London he would run the line himself if the commissioners failed to agree.[123] After persuasion by Prime Minister Balfour, the British commissioner, Lord Chief Justice Alverstone, sided with the Americans, and on October 20, 1903, by a vote of four to two, the commission officially decided for the United States. Canada's claims had not been defeated because they lacked historical foundation. They had been sacrificed as unworthy impediments to improved Anglo-American relations.

Theodore Roosevelt later commented that the final definition "of the Alaskan boundary settled the last serious trouble between the British Empire and ourselves," an observation especially pertinent to Anglo-American policies in the western hemisphere.[124] In February, 1903, shortly after agreeing to the Alaskan commission, British leaders silenced trans-Atlantic criticism of the intervention in Venezuela by accepting international adjudication of the Anglo-German claims and publicly praising the Monroe Doctrine. A month later the British Ambassador, Sir Michael Herbert, half-jocularly admonished President Roosevelt to "be ready to police the whole American Continent" since the United States no longer would permit European nations to collect debts by force.[125] The Roosevelt Corollary therefore neither surprised nor displeased Great Britain, and the same was true of the denouement in Panama in 1903. London declined diplomatic assistance to embattled Colombia prior to its rejection of the Hay-Herrán Treaty, and British observers complacently watched the subsequent revolution lead to the Hay–Bunau-Varilla Treaty.

English acquiescence also characterized another Anglo-American settlement of Roosevelt's presidency, the North Atlantic fisheries dispute. Since 1782 American fishermen, especially those from Massachusetts, had insisted on retaining their pre-Revolutionary privileges along the coasts of Newfoundland. The modus vivendi of 1888, by which they had fished for several years, collapsed in 1905 when Newfoundland's Parliament placed restrictions on American fishing vessels. Senator Lodge cried for warships to protect his constituents' livelihood. To avoid a heated quarrel with Britain over a matter important largely to one state, Roosevelt proposed, and London accepted, arbitration at the Hague Tribunal. In 1910 the tribunal ruled that Britain could oversee fishing off Newfoundland if it established reasonable regulations, that a fisheries commission would hear cases disputing the definition of reasonableness, and that Americans could fish in large bays if they remained three miles from shore. This compromise defused the oldest dispute in American foreign relations and symbolized London's political withdrawal from the western hemisphere.

The naval retreat had occurred earlier, when the Admiralty abolished the North Atlantic station based at Halifax. After 1902 the Royal Navy patrolled the Caribbean only with an annual visit by a token squadron of cruisers. Admiral Sir John Fisher, who oversaw this historic retrenchment, wanted to concentrate his heavy ships in the English Channel and North Sea as monitors of the growing German Navy, but he acted on the dual premise that the United States was "a kindred state with whom we shall never have a parricidal war."[126]

Even the aggressive hemispheric diplomacy of Taft and Wilson did not undermine the Anglo-American rapprochement. Although Britain criticized dollar diplomacy in Latin America, the complaints, in the words of historian Bradford Perkins, "were sporadic and carping rather than a rising crescendo of calls for positive action."[127] Wilson's quixotic efforts to dislodge Huerta from the presidency of Mexico met with little, if any, sympathy in England, but Foreign Secretary Sir Edward Grey tersely laid to rest all talk of a challenge: "His Majesty's Government cannot with any prospect of success embark upon an active counterpolicy to that of the United States, or constitute themselves the champions of Mexico or any of these republics against the United States."[128] In reciprocation, Wilson eliminated the one potentially dangerous British grievance inherited from his predecessor. Late in the Taft Administration, Congress had enacted a measure exempting American intercoastal shippers from payment of tolls at the Panama Canal. British opinion unanimously condemned this shifting of canal maintenance costs to other users. Wilson soon decided that the law unjustly discriminated against foreign shipping, and in June, 1914, Congress revoked the preferential treatment.

In the geographic area of secondary interest to the United States, the Far East, the Anglo-American rapprochement proved less fruitful. London negotiated the alliance with Tokyo in 1902 as a makeweight against Russian pressure upon China and as a means of concentrating more British battleships in home waters. Japan's defeat of Russia in 1904–1905 eliminated the alliance's principal theoretical opponent and removed any serious barriers to Japanese expansionism. The British faced a dilemma. They tried to maintain an alliance now valuable against the mounting German threat without sacrificing the equally vital harmony with the United States, the major power alternately accepting and resisting Japanese expansion. The Taft-Katsura and Root-Takahira exchanges, seemingly exhibiting Washington's acceptance, therefore elicited favorable comment from the British Foreign Office. Secretary of State Knox's neutralization and loan schemes, on the other hand, encountered a mixture of polite discouragement and firm disapproval.

The First World War simply accentuated Anglo-American differences over Japan and China. Britain welcomed Japanese expulsion of Germany from its insular positions in the Pacific and on the Shandong Peninsula of China, and British imperial forces seized all German islands south of the equator. On February 16, 1917, the two allies signed an additional, and secret, treaty pledging reciprocal support for their new territorial claims at the postwar peace conference. This rock lay beneath the deceptively tranquil surface of the Anglo-American wartime coalition, ready to surface when the tides of war receded.

American Foreign Policy on the Eve of the "Great War"

Prior to the outbreak of the First World War, American policymakers largely adhered to the tradition of aloofness from continental European political and military affairs, as prescribed in Washington's Farewell Address and Jefferson's

Naval Arms Race. The vigorous international competition for large navies in the early twentieth century was foreboding. Disarmament talks at The Hague Conferences and arbitration treaties did not curb the arms buildup. Theodore Roosevelt's decision to send the "Great White Fleet" around the world in 1907–1908 may have encouraged both Japan and Germany to speed up their naval programs. (*Detroit News* in *Literary Digest,* 1904)

First Inaugural. Even Theodore Roosevelt, who appeared so impetuous, tampered only once with Europe's balance of power. In 1904 France acquiesced in British control of Egypt, in exchange for primacy in semi-independent Morocco. A year later, Germany decided to test the solidity of the new Anglo-French entente by challenging France's extension of power in Morocco. Speaking at Tangier, the Kaiser belligerently demanded a German political role in Morocco, which France at once refused. After a brief European war scare, in which Britain stood by her ally, Germany asked Roosevelt to induce France and England to convene a conference to settle Morocco's future. On the grounds that world peace was threatened, Roosevelt accepted the personal invitation only after assuring Paris that he was not acting on Berlin's behalf. During the conference, held in early 1906 at Algeciras, Spain, Roosevelt devised a compromise substantively favorable to Paris and persuaded the Kaiser to accept it. This political intervention isolated Germany and reinforced the Anglo-French entente, but it generated criticism at home. Roosevelt's successors made sure they did not violate the American policy of nonentanglement with Europe during the more ominous second Moroccan and Balkan crises preceding the "Great War."

Nonentanglement also doomed the sweeping arbitration treaties that Secretary of State Hay negotiated with several world powers. The Senate, always the jealous guardian of prerogative and aloofness, attached emasculating amendments, leading Roosevelt to withdraw the treaties because they now did "not in the smallest degree facilitate settlements by arbitration, [and] to make them would in no way further the cause of international peace."[129] After 1905 Secretary Root persuaded Roosevelt to accept watered-down bilateral arbitration treaties, and Secretary Bryan later negotiated a series of supplementary "cooling-off" treaties by which nations pledged to refrain from war during international investigations of serious disputes. None of these arrangements, however, effectively bound any of the signatories, and like the Permanent Court of Arbitration at The Hague, they represented a backwater in international diplomacy.

The mainstream of American foreign policy between 1900 and 1914 flowed through the Panama Canal. That momentous political, military, and technological achievement drew the United States physically into the Caribbean and Gulf of Mexico with unprecedented force. After ratification of the Hay–Bunau-Varilla Treaty, the United States became the unchallenged policeman of Central America. For Taft, the treaty "permits us to prevent revolutions" so that "we'll have no more."[130] In East Asia, American power was pale in comparison. The United States was in no position to challenge Japan or England, especially after the formation of the Anglo-Japanese Alliance in 1902 and the defeat of Russia in 1904–1905. As Roosevelt wrote Taft in 1910, the Open Door "completely disappears as soon as a powerful nation determines to disregard it."[131] Nor were American interests in Asia clearly discernible. The vulnerable Philippines needed protection, but diplomatic agreements were the only safeguards that even Theodore Roosevelt could devise, given the remoteness of the islands and congressional distaste for military spending. Beyond the Philippines, many Americans believed in what historian Paul Varg has called "the myth of the China market."[132] Straight, Taft, and Knox conceived of dollar diplomacy as a means of blocking Japanese expansion, sustaining Chinese independence, and stimulating American overseas investments and trade. Wilson's futile revival of the ill-fated consortium was largely a political act aimed at Japan. This persistent but ineffectual opposition to Japanese expansion constituted a most deleterious legacy. To the next generation it bequeathed war in the Pacific.

Another legacy of the 1900–1914 period was less measurable, but nevertheless a long-term consequence: American insensitivity to the nationalism of other peoples. The violent Filipino resistance to American domination, Cuban anger over the interventionist Platt Amendment, Colombian outrage over the "rape" of Panama, and Mexican rejection of Wilsonian meddling, bore witness to the depth of nationalistic sentiments. Like the European powers who were carving up Asia, Africa, and the Middle East, the United States was developing its empire and subjugating peoples and trampling on their sovereignty, especially in Latin America. With the exception of the Virgin Islands, purchased from Denmark for $25 million in 1917 to forestall any wartime German interest in seizing the Danish West Indies, the Latin American empire of the United States grew little from outright territorial aggrandizement. It was, instead, an informal empire administered by Marines and financial advisers who "came to democratize and uplift," as historian Lester Langley has written of the protectorates, "yet in the process they expressed their contempt for Caribbean politics, economic systems, and culture."[133] This North American chauvinism was equally characteristic of Roosevelt's "big stick," Taft's "dollar diplomacy," and Wilson's missionary zeal to remake flawed national characters.

The much heralded rapprochement between Britain and the United States also meant mutual respect for each other's empires. Roosevelt, for example, encouraged London to frustrate native aspirations for independence in India, while the British accepted the American suppression of the Filipinos and United States hegemony in Latin America. American leaders usually spoke favorably of independence for colonial peoples, but independence only after long-term education to make them "fit" and "civilized" enough to govern. In 1910 in Egypt, where Roosevelt applauded Britain's "great work for civilization," the ex-President even lectured restless Moslem nationalists about Christian respect for womanhood.[134]

This United States insensitivity to nationalism in the colonial world was evident express any "scurrilous libels" against America.[135] Newspapers were censored and was captured, Filipino resistance continued for years thereafter. From 1903 to 1914, for example, Artemio Ricarte harassed American military authorities with his hit-and-run tactics. Deported several times, he consistently refused to take an oath of allegiance to the United States. To silence less violent dissenters, the American colonial government imposed the Sedition Act of 1901, which made it unlawful to express any "scurrilous libels" against America.[135] Newspapers were censored and sometimes shut down. Recalcitrant dissidents were jailed. Some economic benefits, improvements in transportation and sanitation, and new educational facilities like the University of the Philippines (1908) accrued to the Filipinos, but American governors helped create an English-speaking, educated elite far removed from the mass of lower-class people. With American direction also came a misplaced pride in things "stateside"—a colonial mentality. Filipino history became "American" history. One Filipino critic wrote that "the history of our ancestors was taken up as if they were strange and foreign peoples who settled in these shores, with whom we had the most tenuous ties. We read about them as if we were tourists in a foreign land."[136]

In 1916, after years of Democratic party pledges, Congress passed and Wilson signed the Jones Act, promising Philippine independence, but setting no date. Thirty years later the United States would in fact relinquish the Philippines, gaining for itself the accolade from apologists of being a "good" imperialist, or—as historian Dexter Perkins has put it—an imperialist with an "uneasy conscience."[137] "Uneasy conscience" or not, Americans as imperialists behaved not unlike the European imperial warriors they so roundly condemned. Indeed, that phrase might better be applied to the American decision to intervene in the "Great War" of 1914–1919—an intervention which permitted the United States to extend further the foreign interests it had cultivated in the previous two decades.

Further Reading for the Period 1900–1914

For general studies of American foreign policy and leaders in this period, see "American Empire, 1898–1903," *Pacific Historical Review* (1979) (entire issue); William H. Becker, *Industry, Government, and Foreign Trade, 1893–1921* (1982); Barton J. Bernstein and Franklin A. Leib, "Progressive Republican Senators and American Imperialism, 1898–1916: A Reappraisal," *Mid-America* (1968); Paolo E. Coletta, *The Presidency of William Howard Taft* (1973) and *William Jennings Bryan* (1964–1969); John M. Cooper, Jr., "Progressivism and American Foreign Policy," *Mid-America* (1969); Norman A. Graebner, ed., *An Uncertain Tradition: American Secretaries of State in the Twentieth Century* (1961); Robert C. Hilderbrand, *Power and the People: Executive Management of Public Opinion in Foreign Affairs, 1897–1921* (1981); Philip C. Jessup, *Elihu Root* (1938); P. C. Kennedy, "LaFollette's Foreign Policy: From Imperialism to Anti-Imperialism," *Wisconsin Magazine of History* (1963); William Leuchtenberg, "Progressivism and Imperialism," *Mississippi Valley Historical Review* (1952); Ralph E. Minger, *William Howard Taft and United States Foreign Policy: The Apprenticeship Years, 1900–1908* (1975); John M. Mulder, *Woodrow Wilson: The Years of Preparation* (1978); Julius W. Pratt, *America's Colonial Experiment* (1950) and *Challenge and Reaction* (1967); Henry F. Pringle, *The Life and Times of William Howard Taft* (1939); Emily S. Rosenberg, *Spreading the American Dream: American Economic and Cultural Expansion, 1890–1945* (1982); Walter V. and Marie V. Scholes, *The Foreign Policies of the Taft Administration* (1970); E. Berkeley Tompkins, *Anti-Imperialism in the United States* (1970); Frank G. Vandiver, *Black Jack: The Life and Times of John J. Pershing* (1977); Richard H. Werking, *The Master Architects: Building the United States Foreign Service, 1890–1913* (1977); Rachel West, *The Department of State on the Eve of the First World War* (1978); and William C. Widenor, *Henry Cabot Lodge and the Search for an American Foreign Policy* (1980).

Theodore Roosevelt and his record in foreign policy are the subject of Howard K. Beale, *Theodore Roosevelt and the Rise of America to World Power* (1956); John M. Blum, *The Republican Roosevelt* (1954); David H. Burton, *Theodore Roosevelt: Confident Imperialist* (1968); Thomas G. Dyer, *Theodore Roosevelt and the Idea of Race* (1980); Raymond A. Esthus, *Theodore Roosevelt and the International Rivalries* (1970); William H. Harbaugh, *The Life and Times of Theodore Roosevelt* (1975); Frederick W. Marks, *Velvet on Iron: The Diplomacy of Theodore Roosevelt* (1979); and Henry F. Pringle, *Theodore Roosevelt* (1956).

United States relations with Latin America are examined in Jose A. Cabranes, *Citizenship and the American Empire* (1979) (on Puerto Rico); David Healy, *Gunboat Diplomacy in the Wilson Era: The U.S. Navy in Haiti, 1915–1916* (1976) and *The United States in Cuba, 1898–1902* (1963); James H. Hitchman, *Leonard Wood and Cuban Independence, 1898–1902* (1971); Warren G. Kneer, *Great Britain and the Caribbean, 1901–1913* (1975); Walter LaFeber, *The Panama Canal* (1978); Lester D. Langley, *Struggle for the American Mediterranean: United States–European Rivalry in the Gulf-Caribbean, 1776–1904* (1976) and *The United States and the Caribbean, 1900–1970* (1980); David McCullough, *The Path Between the Seas: The Creation of the Panama Canal, 1870–1914* (1977); Allan R. Millett, *The Politics of Intervention: The Military Occupation of Cuba, 1906–1909* (1968); Dwight C. Miner, *The Fight for the Panama Route* (1940); Dana Munro, *Intervention and Dollar Diplomacy* (1964); Dexter Perkins, *The Monroe Doctrine, 1867–1907* (1937); Whitney T. Perkins, *Constraint of Empire: The United States and Caribbean Intervention* (1981); and Hans Schmidt, *The United States Occupation of Haiti, 1915–1934* (1971).

Relations with Mexico are treated in Peter Calvert, *The Mexican Revolution, 1910–1914* (1968); Clarence C. Clendenen, *Blood on the Border: The United States Army and the Mexican Irregulars* (1969) and *The United States and Pancho Villa* (1961); Howard F. Cline, *The United States and Mexico* (1963); Jules Davids, *American Political and Economic Penetration of Mexico, 1877–1920* (1976); Mark T. Gilderhus, *Diplomacy and Revolution: U.S.–Mexican Relations Under Wilson and Carranza* (1977); Kenneth J. Grieb, *The United States and Huerta* (1969); Larry D. Hill, *Emissaries to a Revolution: Woodrow Wilson's Executive Agents in Mexico* (1973); Friedrich Katz, *The Secret War in Mexico: Europe, the United States, and the Mexican Revolution*

(1981); Robert E. Quirk, *An Affair of Honor: Woodrow Wilson and the Occupation of Veracruz* (1962); Ramon E. Ruiz, *The Great Rebellion: Mexico, 1905–1924* (1980); and Karl M. Schmitt, *Mexico and the United States, 1821–1973* (1974).

America's interaction with China and Asia in general is the subject of William R. Braisted, *The United States Navy in the Pacific, 1897–1909* (1958) and *1909–1922* (1971); Warren I. Cohen, *America's Response to China* (1980); Roy W. Curry, *Woodrow Wilson and Far Eastern Policy, 1913–1921* (1957); Raymond A. Esthus, "The Changing Concept of the Open Door, 1899–1910," *Mississippi Valley Historical Review* (1959); A. Whitney Griswold, *The Far Eastern Policy of the United States* (1938); Robert A. Hart, *The Great White Fleet* (1965); Akira Iriye, *Across the Pacific* (1967); Jerry Israel, *Progressivism and the Open Door: America and China, 1905–1921* (1971); Delber L. McKee, *Chinese Exclusion versus the Open Door Policy, 1900–1906* (1976); Noel H. Pugach, *Paul S. Reinsch: Open Door Diplomat in Action* (1979); Paul A. Varg, *The Making of a Myth: The United States and China, 1897–1912* (1968); and Charles Vevier, *The United States and China, 1906–1913* (1955).

Japanese-American relations can be studied in Burton F. Beers, *Vain Endeavor: Robert Lansing's Attempt to End the American-Japanese Rivalry* (1962); Raymond A. Esthus, *Theodore Roosevelt and Japan* (1966); Akira Iriye, *Pacific Estrangement: Japanese and American Expansion, 1897–1911* (1972); Charles E. Neu, *An Uncertain Friendship: Theodore Roosevelt and Japan, 1906–1909* (1967) and *The Troubled Encounter* (1975); and Eugene P. Trani, *The Treaty of Portsmouth* (1969).

For American colonial policy in the Philippines, see Glenn A. May, *Social Engineering in the Philippines* (1980); William J. Pomeroy, *American Neo-Colonialism: Its Emergence in the Philippines and Asia* (1970); Bonifacio S. Salamanca, *The Filipino Reaction to American Rule, 1901–1913* (1968); and Peter Stanley, *A Nation in the Making: The Philippines and the United States, 1899–1921* (1974).

The history of United States relations with Europe and Great Britain is discussed in A. E. Campbell, *Great Britain and the United States, 1895–1903* (1960); Charles S. Campbell, *Anglo-American Understanding, 1898–1903* (1957); Raymond A. Esthus, *Theodore Roosevelt and the International Rivalries* (1970); and Bradford Perkins, *The Great Rapprochement: England and the United States, 1895–1914* (1968).

Economic, racial, and military ingredients in American foreign policy are described in Paul P. Abrahams, *The Foreign Expansion of American Finance . . . , 1907–1921* (1976); Richard D. Challener, *Admirals, Generals, and American Foreign Policy, 1898–1914* (1973); Roger Daniels, *The Politics of Prejudice: The Anti-Japanese Movement in California and the Struggle for Japanese Exclusion* (1962); Rubin F. Weston, *Racism in United States Imperialism* (1972); and Mira Wilkins, *The Emergence of Multinational Enterprise: American Business Abroad from the Colonial Era to 1914* (1970).

The peace movement and the role of The Hague are discussed in Peter Brock, *Pacifism in the United States: From the Colonial Era to the First World War* (1968); Merle E. Curti, *Peace or War* (1936); Calvin Davis, *The United States and the First Hague Conference* (1962) and *The United States and the Second Hague Peace Conference* (1976); Charles DeBenedetti, *The Peace Reform in American History* (1980); Sondra R. Herman, *Eleven Against War* (1969); C. Roland Marchand, *The American Peace Movement and Social Reform, 1898–1918* (1973); and David S. Patterson, *Toward a Warless World: The Travail of the American Peace Movement, 1887–1914* (1976).

See also the General Bibliography and the following notes.

Notes to Chapter 7

1. This and previous quotations from U.S. Congress, *Diplomatic History of the Panama Canal*, Senate Document 474 (1914), pp. 345–363.

2. Elting E. Morison, ed., *The Letters of Theodore Roosevelt* (Cambridge: Harvard University Press, 1951–1954; 8 vols.), II, 1185–1187.

3. Quoted in Gerstle Mack, *The Land Divided* (New York: Alfred A. Knopf, 1944), p. 417.

4. Dwight C. Miner, *The Fight for the Panama Route* (New York: Columbia University Press, 1940), p. 75.

5. *Diplomatic History of the Canal,* p. 261.

6. Quoted in Miner, *Fight for the Panama Route,* p. 275.

7. Quoted in Henry F. Pringle, *Theodore Roosevelt* (New York: Harcourt, Brace, 1931), p. 311.

8. Quoted in Howard K. Beale, *Theodore Roosevelt and the Rise of America to World Power* (Baltimore: The Johns Hopkins Press, 1956), p. 33.

9. Quoted in David McCullough, *The Path Between the Seas* (New York: Simon and Schuster, 1977), p. 333.

10. *New York World,* June 14, 1903.

11. Quoted in Pringle, *Roosevelt,* p. 311.

12. Quoted in Tyler Dennett, *John Hay* (New York: Dodd, Mead, 1933), p. 377.

13. Quoted in Walter LaFeber, *The Panama Canal* (New York: Oxford University Press, 1978), p. 30.

14. James D. Richardson, ed., *A Compilation of the Messages and Papers of the Presidents, 1789–1897* (Washington, D.C.: Government Printing Office, 1896–1899; 10 vols.), IX, 6919–6923.

15. Quoted in LaFeber, *The Panama Canal,* p. 38.

16. *New York Times,* March 25, 1911.

17. William H. Harbaugh, *The Life and Times of Theodore Roosevelt* (New York: Oxford University Press, 1975; rev. ed.), p. 197.

18. Ronald H. Spector, *Professors of War: The Naval War College and the Development of the Naval Profession* (Newport, R.I.: Naval War College Press, 1977).

19. Quoted in Kenneth J. Hagan, "Alfred Thayer Mahan: Turning America Back to the Sea," in Frank Merli and Theodore Wilson, eds., *Makers of American Diplomacy* (New York: Charles Scribner's Sons, 1974), p. 298.

20. John M. Cooper, Jr., "Progressivism and American Foreign Policy: A Reconsideration," *Mid-America,* LI (October, 1969), 261.

21. Quoted in John Morton Blum, *The Republican Roosevelt* (New York: Atheneum, 1973 [1954]), p. 127.

22. Quoted in Beale, *Theodore Roosevelt,* p. 77 and G. Wallace Chessman, *Theodore Roosevelt and the Politics of Power* (Boston: Little, Brown, 1969), p. 70.

23. Quoted in Beale, *Theodore Roosevelt,* p. 140.

24. *Ibid.,* p. 13.

25. Quoted in Foster Rhea Dulles, "John Hay," in Norman A. Graebner, ed., *An Uncertain Tradition: American Secretaries of State in the Twentieth Century* (New York: McGraw-Hill, 1961), p. 24.

26. Quoted in Charles W. Toth, "Elihu Root," *ibid.,* p. 41.

27. Quoted in Richard W. Leopold, *Elihu Root and the Conservative Tradition* (Boston: Little, Brown, 1954), p. 50.

28. Quoted in David H. Burton, *Theodore Roosevelt: Confident Imperialist* (Philadelphia: University of Pennsylvania Press, 1968), p. 97, and *Congressional Record, XXXV* (December 3, 1901), 82–83.

29. Quoted in Ralph E. Minger, *William Howard Taft and United States Foreign Policy: The Apprenticeship Years, 1900–1908* (Urbana: University of Illinois Press, 1975), p. 179.

30. Quoted in Ray S. Baker, *Woodrow Wilson: Life and Letters* (Garden City, N.Y.: Doubleday, Doran, 1927–1939; 8 vols.), IV, 289.

31. Jerry Israel, "'For God, for China and for Yale'—The Open Door in Action," *American Historical Review, LXXV* (February, 1970), 807.

32. *Foreign Relations of the United States, 1898* (Washington, D.C.: Government Printing Office, 1901), pp. lxvi–lxvii.

33. Quoted in Philip C. Jessup, *Elihu Root* (New York: Dodd, Mead, 1938; 2 vols.), I, 286–287.

34. Quoted in David F. Healy, *The United States in Cuba, 1898–1902* (Madison: University of Wisconsin Press, 1963), p. 133.

35. *Congressional Record, XXXIV* (February 26, 1901), 3036.

36. Quoted in Healy, *United States in Cuba,* p. 177.

37. Quoted in Hermann Hagedorn, *Leonard Wood, A Biography* (New York: Harper and Brothers, 1931; 2 vols.), I, 362 and Healy, *United States in Cuba,* p. 178.

38. Quoted in Russell H. Fitzgibbon, *Cuba and the United States, 1900–1935* (New York: Russell & Russell, 1964 [1935]), p. 112.

39. Quoted in Allan R. Millett, *The Politics of Intervention* (Columbus: Ohio State University Press, 1968), p. 72.

40. Quoted in Burton, *Theodore Roosevelt,* p. 106.

41. Quoted in Millett, *Politics of Intervention,* p. 78.

42. Richardson, *Messages of the Presidents,* X, 7436–7437.

43. Quoted in Minger, *William Howard Taft,* p. 136.

44. Lawrence F. Abbott, ed., *The Letters of Archie Butt* (Garden City, N.Y.: Doubleday, Page, 1924), p. 325.

45. Fitzgibbon, *Cuba and the United States,* p. 145 and Millett, *Politics of Intervention,* p. 267.

46. Fred L. Israel, ed., *The State of the Union Messages of the Presidents, 1790–1966* (New York: Chelsea House, 1967; 3 vols.), II, 2038.

47. Morison, *Letters of Roosevelt,* III, 116.

48. *Ibid.,* IV, 1156.

49. *Literary Digest, XXV* (December 20, 1902), 823–824.

50. Quoted in Dexter Perkins, *The Monroe Doctrine, 1867–1907* (Baltimore: The Johns Hopkins Press, 1937), p. 358.

51. Quoted *ibid.,* p. 360.

52. Quoted *ibid.,* p. 420.

53. Quoted in Lloyd Gardner, "A Progressive Foreign Policy, 1900–1921," in William A. Williams, ed., *From Colony to Empire* (New York: John Wiley and Sons, 1972), p. 218.

54. Quoted in Perkins, *Monroe Doctrine,* p. 420.

55. Israel, *State of the Union Messages,* II, 2134.

56. Quoted in Jessup, *Root,* I, 471.

57. Elihu Root, *Latin America and the United States* (Cambridge: Harvard University Press, 1917), p. 275.

58. *Foreign Relations, 1912* (Washington, D.C.: Government Printing Office, 1919), p. 1091.

59. *Congressional Record, L* (November 3, 1913), 5845.

60. *Foreign Relations, 1913* (Washington, D.C.: Government Printing Office, 1920), p. 426.

61. Quoted in Dana G. Munro, *Intervention and Dollar Diplomacy in the Caribbean* (Princeton: Princeton University Press, 1964), p. 336.

62. Quoted in David F. Healy, *Gunboat Diplomacy in the Wilson Era* (Madison: University of Wisconsin Press, 1976), p. 109.

63. Quoted *ibid.,* p. 131.

64. *Ibid.,* p. 205.

65. Quoted in Munro, *Intervention and Dollar Diplomacy,* p. 155.

66. *Ibid.,* p. 160.

67. *Ibid.,* p. 181.

68. Quoted in Baker, *Wilson, IV,* 436.

69. Quoted in Paolo E. Coletta, *The Presidency of William Howard Taft* (Lawrence: University Press of Kansas, 1973), p. 176.

70. *Foreign Relations, 1912,* p. 846.

71. Quoted in Howard F. Cline, *The United States and Mexico* (New York: Atheneum, 1963; rev. ed.), p. 144.

72. Quoted in Arthur S. Link, *Wilson: The New Freedom* (Princeton: Princeton University Press, 1956), p. 360.

73. Quoted in Arthur S. Link, *Wilson: Confusions and Crises, 1915–1916* (Princeton: Princeton University Press, 1964), p. 317.

74. Quoted in Link, *Wilson: New Freedom,* p. 358.

75. Quoted *ibid.,* p. 360.

76. Quoted in Kenneth J. Grieb, *The United States and Huerta* (Lincoln: University of Nebraska Press, 1969), p. 137.

77. Quoted in Link, *Wilson: New Freedom,* pp. 386–387.

78. Quoted in Grieb, *United States and Huerta,* p. 137.

79. Quoted *ibid.,* p. 135.

80. Quoted in Robert E. Quirk, *An Affair of Honor* (Lexington: University of Kentucky Press, 1962), p. 26.

81. Quoted *ibid.,* pp. 32, 49.

82. Quoted in Mark T. Gilderhus, *Diplomacy and Revolution: U.S.–Mexican Relations Under Wilson and Carranza* (Tucson: University of Arizona Press, 1977), p. 11.

83. Quoted in Henry C. Lodge, *The Senate and the League of Nations* (New York: Charles Scribner's Sons, 1925), p. 18 and Cary T. Grayson, *Woodrow Wilson: An Intimate Memoir* (New York: Holt, Rinehart and Winston, 1960), p. 30.

84. Quoted in Link, *Wilson: New Freedom,* p. 402.

85. Quoted in Grieb, *United States and Huerta,* p. 160.

86. *Washington Post,* June 3, 1914.

87. Quoted in Arthur S. Link, *Wilson: The Struggle for Neutrality, 1914–1915* (Princeton: Princeton University Press, 1960), p. 239.

88. Quoted *ibid.,* p. 491.

89. Quoted in Friedrich Katz, "Pancho Villa and the Attack on Columbus, New Mexico," *American Historical Review,* LXXXIII (February, 1978), 111, 114.

90. Morison, *Letters of Roosevelt, III,* 497–498.

91. Akira Iriye, *The Cold War in Asia* (Englewood Cliffs, N.J.: Prentice Hall, 1974), p. 35.

92. Morison, *Letters of Roosevelt, IV,* 724, 761.

93. *Ibid.,* p. 1222.

94. Quoted in Raymond A. Esthus, *Theodore Roosevelt and Japan* (Seattle: University of Washington Press, 1966), p. 101.

95. Quoted *ibid.,* p. 103.

96. Quoted in Charles E. Neu, *An Uncertain Friendship* (Cambridge: Harvard University Press, 1967), pp. 36, 47.

97. Quoted in Akira Iriye, *Across the Pacific* (New York: Harcourt, Brace & World, 1967), p. 107.

98. Quoted in Esthus, *Roosevelt and Japan,* p. 149.

99. Quoted *ibid.,* p. 173.

100. Morison, *Letters of Roosevelt, V,* 729–730, 761–762.

101. Quoted in Frederick W. Marks, *Velvet on Iron: The Diplomacy of Theodore Roosevelt* (Lincoln: University of Nebraska Press, 1979), p. 57.

102. Quoted *ibid.*

103. Quoted in Herbert Croly, *Willard Straight* (New York: Macmillan, 1925), p. 276.

104. A. Whitney Griswold, *The Far Eastern Policy of the United States* (New Haven: Yale University Press, 1964 [c. 1938]), p. 157.

105. *Foreign Relations, 1909* (Washington, D.C.: Government Printing Office, 1914), p. 178.

106. Quoted in Croly, *Straight,* pp. 392–393.

107. Quoted in Iriye, *Across the Pacific,* p. 126.

108. *Ibid.,* p. 127.

109. Quoted in Link, *Wilson: New Freedom,* p. 286.

110. *New York Times,* May 5, 1913.

111. Quoted in Roger Daniels, *The Politics of Prejudice* (New York: Atheneum, 1968 [c. 1962]), p. 59.

112. Quoted in David F. Houston, *Eight Years with Wilson's Cabinet* (Garden City, N.Y.: Doubleday, 1926; 2 vols.), I, 66.

113. Quoted in Link, *Wilson: New Freedom,* pp. 300–301.

114. *Foreign Relations, 1915* (Washington, D.C.: Government Printing Office, 1924), p. 146.

115. *Foreign Relations, 1922* (Washington, D.C.: Government Printing Office, 1938; 2 vols.), II, 591.

116. Quoted in Beale, *Theodore Roosevelt,* pp. 81, 152.

117. Morison, *Letters of Roosevelt, II,* 1186–87.

118. Quoted in Beale, *Theodore Roosevelt,* p. 104.

119. Bradford Perkins, *The Great Rapprochement: England and the United States, 1895–1914* (New York: Atheneum, 1968).

120. Quoted in Charles S. Campbell, *Anglo-American Understanding, 1898–1903* (Baltimore: The Johns Hopkins Press, 1957), p. 190.

121. Quoted in Alexander E. Campbell, *Great Britain and the United States* (Westport, Conn.: Greenwood Press, 1974 [c. 1960]), pp. 105–106 and Morison, *Letters of Roosevelt, III,* 66.

122. Quoted in Perkins, *Great Rapprochement,* p. 168.

123. Quoted *ibid.,* p. 169.

124. Morison, *Letters of Roosevelt, VII,* 28.

125. Quoted in Perkins, *Monroe Doctrine,* p. 364.

126. Quoted in Arthur J. Marder, *From the Dreadnought to Scapa Flow: The Royal Navy in the Fisher Era, 1904–1919* (London: Oxford University Press, 1961–1970; 5 vols.), I, 125.

127. Perkins, *Great Rapprochement,* p. 195.

128. Quoted *ibid.,* p. 201.

129. Morison, *Letters of Roosevelt, IV,* 1119.

130. Quoted in Minger, *William Howard Taft,* p. 106.

131. Quoted in Jerry Israel, *Progressivism and the Open Door: America and China, 1905–1921* (Pittsburgh: University of Pittsburgh Press, 1971), p. 96.

132. Paul A. Varg, *The Making of a Myth* (East Lansing: Michigan State University Press, 1968), p. 36.

133. Lester D. Langley, *The United States and the Caribbean, 1900–1970* (Athens: University of Georgia Press, 1980), p. 92.

134. Quoted in Burton, *Theodore Roosevelt,* p. 190.

135. Quoted in Teodoro A. Agoncillo, *A Short History of the Philippines* (New York: New American Library, 1969), p. 156.

136. Quoted *ibid.,* p. 120.

137. Dexter Perkins, *The American Approach to Foreign Policy* (New York: Atheneum, 1968 [c. 1962], rev. ed.), p. 31.

Mass Grave of *Lusitania* Victims. In Queenstown, Ireland, a large burial ground holds more than a hundred victims of the *Lusitania* disaster of 1915, which rudely brought World War I to American consciousness. (U.S. War Department, National Archives)

8 World Reform Through World War, 1914–1920

Diplomatic Crossroad: The Sinking of the *Lusitania*, 1915

"Perfectly safe; safer than the trolley cars in New York City," claimed a Cunard Line official the morning of May 1, 1915.[1] Indeed, the majestic *Lusitania*, with her watertight compartments and swiftness, seemed invulnerable. The coal-burning steamer had already crossed the Atlantic one hundred times, and in 1907, the year of her maiden voyage, the *Lusitania* had set a speed record for transatlantic crossings. The British government, inspired by a German challenge to Britannia's supremacy of the seas, loaned Cunard the money to build this fast passenger liner, over twice as long as an American football field. The British Admiralty dictated many of the ship's specifications, so that the 30,396-ton vessel could be armed if necessary during war, and stipulated that half the *Lusitania*'s crew belong to the naval reserves.

"Lucy's" business was pleasure, not war. Resplendent with tapestries and carpets, the luxurious floating palace dazzled her passengers. One suitably impressed American politician found the ship "more beautiful than Solomon's Temple—and big enough to hold all his wives."[2] The 1,257 travelers were attended by a crew of 702 for the 101st transatlantic voyage, leaving from New York's Pier 54 on May 1; among them were renowned theatrical producer Charles Frohman and the multimillionaire playboy Alfred Vanderbilt. Deep in the *Lusitania*'s storage area rested a cargo of foodstuffs and contraband (4.2 million rounds of ammunition for Remington rifles, 1,250 cases of empty shrapnel shells, and eighteen cases of nonexplosive fuses). The Cunarder thus carried, said a State Department official, both "babies and bullets."[3]

In the morning newspapers of May 1 a rather unusual announcement, placed by the Imperial German Embassy, appeared beside the Cunard Line advertisement. The German "Notice" warned passengers that Germany and Britain were at war and that the waters around the British Isles constituted a war zone wherein British vessels were subject to destruction. One passenger called the warning

"tommy-rot" and only a handful canceled their bookings on the *Lusitania*. Few transferred to the *New York,* ready to sail under the American flag that same day. There was little time to shift vessels. Anyway, the unattractive *New York* was slow and for the American "smart set" socially unacceptable. Cunard officials at dockside reassured voyagers, and the State Department did not intercede to warn the one hundred and ninety-seven American passengers away from the *Lusitania*. Most Americans, in their "business-as-usual" attitude, accepted the statement of the Cunard Line agent: "The truth is that the *Lusitania* is the safest boat on the sea. She is too fast for any submarine. No German war vessel can get her or near her."[4] During this very time, Secretary of State William Jennings Bryan was trying to persuade President Woodrow Wilson that Americans should be prohibited from traveling on belligerent ships. He was making little headway.

Captained by an old sea dog, William T. Turner, the *Lusitania* steamed from New York into the Atlantic at half past noon on May 1. Manned by an ill-trained crew (the best had been called to war duty), "Lucy" enjoyed a smooth crossing in calm water. Perfunctory lifesaving drills were held, but complacency about the submarine danger characterized captain, crew, and passengers alike. Passengers joked about torpedoes, played cards, consumed gallons of liquor, and listened to concerts on deck. During the evening of May 6, as the *Lusitania* neared Ireland, Turner received a warning from the Naval Centre at Queenstown: "Submarines active off south coast of Ireland."[5] Earlier in the day two ships had been sunk in that vicinity. Captain Turner posted lookouts but took no other precautions, even after receiving follow-up warnings. He had standing orders from the Admiralty to take a zigzag path, to stay away from headlands, to steer a midchannel course, and to steam full speed—all to make it difficult for lurking German submarines to zero in on their targets. But Turner ignored these instructions.

May 7 was a beautiful day with unusually good visibility, recorded Lieutenant Walter Schwieger in his log. The young commander was piloting his U-20 submarine along the southern Irish coast. That morning it had submerged because

The *Lusitania* and U-20. The majestic passenger liner was sunk by German submarine U-20 off the coast of Ireland on May 7, 1915. (Peabody Museum of Salem; Bundesarchiv)

Architects of Disaster. Captain William T. Turner (1856–1933), left, of the *Lusitania* and Lieutenant Walter Schwieger (1885–1917) of U-20 never saw one another, but because their nations were at war, they were enemies nonetheless. (U.S. War Department, National Archives; Bundesarchiv)

British ships, capable of ramming the fragile, slender craft, were passing by. Schwieger surfaced at 1:45 P.M. and within a short time spotted a four-funneled ship in the distance. Carrying general orders to sink British vessels, Schwieger quickly submerged and set a track toward the *Lusitania,* eager to take advantage of this chance meeting (his specific orders, had he followed them, would have placed the U-20 near Liverpool). At 700 meters the U-20 released a torpedo. The deadly missile dashed through the water tailed by bubbles. A watchman on the starboard bow saw it and cried out. Captain Turner was unaccountably below deck, where he should not have been in those dangerous waters; and for some reason the bridge did not hear the lookout's warning called through a megaphone one minute before the torpedo struck. Had the message been received, the ship *might* have veered sharply and avoided danger. Thirty seconds before disaster a lookout in the crow's nest spied the torpedo and his frightened message sounded the alarm. Turner rushed to the bridge. He did not see the torpedo, but he heard the explosion as it ripped into the *Lusitania.* Schwieger watched through his periscope as the mighty vessel leaned on its starboard side and its bow dipped. The gold letters "LUSITANIA" became visible to the excited officer. "Great confusion ensues on board," he noted.[6] Panic swept the passengers as they stumbled about the listing decks or groped in the darkness below when the cut-off of electric power stranded elevators. Steam whistled from punctured boilers. Less than half the lifeboats were lowered; some capsized or were launched only partially loaded. Within eighteen minutes the "Queen of the Atlantic" sank, killing 1,198—128 of them Americans. A survivor remembered that when the *Lusitania* went down, "it sounded like a terrible moan."[7]

President Wilson had just completed a Cabinet meeting in the White House when he received the first sketchy news of the disaster. He was stunned, as was his special assistant Colonel Edward House, then dining in London with American Ambassador Walter Hines Page. "We shall be at war with Germany within a month," uttered the pro-British House, who, interestingly enough, had sailed on the *Lusitania* in February and had witnessed, much to his surprise, the hoisting of an American flag as the ship neared the Irish coast.[8] Secretary Bryan worried about war, and two days later he wrote the President that "ships carrying contraband should be prohibited from carrying passengers. . . . Germany has a right to prevent contraband going to the Allies and a ship carrying contraband should not rely upon passengers to protect her from attack—it would be like putting women and children in front of an army."[9] Bellicose ex-President Theodore Roosevelt was in Syracuse when he learned about the tragedy; he soon seared the air with his declaration that "this represents not merely piracy, but piracy on a vaster scale of murder than old-time pirates ever practiced."[10] American after American voiced horror and demanded that the President express the nation's collective moral indignation. But few wanted war. A troubled Wilson secluded himself to ponder an American response to this ghastly event. Just months before, he had warned Berlin that it would be held strictly accountable for the loss of any American ships or lives because of submarine warfare. "For the President of the United States," historian Arthur S. Link has noted, "this was by far the severest testing that he had ever known."[11]

After three days of reflection, which included reading memoranda from Bryan urging warnings to Americans not to travel on Allied ships carrying contraband, Wilson fulfilled a previous commitment and spoke in Philadelphia on May 10. His

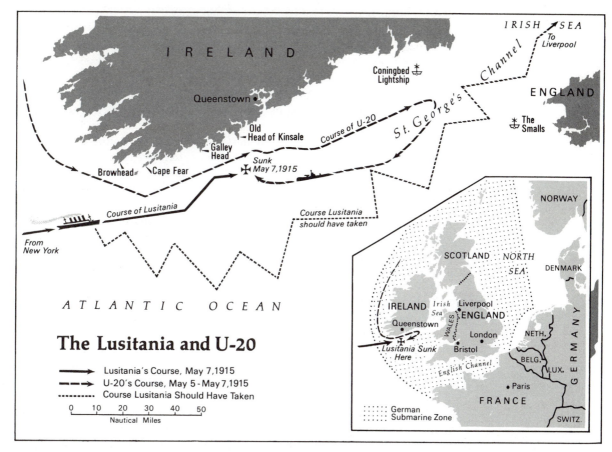

The Lusitania and U-20

→ Lusitania's Course, May 7, 1915
--→ U-20's Course, May 5 – May 7, 1915
········ Course Lusitania Should Have Taken

0 10 20 30 40 50
Nautical Miles

words, much misunderstood, suggested he had no backbone: "There is such a thing as a man being too proud to fight. There is such a thing as a nation being so right that it does not need to convince others by force that it is right."[12] Both cheers and boos echoed across the nation, and Wilson regretted his impromptu choice of words. The next morning he told the Cabinet what he had decided. He would send a note to Berlin insisting that Americans had a right to travel upon the high seas and demanding a disavowal by the German government of the inhumane acts of its submarine commanders. Bryan approved this first "Lusitania note," but with a heavy heart, fearing war. Long upset about an apparent American double standard in protesting more against German than British violations of American neutral rights, the secretary pleaded with Wilson to send a simultaneous protest note to London. But only one note went out on May 13—to Berlin: "The Imperial Government will not expect the United States to omit any word or any act necessary to the performance of its sacred duty of maintaining the rights of the United States and its citizens and of safeguarding their free exercise and enjoyment."[13] In short, end submarine warfare, or else.

The German government was much less ecstatic than the German Navy about the destruction of the Lusitania. Chancellor Theobold von Bethmann-Hollweg had more than once chastised the Navy for inviting war with the United States through submarine attacks on neutral or Allied merchant vessels. On May 28 he sent an evasive reply to Wilson's note. The Lusitania case could not be settled, it read, until certain questions were clarified. The German note claimed that the ship was armed, that it carried munitions, and that it, like other merchantmen, had orders to ram submarines. Germany asked Washington to investigate. One angry American newspaper thought the reply "the answer of an outlaw who assumes no obligation toward society."[14] Nevertheless, the German reply raised serious issues.

Wilson convened the Cabinet on June 1 and asked for advice. When one member recommended a strong note demanding observance of American rights, another suggested as well a note to England to protest British interference with American commerce. Debate became heated. A majority denounced the idea of simultaneous notes. Bryan, obviously under strain, remarked that the Cabinet was pro-Ally. Wilson quickly rebuked him for "unfair and unjust" comments.[15] After this curt exchange, tension grew between Bryan and Wilson. Over the next days Wilson worked on a second "*Lusitania* note." This note, arguing the case for humanity, vigorously called for an end to warfare by submarine, which could not, given its method of attack, abide by the rules of reason and justice. Wilson rejected Bryan's plea for a warning to passengers and a protest note to England. A man of conscience, Bryan could no longer work for a President with whom he so profoundly differed. Realizing he was probably wrecking his own political career, he quietly resigned on June 8. Privately he complained to Wilson that "Colonel House has been Secretary of State, not I, and I have never had your full confidence."[16] Wilson, relieved that he no longer had to face Bryan, went to the golf links to relax and to free himself from the blinding headaches of the past several days. Bryan told a friend: "The President is wrong and history will not sustain him."[17]

Other notes on the *Lusitania* and the question of neutral rights on the seas would follow over the succeeding months. The *Lusitania* disaster was not forgotten, but diplomats in Washington and Berlin permitted it to drop from the front pages of newspapers. The crux of the issue was this: the United States insisted that Germany admit it had committed an illegal act; but Germany, unwilling to abandon one of its few effective weapons against British mastery of the ocean, refused to admit wrongdoing and asked for arbitration. Wilson grew impatient in early 1916, apparently ready to sever diplomatic relations with Berlin. Germany sought a compromise. On February 4 it expressed regret over the American deaths and offered to pay an indemnity (eventually paid in the early 1920s). Semanticists will debate whether this constituted a formal apology, but it surely did not equal an admission of guilt. Nevertheless, Wilson and his new Secretary of State Robert Lansing, eager to drop the *Lusitania* from their list of diplomatic squabbles, accepted what they recognized as a German concession.

Although a diplomatic settlement had been reached, the horrible deaths from the sinking of the *Lusitania* were etched on American memories. The torpedoing of the magnificent Cunarder represented a benchmark in German-American relations and the era of World War I. The Germans suffered a propaganda loss of significant proportions, as Englishmen and Americans alike depicted the "Huns" as depraved. The *Lusitania* disaster became a "naval victory worse than a defeat."[18] The sinking also hardened Wilson's opinion of Germany. The President refused henceforth to make diplomatic life easier for the Germans by simultaneously protesting British infractions. No, Germany could not count on equal treatment. The British were violating property rights, but the Germans were violating human rights. He also refused to warn Americans away from belligerent ships. In short, if a U-boat attacked a British ship with Americans aboard, Germany would have to take the consequences. Wilson did not reveal those consequences exactly, but the logical implication was war—just what Bryan feared. His resignation had placed pro-Ally Robert Lansing in the secretaryship of state. After the *Lusitania* crisis, Lansing recalled, he held the "conviction that we would ultimately become an ally of Great Britain."[19] The sinking of the *Lusitania* pointed up, for all to see, the complexities, contradictions, and uncertainties inherent in American neutrality during the European phase of the First World War, 1914–1917.

The Unreality of Neutrality

Woodrow Wilson was virtually his own secretary of state during those troubled years. His secretary of the interior remarked that the President was "one of those men made by nature to tread the winepress alone."[20] British Prime Minister Lloyd George put it less kindly. Wilson, he said, "believed in mankind but . . . distrusted all men."[21] The President defined the overall character of American foreign policy—what historians call "Wilsonianism." Above all else, Wilson stood for an *open* world unencumbered by imperialism, war, or revolution. Barriers to trade and democracy had to be torn down, and secret diplomacy had to give way to public negotiations. The right of self-determination would force the collapse of empires. Constitutional procedures would replace revolution. A free-market, humanized capitalism would insure democracy. Disarmament programs would restrict the weapons of war. The economic competition that led to war would be harnessed by the Open Door of equal trade and investment opportunity. Wilson, like so many Americans, believed that the United States was exceptional among nations, that it was the redeemer nation. His reformist, inherently expansionist zeal, often called idealism, blended with realism. The President knew the nation's economic and strategic needs and devised a foreign policy that protected them. Yet many Americans questioned his definition of the national interest and feared that his world reforming efforts might invite war, dissipate American resources, and undermine reform at home. Hence Wilson led a divided nation, as his differences with Bryan suggested.

Few Americans, Wilson included, desired war, of course. Most watched in shock as the European nations savagely slashed at one another in 1914. Americans of the progressive reform era found it difficult to argue now that decent men had abolished immoral and barbaric war. The progressive faith in man's ability to right wrongs, the belief that war was part of the decadent past, the conviction that civilization had advanced too far for such blood-letting—all were ruthlessly challenged. It had seemed before 1914 that the new machine guns, howitzers, submarines, and dreadnoughts were simply too awesome to be unleashed by fair-minded human beings. The outbreak of World War I smashed illusions and tested innocence. "We were not used to smelling blood from vast human slaughterhouses," recalled reformer William Allen White.[22] The shock did not become despair, despite the horrible news of poison gas, U-boats, and civilian casualties. The "progressive" era was a time of optimism, and Americans, particularly the crusading Wilson, sought to retrieve the happier moments of the past by assuming the role of civilized instructors. America would help Europe come to its senses by teaching it the rules of humane conduct. The carnage explained why the mission was necessary. In 1915 alone France suffered 1.3 million casualties, 330,000 of whom were deaths. For Germany the figure was 848,000, and 170,000 deaths. Britain followed with 313,000 casualties, and 73,000 deaths.

Woodrow Wilson (1856–1924). Scholar, professor, university president (Princeton), and governor (New Jersey), Woodrow Wilson was usually cocksure once he made a decision. He protested war and imperialism, but as America's chief diplomat he failed to avoid both. (*Cartoons*, 1912)

Makers of American Foreign Policy from 1914 to 1920

Presidents	Secretaries of State
Woodrow Wilson, 1913–1921	William Jennings Bryan, 1913–1915 Robert Lansing, 1915–1920 Bainbridge Colby, 1920–1921

There was good reason, then, for Americans to believe that Europe needed help in cleaning its own house. Furthermore, the outbreak of the war seemed so senseless. By June, 1914, the great powers had constructed two alliances, the Triple Alliance (Germany, Austria, and Italy) and the Triple Entente (France, Russia, and Great Britain). Some called this division of Europe a balance of power, but an assassin's bullet easily unbalanced it. Between Austria and Serbia (part of Yugoslavia today) lay Bosnia, a tiny province annexed by expansionistic Austria in 1909. The nationalistic Serbs had protested this absorption of fellow Slavs, and Bosnia became hotly disputed territory. Young Bosnian assassins, clutching bombs and pistols and apparently egged on by some Serbian officials, precipitated a world conflict. One of their number gunned down the heir to the Hapsburg Crown of Austria-Hungary, Archduke Franz Ferdinand, as his car moved through the streets of Sarajevo, the capital of Bosnia. Austria sent impossible demands to Serbia. The Serbs indignantly rejected them. Austria had already received encouragement from Germany, and Serbia had gotten a pledge of support from Russia, which in turn received backing from France. A chain reaction set in. On July 28 Austria declared war on Serbia; on August 1 Germany declared "preventive" war on Russia and two days later on France; on August 4 Germany invaded Belgium, and Great Britain declared war on Germany. In a few weeks Japan joined the Allies (Triple Entente) and Turkey the Central Powers (Triple Alliance). As Germany's Otto von Bismarck had once predicted, "some damned foolish thing in the Balkans" would start a world war.[23]

The Atlantic seemed at first a solid enough barrier to insulate the United States. In early August, Ambassador Walter Hines Page wrote the President: "Be ready; for you will be called on to compose their huge quarrel. I thank Heaven for many things—first the Atlantic Ocean."[24] Adhering to diplomatic tradition, Wilson on August 4 issued a Proclamation of Neutrality, followed days later by an appeal to Americans to be neutral in thought, speech, and action. It was a request laced with patriotic utterances ("Every man who really loves America . . ."), designed to cool the passions of immigrant groups who identified with the belligerents. Wilson warned that such alignments would be fatal to "our peace of mind." America, he implored, must demonstrate to a troubled world that it was "fit beyond others to exhibit the fine poise of undisturbed judgment, the dignity of self-control, the efficiency of dispassionate action."[25] A lofty call for restraint, an expression of America as the beacon of common sense in a world gone mad, a plea for unity at home—but difficult to achieve.

Few Americans, including officials of the Wilson Administration, were capable of neutral thoughts and deeds. Loyalties to fatherlands and motherlands were understandable. German-Americans naturally identified with the Central Powers.

Many Irish-Americans, nourishing their traditional Anglophobia at a time when Ireland was on the verge of rebellion against London, wished catastrophe upon Britain. But Anglo-American traditions and cultural ties, as well as slogans like "Remember LaFayette," pulled a majority of Americans toward a pro-Allied position. Since the 1890s Anglophobia had weakened in the face of the calming Anglo-American rapprochement. Woodrow Wilson himself harbored some pro-British sentiment, believing as he did that a German victory would constitute a blow against government by law. Then, too, in his days as a scholar, Wilson had affirmed that the British parliamentary system of government was a preferable form of government and had once envisioned himself as a great prime minister. Wilson's advisers, Colonel Edward House and Robert Lansing, were ardently pro-British, as was the American Ambassador to London, Walter Hines Page. Page became so enthusiastic about British-American cooperation that once, after delivering to the British foreign minister an American protest note asserting the rights of neutral traders against British encroachments, he apologized for the American position and sat down to help draft a British reply to his own government.

German war actions, exaggerated by British propaganda, also undermined neutrality. The Germans, led by the boldly moustached, arrogant Kaiser Wilhelm II, were symbols to Americans of the dreaded militarism and conscription of the Old World. Even German Chancellor Theobold von Bethmann-Hollweg admitted that "we often got on the world's nerves."[26] Germany, too, was an upstart nation, an aggressive latecomer to the scramble for imperialist prizes, and appeared to be an intruder in the Caribbean, which even the British had acknowledged as an American lake. Eager to grasp world power and encouraging Austria to war, Berlin certainly had little claim on virtue. The rape of Belgium alone persuaded untold thousands of Americans to hate the "Hun." Belgium's neutrality in war was guaranteed by treaty, but Bethmann-Hollweg dismissed it as a "scrap of

"Sport." After Germany's tragic conquest of Belgium, Berlin drew critical commentary from cartoonists like A. B. Walker, who depicted the "Hun" in 1915 as the executioner of men, women, and children. (Historical Pictures Service, Inc., Chicago)

paper."[27] On August 4, 1914, hoping to get at France easily, the Germans attacked Belgium and, angered that the Belgians resisted, ruthlessly proceeded to raze villages, unleash firing squads against townspeople, and deport young workers to Germany. One current magazine was appalled by the brutality, declaring Belgium "a martyr to civilization, sister to all who love liberty, or law; assailed, polluted, trampled in the mire, heel-marked in her breast, tattered, homeless."[28] American hearts went out in the form of a major relief mission headed by a young, wealthy, and courageous mining engineer, Herbert Hoover. The British did not have to play up these atrocities for them to have an impact, but they undertook a hyperbolic propaganda campaign nevertheless, creating fictional stories of babies at the bloody ends of German bayonets and of Belgian women with breasts hacked off.

American economic links with the Allies also undermined Wilsonian appeals for neutrality. England had always been America's best customer and wartime conditions simply intensified the relationship. The Allies needed both war materiel and consumer goods. Americans, inspired by huge profits, a chance to pull out of a recession, and a "business-as-usual" attitude, obliged. In 1914 United States exports to England and France equaled $754 million; in 1915 the figure shot up to $1.28 billion, and in 1916 the amount more than doubled to $2.75 billion. Comparable statistics for Germany reveal why Berlin believed the United States was taking sides. In 1914 exports to Germany totaled $345 million; in 1915 they plummeted to $29 million, and in 1916 they fell to the negligible figure of $2 million. In 1914–1917 the prestigious banking house of J. P. Morgan Company of New York City served as an agent for England and France and arranged for the shipment of over $3 billion worth of goods. In April, 1915, Britain ordered shells from the American Locomotive Company costing $63.7 million, and that year Bethlehem Steel contracted for about $150 million in ammunition, to cite two examples. American copper, steel, cotton, wheat, oil, and munitions were part of this big business, which became a significant part of the Allied war chest.

Britain and France were hard pressed to pay for these huge shipments. First, they sold many of their American securities and liquidated investments. This netted them several billion dollars. Next, in cooperation with prominent American bankers and Secretary of State Robert Lansing, they appealed for loans. In 1914 Bryan discouraged private American loans to the belligerents, for, as he put it, "money is the worst of all contrabands because it commands everything else."[29] Yet in early 1915 the Wilson Administration did not object to a Morgan credit to France of $50 million. With Bryan's resignation and Lansing's ascent, the practice became common. As Lansing told Wilson in September, if Americans did not extend loans to the Allies, the United States would invite "restriction of output, industrial depression, idle capital, idle labor, numerous failures, financial demoralization, and general unrest and suffering among the laboring classes."[30] The Wilson Administration permitted loans to the Allies amounting to $2.3 billion during the period of American neutrality. Germany could garner only $27 million.

Berlin protested that such Allied-American economic ties were "unneutral." Yet to have curbed trade with Britain, which ruled the seas, would have been an unneutral act in favor of the Germans, for under international law a belligerent could buy, at its own risk, contraband and noncontraband goods from a neutral. Neutral or not, America's large trade with the Allies thoroughly alarmed the

Germans, who understood that the United States had become the arsenal of the Allied war effort. German-American propagandist George S. Viereck bitterly complained that Americans "prattle about humanity, while we manufacture poisoned shrapnel and picric acid for profit. Ten thousand German widows, ten thousand orphans, ten thousand graves bear the legend 'Made in America.'"[31] Berlin, in defining its national interest, felt compelled to interrupt this damaging trade with *unterseebooten.* "Without American assistance to the Allies," historian Ross Gregory has written, "Germany would have had no reason to adopt [a] policy injurious to the interests of the United States."[32]

Murder on the High Seas: Submarines and Neutral Rights

The British planned to strangle Germany economically. They declared a loose and hence illegal economic blockade in 1914, mined the North Sea, defined contraband so broadly that it included foodstuffs and cotton by the end of the war, forced American ships into port for inspection, confiscated contraband from neutral vessels, interrupted American trade with Germany's neutral neighbors Denmark and Holland, armed British merchant vessels, used decoy ships to lure U-boats into traps, flew neutral (often American) flags, and rammed whenever possible any U-boats that complied with international law by surfacing to warn a British merchant vessel of its imminent destruction. The British "ruled the waves and waived the rules," as someone put it.[33] Defending America's traditional principles of neutral rights, the Wilson Administration issued protests, some mild, some tough, against these illegalities. London was not impressed. When it replied, the Foreign Office paid appropriate verbal deference to neutral rights and international law and went right on with its unorthodox behavior. It soothed America's hurt by compensating its businessmen for damages and purchasing large quantities of its goods at inflated prices. Americans thus came to accept the indignities of British economic warfare. Britain managed brilliantly to sever American economic lines to the Central Powers without producing a rupture in Anglo-American relations.

Germans protested vehemently against this seeming American acquiescence in British practice. They considered it a "hunger" or "starvation" blockade. If Germany expected to survive as a nation, to continue the battle against the Allies, it had to have imports. Furthermore, Germany had to curb the flourishing Anglo-American trade that fueled the Allied war machine. The German Navy, most of it bottled up in ports by British vessels, seemed inadequate for the task, so German leaders hesitantly turned to a relatively new experimental weapon of limited maneuverability, the U-boat or submarine. They possessed just 21 of them initially and at peak strength in October, 1917 they had only 127. Only a third of this fleet was at sea at any one time. On February 4, 1915 Berlin announced that it was retaliating against British strangulation by declaring a war zone around Britain. All *enemy* ships in the area would be destroyed. Neutral ships were warned to *stay out* of the zone because of the possibility of mistaken identity, a possibility given the British practice of hoisting neutral flags. Passengers from neutral countries like the United States were urged to *stay off* enemy passenger vessels. Six days later Wilson vigorously instructed Germany that it would be held to a "strict accountability" for the loss of American life and property.[34]

The English continued to arm their merchant vessels, which thereby became warships and theoretically ineligible to frequent neutral territory like the United States. But Washington invoked a fine point of law, made the distinction between offensive and defensive armaments and permitted such "defensively" weaponed British craft to visit American ports. The Germans detected some favoritism. They also thought that old international law, which Wilson piously invoked, did not fit the submarine. Traditional rules held that enemy merchant vessels about to be captured or sunk had to be adequately warned by the attacking cruiser so that the safety of passengers and crew could be insured. The submarine could not fulfill this requirement. If it surfaced in its sluggish fashion, the merchantman's crew might sink it with the blast from a deck gun or even a hand grenade, or ram the vulnerable and slow-moving craft. British vessels like the *Lusitania* had standing Admiralty orders to resist U-boats and to ram them. Before the sinking of the *Lusitania,* the Germans had lost eleven submarines—five by ramming. Imagine the problem for Schwieger of U-20 when he spotted the *Lusitania.* Had he surfaced to warn her, he would have imperiled his boat and crew. The *Lusitania* would probably have attempted to ram U-20 or flee and would have sent distress signals to British warships in the vicinity. Even if the *Lusitania* had submitted to the warning, it would have taken at least an hour for the passengers to be placed in lifeboats before the ship could be sunk, and by then, in all likelihood, British vessels would have closed in upon Schwieger. In short, from the German point of view, it was impossible to comply with an international law that did not include provision for the submarine. Wilson, said Berlin, was attempting to deny Germany the use of the one weapon that might break the British blockade. That weapon, Wilson and other Americans replied, brought horrible death to innocent people.

Secretary Bryan tried diplomacy in early 1915, asking Germany to give up use of unannounced submarine attacks in exchange for a British promise to disarm its merchant carriers and permit food to flow to Germany. The Germans seemed interested, but London, which would have to abandon its successful blockade, demurred. Some critics have stated that at this point Wilson should have been tough in pressuring the belligerents to alter their naval strategies or face the prospect of American warships convoying America's "neutral" ships. Or, he might have launched a vigorous diplomatic offensive to delay explosive events on the seas. Yet the war was still in infancy, its direction and length uncertain, and American armed convoys in the Atlantic could very well draw America into a war it did not want. A diplomatic offensive, given the intensity of nationalism and war fever in Europe, seemed doomed to an early and inglorious failure. Wilson had to ask if he could risk all this. In March, 1915, he did send Colonel House to Europe to sound out possibilities for mediation, but to no avail. Nonetheless, Wilson failed to adjust or shelve ancient international law, which had no provision for the submarine. He was willing to accept British alterations but not German ones, for reasons both of morality and economics.

Between February and early May, 1915, ninety ships were sunk in the war zone by marauding submarines. One American, on the British passenger ship *Falaba,* died in the sinking of that vessel on March 28. Washington did not protest, hoping that a crisis could be avoided and that the belligerents could yet be lured to the conference table. Then came the *Lusitania* in May. Something had to be done. Wilson tried his protest notes, and the American position became defined as uneasy tolerance of the violation of property rights by the British and as rejection of the violation of human rights by the Germans. The Germans, Wilson pointed out, were killing people, whereas the British were inconveniencing them. Secret German orders went out to U-boat commanders to cease sinking passenger liners, but on August 19 the *Arabic,* another British liner, was torpedoed with the loss of two American lives. A worried German ambassador pledged that never again would unarmed passenger ships be attacked without warning.

In early 1916, with the *Lusitania* issue still unresolved, the United States attempted to bring the warring parties to the conference table. In early January Colonel House arrived in London, talked with British officials for two weeks, but left with no promises for peace. He stopped next in Berlin, where the imperial German leaders gave no assurances. Both sides would fight on. "Hell will break loose in Europe this spring and summer as never before," House informed the President.[35] He traveled next to Paris for a round of talks with the French. Indiscreetly showing his pro-Allied colors, House assured them that *"in the event the Allies are successful during the next few months I promised that the President would not intervene. In the event that they were losing ground, I promised the President would intervene."*[36] The French were pleased at the prospect of American participation in the war against Germany. House apparently did not tell the President exactly what he had told the surprised French.

House then returned to London to try to persuade Sir Edward Grey, British foreign secretary, to heed Wilson's call for a peace conference. The colonel recorded his agreements with the British diplomat in the House-Grey Memorandum of February 22, 1916, a document loaded with "ifs." The first paragraph read: "Colonel House told me that President Wilson was ready, on hearing from France and England that the moment was opportune, to propose that a Conference should be summoned to put an end to the war. Should the Allies accept the proposal, and should Germany refuse it, the United States would probably enter the war against Germany." The record of conversation went on to report that House had said that the peace conference would secure terms "not unfavourable to the Allies" and that if the conference failed to achieve peace, "the United States would leave the Conference as a belligerent on the side of the Allies, if Germany was unreasonable."[37] President Wilson pronounced the memorandum a diplomatic triumph, but clouded its meaning all the more by inserting a "probably" before the word "leave" in the sentence quoted above. He took the document much more seriously than did the British or French, who shelved it, snubbed American mediation, and vowed victory over Germany.

Meanwhile, Lansing and Wilson were working on a particular problem: armed merchant vessels and submarines. As House moved about the European capitals, Lansing informed the Allied governments that the United States sought a modus vivendi to defuse naval crises: the Allies would disarm merchant vessels and the Germans would agree to follow international law by warning enemy merchant ships. This suggestion revealed that the Wilson Administration understood the German argument that armed merchantmen were in reality offensive craft, that is, warships. The British and Colonel House were aghast when they received this news, and were further set back when the Germans seemed to endorse the modus vivendi by declaring on February 10 that submarines would henceforth attack only *armed* merchant ships without warning. Suddenly Wilson reversed policy. He

Edward M. House (1858–1938). A Texan who loyally served President Woodrow Wilson, the colonel traveled widely as a special presidential emissary. Wilson called House "my second personality." (Sketch by Anthony Saris, American Heritage Collection)

abandoned the modus vivendi in order to restore his standing with the British and sustain House's efforts at mediation in London. Lansing announced, furthermore, that the United States would not prevent its citizens from traveling on "defensively" armed merchant ships.

Passengers, Perils, and Pledges: Descent into World War I

These diplomatic confusions alarmed many Americans. Why let one American passenger and a trigger-happy U-boat captain bring Germany and the United States to war? asked public critics like Bryan. Why not, they inquired, keep Americans off belligerent ships and require them to sail on American vessels? From August, 1914 to mid-March, 1917 only three Americans (on the American oil tanker *Gulflight,* May 1, 1915) had lost their lives on an *American* ship torpedoed by a U-boat. In contrast, about 190 Americans, including the *Lusitania's* 128, died on belligerent ships. After the *Falaba* was sunk, Bryan, still secretary of state, recognized that Americans had a right to travel on belligerent vessels, but asked Wilson to ask them to forego that right. "I cannot see," Bryan wrote the President, "that he [an American on a belligerent ship] is differently situated from those who by remaining in a belligerent country assume risk of injury."[38] Wilson had, after all, urged Americans to leave war-torn Mexico. The American Ambassador to Germany, James W. Gerard, wrote the President in July, 1915, that "when Americans have reasonable opportunity to cross the ocean [on American ships] why should we enter a great war because some American wants to cross on a ship where he can have a private bathroom?"[39] Senator William J. Stone, chairman of the Foreign Relations Committee, forcefully pointed out that the *Lusitania* passengers, duly warned about the risk, were in essence on "British soil." He continued: "Was not their position substantially equivalent to their being in the walls of a fortified city?"[40]

Wilson did not agree. Americans could not give up one right, or all rights would be jeopardized. In January, 1916, Congressman Jeff: McLemore of Texas introduced a resolution to prohibit Americans from traveling on armed belligerent vessels. In late February Senator Thomas P. Gore of Oklahoma followed with a similar resolution in his chamber. The prohibition demanded by the Gore-McLemore resolution very quickly gained support in both houses. Wilson, a firm believer in presidential supremacy in decisionmaking, was irate that his foreign policy leadership would be challenged by Congress. He attacked Gore-McLemore fiercely, unleashing Cabinet members with patronage muscle on timid congressmen, and suggesting that the resolution was a pro-German ploy. He issued a statement marked by lofty, almost embarrassing, phrases. To halt American passage on belligerent ships, Wilson intoned, would be to accept national humiliation and destruction of the "whole fine fabric of international law."[41] In short, he stuck with rigid, archaic concepts, refusing to adjust to the new factor of the submarine or to appreciate the impact on Germany of the obvious British violations of the same law. In early March, the Gore-McLemore resolution was beaten 68–14 in the Senate and 276–142 in the House. One congressman complained that the "President absolutely dominates Congress."[42] The Gore-McLemore resolution was one of the more sensible proposals for avoiding German-American conflict. It asked America to give up very little; despite Wilson's exaggerated rhetoric, it did not besmudge national honor. Wilson's message to Berlin was unmistakable: do not use your submarines.

In March, 1916, another passenger ship, another U-boat, another torpedo, more American injuries: the French ship *Sussex,* moving across the channel, was badly mangled but not sunk. Aboard her was a young American scholar, Samuel Flagg Bemis, later to become a renowned diplomatic historian but then fresh from archival research on Jay's Treaty. Gazing over the calm sea, Bemis glimpsed the swirling wake of a torpedo moments before impact. "The entire bow was blown off and with it the people who were in the dining room," he recalled.[43] Although four Americans were injured, a wet Bemis escaped serious harm. Fortunately, he also saved his little bag of note cards. The *Sussex* attack violated the *"Arabic* pledge," even though the U-boat commander mistook the ship for a minelayer, and Lansing counseled the President to break diplomatic relations with Berlin. Wilson decided instead upon an ultimatum. He warned the Germans on April 18 that he would sever diplomatic relations if they did not pledge to halt their submarine warfare against passenger and merchant vessels; to emphasize the point he went to Congress the next day and repeated the warning. The German hierarchy was alarmed, fully expecting a rupture if the torpedo bays were not blocked. With the ground war going badly (a German offensive at Verdun was costing thousands of lives), Berlin was not willing to invite war with the United States. In early May Germany promised (the *"Sussex* pledge") that submarines would not attack passenger or merchant ships without proper warning. The Germans also reminded Washington that it should do something about British infractions of international law.

Meanwhile, the British, sensing favorable winds, clamped down even harder on trade with the Central Powers. In July they issued a "blacklist" of firms; over eighty American companies that had traded with the Central Powers were on it, and even Woodrow Wilson now fumed that he was "about at the end of my patience with Great Britain and the Allies."[44] He contemplated a prohibition on loans and exports to them, but he did little. Many Americans also condemned the brutal British success in smashing the Irish Easter rebellion in April of 1916.

Shortly after the presidential election of 1916, punctuated with the Democrats' slogan "He Kept Us Out of War," the President launched another diplomatic offensive. In December Wilson boldly asked the belligerents to state their war aims. Actually, neither Berlin nor London, still seeking elusive military victory, welcomed Wilson's mediation, which would deny them the spoils of war. Germany intended to obtain Poland, Lithuania, Belgium, and the Belgian Congo; Britain sought German colonies; France wanted the return of Alsace-Lorraine. To these ardent war aims, Wilson seemed oblivious, especially when, on January 22, 1917, he called for a "peace without victory" because only through a peace founded on the "equality of nations" could a lasting world order be achieved. He proposed that "nations should with one accord adopt the doctrine of President Monroe as the doctrine of the world."[45] French Premier Georges Clemenceau's newspaper was cynical about Wilson's new appeal: "Never before has any political assembly heard so fine a sermon on what human beings might be capable of accomplishing if only they weren't human." And the radical *L'Oeuvre* contemptuously asked: "What about Cuba?"[46] The grand old man of French letters, Anatole France, revealing the French quest for revenge, put it this way: "Peace without victory is bread without yeast . . . , love without quarrels, a camel without humps, night without moon, roof without smoke, town without brothel."[47]

Woodrow Wilson and the Decision for War, 1917

In early 1917 crises mounted quickly. On January 31 Berlin announced that, starting the next day, German submarines would attack without warning and sink all vessels, enemy and neutral, found near British waters. This declaration of unrestricted submarine warfare expressed Germany's calculated risk that England would be defeated before the United States could mobilize and send its soldiers overseas. The cocky German naval minister was emphatic: "From a military standpoint, America's entrance is as nothing."[48] German naval officers convinced the Kaiser that the U-boats, now numbering about 100, could shrink United States munitions shipments and hence knock Britain out of the war in six months. Army officers, bogged down in trench warfare, were eager to end their costly immobility through a bold stroke. Field Marshal Paul von Hindenburg overcame the arguments of a more cautious Chancellor Bethmann-Hollweg by insisting persuasively that "we are counting on the possibility of war with the United States, and have made all preparations to meet it. Things cannot be worse than they are now."[49] But an adviser to Bethmann-Hollweg fatalistically recorded in his diary that "despite all promises of the navy it remains a leap into the dark."[50]

Wilson still did not want war with Germany, though he was incensed by Berlin's most recent decision. He had become, according to Lansing, "more and more impressed with the idea that 'white civilization' and its domination over the world rested largely on our ability to keep this country intact, as we would have to build up the nations ravaged by the war."[51] Yet Wilson had also committed himself in notes and impassioned rhetoric to a forceful response to unrestricted submarine warfare. So on February 3 Washington severed diplomatic relations with Berlin. Allied and neutral vessels soon succumbed to U-boat torpedoes, and fearful American owners kept their merchant ships in port. Goods stacked up on wharves and many leaders predicted economic doom for the United States.

Added to this threat to America's economic interests and the intense Wilsonian defense of human rights was an implied threat to United States security. In late February the British passed to Ambassador Page an intercepted and decoded telegram sent to Mexico by German Foreign Minister Arthur Zimmermann. The remarkable message proposed a military alliance with the Latin American country. And should war with the United States break out, Germany would help Mexico "gain back by conquest" the territory lost in 1848: Arizona, California, and New Mexico.[52] Wilson read the telegram as a direct slap at American honor and a challenge to American security. Although the threat was potential rather than real, it deeply angered Washington, in large part because the United States was plagued at the time by stormy relations with a revolution-torn Mexico. Germany, it appeared, would stop at nothing. "This wd [would] precipitate a war between almost any 2 nations," Ambassador Page confided to his diary.[53]

One day after Wilson learned of Zimmermann's cable, he asked Congress for authority to arm American merchant vessels. On March 1, to create a favorable public opinion for the request, he released the offensive Zimmermann telegram to the press. But antiwar senators Robert LaFollette and George Norris led a filibuster—a "little group of willful men," said Wilson—that killed the armed ship legislation.[54] Stubbornly ignoring the Senate, Wilson ordered the arming anyway. Nevertheless, ship after ship was sunk by the U-boats: in March 16–18 alone the American ships *City of Memphis, Illinois,* and *Vigilancia* went down. Buttressed by the unanimous support of his Cabinet, the President decided for war.

On April 2 Wilson solemnly addressed a special joint session of Congress and appealed for a declaration of war against Germany—a war that Berlin had "thrust" upon the United States. His words were inspired, moving his audience to nationalistic enthusiasm. The President depicted the "unmanly business" of using submarines as "warfare against mankind." Freedom of the seas, commerce, American lives, human rights—all were challenged by the "outlaw" U-boats. A combination of economic self-interest, morality, and national honor compelled Americans to fight. He characterized the German government as a menacing monster striking at the "very roots of human life." The "Prussian autocracy" was also stirring up trouble through spies and the Zimmermann note. He acknowledged, too, that the Russian Revolution of March made fighting on the Allied side easier because now all the Allies would be democracies. Then came the memorable words: "The world must be made safe for democracy."[55] The address simplified issues and claimed too much for American participation in World War I. But the moment required patriotic fervor, not sophisticated analysis. "It had been a moving oration," Ross Gregory has written, "and when the President had finished, most of his listeners—there remained a few diehard dissenters—were ready to grasp the Hun by the collar, feeling that surely God was on their side, and if He was not, God this one time must be wrong."[56] By votes of 82–6 (Senate, April 4) and 373–50 (House, April 6), Congress endorsed Wilson's appeal for a war for peace.

Most historians agree that submarine warfare precipitated the American decision to enter the war. Such a conclusion is not inaccurate, but it is incomplete. Certainly had there been no submarine to menace American lives, property, and the United States definition of international law, there would have been no American soliders sent to France. From the German perspective, however, use of the submarine was justified by the long list of unfriendly American acts: American acquiescence in the British blockade, part of a general American pro-British bias; large-scale American munitions shipments to, and other commerce with, the Allies; large American loans; an interpretation of neutral rights, which insisted that American passengers could sail anywhere, even into a war zone, and which thereby rendered the submarine an impotent weapon. Take away those acts, which the Germans considered unneutral, and they might not have launched the U-boats. It seems questionable that American ideals and interest could depend so perilously on a ship loaded with contraband, heading for Britain, and steaming through a war zone. Yet that is how Wilson and his advisers defined the problem; dissenters like Gore and McLemore disagreed, but they were in the minority.

Evident in Wilson's policies was the traditional American belief that others must conform to American prescriptions, self-professed as they were, and that America's ideals were a beacon for mankind. "We created this Nation," the President once proclaimed, "not to serve ourselves, but to serve mankind."[57] When the Germans defied America's rules, ideals, and property, and threatened its security through a proposed alliance with Mexico, they had to be punished. Here was an opportunity to protect both humane principles and commercial interests. When Wilson spoke passionately of the right of a neutral to freedom of the seas, he

Jeanette Rankin (1880–1973). Native of Montana, Rankin, in 1916, became the first woman to be elected to the House of Representatives. A lifelong pacifist, she voted against war in 1917, only to lose her seat the following year. In the interwar period she lobbied for peace and was again elected to Congress in 1940. Once again she refused to send American soldiers into "the foreign slaughterhouse" and cast the only vote against war in 1941. She later participated in marches against the Vietnam War. (Montana Historical Society, Helena)

demonstrated how intertwined were American moral, economic, and strategic concerns. Wilson sought the role of peacemaker and he promised to remake the world in the American image: that is, to create a world order in which barriers to political democracy and the "Open Door" were eliminated, in which revolution and aggression were abolished. This missionary zeal served, at least in Wilson's mind, the national interest (trade and the Open Door) and high principles (respect for human rights, self-determination, and democracy). War came to the United States not simply because of German submarines, but because expansionist American leaders were finally willing to fight in order to implant in the Old World the best principles and goods America had to offer.

Preparing for War

Berlin had risked war with the United States because it assumed that American soldiers could not reach France fast enough to reverse an expected German victory. That proved to be a gross misjudgment, for American military muscle and economic power decisively tipped the balance against Germany. Given the information available in early 1917, however, the German assumption does not seem so unrealistic. In April the United States was hardly prepared to send a major expedition to the Western Front. At that date the Regular Army counted only 130,000 officers and men, backed by 180,000 National Guardsmen. Although some American officers had been seasoned by military interventions in Cuba, the Philippines, and recently in Mexico, many soldiers were poorly trained. Weapons such as the machine gun were in short supply. The "Air Service," then part of the Army, did not have a plane of modern design with a machine gun, and some ships in the Navy had never fired a gun. German calculations based upon these facts seemed at the time sensible; what the Germans underestimated badly was American capacity for organization and the intense nationalism and remarkable productive power of the United States.

An American "preparedness movement" had been under way for months, encouraged by prominent Americans like the tough-minded Rough Rider and military evangelist, General Leonard Wood, who overstated the case when he argued that America's military weakness invited attack, but rang true when he noted that the United States was not recognized as an important military power. After 1914, Wood, Theodore Roosevelt, the National Security League, the Army League, and the Navy League lobbied actively for bigger military appropriations. The belief that "preparedness" was an insurance against war grew more popular. One propaganda film, *The Fall of a Nation,* depicted a helpless United States invaded by spike-helmeted attackers. In mid-1915 one hundred of America's wealthiest men pledged thousands of dollars to help the Navy League plead its case before Congress, and by September of that year twenty-eight governors had joined the National Security League.

Wilson himself decided to prepare the nation for possible war. After consulting senior Army and Navy officers, he presented his plan to Congress in December, 1915. He dramatically asked for a half-billion-dollar naval expansion program, including ten battleships and one hundred submarines, to bring the United States to first rank with Britain in five years. Land forces would also be enlarged and reorganized. Perpetuating the antimilitarist tradition of great numbers of Americans, Senator Robert LaFollette, House Majority Leader Claude Kitchin, and such prominent citizens as Jane Addams, William Jennings Bryan, Lillian Wald, and Oswald Garrison Villard spurred a movement against these measures. These peace advocates, the Women's Peace Party, and the League to Limit Armaments argued that war would interrupt reform at home, benefit big business, and curtail civil liberties. Their arguments were formidable and their numerical strength impressive. The President faced a serious test.

In January, 1916, Wilson set out on a two-month speaking tour, often having to criticize members of his own party for their opposition to a military buildup. U-boat sinkings aided the President's message. Finally, in May, 1916, Congress passed the National Defense Act, increasing the Regular Army to over 200,000 men and 11,000 officers, and the National Guard to 440,000 men and 17,000 officers. Provision was made, too, for summer training camps, modeled after one held in 1915 for the social and economic elite in Plattsburg, New York. In June, 1916, Wilson asserted that "mankind is going to know that when America speaks she means what she says."[58] The Navy bill passed in August, 1916 and was followed by the shipping bill providing $50 million to enlarge the merchant marine. With these successes, Wilson entered the presidential campaign under the banner of "reasonable" preparedness and "He Kept Us Out of War." Peace groups thought the measures went too far; Teddy Roosevelt, of course, believed they fell short.

"In the Front Line at Early Morning." A soldier stares across "no-man's-land" from a World War I trench in this painting by Harvey Dunn. American generals vowed to end the stalemate of costly trench warfare. (Smithsonian Institution)

When the United States voted for belligerency in April, 1917, it was preparing for war, but was not yet ready. Wilson requested 500,000 more soldiers in his war message. The Selective Service Act of May, 1917 began a registration process that included all males between the ages of eighteen and forty-five. By the end of the conflict, 4,800,000 soldiers, sailors, and marines had been mobilized. Officer training camps turned out "ninety-day wonders," thousands of commissioned officers drawn largely from people of elite background. One camper remarked about the spirit of his group: "There are so many Roosevelts that you can't turn around without stumbling over one."[59] Actually, Theodore Roosevelt was not there. The old Rough Rider had asked Wilson for permission to recruit and lead a volunteer unit into battle; no doubt taking some revengeful pleasure in denying the request, Wilson argued that special volunteer divisions would raise havoc with military organization. As historian Edward M. Coffman has concluded: "A dilettante at war with a political reputation and political ambitions was out of place in the American army of 1917–18."[60] Roosevelt was to die peacefully in January, 1919, after tragically losing his youngest son in the war.

Right after the American declaration of war, Allied military missions flocked to the White House to beg for soldiers. General John J. "Black Jack" Pershing, veteran fighter against Apaches, Filipinos, and Mexicans, and now head of the American Expeditionary Force to Europe, soon sent a "show the flag" contingent to France to stimulate Allied morale. Neither Wilson nor Pershing would accept, however, the European recommendation that American troops be inserted in Allied units where needed. American units would cooperate in joint maneuvers with other forces, but the United States Army would remain separate and independent. National pride dictated this decision, but so did the realization that Allied commanders had for years wasted the lives of hundreds of thousands in vicious trench warfare. The United States would not supply more bodies for such an unsuccessful strategy. It wanted freedom of choice and no identification with exploitative Allied war aims. Thus the United States insisted on calling itself an "associated" rather than an "allied" power in the war.

Over There: Winning the War

On July 4, 1917, General Pershing reviewed the first unit of American troops to arrive in France. A battalion of the 16th Infantry marched proudly through the streets of Paris, as nearly a million Parisians madly tossed flowers, hugged the doughboys, and cheered wildly. The American soldiers were enthusiastic but ill-trained recruits. One company commander recalled that "these men couldn't even slope arms. They were even more dangerous with a loaded rifle."[61] But to the war-weary French, accustomed to viewing haggard men exhausted by the agony of the trenches, these fresh American troops were inspirational. Speeches were delivered with accustomed Independence Day rhetoric. One colonel proclaimed, "Lafayette, we are here!" and back home the *New York Times* echoed, "the old debt is being paid."[62]

Preparations continued in the United States. To the tune "Johnny Get Your Gun," innocent but eager recruits—draftees and volunteers—were sent from their hometowns with fanfare and full stomachs from church dinners. Many got drunk on the mobilization trains. "Hurry up and wait," a military tradition, greeted the young soldiers in camp. The six-month training program demanded a seven-

Recruiting Poster. James Montgomery Flagg's famous poster urged young people to join the American crusade in World War I. (Library of Congress)

teen-hour day, including "policing the area" (i.e., picking up cigarette butts), a military custom considered instructive for "discipline." The soldiers ate well, slept on straw mattresses and cots, and drilled, often without the benefit of weapons. Some never fired a rifle until stationed in France. War hero Private Alvin C. York, of Tennessee's mountain country, remarked that many of his fellow warriors "missed everything but the sky" during marksmanship training. "Of course, it weren't no trouble nohow for me to hit them big army targets. They were so much bigger than turkey's heads."[63]

To the chagrin of American leaders, taverns and brothels quickly surrounded army camps. Alcohol and prostitution were, of course, taboos during the progressive era. "Fit to Fight" became the government's slogan, as it moved to close down "red-light districts"; "sin-free zones" around camps were declared, and the sale of liquor to men in uniform was prohibited. Secretary of the Navy Josephus Daniels preached that "Men must live straight if they would shoot straight."[64] The military conquered the venereal disease problem in the United States. As historian Allen F. Davis has concluded, "it was a typical progressive effort—a large amount of moral indignation combined with the use of the most scientific prophylaxis."[65] Groups like the YMCA and the Jewish Welfare Board helped work against sin by sending song leaders to camps. Movies, athletic programs, and well-stocked stores were also designed to keep the soldier on the base by making him feel "at home." These activities could not deal with a major flu epidemic, which struck several camps in

1918. The death rate was awesome. At Camp Sherman, Ohio, one of the bases hit hardest, 1,101 men died between September 27 and October 13. According to army records for the war as a whole, 62,000 men died of diseases of many kinds. Battle deaths numbered less—about 51,000.

Approximately 400,000 black troops suffered the intolerance of American racism and discrimination during this war "to make the world safe for democracy." Camps were segregated and "white only" signs posted. In 1917 in Houston, Texas, whites provoked blacks into a riot that left seventeen whites and two blacks dead. Over a hundred black soldiers were courtmartialed; thirteen were executed by hanging. In the army, three out of every four black soldiers were assigned to labor units, where they wielded a shovel, not a gun, or where they cooked or unloaded supplies. They received poor training and became dispirited under the leadership of white officers. Even black officers were assigned second-class quarters during the transatlantic trip. Black troops in France won high praise from French leaders, but Americans insensitively poked fun by quipping that it would be difficult to get a load of watermelons across the Atlantic to reward them. Many black soldiers earned the coveted medal "Croix de Guerre," but Americans preferred to emphasize an uneven performance by two black units in the Meuse-Argonne offensive near the end of the war. To be black in World War I was to be reminded of the

Black "Kitchen Engineers." In Marseilles, France these black members of the United States Army peel potatoes, one of the "service" functions performed by segregated blacks, who ironically participated in a war to "make the world safe for democracy." (U.S. Signal Corps, National Archives)

blotted lives of slave ancestors and the utter contradiction between America's wartime rhetoric and reality. Lynchings revealed the problem: 382 black Americans were so killed in the period 1914–1920.

After training in the Unites States, troops went to France for two more months of preparation. There they endured frequent rain and mud, slept in barns and stables, fought off "cooties" (lice), and ate "monkey-meat" (canned corned beef from Madagascar). One soldier, battling the lice, remarked that he knew full well why Napoleon was always pictured with his hand in his shirt. They made friends, some lasting, with French villagers, although some resented Americans who flaunted their wealth among people who knew only wartime sacrifice. Wine and women occupied spare hours. American reformers in the camps back home had said that they hoped to give the soldiers enough social armor before they reached France so that they would not be tempted by sin overseas. But they either overestimated the self-control of American men or underestimated the power of French women, because the venereal disease rate spiraled up alarmingly. Every morning General Pershing had a venereal disease chart laid on his desk. What to do? French Prime Minister Georges Clemenceau generously offered to supply the American Army with licensed—health-inspected—prostitutes. A cautious Pershing commented that the offer was "too hot to handle," and forwarded it to Raymond Fosdick, Chairman of the Commission on Training Camp Activities. Fosdick carried it to Secretary of War Newton Baker, who in shock expostulated: "For God's sake, Raymond, don't show this to the President or he'll stop the war."[66] Clemenceau's offer was never taken up, but disease prevention programs and the threat of court-martial confronting any infected soldier helped reduce the problem. We shall always remember the problem existed, however, because one of the French ladies of ill repute was immortalized in some of the unprintable words of the popular song "Mademoiselle from Armentières."

Pershing established headquarters outside Paris and tried to acquaint his soldiers with the hardships of trench and gas warfare. The first American deaths came from limited combat in October, 1917. Despite the impatience of the French and British, Pershing was reluctant to commit his green soldiers to full-scale battle. As it was, great numbers of troops were shipped over in British vessels and had to borrow French weapons. And by early 1918 the Allies were mired in a murderous strategy of throwing ground forces directly at other ground forces. German troops were mauling Italian forces, and the French army was still suffering from the mutinies of the year before. In March Germany forced an exhausted and revolution-wracked Russia out of the war in the draconian Brest-Litovsk Treaty, which stripped the victim of valuable land and people. President Wilson, trying to avoid vindictiveness, nevertheless waxed militant. He told a Baltimore audience in April that Americans must employ "Force, Force to the utmost, Force without stint or limit, the righteous and triumphant Force which shall make Right the law of the world, and cast every selfish dominion down in the dust."[67] American soldiers soon trooped into battle.

In March the German armies, swollen by forty divisions from the Russian front, launched a great offensive. Allied forces were hurled back, and by late May the Kaiser's soldiers encamped near the Marne River less than fifty miles from Paris. Saint-Mihiel, Belleau Wood, Cantigny, Château-Thierry—sites where American soldiers shed their blood against Germany—soon became household words at home. In June at Château-Thierry the doughboys dramatically stopped a German advance. From May through September of 1918 over a million American troops went to France; two million would be there by the armistice in November. In mid-July the Allies launched a counteroffensive and nine American divisions fought fiercely near Château-Thierry, helping to lift the German threat from Paris. In the Meuse-Argonne offensive (begun on September 26), over a million American soldiers joined French and British units in penetrating the crumbling German lines.

Preparing for Peace: The Fourteen Points, Armistice, and Allied Competition

In the fall of 1918, German leaders began to think peace, as the Allied offensive steadily struggled forward. On October 4, as American soldiers fought in the thick Argonne Forest, the German chancellor asked Wilson for an armistice. German troops were mutinous; revolution and riots plagued German cities; Bulgaria had left the war in September. Turkey would drop out in late October, and Austria-Hungary would surrender on November 3. Germany had no choice but to surrender. The Kaiser fled to Holland. On November 11, in a railroad car in the Compiègne Forest, German representatives capitulated. At the time, American troops controlled 21 percent of the Western Front: the United States, through its men and supply, had made the difference in defeating Germany. In the sports vernacular of the day, the *Rochester Post-Express* concluded that the "trouble with this war game was that it ran into extra innings and Germany had no relief pitcher or pinchhitters."[68] The Allies had the Americans, and the latter would not let the former forget it.

During the combat, President Wilson had begun to explain in very general terms his plans for the peace. His message of a "peace without victory" was trumpeted most dramatically in his "Fourteen Points" speech before Congress on January 8, 1918. The first five points promised an "open" world after the war, a world distinguished by "open covenants, openly arrived at," freedom of navigation upon the seas, equal trade opportunity and the removal of tariffs, reduction of armaments, and an end to colonialism. Points six through thirteen called for self-determination for national minorities in Europe. Point fourteen was paramount: a "general association of nations" to insure "political independence and territorial integrity to great and small states alike."[69] His Fourteen Points, joined by later elaborations, signaled from the American perspective a generous, nonpunitive postwar settlement. They served as effective American propaganda against revenge-fed Allied aims and Russian Bolshevik appeals for European revolution.

Leaders in France, Britain, and Italy grew angry at Wilson, fearing he would deny them the spoils of war. In 1915 the Allies had signed secret treaties carving up German territories, including colonies in Africa and Asia. Nursing deep war wounds and dreaming of imperial expansion at the expense of a defeated Germany, the Allies sneered at Wilson's prescriptions. They did not appreciate the "modern St. George," as publicist Herbert Croly depicted Wilson, or his attempts to slay the "dragons of reaction" in Europe.[70] Furthermore, Europeans, surveying the comparative wartime suffering and human loss, believed that Wilson "had bought his seat at the peace table at a discount."[71] When, in September and October of 1918, Wilson exchanged notes with Germany and Austria-Hungary about an armistice, the Allied powers grew restless. They expressed strong reservations about the Fourteen Points. General Tasker Howard Bliss, the Ameri-

A German Soldier. This disturbing picture of an unburied German soldier of the First World War, and others like it, convinced many Americans to abstain in the future from European squabbles that might lead to United States military action. (Imperial War Museum, London)

can representative on the Supreme War Council (established in the fall of 1917 to coordinate the Allied war effort), recognized the Allied thirst for revenge. "Judging from the spirit which seems more and more to actuate our European allies," he informed Washington in October, "I am beginning to despair that the war will accomplish more than the abolition of *German* militarism while leaving *European* militarism as rampant as ever."[72] To counter the Allied assault upon the Fourteen Points, presidential aide Colonel Edward House and Wilson hinted that the United States might negotiate a separate peace with the Central Powers. House further warned that the President might go before Congress and publicize the exploitative Allied war aims. The colonel also contemplated economic coercion in the form of a reduction in American shipments to Europe. London, Paris, and Rome reluctantly agreed, in the armistice of November, to begin peace negotiations on the basis of the Fourteen Points.

Wilson, at the peak of his diplomatic career, relished the opportunity to shape the postwar world. The war had been won by the infusion of American arms, and the United States was about to claim a major role in deciding world events. The pictures of dying men dangling from barbed wire fences, and the reality of battle shock victims who staggered home, convinced many Americans of the frightful costs of war and the need to prevent another conflagration. Wilson's call for a just peace commanded the backing of countless foreigners as well. The President thus headed for the Paris Peace Conference at Versailles with a reputation as an apostle of peace.

He also went as a person with human weaknesses and olympian ambitions. It became a personal tragedy that the sacred garb of peace, so carefully tailored by Wilson himself, would be stripped from the President by recalcitrant European leaders, critical senators, and his own disaffected advisers. But, as most historians point out, Wilson invited calamity by compromising too much in Europe and too little at home. A personal tragedy the peacemaking was; whether it was a national tragedy remains an open question.

In telling fashion, the President weakened his position even before he reached the peace conference. Against the advice of many friends he had decided to go personally to Paris to conduct the meetings. Congressional leaders wanted him to stay home to handle domestic problems. Advisers like Lansing feared that in the day-to-day bickering of a conference he would lose his exalted image. He would have only one vote, whereas from Washington he could symbolically marshall the votes of mankind. Wilson retorted that distance contributes to confusion, that he had already pledged the United States to a direct hand in the peacemaking, and that his presence would prevent an Allied retreat from the Fourteen Points. The President rejected the apparently sounder advice that he open the conference, engage in preliminary discussions, and then exit, leaving the daily quarreling to American diplomats. No, this would be Wilson's show: "I must go."[73]

In late October, 1918, Wilson appealed to Americans to return a Democratic Congress loyal to him. Anything less, he said, would be read abroad as a repudiation of his leadership and ideas. Republicans, partisans themselves, were angry that he attempted to identify himself and the Democratic party with the well-being of the nation. The Republicans proceeded to capture the November election and a majority in both houses of Congress; now they would sit in ultimate judgment of Wilson's peacemaking. Not only did Wilson undercut himself at home by arousing partisanship; he also weakened his position at the conference table. European leaders, some of them fresh from political victories, may have agreed with Wilson-baiter Theodore Roosevelt that "Mr. Wilson has no authority whatever to speak for the American people at this time. His leadership has just been emphatically repudiated by them."[74] The President also made the political mistake of not appointing either an important Republican or a senator to the American Peace Commission. Wilson, House, and Lansing sat on it; they were joined by General Bliss and Henry White, seasoned diplomat and nominal Republican. One critical editor listed the members this way:[75]

Name	Occupation	Representing
Woodrow Wilson	President	Himself
Robert Lansing	Sec. of State	The Executive
Henry White	None	Nobody
Edward M. House	Scout	The Executive
Tasker H. Bliss	Soldier	The Commander-in-Chief

It was a handpicked group tied to the President. Wilson also failed to consult with the Senate Foreign Relations Committee before he departed for Paris. Some concessions to his political opposition, and to senatorial prerogatives in foreign affairs, might have smoothed the path later for his peace treaty.

Making the Peace: The Paris Conference at Versailles

On December 4, with great fanfare, Wilson departed from New York harbor aboard the *George Washington.* He settled into a quiet voyage, surrounded by advisers and nearly 2,000 reports produced by "The Inquiry," a group of scholars who for over a year had studied international problems likely to arise at the peace conference. There were many reports, but few plans. In fact, Wilson's friends were alarmed that the President continued to speak in vague terms and still had not produced a blueprint for the League of Nations. Wilson landed in France on

David Lloyd George (1863–1945). One of Wilson's antagonists at Versailles, the British Prime Minister (left) grew annoyed with Wilson's pontificating lectures. (Sketch by Anthony Saris, American Heritage Publishing Company)

Georges Clemenceau (1841–1929). Auguste Rodin's bronze (right) aptly conveys the formidable stature of ''The Tiger'' from France, eager for revenge against Germany. (The Rodin Museum, Philadelphia)

Wilson in Dover, England, 1919. Demonstrations of adulation like this one buoyed Wilson's faith that he represented mankind in the quest for peace. (U.S. Signal Corps, National Archives)

December 13, and soon began a tiring round of receptions and speeches. Enthusiastic Paris crowds cheered him, and thousands in England and Italy greeted him with admiration verging on the religious. Wilson assumed that this generous outpouring meant that *his* version was universally popular and that *he* had a missionary duty to carry it forward. He would soon discover that such ambiguous "man-in-the-street" opinion was not shared by the more sober David Lloyd George, Prime Minister of Britain, by French Premier Georges Clemenceau, or by Italian leader Vittorio Orlando, his antagonists at the Paris Conference.

Germany and Bolshevik Russia were excluded from the conference of January–May, 1919, but thirty-two nations sent delegations, which essentially followed the lead of the "Big Four." Most of the sessions were conducted in secrecy, hardly befitting Wilson's first "point." Clemenceau, dubbed "The Tiger," was imposing—his face masked by a bushy moustache and his mind dominated by French revenge against Germany. He sparred with Wilson, snorting that "God gave us the Ten Commandments, and we broke them. Wilson gives us the Fourteen Points. We shall see."[76] Lloyd George, the "Welsh Witch," was more conciliatory, eager to build a strong France and to head off a reduction in German purchases of British exports. Orlando was a fervent Italian nationalist, concerned primarily with those issues that would enlarge Italian interests. All of them distrusted American power, harbored dreams of bigger empires, sought security and postwar reconstruction, and resented Wilson's "sermonettes." Lloyd George, who complained that the United States was bullying Europe, concluded that Wilson "was the most extraordinary compound I have ever encountered of the noble visionary, the implacable and unscrupulous partisan, the exalted idealist and the man of rather petty personal rancour."[77]

One of the thorniest issues at the conference was the disposition of colonies and the establishment of new countries. Wilson had appealed for self-determination, but the belligerents had already signed secret treaties of conquest. After hard negotiating, the conferees mandated former German and Turkish colonies to the countries which had conquered them, to be loosely supervised under League of Nations auspices. Under the mandate system—a compromise between outright annexation and complete independence—France and Britain obtained parts of the Middle East, and Japan acquired China's Shandong Province and Germany's Pacific islands. After Wilson's reluctant acceptance of the Shandong arrangement, the President lamented to a friend that "the settlement was the best that could be had out of a dirty past."[78] The victimized Chinese were naturally irate. France gained the demilitarization of the German Rhineland and a stake in the coal-rich Saar Basin. Italy annexed South Tyrol and Trieste from the collapsed Austro-Hungarian Empire. A total of 1,132,000 square miles changed hands. Newly formed or independent countries also emerged: Austria, Czechoslovakia, Hungary, Poland, and Yugoslavia. The Allies further exploited nationalism to establish a ring of hostile states around Bolshevik Russia: Finland, Estonia, Latvia, and Lithuania, all formerly part of the Russian Empire. The map of Europe was redrawn. The mandate system smacked of imperialism, in violation of the Fourteen Points. But the new states in Europe were examples of Wilson's self-determination pledge—although some critics argued that the new countries were very weak and vulnerable to outside pressures, thereby inviting international conflict. France itself felt insecure. To assuage French fears of a revived Germany, Britain and the United States signed a security pact with France guaranteeing its border, but the pact was never ratified by the Senate.

Reparations proved a knotty issue. The peace conference, recalled American adviser Bernard Baruch, "was dealing with blood-raw passions still pulsing through people's veins."[79] The United States wanted a limited indemnity for Germany, to avoid a harsh peace that might arouse long-term German resentment or debilitate the German economy and politics. "If we humiliate the German people and drive them too far," Wilson remarked before Versailles, "we shall destroy all form of government, and Bolshevism will take its place."[80] France, hoping to cripple Germany, pushed for a large bill of reparations. Britain, suffering a milder case of revenge, sided with France. The conferees wrote a "war guilt clause," which held Germany responsible for all of the war's damages. Although the reparations settlement was shortsighted, Wilson felt compelled to give in to heavy pressure, always confident that his League of Nations would ameliorate any severity. With little regard for Germany's ability to pay, the Reparations Commission in 1921 presented a hobbled Germany with the outrageous indemnity of thirty-three billion dollars. The Paris reparations agreement plagued international relations for the next decade.

Wilson's primary concern, unlike that of the other participants, was the League of Nations. He directly supervised the drafting of the League's covenant. This charter provided for an influential council of five big powers (permanent) and representatives from smaller nations (by election). An assembly of all nations for discussion was also created. Wilson argued that the heart of the covenant was Article 10, a provision designed to curb aggression and war: "The Members of the League undertake to respect and preserve as against external aggression the territorial integrity and existing political independence of all Members of the League. In case of any such aggression or in case of any threat or danger of such aggression the Council shall advise upon the means by which this obligation shall be fulfilled."[81] Wilson succeeded in persuading the conferees to merge the League covenant and the peace terms in a package. The League charter, then, constituted the first 26 articles of a 440-article Treaty of Paris. The League covenant was the noblest part of all—"It is practical, and yet it is intended to purify, to rectify, to elevate."[82]

The Germans, when first handed the long document, refused to sign, pleading that some of its provisions violated the Fourteen Points. The Allies were not in a forgiving mood, so the losers bowed to the inevitable humiliation on June 28 in Versailles' elegant Hall of Mirrors. Germany was stripped of 13 percent of its territory, 10 percent of its population, and all its colonies. Lansing, believing the harsh peace terms would make the League unworkable, complained: "The League might as well attempt to prevent the growth of plant life in a tropical jungle."[83] A German nationalist bitterly wrote a year later: "Among all those who shoveled at the grave of our people, none was more clever or more successful than Woodrow Wilson."[84]

Principle and Partisanship: The League Fight at Home

Wilson spent almost six months in Europe drawing up his plans for the postwar peace. From February 24 to March 14, he returned to the United States for executive business; during that brief respite from the Paris Conference, Wilson's handiwork came under attack. Upon landing in Boston in late February, he castigated critics. "America is the hope of the world," he lectured. Wilson would not let "minds that have no sweep beyond the nearest horizon" reject the American purpose of making men free. "I have fighting blood in me," he asserted.[85]

Within days he met with the House Foreign Affairs Committee and Senate Foreign Relations Committee. Republicans peppered him with questions about the degree to which the covenant limited American sovereignty. Senator Frank Brandegee of Connecticut was not impressed with Wilson's performance: "I feel as if I had been wandering with Alice in Wonderland and had tea with the Mad Hatter."[86] In early March, Republican Senator Henry Cabot Lodge of Massachusetts engineered a "Round Robin," a statement by thirty-nine senators (enough to deny the treaty a two-thirds vote) that questioned the League covenant and requested that the peace treaty and the covenant be acted upon separately. Many of the signers feared that the League would limit United States freedom to act independently in international affairs.

A defiant Wilson sailed again for France, cocksure that the "pygmy" minds in America would not destroy his precious League. Still, he was politician enough, and stung enough, to seek slight changes in Paris. He did not think his senatorial opponents had much sense, but he knew they had votes. So he amended the covenant, to the effect that League members could refuse mandates, that the League had no jurisdiction over purely domestic issues, and that the Monroe Doctrine was safeguarded against League action. He would not alter Article 10. When he returned to the United States in July, criticism had not subsided; indeed, it was more insistent. Wilson submitted the 264-page Treaty of Paris to the Senate on July 10, with an address that resembled an evangelical sermon: "The stage is set, the destiny disclosed. It has come about by no plan of our conceiving, but by the hand of God, who led us into this way. . . . The light streams upon the path ahead, and nowhere else."[87] There was no doubt about the outcome in Wilson's mind, for as he told a reporter, *"The Senate is going to ratify the treaty."*[88] Asked by the French ambassador if he would accept senatorial "reservations" to the treaty, Wilson snapped: "I shall consent to nothing. The Senate must take its medicine."[89]

Both friends and foes were asking if Wilson could have avoided the compromises, the land-grabbing, the harsh reparations bill, and the less than open diplomacy at the conference. Most historians agree that Wilson, against strong odds, gained a good percentage of his goals as outlined in the Fourteen Points. Self-determination for nationalities was established as never before in Europe, and the League, despite later failings, was a notable achievement. Wilson did compromise, however, especially when faced by formidable opposition like that thrown up by Clemenceau, who spoke for the many Europeans unable easily to forget the war's death count. During the conference, too, both Italy and Japan had threatened to walk out unless they realized some territorial goals. Wilson's problem with his domestic critics was that he had so built up a case for his ability to deliver an unselfish peace that when the conquerors' hard bargaining, rather than charity, characterized the conference, observers could only conclude that the President had failed badly to live up to his own ideals. In short, Wilson, through his pompous and vague rhetoric, had misled. The millenium he promised was obviously unattainable. Some of his critics said that he should have left Paris in protest, refusing to sign, or that he should have threatened the European powers with American economic power by curbing postwar loans and trade. Believing ardently that the League, with Article 10, would rectify all, Wilson instead had accepted embarrassing compromises.

Wilson would not compromise at home, however. Nor would he give systematic technical analysis to the many clauses of the treaty or admit that it might be flawed. He simply expected the Senate dutifully to ratify his masterwork. Yet his earlier bypassing of that body and his own partisan speeches and self-righteousness insured debate with influential critics. Progressives among them, like Senator George Norris, tended to think that the League did not go far enough in reducing the possibility of war, that it was an ill-disguised device to continue great power domination. Conservative critics, like Senator Henry Cabot Lodge, argued on the other hand that the League deprived the United States of too much sovereignty. Senator James Reed of Missouri added a racist touch: "Think of submitting questions involving the very life of the United States to a tribunal on which a nigger from Liberia, a nigger from Honduras, a nigger from India . . . each have votes equal to that of the great United States."[90] Article 10 seemed to bother everybody. Two questions were uppermost: Would League members be obligated to use force? Did the article mean that the status quo would always be upheld? The article did not require members to use force, but it implied they should. Senator William Borah complained that "I may be willing to help my neighbor . . . , but I do not want him placed in a position where he may decide for me when and how I shall act or to what extent I shall make sacrifice."[91] Article 10 also implied that territorial adjustments or rebellions, such as those in Ireland, India, and Egypt, would not be permitted. Senator Robert LaFollette called the League an imperialist club, which would keep colonies in bondage against their will by invoking Article 10. The article was simply too open-ended. Yet Wilson argued that without such a commitment to halt warmakers in the future the League would be feeble. "In effect," historian Roland N. Stromberg has noted, "Wilson and the Democrats wanted to accept an obligation that we might thereafter refuse, while Lodge and the Republicans wanted to refuse an obligation we might thereafter accept."[92]

Wilson's chief legislative obstacle was Henry Cabot Lodge. Chairman of the Senate Foreign Relations Committee, nationalist-imperialist, author, Ph.D., Republican partisan, like Wilson a scholar in politics, Lodge packed his committee with anti-League senators, dragged out hearings for weeks, kept most Republicans together on treaty votes, and nurtured a personal animosity toward Wilson matched only by Wilson's detestation for Lodge. It is frankly unclear whether or not Lodge sought to kill the League in infancy: in any case, his method of attack was indirect. He proposed a series of "reservations" to the League covenant. Although in retrospect these reservations, intended to guard American sovereignty, do not appear to have been death blows to the League, at the time they were hotly debated. They addressed the question of American national interest—the degree to which the United States would limit its freedom of action, the degree to which the United States should engage in collective security. Many of the fourteen reservations stated the obvious—such as, that Congress would retain its constitutional role in foreign policy. Others excluded the Monroe Doctrine from League oversight more explicitly than the covenant's version, and denied the League jurisdiction over American domestic legislation such as immigration laws. The reservation that struck at Article 10 was important: The United States assumed no obligation to preserve the territorial integrity or political independence of another country unless authorized by Congress.

The Senate divided into four groups. Loyal to Wilson were about forty Democrats called the Non-Reservationists. Another group, the Mild-Reservationists, led by Frank B. Kellogg, numbered about thirteen Republicans. The third faction, managed by Lodge, were known as the Strong-Reservationists. They counted in

Henry Cabot Lodge (1850–1924). Wilson's partisan rival complained that the President's speeches in Europe "are all in the clouds and fine sentiments that lead nowhere." As for the League covenant, Lodge ridiculed its scholarship. "It might get by at Princeton," Wilson's alma mater, "but certainly not at Harvard," where the senator had earned a Ph.D. in history. (Library of Congress)

Woodrow Wilson after His Stroke. Throughout his adult life, Wilson suffered cerebral vascular disease, and a series of strokes produced brain damage. After his collapse in September, 1919, he was forced to remain in the White House while his aides and wife tried to keep secret the severity of his physical incapacity. Dr. Edwin A. Weinstein, who has studied the relationship between Wilson's health, personality, and decisionmaking, has noted that the President became unable to keep his train of thought and to sustain work, and was prone to outbursts of temper. (Library of Congress)

their number some twenty Republicans and a handful of Democrats. The fourth group, consisting of sixteen Irreconcilables, ardently opposed the treaty with or without reservations. Most of them were Republicans, including LaFollette, Norris, and Borah.

Wilson refused to accept any reservations whatsoever. He also argued that a treaty ratified with reservations would have to go back to another international conference for acceptance; he was unwilling to invite that possibility, because every nation would then rush in with its pet reservations. Later this argument was weakened when the British announced that they would accept American reservations just so that the League could be launched and the treaty passed. In September, 1919, noting that Lodge was hoping delay would sour the American people on the treaty, Wilson decided to dig his spade into the grass roots. He set off on an 8,000-mile trip across the United States. It was a tragic journey. Weak, tired, irritable, and plagued by severe headaches, he pounded the podium for forty speeches before he collapsed in Pueblo, Colorado. He took the offensive, blasting his traducers as "absolute, contemptible quitters."[93] He also appealed to patriotism by denouncing hyphenated Americans (a response to Irish- and German-American opposition to the treaty) and by comparing his critics to Bolsheviks (both destructive, he said). He confused his audiences when he stated that Article 10 meant that the United States had a moral but not legal obligation to use armed force. He insisted that America could still decide which wars it wanted to enter. Wilson's erratic practice of mixing impassioned rhetoric with occasional sober analysis undercut his effectiveness.

After his collapse, he returned to Washington, where he fell victim to a stroke that paralyzed his left side. Wilson's poor health probably did not affect the outcome; sick or healthy, he was adamant against compromise. After his stroke, however, he isolated himself, apparently ashamed of his physical weakness. The brain damage and impaired vision resulting from the stroke hindered concentration and promoted stubbornness. His wife, Edith Bolling Wilson, helped run his political affairs, screening messages and visitors, and such advocates of conciliation as Colonel House and Secretary Lansing fell from presidential grace. House was unable even to get an appointment with the ailing President, and in February, 1920, Lansing was abruptly dismissed, replaced by the more pliable Bainbridge Colby, a Wilson admirer. "Better a thousand times to go down fighting," Wilson told his wife, "than to dip your colors to dishonorable compromise."[94] Wilson held firm, but so did the critics.

In November, 1919, the Senate balloted on the complete treaty *with* reservations and rejected it, 39–55 (Irreconcilables and Non-Reservationists in the negative). Then it voted on the treaty *without* reservations and also rejected it, 38–53 (Irreconcilables and Reservationists in the negative). The President kept loyal Democrats in line, forbidding them to accept any "reserved" treaty, yet realistically such was the only kind that would have fulfilled his dream of American membership in the League. In March, 1920, another tally saw many Democrats break ranks to vote in favor of reservations. Still not enough, the treaty was rejected 49–35, short of the two-thirds majority required for ratification. "It is dead," Wilson lamented to his Cabinet, "and lies over there. Every morning I put flowers on its grave."[95] Still a fighter, he avowed that the election of 1920 would be a "solemn referendum" on the treaty. It was not. A multitude of other questions blurred the League issue in that campaign, and Warren G. Harding, who as a senator had supported reservations, was elected President. In July, 1921, Congress officially terminated the war, and in August by treaty with Germany the United States claimed as valid for itself the terms of the Treaty of Paris—exclusive of the League articles.

The memorable League fight was over. The negative outcome can be blamed on political partisanship, personal animosities, senatorial resentment at having been slighted in the peacemaking, and disinterest and confusion in the public, which increasingly diverted its attention to the problem of readjusting to a peacetime economy. Then, of course, there was Wilson himself—stubborn, pontificating, and combative. He might have conceded that the peace was imperfect. He might have provided more careful analysis of a complicated document of 264 pages. He might, further, have admitted that his opponents held a respectable intellectual position. Instead he chose an often shrill rhetoric and a rigid self-righteousness, excessively defensive of his authorship of a parchment that he considered almost sacred. Most important, he refused compromise because the difference between himself and his critics was fundamental: whether it was in America's national interest to participate in collective security or seek safety unilaterally. In essence, then, traditional American nationalism and nonalignment, or unilateralism, decided the debate against Wilson.

America's absence from the League was not catastrophic. None of the great powers wished to bestow significant authority on the League. Even if the United States had joined, it too probably would have continued to act outside the League's auspices, especially regarding its own imperialism in Latin America. No international organization at that time could have outlawed war, dismantled empires, or scuttled navies. Wilson overshot reality in thinking that he could reform world politics through a new international organization: certainly the League was a commendable cry for restraint, but it was no panacea for world peace.

Containing the Bolshevik Specter: Intervention in Russia

"Paris cannot be understood without Moscow," wrote Wilson's press secretary in France, Ray Stannard Baker. "Without ever being represented at Paris at all, the Bolsheviki and Bolshevism were powerful elements at every turn."[96] Indeed, throughout the conference "there rose the specter of chaos, like a black cloud out of the east, threatening to overwhelm and swallow up the world."[97] As he traveled to France aboard the *George Washington,* President Wilson complained about the "poison of Bolshevism."[98] Revolutionary and anticapitalist, the Bolsheviks, or Communists, threw fright into the established leaders of Europe and America. David Lloyd George worried that Western statesmen would be unable to dam the "waters of Revolution."[99] At home and abroad the peacemakers battled the radical left. In the United States the Wilson Administration trampled on civil liberties during an exaggerated "Red Scare," which sent innocent people to jail or deported them. Abroad Wilson first hoped to tame the Bolsheviks, to reform them, to contain them; finally he hesitantly aligned with other powers in a futile attempt to destroy them.

Most Americans applauded the Russian Revolution of March, 1917, which toppled Tsar Nicholas II. Wilson himself viewed it as a thrust against autocracy, war, and imperialism. But when the moderate Provisional government under Alexander Kerensky fell to the radical Bolsheviks in October, shocked Americans responded with hostility. American anger was further aroused in March, 1918,

Тов. Ленин ОЧИЩАЕТ
землю от нечисти.

"**Comrade Lenin Sweeps the Globe
Clean.**" Vladimir Ilyich Lenin
(1870–1924) is shown in this Bolshevik art as a revolutionary ridding the
world of monarchs and capitalists. Wilson and the Allies took him for the revolutionary he professed to be and tried
to contain Lenin's Bolshevism through a
variety of hostile acts. (By Mikhail
Cheremnykh and Victor Deni in Mikhail
Guerman, comp., *Art of the October
Revolution,* Leningrad: Aurora Art Publishers, 1979)

when the Bolsheviks signed the Brest-Litovsk Treaty with Germany. It was a harsh
peace for the Russians, for they had to relinquish the territories of the Ukraine and
Finland, among others—a total of 1,267,000 square miles, 62,000,000 people, and
one-third of Russia's best agricultural land. From the Bolshevik perspective, it was
a necessary peace for a nation incapable of continued fighting. From the Allied
point of view, the treaty was a stab in the back, an end to the war's eastern front,
and a victory for Germany. Some irate American officials began to think that the
Bolsheviks were pro-German. V. I. Lenin's travel through Germany in early 1917,
with the apparent permission of German authorities, fed this mistaken notion.

A number of methods were open to Wilson and the Allies to smash Bolshevism:
military intervention, economic blockade, exclusion from the peacemaking, nonrecognition, encirclement with hostile countries (*cordon sanitaire*), food relief, and
aid to anti-Bolshevik forces within Russia. They tried all, but Wilson was never
sure about the viability of the methods. "I have been sweating blood over the
question what it is right and feasible to do in Russia," Wilson wrote Colonel
House. "It goes to pieces like quicksilver under my touch."[100] In June, 1918,
Wilson decided to send American troops to northern Russia. They were ordered to
avoid military action in the Russian civil war, but inevitably they supported French
and British units in military efforts to roll back Bolshevik influence. Wilson
announced that the expedition was authorized only to prevent German seizure of
military supplies and a railroad, but he did not reveal his hope that the venture
would help cripple the Red Army. Eventually 5,000 American soldiers, many
constituting the "Polar Bears," or 339th Infantry Regiment from Michigan, were
stationed there. One hundred and thirty-nine died on Russian soil. They suffered

through a bitter winter of fifty below zero temperatures and few daylight hours. Their morale sagged and mutiny threatened. As George F. Kennan has noted: "They alone had to endure this purgatory, and this for reasons never adequately explained to them."[101] Remaining even beyond the armistice of World War I, they departed in June, 1919.

Wilson had hoped to avoid military action, to draw the Bolsheviks peacefully somehow into a nebulous world order. But the pressure from the deeply anticommunist French and British and expansionist Japanese persuaded him to send another expedition, this time to Siberia, where he envisioned the growth of a non-Bolshevik Russian bastion. In July he approved the expedition, later officially explaining to the American people that the troops (eventually numbering 10,000) were being dispatched to rescue a group of Czechs stranded in Russia. The Czech legion had been organized during the war as part of the Russian army to fight for a Czech homeland in Austria-Hungary, but in 1918 it was fighting the Bolsheviks along the Trans-Siberian Railroad. Wilson said he hoped they could get out and back to central Europe to fight Germans.

Wilson's official explanation masked his more general strategy of opposing Bolshevism. Historians disagree on Wilson's motives. Some argue that the official reason (saving the Czechs) is the only one; others say that he wanted to preserve the "Open Door" against the Japanese, who sent some 72,000 troops to Siberia; still others point to the President's anti-Bolshevik intentions. Whether his inten-

American Troops in Vladivostok, Siberia. A contingent of the 10,000 United States troops sent by President Wilson to Siberia in 1918 during the Russian civil war. (U.S. Signal Corps, National Archives)

tions were anti-Bolshevik or not, his actions certainly became so. The very presence of American troops in Russia during a civil war, and American support for non-Bolshevik groups, constituted hostility to the Communist regime. Then, too, there is no question that the Czechs were anti-Bolshevik and that the other powers intended their military expeditions to crush the radicals. Wilson and the Allies for a time hoped that anti-Bolshevik White Russian leader Admiral A. V. Kolchak would marshal enough strength to form a pro-Western constitutional government. They funneled money and supplies to him, but he proved an immoderate and ineffective leader, and Kolchak's movement collapsed in late 1919. American troops were finally withdrawn in early 1920 after thirty-six deaths.

At the Paris Peace Conference, the victors tried to isolate what they considered a revolutionary contagion. The Bolsheviks were, of course, excluded from the meeting, certainly a serious mistake: a strike against Wilson's own desire for world unity, and a denial of his pledge of self-determination. "Bolshevism is gaining ground everywhere," Colonel House noted in his diary. "We are sitting on an open powder magazine and some day a spark may ignite it."[102] The organization of the Third International in Moscow in early 1919 alarmed postwar leaders, as did Communist Bela Kun's successful revolution in Hungary in March, 1919, which only lasted until August. At Versailles, the conferees granted territory to Russia's neighbors (Poland, Rumania, and Czechoslovakia) and created the nations of Finland, Estonia, Latvia, and Lithuania as a ring of unfriendly states around Russia. During the conference, besides the military interventions, the Allies imposed a strict economic blockade on Russia, continued aid to the White forces, and sent relief assistance to other countries, like Austria and Hungary, to stem political unrest.

Critics protested against these counterrevolutionary efforts and suggested that alternatives were possible. Raymond Robins (a Red Cross official) and Senator Robert LaFollette, among others, called for recognition of Lenin's government and opposed the policy of isolating Russia from the peace conference. Robins, who met frequently with Lenin, urged the Wilson Administration in early 1918 to send aid to the Bolsheviks so that they could resist the German peace terms eventually written into the Brest-Litovsk Treaty. Other critics, like Walter Lippmann, urged a policy of noninterference—let the Russians settle their own affairs. But Wilson could not tolerate the Bolsheviks; they had betrayed the Allies, expropriated commercial and church property, established a dictatorship, denounced capitalism, and planted seeds of revolution elsewhere. Wilson wanted to reform capitalism; Lenin sought to eliminate it. Wilson believed imperialism and war could be contained through an international organization; Lenin was adamant that war and imperialism were an inevitable outgrowth of expansionist capitalist institutions.

Certainly no ideological compromise was possible. But recognition of the Moscow regime and a diplomatic accommodation appear to have been options. Wilson attempted to end the civil war in Russia in January, 1919, when he invited the warring groups to meet on Prinkipo Island in the Sea of Marmara. The Bolsheviks cautiously accepted the invitation, but the anti-Bolsheviks flatly rejected it and the meeting never took place. Next, in February, Colonel House arranged to send William C. Bullitt, a member of the American delegation at Versailles, and Lincoln Steffens, radical muckraking journalist, to Russia to talk with the Soviets. Wilson envisioned a factfinding mission. The ambitious Bullitt, however, dreamed of an agreement whereby Allied troops would be withdrawn from Russia and Lenin would make territorial concessions to his adversaries to end the civil war. Believing that the Moscow government was well established, Bullitt and Steffens returned to Paris convinced they had struck such an agreement. Lloyd George squelched it; Wilson ignored it. Bullitt, already disgusted by Wilson's compromises with the Allies at Paris, resigned in protest.

The Allied counterrevolution was costly to the future of international relations. The scar ran deep. "Few in the West recall the war of East and West of 1918–20," Frederick L. Schuman has written. "Every city, town, and village in Russia preserves momentoes of these tragic years."[103] In 1959, for example, Premier Nikita Khrushchev reminded Americans of their oft-forgotten intervention. At a time when Soviet leaders were locked in a life-or-death struggle against internal enemies, they had to resist a foreign invasion that prolonged the agony of civil war. The blatant Allied tactics ultimately backfired, as the Bolsheviks capitalized on the nationalistic feelings aroused by foreign troops on Russian soil. Wilson's dream of a cooperative and harmonious world was dealt another blow. William Bullitt resolved to lie on the beaches of the Mediterranean and "watch the world go to hell."[104] "He went. And it did."[105]

American Expansion and World War I

About 130,000 Americans died in the First World War and the conflict cost the United States government over thirty billion dollars. A third of the figure was paid through taxes; the other two-thirds represented borrowed money, which would have to be paid off by postwar generations. If one counts the long-term expense of veterans' benefits, the cost to the United States probably equaled three times the immediate direct costs. But the price and consequences of World War I can be reckoned in other ways. What President Dwight D. Eisenhower would later call the "military-industrial complex" had its origins in the government-business cooperation during that war; economic decisionmaking for the nation was centralized as never before, and efficient methods in manufacturing were applied comprehensively, contributing to American economic power. In foreign affairs, the White House, under Wilson's heady leadership, assumed more authority in initiating policy and controlling execution. The State Department read diplomatic messages after Wilson had typed them on his own machine. Wilson bypassed Congress on a number of occasions, failing even to consult that body, for example, about the Fourteen Points, the goals at Versailles, and the intervention in the Russian civil war. He acted, according to his biographer Arthur S. Link, "like a divine-right monarch in the conduct of foreign relations."[106] The Senate finally rebelled by rejecting the League of Nations, but that negative decision did not undercut the trend of growing presidential power in the making of foreign policy.

The era of World War I also witnessed domestic events that in turn affected foreign affairs: racial conflict, evidenced by twenty-five race riots in 1919; suppression of civil liberties under the Espionage and Sedition Acts, by which innocent people who dissented from the war were silenced; the crippling of radical commentary (Socialist party leader Eugene Debs was jailed for opposing the war) and hence the growth of an uncritical consensus; the emasculation of the reform impulse. Wars tend to demand conformity at home because leaders insist on

"We Are Making a New World." British painter Paul Nash rendered this gloomy landscape as a commentary on the ugly devastation wrought by the guns of World War I. (Imperial War Museum, London)

patriotism and commitment to the "crusade." Those who question the foreign venture can face ostracism and harassment.

Over 10 million lives were annihilated in World War I. Russia lost 1.7 million, Germany gave up 1.8 million, and Britain lost 1 million. One out of every two French males between the ages of twenty and thirty-two (in 1914) died during the war. It had been a total war, involving whole societies, not merely their marching armies. Europe's landscape was trampled. Never before had a war left the belligerents so exhausted, so battered. New destructive weapons had been introduced—tanks, airplanes, poison gas, the Big Bertha gun, and submarines. Journalist Hanson Baldwin has commented that World War I "provided a preview of the Pandora's box of evils that the linkage of science with industry in the service of war was to mean."[107] Many Americans turned away in disgust from the slaughter and the new weapons of destruction. The sight of men singing as they marched to their deaths seemed incongruous. The desire to avoid a major war was strong after the European conflict, and Americans would henceforth be cautious about entering a conflagration in Europe. The *New Republic* editorialized: "THIS IS NOT PEACE. Americans would be fools if they permitted themselves to be embroiled in a system of European alliances. . . . America should withdraw from all commitments which would impair her freedom of action."[108] Disillusioned intellectuals like Ernest Hemingway and John Dos Passos mocked the carthaginian peace. E. M. Remarque's *All Quiet on the Western Front* (1929) captured the antiwar mood: "A hospital alone shows what war is."[109]

World War I, as someone remarked, stacked the cards for the future. Empires were broken up—the Turkish, Austro-Hungarian, German, and Russian—creating new and weak nations. Nationalists in Asia, such as Mahatma Gandhi in British-dominated India and Ho Chi Minh in French-controlled Indochina, set goals of national liberation based in part upon Wilson's ideal of self-determination. Sun Yat-sen's Chinese revolution jarred Asian relationships. The rather closed, Europe-oriented diplomatic system of the turn of the century had fragmented and expanded to include the several new states in central and eastern Europe, Japan, and the United States, as well as the new League of Nations. In Latin America, prewar European economic stakes were loosened, inviting the United States to expand its interests there. The international system was quite fluid, made more so by the rise of Bolshevism in Russia. The world had to be put back together again: the adjustments to new relationships would not come easily. Because of fear of communism, leaders tried to isolate Soviet Russia. Because of fear of a revived Germany, leaders tried to strip it of power, creating bitter resentments in the German people. Because the victors faced reconstruction problems at home, they tagged Germany with a huge reparations bill that would disorient European and world economics. Nobody seemed happy with the postwar settlement; many would attempt to recapture lost opportunities or to redefine the terms. Wilsonianism enjoyed but a brief prominence; the lessons Wilson sought to impress upon an offending mankind were taught, but unlearned. World War I had, surely, created as many problems as it solved. "Politically, economically, socially," Wilson informed Congress in 1919, "the World is on the operating table, and it has not been possible to administer any anesthetic."[110] Wilson had his prescription for the cure, but so did others, including the Russians with their competing ideology of communism.

To Americans, World War I bequeathed an unassailable legacy: the United States became the world's leading economic power. As Wilson confidently put it in August, 1919: "The financial leadership will be ours. The industrial primacy will be ours. The commercial advantage will be ours. The other countries of the world are looking to us for leadership and direction."[111] During the war years, to meet the need for raw materials, American companies expanded operations in developing nations. Goodyear went into the Dutch East Indies for rubber, Swift and Armour expanded in South America, tin interests tapped Bolivia, copper companies penetrated Chile, and oil firms sank new wells in Latin America. The government encouraged this economic expansion by building up the merchant marine, which by 1919 was 60 percent over its prewar size. By 1920, the United States produced about 40 percent of the world's coal and 50 percent of its pig iron.

Because the United States government and American citizens loaned heavily to the Allies during the war, the nation shifted abruptly from a debtor to a creditor status, with Wall Street replacing London as the world's financial center. By early 1919 the Allied governments owed the United States government $10 billion. Whereas before the war Americans owed foreigners $3 billion, after the conflict foreigners owed Americans $13 billion. A gradual shift had begun before the war, but the wartime experience accelerated it tremendously. Americans had devised plans to seize the apparent economic opportunities given them by the war—the Edge Act to permit foreign branch banks, and the Webb-Pomerene Act to allow trade associations to continue to combine for export trading without fear of antitrust action, for example—but a key question remained: how could Europeans pay back their debt to the United States? The answer lay somewhere in a complicated tangle of loans, reparations, tariffs, and world trade. "We are on the eve of a commercial war of the severest sort," predicted Wilson in early 1920.[112]

Economic disorder, then, coupled with political instability, was a legacy of the war. Wilson, who tried to plan against it, warned Congress in August, 1919: "We must face the fact that unless we help Europe to get back to her normal life and production a chaos will ensue there which will inevitably be communicated to this country. . . . In saving Europe, she [United States] will save herself. . . . Europe is our best customer. We must keep her going or thousands of our shops and scores of our mines must close. There is no such thing as letting her go to ruin without ourselves sharing in the disaster."[113] Whether this awareness of the interdependence of the world economy would be matched by policies to stabilize economic conditions was the supreme question for postwar leaders. In 1920, as they contemplated the future, it appeared that World War I had made the world safe neither for American democracy nor for American commerce and capital. American diplomats, with a sense of America's new power, would next try nonmilitary methods.

Further Reading for the Period 1914–1920

For the foreign policy of Woodrow Wilson and the era of World War I, see Thomas A. Bailey and Paul B. Ryan, *The Lusitania Disaster* (1975); Paul Birdsall, "Neutrality and Economic Pressure, 1914–1917," *Science and Society* (1939); Edward H. Buehrig, ed., *Wilson's Foreign Policy in Perspective* (1957); John W. Coogan, *The End of Neutrality: The United States, Britain, and Maritime Rights, 1899–1915* (1981); John M. Cooper, *The Vanity of Power: American Isolationism and the First World War* (1969); R. D. Cuff and J. L. Granatstein, *Canadian-American Relations in Wartime* (1975); Patrick Devlin, *Too Proud to Fight: Woodrow Wilson's Neutrality* (1975); Jean-Baptiste Duroselle, *France and the United States* (1978); Ross Gregory, *The Origins of American Intervention in the First World War* (1971); Sondra Herman, *Eleven Against War* (1969); Burton I. Kaufman, *Efficiency and Expansion: Foreign Trade Organization in the Wilson Administration, 1913–1921* (1974); Arthur S. Link, *Wilson* (1960–1965), *Wilson the Diplomatist* (1963), and *Woodrow Wilson: Revolution, War, and Peace* (1979); Ernest R. May, *The World War and American Isolation, 1914–1917* (1959); Emily S. Rosenberg, *Spreading the American Dream: American Economic and Cultural Expansion, 1890–1945* (1982); Jeffrey J. Safford, *Wilsonian Maritime Diplomacy, 1913–1921* (1978); Clara E. Schieber, *The Transformation of American Sentiment Toward Germany 1870–1914* (1923); Daniel M. Smith, *The Great Departure* (1965); Charles C. Tansill, *America Goes to War* (1938); Barbara Tuchman, *The Zimmermann Telegram* (1958); and Edwin A. Weinstein, *Woodrow Wilson: A Medical and Psychological Biography* (1981).

For Americans at home and abroad during the First World War, consult George T. Blakey, *Historians on the Homefront: American Propagandists for the Great War* (1970); J. Garry Clifford, *The Citizen Soldiers: The Plattsburg Training Camp Movement, 1913–1920* (1972); Edward M. Coffman, *The War To End All Wars* (1968); Charles DeBenedetti, *Origins of the Modern American Peace Movement, 1915–1929* (1978); Harvey A. DeWeerd, *President Wilson Fights His War* (1968); David M. Kennedy, *Over Here: The First World War and American Society* (1980); Thomas C. Leonard, *Above the Battle: War-Making in America from Appomattox to Versailles* (1978); Seward W. Livermore, *Politics is Adjourned: Woodrow Wilson and the War Congress, 1916–1918* (1966); Paul L. Murphy, *World War I and the Origin of Civil Liberties* (1979); Horace C. Peterson and Gilbert C. Fite, *Opponents of War, 1917–1918* (1957); David

F. Trask, *Captains & Cabinets: Anglo-American Naval Relations, 1917–1918* (1972) and *The United States in the Supreme War Council* (1961); and Stephen Vaughn, *Holding Fast the Inner Lines: Democracy, Nationalism, and the Committee on Public Information* (1980).

The peacemaking at Versailles and the fate of the League of Nations in the Senate are discussed in Thomas A. Bailey, *Woodrow Wilson and the Lost Peace* (1944) and *Woodrow Wilson and the Great Betrayal* (1945); Inga Floto, *Colonel House in Paris* (1973); Lawrence E. Gelfand, *The Inquiry: American Preparations for Peace* (1963); Herbert Hoover, *The Ordeal of Woodrow Wilson* (1958); Warren F. Kuehl, *Seeking World Order: The United States and International Organization to 1920* (1969); Keith Nelson, *Victors Divided: America and the Allies in Germany, 1918–1923* (1973); Joseph P. O'Grady, ed., *The Immigrants' Influence on Wilson's Peace Policies* (1967); Robert E. Osgood, *Ideals and Self-Interest in American Foreign Relations* (1953); Stuart I. Rochester, *American Liberal Disillusionment in the Wake of World War I* (1977); Ralph A. Stone, *The Irreconcilables* (1970); and Seth P. Tillman, *Anglo-American Relations at the Paris Peace Conference, 1919* (1961).

America's response to the Bolshevik Revolution in Russia is treated in John L. Gaddis, *Russia, the Soviet Union, and the United States* (1978); Lloyd C. Gardner, ed., *Wilson and Revolutions, 1913–1921* (1976); Richard Goldhurst, *The Midnight War: The American Intervention in Russia, 1918–1920* (1978); George F. Kennan, *Russia Leaves the War* (1956) and *The Decision to Intervene* (1958); N. Gordon Levin, *Woodrow Wilson and World Politics* (1968); Arno Mayer, *Politics and Diplomacy of Peacemaking* (1967); Robert K. Murray, *Red Scare* (1955); John Thompson, *Russia, Bolshevism, and the Versailles Peace* (1966); and Betty M. Unterberger, *America's Siberian Expedition* (1956).

The following works study prominent individuals: Paolo Coletta, *William Jennings Bryan* (1965–1969); John M. Cooper, Jr., *Walter Hines Page* (1977); Allen F. Davis, *American Heroine: The Life and Legend of Jane Addams* (1974); John A. Garraty, *Henry Cabot Lodge* (1953); Ross Gregory, *Walter Hines Page* (1970); Lawrence W. Levine, *Defender of the Faith* (1965) (on Bryan); Daniel M. Smith, *Robert Lansing and American Neutrality* (1958); David P. Thelen, *Robert M. LaFollette and the Insurgent Spirit* (1976); and William C. Widenor, *Henry Cabot Lodge and the Search for an American Foreign Policy* (1980).

See also the General Bibliography and the following notes.

Notes to Chapter 8

1. Quoted in Thomas A. Bailey and Paul B. Ryan, *The Lusitania Disaster* (New York: The Free Press, 1975), p. 81.

2. Quoted in Edward Robb Ellis, *Echoes of Distant Thunder: Life in the United States, 1914–1918* (New York: Coward, McCann & Geoghegan, 1975), p. 195.

3. Quoted in Bailey and Ryan, *Lusitania Disaster*, p. 94.

4. *Ibid.*, p. 82.

5. *Ibid.*, p. 133.

6. *Ibid.*, p. 150.

7. Quoted in C. L. Droste and W. H. Tantum, eds., *The Lusitania Case* (Riverside, Conn.: 7 C's Press, 1972), p. 172.

8. Quoted in Burton J. Hendrick, *Life and Letters of Walter Hines Page* (Garden City, N.Y.: Doubleday, Page, 1922–1925; 3 vols.), II, 2.

9. William Jennings Bryan and Mary B. Bryan, *Memoirs* (Chicago: John C. Winston, 1925), pp. 398–399.

10. Quoted in William H. Harbaugh, *The Life and Times of Theodore Roosevelt* (New York: Oxford University Press, 1975; rev. ed.), p. 448.

11. Arthur S. Link, *Wilson: The Struggle for Neutrality, 1914–1915* (Princeton: Princeton University Press, 1960), p. 379.

12. Ray Stannard Baker and William E. Dodd, eds., *Public Papers of Woodrow Wilson: The New Democracy* (New York: Harper and Brothers, 1926; 2 vols.), I, 321.

13. U.S. Department of State, *Foreign Relations of the United States, 1915, Supplement* (Washington: Government Printing Office, 1928), p. 396.

14. *New York World*, quoted in Link, *Wilson: Struggle for Neutrality*, p. 410.

15. David F. Houston, *Eight Years with Wilson's Cabinet, 1913 to 1920* (Garden City, N.Y.: Doubleday, Page, 1926; 2 vols.), I, 137.

16. Quoted in Ernest R. May, *The World War and American Isolation, 1914–1917* (Chicago: Quadrangle Books, [1959], 1966), p. 155.

17. Quoted in Paolo E. Coletta, *William Jennings Bryan* (Lincoln: University of Nebraska Press, 1964–1969; 3 vols.), II, 343.

18. Bailey and Ryan, *Lusitania Disaster*, p. 340.

19. Robert Lansing, *War Memoirs* (Indianapolis: Bobbs-Merrill, 1935), p. 128.

20. Franklin K. Lane, quoted in Robert E. Osgood, *Ideals and Self-Interest in American Foreign Relations* (Chicago: University of Chicago Press, 1953), p. 173.

21. Quoted in Rohan Butler, "The Peace Settlement of Ver-

sailles, 1918–1933," in C. L. Mowat, ed., *The New Cambridge Modern History*, vol. XII: *The Shifting Balance of World Forces, 1898–1945* (Cambridge: Cambridge University Press, 1968), p. 214.

22. Quoted in George H. Knoles, "American Intellectuals and World War I," *Pacific Northwest Quarterly*, LIX (October, 1968), 203.

23. Quoted in Barbara Tuchman, *The Guns of August* (New York: Dell, [1962], 1963), p. 91.

24. Quoted in Hendrick, *Life and Letters of Walter Hines Page*, I, 310.

25. Baker and Dodd, *Public Papers: The New Democracy*, I, 157–159.

26. Quoted in Tuchman, *Guns of August*, p. 349.

27. *Ibid.*, p. 153.

28. Quoted from *Life* magazine, in Mark Sullivan, *Our Times* (New York: Charles Scribner's Sons, 1926–1937; 6 vols.), V, 59.

29. Quoted in Ray Stannard Baker, *Woodrow Wilson: Life and Letters* (New York: Doubleday, Doran, 1927–39; 8 vols.), V, 175.

30. Quoted in Paul Birdsall, "Neutrality and Economic Pressures, 1914–1917," *Science and Society*, III (Spring, 1939), 221.

31. Quoted in Bailey and Ryan, *Lusitania Disaster*, p. 99.

32. Ross Gregory, *The Origins of American Intervention in the First World War* (New York: W. W. Norton, 1971), p. 131.

33. Quoted in Bailey and Ryan, *Lusitania Disaster*, p. 29.

34. *Foreign Relations, 1915, Supplement*, p. 99.

35. Quoted in Arthur S. Link, *Woodrow Wilson and the Progressive Era, 1910–1917* (New York: Harper & Row, 1954), p. 203.

36. Quoted in Arthur S. Link, *Wilson: Confusions and Crisis, 1915–1916* (Princeton: Princeton University Press, 1964), p. 125n. Italics in original.

37. *Ibid.*, pp. 134–135.

38. Bryan and Bryan, *Memoirs*, p. 397.

39. *Foreign Relations, 1915, Supplement*, p. 461.

40. Quoted in Bailey and Ryan, *Lusitania Disaster*, p. 128.

41. Baker and Dodd, *Public Papers: The New Democracy*, II, 122–124.

42. Claude Kitchin, quoted in May, *World War and American Isolation*, p. 189.

43. Samuel Flagg Bemis, "A Worcester County Student in Wartime London and Paris (via Harvard): 1915–1916," *New England Galaxy*, XI (Spring, 1970), 20.

44. Quoted in Patrick Devlin, *Too Proud to Fight: Woodrow Wilson's Neutrality* (New York: Oxford University Press, 1975), p. 517.

45. Baker and Dodd, *Public Papers: The New Democracy*, II, 407–414.

46. Quoted in Jean-Baptiste Duroselle's essay in *Wilson's Diplomacy: An International Symposium* (Cambridge, Mass.: Schenkman, 1973), p. 21.

47. Quoted in Arthur S. Link, *Wilson: Campaigns for Progressivism and Peace, 1916–1917* (Princeton: Princeton University Press, 1965), p. 274.

48. *Ibid.*, p. 289.

49. Quoted in May, *World War and American Isolation*, p. 414.

50. Quoted in Konrad H. Jaransch, *The Enigmatic Chancellor:*

Bethmann Hollweg and the Hubris of Imperial Germany (New Haven: Yale University Press, 1973), p. 301.

51. Lansing, *War Memoirs*, p. 212.

52. Quoted in Link, *Wilson: Campaigns*, p. 343.

53. Quoted in John M. Cooper, Jr., *Walter Hines Page* (Chapel Hill: University of North Carolina Press, 1977), p. 369.

54. Quoted in Baker, *Woodrow Wilson: Life and Letters*, VI, 481.

55. Ray Stannard Baker and William E. Dodd, eds., *Public Papers of Woodrow Wilson: War and Peace* (New York: Harper & Brothers, 1927; 2 vols.), I, 6–16.

56. Gregory, *Origins of American Intervention*, p. 128.

57. Quoted in Osgood, *Ideals and Self-Interest*, p. 177.

58. Quoted in May, *World War and American Isolation*, p. 337.

59. Quoted in J. Garry Clifford, *The Citizen Soldiers: The Plattsburg Training Camp Movement, 1913–1920* (Lexington, Ky.: University Press of Kentucky, 1972), p. 234.

60. Edward M. Coffman, *The War To End All Wars: The American Military Experience in World War I* (New York: Oxford University Press, 1968), p. 27.

61. Quoted *ibid.*, p. 4.

62. *Ibid.*

63. *Ibid.*, p. 67.

64. Quoted in Allen F. Davis, "Welfare, Reform, and World War I," *American Quarterly*, XIX (Fall, 1967), 530.

65. *Ibid.*

66. *Ibid.*, p. 531.

67. Baker and Dodd, *Public Papers: War and Peace*, I, 202.

68. Quoted in *Literary Digest*, LIX (November 30, 1918), 15.

69. Baker and Dodd, *Public Papers: War and Peace*, I, 159–161.

70. Quoted in Selig Adler, *The Isolationist Impulse* (New York: Collier Books [c. 1957], 1961), pp. 60–61.

71. H. G. Nicholas' essay in *Wilson's Diplomacy*, p. 81.

72. Quoted in David F. Trask, *The United States in the Supreme War Council: American War Aims and Inter-Allied Strategy, 1917–1918* (Middletown, Conn.: Wesleyan University Press, 1961), p. 155.

73. Quoted in Daniel M. Smith, *The Great Departure* (New York: John Wiley and Sons, 1965), p. 115.

74. Quoted in Julius W. Pratt, *America and World Leadership, 1900–1921* (New York: Collier Books [c. 1967], 1970), p. 175.

75. George Harvey, quoted in Ralph Stone, *The Irreconcilables* (Lexington, Ky.: University Press of Kentucky, 1970), p. 35.

76. Quoted in Smith, *Great Departure*, p. 109.

77. Quoted in Herbert Hoover, *The Ordeal of Woodrow Wilson* (New York: McGraw-Hill, 1958), p. 254.

78. Quoted in Ross Gregory, "To Do Good in the World: Woodrow Wilson," in Frank Merli and Theodore Wilson, eds., *Makers of American Diplomacy* (New York: Scribner's, 1974), p. 380.

79. Bernard M. Baruch, *The Making of the Reparation and Economic Sections of The Treaty* (New York: Harper & Brothers, 1920), p. 7.

80. Quoted in N. Gordon Levin, Jr., *Woodrow Wilson and World Politics: America's Response to War and Revolution* (New York: Oxford University Press, 1968), p. 134.

81. Article 10 of the League covenant.

82. Baker and Dodd, *Public Papers: War and Peace*, I, 428.

83. Quoted in Hoover, *Ordeal of Woodrow Wilson*, p. 239.

84. Quoted in Ernst Fraenkel's essay in *Wilson's Diplomacy*, p. 65.

85. Baker and Dodd, *Public Papers: War and Peace, I*, 432–440.

86. Quoted in D. F. Fleming, *The United States and the League of Nations, 1918–1920* (New York: Russell & Russell, 1968), p. 134.

87. Baker and Dodd, *Public Papers: War and Peace, I*, 551–552.

88. Quoted in Thomas A. Bailey, *Woodrow Wilson and the Great Betrayal* (Chicago: Quadrangle Books [1945], 1963), p. 9.

89. Quoted in Arthur S. Link, *Wilson the Diplomatist* (Chicago: Quadrangle Books [1957], 1963), p. 131.

90. Quoted in Stone, *Irreconcilables*, p. 88.

91. Quoted in Osgood, *Ideals and Self-Interest*, p. 286.

92. Roland N. Stromberg, *Collective Security and American Foreign Policy* (New York: Frederick A. Praeger, 1963), p. 37.

93. Baker and Dodd, *Public Papers: War and Peace, I*, 624.

94. Quoted in Hoover, *Ordeal of Woodrow Wilson*, p. 281.

95. Quoted in E. David Cronon, ed., *The Cabinet Diaries of Josephus Daniels, 1913–1921* (Lincoln: University of Nebraska Press, 1963), p. 520.

96. Quoted in John M. Thompson, *Russia, Bolshevism, and the Versailles Peace* (Princeton: Princeton University Press, 1966), pp. 3–4.

97. Quoted in Arno J. Mayer, *Politics and Diplomacy of Peacemaking* (New York: Vintage Books [c. 1967], 1969), p. 10.

98. *Ibid.*, p. 21.

99. Quoted in Hoover, *Ordeal of Woodrow Wilson*, p. 168.

100. Quoted in Charles Seymour, *The Intimate Papers of Colonel House* (Boston: Houghton Mifflin, 1926–1928; 4 vols.), *III*, 415.

101. George F. Kennan, *Russia and the West under Lenin and Stalin* (Boston: Little, Brown, 1960), pp. 88.

102. Quoted in Thompson, *Russia, Bolshevism, and the Versailles Peace*, p. 389.

103. Frederick L. Schuman, *Russia Since 1917* (New York: Alfred A. Knopf, 1957), p. 109.

104. Quoted in Beatrice Farnsworth, *William C. Bullitt and the Soviet Union* (Bloomington: Indiana University Press, 1967), p. 70.

105. Walter LaFeber and Richard Polenberg, *The American Century* (New York: John Wiley & Sons, 1975), p. 127.

106. Arthur S. Link, *The Higher Realism of Woodrow Wilson* (Nashville: Vanderbilt University Press, 1971), p. 83.

107. Quoted in Gordon A. Craig, "The Revolution in War and Diplomacy," in Jack J. Roth, ed., *World War I: A Turning Point in Modern History* (New York: Alfred A. Knopf, 1967), p. 12.

108. Quoted in Arthur A. Ekirch, Jr., *Ideas, Ideals, and American Diplomacy* (New York: Appleton-Century-Crofts, 1966), p. 121.

109. E. M. Remarque, *All Quiet on the Western Front* (London: Putnam, 1929), p. 224.

110. Baker and Dodd, *Public Papers: War and Peace, I*, 560.

111. *Ibid.*, p. 640.

112. Quoted in John A. DeNovo, "The Movement for an Aggressive American Oil Policy Abroad, 1918–1920," *American Historical Review*, LXI (July, 1956), 858.

113. Baker and Dodd, *Public Papers: War and Peace, I*, 568–569.

Franklin D. Roosevelt (1882–1945). "Happy Days Are Here Again" was his campaign song. Although crippled by polio, Roosevelt was an activist President who preferred to deal with people directly. His personal style of diplomacy could be unsettling, as State Department officials learned. British diplomat Lord Halifax once likened FDR's administration to "a disorderly line of beaters out shooting; they do put the rabbits out of the bracken, but they don't come out where you expect." (United Press International)

9 Power Without Punch: Relations with Europe, 1920–1939

Diplomatic Crossroad: Franklin D. Roosevelt and the Recognition of Russia, 1933

"Gosh, if I could only, myself, talk to some one man representing the Russians," remarked the President to his close friend and soon-to-be Secretary of the Treasury Henry Morgenthau, Jr., "I could straighten out this whole question."[1] The problem was the sixteen-year-old American policy of nonrecognition of Soviet Russia. Franklin D. Roosevelt decided in early 1933 to bring "this whole Russian question into our front parlor instead of back in the kitchen."[2] The tall, balding, inarticulate, but forceful Morgenthau wanted to sell surplus American cotton to the Russians, and in union with such advocates as Senator William Borah and Colonel Edward House, he encouraged the shift toward recognition. Rather than use the services of the Department of State, which Roosevelt considered still in the "horse and buggy age,"[3] the President preferred personal emissaries like Morgenthau and William C. Bullitt. Bullitt, who had undertaken the abortive mission to Lenin in 1919, was considered a friend of Russia. Ambitious, headstrong, and irascible, Bullitt in 1933 served as special assistant to the secretary of state. In reality, he represented Roosevelt—a "Colonel House in disguise," as one senator put it.[4]

In early October, 1933, at Roosevelt's request, Bullitt began meeting with Boris Skvirsky, director of the Soviet Information Bureau in Washington. He handed Skvirsky a presidential invitation to open discussions "to end the present abnormal relations." But, Bullitt hastened to add, the President's note was only a draft, not a formal document. He instructed the somewhat surprised Russian official to send the invitation to Moscow "by your most confidential code, and learn if it is acceptable to your people." If Russian leaders found it acceptable, they should forward a draft response and, when approved in Washington, both the invitation and Soviet answer would be made public. However, if the Soviet reply should be negative, "Will you give me your word of honor that there will never be any publicity in regard to this proposed exchange of letters and that the whole matter will be kept a secret?"[5] Secrecy being nothing new to Soviet diplomacy, Skvirsky gave his word.

Moscow responded favorably and on October 20 Roosevelt, who liked surprises, published his letter to Russian titular head Mikhail Kalinin, as well as Kalinin's missive to the President. The letters were purposely vague, although the often hyperbolic FDR managed to say at his press conference that "they describe the situation 100 per cent."[6] The President's cordial letter invited the Russians to engage in "frank, friendly conversations" with him "personally." Kalinin responded that he too sought to end the abnormality of nonrecognition, which had an "unfavorable effect not only on the interests of the two states concerned, but also on the general international situation, increasing the element of disquiet, complicating the process of consolidating world peace and encouraging forces tending to disturb that peace."[7]

The last, oblique reference to Japanese aggression in China suggested that the Russians, as well as the Americans, placed the upcoming negotiations in a global context. Since 1917 the Soviets had unsuccessfully sought recognition from the United States, but had been told repeatedly that they must first assume their "international obligations." A world depression and Japanese aggression along Russia's Far Eastern border—trade and security questions—changed attitudes. In early 1933, American officials like Bullitt met informally with Russian diplomats in Europe, and both sides intimated interest in opening diplomatic relations. Bullitt assured Commissar for Foreign Affairs Maxim Litvinov in London that Americans were talking with him "as if he were a human being and not a wild man," and Bullitt advised the President to recognize the Soviet Union because "the two

"**So You're the Big Bad Bear!**" Roosevelt and Soviet Commissar for Foreign Affairs Maxim Litvinov met in Washington in 1933. The atmosphere was friendly. (*Washington Evening Star*, Library of Congress)

countries will henceforth be intimately related in their policy towards Japan and if we should have first-rate men in both countries we might to a large extent control their common actions or at least prevent their acting in a way of which we disapprove."[8] Litvinov likewise hoped American recognition would stand as a warning to Tokyo, which might wonder whether the United States would join forces with Russia if war broke out. Litvinov may even have wanted something approximating an alliance. The fact that Moscow later named its foremost expert on Japan, Alexander Troyanovsky, as the first ambassador to the United States further suggests the Russian preoccupation.

Russia's chief diplomat, Litvinov himself, came to Washington for the negotiations in November, 1933. The chubby round-faced commissar was "regarded as the sharpest trader in Europe," according to Under Secretary of State William Phillips.[9] Morgenthau found him a "warm, friendly man, sparkling in conversation, abundant in hospitality," and Louis Fischer, considered one of the most knowledgeable journalists on Soviet affairs, commented that the intelligent, English-speaking Litvinov "talks quickly on the platform and swallows at least one syllable in each word."[10] On his arrival in the United States on November 7, Litvinov amused reporters when he said that the negotiations would take less than half an hour. In Washington Secretary of State Cordell Hull greeted the visiting envoy and grumbled privately that the President should have used State Department machinery to contact Russia. Actually this was one of the few functions Hull would undertake during the Litvinov visit, because Roosevelt had deliberately scheduled the negotiations knowing full well that his silver-haired secretary would soon be departing for a Pan American Conference in Montevideo, Uruguay. The show would belong to the charming and self-confident Roosevelt, an example of his "personal diplomacy." When the President first met Litvinov in the Blue Room of the White House, he tried to humor the Russian by cracking that the Red Room would be a more appropriate site.

Humor aside, the United States had serious reasons for a turnaround on the question of recognition. Nonrecognition of a major country simply made no diplomatic sense. It had not altered the Soviet system or foreign policy. Fischer summarized widespread opinion when he said it was wrong "not to be in touch with a power which was half of Europe and which occupied a most important strategic position in relation to Japan and China."[11] Phillips concluded that, "since most of the other great powers had already taken the step, to continue to be not on speaking terms had become an absurdity."[12] Although they were divided on the issue, with the American Federation of Labor and the American Legion, among other groups, opposed, more Americans favored recognition in 1933 than ever before. Opening relations, then, might even prove a political success at home. Also, increased trade with Russia beckoned in the hard days of the depression. Many businessmen sought Russian markets, and humorist Will Rogers quipped that "we would recognize the Devil with a false face if he would contract for some pitchforks."[13] Furthermore, of prime strategic importance in American calculations was Japan, recent conqueror of Manchuria: as an Asian power itself, the Soviet Union was a potential bulwark against further Japanese expansion. "The world is moving into a dangerous period both in Europe and Asia," Hull once told the President. "Russia could be a great help in stabilizing this situation as time goes on and peace becomes more and more threatened."[14] No American official ever precisely explained how Russia and the United States might cooperate to tame

Japan, but the common assumption prevailed that somehow Japan would think recognition implied something formal, hence dictating caution in Asia.

A number of Russian-American issues from the past also claimed attention in 1933. This "rich food for debate," as Hull put it, included the debts-claims question.[15] By American accounts Russia owed Americans and the United States government about $636 million for loans extended during World War I and compensation for property confiscated during the Bolshevik Revolution. Moreover, Russia was to many Americans the epitome of anti-God; to gain support from American religious leaders, most notably Father Edmund Walsh of Georgetown University, Roosevelt promised to seek Soviet pledges guaranteeing religious freedom for Americans in Russia. Anticapitalist propaganda directed at the United States also aroused antagonism to communism, as did the uncertainty of legal rights for Americans charged with crimes in Russia. The State Department, which for years had been collecting data and formulating arguments against recognition, was now directed to shift its position, much against its will. It prepared documents on these outstanding questions, making the case that solutions should precede the extension of recognition. Secretary Hull himself seemed lukewarm toward recognition, not simply because Roosevelt was bypassing him, but because he thought Moscow-directed Communists were fomenting revolution in Cuba. His attitudes did not command presidential notice. Anyway, Hull was packing his bags for Montevideo.

The first serious talks, dealing with what Roosevelt called the "mechanical procedure" of sifting through hundreds of "details and figures," went badly.[16] Litvinov insisted on recognition before negotiations. Roosevelt broke the impasse on November 10 when he again humored the commissar by suggesting they meet alone so that "they could, if need be, insult each other with impunity."[17] In subsequent tête-à-tête meetings on the 12th, 15th, and 16th, the two amiable negotiators moved like two bookworms eating toward one another from opposite ends of the shelf, as Bullitt put it. The knottiest question was debts-claims. Much of the amount, Litvinov insisted, was owed by the defunct Tsarist and Provisional governments, not by the Bolsheviks. That amount would never be paid. Unable to resolve their differences, the parties initialed a "gentleman's agreement" acknowledging that they would discuss debts and claims in the future.

Shortly after midnight, on November 17, Roosevelt and Litvinov signed agreements: establishment of diplomatic relations, cessation of Soviet subversive activities and propaganda against the United States, religious freedom and legal rights for Americans in Russia, settlement of debts and claims through future negotiations, and an American loan to finance trade. Although they talked about Japan and Germany as military threats and FDR even suggested that Moscow and Washington together ward them off, the documents never mentioned this subject. The agreements were written in imprecise language. State Department officials, who were not invited to the final talks, predicted future squabbling over meaning. For example, no interest rate was set for the loan, and Comintern, the Soviet propaganda agency, was not specifically named.

When Josef Stalin heard about recognition he uttered *"Ne Razkhlebasta"* or "Keep your shirt on. Don't display our excessive glee."[18] Russian and American expectations for healthy relations *at the time* ran high, despite the Department of State's lack of optimism. Soviet expert George F. Kennan complained later that the popular "idea of trying to enlist Soviet strength in a cause [against Japan] for which we were unwilling to develop and mobilize our own seemed to me particularly dangerous."[19] Kennan's harsh criticism suggests an important consideration: America and Russia were using one another against a third power because alone each was too weak. For the rest of the decade each would attempt to increase its own strength, but in 1933 both looked upon recognition as a stopgap solution to the Asian crisis and depression-plagued trade. "I hope it lasts," Hull remarked when he heard about the Litvinov-Roosevelt accord.[20] It did not, for both Moscow and Washington pursued independent foreign policies that obstructed cooperation against what Morgenthau called the "roughnecks" of international relations.[21]

Independent Internationalism: Diplomats and Diplomacy Between the Wars

The history of the 1933 recognition of Russia illustrates well some of the key themes of interwar diplomacy. It demonstrates that the United States was seeking nonmilitary methods to implement its foreign policy of thwarting hostile powers in traditionally significant areas. It reveals the importance of trade questions and the impact of the Great Depression on diplomacy. It suggests that at times ideological differences, or emotional dislike for a dreaded and alien social-political system, could be subordinated to the national interest. It demonstrates how a President, if an activist, can master the foreign affairs process, even using such devices as isolating his own State Department and signing vague agreements. The recognition of Soviet Russia, finally, proves that the United States in the interwar years was not following a course of simple "isolationism."

The United States had emerged from World War I a recognized world power. Postwar American diplomats, closer to a global perspective than ever before, knew that the American frontier had been extended, that even if they wanted to, Americans could not be bystanders in world affairs. True, between the First and Second World Wars Americans hoped to avoid foreign entanglements and concentrate on domestic matters. But, within the limits of United States power, American leaders largely pursued an active foreign policy befitting their nation's high international status. On the whole, they did not put themselves helplessly at the mercy of events, but worked to create a world of peaceful nations characterized by legal and orderly processes, the Open Door, and economic and political stability. Washington emphasized nonmilitary means—treaties, conferences, disarmament, economic and financial arrangements—in its pursuit of that elusive order. One President pointed to this attempted retreat from military methods when he observed that "we can never herd the world into the paths of righteousness with the dogs of war," and a secretary of state remarked that the United States championed a "commercial and non-military stabilization of the world."[22]

America was "isolationist" between the wars only in the sense that it wanted to isolate itself from war, to scale down foreign military involvements, and to preserve the freedom to make independent decisions in international affairs in order to serve the national interest of prosperity and security. Historian Joan Hoff Wilson's apt phrase, "independent internationalism," rather than "isolationism," characterized American practice and attitude—active on an international scale, but independent in action.[23] There was some recognition in the United States that its influence abroad had limits: where the United States lacked viable power, such as in Asia, it moved haltingly. Where it possessed power, as in Latin America, it moved vigorously. As for Europe, where United States influence was extensive, Americans ultimately concluded they could not solve Europe's problems if Europeans themselves would not do so, and Congress adopted "neutrality" legislation.

Charles Evans Hughes (1862–1948) and Warren G. Harding (1865–1923). The secretary of state and President were quite different in background and intelligence, but as conservatives both sought a stable nonrevolutionary world order. (Ohio Historical Society)

Unwilling to become entangled once again in European military squabbles and balance-of-power machinations, the United States did try, however ineffectually, to heal the wounds of World War I through economic diplomacy, disarmament, and the outlawry of war. Yet, by 1939, Washington had decided again that risking war was necessary to achieve world order.

After Woodrow Wilson's Administration and until that of Franklin D. Roosevelt, the American foreign policy process was characterized by weak presidential leadership, congressional-executive competition, and increased professionalism in the Foreign Service. Presidents Warren G. Harding and Calvin Coolidge gave minimal attention to foreign affairs, leaving that field to their secretaries of state. Harding's world was his hometown of Marion, Ohio. He was "most comfortable in the realm of clichés and maxims, and left it to others to supply the necessary intellectual content."[24] Furthermore, Wilson's League of Nations fiasco at home persuaded Harding to eschew a conspicuous role in foreign policy. On one occasion, when a European correspondent for the *New York Times* talked with Harding, the President cut him short: "I don't know anything about this European stuff."[25]

Calvin Coolidge managed in his autobiography to avoid mentioning foreign policy, although as a politician he had often waxed noisy on the issue of Bolshevism. Congressman Lewis Douglas described the taciturn Coolidge as "much like a wooden Indian except more tired looking."[26] Coolidge could deflate anybody's interest in most topics. His relaxed approach to problems, exemplified by the long afternoon naps he took in the White House and by his fawning worship of American business, created a deceptively passive image. Compared to Franklin D. Roosevelt, he certainly was passive—but Coolidge was not withdrawn from foreign policymaking as much as Harding was. The simple man from Vermont, preaching the virtues of self-reliance, did grow impatient with Europeans—who, he believed, always looked to the United States to bail them out. "I think I have stated in some of my addresses," he noted in 1926, "that we couldn't help people very much until they showed a disposition to help themselves."[27]

Herbert Hoover held much the same philosophy, but he was knowledgeable about foreign affairs and committed to an active presidential role. He was a practitioner of independent internationalism. His distinguished career included experience in international business (mining), food relief (Belgium and Russia), and diplomacy (reparations adviser at Versailles). As secretary of commerce under Harding and Coolidge, he used his office energetically to expand American economic interests abroad. Coolidge had considered his millionaire deputy the "smartest 'gink' I know."[28] Known as the "Great Engineer," Hoover had a telephone installed at his elbow in the White House, further contributing to his reputation as a specialist in administrative efficiency. A plodding speaker with a shy personality, Hoover had the misfortune to enter the presidency as the Great Depression struck, thereby wrecking his political career. True to his Quaker background, he sought nonmilitary, noncoercive solutions to international crises. He believed that world order could be maintained largely through stable economic relations.

The secretaries of state in the 1920s often compensated for some of the presidential shortcomings. Majestical Charles Evans Hughes, facetiously called by Louis Brandeis the "most enlightened mind of the eighteenth century," was a distinguished jurist (Supreme Court), an experienced politician (governor of New York and unsuccessful candidate for President in 1916), and a confirmed nationalist and expansionist.[29] Under Harding and Coolidge, the patient and pragmatic Hughes enjoyed considerable freedom in diplomacy, receiving little presidential instruction. The observance of international law and the sanctity of treaties were his primary guides to the attainment of world order. Still, "foreign policies are not built upon abstractions," he said. "They are the result of practical conceptions of national interest arising from some immediate exigency or standing out vividly in historical perspective."[30] Hughes's successor was Frank B. Kellogg, ingloriously called "Nervous Nellie" because of his shaky appearance (one blind eye and a trembling hand). A former senator and ambassador to Britain, Kellogg was cautious, often consulting a major critic of interventionism, the irrepressible "Lion"

Herbert Hoover (1874–1964). Graduate of Stanford University, mining engineer, millionaire, and secretary of commerce before he became the thirty-first President, the cautious and stubborn Hoover advocated healthy trade relations as a route to peace. (*The Reporter*, 1953, Copyright 1953 by Fortnightly Publishing Co., Inc.)

Makers of American Foreign Policy from 1920 to 1939

Presidents	Secretaries of State
Woodrow Wilson, 1913–1921	Bainbridge Colby, 1920–1921
Warren G. Harding, 1921–1923	Charles E. Hughes, 1921–1925
Calvin Coolidge, 1923–1929	Frank B. Kellogg, 1925–1929
Herbert C. Hoover, 1929–1933	Henry L. Stimson, 1929–1933
Franklin D. Roosevelt, 1933–1945	Cordell Hull, 1933–1944

from Idaho, Senator William Borah. Kellogg broke no new ground in diplomacy, leaving only the much derided Kellogg-Briand peace pact as a legacy. Both he and Hughes had to contend with jurisdictional disputes as Hoover expanded the international offices and functions of the Department of Commerce.

President Hoover's secretary of state was the trim, moustachioed Henry L. Stimson, one of America's distinguished public servants. The strong-willed, wealthy lawyer lived on his Long Island estate like an English squire. His social pedigree included Phillips Andover Academy, Yale University, Harvard Law School, and tutelage under the eminent Elihu Root. Tenacious, cold, confident, aloof, reserved, punctual, mannered, stern—his characteristics befitted an American aristocrat. Before becoming secretary of state, Stimson had served as secretary of war under Taft, as a diplomatic troubleshooter in Nicaragua in 1927, and during 1927–1929 as governor-general of the Philippines. He had been Colonel Stimson in World War—and let few forget it. Indeed, his athletic and strenuous life style reminded many of Theodore Roosevelt. Hoover apparently did not like the man, finding his personality too combative and disapproving of his eagerness to use force in foreign affairs.

That kind of strong personality was just what Franklin D. Roosevelt did not want for his secretary of state. Roosevelt, like Theodore Roosevelt and Woodrow Wilson before him, wanted foreign policymaking in his own hands. FDR came to office with some foreign affairs experience, having served in the Navy Department under Wilson, and unlike the Republican Presidents of the 1920s, he was an activist diplomat. He admired both the big-sticking of his cousin Theodore and the liberal internationalism of Wilson. As a vice-presidential candidate in 1920, Roosevelt had defended the new League and the Versailles treaty, but in the 1932 campaign he abandoned support for the League in order to garner the endorsement of influential newspaper magnate William Randolph Hearst. Considerable debate has centered on whether Roosevelt was an "isolationist." Without contradiction, the historian can conclude that he was both a Wilsonian and an "isolationist." That is, he was Wilsonian because he believed that collective security through an international organization directed by the large powers would help stabilize world politics, and that the world should be "democratized." He was an isolationist because he shared, although in differing degrees, the basic components of isolationist thought: (1) abhorrence of war; (2) limited *military* intervention abroad; (3) freedom of action in international relations. He was very much part of the age of independent internationalism.

Roosevelt conducted personal diplomacy, often taking command of negotiations and appointments and more than once failing to tell the Department of State what he was doing. He centralized decisionmaking in the White House, but, because too often he possessed only a superficial understanding of other national cultures and histories, dangers lurked in his methods. Sometimes he misled diplomats with his easy smile and tendency to be agreeable at the moment; sometimes his agreements were imprecise, depending for their authority on the honor of gentlemen's words; sometimes the "spirit" of a meeting was not properly captured in the formal diplomatic document; sometimes American diplomacy moved forward with the dizziness of a confused bureaucracy. Then, too, as a consummate politician always conscious of hostile opinion, he compromised frequently, leaving his ideals a bit tattered. Roosevelt was not above deception when he believed it would serve his goals. He has been likened to a physician who lies to the patient for his own good. Historian Willard Range has noted that FDR was "something of an intellectual jumping-jack and was often guilty of hopping helter-skelter in several directions at once."[31]

Roosevelt's secretary of state was Tennesseean Cordell Hull. A powerful senator whose primary interest was the improvement of international trade, the sixty-one-year-old Hull accepted the assignment reluctantly. FDR picked him not for his foreign views (Roosevelt knew little about them), but because the appointment would be popular with old Democratic party members, southern conservatives, and unreconstructed Wilsonians. Once Hull was appointed, Roosevelt often ignored him, although he and the State Department did influence Asian and Latin American policy. Rexford Tugwell, a presidential assistant, noted in 1933 that "I'm sure Hull doesn't know half of what goes on."[32] For example, Roosevelt sent Hull to the World Economic Conference in London that year without consulting him on the makeup of the delegation, and then embarrassed him by suddenly withdrawing the United States from the meeting. Once dubbed "Miss Cordelia Dull" for being so distant from the center of American foreign policymaking, Hull had contemplated resigning even before the conference broke up, because the President had decided to delay sending Hull's pet project, the reciprocal trade bill, to Congress. Hull possessed a deliberate style that annoyed the President, who preferred quickness of thought and decision. The secretary resented the President's practice of sending personal envoys like Harry Hopkins overseas, of conspicuously excluding Hull from important conferences, and of consulting with friends like Sumner Welles (after 1937 under-secretary of state), Morgenthau, and Bullitt, instead of Hull himself. Hull nevertheless stayed on until 1944, the longest tenure of any secretary of state, forever disliking the pomp of official dinners and receptions, always charming his listeners with his hill-country drawl and lisp, and impressing all with his personal dignity, hard work, and deep commitment to the premise that wars grew out of international economic competition. The loyal Hull recalled later that he suffered "humiliations" but "just kept right on."[33]

The Foreign Service over which Hull presided made important strides toward professionalism in the interwar period, reflecting the increased involvement of the United States in world affairs. It had certainly needed reform. Frequenting the dark corridors, black leather rocking chairs, and Victorian furnishings of the old State, War, and Navy Building on Pennsylvania Avenue were American diplomats noted for their elite backgrounds (urban, wealthy, eastern, and Ivy League-educated) and their loyalty to the diplomatic club. Roosevelt thought them snobbish and too preoccupied by social amenities. Often derided as "cookie pushers" and "striped pants," as purveyors of "pink peppermint and protocol," they were paid insufficient salaries, thereby insuring that only people of independent means would seek diplomatic posts. President Coolidge, who knew little about the Foreign Service and its responsibilities, met in 1925 with his new Ambassador to Argentina, Peter Jay. The exchange is illustrative, if exaggerated: *Jay:* "You know Mr. President that my salary as Ambassador is $17,500, and I will have to spend $15,000 on my rent." *Coolidge:* "What are you going to do with the other $2,500?"[34] Many appointees were unqualified, unable to speak the language of the country to which they were assigned. Under the spoils system, faithful politicians were given diplomatic posts.

The heavy work load imposed on Foreign Service personnel during World War I had exposed the shortcomings. Congressman John J. Rogers concluded after the war that, "as adequate as [the Foreign Service] may have been when the old order prevailed and the affairs of the world were free from the present perplexities, it has ceased to be responsive to present needs."[35] The immigration laws of 1921 and

Cordell Hull (1871–1955). A politician from Tennessee, the long-tenured secretary of state (1933–1944) was often left out of diplomatic decisions by President Roosevelt. On trade questions, however, Hull was central. He firmly believed that "we cannot have a peaceful world . . . until we rebuild the international economic structure." (Franklin D. Roosevelt Library)

1924, establishing quotas for nationals from abroad, demanded a more efficient consular staff; the revolution in China required observers who could intelligently report on that major event; and economic expansion depended upon efficient reporting abroad. The Rogers Act of 1924 brought some improvements. It merged the previously unequal consular and diplomatic corps into the Foreign Service of the United States and provided for examinations, increased salaries, promotion by merit, and living expense allowances abroad. It also created the Foreign Service School. At about the same time, the State Department began training specialists in Soviet affairs, with George F. Kennan and Charles E. Bohlen (both later to serve as ambassadors to Russia) as initiates who mastered the language and culture of Russia. President Roosevelt, however, desiring to keep the instruments of foreign policymaking in the White House, weakened the influence of the Foreign Service by simply not utilizing it in key policy formulation. The depression forced salaries down and the service became badly understaffed. Politics still intruded, and aristocratic pretensions still characterized the Foreign Service, but overall it was becoming more efficient and professional in handling the global questions facing the United States.

American Expansion and the Shaky World Economy

The Foreign Service helped facilitate the conspicuous American economic expansion abroad in the 1920s, since the developing economic ties frequently required American diplomats to protect "American lives and property." After World War I, measured by statistics, the United States was the most powerful nation in the world, accounting for 70 percent of the world's petroleum and 40 percent of its coal production. Most impressive, the United States produced 46 percent of total world industrial goods (1925–1929 figures). It also ranked first as an exporter, shipping over 15 percent of total world exports in 1929, and it replaced Great Britain as the largest foreign investor and financier of world trade. Throughout the decade the United States enjoyed a favorable balance of trade, exporting more than it imported. In the period 1914–1929, the value of exports more than doubled, to $5.4 billion, and American private investments abroad grew fivefold—from $3.5 billion in 1914 to $17.2 billion by 1930.

"The growth of U.S. stakes abroad during the 1920s represented not simply an increase in scale," historian Mira Wilkins has noted. "Rather, U.S. companies were (1) going to *more countries*, (2) building *more plants* in a particular foreign country, (3) manufacturing or mining *more end products* in a particular foreign land, (4) investing in a single alien nation in a *greater degree* of integration, and (5) diversifying on a *worldwide* basis."[36] U.S. Rubber bought its first Malayan plantation; Anaconda moved into Chilean copper mining; General Electric joined international cartels and invested heavily in Germany; oil companies began to penetrate the Middle East; Radio Corporation of America built high-power radio stations in Poland; General Motors purchased Opel, by 1929 the best-selling automobile in Germany; Henry Ford helped build an automobile plant in Russia; Borden and International Telephone and Telegraph expanded in England; and American firms handled about one-third of oil sales in France. Direct American investments in Europe more than doubled during the 1920s.

This economic surge on a worldwide basis had to overcome adversities at the beginning of that decade. Mexican nationalism, confiscation of property in Russia, European resentment over American prosperity, a wrecked German economy,

The Weight of the United States in the World Economy:
Relative Value of Industrial Production, 1925–1929*

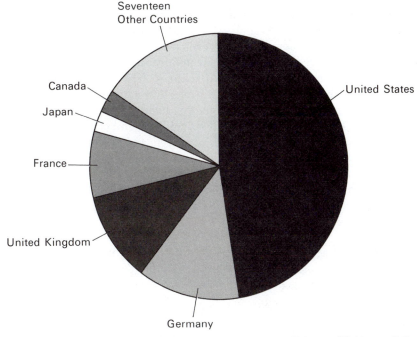

Source: U.S. Department of Commerce, *The United States in the World Economy* (Washington, D.C.: Government Printing Office, 1943), p. 28.

wartime destruction in Europe, growing tariff walls, and the nightmarish dislocation of international finance caused by World War I debts and reparations—all placed hurdles before enterprising American businessmen and American diplomats. The recession of 1920–1921 further disrupted commerce and investments. Some of these obstacles soon disappeared; expansion was spurred by need for capital, by the availability of rich raw materials and growing markets in Latin America (where competing Europeans were nudged out), by aggressive American entrepreneurs, and by the active encouragement of the United States government. New tools, which proved to be of welcome but limited help, were provided by the Webb-Pomerene Act (1918), which permitted American companies to combine for purposes of foreign trade without prosecution under the antitrust laws; the Edge Act of 1919, which legalized branch banks abroad; and the Merchant Marine Act of 1920, which authorized the federal government to sell vessels to private companies and to make loans for the construction of new ships. Useful also were American tax laws that permitted foreign tax credits for American investors abroad. Secretary Hoover put the Department of Commerce behind trade expansion by providing businessmen with research data and advice. To help financiers avoid unproductive foreign lending and the purchase of risky foreign bonds, official Washington tried to oversee loans and bond sales, but the practice was never consistent or thorough. Businessmen were granted considerable freedom to make their own lending choices. For example, the government discouraged the sale in the United States of the bonds of a Czech brewery because it would violate the "spirit" of prohibition laws, but tolerated an unproductive loan for a sports palace in Germany. Overall, American leaders considered foreign economic expansion essential for prosperity at home.

The United States continued to proclaim the Open Door policy, but applied it selectively and imperfectly. It was usually invoked where the United States faced vigorous competition, as in Asia and the Middle East. In Latin America and the Philippines, however, where American capital and trade dominated, something approximating a "closed door" was in effect. Europeans complained bitterly that the United States was following a double standard. They also resented American tariff policy, which made it more difficult for other nations to sell to the United States—as they had to do in order to get the dollars necessary to buy from the United States. The tariff acts of 1922 (Fordney-McCumber) and 1930 (Hawley-Smoot) raised duties to protect domestic producers and invited retaliation against American products. A group of over a thousand economists protested the Hawley-Smoot Tariff: "There are few more ironical spectacles than the American Government as it seeks, on the one hand, to promote exports . . . , while, on the other hand, by increasing tariffs it makes exportation ever more difficult." More generally, they concluded, "a tariff war does not furnish good soil for the growth of

The Contracting Spiral of World Trade:
January, 1929 to March, 1933*
(Total imports of 75 countries in millions of dollars)

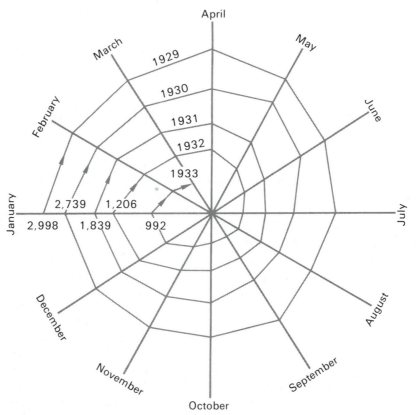

*Source: Charles P. Kindleberger, *The World in Depression, 1929–1939* (Berkeley and Los Angeles: University of California Press, 1973), p. 172. Copyright © 1973 by The Regents of the University of California; reprinted by permission of the University of California Press.

world peace."[37] Some twenty-five nations by 1932 had indeed retaliated against American imports; even some Latin American countries imposed trade controls. Hoover and others in authority held that high tariffs and overseas economic expansion could proceed hand in hand, and until the Great Depression struck in 1929 the seeming contradiction appeared to work.

The depression raised havoc with the international economy. Economic nationalism guided most countries as they tried to protect themselves from the cataclysm with higher tariffs, import quotas, and preferential and discriminatory trade agreements. World trade declined 40 percent in value and 25 percent in volume from 1929 to mid-1933. In 1933 the United States exported goods worth $2.1 billion, down from the 1929 figure of $5.4 billion. American capital stayed at home and foreign holders of American loans defaulted. American private investments abroad slumped to $13.5 billion, down from the $17.2 billion figure of 1930. Hoover simply blamed the economic trouble on the rest of the world. His successor, Franklin D. Roosevelt, facing the problem of 13 million unemployed Americans when he took office in 1933, also succumbed to economic nationalism as he created his New Deal recovery program at home. He abruptly withdrew the United States from the London Economic Conference. But gradually Hull persuaded him that lowered tariffs would spur American foreign trade and hence spark recovery at home. Furthermore, argued Hull, healthy world trade would contribute to stable politics and peace at a time when Japan, Germany, and Italy were turning to political extremes and aggressive foreign policies. It was feared, furthermore, that Bolshevism might exploit Europe's economic and social disequilibrium. "International commerce conducted on a fair and mutually profitable basis," the inspired secretary told a congressional committee, "is not only calculated to aid materially in the restoration of prosperity everywhere, but it is the greatest civilizer and peacemaker in the experience of the human race."[38]

In 1934 Hull piloted through Congress the Reciprocal Trade Agreements Act, which empowered the President to reduce tariffs by as much as 50 percent after making agreements with other nations under the doctrine of the most-favored nation. This principle, which had traditionally guided American trade, did not mean that one nation was more favored than another. Rather, it meant that the United States was entitled to the lowest tariffs imposed by a country (in short, the best favor that country granted any other nation) with which the United States had a reciprocal agreement, and vice versa. The reciprocal trade program did not bring immediate results, but it did slow the deterioration of world trade and placed it on a path toward freer commercial intercourse. Hull also created in 1934 the Export-Import Bank, a governmental agency designed to provide loans to expand foreign trade. It not only assisted in commercial expansion; it also became an important diplomatic weapon, as Washington gave or withdrew credits to satisfy foreign policy goals.

The reciprocal trade program and the bank, however, came too late to help solve one of the major troubling legacies of World War I and Versailles—the debts-reparations tangle. Whereas before the war United States citizens owed some $3 billion to Europeans, after the war European citizens owed private Americans $3 billion and their governments owed another $10 billion, largely because of wartime loans. America had gone dramatically from a debtor to a creditor nation. But how would the European countries pay such a huge sum? Besides American dollar investments and the sale of goods to the United States to raise dollars, there was the income from German reparations payments. But the Germans were incapable of meeting the indemnity of $33 billion, so in the early 1920s the British began asking for a cancellation of the debts, arguing that they should be considered an American contribution to the Allied victory. Europeans, then, looked upon the war loans as essentially political in character, rather than as normal business transactions. Anyway, they pointed out, they had given lives and had endured destruction and damage of property. The United States, on the other hand, had not suffered military trampling and had enjoyed unprecedented profits from the sale of goods to the Allies. America indignantly rejected this argument and soon earned the label "Uncle Shylock." Coolidge complained that "this money has to be paid by our taxpayers unless it is paid by the taxpayers [of the debtor nations]."[39] He also reportedly snapped, "They hired the money, didn't they?"[40] Will Rogers captured the American mood in a joke: "There is only one way we could be worse with the Europeans, and that is to have helped them out in two wars instead of one."[41] Congress created the War Debt Commission in 1922 to negotiate for full payment. The commission ultimately forgave or canceled about half of the Allied debts. From 1918 to 1931 the United States actually received only $2.6 billion in debts payments from the Allies.

Germany held a key place in the debts-reparations tangle. Wild inflation, a crippled economy, inadequate exports, and anti-Versailles hostility prompted the Germans to default on reparations payments in 1922–1923. France and Belgium thereupon aggravated Germany's plight by seizing the rich Ruhr Valley. Britain called again for cancellation of debts. To alleviate the German economic crisis, Americans had been for years pumping millions in capital into the struggling nation. In 1924 the State Department sponsored the Dawes Plan, whereby American investors like the J. P. Morgan Company loaned millions to Germany. A systematic reparations payment schedule was also devised. It proved to be a superficial solution, for the European economy simply could not bear the heavy debts (Europeans also owed money to other Europeans) and the reparations. Nor could American capital continue to keep Europe afloat. Under the Young Plan of 1929, another salvaging effort was made: German reparations were reduced to nine billion dollars. That year too, President Hoover informed the British that he would cancel their debt if they transferred Bermuda, British Honduras (Belize), and Trinidad to the United States. London refused. In 1931 Hoover declared a one-year moratorium on debts payments. But thereafter only Finland met its debt obligations, forever winning a place in American hearts. Debtors defaulted, Germany stopped paying reparations, and the world settled into the devastating depression of the 1930s. The great powers had failed to resolve the debts-reparations problem, to prevent a profound economic downturn, and to contain the political chaos that sprang from the economic calamity.

Peace, the League, and Disarmament: The Failed Alternatives

If Europeans and Americans failed to resolve the mammoth problems plaguing the international economy, they also failed to curb a growing arms race. Peace sentiment ran high, but it seldom found its way into formal treaties. In 1922, when publisher Edward Bok sponsored a contest for the best peace plan, over 22,000 entries were filed. The winner of $100,000 was a member of the New York Peace Society who recommended entry into the World Court and partial participation in

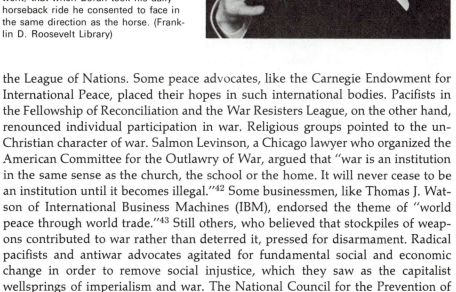

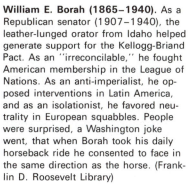

William E. Borah (1865–1940). As a Republican senator (1907–1940), the leather-lunged orator from Idaho helped generate support for the Kellogg-Briand Pact. As an "irreconcilable," he fought American membership in the League of Nations. As an anti-imperialist, he opposed interventions in Latin America, and as an isolationist, he favored neutrality in European squabbles. People were surprised, a Washington joke went, that when Borah took his daily horseback ride he consented to face in the same direction as the horse. (Franklin D. Roosevelt Library)

the League of Nations. Some peace advocates, like the Carnegie Endowment for International Peace, placed their hopes in such international bodies. Pacifists in the Fellowship of Reconciliation and the War Resisters League, on the other hand, renounced individual participation in war. Religious groups pointed to the un-Christian character of war. Salmon Levinson, a Chicago lawyer who organized the American Committee for the Outlawry of War, argued that "war is an institution in the same sense as the church, the school or the home. It will never cease to be an institution until it becomes illegal."[42] Some businessmen, like Thomas J. Watson of International Business Machines (IBM), endorsed the theme of "world peace through world trade."[43] Still others, who believed that stockpiles of weapons contributed to war rather than deterred it, pressed for disarmament. Radical pacifists and antiwar advocates agitated for fundamental social and economic change in order to remove social injustice, which they saw as the capitalist wellsprings of imperialism and war. The National Council for the Prevention of War, founded in 1921, served as an organizational umbrella for the divergent peace groups.

One of the few achievements of the peace people was the Kellogg-Briand Pact of 1928. The French, prodded by James T. Shotwell, a Columbia University professor and trustee of the Carnegie Endowment for International Peace, asked the United States to sign a bilateral treaty outlawing war. The security-conscious French, ever worried about a revived Germany, were hoping that an alliance with the United States would prevent any rebirth of German militarism. The invitation met

Most peace activists or peace-conscious citizens were strong nationalists who believed that the United States, because of its basically democratic and pacific intents, could regenerate habitually war-prone Europe. At the time, such reformist ideas did not seem farfetched: arms seemed controllable (technology had not yet produced global bombers or atomic weapons); domestic economies did not yet rely heavily for their prosperity on defense production; the revulsion against World War I was intense; and few warmongers were in immediate sight. Still, most Americans were more interested in sports, movies, and the radio in the "roaring twenties" than in questions of peace. The peace advocates were, as historian Merle Curti has noted, "mere chips and foam on the surface of the stream of American life."[44]

with a cool reception in Washington. But a publicity campaign for a multilateral treaty launched by Shotwell, Levinson, and Senator William Borah put the State Department on the spot. Something had to be done. At first reluctant, Kellogg soon took the lead. In February of 1928 he sent a draft treaty to France and other powers. Foreign Minister Aristide Briand felt betrayed; he had wanted a Franco-American treaty for security, much like the abortive one Wilson devised at Versailles. Kellogg and the peace advocates had converted his idea into a universal declaration against war. That August in Paris, the signatories, eventually numbering sixty-two, agreed to "condemn recourse to war for the solution of international controversies, and renounce it as an instrument of national policy."[45] Occasional poet Robert Underwood Johnson struck the euphoric moment for some Americans:[46]

> Lift up your heads, ye peoples,
> The miracle has come
> No longer are ye helpless,
> No longer are ye dumb.

The Kellogg-Briand Treaty was a harmless, feeble document, a statement of principle, requiring no real sacrifices and establishing no precise responsibilities. In January, 1929, the Senate approved it 85-1, the lone dissenter being John J. Blaine of Wisconsin, a confirmed Anglophobe. Senator Hiram Johnson of California who voted "aye," parodied the treaty's lack of enforcement authority by quoting François Villon:[47]

> To Messur Noel, named the neat
> By those who love him, I bequeath
> A helmless ship, a houseless street
> A wordless book, a swordless sheath
> An hourless clock, a leafless wreath
> A bell sans tongue, a saw sans teeth,
> A bed sans sheet, a board sans meat,
> To make his nothingness complete.

Senator Carter Glass of Virginia also voted for the treaty, after belittling it as worth no more than a postage stamp. American statesmen were not lulled into a sense of security by the treaty; indeed, on the same day the Senate approved funds for fifteen new cruisers. Peace advocates were not so naive as to think that Kellogg-Briand guaranteed a peaceful world. They saw it as only a first step in a long process toward peace and championed the pact as a way of alerting the American people to think once again of the costs of war. Thus it held educational value. And the pact was revived after World War II by the Allies to punish German leaders at the Nuremburg Trials.

The League of Nations, itself designed to check wars, opened in Geneva without the United States, and Washington at first impolitely ignored communications from the League. But by 1925 American diplomats were quietly attending and discreetly participating in League functions. By 1930, unofficial American "observers" had participated in over forty League conferences on such questions as health, prostitution, suppression of obscene materials, codification of international law, and opium. In October, 1931, an American diplomat participated in League discussions of Japanese thrusts into China, but Washington would not push the League to do any more than timidly invoke the Kellogg-Briand pact and condemn

Japan for aggression. The United States almost joined the League-sponsored Permanent Court of International Justice. This Geneva-based World Court sought to arbitrate international disputes when requested to do so. In 1926 the Senate approved American membership, but so qualified it that the court could not accept the American proposal. Finally, in 1935, a treaty of membership was defeated in the Senate and hopes for a World Court–United States linkage were daunted. Nevertheless, outstanding jurists like Charles Evans Hughes sat as judges in the international body.

American participation in disarmament conferences in 1922 (Washington), 1927 (Geneva), 1930 (London), 1932–33 (Geneva), and 1935–36 (London) also demonstrated America's international but independent diplomatic course. At those conferences, the United States sought limitations especially on navies, in part because it hoped to restrain others at a time when Congress restrained American growth. Except for some naval restrictions imposed by the Washington Treaty of 1922 (discussed in the next chapter) and the London Conference of 1930, little was accomplished. The reasons are clear. The United States, a leading naval power, was seeking to check the quantitative growth of others; France would not endorse disarmament until its security was guaranteed; the British had a huge empire to protect and police by sea; Italy and Germany under dictators Benito Mussolini and Adolf Hitler were bent on military expansion; Japan eyed naval expansion in the Pacific. German rearmament under Hitler in the early 1930s and Japanese renunciation of the Washington Treaty restrictions in 1934 provided stark evidence not only that arms limitation efforts had failed, but also that the Versailles treaty and the League of Nations had proven impotent.

The Uncertainty of Soviet-American Relations

The Russians were the first to sign the Kellogg-Briand Treaty and were permitted to join the League of Nations in 1934. Yet these acts did not nullify the fact that between the wars most European nations and the United States treated Bolshevik Russia as an outsider, a revolutionary disease to be isolated. Only when Europe tottered on the brink of war in 1939 did Germany on the one hand and France and Britain on the other seriously woo the Soviet Union. Nevertheless, most powers grudgingly established diplomatic and commercial contact with the Soviet Union in the interwar years, unable any longer to nurse their fantasies that somehow Bolshevism would be tossed out of Moscow, or to ignore a country that figured in both European and Asian politics. The roller-coaster characteristic of ups and downs in Soviet-American relations was typical of Western relations with the Soviets.

Despite Russian interest in gaining official diplomatic recognition from Washington in the 1920s, the Republican administrations adhered to the nonrecognition policy set by Woodrow Wilson. The Bolsheviks, they pointed out, had confiscated American-owned property valued at $336 million and had rejected compensation. Russia owed another $192 million to the United States government and still another $107 million to American nationals (Tsarist and Provisional government debts). Until the roughly $636 million was paid, until Moscow met its obligations, recognition would be denied. Behind this official position lay an antiradical sentiment, harshly expressed in the Red Scare of 1919-1920, and an attitude among many prominent Americans in the 1920s that the threatening Bolsheviks were godless, uncivilized, anticapitalist, violent, destructive revolutionaries who chained their workers like slaves to an authoritarian system. The *New York Times* and the American Federation of Labor, among others, bitterly castigated the Soviet experiment. President Samuel Gompers of the AFL thought Soviet Russia a "villainous despotism."[48] Secretary Stimson, like other Americans annoyed by the rantings of the American Communist party, declared in 1930 there would be no recognition until Russia "ceased to agitate for the overthrow of American institutions by revolution."[49] Only a few Americans, like Senator Borah and the International Ladies Garment Workers Union, urged tolerance and recognition, although even they did not admire the Soviet system.

If most Americans kept at arm's length from the dreaded Bolsheviks, others, for a variety of reasons, got closer. In 1921 Russia suffered a devastating famine. When writer Maxim Gorky appealed for help, Secretary of Commerce Herbert Hoover began to mobilize support for assistance. In 1919 Hoover had told President Wilson that relief aid to Russia would be more humane than military intervention, and that it would bring about Russian political stability by weakening the authority of the Bolsheviks. For both humanitarian and anti-Soviet purposes, Hoover signed an agreement with Moscow in 1921 and organized the shipments of valuable food and medicine to needy areas of Russia. Hoover believed that food would help implant American influence in Russia and serve as a counterrevolutionary force. From 1921 to 1924 the American Relief Administration collected $50 million from the federal government and private citizens for assistance to approximately 10 million Russians. Colonel William Haskell, who headed the effort in Russia, reported his accomplishment in 1923: the relief mission, he concluded rather incorrectly, had left communism "dead and abandoned."[50]

Businessmen, for profit and adventure, sought commercial contacts. The State Department divorced its distaste for Bolshevism from its desire for economic expansion and permitted important commercial relations to develop. Companies like International Harvester, General Electric, and DuPont signed trade and technical assistance contracts with the Soviet government, often through its purchasing agency in New York, the Soviet-owned Amtorg Trading Corporation. By 1924 Soviet purchases of American products had jumped seven times over the 1923 figure. In 1925 W. Averell Harriman, two decades later an ambassador to Russia, received monopolistic rights to rich manganese deposits valued at a billion dollars, although the project never got under way. In 1928, 24 percent of all foreign investment in Russia was American. Russia's plans for industrialization and collectivization could not have moved forward without the influx of American machinery, technology, and engineers (1000 by 1931). Improvements in steel and agriculture in particular depended upon American businessmen and technicians, although German trade and investments also figured heavily in Soviet economic growth.

To people who believed that capitalism and communism could never meld, these economic ties were eyeopening. Surprising too was the news in 1929 that business hero Henry Ford had signed a Soviet contract. He agreed to give technical information needed to build the large Nizhni-Novgorod automobile factory near the Volga River, which would buy Ford parts and produce a car like the Model A and a truck like the Model AA. It was a multimillion-dollar venture, and Ford eventually lost $578,000 (the arrangement terminated in 1934). Nevertheless, conclude two Ford biographers, "to give his ideas a practical illustration on the world stage, Henry Ford would gladly have sacrificed twice that sum."[51] Ford was attracted to the Soviets because they were enthusiastic about his mass production methods (*Fordizatsia*). The Russians saw him as a radical individual, an efficiency expert who could speed up industrial production and reduce drudgery in the fields. By 1927, 85 percent of the Soviets' tractors were "Fordsons." One American returned from a tour of Russian villages to report that "next to Lenin, Trotsky, and Kalinin, Ford is possibly the most widely known personage in Russia."[52] To Ford, Russia looked like an engineer's dream: central planning, regulated materials and work force, and a zeal for efficiency. So in their respect for the wonders of machine and man in harmony, capitalists and Bolsheviks embraced.

American-Russian economic ties began to loosen in the early 1930s. The Great Depression had sent capitalism to its knees, and government and business officials were not amused by Soviet announcements in the United States that jobs were available in Russia. Most important, Russia began selling goods in the world market below American prices, and the United States charged Moscow with "dumping." In mid-1930 Soviet paper pulp was denied entry into the United States because the material was allegedly produced by convict labor. In retaliation and because of inadequate American capital to fund purchases, the Soviets reduced drastically their buying of American goods. In 1932 American exports to Russia declined 90 percent from the 1931 trade. Businessmen eager for markets began to argue that official diplomatic recognition might restart stalled commercial relations. The Reconstruction Finance Corporation, a government agency set up to battle the depression, helped some by extending Russia a $4 million credit for the purchase of American cotton.

Ford in Russia. Under a banner of Josef Stalin, a 1929 Model A Ford automobile rolls from a Russian assembly line. Henry Ford's contract with the Soviets proved a losing investment, but the venerable auto king nevertheless relished the experiment. Stalin agreed with Ford, saying, "We would like the scientific and technical people in America to be our teachers." (*Tass* from Sovfoto)

The Roosevelt Administration, because it wanted to improve trade and stop Japan, and simply because nonrecognition served no useful purpose, recognized the Soviet Union in November, 1933. But the exchange of embassies did not smooth relations or halt Japan. American trade with Russia did not improve very much, despite the signing of a trade treaty in 1935, its renewal in 1937, and the establishment of the Export-Import Bank, which was in fact ordered to refrain from extending credits to the Soviets. The loan or credit Litvinov and Roosevelt had agreed upon in 1933 never materialized, because the debts issue went unsolved. When some American Communists spoke critically of the United States at Moscow's Seventh International Communist (Comintern) Congress in 1935, Secretary of State Hull protested, charging a violation of Russia's no-propaganda pledge. To many Americans, the squabbling and dashed hopes meant that the United States could not trust the Russians. President Roosevelt was disappointed, but he continued to seek reconciliation.

After recognition other issues disrupted Soviet-American relations. William Bullitt was named the first ambassador to Moscow; he left America in 1933 as a friend of Russia. Two years later an embittered Bullitt preached the "hard line" and resigned his post. Difficult living conditions in Moscow, spies among his servants, daily indignities at the hands of rude Soviet bureaucrats, and the conspicuous Soviet tyranny—all helped change his mind. The Comintern Congress of 1935 angered him, because it seemed to violate Russia's promise not to permit propaganda activities to originate from its soil. "Honor" and "fair dealing" were at stake; "friendly" relations with Russia could not be expected. With pride the often hotheaded Bullitt in later years recalled that "I deviled the Russians. I did all I could to make things unpleasant."[53] American correspondent Louis Fischer, who frequented the embassy rooms in Moscow, remembered that the ambassador urged reporters every day to "fan the flames of anti-Sovietism in America."[54] Bullitt did just that himself in the years ahead. In 1946 he had this exchange with Congressman John Rankin:[55]

RANKIN: Is it true that they eat human bodies in Russia?
BULLITT: I did see a picture of a skeleton of a child eaten by its parents.
RANKIN: Then they're just human slaves in Russia?
BULLITT: There are more human slaves in Russia than ever existed anywhere in the world.

Bullitt was also moved toward the "hard line" by the ghastly purges, which began in earnest in 1935. George F. Kennan, a member of the embassy staff and later ambassador to Russia, found those days "a sort of liberal education in the horrors of Stalinism."[56] For Kennan, who attended many of the purge trials in person, Russia had become a nightmarish scene of political murders, secretiveness, conspiratorial thinking, cruelty, and opportunism. Like most diplomats who have been stationed in the suspicious, isolated environment forced on foreigners in Moscow, Bullitt and Kennan became intense in their rejection of things Soviet. So did some liberal and leftist Americans who had previously urged tolerance for the Soviet experiment. Journalist Eugene Lyons, for example, a United Press correspondent in Russia from 1928 to 1934, became sickened by the callousness of the Soviet regime. When he returned to the United States he wrote a controversial article for *Harper's* magazine (1935) titled "To Tell or Not to Tell," an anguished autobiography which did the former. "The great tragic themes of peasant liquidation, persecution of intellectuals, tightening food shortage were bodied forth in hundreds of individual tragedies," he sadly wrote.[57]

If the ugly purges stunned many Americans, the Nazi-Soviet pact of August, 1939 outraged them. Premier Stalin believed he had no choice but to sign this agreement in order to protect his country from a menacing Germany. From the Russian point of view the Western European powers and the United States had let Hitler expand uninhibited, because he harbored conquerer's designs toward Russia. Moscow believed itself abandoned by others to face alone the German military onslaught. And Stalin had so depleted the officer ranks of his army through the purges that he was in no position to stave off an expected German attack. In the United States, the nonaggression pact, which secretly divided Poland, proved charges that Hitler and Stalin were one and the same, even that fascism and communism were similar ideologies. When World War II erupted in September, 1939, many Americans blamed Russia.

There were some light moments during the deterioration of Soviet-American relations. Shortly after Bullitt's arrival in Russia, the ambassador threw a party for Red Army generals. Amidst the tables covered with plates of caviar, duck, pheasant, and the usual bottles of vodka sat Bullitt and the Soviet commissar of war. With the help of Charles Thayer, a prank-prone interpreter bored with his job, the conversation turned to polo. The Russians enthusiastically requested American polo instruction, having learned that the sport was good for the cavalry, and in due course the American embassy imported the necessary balls and mallets. The Russians selected their best horsemen and sent them to an open field near the Moscow River, where Bullitt tried desperately to explain the game. Once the match started, the refereeing ambassador lost control over the fierce competitors, who paid little attention to fouls as madly galloping men and horses collided. Then, of course, Thayer had forgotten to translate Bullitt's words regarding the relationship between the whistle and the end of the game. Finding no other way to halt the thundering mob of players, Thayer dashed on the field and sent the ball into the Moscow River. It was an unsuccessful effort, for an exuberant Russian rider retrieved it and the melee went on. Thayer then lunged at the ball, tucked it under his arm, and begged the horsemen to stop. Weeks later, after Moscow ordered the best ponies shipped to its polo teams, the first formal match was staged before the elite of the Soviet government. As Europe moved toward war, however, the Russian cavalrymen went off on maneuvers, abandoning their "polo for the proletariat."[58]

Hitler's Germany, Appeasement, and the Coming of War

By exploiting the depression-afflicted economy and the vehement attitudes against the Versailles treaty in Germany, Nazi leader Adolf Hitler came to power in January, 1933. Racist toward Jews, emphatically anti-Bolshevik, and fanatical in his quest for personal power, Hitler created a regime that set out to recapture past glory through the expansionist concept of Pan Germanism. In October, 1933, Hitler withdrew Germany from the faltering League of Nations and denounced disarmament talks. Defiantly, he told an associate that the European powers would "never act! They'll just protest. And they will always be too late."[59] Indeed, France and Britain settled upon a timid policy, ultimately called "appeasement," hoping thereby to satisfy what they thought were Hitler's limited goals and to

Adolf Hitler (1889–1945). The anti-Communist, anti-Semitic Nazi leader, here reviewing German youth, catapulted Europe into war after securing control of Germany through nationalistic appeals. Hitler saw the United States as a "mongrel society" that was "hopelessly weak." (Library of Congress)

avert another European war. By 1935 Hitler was rearming Germany, building an air force and a huge army. Britain, France, Italy, and the League of Nations censured Germany in April, 1935. Yet at the same time, Britain agreed that Germany should be permitted to rebuild its navy to 35 percent of the size of the British Navy. It proved a costly concession to German militarism.

Hardly adjusted to the rise of Nazi Germany, the world was shocked by another example of military extremism when Italy invaded the African state of Ethiopia in October, 1935. Fascist Benito Mussolini had governed Italy since 1922, and had long dreamed of creating an Italian empire. Already holding Somaliland and Eritrea as African colonies, Mussolini gradually built up pressure on Ethiopian leader Haile Selassie until military skirmishes broke out. Then he struck in a bold invasion and annexation of Ethiopia that encouraged new European appeasement. The League did impose an embargo on the shipment of war-related goods (except oil) to Italy. But the French, with their own empire in Africa, and the British, fearful that Italy might impede their imperial lifeline in the Mediterranean, seemed willing to sacrifice Ethiopia, a mere "corridor for camels."[60] Also, they hoped that Italy might stand with them against German expansion.

Apparently encouraged by Anglo-French docility over Ethiopia, Hitler in March, 1936 ordered his goose-stepping troops into the Rhineland, the area bordering Belgium and France that the Versailles treaty had declared permanently demilitarized. Gambling that the French would not resist this audacious act, Hitler envisioned a potential military avenue through Belgium into France. After World War I, the French had erected the Maginot Line, a series of large gun emplacements and defensive bunkers along the German-French border. By seizing the Rhineland, Germany was now in a position to skirt the supposedly impregnable Maginot. The French, fearful of igniting another war, did not resist the German advance into the Rhineland. Meanwhile, in June, the League of Nations lifted the economic sanctions against Italy. In October, 1936, Germany and Italy arranged a tenuous alignment, the Rome-Berlin Axis; and a month later Germany and Japan, then deep into China, joined in the Anti-Comintern Pact aimed at Russia. The aggressors had joined hands.

Spain provided another battleground. "Nationalist" soldiers under General Francisco Franco started the Spanish Civil War in July of 1936 by attacking the "Loyalist" Republican government in Madrid. Eager to mold in Spain a Franco government hostile to France, Hitler and Mussolini poured military equipment and troops into the Nationalist effort. The Anglo-French response was the tepid International Non-Intervention Committee of twenty-seven nations, remarkably including Germany and Italy. Although the signatories pledged to stay out of the Spanish conflict, Hitler and Mussolini continued covert aid, and France and Britain lived with the fiction that the Spanish Civil War had been isolated. Russia and Mexico sent help to the Republicans, and some Americans volunteered and fought alongside them in the Lincoln Brigade, but Franco battled his way to bloody victory in early 1939.

The mid-1937 election of Neville Chamberlain as British Prime Minister enshrined the "appeasement" policy. Chamberlain believed that Germany had good reason to want to throw off the humiliating Versailles treaty (Hitler called it a "dictated treaty"[61]) and to claim status as a major power. He was resigned to German dominance of Central Europe and tolerant of Hitler's demand for mastery over people of German descent living in Austria, Czechoslovakia, and Poland. Historian Raymond J. Sontag has described Chamberlain's view: "As Germany became economically prosperous, as Germany attained equality as a colonial power, and as Germans lost the feeling their fellow Germans in other countries were treated unjustly, the neurotic excitability which made Germany a difficult neighbor would subside."[62] Furthermore, an appeased Germany could serve as a useful restraint on communist Russia.

Benito Mussolini (1883–1945). The Fascist dictator who apparently made the trains run on time in Italy, "Il Duce" excited a revival of Italian imperial grandeur by attacking Ethiopia in 1935. (U.S. Information Agency, National Archives)

Chamberlain's ideas were tested in 1938. In March, German troops crossed into Austria and annexed it to the German Reich. Months of terrorism against Jews and opponents of Nazism in Austria followed. Hitler next demanded the Sudeten region of Czechoslovakia, where three million ethnic Germans lived. Hitler assured Chamberlain that this was Germany's last territorial demand. Britain and France (which had a defense treaty with Prague) granted the Nazi this additional prize. The Czechs had to capitulate. The end of Czechoslovakia's independence was confirmed at the Munich Conference of September 29-30, 1938, where Italy, Germany, France, and Britain agreed never to make war against one another and to sever the Sudetenland from Czechoslovakia. The Munich agreement was negotiated without consulting the Czechs themselves. They were not invited to the conference. Nor were the Russians or Americans. Chamberlain proclaimed "peace with honour" and "peace for our time," but as a precaution Britain launched a rearmament program.[63] Hitler soon initiated a brutal program against German Jews and in March of 1939 swallowed the rest of Czechoslovakia. The following month Italy absorbed Albania.

Poland came next. Refusing Hitler's demands for the city of Danzig, the Poles soon suffered German pressure. But London and Paris, questioning Hitler's professions about limited goals, announced in March, 1939, that they would stand behind an independent Poland. "Hitler is highly intelligent," mused Chamberlain, "and therefore would not be prepared to wage a world war."[64] Hitler commented privately that "while England may talk big . . . she is sure not to resort to armed intervention in the conflict."[65] Russia then emerged as a central actor in the European tumult. Germany, Britain, and France opened negotiations with Moscow in attempts to gain Russia's allegiance. Germany won. On August 23, Nazi Germany and Soviet Russia signed the nonaggression pact, essentially assuring Berlin that Russia would remain neutral and not align with an Anglo-French coalition. Poland, the immediate victim, was to be divided between the two powers. Hitler had accomplished another stunning feat—in this case cavorting with the Bolshevik devil itself. So much for Stalin's denunciations of Nazism and Hitler's shrill harangues against Bolshevism. Yet Western outcries against the Nazi-Soviet pact seemed hypocritical, for Russia had done much the same thing that Britain and France had done at Munich. Hypocrisy or not, Germany was ready for another conquest. On September 1, German soldiers invaded Poland. Two days later, Britain and France buried appeasement and declared war against Germany. On the 17th, Soviet troops struck Poland, engulfing half the nation. "Everything that I have worked for," cried Chamberlain, "has crashed into ruins."[66]

Throughout these years of descent into World War II, Hitler apparently did not consider the United States a nation of much consequence. In his warped view, shaped by limited knowledge, the United States could not and would not be a vital factor in international affairs. Although his diplomatic advisers, including German Ambassador to the United States Hans Dieckhoff, warned the Fuehrer that American "isolationism" was not permanent and could not be counted upon, Hitler believed that America could be nothing else than a weak, noninterventionist nation. Even in the period 1939-1941, when the United States took measures to aid the Allies, he did not alter his view. The United States, he said, "was incapable of conducting war." It was a "Jewish rubbish heap," incapacitated by economic and racial crisis, crime, and inept political leadership. "The inferiority and decadence of this allegedly new world is evident in its military inefficiency," he claimed. For

**Neville Chamberlain
(1869–1940).** The British Prime Minister (1937-1940), a Conservative party member from a wealthy, elite family, became the architect of the ill-fated appeasement policy. He resigned from office in May of 1940. (U.S. Information Agency, National Archives)

Joachim von Ribbentrop (1893–1946) and Josef Stalin (1879–1953). The German foreign minister and Soviet Premier smile their approval of the Nazi-Soviet nonaggression pact signed in August, 1939. The news angered but did not surprise American officials, who monitored the secret negotiations through reports from a cooperative German diplomat in Moscow. (World War II Collection of Seized Enemy Records, National Archives)

Hitler a nation was powerful, and thus to be taken seriously, if its racial composition was pure and if it was a land power. Because the United States was a so-called "melting pot" of ethnic diversity, "half Judaized, half negrified," and because it was largely a sea power, Hitler underestimated it.[67] This gross misperception, this subjective view, would ultimately mean his undoing, as the United States after 1938 increasingly tied its fortunes to Britain and France in the European squabbles.

American "Isolationism" and the Neutrality Acts

"This nation will remain a neutral nation," the President announced on September 3, 1939, "but I cannot ask that every American remain neutral in thought as well."[68] Actually, at the start of the war, the United States was not quite neutral in thought or deed. But this nascent unneutrality was a recent phenomenon. During the early 1930s the United States attempted to shield itself from conflict in Europe, to let Europeans settle their own political differences, and to remain neutral.

Although most Americans responded to the rise of Nazism with hostility, and strongly disapproved of Hitler's machinations at home and abroad, they tried to isolate themselves politically from what they considered European decadence, from a continent prone to self-destruction. If Britain and France could not handle German aggression in their own backyards, America could not do the job for them.

Americans also drew lessons from the bloody experiences and inconclusive peace of World War I. Disillusioned writers and "revisionist" historians argued that Germany was not alone to blame for the outbreak of war in 1914, that Wilson was pro-British and influenced by businessmen and propagandists, and that the costs and results of war—the national interest—would not justify American involvement. In 1934 a best-selling book titled *Merchants of Death* (by Helmuth Englebrecht and Frank Hanighen) was offered by the Book-of-the-Month Club. Its message, that profiteering manufacturers of armaments were active members of the American economic and political system and had helped compromise American neutrality during the First World War, reflected popular opinion. A Senate committee under the leadership of Gerald P. Nye held hearings during 1934–1936 to determine if munitions makers and bankers had lobbied Wilson into war. The committee never proved the allegation, but did uncover substantial evidence that these entrepreneurs were hardly agents of peace. As John Wiltz, historian of the investigation, has concluded, the Nye Committee "exhibited documents which shocked Americans into the realization that there was a difference between selling instruments of human destruction and selling sewing machines or automobiles."[69] Nye wailed against "rotten commercialism."[70] Such revelations fed popular sentiment that World War I had been a tragic blunder—Americans would stay out of the next one. Historian and isolationist Carl Becker complained that, in regard to the First World War, the United States, rather than defending its property or making the world safe for democracy, had actually lost millions of dollars in bad debts and helped make the world safe for dictators.

Peace groups, scientist Albert Einstein, celebrated pilot Charles Lindbergh, Herbert Hoover, anti-Semite Father Charles E. Coughlin, historian Charles Beard, President Robert Hutchins of the University of Chicago, and senators like William Borah and George Norris shared some of these ideas. The antiwar movement was particularly strong on college campuses and among women. Princeton University students organized the Veterans of Future Wars in 1936 and demanded $1000 each as a bonus *before* going into battle, because few, they predicted, would live through the next war. "Hello Sucker" posters picturing maimed soldiers aroused antiwar consciences. In 1938, Congressman Louis Ludlow introduced a constitutional amendment calling for a national referendum on decisions for war. A motion to discharge his resolution from the Rules Committee failed by only twenty-one votes, 209–188. Warned Ludlow: "The art of killing people en masse and maiming and wrecking human bodies has been perfected until it is impossible to imagine the next large-scale war being anything less than a vast carnival of death."[71] Roosevelt had worked against the referendum, claiming that it "would cripple any President in his conduct of our foreign relations," and isolationist Senator Arthur Vandenberg protested that it "would be as sensible to require a town meeting before permitting the fire department to put out the blaze."[72]

Many of the so-called "isolationists" were liberal reformers who believed that American involvement in a European war would undercut the New Deal's attempts to recover from the depression. They remembered how Wilson had turned against critics in World War I, suppressing civil liberties. They remembered, too, that he cooperated with big business to win the war. Some reformers were convinced that businessmen were harbingers of war; hence they sought to curb business adventures abroad that entangled the United States and compromised what they believed to be the national interest. The statistics were not as readily available to them as they are now to historians. In 1937, for example, 20 of the top 100 American corporations were involved in important agreements with Nazi Germany, some of them with the backbone of the German military machine, the I. G. Farben Company. Companies like DuPont, Union Carbide, and Standard Oil were closely tied to Germany through contracts. Standard Oil helped Germany develop both synthetic rubber and hundred-octane aviation fuel, and, true to its arrangement with Farben, refused to develop the fuel for the United States Army. As historian Arnold A. Offner has concluded: "American businessmen publicly opposed war as much as anyone else. But it would seem that the one price they would not pay for peace was private profit."[73] A notable exception was the Wall Street law firm of Sullivan and Cromwell, which severed profitable ties with Germany in protest against the persecution of Jews.

The abhorrence of war and its potential for harm in the United States, the desire to avoid intervention in another European squabble, and the nationalist conviction that the United States should find a way to protect its freedom of action, all contributed to the passage of the Neutrality Acts of 1935–1937. Roosevelt, sharing much of the isolationist thought, wanted a neutrality act, but he sought the discretionary power to decide to which belligerent in a war an embargo on arms shipments should be applied. Suspicious of presidential power in foreign policy-making, Congress refused and passed the Neutrality Act of 1935. It required an American arms embargo against all belligerents, after the President had officially declared the existence of war. The President could not, in short, designate and punish the aggressor. Subsequent acts added that loans were forbidden to the belligerents (Act of 1936), that the United States was neutral in the Spanish Civil War (Amendment of 1937), and that belligerents wishing to trade with the United States would have to come to this country and carry away the goods in their own ships ("cash and carry"), after payment upon delivery (Act of 1937). The last legislation also forbade American citizens to travel on belligerent vessels.

The Neutrality Acts were a mistake; they provided for no discrimination among the belligerents, no punishment of the aggressor. They denied the United States any forceful word in the cascading events in Europe. They amounted to an abdication of power. Yet, at the same time, much of what the isolationists said about the fruits of war was true. Their criticisms of imperialism and business expansion were honest and telling. They scored the British Empire and American intervention in Latin America. They compared Italy's subjugation of Ethiopia to Britain's supremacy in India. Many of them warned about increasing the power of the President in foreign affairs beyond congressional reach. Their commitment to peace, and their rejection of war as a solution to human problems, were compelling and ennobling. They cannot simply be dismissed as obstructionist crackpots who left the nation unprepared for war, for many were nationalists who did vote defense funds. "Isolationism was," historian Manfred Jonas has written, "the considered response to foreign and domestic developments of a large, responsible, and respectable segment of the American people."[74] In condemning all imperialism—American, British, or German—the isolationists often refused to make the choice of the lesser of two or three evils, as human necessity requires. However praiseworthy some components of their thought (and later generations have learned to heed many of their criticisms about intervention abroad), their formulas for the 1930s were mistaken—as mistaken, certainly, as Britain's appeasement policy.

Roosevelt and the United States on the Eve of War

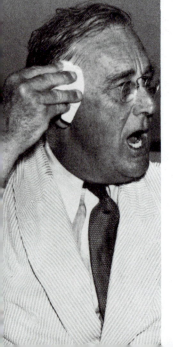

Franklin D. Roosevelt in Hot Times. After re-election in 1936, the President moved haltingly away from neutrality and isolationism as he reacted to war clouds abroad. Domestic issues still claimed high priority and aroused opposition to his leadership, as evidenced by his efforts to "pack" the Supreme Court in 1937 and to "purge" conservative Democrats in 1938. Here Roosevelt is mopping his brow after a cruise in the hot sun aboard the U.S.S. *Houston,* one ship in the Navy that he was enlarging. (United Press International)

President Franklin D. Roosevelt, sensitive to the political weight of the prevailing American sentiment against involvement in European bickering and territorial rearrangements and sharing much of the isolationist loathing of war, responded haltingly to the events of the 1930s. His foreign policy fed appeasement. When Germany began to rearm and when Italy attacked Ethiopia, Roosevelt stated that the United States sought above all to avoid war. America would set a peaceful example for other nations to follow. The idea of the United States as a "showcase" of righteousness drew upon American tradition. He and Hull invoked the Neutrality Act in the Italo-Ethiopian conflict, warned Americans not to travel on belligerent ships, and suggested a moral embargo against trade with the warring parties. Actually American businessmen ignored the moral embargo and increased commerce with Italy, especially in oil. In August of 1936 the President gave a stirring speech at Chautauqua, New York, recalling memories of World War I: "I have seen war. . . . I have seen blood running from the wounded. I have seen men coughing out their gassed lungs. I have seen the dead in the mud. . . . I have seen the agony of mothers and wives. I hate war. I have passed unnumbered hours, I shall pass unnumbered hours, thinking and planning how war may be kept from this nation."[75]

In January, 1937, the Roosevelt Administration asked Congress for an arms embargo against Spain, then wracked by civil war. Congress obliged, but the decision sparked considerable debate, because the embargo clearly worked against the "Loyalist" Republican government and in favor of Franco, who received arms from Germany and Italy. Many isolationists protested neutrality—the sacrifice of Spanish democracy—in this case. The issue was agonizing: How can one be committed to both peace and liberty? Roosevelt and Hull chose strict neutrality, in essence backing feeble British-French efforts to contain the civil war and aligning themselves with the pro-Franco views of the Catholic hierarchy at home. Yet FDR privately pondered ways to curb the aggressors. In the summer of 1937, Roosevelt thought vaguely about calling an international conference, but he took no action, uncertain that the United States could perform any magic. "I haven't got a hat and I haven't got a rabbit in it," he sighed.[76] In July, when Japan plunged into undeclared war against China, Roosevelt favored China by not invoking the Neutrality Act, thereby permitting the Chinese government to buy and import American war goods. Then in October he delivered his famous "quarantine" speech, calling for the isolation of international lawbreakers, the disease carriers. FDR began vague talks with the British ambassador about a joint cruiser blockade against Japan and sent a naval officer to London for secret staff talks. Under Secretary of State Sumner Welles also proposed a world conference on disarmament and international law in Washington, at which Roosevelt might quietly stiffen British diplomacy. Neville Chamberlain, however, blocked the meeting in early 1938, because it "cut across efforts to negotiate on immediate issues with the dictators."[77] Convinced that he could "count on nothing from the Americans but words," and that FDR's words on quarantines were the "utterings of a hare-brained statesman," Chamberlain continued to pursue appeasement.[78]

During the Czech crisis of 1938 the United States kept at a safe distance. The President appealed for negotiations to head off war, but he informed Hitler that the United States had "no political involvements in Europe and will assume no obligations in the conduct of the present negotiations."[79] He refrained from criticizing Germany for fear that Czechoslovakia would be encouraged to resist. "Good man," Roosevelt cabled Chamberlain when he heard that the Prime Minister would go to Munich.[80] When the Munich accord was announced, Roosevelt accepted it as a measure for peace and Hull remarked that Munich provided "a universal sense of relief."[81] Yet the dismemberment of Czechoslovakia, combined with the Japanese terror in China, profoundly troubled the President. To stop the lawlessness he began to shed his isolationist proclivities; within months after Munich, he admitted privately that he was ashamed of his earlier response. He got encouragement for this shift in attitude from former ambassador to Germany William Dodd and Assistant Secretary of State George Messersmith, both of whom roundly condemned appeasement.

In October of 1938 Roosevelt asked Congress for $300 million for national defense. He encouraged the State Department and Senator Key Pittman, that hard-drinking, gun-packing, incompetent chairman of the Foreign Relations Committee, to lobby for the repeal of the arms embargo law. In November, in protest against Hitler's vicious persecution of the Jews, he recalled Ambassador Hugh Wilson from Berlin and never let him return. Wilson had endorsed the appeasement policy, applauding Munich as opening the way "to a better Europe."[82] He, like many other Americans, hoped that a strong Germany would stand as a bulwark against Bolshevik Russia. That same month, FDR initiated a program to build more than 10,000 warplanes per year, in order "to have something to back up my words."[83] He also secretly arranged for the French government to place orders for 555 planes, including the latest fighters and bombers. In December, the administration rallied behind a declaration of joint defense against aggression in the western hemisphere and loaned $25 million to China.

In his annual message to Congress in January, 1939, Roosevelt again urged revision of the Neutrality Act so that it would not "actually give aid to an aggressor and deny it to the victim."[84] This initiative stalled three weeks later when a Douglas DB-7 bomber crashed in California with a French officer on board. To squelch a full investigation, the President tried to persuade key senators of the need to deter German aggression by selling arms to friendly nations. Word leaked, however, that FDR had said that America's frontier was "on the Rhine," a charge he hotly branded "a deliberate lie."[85] Isolationists who had heard him say almost those very words grew even more suspicious of his intentions. "Get the uniforms ready for the boys," complained Senator Nye.[86] The President thus delayed until March the introduction of a bill specifically repealing the arms embargo, and throughout the spring he allowed the erratic Pittman to direct legislative strategy. Reluctant to risk battle against sizable political odds, FDR failed to lead at a critical time. In April he asked Hitler and Mussolini to refrain from attacking countries named on a list, but his request met open derision, Il Duce saying that Italy would not respond to "convivial vociferations, or Messiah-like messages."[87] The Senate Foreign Relations Committee, by a 12–11 vote, refused in

July to report out a bill repealing the arms embargo. "I've fired my last shot," the President groaned.[88] Not until November, 1939—after Germany's conquest of Poland—did Congress finally revise the Neutrality Act so that England and France, as belligerents, could purchase American arms on a cash-and-carry basis.

Even in the fall of 1939, however, most Americans joined their President in wanting to avoid participation in World War II. "We cannot expect . . . the United States to evolve quicker than we did," the British ambassador reported.[89] Americans still hoped they could remain above the melee, to avoid being sucked in. FDR, by sending Sumner Welles to Berlin, London, Paris, and Rome in the winter of 1939–1940, evidently thought he might somehow mediate the conflict. Hitler's *blitzkrieg* in the west that spring killed any such possibility. The Democratic party platform of 1940 reflected the American desire to avoid war, but to prepare for it: "We will not participate in foreign wars, and we will not send our army, naval or air forces to fight in foreign lands outside of the Americas except in case of attack." Still, it also promised "an invincible air force, a navy strong enough to protect all our seacoasts and our national interests, and a fully equipped and mechanized army."[90] As in the era of the First World War, because of their international interests, because American power became intricately involved in the war, and because they gradually abandoned neutrality to aid the Allies, Americans once again found themselves risking war to serve peace. The interwar quest for order had failed; the Neutrality Acts had failed; independent internationalism had failed. The time was ripe for changes in foreign policy.

Further Reading for the Period 1920–1939

For general studies, see Selig Adler, *The Isolationist Impulse* (1957) and *The Uncertain Giant* (1965); Robert A. Divine, *The Reluctant Belligerent* (1979); Jean-Baptiste Duroselle, *From Wilson to Roosevelt* (1963); L. Ethan Ellis, *Republican Foreign Policy, 1921–1933* (1968); William E. Leuchtenburg, *Franklin D. Roosevelt and the New Deal* (1963); Sally Marks, *The Illusion of Peace* (1976); Arnold Offner, *The Origins of the Second World War* (1975); Emily S. Rosenberg, *Spreading the American Dream: American Economic and Cultural Expansion, 1890–1945* (1982); Robert Freeman Smith, "American Foreign Relations, 1920–1942," in Barton J. Bernstein, ed., *Towards a New Past* (1968); Raymond Sontag, *A Broken World, 1919–1939* (1971); William A. Williams, *Tragedy of American Diplomacy* (1962); and John Wiltz, *From Isolation to War, 1931–1941* (1968).

Leading participants and their diplomacy are treated in McGeorge Bundy, *On Active Service in Peace and War* (1948) (on Stimson); Wayne S. Cole, *Senator Gerald P. Nye and American Foreign Relations* (1962); Richard Current, *Secretary Stimson* (1954); Robert Dallek, *Democrat and Diplomat: The Life of William E. Dodd* (1968); L. Ethan Ellis, *Frank B. Kellogg and American Foreign Relations, 1925–1929* (1961); Robert H. Ferrell, *American Diplomacy in the Great Depression* (1957) and *Frank B. Kellogg and Henry L. Stimson* (1963); Betty Glad, *Charles Evans Hughes and the Illusions of Innocence* (1967); Ellis W. Hawley, ed., *Herbert Hoover, Secretary of Commerce, 1921–1928* (1981); Waldo Heinrichs, *American Ambassador* (1966) (on Joseph C. Grew); Kenneth P. Jones, *U.S. Diplomats in Europe, 1919–1941* (1981); Richard Lowitt, *George W. Norris* (1963–1978); Robert James Maddox, *William E. Borah and American Foreign Policy* (1969); Elting E. Morison, *Turmoil and Tradition: A Study of the Life and Times of Henry L. Stimson* (1960); Robert K. Murray, *The Harding Era* (1969); Dexter Perkins, *Charles Evans Hughes and American Democratic Statesmanship* (1956); Julius Pratt, *Cordell Hull* (1964); Merlo J. Pusey, *Charles Evans Hughes* (1951); essays on Hughes, Kellogg, and Stimson by John C. Vinson, L. Ethan Ellis, and Richard Current in Norman A. Graebner, ed., *An*

Uncertain Tradition (1961); and Joan Hoff Wilson, *Herbert Hoover* (1975). See also Robert Schulzinger, *The Making of the Diplomatic Mind: The Training, Outlook, and Style of United States Foreign Service Officers, 1908–1931* (1975).

For studies of Franklin D. Roosevelt, see James M. Burns, *The Lion and the Fox* (1956); Robert Dallek, *Franklin D. Roosevelt and American Foreign Policy, 1933–1945* (1979); Robert A. Divine, *Roosevelt and World War II* (1969); Frank Freidel, *Franklin D. Roosevelt* (1953–1973); William E. Kinsella, Jr., *Leadership in Isolation* (1978); Willard Range, *Franklin D. Roosevelt's World Order* (1959); and Arthur M. Schlesinger, *The Age of Roosevelt* (1957–1960). See also Jason Berger *A New Deal for the World: Eleanor Roosevelt and American Foreign Policy 1920–1962* (1981).

Problems of economic diplomacy receive attention in Frederick Adams, *Economic Diplomacy: The Export-Import Bank and American Foreign Policy, 1934–1939* (1976); Derek H. Aldcroft, *From Versailles to Wall Street, 1919–1929* (1977); Joseph Brandes, *Herbert Hoover and Economic Diplomacy* (1962); Herbert Feis, *The Diplomacy of the Dollar* (1950); Lloyd C. Gardner, *Economic Aspects of New Deal Diplomacy* (1964); Michael J. Hogan, *Informal Entente: The Private Structure of Cooperation in Anglo-American Economic Diplomacy* (1977); Burton I. Kaufman, *Efficiency and Expansion: Foreign Trade Organization in the Wilson Administration, 1913–1921* (1974); Richard N. Kottman, *Reciprocity and the North Atlantic Triangle, 1932–1938* (1968);Cleona Lewis, *America's Stake in International Investments* (1938); Carl Parrini, *Heir to Empire: United States Economic Diplomacy, 1916–1923* (1969); George Soule, *Prosperity Decade* (1947); Harris G. Warren, *Herbert Hoover and the Great Depression* (1959); Mira Wilkins, *The Maturing of Multinational Enterprise: American Business Abroad from 1914 to 1970* (1974); and Joan Hoff Wilson, *American Business and Foreign Policy, 1920–1933* (1971).

For questions of peace, the League of Nations, and disarmament, see Thomas Buckley, *The United States and the Washington Conference, 1921–1922* (1970); Charles Chatfield, *For Peace and Justice* (1971); Merle Curti, *Peace or War* (1936); Charles DeBenedetti, *Origins of the Modern American Peace Movement, 1915–1929*(1978), and *The Peace Reform in American History* (1980); Roger Dingman, *Power in the Pacific: The Origins of Naval Arms Limitation, 1914–1922* (1976); Robert Ferrell, *Peace in Their Time* (1952); D. F. Fleming, *The United States and World Organization, 1920–1933* (1938); Harold Josephson, *James T. Shotwell and the Rise of Internationalism in America* (1976); Gary B. Ostrower, *Collective Insecurity: The United States and the League of Nations during the Early Thirties* (1979); and Stephen Pelz, *Race to Pearl Harbor: The Failure of the Second London Naval Conference and the Onset of World War II* (1974). See also Arnold H. Taylor, *American Diplomacy and the Narcotics Traffic, 1900–1939* (1969).

Soviet-American relations and recognition are discussed in Edward Bennett, *Recognition of Russia* (1970); Donald G. Bishop, *The Roosevelt-Litvinov Agreements* (1965); Robert Browder, *The Origins of Soviet-American Diplomacy* (1953); Beatrice Farnsworth, *William C. Bullitt and the Soviet Union* (1967); Peter Filene, *Americans and the Soviet Experiment, 1917–1933* (1967); John L. Gaddis, *Russia, the Soviet Union, and the United States* (1978); George F. Kennan, *Russia and the West under Lenin and Stalin* (1960); James K. Libbey, *Alexander Gumberg and Soviet-American Relations, 1917–1933* (1977); Thomas R. Maddux, *Years of Estrangement: American Relations with the Soviet Union, 1933–1941* (1980); Anthony Sutton, *Western Technology and Soviet Economic Development, 1917–1930* (1968); Robert C. Williams, *Russian Art and American Money, 1900–1940* (1980); William A. Williams, *American-Russian Relations, 1781–1947* (1952); and Joan Hoff Wilson, *Ideology and Economics: U.S. Relations with the Soviet Union, 1918–1933* (1974).

American "isolationism," neutrality, European questions, the rise of fascism, and the coming of World War II are treated in many of the works cited above and in James J. and Patience P. Barnes, *Hitler's Mein Kampf in Britain and America* (1980); Edward W. Bennett, *German Rearmament and the West, 1932–1933* (1979); Warren Cohen, *The American Revisionists* (1967); James V. Compton, *The Swastika and the Eagle: Hitler, the United States and the Origins of World War II* (1967); David H. Culbert, *News for Everyman: Radio and Foreign Affairs in Thirties America* (1976); Robert A. Divine, *The Illusion of Neutrality* (1962); Jean-Baptiste Duroselle, *France and the United States* (1978); George Q. Flynn, *Roosevelt and Ro-*

manism: *Catholics and American Diplomacy, 1937–1945* (1976); Thomas N. Guinsburg, *The Pursuit of Isolationism in the United States Senate from Versailles to Pearl Harbor* (1981); Allen Guttmann, *The Wound in the Heart: America and the Spanish Civil War* (1962); John M. Haight, Jr., *American Aid to France, 1938–1940* (1970); Manfred Jonas, *Isolationism in America* (1966); Thomas C. Kennedy, *Charles A. Beard and American Foreign Policy* (1975); Lawrence Lafore, *The End of Glory* (1971); Melvyn Leffler, *The Elusive Quest: America's Pursuit of European Stability and French Security, 1919–1933* (1979); Arnold Offner, *American Appeasement* (1969); Thomas G. Paterson, "Isolationism Revisited," *The Nation* (1969); Dan P. Silverman, *Reconstructing Europe after the Great War* (1982); David Strauss, *Menace in the West: The Rise of French Anti-Americanism in Modern Times* (1978); Richard Traina, *American Diplomacy and the Spanish Civil War* (1968); and John Wiltz, *In Search of Peace: The Senate Munitions Inquiry* (1963).

See also the "Further Reading" sections for Chapters 10 and 11, the General Bibliography, and the following notes.

Notes to Chapter 9

1. Quoted in John M. Blum, *From the Morgenthau Diaries: Years of Crisis, 1928–1938* (Boston: Houghton Mifflin, 1959–1967; 3 vols.), I, 55.
2. *Ibid.*
3. Quoted in Dean Acheson, *This Vast Eternal Realm* (New York: W. W. Norton Company, 1973), p. 288.
4. Quoted in Beatrice Farnsworth, *William C. Bullitt and the Soviet Union* (Bloomington: Indiana University Press, 1967), p. 86.
5. Quoted in Edward M. Bennett, *Recognition of Russia* (Waltham, Mass.: Blaisdell, 1970), pp. 111–112.
6. Edgar B. Nixon, ed., *Franklin D. Roosevelt and Foreign Affairs* (Cambridge: Harvard University Press, 1969; 3 vols.), I, 434n.
7. U.S. Department of State, *Foreign Relations of the United States, 1933, II* (Washington: Government Printing Office, 1949), 794–795.
8. Nixon, *Roosevelt and Foreign Affairs*, I, 293–294.
9. William Phillips, *Ventures in Diplomacy* (Boston: Beacon Press, 1952), pp. 156–157.
10. Blum, *From the Morgenthau Diaries*, I, 57 and Louis Fischer, *Men and Politics: An Autobiography* (New York: Duell, Sloan and Pearce, 1941), p. 130.
11. Fischer, *Men and Politics*, p. 211.
12. Phillips, *Ventures in Diplomacy*, p. 156.
13. Will Rogers, *How We Elect Our President* (Boston: Little, Brown, 1952), p. 148.
14. Cordell Hull, *Memoirs* (New York: Macmillan, 1948; 2 vols.), I, 297.
15. *Ibid.*, p. 292.
16. Nixon, *Roosevelt and Foreign Affairs*, I, 468.
17. Robert P. Browder, *The Origins of Soviet-American Diplomacy* (Princeton: Princeton University Press, 1953), p. 133.
18. Quoted in Fischer, *Men and Politics*, p. 299.
19. George F. Kennan, *Memoirs, 1925–1950* (Boston: Little, Brown, 1967), p. 57.
20. Hull, *Memoirs*, I, 302.
21. Blum, *From the Morgenthau Diaries*, I, 57.
22. Herbert Hoover, quoted in Robert F. Smith, "Republican Policy and the Pax Americana, 1921–1932," in William A. Williams, ed., *From Colony to Empire* (New York: John Wiley and Sons, 1972), p. 292; and Henry L. Stimson, quoted in Melvyn P. Leffler, "Political Isolationism: Economic Expansionism or Diplomatic Realism? American Policy toward Western Europe, 1921–1933," *Perspectives in American History*, VIII (1974), 419.
23. Joan Hoff Wilson, *American Business and Foreign Policy, 1920–1933* (Boston: Beacon Press, 1973 [c. 1971]), p. x.
24. Robert K. Murray, *The Politics of Normalcy* (New York: W. W. Norton, 1973), p. 21.
25. Quoted in L. Ethan Ellis, *Republican Foreign Policy, 1921–1933* (New Brunswick, N.J.: Rutgers University Press, 1968), p. 40.
26. Diary, December 9, 1927, Box 87, Lewis W. Douglas Papers, University of Arizona Library (from the notes of Professor Thomas G. Smith).
27. Howard H. Quint and Robert H. Ferrell, eds., *The Talkative President: The Off-the-Record Press Conferences of Calvin Coolidge* (Amherst: University of Massachusetts Press, 1964), p. 298.
28. Quoted in Joan Hoff Wilson, *Herbert Hoover: Forgotten Progressive* (Boston: Little, Brown, 1975), p. 122.
29. Quoted in John Chalmers Vinson, "Charles Evans Hughes," in Norman A. Graebner, ed., *An Uncertain Tradition: American Secretaries of State in the Twentieth Century* (New York: McGraw-Hill, 1961), p. 133.
30. *Ibid.*, p. 132.
31. Willard Range, *Franklin D. Roosevelt's World Order* (Athens: University of Georgia Press, 1959), p. xii.
32. Quoted in Frank Freidel, *Franklin D. Roosevelt: Launching the New Deal* (Boston: Little, Brown, 1973), p. 459.
33. Quoted in Louis B. Wehle, *Hidden Threads of History* (New York: Macmillan, 1953), p. 131.
34. Quoted in Lewis Einstein, *A Diplomat Looks Back* (New Haven: Yale University Press, 1968; ed. by Lawrence E. Gelfand), p. 29.
35. Quoted in William Barnes and John H. Morgan, *The Foreign Service of the United States* (Washington: Department of State, 1961), p. 203.
36. Mira Wilkins, *The Maturing of Multinational Enterprise: Ameri-*

can Business Abroad from 1914 to 1970 (Cambridge: Harvard University Press, 1974), p. 138.

37. *New York Times,* May 5, 1930.

38. Quoted in Julius W. Pratt, *Cordell Hull* (New York: Cooper Square, 1964; 2 vols.), I, 112.

39. Quint and Ferrell, *Talkative President,* p. 196.

40. Quoted in John D. Hicks, *Republican Ascendancy, 1921–1933* (New York: Harper and Row, 1960), p. 136.

41. Will Rogers, *Letters of a Self-Made Diplomat to His President* (New York: A. & C. Boni, 1926), p. xii.

42. Quoted in Harold Josephson, *James T. Shotwell and the Rise of Internationalism in America* (Rutherford, N.J.: Fairleigh Dickinson University Press, 1975), p. 140.

43. Quoted in Charles DeBenedetti, "Peace Was His Profession: James T. Shotwell and American Internationalism," in Frank Merli and Theodore A. Wilson, eds., *Makers of American Diplomacy* (New York: Charles Scribner's Sons, 1974), p. 390.

44. Merle Curti, *Peace or War: The American Struggle, 1636–1936* (New York: W. W. Norton, 1936), p. 262.

45. *The General Pact for the Renunciation of War* (Washington: Government Printing Office, 1928).

46. Quoted in Robert H. Ferrell, *Peace in Their Time* (New York: W. W. Norton, [c. 1952], 1969), p. 201.

47. Quoted in L. Ethan Ellis, "Frank B. Kellogg," in Graebner, *Uncertain Tradition,* p. 166.

48. *Foreign Relations, 1923, II* (Washington: Government Printing Office, 1938), 760.

49. Quoted in David J. Danelski and Joseph S. Tulchin, eds., *The Autobiographical Notes of Charles Evans Hughes* (Cambridge: Harvard University Press, 1973), p. 262.

50. Quoted in Peter G. Filene, *Americans and the Soviet Experiment, 1917–1933* (Cambridge: Harvard University Press, 1967), p. 82.

51. Allen Nevins and Frank E. Hill, *Ford: Expansion and Challenge, 1915–1933* (New York: Charles Scribner's Sons, 1952), p. 683.

52. Maurice Hindus (*The Outlook*) quoted *ibid.,* p. 603.

53. Quoted in Farnsworth, *Bullitt and the Soviet Union,* p. 153.

54. Fischer, *Men and Politics,* p. 308.

55. Quoted in James Aronson, *The Press and the Cold War* (Indianapolis: Bobbs-Merrill, 1970), p. 32.

56. Kennan, *Memoirs, 1925–1950,* p. 67.

57. Eugene Lyons, "To Tell or Not to Tell," *Harper's, CLXXI* (June, 1935), 102.

58. Charles W. Thayer, *Bears in the Caviar* (Philadelphia: Lippincott, 1951), p. 115.

59. Quoted in Arnold A. Offner, *American Appeasement: United States Foreign Policy and Germany, 1933–1938* (New York: W. W. Norton, 1976 [c. 1969]), p. 50.

60. Quoted in Raymond J. Sontag, *A Broken World, 1919–1939* (New York: Harper and Row, 1971), p. 290.

61. Quoted in Lawrence Lafore, *The End of Glory: An Interpretation of the Origins of World War II* (Philadelphia: J. B. Lippincott, 1970), p. 158.

62. Sontag, *A Broken World,* p. 316.

63. Quoted in A. J. P. Taylor, *The Origins of the Second World War* (New York: Fawcett Publications, 1966 [c. 1961]), p. 181.

64. *Foreign Relations, 1939, I* (Washington: Government Printing Office, 1956), 288.

65. Quoted in Sontag, *A Broken World,* p. 374.

66. *Ibid.,* p. 381.

67. Quoted in James V. Compton, *The Swastika and the Eagle: Hitler, the United States, and the Origins of World War II* (Boston: Houghton Mifflin, 1967), pp. 17, 25, 33.

68. Samuel I. Rosenman, ed., *Public Papers and Addresses of Franklin D. Roosevelt, 1939* (New York: Macmillan, 1938–50; 13 vols.), VIII, 463.

69. John E. Wiltz, "The Nye Committee Revisited," *The Historian, XXIII* (February, 1961), 232.

70. Quoted in Wayne S. Cole, *Senator Gerald P. Nye and American Foreign Relations* (Minneapolis: University of Minnesota Press, 1962), pp. 126–127.

71. Quoted in Thomas G. Paterson, "Isolationism Revisited," *The Nation, CCIX* (September 1, 1969), 167.

72. Quoted in Robert A. Divine, *The Reluctant Belligerent* (New York: John Wiley and Sons, 1979; 2nd ed.), p. 52; and in John E. Wiltz, *From Isolation to War, 1931–1941* (New York: Thomas Y. Crowell, 1968), p. 16.

73. Offner, *American Appeasement,* p. 103.

74. Manfred Jonas, *Isolationism in America, 1935–1941* (Ithaca, New York: Cornell University Press, 1966), p. viii.

75. Rosenman, *Public Papers, 1936, V,* 289.

76. Quoted in Dorothy Borg, *The United States and the Far Eastern Crisis of 1933–1938* (Cambridge: Harvard University Press, 1964), p. 374.

77. Quoted in James R. Leutze, *Bargaining for Supremacy* (Chapel Hill: University of North Carolina Press, 1977), p. 26.

78. Quoted in Christopher Thorne, *Allies of a Kind* (New York: Oxford University Press, 1978), p. 38.

79. *Foreign Relations, 1938, I* (Washington: Government Printing Office, 1955), 685.

80. *Ibid.,* p. 688.

81. *Ibid.,* p. 703.

82. Quoted in Offner, *American Appeasement,* p. 215.

83. Quoted in Blum, *From the Morgenthau Diaries: Years of Urgency, 1938–1941, II,* 49.

84. Rosenman, *Public Papers, 1939, VIII,* 4.

85. *New York Times,* February 1, 1939.

86. Memorandum, January 31, 1939, Box 37, Gerald P. Nye Papers, Herbert H. Hoover Library, West Branch, Iowa.

87. Quoted in William L. Langer and S. Everett Gleason, *The Challenge to Isolation, 1937–1940* (New York: Harper and Brothers, 1952), p. 87.

88. Quoted in Robert Dallek, *Franklin D. Roosevelt and American Foreign Policy, 1932–1945* (New York: Oxford University Press, 1979), p. 192.

89. Lord Lothian to Lord Halifax, September 27, 1939, vol. 24, Halifax Papers, FO/800, Public Record Office, Kew, England.

90. Kirk H. Porter and Donald B. Johnson, eds., *National Party Platforms, 1840–1972* (Urbana: University of Illinois Press, 1973), p. 382.

"The Open Door." The Japanese thrust into Manchuria in 1931 called into question the peace and disarmament agreements of the previous decade. (*The Outlook,* 1931)

10 A Question of Power: Relations with Asia and Latin America, 1920–1939

Diplomatic Crossroad: The Manchurian Crisis, 1931–1932

It apparently started with thirty-one inches of steel. At 10:30 P.M., a few miles outside the Manchurian capital of Mukden during the night of September 18, 1931, an explosion apparently blasted a short section from the South Manchurian Railway. Apparently Japanese soldiers shot and killed some Chinese attempting to escape from the area. Apparently? Yes, because Japanese army officers had a most difficult time explaining the events of that dark night. The Mukden Express had somehow managed to cross over that very section of track *after* the alleged explosion. The train must have jumped the gap, the Japanese lamely answered. American officials who inspected the steel fragments noted that they did not carry the imprint of the Carnegie Steel Works as did the track still in place. Indeed, it appears compelling that the "Mukden Incident" of September 18 was fabricated by young Japanese officers of the Guandong (Manchurian) Army. They had plotted for months to seize Manchuria and sever it permanently from China. Feverish in their quest for Japanese grandeur and Asian power, they or their followers had already, in 1930, assassinated the Japanese premier. So when the news from Mukden reached Tokyo, one civilian official remarked with resignation, "They've done it at last."[1]

Manchuria was to Tokyo, civilian and military alike, a vital Japanese interest. It served as a defensive buffer against the hated Russians and their communism. More important, it teemed with the raw materials (coal, iron, timber, soybeans) so desperately needed by the import-hungry Japanese islands. More than half of Japan's foreign investments were in Manchuria. The Japanese-run South Manchurian Railway served as the nerve center of these large economic holdings. Ever since their victory in the Russo-Japanese War, the Japanese had been driving in their imperial stakes. By treaty they had acquired the right to station troops along the railroad. The United States had recognized Japan's primacy in Manchuria through the Root-Takahira and Lansing-Ishii agreements.

Chinese nationalists throughout the 1920s had harassed their Asian brethren. Nationalist leader Jiang Jieshi (Chiang Kai-shek) encouraged Chinese to move to Manchuria and sought to build a railroad to compete with the South Manchurian. The Chinese boycotted Japanese products, a particularly alarming practice during the Great Depression, when Japan's foreign trade faced a serious slump. Both Chinese and Japanese blood was spilled in isolated incidents. Such cumulative provocations amounted to "a case where a thousand pinpricks equalled a slash of the saber,"[2] and the haughty Japanese response came in the darkness of September 18, 1931.

The Mukden news reached an irritable Secretary of State Henry L. Stimson, worn low by Washington's exceedingly hot, humid temperatures before the age of the air conditioner. The weather accentuated a Stimsonian personality trait. President Herbert Hoover thought the moustachioed Stimson "more of a warrior than a diplomat," and Stimson himself pointed to his "combat psychology."[3] The forthright secretary shared prevalent American attitudes toward "inferior" races and believed that he understood the "Oriental mind."[4] He also embraced the Open Door policy and the sanctity of law. "Respect for treaties was the very foundation of peace," he said.[5] Japanese aggression in Manchuria violated treaties signed at the Washington Conference (1922), which endorsed the Open Door, and the Kellogg-Briand Pact (1928), which outlawed war. Thus, Stimson concluded that the Manchurian crisis was "an issue between the two great theories of civilization and economic methods."[6]

Stimson hoped at first that the "Mukden Incident" was a localized mutiny of the Japanese army. No American wanted the United States to become ensnarled "'all

Henry L. Stimson (1867–1950) and Herbert Hoover (1874–1964). The secretary of state (left) and President differed on how the United States should protest Japanese machinations in Manchuria. Hoover opposed force because it was "contrary to the policy and best judgment of the United States to build peace on military sanctions." (Herbert Hoover Presidential Library)

by itself' in the jungle of this Chinese-Japanese-Manchurian mixup—which is full of hidden explosives, dense underbrush, [and] quicksand," noted Chief of the State Department's Division of Far Eastern Affairs Stanley K. Hornbeck.[7] One of Stimson's aides depicted the secretary as "a small boy at the edge of a pool which is cold, just not quite willing to get in there in one plunge and swim."[8] Caution was quite in order. The United States possessed little power in Asia. The British, interested in preserving their own Asian empire and hobbled by economic crisis at home, preferred to appease their former ally Japan. The French were caught in their usual domestic political confusion. Soviet Russia, still not recognized by the United States, could hardly be called upon for help. The League of Nations was notably feeble, its big power members openly contemptuous of Wilson's creation. Neither the United States nor Russia belonged to it.

Stimson decided on a meek policy of letting "the Japanese know we are watching them."[9] On September 24, 1931, he gently urged the Chinese and Japanese to cease hostilities. A few days later the League began to discuss the Manchurian crisis, and the United States permitted an American representative to sit at the League table only as an "observer." Stimson and Hoover feared that the international organization would "dump" the "Manchurian baby" in Washington's lap,[10] but the League passed meaningless resolutions for peace and set up the Lytton Commission to investigate. Japanese soldiers kept marching, meeting little resistance from ineptly led Chinese forces, and within months they had seized all of Manchuria. Humorist Will Rogers quipped that nations would run out of stationery for their many protest notes before the Japanese ran out of soldiers.

The secretary of state did not have many diplomatic tools with which to work. He could not intervene militarily. He could not call on Britain, France, Russia, or the tepid League. And when he suggested to Hoover, in December, 1931, that the United States and others impose economic sanctions on Japan, the President strongly rejected the idea. Stimson knew that Japan depended upon imports of American oil, that it was the third largest buyer of American exports, and that the United States took about 40 percent of Japan's exports. Maybe economic pressure would force Tokyo to reverse its military thrust through Manchuria. Hoover, however, responded that the United States should not venture forth alone "sticking pins in tigers."[11] The risk of war was too great, the President cautioned.

Thus, nonrecognition. Drawing upon Secretary of State William Jennings Bryan's protest in 1915 against the Japanese Twenty-One Demands on China, Stimson on January 7, 1932 issued what became known as the "Stimson Doctrine." (Hoover, his political fortunes flagging at home, thought it should be called the "Hoover Doctrine.") Stimson threw tradition and law against Japan: the United States would not recognize any arrangements in China that might impair American treaty rights, violate the Open Door policy, or subvert the Kellogg-Briand Pact. Defiantly, on January 28, the Japanese marched into Shanghai. Stimson grew belligerent and convinced Hoover to reinforce the American military garrison in that city. Reminded of the German attack on Belgium in 1914, the secretary drew an historical lesson and set his jaw against this new aggressive outrage.

There was nothing left to try but bluff. He wanted to frighten Japan without its knowing that it had no reason to be afraid. On February 23, 1932, Stimson sent a public letter to Senator William Borah, chairman of the Senate Foreign Relations Committee. Privately the secretary hoped it would "encourage China, enlighten the American public, exhort the League, stir up the British, and warn Japan."[12] A rather ambitious set of goals, for sure. Employing the Open Door policy as an instrument, Stimson chastised Japan for violating the administrative and territorial integrity of China and the Kellogg-Briand agreement. He repeated his earlier denial of recognition and threatened to fortify Guam and build up the American Navy in the Pacific if Japan did not halt its aggression. The protest letter made little impact, although Japan soon signed an armistice in Shanghai and the League endorsed nonrecognition. In February, Japan actually reconstituted Manchuria as the puppet state of Manchukuo, and in September recognized it. The next month the Lytton Commission chided the Japanese for misconduct in Manchuria. Perturbed but unchecked, Japan resigned from the League of Nations in early 1933, claiming it was being crucified like Christ on the cross. Stimson's bluff had failed. The secretary, biographer Elting E. Morison concludes, "wound up like a man before a breaking dam with a shovel in his hands." Stimson himself remarked that he was armed only with "spears of straw and swords of ice."[13]

The Quest for a Nonmilitary Foreign Policy

Stimson's diplomacy raises questions that help us understand the 1920–1939 period. Was it wise for Stimson to rail so vigorously against Japanese machinations in Manchuria? Did it do any good? Did it help the Japanese military faction gain support from other nationalists who also considered Manchuria of supreme importance? Did the policy of nonrecognition reveal how weak the United States was in Asia? Was it read as bluff? Did it not also expose China's vulnerability, its abandonment by other nations? Should Stimson have ignored the violations of the treaties? Would it have been wiser to let the Asians settle their own differences—especially since the United States lacked sufficient naval and military power to intervene in the area? Was America's national interest affected by the Manchurian crisis?

Years after 1931, Stimson admitted that nonrecognition had not worked. It did not alter the balance of power in Asia. Japan was not cowed. Moral exhortation and lecturing may only have soothed the American conscience and stirred up the aggressor, to nobody's benefit. Diplomat Hugh Wilson reflected on Stimson's tactics: "If the nations of the world feel strongly enough to condemn, they should feel strongly enough to use force. . . . To condemn only merely intensifies the heat." He went on: "Condemnation creates a community of the damned who are forced outside the pale, who have nothing to lose by the violation of all laws of order and international good faith."[14]

Stimson tried lecture and bluff because he had no other viable options. As an aristocrat committed to law and order, it seemed to him natural and gentlemanly to isolate the disorderly and to identify the damned. Further, although American economic interests in Manchuria were small, the cherished principle of the Open Door, both as diplomatic tool and as ideology, was at stake. The Japanese were shutting the door. If the Open Door could be violated so callously in Manchuria, it could be jeopardized elsewhere. Stimson spoke out for the principle that bolstered American economic interest overseas—hence his reference to the struggle in Manchuria as one between different economic methods.

America's timid response to the Manchurian crisis demonstrated that the United States, because it lacked power, could not manage affairs in Asia. United States gunboats still chugged on Chinese rivers, American troops were garrisoned on

Makers of American Foreign Policy from 1920 to 1939

Presidents	Secretaries of State
Woodrow Wilson, 1913–1921	Bainbridge Colby, 1920–1921
Warren G. Harding, 1921–1923	Charles E. Hughes, 1921–1925
Calvin Coolidge, 1923–1929	Frank B. Kellogg, 1925–1929
Herbert C. Hoover, 1929–1933	Henry L. Stimson, 1929–1933
Franklin D. Roosevelt, 1933–1945	Cordell Hull, 1933–1944

Chinese soil, and the Philippines remained a colony, but in the Pacific the Japanese were far superior. America could lecture, but not enforce. By contrast, the United States held considerable power—economic, naval, military, political—in Latin America. It was to the United States what China, especially Manchuria, was to Japan. The Japanese, in fact, often commented that what they were doing in China was what the United States had been doing for decades in Latin America. In Latin America the United States practiced the "closed door"; in Asia it appealed for the "Open Door." In both areas, the viability of American foreign policy depended upon power.

The Manchurian crisis also revealed the feebleness of the treaties of the 1920s and the reluctance of the European powers to check aggression in the 1930s, when appeasement was the policy of the day. Britain and France would not act; the League of Nations was weak and devoid of commitment from its chief members. Under these circumstances, and under the debilitating effects of the Great Depression, Americans understandably nurtured their independent internationalism. Given the timid policies of the Europeans and the League, Americans seemed to recognize the limits of their own power and the difficulty of taking unilateral action. They may have overextended themselves in words, but not in deeds. Their power did not reach as far as their desires. Still they did not withdraw from international events. Rather, the United States sought to create with nonmilitary means a world characterized by legal, orderly processes, the Open Door, and economic and political stability. The Hoover-Stimson response to the Manchurian episode typified these goals and methods. To quote Hoover again: "we can never herd the world into the paths of righteousness with the dogs of war."[15] Practicing "independent internationalism," America hoped to muzzle the dogs of war, not solely in the abstract, but to stimulate domestic prosperity, expand foreign trade, and insure national security.

The Washington Conference: Navies and Asia

The American pursuit of independent internationalism and a nonmilitary foreign policy was evident at the Washington Naval Conference of November 12, 1921 through February 6, 1922. After World War I a naval arms race loomed between the United States, Britain, and Japan. None of the parties really welcomed the spiraling financial costs of such a contest. Japan was pumping as much as one-third of its national budget into naval construction. The United States, possessing the second largest navy in the world, alarmed third-ranked Japan by shifting the main part of its battle fleet to the Pacific, by developing the base at Pearl Harbor, and by talking about fortifying the Philippines and Guam. First-ranked Britain already had Singapore, but lacked funds to engage in a naval arms race. The United States Congress might not appropriate funds either. Thus all three powers embraced arms control in order to check one another. With some prodding from Senator William Borah, the Harding Administration invited eight nations (Britain, France, Italy, Japan, China, Belgium, Netherlands, and Portugal) to Washington to discuss with the United States naval arms limitations and competition in Asia.

The Washington Conference opened with dramatic words from bewhiskered Secretary of State Charles Evans Hughes. Disdaining the usual generalities of welcoming statements, Hughes cut quickly to the problem. Calmly but deliberately he announced that the United States would scrap thirty ships. Then he turned to the British delegation and sank twenty-three of its ships. British Admiral Lord David Beatty, noted a reporter, leaned forward like a "bulldog, sleeping on a sunny doorstep, who has been poked in the stomach by the impudent foot of an itinerant soap canvasser." Spellbound now, the delegates heard Hughes scuttle twenty-five Japanese vessels. One commentator wrote that "Hughes sank in thirty-five minutes more ships than all the admirals of the world have sunk in a cycle of centuries."[16]

Despite grumblings of doom from naval advisers, the diplomats hammered out a naval limitations pact—the Five Power Treaty. It set a ten-year moratorium on the construction of capital vessels, defined as warships of more than 10,000 tons displacement or carrying guns larger than eight inches in bore diameter. The treaty also limited the tonnage for aircraft carriers, and established a tonnage ratio for capital ships of $5:5:3:1.75:1.75$ (United States:Britain:Japan:France:Italy; $1 =$ approximately 100,000 tons displacement). The top three naval powers agreed to dismantle a total of seventy ships. They also pledged not to build new fortifications in their Pacific possessions, such as the Philippines and Hong Kong, thus giving protection to the Japanese, who had sarcastically accepted naval inferiority by translating $5:5:3$ as Rolls Royce:Rolls Royce:Ford. Another treaty—the Four Power—abolished the Anglo-Japanese Alliance and stated simply that the signatories would respect each other's Pacific territories. All delegations also signed the Nine Power Treaty, a polite endorsement of the Open Door for the preservation of China's sovereignty and equal trade opportunity there. Other agreements were struck. Japan consented to evacuate troops from the Shandong Peninsula; the United States was given cable rights to the Pacific island of Yap; and Japan agreed to end its occupation of parts of Russian Siberia and the northern half of Sakhalin Island. President Harding, who had little to do with the conference, claimed these results as a political achievement, demonstrating, he said, that he was "not so much of a duffer as a good many people expected me to be."[17]

The treaties signed in Washington essentially recognized the status quo in Asia. Japan had the upper hand, and the other powers were in no position to challenge it without undertaking massive naval construction and prohibitively expensive fortifications. Hughes knew he could not drive the Japanese out of Manchuria, so he skirted that issue. Geography clearly worked in Japan's favor in Asia, as it did for the United States in Latin America. The United States gave up little in the treaties, except the *potential* of naval superiority. It secured temporary protection of the vulnerable Philippines and abolition of the Anglo-Japanese Alliance, a threatening vestige of the old imperialism against which the Open Door was aimed. Each power accepted some naval disarmament in its national interest, as a way of checking a costly arms race and protecting its Asian interests. But as the Japanese prime minister noted: "While armed conflict has cooled off, economic competition is becoming more and more intense."[18]

There were shortcomings. The Five Power Treaty did not limit submarines, destroyers, or cruisers, thus permitting an arms race in those categories, which was only partially checked by agreements at the London Conference of 1930. Russia, which had stakes in Asia, was not invited to the Washington Conference, since the major powers were still attempting to isolate the Bolsheviks. There was no enforcement provision in the Nine Power Treaty. China, torn by factionalism and civil war, was a loser at the conference. It was represented by the feeble Beijing regime, rather than Sun Yat-sen's Guomindang government in Canton, although the latter sent a watchdog. Most Chinese groups resented the Western powers' maintenance of imperial privileges, the very symbols of China's inferiority. As historian Warren Cohen has written: "In answer to China's demand to be allowed to set its own tariff rates, the powers offered a five-percent increase on imports and a promise of subsequent discussion. In answer to the Chinese demand for an end to extraterritoriality, the powers offered only a commission to study the problem. In answer to the Chinese demand for the withdrawal of foreign troops from Chinese soil, nothing was done."[19] The United States did help China negotiate the Japanese out of Shandong, but the imperial powers, including the United States, resisted Chinese nationalist calls for full sovereignty. The Washington Conference constituted a worthy step toward disarmament, but it still left China at the mercy of foreigners. Hence Japan in 1931, without any countervailing power from foreign nations or China itself, could easily emasculate the generalities of the Nine Power Treaty.

The Rise of Chinese Nationalism

United States policy toward Asia had to contend not only with expansionist Japan, but also with anti-imperialist, nationalist Chinese. In 1898 the Philippines had been seized in large part because they were perceived as steppingstones to China; three decades later, in an historical flipflop, a strong China friendly to the United States seemed necessary to protect those defenseless islands. China thus took on some strategic importance for Americans in the 1920s and 1930s. Also, many Americans were still mesmerized by the mirage of the China market and the ostensible inviolability of the Open Door principle. Stanley K. Hornbeck affirmed that "our people and our Government have, from the beginning of our national life, asserted that in the commercial relationships of sovereign states there should *not* be a 'closed door' *anywhere*."[20] Sentimental considerations partially accounted for the American attachment to China, especially in the 1930s. Pearl Buck's best-selling *The Good Earth* (1931), made into a powerful movie six years later, captured for Americans the romance of the hard-working, persevering Chinese peasants. This Sinophile's book humanized the people then being victimized by the Japanese. John Paton Davies, a young Foreign Service officer in China during the depression decade, has commented that Americans held a "righteous infatuation" with China, stemming from years of missionary activity and a misguided and self-congratulatory belief that America was China's special friend by virtue of the Open Door Notes. In Asia, Davies has concluded, "Washington preached to everyone, including the Chinese."[21]

Washington directed its preaching at the principal activists in Asia between the world wars: Japan, Russia, and the Chinese Nationalists. Each defined a new "order" that excluded the United States and the other Western imperialists. For the United States, "order" meant peaceful change or "orderly processes," in the words of Cordell Hull.[22] It meant the Open Door, protection of American property and citizens, and the treaty rights of trade and judicial extraterritoriality (criminal trials for its nationals in American rather than Chinese courts). To protect its interests and to preserve order, the United States maintained troops on Chinese soil and gunboats on Chinese rivers. What would Americans think, someone asked, if China sent armed junks up the Mississippi River to "protect" Chinese laundrymen in Memphis? Sun Yat-sen, the leader of the Chinese Revolution from its outbreak in 1911 until his death in 1925, bristled when American gunboats from the South China Patrol visited Canton in 1923 to halt a potential Chinese takeover of foreign-dominated customs houses. After declaring that the Chinese Revolution took its inspiration from America, Sun lamented that "we might well have expected that an American Lafayette would fight on our side in this good cause. In the twelfth year of our struggle towards liberty there comes not a Lafayette but an American Admiral with more ships of war than any other nation in our waters."[23]

There were two roadblocks to Japanese expansion—Russia and the Chinese Nationalists—but the United States did not cooperate with or strengthen either. Few American leaders paid heed to the 1921 prophecy of Minister to China Jacob G. Schurman that "only the Chinese can solve China's problems and they will do it in a Chinese way."[24] Americans applauded the Chinese nationalistic spirit, preached the Open Door, but then asked that American treaty privileges be perpetuated. Finding minimal sympathy in Washington, the Chinese turned to another possible means of support, Bolshevik Russia; and Moscow, seeking to restrain Japan, spank imperialist capitalists, and implant communism, sent advisers to China. Under the guidance of agent Michael Borodin, the Soviets helped the Nationalists centralize the structure of the Guomindang party. Americans understood neither the depth of Chinese nationalism nor Sun Yat-sen's use of Russians for Chinese purposes; Americans at first compared Sun with the unruly Chinese warlords he was fighting, and when that analogy collapsed, they attributed China's intense antiforeign sentiment to Bolshevik agitation. A lucid understanding of Chinese nationalism was made extremely difficult by the tumult and factionalism of the Chinese Revolution. Although Sun was the recognized Nationalist leader, he by no means had firm control of China. Events were confusing and moved quickly. Few Americans could foresee who would win.

In 1925, Sun died and the Nationalist outpouring in the May 30th Movement of that year led to attacks on American and other foreign property and citizens. The 10,000 Christian missionaries who lived in China were subjected to threats and violence. Anti-imperialist opinion at home, and Chinese determination to gain control of their own country, combined to prompt a reconsideration of American treaty privileges by Washington. The outbreak of civil war within the Nationalist ranks also dictated a re-evaluation. The clever and ambitious Guomindang leader, Jiang Jieshi, turned fiercely on his Communist allies in 1926–1927. Borodin was booted ingloriously from China. Chinese Communists were murdered by the thousands or chased into the hills; their leader, Mao Zedong, fled south to Kiangsi Province, where he set up a rebel government. Although the United States used gunboats in 1927 to protect its nationals and property in Nanjing, it did respond

Jiang Jieshi (Chiang Kai-Shek) (1887–1975). Ambitious and often ruthless, Jiang took command of the Nationalist movement in China, drove the Communists into the hills, and cultivated cordial relations with the United States in the 1920s. (Library of Congress)

to Jiang's assertion of power by signing in 1928 a new treaty restoring tariff autonomy to China and providing for most-favored-nation treatment. Still, Sino-American trade and investment remained in a category labeled "potential." By 1930 over 500 American companies were operating in China, with investments amounting to $155 million, yet they represented only 1 percent of total American foreign investments. From 1923 to 1931 the United States sent only 3 percent of its total exports to China. American trade with Japan totaled twice as much.

Despite minimal trade and the continued elusiveness of the mythical China market, Americans warmed toward Jiang. He had joined their crusade against communism, and in 1930 he announced that he had been converted to Christianity. Furthermore, and quite important, he gave up a previous wife and two concubines and married Meiling Soong, the ambitious daughter of American-educated Chinese businessman Charles Soong. A Wellesley College honors graduate, she spoke flawless English and soon established ties with prominent Americans in the United States, later called the "China Lobby." Madame Jiang was beautiful, intelligent, poised, and "westernized." Americans were captivated by her. She was the right Chinese woman in America's dream of a stable, God-fearing, and Open Door China.

The "New Order" and Japanese-American Conflict

The Japanese were motivated by an intense nationalism of their own. They were driven by a fear of inferiority spawned by a shortage of land for a growing population (in 1931, 65 million lived in an area smaller than Texas), by a dependence upon outside sources for raw materials, and by an awareness that Western nations had for years intruded into their sphere of influence and come to control products like oil vital to their economy. Japan sought self-sufficiency. One Japanese leader argued that a "tree must have its roots," and cited the United States "roots" in Latin America as an example.[25] Without an empire, it was believed, Japan could not survive as a nation. A Monroe Doctrine for Asia, or "Greater East Asia Co-Prosperity Sphere," would insure the Japanese full stomachs and satiated egos. They were compulsive about seeking "equality" with the Occidental powers, and they often explained their expansion and rationalization of the Asian sphere in the broadest terms: all major powers were doing it. With a high degree of fatalism, the Japanese recognized that an imperialist thrust into Manchuria and China could very well bring them into war with the United States or Russia.

Despite past efforts to defuse their rivalry, in the 1920s and 1930s Tokyo and Washington took actions that intensified their differences. Indeed, in 1923 Japan ranked the United States first in its list of potential enemies. A Japanese Navy War College study of 1936 stated that "in case the enemy's [America's] main fleet is berthed at Pearl Harbor the idea should be to open hostilities by surprise attacks from the air."[26] Naval competition, despite the Washington Conference, continued. Historian Waldo Heinrichs has noted that American naval leaders of the interwar years "regarded war with Japan as practically inevitable some day," and used Japan as the enemy on the war game board at the Naval War College.[27] The limits were taken off that rivalry in 1935-36 when the London Conference broke up without agreement and Japan announced its abrogation of the Washington and London treaties. The American Immigration Act of 1924, blatantly discriminatory in excluding Japanese citizens from entering the United States, rankled the sensitive Japanese. Secretary of State Hughes, less alarmed than West Coast racists about the threat of a domestic "Yellow Peril" to American institutions, lamented that the legislation had "undone the work of the Washington Conference and implanted the seeds of an antagonism sure to bear fruit in the future."[28] Angry Japanese, as if to emphasize their power in Asia, contemptuously remarked that, although they could not enter America, they could still go to China. Commercial rivalry also increased. Inexpensive Japanese goods, especially textiles, entered the American market to bring havoc to some domestic producers. "Buy America" campaigns and public boycotts of Japanese goods followed. Japan began to close the trade and investment door in China and that angered Washington. The Japanese considered Western lecturing against expansion a double standard. One diplomat complained that the Western powers taught Japan the game of poker, but after acquiring most of the chips they pronounced the game immoral and took up contract bridge. Japan and the United States did have two common interests: their mutual trade continued at high levels, and both feared communism and Soviet Russia (Japan joined the Anti-Comintern Pact with Germany in 1936).

When Roosevelt took office in early 1933, his Administration continued Stimson's nonrecognition policy. The British ambassador, after a conversation with the President, reported to London that FDR's "view is that there is nothing to be done at present to stop [the] Japanese government and that the question can only be solved by the ultimate inability of Japan to stand the strain any longer. His policy would be to avoid anything that would tend to relieve that strain."[29] This nonintervention attitude was necessitated by American weakness in Asia and was made possible, at least until 1937, by the long lull in fighting between China and Japan. Little American action seemed required.

Through the 1930s, the Roosevelt Administration did improve the Navy and take other steps to increase the "strain" on Japan. Shortly after taking office, Roosevelt moved to bring the Navy up to the strength permitted by the Washington and London conference treaties. Under New Deal relief programs in 1933, the President allocated funds for thirty-two new vessels, including two aircraft carriers, and by 1937 naval appropriations had doubled. Two years earlier large-scale naval maneuvers near Midway Island in the Pacific alarmed the Japanese. American leaders believed that a large and conspicuous navy would help deter Japanese expansion, because, some argued, the Japanese were a military people who respected military might. Actually, the American naval buildup convinced the Japanese in 1936 to terminate the treaty limitations, thus setting off a vigorous naval arms race. Roosevelt's diplomatic recognition of Soviet Russia in 1933 was in part an effort to frighten Japan with the suspicion that Russia and America were teaming up in Asia. Four years later, Captain Claire Chennault, retired from the United States Army Air Corps, joined the Chinese air force as chief adviser. His "Flying Tigers" unit was staffed by mercenary American pilots and tolerated by American officials. These efforts, official and unofficial, to strengthen both the United States and China did not risk war for the former. Washington sought to *alert* the Japanese to American disapproval, but not to *threaten* them.

A more interventionist American policy developed after the eruption of new Sino-Japanese warfare in 1937. During the evening of July 7, Japanese and Chinese units clashed at the Marco Polo Bridge near Beijing. This skirmish grew quickly into the "China Incident" (it was not called a "war" because the Kellogg-Briand Pact outlawed wars), with fighting throughout China. Shanghai fell to Japan in November after a costly battle and the cruel bombing of helpless civilians. A

Shanghai, China, 1937. This photograph of a baby amidst the ruins of North Station after Japanese bombing galvanized American opinion. Senator George Norris, who gradually abandoned his isolationism because of scenes like this, denounced the Japanese as "disgraceful, ignoble, barbarous, and cruel, even beyond the power of language to describe." (United Press International)

stirring United Press International photograph of a crying baby in the midst of the bombed ruins of Shanghai aroused American emotions and, as Barbara Tuchman has written, the picture "humanized the war for Americans. . . . Journalists flocking to the drama . . . reported tales of heroism, blood and suffering. China was seen as fighting democracy's battle and personified by the steadfast Generalissimo and his marvelously attractive, American-educated, unafraid wife."[30] President Roosevelt responded at first by refusing to invoke American neutrality, thereby permitting valuable trade to continue with the beleaguered Chinese. It was hardly enough to save China. To make matters worse, the civil war between Jiang's Guomindang forces and Mao Zedong's Communists further sapped China. The Communists had declared war on Japan in 1932 and had charged Jiang with appeasing Tokyo. And until 1937 Jiang fought the Communists more than the Japanese. From 1935 to 1937, the Communists took the dramatic "Long March" from their southern haven to Yan'an (Yenan) in the north—an expedition of 6,000 miles. In late 1936 Jiang was actually kidnapped by dissident army forces in Manchuria. They wanted to end the civil war by creating a coalition government. Russia and the Chinese Communists persuaded them to release Jiang, for they saw him as a bulwark against Japan. The outcome was a tenuous and largely ineffective united front against Japan in 1937.

Roosevelt addressed a Chicago audience on October 5, 1937 and used a medical metaphor to describe American "policy" after the China Incident. He called vaguely for a "quarantine" on aggressors to check the "epidemic of world lawlessness." Americans, he declared, could not be safe in a "world of disorder."[31] After the speech the President admitted he had no plan; indeed, it was an attitude more than a "policy." Privately he toyed with economic warfare—a naval blockade or embargo—but American isolationists responded to the speech by warning him against any bold action. Senator Gerald P. Nye, citing historical lessons, complained that "we are once again being caused to feel that the call is upon the United States to police a world that chooses to follow insane leaders. Once again we are baited to thrill to a call to save the world. We reach a condition on all fours with that prevailing just before our plunge into the European war in 1917."[32] In November Roosevelt sent American representatives to a conference in Brussels, but it disbanded without taking a stand—only the Soviet Union pushed for reprisals against Japan. The following month the war came closer to America. The American gunboat *Panay,* escorting on the Yangtze River three small Standard Oil Company tankers flying American flags and well-marked with the symbol "S," was sunk by zealous Japanese pilots. Under pressure from Ambassador Joseph Grew, Tokyo quickly apologized and offered reparations. Many Americans were relieved, some remembering the war fevers aroused by the sinking of the *Maine* in 1898 and others suggesting that the vessel should not have been there in the first place.

As Japan tightened its grip on China in 1938, the Roosevelt Administration cautiously initiated new measures designed to strengthen both China and American defenses in Asia. First, through the purchase of Chinese silver, the United States gave China dollars with which to buy American military equipment. Second, Secretary Hull imposed a "moral embargo" on the sale of aircraft to Japan. Third, the United States extended technical assistance to improve the Chinese transportation system. Fourth, a naval bill authorized the construction of two new carriers and the doubling of naval airplanes. Fifth, the United States occupied

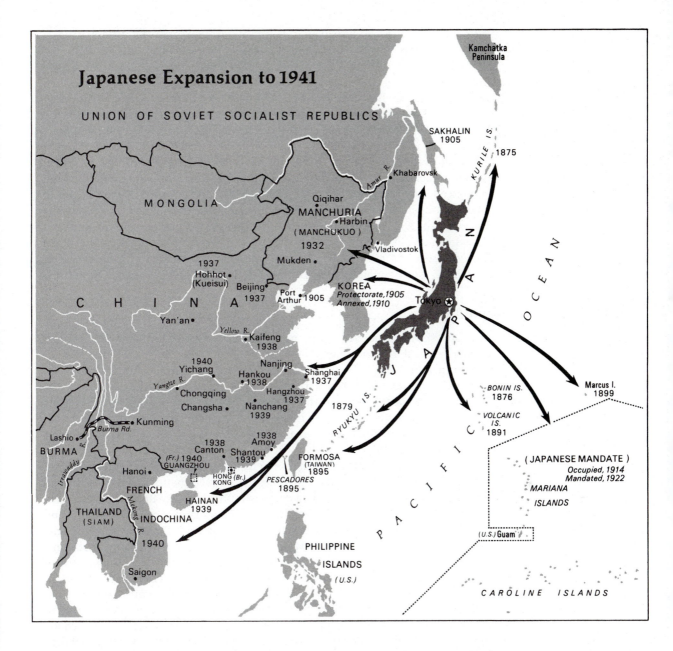

Japanese Expansion to 1941

several Pacific islands (Enderbury, for example) as potential naval bases. These actions of 1938 did not deter the brazen Japanese, who by the end of that year had gained authority in almost all major Chinese seaports, declared a "New Order" for Asia, and established exploitative development companies. An American trade commissioner in Shanghai charged quite correctly that the "Open Door" was being "banged, barred, and bolted."[33] The "New Order" meant the ouster of Western imperialism and the creation of a self-sufficient Asian bloc united economically and racially.

In 1939 Roosevelt and Hull remained cautious, unwilling to take steps that might risk war in Asia. Events in Europe were more significant for the American national interest. In mid-1939 the United States abrogated the 1911 Japanese-American Treaty of Commerce and Navigation, hoping this application of economic leverage would shock the Japanese into tempering their onslaught in China. In 1938 the United States had supplied Japan with 44 percent of its imports, a sizable portion of which consisted of automobiles, machinery, copper, oil, iron, and steel. The abrogation, effective January, 1940, by no means ended trade, for the Roosevelt Administration remained reluctant to impose a rigid trade embargo. Grew's talks with the Japanese foreign minister in the fall of 1939 failed to secure American trading rights in China, but did elicit a Japanese pledge to curtail brutalities against foreigners. In November of 1939 another American naval bill authorized two more battleships. By then the Second World War had begun to bloody Europe, and Japanese-American relations were stalemated, with every new Japanese jab into the "sick man of Asia" convincing American diplomats that a showdown was in the offing. By late 1939, with Pearl Harbor two years ahead, the United States had moved in Asia a considerable distance from its weakness of 1931–1932, but its methods remained timid and its power limited.

Good Neighbors in Latin America

In contrast with Asia, American power in the western hemisphere remained unmatched and American methods bold. Indeed, shortly after World War I, American armed forces used the Caribbean for maneuvers and planning—as preparation for a possible war with Japan in the Pacific. And when Germany and Japan marched aggressively in the 1930s, the United States brought most of the Latin American states into a virtual alliance to resist any foreign intrusions in the United States sphere of influence. Earlier, Japanese leaders observed that their "New Order" in Asia was simply a copying of United States hegemony in Latin America. The United States imperial net in Latin America had been stitched before and during the First World War, especially in Central America and the Caribbean, through military occupations, naval demonstrations, the Panama Canal, the management of national finances, the threat of intervention, nonrecognition, and economic ties. The Roosevelt Corollary to the Monroe Doctrine provided the overriding justification. In the 1920 presidential campaign, after some Republicans insisted that the United States reject League membership because the British controlled six votes, Democratic vice-presidential candidate Franklin D. Roosevelt rebutted happily that the United States would control twelve votes—eleven from Latin America. The chief of the State Department's Division of Latin American Affairs expressed a typical attitude in a 1925 speech to the Foreign Service School. He mentioned the "low racial quality" of Latin Americans, but concluded that they were "very easy people to deal with if properly managed."[34] The sight of swaggering American Marines in the streets of Havana, Managua, or Port-au-Prince represented only the most conspicuous evidence of the United States' imperial management.

The use of Marines as instruments of policy, however, was becoming unpopular and counterproductive, and some limitations were placed on United States power by nationalist sentiment, especially in Mexico and Argentina. Anti-imperialists like Senators George Norris and William Borah, citing the Wilsonian ideal of self-determination, demanded it for Latin Americans. Congressmen increasingly resented the costs of military interventions, as well as the President's usurpation of

Uncle Sam as Seen by Latin America. This angry cartoon from *Critica* (Buenos Aires) represented one view of the United States in the western hemisphere. (*Current History and Forum,* 1927)

their power to declare war when as Commander-in-Chief he unilaterally dispatched soldiers to the Caribbean. Businessmen came to believe that military expeditions, because they aroused anti-United States sentiment and violence, endangered rather than protected their properties. The United States was also caught in its own imperialist posture in Latin America when Japan seized Manchuria in 1931. The double standard was embarrassing. Henry L. Stimson, who had supported American occupation before, commented in 1932: "If we landed a single soldier among those South Americans now . . . it would put me absolutely in the wrong in China, where Japan has done all this monstrous work under the guise of protecting her nationals with a landing force."[35] Pragmatic American diplomats recognized that armed interventions generated hostile nationalism and violence, and thereby undermined the basic American goal of tranquil order.

Between the world wars, therefore, the United States attempted to find means other than direct military intervention to continue its influence over Latin America. Increasingly Washington foreswore armed interference and employed the methods of economic penetration, political subversion, nonrecognition, support for stable dictators, arbitration treaties, Pan Americanism, Export-Import Bank loans, and the training of national guards. These tactics were summarized in a catchy phrase popularized, but not invented, by Franklin D. Roosevelt—the Good Neighbor policy. The President declared in early 1933 that "I would dedicate this Nation to the policy of the good neighbor—the neighbor who resolutely respects himself and, because he does so, respects the rights of others—the neighbor who respects his obligations and respects the sanctity of his agreements in and with a world of neighbors."[36] Some observers quickly declared a new era in inter-American relations, and Latin Americans welcomed the seemingly new spirit. What had changed was not the goal of United States hegemony over Latin America, but the methods for insuring it. After the Good Neighbor policy, however, Washington was more hesitant to defend exploitative American companies and more willing to entertain mutual decisionmaking. Roosevelt defined the "new approach" toward Latin America: "Give them a share. They think they are just as good as we are, and many of them are."[37] And as an Axis threat was perceived in the late 1930s, the Good Neighbor policy came to mean close cooperation against the European totalitarians.

The history of the famous 1928 memorandum by Under Secretary of State J. Reuben Clark illustrates that the Good Neighbor policy meant new tactics, not new goals. This report repudiated the Roosevelt Corollary by stating that the Monroe Doctrine could not be cited as a rationale for American intervention in Latin America, for that doctrine referred specifically to European intrusions, not to the right of the United States to intervene. Many contemporaries and historians have applauded the Clark Memorandum as a forerunner of the Good Neighbor policy. Yet the report did not denounce the right of intervention, only its sanction by the Monroe Doctrine. Furthermore, neither the Hoover nor Roosevelt administrations paid much attention to the memorandum. For many Latin Americans it simply meant that Washington would find other explanations for intervention. The imperialist elements of coercion, imposition, and external authority largely remained.

The Annexation of Wealth: Economic Ties with Latin America

Economic decisions made by American leaders, private and governmental, held immense importance for the life of Latin American nations, especially in the Caribbean, Mexico, and Central America. In the Dominican Republic, Cuba, and Haiti, for example, officials had to obtain United States consent before borrowing foreign capital. The Chilean ambassador to Washington in the early 1930s spent much of his time trying to anticipate American decisions on copper purchases and Chilean bonds, both essential to his nation's livelihood. In that decade "never had Chile felt so totally controlled by the unpredictable attitudes of a foreign power."[38] In Cuba, where American interests accounted for about two-thirds of sugar production, American investments helped lock the country into a risky one-crop economy subject to fluctuating world sugar prices. Sumner Welles reported in 1924 that in Honduras, where the United Fruit Company and Standard Fruit Company accounted for most of the country's revenue, American interests provided essential cannon and machine guns to one political group that conducted a successful coup. In Venezuela, one-half of the nation's tax revenues came from oil taxes—hence from foreign-owned oil companies. In 1929 American firms produced more than one-half of Venezuela's oil. Their bribery of Venezuelan government officials, including the President, was not uncommon. Over 1,000 American-controlled businesses exercised significant influence in at least three-fourths of the Latin American countries by 1920. As historian J. Fred Rippy has noted: "The operation of these numerous business enterprises requires many intimate associations and a multitude of contacts. . . . Thousands of businessmen and technicians from the United States were brought into close touch with millions of Latin Americans almost every day in the year."[39]

Argentine writer Manuel Ugarte was blunt in the mid-1920s when he tagged the United States a "new Rome." The United States, he complained, annexed wealth rather than territory, and thereby enjoyed the "essentials of domination" without the "dead-weight of areas to administrate and multitudes to govern." He deplored the consequences of America's economic penetration: "Its subtle intrusion into the private affairs of each people has always in consecrated phrase invoked peace, progress, civilization, and culture; but its motives, procedure, and results have frequently been a complete negation of these premises."[40] Latin American leaders, when making economic, political, and diplomatic decisions, had to consider what

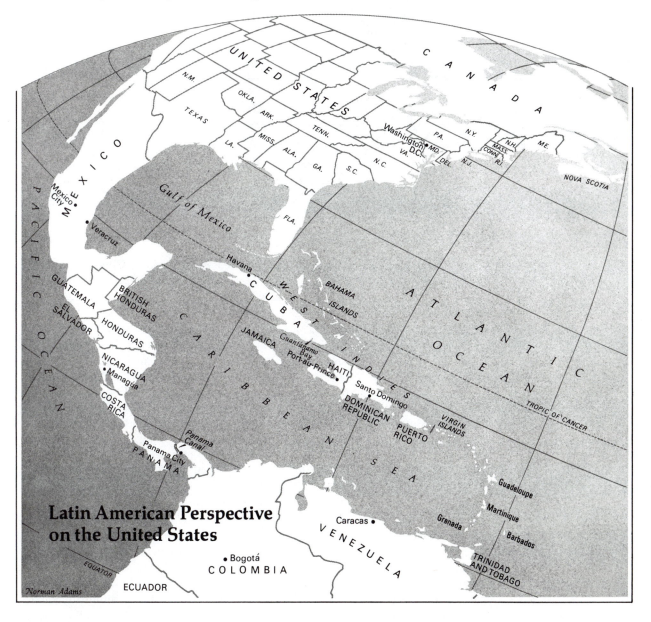

**Latin American Perspective
on the United States**

Norman Adams

Herbert Hoover, Good Neighbor. As secretary of commerce and President, Hoover improved trade relations with Latin America and spawned the Good Neighbor policy before Roosevelt popularized the phrase. Shortly after his election as President, Hoover traveled for several weeks on a "good will" tour of Latin American states. (*La Nacion,* Santiago, Chile in *American Review of Reviews,* 1929)

North Americans thought and what they owned. Ambassador to Chile William D. Culbertson made no apologies in 1930: "American capital will be the controlling factor in public and private finance in these [South American] countries. . . . Opposition and criticism may divert or slow down these tendencies but they cannot defeat the final result, namely, that American civilization, material and cultural, is bound to impress itself upon, and I believe, benefit these peoples. If anti-American critics wish to describe this as our 'imperialism' let them make the most of it." [41]

Economic expansion characterized United States foreign relations after World War I, and investments in and trade with Latin America reached a "boom" stage. Although European, especially British, interests remained important there, United States businessmen gradually nudged them out of first rank. The direct investments of United States citizens (excluding bonds and securities) jumped from $1.26 billion in 1914 to $3.52 billion in 1929, mostly in electric power, railroads, bananas, sugar, oil, and minerals. By 1936, because of the devastating impact of the worldwide depression on economic relations, the amount dropped to $2.77 billion. These figures represented about one-third of total United States investments abroad. One of the nation's largest corporations, Standard Oil of New Jersey, was active in eight countries, and the United Fruit Company held a large stake in the "banana republics" of Central America. International Telephone and Telegraph controlled communications in Cuba, where, between 1919 and 1933, overall American investments increased 536 percent. Worried about diminishing oil reserves in the United States after World War I, the Harding Administration, particularly under the leadership of Secretary of State Charles E. Hughes and Secretary of Commerce Herbert Hoover, decided to "urge our oil companies to acquire oil territory in South America and elsewhere before the European companies preempted all of it." As Hoover further recounted, "a conference of the leading oil producers was called and such action taken that most of the available oil lands in South America were acquired by Americans."[42] Then, too, fourteen Latin American nations floated bonds in the United States in the 1920s, many of them for unproductive public works, such as a marble palace for the Peruvian President. This "easy money" returned a respectable profit for North Americans, but generally had a damaging effect upon Latin American economies. Latin American nationalists also complained that large profits went back to the United States. In the period 1925–1929, the average annual income outflow from United States investments was $100 million more than the United States capital inflow.

"Trade follows investments" was a popular slogan of the time. From 1914 to 1929 United States exports to Latin America tripled in value, reaching the billion dollar figure, representing about 20 percent of total United States exports. Although trade declined in the 1930s and most United States commerce continued to be with Europe, for many Latin American countries commercial relationships with the United States were vital. Nicaragua, for example, shipped 96 percent of its exports to the United States by 1941. In 1920 the United States supplied Cuba with 73 percent of its imports; that trade shrank to 59 percent in 1929 because of the depressed state of the Cuban sugar economy. Cuba's exports to the United States also dropped off, although they remained at the high level of 68 percent of all the island's exports. If trade with Cuba was declining, it improved with other nations farther south. Large American investments in and trade with Venezuela moved the British out and helped that country to become the world's leading exporter of oil and the second-ranked oil producer, behind only the United States. Trade with Chile in nitrates and copper jumped after American investments there doubled from $200 million in 1920 to $400 million in 1928. United States capital represented 92 percent of the total amount invested in Chilean copper mining by the mid-1920s. Worried by declining world trade during the crippling depression of the 1930s, Secretary of State Cordell Hull was alive to the possibilities of increasing markets in Latin America when he launched the Export-Import Bank (and directed some of its loans to inter-American commerce) and the Reciprocal Trade Agreements Program. His efforts helped increase the value of exports to Latin America from $244 million in 1933 to $642 million in 1938.

Santo Domingo and Nicaragua: Learning New Methods

After Spain left the Dominican Republic in 1865 and until the American military occupation began in 1916, that impoverished Caribbean country knew little peace. Corrupt politics and the mismanagement of the national revenues produced economic stagnation, political factionalism, and foreign indebtedness. Americans had long been interested in the Dominican Republic. Since the nineteenth century businessmen were active in sugar and finance there, and the Navy had its eye on the harbor of Samaná Bay. President Theodore Roosevelt seized control of Dominican finances in 1905, but for years insurrections fractured Dominican order. In May of 1916, when a contest between the Dominican Congress and President threatened to postpone American demands for expanded United States authority, American Marines went ashore. Within months they had subdued embittered Dominicans, occupied major cities, and established martial law. Sumner Welles, American commissioner to the Dominican Republic (1922–1924), later observed that a new government began to function, "headed by an officer of the American Navy, with a cabinet composed of officers of the United States Navy or Marine Corps, none of whom had any knowledge or experience of Dominican affairs or problems, and the great majority of whom could not even speak the language of the country."[43]

The military intervention in the Dominican Republic, more so than other American interventions, became a hot political issue in the United States and abroad. The Republicans went on record in 1920 as favoring withdrawal. *The Nation* (1920), in denying the imperialist argument that occupation was justified because the United States had improved educational facilities and health, wrote that the "Germans improved sanitation during their occupation of some of the villages of northern France, but no officer of the Marine Corps ever suggested that these reforms justified German presence in France."[44] Washington decided to make a virtue out of adversity and to withdraw in 1924. The United States soon cited the Dominican occupation, and withdrawal, as an example of its good intentions toward Latin America. As Hughes ingeniously argued in 1928, the departure proved that the United States was "anti-imperialistic."[45] Franklin D. Roosevelt agreed, in a 1928 article in *Foreign Affairs:* "We accomplished an excellent piece of constructive work, and the world ought to thank us."[46] Happy with its newfound showcase, the United States continued to manage fiscal matters until 1941, aligning itself with a dictator who served American interests.

Rafael Leonidas Trujillo was an offspring of the American occupation. In early 1919 he was commissioned a second lieutenant in the United States–created national constabulary; he earned high marks from American military officers and became chief of staff of the reorganized National Army in 1928. Through the election of 1930, characterized by violence, fraud, and a boycott by political opponents, Trujillo became President. The vote, roughly 224,000 to 1,900, demonstrated that he held a firm grip on the country. Washington was wary, fearing that his authoritarian methods would spawn new insurrections, but gradually warmed to him when it became clear that his strong-arm tactics would create internal order and thereby eliminate the need for American military intervention. Thanks to beneficent American control of the customs, Trujillo was able to divert considerable funds to his army for the suppression of internal dissent. Political corruption, military muscle, torture, murder, nepotism, commercial monopolies, and raids on the national treasury permitted Trujillo to quiet all opposition and increase his fortune to $800 million.

From 1930 until his assassination in 1961, sometimes as President, sometimes through puppets, "Benefactor of the Nation" Trujillo ruled the Dominican Republic. American military arms filled Dominican arsenals. American businessmen, who dominated the sugar production of the country, endorsed him. Most imports came from the United States, and the economic links were profitable. The National City Bank was designated the official depository for Dominican revenues. In July of 1939, Trujillo traveled to the United States, not as President, but as commander of the armed forces. FDR greeted him in good neighborly fashion. By World War II the Dominican Republic stood as a success story for the new Good Neighbor policy. But, asked many critics, pointing to the brutalities and poverty of Dominican life, good neighbors with whom? Roosevelt gave an answer in reference to Trujillo: "He may be an S.O.B., but he is our S.O.B."[47]

Nicaragua, like the Dominican Republic, developed in the twentieth century under the weight of American military occupation and the Good Neighbor policy. From 1912 to 1925 the United States ruled Nicaragua and kept in power its favorite group, the Conservative party. Nicaragua by 1925 appeared to be solvent, secure, and stable. The Marines departed, but in late 1926 they returned. Even ardent imperialists found it hard to swallow the explanation for this intervention given by the Coolidge Administration. It charged, in an exaggerated report titled "Bolshevik Aims and Policies in Mexico and Latin America," that Communists were fomenting trouble in Nicaragua. It had no evidence of such activity and historians can find none, but such rhetorical rationalization was typical in that era of prevailing anti-Bolshevism. Actually the Nicaraguan Liberals had used Mexico as a sanctuary to organize a countermovement against the Conservatives. "We are not making war on Nicaragua," Coolidge opined, with tones of the Roosevelt Corollary, "any more than a policeman on the street is making war on passersby."[48]

The Nicaraguan intervention generated heated debate in the United States. The assertion of a Communist plot convinced few. Congress again resented a military action taken by the executive, which bypassed its power to declare war. Senator George Norris suggested critically that, if the Coolidge Administration thought Marines could insure honest elections, they should be sent first to Philadelphia and Pittsburgh, cities notorious for their political corruption. Bloodshed and destruction in Nicaragua raised further outcries after Secretary of the Navy Curtis D. Wilbur matter-of-factly reported in 1928: "Several houses were destroyed in the village of Quilali in order to prepare a landing field for airplanes so that 19

Rafael Trujillo (1891–1961). The strong man of the Dominican Republic graduated from an American military training school and went on to rule his nation from 1930 to 1961, when he was assassinated. (*The Reporter,* 1961. Copyright 1961 by The Reporter Magazine Co.)

"The Congressional Castigator." The intervention in Nicaragua sparked considerable debate in the United States. Uncle Sam is beleaguered by the terrain, a sniping congressman, and the bite of the rebel Sandino. (*The Outlook*, 1928)

wounded Marines could be evacuated to a hospital."[49] Despite extensive American military operations, Liberal leader César Augusto Sandino escaped subjugation; his flight to the hills and his daring struggles against some 5,000 American troops gained him an international reputation as a battler against "Yankee imperialism."

Sensitive to the large-scale criticism of and resistance to the American presence in Nicaragua, special emissary Henry L. Stimson engineered withdrawal (1933). He brought Liberals and Conservatives together in the "Peace of Tipitapa" (1927) and provided for United States supervision of the election of 1928. Most important, he helped create an American-trained national guard to insure the domestic order which American Marines had imposed. Shortly after withdrawal, Sandino signed a truce with the Nicaraguan government. But he was assassinated by the new American-instructed constabulary; the United States, historian Neill Macaulay has written, supplied the "murder weapon."[50] The Guardia Nacional came under the control of a former Liberal rebel, General Anastasio Somoza, who seized power in 1936 and established a family dictatorship which lasted until 1979. Somoza and the United States struck an uneasy alliance. An American collector-general remained to handle customs collections until 1944, and the United States retained canal rights and a naval base. In the late 1930s Somoza complained that the United States was undermining the economic development of his country by

César Augusto Sandino (1895–1934).
The Nicaraguan rebel and Latin American hero battled American Marines for years before his death. In his honor, the revolutionaries who overthrew the Somoza dictatorship in 1979 called themselves "Sandinistas." (Marine Corps, National Archives)

not building a canal. To assuage the dictator's discontent, the Roosevelt Administration in 1939 offered to build an interoceanic highway (Rama Road) for several million dollars. Somoza also used the road for moving the guardsmen who suppressed the critics of his self-enriching, corrupt, and brutal regime.

Few benefits accrued to the United States from its years of interference in Nicaragua. Trade and investments never reached important levels. From 1914 to 1930 American investments grew from $4.5 million to $13 million, the latter a miniscule part of overall investments in Latin America. Although the occupation of Nicaragua sparked strong resentment and helped foster the Good Neighbor policy, for Nicaragua that policy meant continued foreign financial management and replacement of the United States Marine Corps by a home-grown dictator and a constabulary traveling the Rama Road.

Comic Strips in Nicaragua. In this 1927 photograph of the tranquil side of American intervention, American Marines read comic strips to appreciative Nicaraguan children. (Marine Corps, National Archives)

When the Marines Ran Haiti

A Marine officer depicted the Haitians as "real nigger and no mistake—there are some very fine looking, well educated polished men here but they are real nigs beneath the surface."[51] When American soldiers went abroad, of course, they carried American prejudices as well as canteens. For nineteen years, from 1915 to 1934, United States Marines governed the tiny black French-speaking nation of Haiti in the Caribbean. The occupation hardly stood as an example of benevolent imperialism, and even the most charitable historian is taxed to salvage much good from the venture. The Wilson Administration ordered the Marines into Haiti on July 28, 1915, after a civil war had erupted there. The United States was interested in the fine harbor at Môle Saint Nicolas, fearful of suspected German intrigue during World War I, protective of American financial interests (largely those of the National City Bank of New York), and insistent, in general, on establishing order in the Caribbean. Franklin D. Roosevelt figured prominently in the story: as assistant secretary of the Navy, he helped write the 1918 Haitian Constitution, and in 1934, as President, he oversaw the evacuation.

The United States occupation touched every aspect of Haitian life. Americans built roads, technical schools, lighthouses, a telephone network, hospitals, and railroads. They improved public health and sanitation. Contemporary critics complained that Haitians could have undertaken most of these projects on their own with some American assistance and without American military subjugation. The improvements never eradicated Haiti's profound human squalor. By the mid-1960s Haiti had the lowest life expectancy (35 years) and the lowest literacy rate (10 percent) in Latin America. Even the new highways soon fell into disrepair, for Americans failed to impart maintenance skills to the Haitians. Many of the roads had been built in 1916–1918 by forced labor—the *corvée* system under which Admiral William Caperton ordered workers into labor gangs and treated them like prisoners. NAACP official James Weldon Johnson, who toured Haiti in 1920, protested: "They were maltreated, beaten and terrorized. In fact, they were in the same category with the convicts in the Negro chain gangs that are used to build roads in many of our southern states."[52] Haitians rebelled against the *corvée*; in 1919 alone the Marines had to kill some 2,000 to quell the insurrection.

American racism and Jim Crow reached into Haiti. American personnel introduced to Haitians the words "nigger," "gook," and "coon" and enforced segregation between blacks and whites. Americans favored mulattoes (the "elite") over the *authentique* (black), but treated all with utter disregard for human dignity. For many Haitians the Marine initials U.S.M.C. meant *Un Salaud Mal Costume*, a sloppy bum. Racism was not the property solely of American soldiers stationed in the field: officials in Washington shared the prevalent view of blacks as inferiors. Secretary of State Robert Lansing, three years after sending the Marines to Haiti, wrote that the "African race" had an "inherent tendency to revert to savagery and to cast aside the shackles of civilization which are irksome to their physical nature. Of course there are many exceptions to this racial weakness but it is true of the mass, as we know from experience in this country."[53] To Americans, if the Haitians were not savage, they were indolent or capable of mastering only menial tasks.

The United States also meddled in the economic affairs of Haiti, sometimes beneficially. New highways, railroads, and bridges expanded commercial contacts between cities and rural farmers. Pan American Airways began flights between Miami and Port-au-Prince. Irrigation systems and a telephone network contributed to economic growth. Sugar and cotton exports increased, although the heavy dependence on one crop, coffee, left Haiti susceptible to fluctuations in world coffee prices. The United States became Haiti's largest trading partner. American capital investments grew from $11.5 million in 1914 to $28.5 million in 1930. The Banque Nationale was owned by the National City Bank of New York. Under American financial supervision, Haiti actually paid its foreign debts (largely

French) ahead of schedule, causing some to complain that the money might have been better spent on economic improvements at home. Haiti's economic life was determined in the United States—although the economic rewards for Americans (or Haitians) hardly justified the occupation.

United States military authorities trained a national guard, the *Garde d'Haiti*, to keep domestic order—to quell revolutions. A majority of the officers of this gendarmerie were actually Americans and no Haitian had reached captain's rank by 1930. The first commandant was Marine Major Smedley D. Butler, a brash veteran previously experienced in putting down "natives" in China, Honduras, Nicaragua, Panama, and Mexico. Mothers in Nicaragua used to discipline their children by warning, "Hush! Major Butler will get you."[54] The national guardsmen enforced the rules of American occupation, served as judges, tax collectors, and paymasters for teachers, and enforced the frequent declarations of martial law. For over two decades after the American military withdrawal in 1934, the *Garde d'Haiti* was the deciding political force.

The United States failed in its years of occupation to establish respect for honest government by law and neglected to train efficient civil servants. The 1918 constitution was drafted in Washington and forced on the Haitians; local elections were rigged, and the press censored. When President Philippe Sudre Dartiguenave's term ended in 1922, he was jilted in favor of wily Louis Borno, a lawyer and perfect stage villain more favorable to the American presence. Borno teamed up with the American High Commissioner, General John H. Russell of Georgia, to rule Haiti from 1922 to 1930. Borno "has never taken a step without

"The Rights of Small Nations: Haiti." A harshly critical view of the American military occupation of Haiti, 1915–1934. (*Good Morning,* 1921)

first consulting me," Russell boasted.[55] The American general wrote Haitian legislation, took personal command of public projects, and when Borno seemed unduly obstinate, ordered the American financial adviser to withhold the President's salary. The Department of State in Washington criticized Russell's authoritarian rule, but accepted it as necessary for maintaining order.

Haitians resented their colonial status. The peaking of resentment in 1929 coincided with a slump in coffee prices and exports during the Great Depression and with exposure of Borno's political machinations. Protests and strikes spread across the country. President Hoover rejected a full-scale military response and appointed instead an investigating commission. Chaired by W. Cameron Forbes, former governor-general of the Philippines, the commission's report of 1930 combined a delicate mixture of praise and criticism: "The failure of the Occupation to understand the social problems of Haiti, its brusque attempt to implant democracy by drill and harrow, its determination to set up a middle class—however wise and necessary it may seem to Americans—all these explain why, in part, the high hopes of our good works in this land have not been realized."[56] The Forbes Commission promoted a "Haitianization" process to ease Haitians into positions of responsibility. Hoover started the withdrawal; Roosevelt completed it in 1934.

After American Marines left Haiti, Haitians celebrated a "Festival of the Second Independence." Thereafter, however, Haiti was ruled by strong-arm presidents with the help of Export-Import Bank loans and ties with Washington. During World War II the United States used Haitian bases, and until 1947 American officials supervised Haitian national finances. A revolution in 1946 placed the government in the hands of the *Garde,* and the revolution of 1956–1957 produced one of the most callous dictatorships in hemispheric history, that of Dr. François ("Papa Doc") Duvalier. He ruled until his death in 1971, when his rotund son "Baby Doc" assumed power. The Duvaliers were not American creations or creatures. As historian Rayford Logan has noted, however, the "American occupation contributed little to the amelioration of Haiti's plight, rooted in poverty, illiteracy, overpopulation, excessive reliance upon a single crop, and a lack of sturdy democratic political and social traditions and institutions."[57] A Haitian nationalist in 1927 summarized the impact of the American occupation: "They have made themselves the allies of the evil past of oppression and tyranny; they have abolished liberty, justice, independence; they are bad administrators of the public funds. . . . They push forward like the rising tide; they attack our traditions, our soul. . . . They are exploiters." He concluded bitterly: "How can they teach us when they have so much to learn themselves?"[58]

The Subversion of Cuban Nationalism

Many Cubans thought similarly, as they bristled under the Platt Amendment and American military interventions. Through the 1920s and into the 1930s the United States helped conduct strife-torn elections, enlarged the national army, managed the national budget, and maintained economic control over Cuba. American investments, particularly in sugar, equaled $50 million in 1895; they jumped to $220 million in 1913, and to $1.5 billion in 1929. With the help of a commercial treaty with the United States, Cuba shipped most of its valuable sugar there.

Gerardo Machado, an admirer of Italy's Benito Mussolini, became President in 1924 and conducted national affairs through corruption and brutality. During his rule from 1924 to 1933, he suppressed free speech, jailed or murdered political leftists, journalists, labor leaders, and students, and used the army as a political weapon. He received loans from American bankers and gained the approval of American businessmen by prohibiting strikes.

Cuban resentment against Machado intensified in the late 1920s when sugar prices began to drop. Dependent upon sugar and exports to the United States, Cuba sank further into economic crisis when the United States imposed the restrictive Smoot-Hawley Tariff of 1931. Unemployment rates shot up. Protests and violence spread. Machado sent his soldiers to club the dissenters, closed Havana University, and generally defied his growing opposition. American officials grew disenchanted—he had become an obvious source of disorder. Shortly after entering office, Roosevelt and his advisers decided that an armed American intervention would be blatantly contrary to the newly stated Good Neighbor policy, so Machado had to be eased out.

Suave Sumner Welles, a Groton school friend of Roosevelt and already experienced in the Dominican Republic, was sent as ambassador to Havana in 1933. While American warships patrolled Cuban waters, Welles began to subvert the Machado regime. Fearful that students and leftists might gain authority once Machado stepped down, the ambassador organized a group of old-style politicians. Welles's pressure, a general strike, and more violence convinced Machado to flee. But Welles lost control of the revolution; "his" government, led by Carlos Manuel de Céspedes, lasted less than a month. Céspedes was, said Welles, a "most sincere friend of the United States,"[59] but he was also a lackluster, relatively unknown leader. On September 4, 1933, army men, commanded by Sergeant Fulgencio Batista, staged the "Sergeants' Revolution," deposed the hapless Céspedes, and installed Professor Ramón Grau San Martín as President.

An exile under Machado, a strong critic of the Platt Amendment, and a friend of the left, Grau, according to scholar Luis Aguilar, stood as "the hope and the symbol of the forces of nationalism, patriotism, and reform."[60] But the American ambassador would not suffer him, and "no government here can survive for a protracted period without recognition by the U.S.," Welles bragged.[61] He contemplated landing troops, but Secretary Hull vetoed that unneighborly suggestion in preference for visits by a few warships. In September, Grau abrogated the Platt Amendment and promulgated a host of economic and social reforms to "liquidate the colonial structure that has survived in Cuba since independence."[62] His government suspended payment on Chase National Bank loans, seized some American-owned sugar mills, and threatened a Cuban takeover of all land. The timid in Grau's revolutionary following began to drop off, as it seemed that his economic nationalism might invite American intervention. Army leaders especially were critical of the revolutionary measures. The Communists, on the other hand, considered Grau's government too moderate. Welles began to talk with Batista, the one man who seemed to represent authority in Cuba. To Washington Welles reported that Communists were taking over the Grau government, a patently erroneous depiction. Although Welles left Cuba in December, 1933 (he later became under secretary of state for Latin American affairs), United States pressure continued. In January, 1934, Batista moved against Grau, who fled to Mexico. A

Fulgencio Batista (1901–1973). Cuban dictator and American friend, Batista (second from right) was driven from power in early 1959 by Fidel Castro. He died in exile in Portugal. Here he and his family and friends arrive in Miami, 1938. (U.S. Information Agency, National Archives)

Batista-backed President took over, and the United States quickly granted recognition.

Batista ruled Cuba, sometimes as President, sometimes from the shadows, from 1934 to 1959. At the start of the "Era of Batista," the United States abrogated the unpopular Platt Amendment (1934), lowered the sugar tariff, granted a favorable quota to Cuban sugar imports (1934), and issued Export-Import Bank loans ($8 million in 1934). In 1940, Cuba granted American armed forces the use of ports and airfields (besides Guantánamo) in exchange for military aid. An angry Cuban revolutionary, Julio Cesar Fernández, wrote in reflection on the lost opportunity of 1933: "American diplomacy has many resources; when the steel of her warships is not convenient, she uses the docile backbone of her native lackeys."[63] Indeed, the American subversion of the Cuban government and United States economic domination provided an example of the nonmilitary tactics of the Good Neighbor policy.

A Different Case: Compromise with Mexican Nationalism

The ongoing Mexican Revolution, which began in 1910, presented the United States with one of its few serious obstacles in Latin America and in the 1930s a test of the nonmilitary emphasis of the Good Neighbor policy. Before the 1920s it had appeared that Mexico would be treated like some of America's other neighbors—invaded, occupied, and owned by Americans, who by 1910 controlled 43 percent of Mexican property and produced more than half of Mexico's oil. In 1914,

American sailors bombarded Veracruz, and two years later General John Pershing crossed into Mexico to chase that colorful bandit Pancho Villa. Pershing ran into the Mexican army instead. Mexican nationalists resented *el peligro yanqui*, the Yankee peril.

The Mexican Constitution was proclaimed the same day the last American soldier withdrew from Mexico—February 5, 1917. The radical document alarmed capitalist Americans, because its Article 27 held that all "land and waters" and all subsoil raw materials belonged to the Mexican nation. Three hundred million dollars in American investments in oil and mines were jeopardized. Mexico also began to tax American oil producers heavily. As historian Karl M. Schmitt has written, "for the first time in the modern industrial age a weak, underdeveloped, and economically penetrated state insisted on modifying if not abolishing its dependence on a highly industrialized, militarily powerful overlord."[64]

The United States continued to claim economic rights for its nationals in Mexico and refused to recognize the Mexican government. In 1923, however, Mexico and the United States signed the Bucareli Agreements. In exchange for American recognition, Mexico agreed that Americans who held subsoil rights before the 1917 Constitution could continue those concessions and that Americans who had their agricultural lands expropriated would receive Mexican bonds in compensation. At the time Americans owned about 60 percent of Mexico's oil industry. But a new law passed by the Mexican Congress in 1925 stated that oil lands secured before 1917 could only be held for a maximum of fifty years. Despite vigorous appeals from American special interest groups to intervene, Washington demonstrated its movement toward nonmilitary methods.

In early 1927, Calvin Coolidge selected an old college chum, a partner in the elite Wall Street firm of J. P. Morgan and Company, as the new ambassador to Mexico City. "After Morrow come the Marines," chanted some Mexicans, but Dwight W. Morrow personified the nonmilitary solutions typical of American foreign policy of that period.[65] Learning a little Spanish, having "Lone Eagle" Charles Lindbergh fly nonstop from Washington, D.C., and even bringing humorist Will Rogers to the Mexican capital, Morrow ingratiated himself with officials. He then negotiated an agreement which confirmed *pre-1917* ownership of petroleum lands. Thus in 1927–1928, the oil controversy seemed defused through compromise: the United States protected the oil investments of its citizens, and Mexico received a tacit American concession that Mexico legally controlled its own raw materials. This arrangement lasted until 1938, when Mexican President Lázaro Cárdenas defiantly expropriated the property of all foreign oil companies, which had grown haughtily obstinate during an oil workers' strike for higher wages. United States economic expansion and Mexican nationalism clashed again, posing a major question for the twentieth century: What were the rights of American businessmen in foreign countries?

The American ambassador in Mexico City in 1938 was Josephus Daniels, who as secretary of the Navy in 1914 had ordered the Marines to occupy Veracruz. Committed to temperance (the embassy served mineral water) and the Golden Rule in diplomacy, the mild-mannered Daniels had dispelled early suspicions and won the admiration of leading Mexicans since his appointment in 1933. "The oil and other big interests here have no sympathy with the Good Neighbor policy," Daniels informed Hull in early 1938. "They go to bed every night wishing that

Díaz were back in power and we carried the Big Stick and had Marines ready to land at their beck and call."[66] Daniels would not tolerate such behavior. Nor would he accept Hull's "get tough" policies, although he disapproved of expropriation. Daniels softened an intemperate State Department blast when he delivered it to the Mexican foreign minister. He ignored Hull's instructions to return to Washington. Hull grew furious with this insubordination. Meanwhile, Washington tried economic coercion by reducing American purchases of Mexican silver, a step Daniels characterized as Big Stick. He urged a reconsideration, and wrote the President that "We are strong. Mexico is weak. It is always noble in the strong to be generous and generous and generous."[67] For their part the American oil companies refused to sell petroleum equipment to Mexico, and they persuaded shipping companies not to carry Mexican oil. Standard Oil of New Jersey financed utterly false propaganda in the United States with the message that Cárdenas was a Communist bent on creating a Soviet Mexico. *Atlantic Monthly* magazine ran a pro-Standard Oil article in its July, 1938, number, and soon admitted with some embarrassment that the issue had been financed by the oil companies. "Rotten oil propaganda," Daniels snarled.[68]

FDR ruled out United States intervention and decided on negotiations to gain compensation for lost properties. That choice was prompted in part by fears that Mexico was moving toward fascist Germany and Italy, which had increased their purchases of Mexican oil during the controversy. Japan too increased trade with Mexico. If the Americans would not sell them equipment or ship their oil, the Mexicans argued, their only chance of economic survival rested in such sales. Long and difficult Mexican-American talks resulted in an agreement in 1941. The United States conceded the principle that Mexico owned its own raw materials, and Mexico promised to pay the oil companies and other Americans for expropriated properties. The Export-Import Bank prepared to extend a $30 million loan. Although Washington's ultimate compromise with Mexican nationalism was an exceptional case, the nonmilitary methods used were typical of the Good Neighbor policy. Mexico remained one of the United States' leading trading partners and loyally joined the United States' fight against the Axis powers in World War II.

Pan Americanism and the Approach of War

In 1889, under Secretary of State James G. Blaine's initiative, the International Bureau of American Republics was created. In 1910 it was renamed the Pan American Union, and the United States secretary of state became its permanent chairman. "Pan Americanism" was at first concerned with the improvement of trade in the western hemisphere and symbolized a mythical inter-American unity. The union's elegant quarters, financed by steel baron Andrew Carnegie, stood, significantly, a short distance from the Department of State Building. One Argentine diplomat sneered that "there is no Pan Americanism in South America; it exists only in Washington."[69] The declarations of neutrality during World War I by seven Latin American governments annoyed Washington and exposed the shallowness of Pan American solidarity.

In 1923 the Fifth Pan American Conference met in Santiago, Chile. The United States controlled the agenda, and the delegates endorsed a Treaty to Avoid or Prevent Conflicts Between the American States (Gondra Treaty). The Havana

Conference of 1928, however, was quite a different matter. Arriving at Havana shortly after American troops were landed in Nicaragua, the conferees assembled in a rebellious mood. American officials had anticipated trouble and had thus appointed former Secretary of State Hughes to head the American delegation. Even President Coolidge traveled to Cuba to address the conference with commonplaces. The cooperative Machado dictatorship ordered newspapers to abstain from critical comment about the United States.

At the conference, the delegate from tiny El Salvador rose and moved that "no state has the right to intervene in the internal affairs of another."[70] Mexico and Argentina backed this challenge to the United States. Hughes had the resolution sent to a study committee chaired by himself. The committee recommended that the question of intervention be considered at the *next* conference. Yet El Salvador's courageous Dr. Gustavo Guerrero reintroduced his nonintervention resolution at the plenary meeting, forcing Hughes to defend the right to intervene with language not altogether dissimilar from that of the Roosevelt Corollary: "We do not wish to intervene in the affairs of any American Republic. We simply wish peace and order and stability and recognition of honest rights properly acquired so that this hemisphere may not only be the hemisphere of peace but the hemisphere of international justice."[71] His words did not persuade many, but the power of the United States did, and the issue of intervention was tabled until the next conference. Professor Samuel Guy Inman of the American delegation critically assessed the meaning of the conference: "We still hold to the old pre-war diplomacy. And the United States still calls for more volunteers to hunt Sandino in Nicaragua and to be ready to act in any country near the Panama Canal where we have a 'moral mandate' to see that they conduct elections as we do in Pennsylvania, Illinois, or Oklahoma. And Latin America still holds her protest meetings . . . , while her officials float new loans in New York to pay their way to the numerous new Pan American conferences."[72]

The Seventh Pan American Conference, in Montevideo, Uruguay (1933), convened with considerable optimism, for it followed Roosevelt's inauguration and met amidst the aura of the Good Neighbor policy. The expected resolution was introduced ("No state has the right to intervene in the internal or external affairs of another"), and Cordell Hull cast an affirmative vote. The jubilation was not uniform, however, for Hull announced that the United States would reserve its right to intervene "by the law of nations as generally recognized and accepted."[73] In other words, the United States still held to intervention as a right. Further confusion about the meaning of the nonintervention pledge was added at the 1936 Buenos Aires Conference, where the United States seemingly endorsed an unequivocal statement of nonintervention. The American definition, however, was that *military* intervention was outlawed, whereas many Latin American countries (especially Mexico) interpreted it to mean that the United States could not interfere through economic or political pressure when countries nationalized American-owned property.

Pan Americanism took a decided turn toward continental solidarity and hemispheric security in the late 1930s, as Germany, Italy, and Japan attempted to improve their economic and political standing in Latin America. "To me the danger to the Western Hemisphere was real and imminent," Cordell Hull recalled. "It was not limited to the possibility of a military invasion. It was more acute in its indirect form of propaganda, penetration, organizing political parties, buying some adherents, and blackmailing others. We had seen the method employed with great success in Austria and in the Sudetenland."[74] Nazi activists were evident in Argentina, Uruguay, Brazil, and Guatemala. Although the United States clearly exaggerated the Nazi threat to the western hemisphere, the fears were nevertheless real, and Washington moved to squash the perceived danger at the Lima Conference of 1938. Argentina, Uruguay, and Chile provided opposition at Lima to United States efforts to knit the Latin American countries together in a quasi-alliance. They argued that they should not break their ties with Europe and become more dependent upon the United States. Hull, through extensive lobbying, beat back attempts to undermine his plan for solidarity. The evident anti-German sentiment of most of the delegates, aroused by the recent Munich crisis, made his task easier. Hence the conference strongly endorsed the Declaration of Lima, wherein the "American Republics" pledged to cooperate in resisting any "foreign intervention or activity that may threaten them."[75] A year later, in the Declaration of Panama, they established a security belt around the western hemisphere to rebuff potential Axis intrusions. At the same time, the United States persuaded Latin American nations to reduce or cease trade with the Axis powers and to ship valuable raw materials to the United States. So, through the late 1930s and into World War II, a perceived threat encouraged methods that continued United States hegemony in Latin America.

On the Eve of War

Japan was still marching in Asia, violating the Open Door and audaciously denying the United States a place in China's destiny. Unintimidated Mexican nationalism had just dealt the United States a rude setback through the expropriation of large American oil properties. Argentina was flirting with Nazi Germany. The post-World War I search for order in international relations had indeed broken down by 1939. In both Asia and Latin America, nationalists challenged the United States. In both areas the success and viability of American diplomacy was determined by the power the United States possessed and exercised. In Asia, after the Manchurian crisis of 1931–1932, the United States sought, without success, to build a counterforce to Japan. Even the Philippines became a virtual hostage that the military said it could not defend. In the Tydings-McDuffie Act of 1934, the United States promised the Philippines independence in ten years. Major backing for the bill came from American economic interests who sought to stop imports of competitive islands' goods. Some observers read the act as a sign of American weakness in Asia. By contrast, the United States enjoyed superior power and suffered few competitors in Latin America.

In both Asia and Latin America the United States looked down on "inferiors" from the grand heights of paternalism. America thought it was China's best friend, even though little could be done to save that friend. In Latin America the long-standing paternalistic attitude was enhanced by the lofty language of the Good Neighbor. Historian Paul A. Varg has noted that the "phrase 'Good Neighbor Policy,' carrying with it the same kind of philanthropic ring as the earlier 'Open Door Policy,' appealed to the public's illusory wish to believe that foreign policy could be altruistic."[76] The self-determination principle was much abused in practice, for the United States acted on the premise that it knew what was best for its southern neighbors. Despite Pan Americanism, Washington still treated Latin Americans as protégés rather than as associates.

American paternalism, however, was being challenged by militant nationalism, a force of considerable power, defining new "orders" that excluded American influence. Cuban nationalism, Mexican nationalism, Chinese nationalism, Japanese nationalism—all demanded the exclusion of imperialists, including (and in some cases especially) the United States. Nationalism was becoming contagious. After the First World War, when the Mexican government and American oil interests tangled, the latter began to invest more heavily in Venezuelan petroleum. But, "what if Mexican nationalism spilled over into Venezuela?" pondered a worried Secretary Hull.[77] Already it had touched Bolivia, which in 1937 confiscated the holdings of the Standard Oil Company. Intolerant of nationalism and its accompanying anti-Yankeeism, yet not altogether able to check it, Washington made compromises. The Big Stick was shelved during the Mexican oil controversy, and in 1942 Standard Oil settled with the Bolivian government. (Ten years later Bolivia invited American companies back.)

The Great Depression had helped undermine American authority in world affairs. That economic catastrophe worked gouging damage on international relations. World trade and investment collapsed; tariffs went up. The island-bound and trade-conscious Japanese were encouraged to seek a "co-prosperity" sphere in Asia. In Latin America, many of whose states depended upon the exportation of one crop for economic survival, revolutions and coups erupted, feeding on incipient nationalism. Social unrest and political instability rocked the area from which the United States was withdrawing its Marines. Santo Domingo, Argentina, Brazil, and Chile in 1930, Peru in 1931, Cuba in 1933 . . . The political upheavals in the United States' sphere of influence were met with the new nonmilitary tactics of the Good Neighbor. Hegemony was maintained, yet compromises with nationalism jeopardized Washington's authority. Latin Americans, devastated by the depression, gained a new awareness of the extent to which their national choices were made by foreigners, and the degree to which foreign companies drained profits from them. By World War II, Latin Americans held a more favorable image of the United States, because the latter had seemingly abandoned military intervention. But they harbored fresh suspicions that inter-American economic relations would continue United States hegemony. Yankeephobia simmered, while the United States continued largely to take Latin American subservience for granted.

On the eve of World War II many Americans were less certain about the wisdom of continuing nonmilitary methods in diplomacy. Of course Americans wanted no part of war in Europe or Asia, but increasing numbers came to believe that more forceful diplomacy and military preparedness would prevent American involvement in the conflagration. Should those tougher methods fail to deter adversaries bent on aggression that endangered American interests, war was the next step. The lessons of the 1930s, then, became clear to reflective American leaders. Interests and commitments, like the Philippines or American commerce, must be defended with power; principles like the Open Door must be buttressed by muscle; power and order go hand in hand; treaties must have enforcement clauses; an international organization, like the League of Nations, unless its members desire to utilize it, is a weak instrument of peace; the United States cannot count on other nations to maintain the peace; nonmilitary tactics must be joined by the willingness to use force. Never again, reasoned American diplomats, would they permit American principles to be so callously trampled or American interests to be jeopardized. Never again would the United States be caught short on power, for persuasive diplomacy hinged on it. One day after Pearl Harbor, the President asserted that Americans "will make it very certain that this form of treachery shall never again endanger us."[78]

Noting the integral relationship between economics and politics, American leaders also vowed to create a healthy world economy and hence a stable political order. Near the end of World War II, Hull identified one of the chief lessons of the 1930s and a core idea of the American outlook: "A world in economic chaos would be forever a breeding ground for trouble and war."[79] Vice-President Henry A. Wallace reflected a few months after Pearl Harbor that "We failed our job after World War I. . . . But by our very errors we learned much, and after this war we

FDR Reviews the Fleet. Aboard the U.S.S. *Houston* with Admiral Claude Bloch, the President, always a "big Navy" man, plays Commander-in-Chief for a day, July 14, 1938, at a time when the United States began to beef up its military status. (Franklin D. Roosevelt Library)

shall be in position to utilize our knowledge in building a world which is economically, politically, and, I hope, spiritually sound."[80] Two days after Pearl Harbor, FDR expressed a similar attitude when he said in a fireside chat that the future would be different, indeed: "We are going to win the war, and we are going to win the peace that follows."[81]

Further Reading for the Period 1920–1939

For general studies of this period and for biographies, see some of the works listed in the "Further Reading" section of Chapter 9.

Tumultuous events in Asia leading to conflict with Japan are studied in Irvine H. Anderson, *The Standard–Vacuum Oil Company and United States East Asia Policy, 1933–1941* (1975); Dorothy Borg, *The United States and the Far Eastern Crisis of 1933–1938* (1964); Dorothy Borg and Shumpei Okamoto, eds., *Pearl Harbor as History: Japanese-American Relations, 1931–1941* (1973); Russell D. Buhite, *Nelson T. Johnson and American Policy Toward China, 1925–1941* (1968); Richard Dean Burns and Edward M. Bennett, eds., *Diplomats in Crisis* (1974); Warren I. Cohen, *America's Response to China* (1980) and *The Chinese Connection* (1978); Roger Dingman, *Power in the Pacific: The Origins of Naval Arms Limitations, 1914–1922* (1976); Herbert Feis, *The Road to Pearl Harbor* (1950); Saburō Ienaga, *The Pacific War: World War II and the Japanese, 1931–1945* (1978); Akira Iriye, *Across the Pacific* (1967) and *After Imperialism* (1969); Manny T. Koginos, *The Panay Incident* (1967); James W. Morely, ed., *Deterrent Diplomacy: Japan, Germany and the U.S.S.R., 1934–1940* (1977); Charles E. Neu, *The Troubled Encounter* (1975); William L. Neumann, *America Encounters Japan* (1963); Armin Rappaport, *Henry L. Stimson and Japan, 1931–1933* (1963); Barbara Tuchman, *Stilwell and the American Experience in China, 1911–45* (1971); and Gerald Wheeler, *Prelude to Pearl Harbor: The United States Navy and the Far East, 1921–1931* (1963).

United States relations with Latin America are treated in Richard Abrams, "United States Intervention Abroad: The First Quarter Century," *American Historical Review* (1974); G. Pope Atkins and Larman C. Wilson, *The United States and the Trujillo Regime* (1972); Glen Barclay, *Struggle for a Continent: The Diplomatic History of South America, 1917–1945* (1972); Cole Blasier, *The Hovering Giant: U.S. Responses to Revolutionary Change in Latin America* (1976); Alexander DeConde, *Herbert Hoover's Latin American Policy* (1951); Donald Dozer, *Are We Good Neighbors?* (1959); Alton Frye, *Nazi Germany and the American Hemisphere, 1933–1941* (1967); Irwin F. Gellman, *Good Neighbor Diplomacy: United States Policies in Latin America, 1933–1945* (1979); Kenneth J. Grieb, *The Latin American Policy of Warren G. Harding* (1976); David Green, *The Containment of Latin America* (1971); Stanley Hilton, *Brazil and the Great Powers, 1930–1939* (1975); Michael Grow, *The Good Neighbor Policy and Authoritarianism in Paraguay* (1981); William Kamman, *A Search for Stability: United States Diplomacy Toward Nicaragua, 1925–1933* (1968); Thomas L. Karnes, *Tropical Enterprise: The Standard Fruit and Steamship Company in Latin America* (1978); Lester D. Langley, *The United States and the Caribbean, 1900–1970* (1980); Neil Macaulay, *The Sandino Affair* (1967); Frank McCann, *The Brazilian-American Alliance, 1937–1945* (1973); Richard Millett, *Guardians of the Dynasty* (1977) (on the Somozas); Michael Montéon, *Chile in the Nitrate Era: The Evolution of Economic Dependence, 1880–1930* (1982); Dana Munro, *United States and the Caribbean Republics, 1921–1933* (1974); Whitney T. Perkins, *Constraint of Empire: The United States and Caribbean Intervention* (1981); Stephen G. Rabe, *The Road to OPEC: United States Relations with Venezuela* (1982); Stephen J. Randall, *The Diplomacy of Modernization: Colombian-American Relations, 1920–1940* (1977); Robert I. Rotberg, *Haiti* (1971); Hans Schmidt, *The United States Occupation of Haiti* (1971); Dick Steward, *Trade and Hemisphere* (1975); Joseph Tulchin, *The Aftermath of War: World War I and U.S. Policy Toward Latin America* (1971); and Bryce Wood, *The Making of the Good Neighbor Policy* (1961).

Specific studies of United States–Mexican relations include E. David Cronon, *Josephus Daniels in Mexico* (1960); Lorenzo Meyer, *Mexico and the United States in the Oil Controversy, 1917–1942* (1977); Ramon E. Ruiz, *The Great Rebellion: Mexico, 1905–1924* (1980); and Robert F. Smith, *The United States and Revolutionary Nationalism in Mexico, 1916–1932* (1972).

Cuba's relationship with the United States is studied in Jules R. Benjamin, *The United States and Cuba: Hegemony and Dependent Development, 1880–1934* (1978); Irwin F. Gellman, *Roosevelt and Batista* (1973); Lester D. Langley, *The Cuban Policy of the United States* (1968); Louis A. Perez, Jr., *Intervention, Revolution, and Politics in Cuba, 1913–1921* (1978); Ramon Ruiz, *Cuba: The Making of a Revolution* (1968); and Robert F. Smith, *The United States and Cuba* (1960).

See also the General Bibliography and the following notes.

Notes to Chapter 10

1. Quoted in Elting E. Morison, *Turmoil and Tradition: A Study of the Life and Times of Henry L. Stimson* (New York: Atheneum, 1964), p. 312.

2. Robert H. Ferrell, "The Mukden Incident: September 18–19, 1931," *Journal of Modern History*, XXVII (March, 1955), 67.

3. Quoted in Morison, *Turmoil and Tradition*, p. 308.

4. Quoted in Richard N. Current, "Henry L. Stimson," in Norman A. Graebner, ed., *An Uncertain Tradition* (New York: McGraw-Hill, 1961), pp. 171, 169.

5. Quoted in John E. Wiltz, *From Isolation to War, 1931–1941* (New York: Thomas Y. Crowell, 1968), p. 39.

6. Quoted in Frank Freidel, *Franklin D. Roosevelt: Launching the New Deal* (Boston: Little, Brown, 1973), p. 120.

7. Quoted in Richard Dean Burns, "Stanley K. Hornbeck: The Diplomacy of the Open Door," in Richard Dean Burns and Edward M. Bennett, eds., *Diplomats in Crisis* (Santa Barbara, Cal.: ABC-CLIO Press, 1974), p. 103.

8. Quoted in Morison, *Turmoil and Tradition*, p. 306.

9. Quoted in Christopher Thorne, *The Limits of Foreign Policy: The West, the League and the Far Eastern Crisis of 1931–1933* (New York: Capricorn Books edition, 1973), p. 158.

10. Quoted in Morison, *Turmoil and Tradition*, p. 310.

11. *Ibid.*, p. 315.

12. Quoted in Norman A. Graebner, "Hoover, Roosevelt, and the Japanese," in Dorothy Borg and Shumpei Okamoto, eds., *Pearl Harbor as History* (New York: Columbia University Press, 1973), p. 30.

13. Morison, *Turmoil and Tradition*, p. 332.

14. Hugh R. Wilson, *Diplomat Between the Wars* (New York: Longmans, Green, 1941), p. 280.

15. Quoted in Robert F. Smith, "Republican Policy and the Pax Americana, 1921–1932," in William A. Williams, ed., *From Colony to Empire* (New York: John Wiley & Sons, 1972), p. 292.

16. Quoted in Thomas H. Buckley, *The United States and the Washington Conference, 1921–1922* (Knoxville: University of Tennessee Press, 1970), pp. 72–73.

17. Quoted in Roger Dingman, *Power in the Pacific: The Origins of Naval Arms Limitations, 1914–1922* (Chicago: University of Chicago Press, 1976), p. 212.

18. Quoted in Akira Iriye, *The Cold War in Asia* (Englewood Cliffs, N.J.: Prentice-Hall, 1974), p. 18.

19. Warren I. Cohen, *America's Response to China* (New York: John Wiley & Sons, 1980; 2nd ed.), p. 106.

20. Stanley K. Hornbeck, *The United States and the Far East* (Boston: World Peace Foundation, 1942), p. 10.

21. John Paton Davies, *Dragon by the Tail* (New York: W. W. Norton, 1972), p. 95.

22. Quoted in Hornbeck, *United States and Far East*, pp. 3–4.

23. Quoted in Akira Iriye, *Across the Pacific* (New York: Harcourt Brace & World, 1967), p. 148.

24. Quoted in Cohen, *America's Response to China*, p. 104.

25. Quoted in Wiltz, *From Isolation to War*, p. 25.

26. Quoted in Asado Sadao, "The Japanese Navy and the United States," in Borg and Okamoto, *Pearl Harbor as History*, p. 238.

27. Waldo Heinrichs, Jr., "The Role of the U.S. Navy," *ibid.*, pp. 202–203.

28. Quoted in William L. Neumann, *America Encounters Japan* (Baltimore: The Johns Hopkins Press, 1963), p. 176.

29. Quoted in Freidel, *Franklin D. Roosevelt: Launching*, p. 104.

30. Barbara W. Tuchman, *Stilwell and the American Experience in China, 1911–45* (New York: Bantam Books, 1972 [c. 1971]), p. 214.

31. Samuel I. Rosenman, ed., *Public Papers and Addresses of Franklin D. Roosevelt* (New York: Macmillan, 1938–1943; 13 vols.), VI, 406–411.

32. Quoted in Wayne S. Cole, "The Role of the United States Congress and Political Parties," in Borg and Okamoto, *Pearl Harbor as History*, p. 314.

33. Quoted in Frederick C. Adams, *Economic Diplomacy: The Export-Import Bank and American Foreign Policy, 1934–1939* (Columbia: University of Missouri Press, 1976), p. 233.

34. Quoted in Robert D. Schulzinger, *The Making of the Diplomatic Mind: The Training, Outlook & Style of United States Foreign Service Officers, 1908–31* (Middletown, Conn.: Wesleyan University Press, 1975), p. 95.

35. Quoted in Arthur P. Whitaker, "From Dollar Diplomacy to the Good Neighbor Policy," *Inter-American Economic Affairs*, IV (Spring, 1951), 18.

36. Rosenman, *Public Papers*, II, 14.

37. Quoted in David Green, *The Containment of Latin America* (Chicago: Quadrangle Books, 1971), p. 38.

38. Frederick B. Pike, *Chile and the United States, 1880–1962*

(South Bend, Ind.: University of Notre Dame Press, 1963), p. 236.

39. J. Fred Rippy, *Globe and Hemisphere* (Chicago: Henry Regnery Company, 1958), pp. 46–47.

40. Quoted in C. Neale Ronning, ed., *Intervention in Latin America* (New York: Alfred A. Knopf, 1970), pp. 42–49.

41. Quoted in Joan Hoff Wilson, *American Business & Foreign Policy, 1920–1933* (Boston: Beacon Press, 1973 [c. 1971]), p. 160.

42. Herbert Hoover, *Memoirs: The Cabinet and the Presidency, 1920–1933* (New York: Macmillan, 1952), p. 69.

43. Sumner Welles, *Naboth's Vineyard* (New York: Payson and Clark, 1928; 2 vols.), II, 797–798.

44. Quoted in Joseph R. Juarez, "United States Withdrawal from Santo Domingo," *Hispanic American Historical Review*, XLII (May, 1962), 180.

45. *Ibid.*

46. Franklin D. Roosevelt, "Our Foreign Policy: A Democratic View," *Foreign Affairs*, VI (July, 1928), 583.

47. Quoted in Robert F. Smith, *The United States and Cuba: Business and Diplomacy, 1917–1960* (New York: Bookman Associates, 1960), p. 184.

48. Quoted in Albert K. Weinberg, *Manifest Destiny* (Chicago: Quadrangle Books, 1963 [c. 1935]), p. 441.

49. United States Department of the Navy, *Operation of Naval Service in Nicaragua* (Senate Doc. No. 86, 70th Cong., 1st Sess., 1928), pp. 5–6.

50. Neill Macaulay, *The Sandino Affair* (Chicago: Quadrangle Books, 1967), p. 257.

51. Colonel Littleton Waller, quoted in Robert I. Rotberg, *Haiti: The Politics of Squalor* (Boston: Houghton Mifflin, 1971), pp. 137–138.

52. James Welton Johnson, "The Truth About Haiti," *The Crisis*, XX (September, 1920), 223.

53. Quoted in Rayford W. Logan, *Haiti and the Dominican Republic* (New York: Oxford University Press, 1968), p. 126.

54. Quoted in Hans Schmidt, *The United States Occupation of Haiti, 1915–1934* (New Brunswick: Rutgers University Press, 1971), p. 81n.

55. Quoted in Donald B. Cooper, "The Withdrawal of the United States from Haiti, 1928–1934," *Journal of Inter-American Studies*, V (January, 1963), 83.

56. Quoted in Dana G. Munro, *The United States and the Caribbean Republics, 1921–1933* (Princeton: Princeton University Press, 1974), pp. 314–315.

57. Logan, *Haiti and Dominican Republic*, pp. 141–142.

58. Quoted in Emily Greene Balch, ed., *Occupied Haiti* (New York: Winters, 1927), pp. 179–180.

59. Quoted in Luis E. Aguilar, *Cuba 1933: Prologue to Revolution* (New York: W. W. Norton, 1974 [1972]), p. 150.

60. *Ibid.*, p. 167.

61. Quoted in Hugh Thomas, *Cuba: The Pursuit of Freedom, 1762–1969* (New York: Harper and Row, 1971), p. 655.

62. Quoted in Aguilar, *Cuba 1933*, p. 175.

63. *Ibid.*, pp. 228–229.

64. Karl M. Schmitt, *Mexico and the United States, 1821–1973* (New York: John Wiley & Sons, 1974), p. 158.

65. Quoted in John W. F. Dulles, *Yesterday in Mexico* (Austin: University of Texas Press, 1961), pp. 324–325.

66. Quoted in E. David Cronon, *Josephus Daniels in Mexico* (Madison: University of Wisconsin Press, 1960), p. 185.

67. *Ibid.*, p. 198.

68. *Ibid.*, p. 210.

69. Quoted in J. Lloyd Mecham, *A Survey of United States–Latin American Relations* (Boston: Houghton Mifflin, 1965), p. 100.

70. Quoted in Samuel Guy Inman, *Inter-American Conferences, 1826–1954* (Washington, D.C.: University Press, 1965; ed. by Harold E. Davis), p. 117.

71. Quoted in Mecham, *Survey of United States–Latin American Relations*, p. 107.

72. Inman, *Inter-American Conferences*, pp. 118–119.

73. Quoted in Bryce Wood, *The Making of the Good Neighbor Policy* (New York: Columbia University Press, 1961), p. 119.

74. Cordell Hull, *Memoirs* (New York: Macmillan, 1948; 2 vols.), I, 602.

75. *Ibid.*, I, 608.

76. Paul A. Varg, "The Economic Side of the Good Neighbor Policy: The Reciprocal Trade Program and South America," *Pacific Historical Review*, XLV (February, 1976), 49.

77. Quoted in Lloyd C. Gardner, *Economic Aspects of New Deal Diplomacy* (Madison: University of Wisconsin Press, 1964), pp. 117–118.

78. Rosenman, *Public Papers*, X, 515.

79. Hull, *Memoirs*, II, 1681.

80. Quoted in John L. Gaddis, *The United States and the Origins of the Cold War* (New York: Columbia University Press, 1972), p. 2.

81. Rosenman, *Public Papers*, X, 530.

Church Service, *Prince of Wales.* On August 10, 1941, President Franklin D. Roosevelt and Prime Minister Winston S. Churchill, with their staffs, attended a memorable church service aboard the British vessel during the Atlantic Charter Conference. (Franklin D. Roosevelt Library)

11 World War II: The Ordeal of Allied Diplomacy, 1939–1945

Diplomatic Crossroad: The "Atlantic Charter" Conference, 1941

It was the longest walk that the tall, greying man had attempted since being stricken by polio twenty years earlier. Holding a cane in his right hand and helped by his son Elliott, President Franklin D. Roosevelt slowly limped the entire length of the battleship H.M.S. *Prince of Wales* to take his place of honor on the quarterdeck. More than fifteen hundred men, including British Prime Minister Winston S. Churchill, stood at rigid attention as the President took his tortured steps. "He was making a tremendous effort," observed a Britisher, and "he was determined to walk along that deck even if it killed him."[1] Finally, Roosevelt reached his seat near the bow, side-by-side with Churchill. British and American chiefs of staff stood behind them, with impressive ranks of sailors and marines on each side. Facing them was the *Prince of Wales'* forward turret, its fourteen-inch guns protruding "like rigid pythons."[2] Roosevelt and Churchill were attending church services together in the quiet waters of Placentia Bay near the harbor of Argentia, Newfoundland that Sunday of August 10, 1941.

Sunday services aboard the *Prince of Wales* marked the high point of the four-day summit meeting between the two leaders (August 9–13, 1941), some four months before Pearl Harbor catapulted the United States into World War II as a formal belligerent. The text of the sermon, from Joshua 1:1–9, seemed directed at the President: "There shall not any man be able to stand before thee all the days of thy life; as I was with Moses, so I will be with thee: I will not fail thee, nor forsake thee." Also suggesting the need for the United States to aid its sister democracy in the war against Hitler was the stirring hymn, "Onward Christian Soldiers," with its call for volunteers "marching as to war." For Roosevelt, who had already assisted the British with destroyers, Lend-Lease, and other aid short of war, the moment evoked a rush of emotion. His handkerchief dabbed at his eyes. "If nothing else had happened," he later told his son, "that would have cemented us. 'Onward Christian Soldiers.' We *are*, and we *will*, go on, with God's help."[3] Churchill later wrote of the symbolism of that Sunday morning—"the Union Jack and the Stars and Stripes draped side by side on the pulpit; . . . the highest naval, military, and air officers of Britain and the United States grouped together behind the President and me; the close-packed ranks of British and American sailors, completely intermingled, sharing the same books and joining fervently in the prayers and hymns familiar to both."[4] None of those praying on the *Prince of Wales* could know, of course, that the majestic battleship would be destroyed by Japanese bombs off the coast of Malaya on December 10, 1941.

The four-day meeting in Placentia Bay was the first of many conferences between Roosevelt and Churchill during World War II; altogether, the two leaders would spend some 120 days in each other's company. Notwithstanding the fears of presidential assistant Harry Hopkins that the meeting foreordained a clash of "prima donnas," the personalities blended nicely.[5] "I am sure I have established warm and deep personal relations with our great friend," Churchill cabled London.[6] The tactful British leader's willingness to pay deference to a man he regarded "almost with religious awe" and his own pride in being half-American (his mother) made Churchill an ardent advocate of Anglo-American solidarity.[7] Roosevelt, although he sometimes saw the Prime Minister as the last of the Victorians, reciprocated Churchill's friendship, and the two heads of government built over the next four years a degree of cooperation unmatched in modern times. "It is fun to be in the same decade with you," FDR wrote his British partner in early 1942.[8]

Aside from the personal equation, the other results of Argentia were less clear-cut. The British asked for men, ships, planes, and tanks. Churchill urged that the American Navy extend its convoying of British vessels farther into the German submarine–infested North Atlantic. The British military chiefs, remembering the frightful casualties of World War I, and perhaps hoping to make military intervention more palatable to the Americans, argued that bombing, blockades, and propaganda might so weaken the Germans that they would surrender without a cross-channel operation. Even with landings, said the British, the burden of fighting would be carried by armored units rather than the large infantry forces of 1914–1918. The Americans, particularly Army Chief of Staff General George C. Marshall, favored a more direct strategy, insisting on large ground armies. Marshall declared further that an American military buildup had to take priority over British demands for weapons and equipment; "the hungry table," as Churchill once described American defense production, simply did not have enough for all who wanted to eat.[9] The one tangible military commitment at Argentia was Roosevelt's promise to order his Navy to convoy British merchant ships as far as Iceland. The President delayed any public declaration until September, when a German submarine torpedoed the American destroyer *Greer* off the coast of Iceland. Neglecting to mention that the *Greer* had been shadowing the U-boat for three hours prior to the attack, Roosevelt announced over worldwide radio on September 11 that henceforth American naval vessels would shoot at German submarines, "the rattlesnakes of the Atlantic."[10] An undeclared naval war was as far as Roosevelt would go in the months before Pearl Harbor.

Discussions about Japan exposed British and American differences at Argentia. Sir Alexander Cadogan of the Foreign Office argued that Japan, which had recently occupied the southern half of French Indochina, should receive an explicit American warning against further encroachments, and that the United States should commit itself to war if the Japanese attacked British or Dutch territory in Southeast

Winston S. Churchill (1874–1965) at Placentia Bay, August, 1941. After the seaborne conference near Newfoundland, Prime Minister Churchill told his war cabinet that President Roosevelt had promised to "wage war" against Germany, "but not declare it" and to do "everything" to "force an 'incident.'" Although these words forecast FDR's policies for the remainder of 1941, they stopped short of a firm American commitment to war. (Franklin D. Roosevelt Library)

Asia. Under Secretary of State Sumner Welles avoided any definite commitment. The best that the British could get was a Rooseveltian promise to deliver a "mighty swat" to Japan. When the President returned to Washington, however, Secretary of State Cordell Hull watered down the proposed statement. Whereas the original draft had stated that further Japanese aggression would cause the United States to take measures that "might result in war," the actual postconference warning to the Japanese ambassador merely read that Washington would take steps necessary "toward insuring the safety and security of the United States."[11] Despite British pressures for a hard line and despite the American embargo of oil to Japan the previous month, Roosevelt preferred to delay a confrontation in the Pacific until his Army and Navy were stronger, public opinion more favorable, and two-front war more advantageous. Roosevelt's policy was to beat Hitler first.

The most famous product of the Churchill-Roosevelt summit conference was the eight-point statement of war aims—the Atlantic Charter. Reminiscent of Woodrow Wilson's Fourteen Points, the Atlantic Charter, in deliberately vaguer terms, reaffirmed the old Wilsonian principles of collective security, national self-determination, freedom of the seas, and liberal trading practices. The signatories also denied themselves any territorial aggrandizement and pledged economic collaboration leading to "social security." Behind the vision of a postwar world in which "all the men in all the lands may live out their lives in freedom from fear and want," however, lay Anglo-American differences. The Americans, particularly Sumner Welles, whom Cadogan said had "swallowed a ramrod in his youth," pressed for a statement explicitly endorsing freer trade.[12] The British wanted to protect their discriminatory system of imperial preferences. The compromise called for "access, on equal terms, to the trade and to the raw materials of the world which are needed for their economic prosperity," leaving the British an escape clause that promised "due respect for their existing obligations." Hull, when he read this vague language later, was "keenly disappointed."[13] Churchill failed to gain Roosevelt's backing for a new League of Nations. The President said that he did not favor a new League Assembly, at least not until England and the United States, acting as policemen, had time to pacify and disarm international troublemakers. Not wishing to arouse either isolationists or fervent internationalists, Roosevelt accepted only "the establishment of a wider and permanent system of general security."[14] As "both realist and idealist, both fixer and preacher, both a prince and a soldier," the President wanted to be as cautious as he was eloquent about postwar goals.[15] "I have not the slightest objection toward your trying your hand at an outline of the post-war picture," he had told an assistant secretary of state in June, 1941. "But for Heaven's sake don't ever let the columnists hear of it."[16]

The Atlantic Charter became a moral and ideological propaganda tool for the war against the Axis. "Every one of the eight points . . . was a challenge to the practice of the Axis Powers, and a challenge to which they could give no effective answer."[17] In September, 1941, at an Inter-Allied meeting in London, representatives of the nations battling Hitler formally adhered to the "common principles" set forth in the Atlantic Charter.[18] The Soviet Union also gave qualified approval. Twenty-six nations, on January 1, 1942, signed the Declaration of the United Nations, which pledged cooperation in achieving the aims of the Atlantic Charter. Churchill and Roosevelt, however, provided no procedures for enforcement or implementation of the principles. Indeed, on September 9, in the House of Commons, the Prime Minister insisted that the charter applied only to "nations of Europe now under the Nazi yoke," not to "the regions and peoples which owe allegiance to the British Crown."[19] As early as December, 1941, Josef Stalin, when rebuffed in his call for Polish territory, remarked: "I thought that the Atlantic Charter was directed against those people who were trying to establish world dominion. It now looks as if the Charter was directed against the USSR."[20] As for Roosevelt, he came to view the principles as guides or inclinations rather than set rules. However much the President believed in the ideals set forth at Argentia, he was always willing to postpone their application or compromise them to accommodate pressing military and diplomatic priorities. "I dream dreams but am, at the same time, an intensely practical person," he once said.[21]

By meeting secretly with Winston Churchill on board a British battleship, President Roosevelt demonstrated America's commitment to the defense of Britain by all means short of war. Notwithstanding outcries from American isolationists, and whatever hopes he might have held that the theatrics of Argentia would galvanize American opinion for a firmer policy, Roosevelt could not commit the United States to war prematurely. "There isn't the slightest chance of the U.S. entering the war until compelled to do so by a direct attack on its own territory," reported one British participant shortly after the conference.[22] Yet the Atlantic Charter, the Churchill-Roosevelt friendship, the Anglo-American strategic conversations, even the divergent views with respect to international organization and postwar economic policy—all struck chords that would echo through the next four years of war. The fact that the Soviet Union, which had been invaded by Germany some six weeks earlier, was not represented at Argentia did not mean that the question of Russian cooperation against the Axis was absent from discussions. Harry Hopkins, Roosevelt's good friend and Churchill's "Lord Root of the Matter," had visited Moscow some two weeks before the Argentia conference, and his assurances that the USSR would withstand the Nazi onslaught were a constant topic of conversation for the two leaders. In a joint communication to Stalin from Argentia, Churchill and Roosevelt hailed "the splendid defense that you are making against the Nazi attack" and promised the "very maximum" of supplies.[23] This Anglo-American commitment to cooperation with the Soviet Union against Hitler also carried large implications for the future.

Step by Step Toward War with Germany, 1939–1941

The conversations at Placentia Bay exemplified Roosevelt's distinctly personal approach to diplomacy during World War II. The President delighted in face-to-face confrontations, always confident in his ability to charm and understand foreign leaders. The meeting with Churchill whetted his appetite for more. It mattered little to Roosevelt that Secretary of State Cordell Hull learned of the conference when he read about it in the newspapers. The President did not mind that his military and naval advisers were often given short notice to prepare for meetings. Roosevelt kept close aides like Harry Hopkins and Sumner Welles nearby and watched the spotlight focus on himself. His cigarette holder omnipresent, the buoyant Roosevelt reveled in the power and drama that were his to command. If not the evil Machiavelli of isolationist fantasy, the President, with his formidable style and strong personality, could be unsettling. As British Foreign Secretary Anthony Eden later put it: "[Roosevelt] seemed to see himself disposing of the fate of so many lands, allied no less than enemy. He did all this with so much grace that it was not easy to dissect. Yet it was too like a conjurer, skillfully juggling with balls of dynamite, whose nature he failed to understand."[24]

The juggling act had begun some two years before the "Atlantic Charter" Conference, when Germany started World War II by attacking Poland. On September 3, 1939, two days after the German invasion, FDR spoke to the American people in a fireside chat. "This nation will remain a neutral nation," he declared, "but I cannot ask that every American remain neutral in thought as well."[25] Thus, in words pointedly different from Woodrow Wilson's in 1914, did Roosevelt project for the next twenty-six months American policy toward the war in Europe. Historian Robert A. Divine has compared the evolution of that policy to a game of giant steps, where the President always "moved two steps forward and one back before he took the giant step ahead."[26] Roosevelt proceeded from neutrality to nonbelligerency to undeclared war in the Atlantic and finally, after Pearl Harbor, to full-scale war against the Axis powers. Hoping to avoid war, while at the same time giving as much aid as possible to Hitler's opponents, the President was not always candid with the public about the possible and ultimate contradiction between these two goals.

Makers of American Foreign Policy from 1939 to 1945

Presidents	Secretaries of State
Franklin D. Roosevelt, 1933–1945	Cordell Hull, 1933–1944
	Edward R. Stettinius, Jr., 1944–1945
Harry S Truman, 1945–1953	James F. Byrnes, 1945–1947

On September 21, 1939 Roosevelt requested that Congress repeal the arms embargo in the Neutrality Act as the best way to keep the United States from entering the war. He stressed this deceptive argument, knowing that the real purpose of the repeal was to permit England and France, with their superior sea power, to purchase arms and munitions on a cash-and-carry basis. He persuaded William Allen White, the Republican sage from Emporia, Kansas, to form a Non-Partisan Committee for Peace through Revision of the Neutrality Act. Although isolationists like Republican Senator Arthur H. Vandenberg of Michigan fumed that the United States could not be "an arsenal for one belligerent without becoming a target for the other," the President's tactics worked.[27] By a vote of 63–30 in the Senate and 243–181 in the House, the revised Neutrality Act became law on November 4.

The Pan American Conference at Panama City (September 23–October 3, 1939) also signaled the pro-Allied emphasis of United States policy. The conferees proclaimed neutrality, established a hemispheric committee for economic coordination, and created a neutral zone three hundred miles wide along the entire coast of the western hemisphere (except Canada), in which belligerent naval operations were prohibited. Roosevelt had told his Cabinet as early as April, 1939, that the United States Atlantic fleet would patrol such areas and "if we fire and sink an Italian or German [submarine] . . . we will say it the way the Japs do, 'so sorry.' 'Never happen again.' Tomorrow we sink two."[28] These "neutrality patrols" actually became the first step toward Anglo-American naval cooperation. By the late summer of 1940 conversations between staff officers began in London, soon to be followed by exchanges of personnel, actual coordination against German naval operations (such as the sighting and sinking of the battleship *Bismarck* in May, 1941), and, in the autumn of 1941, the convoying of merchant ships across the Atlantic. Justified in terms of contingency planning and aid short of war, such naval measures nonetheless led the Chief of Naval Operations, Admiral Harold R. Stark, to conclude early in 1941: "The question as to our entry into the war seems to be *when* and not *whether*."[29]

Germany's *blitzkrieg* humbled Poland in two weeks, and then came, in the winter of 1939–1940, a period of some quiet called the "phony war" or *sitzkrieg*. Most battle news, from November to March, flowed from Northern Europe, where Russia defeated Finland in the "Winter war." Roosevelt sent his sympathies but little else to Finland. The fall of France in June, 1940, stung FDR into bold measures. In a speech of June 10 Roosevelt condemned Italy for holding the dagger that "struck . . . the back of its neighbor," and pledged to England "the material resources of this nation."[30] A week later he named prominent Republicans Henry L. Stimson and Frank Knox, both ardent advocates of aid to Britain, as secretary of war and secretary of the navy, respectively. Then, after careful preparations and intricate negotiations, the President announced on September 3, 1940, that he was, by executive agreement, transferring to England some fifty old destroyers in exchange for leases to eight British bases stretching from Newfoundland to British Guiana. Two weeks later, he signed into law the Selective Training and Service Act of 1940, the first peacetime military draft in American history.

That Roosevelt could accomplish so much in the summer of 1940, at a time when isolationist sentiment still prevailed and he was seeking a controversial third term as President, testifies to his political astuteness. As to both selective service

The German Onslaught 1939–1942

and the destroyers-for-bases agreement, FDR ascertained through intermediaries that his Republican presidential opponent, Wendell L. Willkie, would not make a campaign issue of either measure. Also, in both cases Roosevelt encouraged influential private citizens (the Century Group for the destroyer deal and the Military Training Camps Association for selective service) to lobby for his objectives. That summer the larger Committee to Defend America by Aiding the Allies, headed by William Allen White, rallied behind the President and served as a counter to the isolationist America First Committee set up in September, 1940. FDR avoided congressional scrutiny of the destroyer deal by negotiating it as an executive agreement rather than a treaty, and he deflected political opposition to conscription by having men of integrity, such as Secretary Stimson and Army Chief of Staff General George C. Marshall, attest to the military need for a draft. Public sympathy for beleaguered Britain also helped. "Every time Hitler bombed

London we got another couple of votes," noted future Selective Service Director Lewis W. Hershey.[31] Furthermore, Roosevelt continued to promise that his policies would keep America out of war. Although the destroyers-for-bases agreement could be considered a *casus belli* by Germany, FDR called it instead "the most important action in the reinforcement of our national defense . . . since the Louisiana Purchase."[32] Churchill privately considered it a "decidedly unneutral act" vital to British survival.[33] The President defended his pro-Allied foreign policy in the fall campaign. When Willkie made last-minute charges that Roosevelt secretly sought war, the White House unequivocally struck back: "Your boys are not going to be sent into any foreign wars." Willkie exploded: "That hypocritical son of a bitch! This is going to beat me!"[34] He was right.

While Roosevelt was celebrating victory on a postelection cruise in the Caribbean, Churchill spelled out Britain's desperate need for arms and munitions and concluded that "the moment approaches when we shall no longer be able to pay cash for shipping and other supplies."[35] On returning to Washington Roosevelt held one of his breezy, jaunty press conferences, telling reporters that he favored a policy of lending or leasing to Britain whatever supplies it needed. Saying that "I am trying to . . . eliminate the dollar sign," he likened his policy to lending a garden hose to a neighbor whose house was burning. Once the fire is out, "he gives it back to me and thanks me very much for the use of it," or, if damaged, he replaces it with a new product.[36] In a fireside chat on December 29, FDR admitted that sending armaments to Britain risked involvement in the war, but "our national policy is not directed toward war. Its sole purpose is to keep war away from our country and our people." Then, in a ringing phrase, Roosevelt called upon the United States to "become the great arsenal of democracy."[37]

Over the next two months, as FDR later put it, the Lend-Lease Bill was debated in Congress, "in every newspaper, on every wave length—over every cracker barrel in all the land."[38] Although the final victory of 60–31 in the Senate and 317–71 in the House was substantial, the White House did not win without a struggle. Isolationist Senator Burton K. Wheeler, a Democrat from Montana, immediately labeled the bill "the New Deal's triple A foreign policy; it will plow under every fourth American boy." Roosevelt shot back at a press conference, calling Wheeler's statement "the rottenest thing that has been said in public life in my generation."[39] A bit of benevolent deception occurred in the numbering of the bill in the House. The Administration's floor manager, Representative John W. McCormack, worried because the Irishmen of his South Boston constituency were sure to protest any "McCormack Bill" designed to aid the British Empire, induced the House parliamentarian to tag the Lend-Lease Bill H.R. 1776. McCormack was relieved. Nonetheless, one irate constituent berated him on the street later that winter. The future Speaker of the House thought quickly: "Madam, do you realize that the Vatican is surrounded on all sides by totalitarianism? Madam, this is not a bill to save the English, this is a bill to save Catholicism."[40]

Formally titled "An Act to Promote the Defense of the United States," the bill was signed into law on March 11, 1941. Under its terms the President was permitted "to sell, transfer title to, exchange, lease, lend, or otherwise dispose of" defense articles to "any country whose defense the President deems vital to the defense of the United States."[41] Although the initial appropriation totaled $7 billion, by the war's end the United States had expended more than $50 billion on Lend-Lease. Fittingly enough, the United States included 900,000 feet of fire-hose in the first shipment of goods to England, which was to receive $31.6 billion in Lend-Lease assistance during the war. "We have torn up 150 years of traditional American foreign policy," cried Senator Vandenberg. "We have tossed Washington's Farewell Address in the discard."[42]

With German U-boats operating in wolf packs and sinking more than 500,000 tons of shipping a month, it seemed likely that the United States would use its Navy to see that Lend-Lease supplies reached England safely. But Roosevelt hesitated, because "public opinion was not yet ready."[43] The President compromised in April by extending naval "patrols" halfway across the Atlantic, announcing publicly that American vessels would watch for German warships and monitor their movements. American troops also occupied Greenland the same month. Stimson, Knox, Treasury Secretary Henry Morgenthau, Jr., and Interior Secretary Harold Ickes all urged the President to speak out candidly for convoys of British ships. The impatient Stimson thought his chief was "tangled up in the coils of his former hasty speeches on possible war and convoying as was Laocoon in the coils of the boa constrictors."[44]

When Hitler occupied the Balkans and launched his attack on the USSR in June, 1941 Roosevelt acted decisively. The President announced the next month that some 4,000 American Marines would occupy Iceland for hemispheric defense—surely the first time anyone had placed Iceland within the western hemisphere. He also began military Lend-Lease aid to Russia in November, notwithstanding opinions from the State Department and his military advisers that the Soviet Union would quickly fall. (By the end of the war Russia received $11 billion in

Lend-Lease to Russia. An American Lend-Lease official checks a shipment of American food destined for Russia's hard-pressed people. The Russians, who eventually lost 15–20 million people, received over $11 billion in Lend-Lease aid, which the President defended as necessary to an Allied victory. (U.S. Information Agency, National Archives)

Lend-Lease.) Roosevelt also ignored the suggestion of Democratic Senator Harry S Truman of Missouri: "If we see that Germany is winning the war we ought to help Russia and if Russia is winning we ought to help Germany, and . . . let them kill as many as possible."[45] As for Churchill's remarks on his new ally Russia: "If Hitler invaded Hell I would make at least a favorable reference to the Devil in the House of Commons."[46] When bureaucratic tangles and military lethargy inhibited the flow of goods to Russia, a short-tempered Roosevelt lectured his Cabinet that "the only answer I want to hear is that it is under way."[47] Then the President held his dramatic meeting with Churchill at Placentia Bay, and in early September, after a German submarine fired torpedoes at the *Greer,* he publicly ordered naval convoys as far as Iceland and issued a "shoot-on-sight" command to the Navy.

By the autumn of 1941, Roosevelt, even though he wanted to limit American military efforts to naval and air support, probably sought an "incident" to induce American entry into the war against Hitler. After the Placentia Bay conference, Churchill told the British War Cabinet that the President "had said that he would wage war, but not declare it, and that he would become more and more provocative. If the Germans did not like it, they could attack American forces."[48] When a U-boat torpedoed the destroyer *Kearny* off Iceland, killing eleven men on October 17, the President seized the moment. "The shooting has started. And history has recorded who fired the first shot," he intoned on October 27. "The U.S.S. *Kearny* is not just a Navy ship. She belongs to every man, woman, and child in this Nation. Hitler's torpedo was directed at every American, whether he lives on our sea coasts or in the innermost part of the country."[49] Roosevelt then flourished a map which purportedly showed how Nazi henchmen planned to reorganize Central and South America as vassal states. Through these histrionics the President hoped to persuade Congress to repeal the sections of the 1939 Neutrality Act that prohibited the arming of merchant ships and banned such vessels from war zones. After the destroyer *Reuben James* was sunk, with the loss of over 100 men, on October 31, the isolationist America First Committee charged that the White House was "asking Congress to issue an engraved drowning license to American seamen."[50] Following a very bitter debate, repeal passed in November by narrow margins, 50–37 in the Senate and 212–194 in the House. For the first time since the outbreak of war in 1939, American merchant vessels were permitted to carry arms and munitions to England. Roosevelt must have suspected that Hitler, unless he courted defeat, could not allow American cargo ships to cross the Atlantic unmolested. American naval escorts were provocative enough. Hitler himself had said on October 3: "When I see the enemy leveling his rifle at me, I am not going to wait till he presses the trigger. I would rather be the first to press the trigger."[51]

Roosevelt charted an oblique path toward war because he believed he had no other choice. The President "devoted considerable time and energy to assessing public opinion"[52] and was particularly impressed by the scientific polling of Gallup, Roper, and others, a new technique based on representative samples of the population. Every poll showed a manifest desire to stay out of the war. In September, 1941, nearly 80 percent of the American people opposed participation in the war. At the same time they strongly wished to defeat Hitler. Thus, so long as Roosevelt defined American policy as building the arsenal of democracy, saying that this would be the best way to avoid war, the American people could have both of their wishes fulfilled. The narrow vote over repeal of the Neutrality Act in November dramatized the power of isolationist sentiment and reinforced the

President's reluctance to ask for outright intervention. As Robert E. Sherwood put it, "he had no more tricks left. The hat from which he had pulled so many rabbits was empty."[53] This inability to go to Congress for a declaration of war was to some extent self-inflicted: that is, FDR had said for months that the United States would not enter the war, that aiding the Allies would prevent the need for American military intervention; now he could not easily reverse his opinions without appearing a hypocrite. The only recourse was to wait for the Germans to fire the first shot. Hitler was slow to oblige, restraining his admirals from all-out war in the shipping lanes while he tried on land to knock Russia out. News of the Japanese attack at Pearl Harbor reached Berlin at a time when German armies had bogged down short of Moscow. In the mistaken belief that Japanese intervention would keep Americans occupied in the Pacific, the Fuehrer jubilantly announced war against the United States on December 11, 1941, saving Roosevelt himself from the difficult task of first having to pilot through Congress a declaration of war against Berlin.

Toward Pearl Harbor: Japanese-American Relations, 1939–1941

Events in Asia, not Europe, plunged the United States into World War II. Ambassador Joseph C. Grew, the grizzled diplomat with the fierce, bushy eyebrows, was surprised at the increased signs of anti-Japanese sentiment during a trip home in the summer of 1939. The ambassador listened to his old Groton and Harvard friend Franklin Roosevelt talk truculently of intercepting the Japanese fleet if it moved against the Dutch East Indies. When the State Department gave formal notice in July that the 1911 commercial treaty with Japan would be terminated in six months, Grew feared that economic sanctions would follow, and perhaps war as well. "[It] is going to be up to me," he noted, "to let this American temper discreetly penetrate into Japanese consciousness. Sparks will fly before long."[54]

Grew, with his Far Eastern preoccupation, had failed to grasp the Europe-first emphasis of Roosevelt's foreign policy. After 1937, when Japan marched deep into the "stubble" of China, Washington angrily reacted with protests, but limited its intervention on behalf of China.[55] As in the 1920s and early 1930s, American power was insufficient to challenge Japanese predominance in East Asia. Even Roosevelt's much-heralded tactic of refusing to apply the Neutrality Act to the "incident" in China, thus making it legal to sell arms and munitions to Jiang Jieshi's government, could not obscure the preponderance of American trade with Japan. As late as 1940, $78 million in American exports went to China, whereas $227 million were shipped to Japan. Abrogation of the 1911 commercial treaty permitted economic sanctions against Japan, but oil, the most vital ingredient in Japan's war machine, was not withheld until July, 1941. In keeping with Roosevelt's policy of all-out aid to England short of war, the Navy revised its strategic thinking in November, 1940. "Plan Dog" called for a defensive posture in the Pacific, depicted Germany as the country's number one enemy, and made preservation of England its principal goal. Opposed to any appeasement of Japan, Roosevelt still hoped to avoid a confrontation, because "I simply have not got enough Navy to go around—and every little episode in the Pacific means fewer ships in the Atlantic."[56]

Japanese movement into Southeast Asia, in apparent coordination with Hitler's *blitzkrieg* in Europe, placed Washington and Tokyo on a collision course. With the

Asian colonies of France and the Netherlands lying unprotected, Japanese expansionists demanded a thrust southward, thus completing the strangulation of China and transforming the whole region into the Greater East Asia Co-Prosperity Sphere. Japan pressed England and France to close supply routes to the Guomindang through Burma and Indochina. Tokyo also demanded economic concessions from the petroleum-rich Dutch East Indies. Then came the shocking news of late September, 1940. Just four days after Vichy French representatives allowed Japanese troops to occupy northern Indochina, Japanese Foreign Minister Yosuke Matsuoka, on September 27, signed the Tripartite Pact with Germany and Italy. Each signatory pledged to aid one another if attacked by a nation not currently involved in the war. Since the Soviet Union was explicitly exempted by the pact, Washington had no doubt about being its target. "This is not the Japan I have known and loved," wrote a disgruntled Ambassador Grew.[57] The aggressors of Europe and Asia had apparently banded together.

A new more militant Japanese government, with Prince Fumimaro Konoye as prime minister and General Hideki Tojo as war minister, took the fateful steps. Matsuoka, who had spent nine years in America as a youth and thought he understood Americans, articulated the advantages of boldness—"one cannot obtain a tiger's cub unless he braves the tiger's den."[58] The intent of the Tripartite Pact, as Matsuoka saw it, was to deter the United States from intervening in either the Atlantic or Pacific, and to facilitate a rapprochement between Japan and the Soviet Union, which was still aligned with Germany in the Nazi-Soviet Pact. Jiang Jieshi might then be induced to accept a reasonable settlement, after which Japanese troops could be gradually withdrawn and Tokyo's civilian control over the army finally reasserted. Japan, moreover, could peacefully carve out its East Asian Co-Prosperity Sphere. "Held together by a long chain of 'ifs,'" as historian Barbara Teters has written, Matsuoka's scenario could also lead to war.[59] The Japanese Navy, which would bear the brunt of any war with England and the United States, fought against the Tripartite Pact. "Our opposition," wrote one admiral, "was like paddling against the rapids only a few hundred yards upstream from Niagara Falls."[60]

Washington flashed warning signals. In July, 1940, Roosevelt clamped an embargo on aviation fuel and top-grade scrap iron sought by Japan. In September, at the time of the Tripartite Pact, he extended the embargo to all scrap metals. Even Grew urged firmness. His famous "green light" telegram of September 12, 1940 labeled Japan "one of the predatory powers," lacking "all moral and ethical sense . . . frankly and unashamedly opportunist, seeking at every turn to profit by the weakness of others."[61] Administration "hawks" like Stimson, Knox, Ickes, Morgenthau, and even Eleanor Roosevelt, pressed the President to shut off oil exports as well. Backed by Secretary Hull and the joint chiefs, however, Roosevelt, in historian Charles Neu's phrase, "swallowed hard and remained in touch with reality."[62] As FDR wrote Grew in January, 1941: "We must recognize that hostilities in Europe, in Africa, and in Asia are all parts of a single world conflict. . . . Our policy of self-defense must be a global strategy."[63] Within this global strategy, however, the President still hoped to aid England, while avoiding a showdown in the Pacific.

The first six months of 1941 saw vigorous private and official transpacific efforts to avoid war. In February, Admiral Kichisaburo Nomura became ambassador to Washington. Well-known for his pro-Western opinions and a personal friend of

Franklin Roosevelt, Nomura accepted the appointment only when assured by Konoye and Matsuoka that peace with the United States took precedence over Japan's commitment to the Axis. Otherwise, he said, his task would be "like chasing two rabbits in different directions."[64] A group of private citizens known as the "John Doe Associates" and led by two Catholic missionaries, Father James M. Drought and Bishop James E. Walsh, also tried to effect conciliation. They held interviews with Prince Konoye, Hull, and Roosevelt. Having a vague understanding of the issues and a strong desire for peace, the John Doe intermediaries told each government what it wanted to hear. Father Drought enthusiastically forwarded a "Draft Understanding" to Secretary Hull on April 9, which, among other points, called for a Konoye-Roosevelt meeting in Hawaii and American pressure on China to recognize the Japanese domination of Manchuria, in exchange for a virtual Japanese disavowal of the Tripartite Pact. Hull, who thought the "Understanding" was a Japanese proposal, accepted it as a basis of discussion, but told Nomura that any Japanese-American agreement had to satisfy four basic principles: respect for the territorial integrity and sovereignty of all nations; noninterference in the internal affairs of other nations; respect for the equality of commercial opportunity, or Open Door; and support for only peaceful change of the status quo in the Pacific. Japan, on the other hand, thought the "Draft Understanding" an American proposal, and Nomura failed to attach appropriate importance to Hull's four points when he reported to Tokyo. Not until September did Tokyo learn that Hull's four principles were crucial and a major obstacle to any settlement of the China war. The amateur diplomatic activities of the Doe Associates had confused Japanese-American relations. The question of a Pacific meeting between Konoye and Roosevelt was a case in point. The "Draft Understanding" of April recommended such a conference; Japan initially indicated that an agreement in principle on key issues was required before a Konoye-Roosevelt meeting could be held. But in August the Japanese reversed themselves and asked for the meeting they thought the Americans had proposed in April. The Doe Associates, of course, not the Americans, had originally urged the conference. By August, however, Washington first wanted assurances from Tokyo on outstanding problems and hence rejected a high-level meeting. Japan then grew annoyed, sure that the United States was retreating from an original position. "The fundamental misconception that had been planted in April," Professor Robert J. C. Butow has written, "had become a tangled, impenetrable growth by August."[65]

The efforts of diplomats, including the Doe Associates, were ultimately doomed by Japan's determination to hold China and to expand farther. "The Japs are having a real drag-down," Roosevelt told Ickes in early July, 1941, "trying to decide which way they are going to jump—attack Russia, attack the South Seas . . . or whether they will sit on the fence and be more friendly with us."[66] When word reached Washington on July 24 that troop transports bearing the Rising Sun were steaming toward Camranh Bay and southern Indochina, FDR signed an executive order freezing all Japanese funds in the United States. In practice, this meant stopping all trade with Japan—including oil. "From now on," Herbert Feis has noted, "the oil gauge and the clock stood side by side. Each fall in the level brought the hour of decision closer."[67]

The diplomacy of proposals and counterproposals in the remaining months of 1941 proved ineffective. Unless the flow of American oil resumed, Japan determined to seize Dutch and British oil fields. But the United States would not turn on the oil spigot until Tokyo agreed to Hull's four principles, especially the pledge to respect China's sovereignty and territorial integrity. Key American officials also knew from cracking the Japanese code ("Operation Magic") that the forces of Nippon were massing to strike southward after mid-November. But many in the Roosevelt Administration did not think Japan would battle the United States. Hard-liners like Henry L. Stimson had advocated embargoes for more than a year, arguing that the Japanese were "notorious bluffers" who backed down when confronted firmly.[68] As late as November 27, when "Magic" was reporting a Japanese strike somewhere very soon, State Department Asian expert Stanley K. Hornbeck, who probably did not know about the intercepts, offered odds of five to one that war with Japan would not occur by December 15. "Tell me of one case in history," he challenged his colleagues, "when a nation went to war out of desperation."[69] Amid such an atmosphere, the urging of Army and Navy leaders to string out negotiations until the Philippines could be reinforced went unheeded. An eleventh-hour modus vivendi proposed a small trickle of oil to Japan and negotiations between Chongqing and Tokyo, while maintaining American aid to China; Japan would have to abrogate the Tripartite Pact and accept basic principles of international conduct. Not trusting the Japanese, Hull and Roosevelt decided to shelve the proposal. "I have washed my hands of it," muttered Hull on November 27, "and it is now in the hands of . . . the Army and Navy."[70]

The Japanese attack on Pearl Harbor, as political scientist Bruce M. Russett has written, cannot "be explained simply as an act of 'irrationality,' an impulsive act by an unstable leader."[71] After months of discussion among civilian and military leaders, a commitment was made at the Imperial Conference of September to fight Americans if the life-strangling embargo on strategic materials was not lifted by October 15. The date was later extended to November 25, then November 30. With 12,000 tons of oil used each day by Japan, moderates and militants alike saw American pressure as provocative. The choices were fighting the United States or pulling out of China, and no Japanese leader counseled the latter. American power and industrial potential were well known, but, as General Tojo put it, "sometimes a man has to jump with his eyes closed, from the veranda of Kiyomizu Temple."[72] The man ordered to plan the Pearl Harbor attack, Admiral Isoroku Yamamoto, had no illusions about ultimate victory. "If told to fight regardless of consequence," he said, "I shall run wild considerably for the first six months or a year, but I have utterly no confidence for the second and third years."[73] At dawn on November 25, 1941, a task force that included six carriers and two battleships headed across three thousand miles of open sea. The planes struck on Sunday, December 7, 1941 a few minutes before eight o'clock, Hawaiian time. Within two hours eight American battleships sank to the bottom of Pearl Harbor and more than 2,400 Americans died.

"Millions of words," Robert E. Sherwood has written, "have been recorded by at least eight official investigating bodies and one may read through all of them without arriving at an adequate explanation of why, with war so obviously ready to break out *somewhere* in the Pacific, our principal Pacific base was in a condition of peacetime Sunday morning somnolence instead of in Condition Red."[74] After World War II, critics argued that Roosevelt, aided by his top advisers, had deliberately sacrificed the Pacific fleet to get into the war against Hitler via the "back door."[75] Most scholars reject the conspiracy theory and explain the Pearl

Harbor disaster as the consequence of mistakes, missed clues, overconfidence, and plain bad luck. American leaders, partly due to the "Magic" intercepts, thought that the Japanese would strike in Southeast Asia, for troop transports were sighted heading for Thailand, and underestimated Japan's capacity to undertake two major operations at once. As to the many hints of major Japanese interest in Pearl Harbor, including Ambassador Grew's warning in February, 1941, of a possible sudden attack, historian Roberta Wohlstetter has written: "After the event a signal is always crystal clear; we can now see what disaster it was signalling, since the disaster has occurred. But before the event it is obscure and pregnant with conflicting meanings. . . . In short, we failed to anticipate Pearl Harbor not for want of the relevant materials, but because of a plethora of irrelevant ones."[76] Many "ifs" cloud the question. If the radar operator had been able to convince his superiors on Oahu that the blips were really planes, if General Marshall's last-minute warning had been sent by Navy cable instead of Western Union telegraph, if a "Magic" decoding machine had been at Honolulu, if . . . .

The attack on Pearl Harbor gave Japan a smashing tactical victory. Yet it was a strategic disaster. In Samuel Eliot Morison's words, "one can search military history in vain for an operation more fatal to the aggressor."[77] When Roosevelt, referring to the "date which will live in infamy," asked for a declaration of war,

Pearl Harbor. A Japanese pilot's perspective on Ford Island, Pearl Harbor, Hawaii. On December 7, 1941, a "date which will live in infamy," the Japanese attackers sank much of the United States Pacific fleet. (Navy Department, National Archives)

Congress responded on December 8 with a unanimous vote in the Senate and only one dissent in the House—that of Jeanette Rankin, who had also voted "no" in 1917.[78] For Vandenberg, Pearl Harbor "ended isolationism for any realist."[79]

The Character of Wartime Diplomacy

The "Atlantic Charter" Conference and the events of 1939–1941 illustrate well some of the themes of wartime diplomacy. The emphasis on giving material aid to Hitler's opponents through the "arsenal of democracy" foreshadowed the main American contribution to victory over the Axis. Washington's commitment to a "Europe First" strategy derived from Anglo-American staff discussions prior to Pearl Harbor, as did the different American and British conceptions of that strategy. Americans favored a "massive thrust at the enemy's heart" and the British preferred "successive stabs around the periphery . . . like jackals worrying a lion before springing at his throat."[80] During the war Americans also revived Wilsonianism, but combined it with a pragmatic determination to avoid Wilson's

"**Jap . . . You're Next!**" James Montgomery Flagg, already famous for his "I Want You" poster of the First World War, offered this version of Uncle Sam in 1942. After Pearl Harbor posters such as Flagg's helped focus public resentment on Japan, rather than on Hitler. Yet Roosevelt did not want to adopt a "Pacific First" strategy and kept his "Europe First" strategy alive by supporting British proposals to invade North Africa in November, 1942. (National Archives)

mistakes. This time the United States would join an international organization to maintain peace, even if it meant adding balance-of-power features to the institution and paying court to sensitive Republican senators. There would be no debts-reparations tangle because Lend-Lease would eliminate the dollar sign. This time, too, the enemy would have to surrender unconditionally. Particularly evident during the war years was the State Department's desire to reduce tariffs abroad and to create an open world, reflecting Secretary Hull's Wilsonian belief that trade discrimination was one of the prime causes of war.

If total war inspired visions of total peace, victory over the Axis also required compromises and short-term decisions that were not always Wilsonian. The marriage of convenience with the Soviet Union involved perhaps the most serious departure from Wilsonian ideals, if only because Russian security needs and drives in Eastern Europe clashed with the principle of national self-determination. But Franklin Roosevelt had learned as much about statecraft from his cousin Theodore as from Woodrow Wilson. His vision of the "Four Policemen" (Russia, China, Britain, and the United States) maintaining world peace implied spheres of influence more than true collective security. Roosevelt was committed, with some precautions, to continuing Soviet-American cooperation into the postwar world. Because the Red Army bore the brunt of the fighting until mid-1944, and because the Kremlin ostentatiously played down its commitment to world revolution after June 22, 1941, it thus became prudent, even necessary, to postpone difficulties with Moscow until the end of the war. Despite wartime propaganda about the similar revolutionary and anti-imperialist pasts, Soviet-American differences remained profound. Fears on both sides that the other would make a separate peace with Germany provided sufficient evidence of the continued tension between the two nations.

The growing influence of the military was another wartime characteristic. That Roosevelt took his joint chiefs, not Secretary Hull, to Argentia and other wartime conferences symbolized the extent to which military decisions determined foreign policy. As a former Assistant Secretary of the Navy, FDR delighted in the duties of Commander-in-Chief. He liked to concentrate on grand strategy, enjoyed the company of admirals and generals, made the joint chiefs principal advisers during the war, and generally left postwar planning and congressional liaison to the State Department. Cordell Hull, although influential in formulating Japanese policy before Pearl Harbor, grudgingly acquiesced because he had never been Roosevelt's "complete agent."[81] The Tennessean complained: "If the President wishes to speak to me all he has to do is pick up that telephone, and I'll come running. It is not for me to bother the President."[82] Frequently Hull did not learn of Roosevelt's decisions until Secretary of War Stimson told him. So confusing did procedures become that at one point in 1944 the State Department was formulating plans for the occupation of Germany that contradicted decisions the President had made at the Teheran Conference a few months earlier. Roosevelt did not tell Hull what happened at Teheran and Hull apparently never asked.

The ordeal of global war brought new power and confidence to American diplomacy. The Atlantic Charter reflected a commitment to shaping the postwar world in an American image. As Henry Luce's best-selling *American Century* phrased it in 1941, the United States must "exert upon the world the full impact of our influence, for such purposes as we see fit and by such means as we see fit."[83] By rearming, acquiring new bases, raising an army of over two million, welding hemispheric unity, and revving up its industries, the United States possessed the sinews of global power even before Pearl Harbor. "The United States was now pursuing an imperialist policy," complained Adolf Hitler in November, 1940. "It was not fighting for England, but only trying to get the British Empire into its grasp, helping England at best to further its own rearmament and to reinforce its military power by acquiring bases. . . . The United States have no business in Europe, Africa, or Asia."[84] Winston Churchill himself told Roosevelt in 1944: "You have the greatest navy in the world. You will have, I hope, the greatest air force. You will have the greatest trade. You have all the gold." But Churchill hoped that the Americans "will not give themselves over to vainglorious ambitions, and that justice and fair-play will be the lights that guide them."[85] The United States used its power for both political and military purposes, but, as Roosevelt told Churchill, postwar political settlements and other issues "must be definitely secondary to the primary operations of striking at the heart of Germany."[86]

The Grand Alliance: Strategy and Fissures, 1941–1943

The diplomacy of the "Grand Alliance" of the United States, Britain, and the Soviet Union centered on two issues: boundaries in Eastern Europe, and the timing of an Anglo-American "second front" in Western Europe. When Anthony Eden went to Moscow just after Pearl Harbor, Premier Stalin said he had no objections to declarations like the Atlantic Charter, which he regarded as "algebra," but he preferred "practical arithmetic"—that is, an agreement guaranteeing Soviet boundaries with Eastern Europe as they stood prior to Hitler's attack in 1941.[87] The British, after an initial refusal, were inclined to grant what Stalin wanted. The Americans, particularly Cordell Hull and most officers of the State Department, worked to postpone such issues until postwar conferences and plebiscites. The second front was another matter. The Russians, fighting some two hundred German divisions and dying by the hundreds of thousands, urged a cross-channel attack as quickly as possible, and the American military, despite British reluctance, wished to comply. "We've got to go to Europe and fight," an American staff officer noted as early as January, 1942. "If we're to keep Russia in, save the Middle East, India and Burma; we've got to begin slugging with air at West Europe; to be followed by a land attack as soon *as possible*."[88] When the Soviet foreign minister visited Washington that May, Roosevelt, partly to defer the question of Russian frontiers, "authorized Mr. Molotov to inform Mr. Stalin that [the President] expected the formation of a second front this year."[89] But the Anglo-American invasion of France did not take place until June 6, 1944, and during the interim, as FDR said, "the Russian armies are killing more Axis personnel and destroying more Axis material than all other twenty-five United Nations put together."[90] The delay, to say the least, produced fissures in the Grand Alliance.

American military leaders urged a cross-channel attack by the spring of 1943 at the latest, but the British, with Roosevelt's compliance, decided otherwise. A new plan, Operation TORCH, called for the invasion of French North Africa in November, 1942, a decision that led logically to operations against Sicily and Italy in the summer of 1943 and effectively postponed a cross-channel attack (later dubbed Operation OVERLORD) until 1944. American generals were bitter. When General Dwight D. Eisenhower learned that the second front had been postponed, he muttered that it might be the "blackest day in history" if Russia were not kept in the war.[91] At numerous military conferences in 1942–1943, from Quebec to Cairo, the Americans argued with their British counterparts, always suspicious that fixation on the Mediterranean reflected a British desire to shore up imperial lifelines, and not, as the British said, a coherent strategy to bloody Germany on the periphery before launching a full-scale invasion of France. Sometimes there was real acrimony, as described by one American general at the Cairo Conference of November, 1943, when British Chief of Staff Alan Brooke exchanged heated words with American Admiral Ernest J. King: "Brooke got nasty and King got good and sore. King almost climbed over the table at Brooke. God, he was mad. I wished he had socked him."[92] Apart from Roosevelt's desire to have Americans fighting Germans somewhere in 1942, the main reason that British strategy predominated in the two years after Pearl Harbor was that England was fully mobilized, while America was not, and any combined operation had to depend largely on British troops, British shipping, and British casualties. Once American production and manpower began to predominate in 1943, combined strategy gradually shifted toward Operation OVERLORD. FDR, according to historian Brian Villa, also "enticed" Churchill toward the cross-channel commitment by temporarily withholding agreement on a postwar atomic partnership.[93] A symbolic clash between the two competing strategies occurred in early 1944. Churchill insisted on an invasion of Rhodes, off the Turkish coast. "No American is going to land on that god-damn island," barked General Marshall.[94] None did.

Roosevelt and Churchill knew how intensely Marshal Stalin wanted a full-scale second front in France, not in North Africa or Italy. The Red Army had stopped the Germans short of Moscow in 1941, but in the summer of 1942 German *panzers* drove into the Caucasus oil fields and laid siege to Stalingrad on the Volga River. Churchill told Stalin in August, 1942 that a cross-channel attack was planned for the spring of 1943. Yet a few months later Stalin was informed that the attack was postponed until August, 1943. Not until June, 1943, did the Russians learn officially that there would be no cross-channel assault at all that year. "Need I speak of the dishearteningly negative expression that this fresh postponement of the second front . . . will produce in the Soviet Union?" Stalin wrote Roosevelt on June 11.[95] Tensions increased that summer, when the Soviet Union broke off diplomatic relations with the Polish exile government in London after the Poles had asked the International Red Cross to investigate charges that the Russians had murdered some 15,000 Polish prisoners in the Katyn Forest in 1941. The Russians also complained when Allied convoys carrying valuable Lend-Lease supplies to Murmansk had to be suspended because of shipping needs in the Mediterranean and Pacific. In August, 1943 Stalin sent a sharp message to Roosevelt, complaining about the separate peace negotiations that the American and British were conducting with Italy. (The Italians formally surrendered in early September, then declared war against Germany, only to have German forces occupy most of the peninsula before Anglo-American troops could be reinforced.) "To date it has been like this," accused the Soviet leader, "the U.S.A. and Britain reached agreement between themselves while the U.S.S.R. is informed . . . as a third party looking passively on. I must say that this situation cannot be tolerated any longer."[96]

Roosevelt and Churchill did what they could to conciliate their testy ally. The Prime Minister urged the Poles not to protest the Katyn massacre because "nothing you can do will bring them [the dead officers] back."[97] The President expedited

Lend-Lease supplies to Russia without the usual quid pro quo arrangements. Probably the most controversial attempt to reassure the Russians came at the Casablanca Conference in January, 1943, when Roosevelt announced that "the elimination of German, Japanese, and Italian war power means the unconditional surrender by Germany, Italy, and Japan." He added, "it does not mean the destruction of the population [of these countries], but it does mean the destruction of the philosophies in those countries."[98] Coming shortly after the so-called Darlan Deal, wherein the Anglo-Americans made an agreement with the Vichy French collaborator Admiral Jean-François Darlan to gain French cooperation in North Africa, Roosevelt's "unconditional surrender" announcement was meant as a signal to a suspicious Stalin that England and the United States would not make a separate peace with one of Hitler's subordinates. Although the doctrine may have encouraged German soldiers to fight harder, as Eisenhower later claimed, its enunciation brought a modicum of Allied unity by concentrating on a total military victory over Hitler, deferring troublesome peace terms until afterward. As long as the United States had to rely on Soviet troops in Europe, however, FDR was in no position to confront the Soviets over political issues like the Polish border.

The Russians became less contentious in late August, 1943, and called for a Big Three foreign ministers' conference in Moscow. Stalin apparently feared that the Italian surrender might bring the Anglo-Americans quickly into Central Europe at a time when, with postwar boundaries unsettled, the advancing Russian armies were still six hundred miles from the 1941 frontiers. The foreign ministers' meeting in Moscow (October 19–30) established an Advisory Council for Italy to coordinate Allied policy and a European Advisory Commission to make recommendations for a final peace settlement. The conferees also called for "a free and independent Austria." The Russians told Secretary of State Cordell Hull that the 200,000 American battle casualties were insignificant—"we lose that many each day before lunch. You haven't got your teeth in the war yet."[99] Hull in turn lectured Commissar for Foreign Affairs V. M. Molotov against gobbling up neighbors: "When I was young I knew a bully in Tennessee. He used to get a few things his way by being a bully and bluffing other fellows. But he ended up by not having a friend in the world."[100] The high point for the ill, seventy-two-year-old Hull, who was "almost mystical in his approach," was a Declaration of Four Nations on General Security (China was included).[101] This was the first definite statement about a postwar replacement for the defunct League of Nations. Hull thereafter exulted to Congress rather naively that "there will no longer be need for spheres of influence, for alliances, for balance of power, or any other of the special arrangements through which, in the unhappy past, the nations strove to safeguard their security and promote their interests."[102]

Moscow seemed a mere appetizer for the first Big Three summit meeting at Teheran, Iran, November 28–December 1, 1943. "The eternal triangle is perhaps as much a threat to politicians as it is to lovers," historian Warren F. Kimball has written, and Teheran proved it as far as the Churchill-Roosevelt relationship was concerned.[103] Meeting the moustachioed Russian leader for the first time, FDR came away from an early conversation thinking Stalin "very confident, very sure of himself, moves slowly—altogether quite impressive, I'd say."[104] At the first plenary session, as an American Army Air Force general recalled, "Uncle Joe had talked straight from the shoulder about how to carry on the war against Germany," telling Churchill and Roosevelt that he favored a firm commitment to OVERLORD as

Major Wartime Conferences, 1941–1945

Conference	Date	Participants	Results
Argentia, Newfoundland	August 9–12, 1941	Roosevelt, Churchill	Atlantic Charter
Washington, D.C.	December 22, 1941– Jan. 14, 1942	Roosevelt, Churchill	Combined Chiefs of Staff; priority in war effort against Germany; United Nations Declaration
Washington, D.C.	June 19–25, 1942	Roosevelt, Churchill	North African campaign strategy
Moscow, USSR	August 12–15, 1942	Churchill, Stalin, Harriman	Postponement of Second Front
Casablanca, Morocco	January 14–24, 1943	Roosevelt, Churchill	Unconditional surrender announcement; campaign against Sicily and Italy
Washington, D.C.	May 12–25, 1943	Roosevelt, Churchill	Schedule for cross-channel landing set as May 1, 1944
Quebec, Canada	August 14–24, 1943	Roosevelt, Churchill	Confirmation of cross-channel landing (OVERLORD); Southeast Asia Command established
Moscow, USSR	October 19–30, 1943	Hull, Eden, Molotov	Postwar international organization to be formed; Russian promise to enter the war against Japan after Germany's defeat; establishment of European Advisory Commission
UNRRA, Washington, D.C.	November 9, 1943	44 nations	Creation of UNRRA
Cairo, Egypt	November 22–26, 1943	Roosevelt, Churchill, Jiang Jieshi	Postwar Asia: China to recover lost lands; Korea to be independent; Japan to be stripped of Pacific Islands
Teheran, Iran	November 27–December 1, 1943	Roosevelt, Churchill, Stalin	Agreement on cross-channel landing and international organization; Soviet reaffirmation of entry into war against Japan
Bretton Woods, New Hampshire	July 1–22, 1944	44 nations	Creation of World Bank and International Monetary Fund
Dumbarton Oaks, Washington, D.C.	August 21–Oct. 7, 1944	U.S., Britain, USSR, China	United Nations Organization
Quebec, Canada	Sept. 11–16, 1944	Roosevelt, Churchill	"Morgenthau Plan" for Germany
Moscow, USSR	October 9–18, 1944	Churchill, Stalin	Spheres of influence in Balkans (percentage scheme)
Yalta, USSR	February 4–11, 1945	Roosevelt, Churchill, Stalin	Polish governmental structure, elections, and boundaries; United Nations; German reparations; USSR pledge to declare war against Japan and to recognize Chiang's government; Asian territories to USSR
San Francisco, California	April 25–June 26, 1945	50 nations	United Nations Organization Charter
Potsdam (Berlin), Germany	July 16–August 2, 1945	Truman, Churchill/ Attlee, Stalin	German reconstruction and reparations; Potsdam Declaration to Japan; Council of Foreign Ministers established

opposed to any Anglo-American operations in the Balkans.[105] When Churchill persisted in cataloguing the advantages of an Adriatic landing, Stalin broke in with a blunt question: "Do the British really believe in OVERLORD or are they only saying so to reassure the Russians?" Churchill lamely retorted that "it was the duty of the British Government to hurl every scrap of strength across the channel."[106] At a dinner party two nights later Stalin playfully baited Churchill further by calling for the summary execution of 50,000 German officers. The Prime Minister protested that the British would "never tolerate mass executions."[107] Roosevelt interceded by joking that only 49,000 should be shot. Churchill walked out in a huff. As General Marshall recalled, Stalin "was turning the hose on Churchill all the time, and Mr. Roosevelt, in a sense, was helping him."[108]

At Teheran, Roosevelt refused to meet with Churchill alone lest the Russians suspect an Anglo-American deal. Yet the President had three conferences à *deux* with Stalin. FDR called for an international organization to be dominated by the "Four Policemen," who would deal immediately with any threat to the peace. Stalin commented that Europe might not like domination by the "Four Policemen," and that China was too weak to be of much use as a policeman. He suggested two regional committees—in Europe, the Big Three and one other power, and in Asia, the Big Three and China. The President also told Stalin that the United States would supply only air and naval support in the event of a crisis in postwar Europe; troops would have to come from Britain and Russia. The Russian agreed with Roosevelt that the future United Nations Organization "should be world-wide and not regional" and that France should be treated as an inconsequential power in the postwar world.[109]

The subjects of Eastern Europe and Germany also came up. Earlier in the conference Churchill, pushing three matchsticks, had proposed moving Poland's boundaries a considerable distance to the west, incorporating German lands. Polish territory in the east would be transferred to the Soviets for the security of their western frontier. Roosevelt told Stalin that he acquiesced in these plans for Poland, but he could not "publicly take part in any such arrangement at the present time." The election of 1944 loomed ahead, and FDR, "as a practical man," did not want to risk losing the votes of six to seven million Polish-Americans. Roosevelt mentioned that there were also many Americans of Lithuanian, Latvian, and Estonian origin who wanted the right of self-determination in the Baltic states. Stalin bristled. Those states, he insisted, were part of the Soviet Union. Roosevelt replied that the American people "neither knew nor understood." Stalin shot back that they "should be informed and some propaganda work should be done."[110] But in the remaining months of the war the President never tried to explain publicly the differences between the Atlantic Charter and Russian desires for security in Eastern Europe. On the subject of Germany, Stalin said he favored dismemberment. Roosevelt suggested the division of Germany into five autonomous regions and international control of the Ruhr and Kiel Canal. "To use an American expression, the President has said a mouthful," observed a disconcerted Churchill, who then proposed a solution that reduced Prussia to impotence and linked the rest of Germany to Austria and Hungary in a Danubian confederation.[111] Stalin objected to Churchill's plan, saying that all Germans, not just the Prussians, fought like devils. Specific postwar plans for Germany were recommended for future consideration.

Even though many of the discussions were inconclusive, the Americans were pleased with Teheran, especially because Stalin had confirmed a previous promise to Secretary Hull that, once Hitler was defeated, Russia would help the United States defeat Japan. In response to this good news, Roosevelt suggested that the Russians might be rewarded with a Chinese "free port" at Dairen. Stalin's preference for OVERLORD instead of a Balkans operation also gratified the American joint chiefs and seemed to clinch their position in the interminable debate with the British. General sentiment in favor of a peace dictated by the big powers, an international organization, and a weakened postwar Germany represented important Allied cohesion. Roosevelt was also impressed when Stalin paid tribute to Lend-Lease and the United States manufacture of 10,000 aircraft a month: "Without these planes from America the war would have been lost."[112] At a Teheran dinner in celebration of Churchill's sixty-ninth birthday, Roosevelt toasted the Big Three: "We can see in the sky, for the first time, that traditional symbol of hope, the rainbow." Churchill drank to "Stalin the Great." Stalin hailed his "fighting friend Churchill," adding one last jibe, "if it is possible for me to consider Churchill my friend."[113] On his return to Washington the President optimistically told a national radio audience: "I 'got along fine' with Marshal Stalin. . . . I believe that we are going to get along very well with him and the Russian people—very well indeed."[114] The Grand Alliance had temporarily closed some of its fissures.

Problem Client: China and the War in Asia

When Winston Churchill journeyed to Washington in December, 1941 to discuss grand strategy, he was astonished at "a standard of values which . . . rated the Chinese armies as a factor to be mentioned in the same breath as the armies of Russia."[115] America's romanticized infatuation with China, its support for the Open Door, the false image of Jiang Jieshi as a democratic leader—all had persisted in American policy during the months before Pearl Harbor. Some Americans, President Roosevelt included, even envisioned a strong, united China as a postwar client of the United States. China's military importance soon diminished, however, as Japanese victories in early 1942 sent the British and Americans reeling. The fall of Burma in May closed the last remaining land route to Generalissimo Jiang Jieshi's capital at Chongqing. Thereafter the only way to send supplies was by flying them over the "hump" of the Himalayas. And given available resources and military priorities, "hump" transport was pitifully small—less than one hundred tons a month during the summer of 1942. The Americans wanted to keep China in the war, yet Roosevelt could not send troops because they were needed elsewhere. He sent General Stilwell instead.

Joseph W. Stilwell was fifty-eight years old when he arrived in Chongqing with the impressive titles of Chief of Staff to Generalissimo Jiang Jieshi and Commanding General of the United States Forces in India, Burma, and China. An aggressive soldier, "diplomacy was not his long suit."[116] As a junior officer he had served two tours of duty in China, had become fluent in Chinese, and had developed great admiration for the Chinese people. But he thought Jiang an untrustworthy scoundrel. Blunt to reporters, Stilwell was even blunter in his diary, where he referred to Jiang as "the Peanut," the British as "pigfuckers," and President Roosevelt as "just a lot of wind."[117] "Vinegar Joe's" principal task in Chongqing was to train and equip Chinese divisions. With these modernized forces, plus British help from India, Stilwell planned to reopen Burma, increase supplies to China, and thus make the mainland the staging point for the final invasion of Japan.

Stilwell's plans for military reform cut at the core of Jiang Jieshi's power structure. The general sputtered in his diary: "Why doesn't the little dummy [Jiang] realize that his only hope is the 30-division plan, and the creation of a separate, efficient, well-equipped, and well-trained force?"[118] In actuality, most of Jiang's armies were controlled by twelve commanders, virtually autonomous warlords whose loyalties were manipulated by the Generalissimo in masterful Byzantine fashion. Jiang wanted Stilwell's equipment, but not his advice. Nor did the Chinese leader want to commit his own forces to battle. Perhaps 500,000 of the Guomindang's best troops were blockading the Communists in Yan'an. Jiang wanted to wait out the war, play one barbarian off against the other, and then muster his strength for the final showdown with Mao Zedong. He would not fight in Burma unless the British and Americans gave more support. Much to Stilwell's chagrin, the "hump" tonnage that Washington promised came in trickles, and the British continually balked at a Burma campaign. "That China is one of the world's four great powers is an absolute farce," said Churchill privately, as he pushed for higher Anglo-American priorities in the Mediterranean.[119] Shortly after the landings in North Africa, Stilwell described his strategic dilemma bitterly: "Peanut and I are on a raft, with one sandwich between us, and the rescue ship is heading away from the scene."[120]

President Roosevelt urged a more conciliatory diplomacy toward China. He warned that Jiang was "the Chief Executive as well as the Commander-in-Chief, and one cannot speak sternly to a man like that or exact commitments from him the way we might do from the Sultan of Morocco."[121] To Chongqing the President sent a stream of personal emissaries to buoy up Chinese morale and listen to complaints about Stilwell. Jiang was given a half-billion dollar loan in 1942, and in January, 1943, the State Department negotiated a treaty abolishing the American right of extraterritoriality in China. The following month Roosevelt hosted Madame Jiang Jieshi at the White House; the immaculately attired Wellesley College alumna also addressed Congress, where she was received as enthusiastically as Churchill. At the Cairo Conference in November, 1943, Churchill and Roosevelt met with Jiang and formally pledged the return of all Japanese-held territories after the war. In December Congress repealed the exclusion laws, which had prohibited Chinese immigration. Roosevelt talked confidently of postwar China, one of his "Four Policemen" to keep the peace. Such sentiment derived partly from sincerity, partly from a felt need to compensate China for wartime neglect, and partly from the assumption that the Chinese would be grateful to the United States. As historian Warren Cohen has written, "Roosevelt was almost Oriental in his attempts to give Chiang [Jiang] 'face' when he could not or would not give anything more substantial."[122]

Roosevelt also endorsed a plan of General Claire Lee Chennault. The organizer of the famed "Flying Tiger" volunteers boasted that with 105 fighters and 42 bombers he could "destroy the effectiveness of the Japanese Air Force" and thereby achieve "the downfall of Japan."[123] Building up air forces in China did not require large numbers, nor did it disturb Jiang's juggling act, so Roosevelt gave the older flyer the wares. The result was near disaster. As Stilwell and Marshall had predicted, when Chennault's bombers began to draw blood in the spring of 1944, Japanese armies launched a massive counterattack and nearly overran all the

The Cairo Conference. Jiang Jieshi, FDR, Churchill, and Madame Jiang pose for photographers at the Cairo Conference of November, 1943, where they agreed that China would be restored territorially after the war. (Franklin D. Roosevelt Library)

American air bases. Jiang then balked at fighting. This time Roosevelt made the extraordinary proposal that Jiang give Stilwell unrestricted command of all forces, Chinese and foreign, in China. The Generalissimo stalled for two months; then Roosevelt sent an ultimatum that Stilwell gleefully delivered in person. "Mark this day in red on the calendar of life," he wrote in his diary on September 19, 1944. "A hot firecracker. I handed this bundle of paprika to the Peanut and then sank back with a sigh. The harpoon hit the little bugger right in the solar plexus, and went right through him."[124] Jiang was never to forgive Stilwell for such a personal humiliation. The vain Chinese leader's reply to Roosevelt hinted that he might accept some other American in command of Chinese forces, but not Stilwell. The President, after some hesitation, decided to replace his unpopular commander. By the autumn of 1944, following the Navy's capture of the Marianas and MacArthur's landings in the Philippines, the likelihood that China would play a major role in the defeat of Japan seemed minimal. The Russians had promised at Teheran that they would enter the Pacific war after the defeat of Hitler, and Roosevelt was counting on Soviet armies, not Chinese, to neutralize Japanese forces on the mainland. It was better not to antagonize an ally by insisting on Stilwell.

Enter General Patrick J. Hurley, a sixty-one-year-old Oklahoma Republican sent by Roosevelt to facilitate Stilwell's appointment as full commander. Actually the Generalissimo persuaded Hurley to support Stilwell's recall. Hurley then became the American ambassador, in November, 1944, replacing Clarence Gauss, a career diplomat known for his disdain toward the corruption in Jiang's government. In his own way every bit as much a bull in the china shop as Stilwell had been, Hurley concentrated his energies on forming a coalition between Jiang's government and the Communists. The Americans had sent an "Observer Mission" to Yan'an in July, 1944, and its members liked what they saw. Using guerrilla tactics, the People's Liberation Army had achieved successes against the Japanese, in marked contrast to the inaction of Jiang's forces. Morale seemed excellent, and Mao's followers possessed a remarkable intelligence network extending behind Japanese lines. One downed American pilot was able to hike more than a thousand miles from eastern Hebei to Yan'an with the aid of "Red" guides. Mao Zedong, Zhou Enlai, and other Communist leaders welcomed the American observers and requested direct military aid. The Communist revolutionary leadership, according

The United States Pushes Japan Back 1942-1945

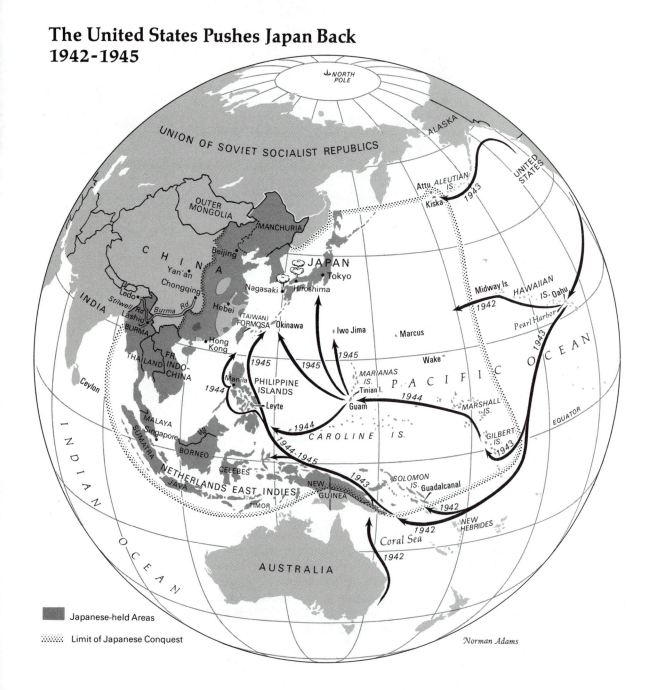

Japanese-held Areas

Limit of Japanese Conquest

Norman Adams

General Patrick J. Hurley (1883–1963) in Yan'an, China. At Communist headquarters, the rambunctious anti-Communist ambassador to China met with Mao
Zedong, Lin Zehao, Zhu De (Chu Teh), and Zhou Enlai (left to right) in his vain effort
to create a coalition government. The time was November, 1944. (Western History
Collections, University of Oklahoma Library)

to Foreign Service Officer John S. Service in October, 1944, "has improved the
political, economic and social status of the peasant. . . . As the Japanese cannot
defeat these forces of the people, neither can the Kuomintang. . . . The Communists are certain to play a large, if not dominant, part in China's future."[125] This
belief—that the Communists might win in a postwar struggle for power—was
widespread among Americans in China, and so Hurley had unified support for his
initial attempts at coalition.

The "Genbassador's" first visit to Communist Yan'an, in November, 1944, was a
grand spectacle. Hurley alighted from his plane "with enough ribbons on his chest
to represent every war . . . in which the United States had ever engaged except
possibly Shays' Rebellion."[126] Then he completely discombobulated Zhou Enlai
by letting out Choctaw war whoops. Later, after the Communists rejected Jiang's
offer of a virtually worthless seat on the National Military Council in return for
merging the Yan'an army under Nationalist control, Hurley accepted Mao's coun-
terproposal for full coalition and a Communist sharing in Lend-Lease supplies.
Back in Chongqing, however, Jiang continued to insist on merger of the two
armies without real coalition, and Hurley seemed to acquiesce. Mao exploded,
calling Jiang and Hurley "turtle eggs," whereupon Hurley called Mao a
"mother——" who "tricked meh!"[127]

At this point Hurley began to diverge markedly from his subordinates, including
the young Foreign Service Officers. Without ever having been so instructed by
either Roosevelt or the State Department, the ambassador decided that his mission
was not to mediate, but rather to "sustain" Jiang Jieshi and "to prevent the
collapse of the Nationalist government."[128] The Communists would undoubtedly
come to terms eventually. Hurley was encouraged in these beliefs by an earlier

visit to Moscow in August, 1944, when Molotov had told him that the Chinese Communists "had no relation whatever to Communism" and the Russians would support Jiang Jieshi.[129] The other Americans in China (representatives of the Army, Office of Strategic Services, and Treasury, as well as Foreign Service Officers) knew that Mao's followers were agrarian-based Communists, and they feared that if the United States denied him aid, Mao would obtain assistance from Moscow and thus create a postwar squabble between the United States and Russia over China. Contrary to Hurley, these "China hands" believed that the rifts between the Communists and Guomindang were deep and long-standing, and that the only way to obtain unity was to pressure Jiang Jieshi by dealing with Yan'an separately. Preliminary talks had already begun in Yan'an, and on January 9, 1945, the head of the American Military Observers Mission cabled that "Mao and Zhou will be immediately available either singly or together for exploratory conference at Washington should President Roosevelt express desire to receive them at White House as leaders of a primary Chinese party."[130] Hurley ignored his staff, and when Guomindang-Communist negotiations stalled, he became convinced that disloyal subordinates were undermining his position by encouraging the Communists. He quickly blocked any meeting between Mao and Roosevelt. "You want me to pull the plug on Chiang Kai-shek," he bellowed to his startled embassy assistant, John Paton Davies.[131]

The predictable explosion occurred when Hurley returned to Washington in February, 1945 for consultations following the Yalta Conference, where Roosevelt had made concessions to Stalin regarding China without consultation with the Guomindang government. In Hurley's absence, the embassy officers at Chongqing sent a long telegram to Washington urging the President to "inform Chiang Kai-shek in definite terms that we are required by military necessity to cooperate with and supply the Communists and other suitable groups who can aid in this war against the Japanese."[132] These young "China hands" did not know that Stalin had reaffirmed Russian entry into the Japanese war at Yalta and, accordingly, that the military rationale for a Guomindang-Communist coalition now became less urgent. Hurley roared like a wounded lion when he read the telegram. He stormed about Washington telling all who would listen that his subordinates were treasonous and that he would get an agreement between Mao and Jiang by April. He called on Roosevelt, then about to take what would be his final journey to Warm Springs, and the weary President gave him what he wanted—unqualified backing for Jiang's regime. The disputatious diplomats, including Service and Davies, were transferred out of China as a frightened State Department kowtowed to the rambunctious ambassador.

Roosevelt's wartime policy toward China exposed the disparity between his military strategy and postwar political goals. When it became obvious in 1944 that China would not play a major role in the Japanese war and hardly deserved rank as one of the "Four Policemen," Roosevelt faced a choice. He could accelerate American military activities in China and press Jiang to undertake the reforms necessary to maintain him in power. Or the President could scale down his political expectations for China and limit his military operations there. In fact, as James MacGregor Burns has pointed out, Roosevelt "tried to do both and ran the risk of succeeding in neither. He kept talking to and about China as a great power even while he was giving higher and higher military priorities to other military theaters."[133] Similarly, when the feud between Hurley and the China hands ignited, Roosevelt chose to drift with existing policy rather than take a hard look at Chinese politics. As happened often, when the smiling squire of New York could not easily resolve dichotomies, he left them to the future. In this case delay raised the ominous prospect of a full-fledged civil war between the Guomindang and the Communists.

Witness to the Holocaust: Americans and the Plight of the European Jews

Another problem left to the future was that of the refugees, hundreds of thousands of them Jews from Nazi-occupied territories. Many sought asylum in the United States. Although most Americans denounced Hitler's drive to preserve the purity of the "Aryan race" through the persecution and extermination of European Jews, translating moral revulsion into policy proved difficult. United States immigration laws, traditional anti-Semitism, the depression, bureaucratic procedures, wartime fear of spies, and domestic politics shaped the timid American response.

The dark story began in 1933 when Hitler initiated his attacks upon "non-Aryans." Throughout the 1930s, they were systematically eliminated from the professions and denied their businesses. In 1935, under the Nuremberg Laws, Jews were stripped of their civil and political rights, in essence becoming stateless beings. Signs reading "whoever buys from a Jew is a traitor" were plastered on buildings.[134] In November, 1938, a young, distraught Jewish boy living in Paris entered the German embassy and shot and killed a German official. He had learned that his parents had been placed in a boxcar for shipment to a concentration camp. Germany erupted in anti-Semitic violence. Several hundred synagogues were sacked and burned; Jews were beaten in the streets; Jewish shops were destroyed. After this *Kristallnacht* or "Night of the Breaking Glass," the German government fined its Jewish subjects $400 million. Fifty thousand Jews were sent to concentration camps at Dachau and Buchenwald, then detention centers later fitted with equipment for extermination. President Roosevelt called the American ambassador home in protest against the blatant persecutions, remarking, "I myself could scarcely believe that such things could occur in a twentieth century civilization."[135]

The brutal events were repeated in Austria, Czechoslovakia, Poland, Hungary, and elsewhere as the Third Reich overran Europe. Americans read about the cruelties in their newspapers. Unprecedented numbers of urgent requests for transit to the United States flooded American embassies and consulates. American immigration law, however, prescribed a quota for each country. Openly discriminatory, the National Origins Act of 1924 was designed to limit immigration from eastern and southern Europe, home, as Congressman J. M. Tincher of Kansas crudely put it, of "Bolshevik Wops, Dagoes, Kikes and Hunkies."[136] The annual quota for Great Britain and Ireland was 83,575, for Germany and Austria 27,370, for Poland 6,000, for Italy 5,500, and for Rumania 300. American consular officers also inhibited easy immigration to the United States from areas overrun by Nazism by strictly enforcing procedures. Potential immigrants had to present as many as fifty pages of documents attesting to their crime-free background, birth, health, and financial status. Many of these papers had to be obtained from Nazi officials. Furthermore, Americans rigidly denied entry to people "likely to become a public charge." This clause meant that persons could gain a place on the quota list only if they proved that they could support themselves once in the United States. Yet under Nazi law Jews could not take their property or savings from Germany. These restrictions, combined with the evaporation of American jobs during the depression, created a revealing statistic for the period 1933–1938: 174,067 people entered the United States and 221,239 departed, or a net *loss* of 47,172. To have opened America's doors to the persecuted abroad, in short, would not have inundated the United States. For a nation of 130 million the admission of several hundred thousand refugees should have been inconsequential.

Not so, said the restrictionists in the interwar years. The American Federation of Labor and patriotic groups lobbied against any revision in the quotas or relaxation of the visa requirements. Foreigners, they argued, should not be permitted to enter the United States to compete with American citizens for scarce jobs—a telling argument during the depression. Long-standing anti-Semitism fed such nativist thought. Father Charles E. Coughlin, the fiery Catholic priest from Michigan, led the anti-Semitic forces. He equated Judaism and communism in his radio broadcasts, which reached 3.5 million listeners a week. Even distinguished diplomat George Messersmith, who was outraged over Hitler and Nazism, opposed the establishment of a University of Exile at the New School for Social Research in New York because he feared that Jews hired there would undermine the basic Anglo-Saxon Protestant nature of American society. Opinion polls in the 1930s revealed that over 80 percent of Americans opposed revision of the quotas to admit European refugees. Although the *New Republic* magazine appealed for "common decency," Congress stood firmly behind the quota system.[137] Roosevelt was sensitive to political realities. Already blistered by charges that his domestic reform program was a "Jew Deal," a label attached because Jews like Henry Morgenthau, Jr. and Felix Frankfurter were prominent in his Administration, the President played it safe. Thwarted in his ill-fated "court-packing" attempt in 1937 and his futile effort to purge conservatives from the Democratic party in 1938, Roosevelt did not wish to risk another political setback. "For God's sake," insisted a congressional spokesman, "don't send us any more controversial legislation!"[138]

Roosevelt left the refugee problem to the Department of State, which "clung to a policy that was timid, rigidly legal, and without innovation."[139] In 1934 the department lobbied successfully against a Senate resolution condemning Germany's treatment of the Jews, fearful that the resolution would spark German comment about the segregation of black Americans. Secretary Hull also opposed boycotts organized by American Jews against German products because such behavior interrupted normal trade channels. Although he did relax enforcement of the "likely to become a public charge" clause, many Jews, caught in circumstances of fear and chaos, still could not obtain the necessary documents. The result: the German-Austrian quota went unfilled in 1933–1938 and 1940–1945; only in 1939 was it filled. For the entire period 1933–1945, only 35.8 percent of the German-Austrian quota was used. Congressman Emanuel Celler of New York thought the State Department a "heartbeat muffled in protocol."[140]

In 1938 Roosevelt called for an international meeting on refugees, which met in Evian, France and established an Intergovernmental Committee on Refugees. No real plans emerged and the committee proved ineffective. Hitler sneered: "It is a shameful example to observe today how the entire democratic world dissolves in tears of pity, but then, in spite of its obvious duty to help, closes its heart to the poor, tortured people."[141] In early 1939 Senator Robert Wagner of New York introduced a bill to allow 20,000 German refugee children to enter above the quota as a "symbol of our faith in the ideals of human brotherhood."[142] The Roosevelt

Administration remained silent. The bill died in committee. In mid-1939 the ship *St. Louis* steamed toward Cuba from Hamburg carrying 930 Jewish refugees. Havana officials, however, would not permit them to land because their visas had not been obtained properly. The ship headed for Miami, tailed by Coast Guard cutters. American immigration officials would not let the passengers disembark. Despite appeals to Washington from concerned American liberals, the *St. Louis* was forced to return to Europe, its passengers ultimately scattered to Britain, the Netherlands, Belgium, and France after refugee societies pressured their governments. "The cruise of the *St. Louis*," editorialized the *New York Times*, "cries to high heaven of man's inhumanity to man."[143]

The plight of Jewish refugees did not improve after the outbreak of war. The State Department actually tightened visa requirements because it feared refugees might include Nazi or Communist spies. American consuls increasingly rejected applications for visas, and ships headed to American shores half empty. Washington tried futilely to persuade Latin American countries to take refugees. When the State Department asked the British to approach Portugal about opening its African colony of Angola, Lord Halifax snapped: "Let the Americans do it."[144] Schemes to provide havens in British Guiana and French Madagascar fell through. Britain also restricted the movement of Jews to Palestine. The record of other countries, in other words, was as bad as that of the United States. In the State Department, refugee questions fell under the authority of Breckinridge Long, a Southern aristocrat, old Wilsonian, former ambassador to Italy, and large financial contributor to the Democratic party. Believing that refugees might become a fifth column of spies in the United States, he and other officials blocked numerous private efforts to save them and actually suppressed information about Hitler's plan to exterminate European Jewry.

In early 1942 reliable evidence reached the State Department that Germany planned to exterminate the entire Jewish population of Europe. The information seemed beyond imagination, too cruel to be true. The thought of Jews being sent by cattle car to extermination camps, gassed, and then burned in crematoria seemed too farfetched. Yet the evidence mounted. After invading Russia in 1941, special German squads rounded up Jews and massacred them. In two days in September, 33,000 were murdered in Kiev. One of the first extermination camps was built at Auschwitz, Poland, where one million people died. At its peak, Auschwitz executed 12,000 people a day. Using Zyklon B gas and large crematoria, German officials competed for efficiency ratings in human destruction. The Jewish ghetto in Warsaw became a target of German barbarity; by the fall of 1942 only 70,000 of its 380,000 residents remained, and they desperately rebelled in the spring of the next year. Italian and Greek Jews were shipped by rail to Auschwitz. Of the ten million Jews who lived in 1939 in areas overrun by the Nazis, an estimated six million had died by the end of the war. Appeals throughout the war years for American planes to bomb the rail lines leading to the death camps and the crematoria went unheeded by the War Department, on the grounds that such diversions would delay victory, itself the best hope for the Jews. Ultimately, two scholars have concluded, "Hitler was able to exult that nobody wanted the Jews and so, since there was nowhere for them to go, he had no option but to destroy them."[145]

In early 1943 representatives of Britain and the United States met in Bermuda to discuss the refugee problem; in essence they reported that they had done all they could to help. After the conference, Hull informed the President: "The unknown cost of moving an undetermined number of persons from an undisclosed place to an unknown destination, a scheme advocated by certain pressure groups, is, of course, out of the question."[146] Hull never sought to solve the unknowns. Secretary of the Treasury Henry Morgenthau, Jr. did. He asked his general counsel, Randolph Paul, to prepare a study of the State Department's handling of the refugee crisis. Paul turned in a *Report to the Secretary on the Acquiescence of This Government in the Murder of the Jews*, a startlingly frank critique of Breckinridge Long and the State Department. "It takes months and months to grant the visa and then it usually applies to a corpse." Morgenthau reported directly to Roosevelt that the rescue of Jews "is a trust too great to remain in the hands of men indifferent, callous and perhaps hostile."[147] In January, 1944, the President created the War Refugee Board, outside the auspices of the State Department. Using private and public funds, board operatives established refugee camps in Italy, Morocco, Hungary, Italy, Sweden, Palestine, and Switzerland. Thousands were saved from the gas chambers. Still, the War Refugee Board had come too late, eleven years after Hitler's first efforts to persecute the Jews. Cordell Hull, after leaving office, could accurately say that "President Roosevelt at no time complained to me that the Department had not done enough."[148] The quota system lasted until 1965. In

Freeing Prisoners at the Wobbelin Concentration Camp. This prisoner near Berlin escaped the ghastly mass murder perpetrated by the Third Reich. (U.S. Office of War Information)

large measure the Jewish refugees themselves took command of their survival after the war by leading the "exodus" to Palestine and creating the new nation of Israel in 1948.

Planning for the Postwar Peace, 1943–1945

American leaders began thinking about the contours of the postwar world early in the war. Interdepartmental committees identified potential problems and suggested courses of action. Determined that never again would isolationism, economic depression, and war threaten American interests, the United States cooperated with other nations to devise a number of international organizations to secure peace and prosperity. The oft-repeated principles of the Atlantic Charter provided useful guides, but, as always, principles were modified in practice and after compromise. During 1943–1945 the United Nations Relief and Rehabilitation Administration (UNRRA), World Bank, International Monetary Fund, and United Nations Organization took form. Unlike World War I, this time the establishment of postwar institutions would not await the grand deliberations of one conference. Nor would plans to reform Germany.

On November 9, 1943, at the White House, forty-four nations signed the UNRRA Agreement to plan and administer "measures for the relief of victims of war . . . through the provision of food, fuel, clothing, shelter and other basic necessities, medical and other essential services."[149] The humanitarian relief program would, said a State Department official, help create "a more stable world order."[150] Some leaders feared that the millions of hungry displaced people might, in desperation, turn to political extremes like communism. Food and medicine would help stem postwar political chaos. The Department of State successfully insisted throughout the negotiations that an American be named head of UNRRA. In existence until mid-1947, UNRRA enjoyed a budget of $4 billion, $2.7 billion of which was donated by the United States. UNRRA dispensed nine million tons of food, built hundreds of hospitals, administered medicine to prevent epidemics of diphtheria, typhoid, cholera, and venereal disease, revived transportation systems, and cared for over one million displaced persons. China, Italy, Greece, and Austria absorbed about half of UNRRA's assistance. The other half was spent in Poland, other Eastern European nations, and the Soviet Union. Therein lay American criticism after the war that American money was being spent through an international organization to shore up Communist governments. In fact, UNRRA tried to avoid politics and to help anybody who was destitute, whether that person lived in a Communist country or not. As part of American foreign aid, however, food was expected to bring political returns. When it did not, Washington killed UNRRA in 1947 by cutting off funds.

Two other organizations proved more permanent. From July 1 to 22, 1944, the delegates of forty-four nations negotiated at Bretton Woods in the scenic White Mountains of New Hampshire. Working from an Anglo-American proposal, the conferees created the International Bank for Reconstruction and Development or World Bank and the International Monetary Fund. The World Bank was designed to extend loans to "assist in the reconstruction and development" of members, to "promote private investment," and to "promote the long-range balanced growth of international trade."[151] The fund was designed to grease world trade by stabilizing the international system of payments through currency loans. "The question," Senator Robert Wagner of New York declared in support of the Bretton Woods agreements, "is whether by default we allow the world to repeat the tragic blunders of the 1920s and 1930s."[152] After much debate, with critics worried about America's possible loss of sovereignty to international organizations, Congress passed the Bretton Woods Agreements Act in July of 1945.

From the start the two organizations were dominated by the economic power of the United States. They were located in Washington, D.C., top posts went to Americans (an American has been president of the World Bank since its formation), and the United States possessed one-third of the votes in the bank by subscribing $3.175 billion of the total of $9.100 billion. The United States also held one-third of the votes in the fund. As payer of the "piper," complained the *Manchester Guardian,* the United States would "call the tune."[153] Britain begrudged American control but joined. Although Russia attended the Bretton Woods Conference, it did not join the bank or fund, because the Soviets practiced state-controlled trade and finance, feared having to divulge economic data, and could not accept the emphasis on "private" enterprise or the American domination. Russia's absence did not prove disruptive, but it augured poorly for postwar Allied cooperation.

From August to October, 1944, representatives of the United States, Britain, Russia, and China met in the handsome Georgetown mansion at Dumbarton Oaks in Washington, D.C. Cordell Hull had been tooling up for this conference since early in the war. Public opinion polls indicated that Americans strongly endorsed a new world organization, and Congress had passed favorable resolutions. Roosevelt had spoken of the "Four Policemen" as guardians of the peace, and at the conference the American delegation helped shape the United Nations Organization (UN) under this concept. The Big Four, with considerable unanimity, hammered out the UN's preliminary charter, providing for a powerful Security Council dominated by the great powers and a weak General Assembly. The Security Council, empowered to use force to settle crises, had five permanent members. When the United States pushed China as a permanent member, Britain proposed France. Churchill had protested that China was not a world power, but a "faggot vote on the side of the United States."[154] Russia, after some grumbling, accepted both China and France, feeling secure in the veto power that each permanent member of the Security Council possessed.

Two issues dogged the conferees: the voting procedure in the Security Council and membership in the Assembly. Russia advocated an absolute veto for permanent members, whereas the United States argued that parties to a conflict should not be in a position to veto discussion or action. The issue was left unsettled. (At the Yalta Conference in early 1945 the Allies agreed to a compromise whereby the veto could not be used for procedural questions but could be applied to substantive questions like economic or military sanctions.) As for membership in the Assembly, Russia at Dumbarton Oaks boldly requested seats for all sixteen Soviet republics. That outlandish request derived from Moscow's fear of being badly outnumbered in the Assembly by the British Commonwealth "bloc" and the United States–Latin American "bloc." The Soviet Union, like Britain and the United States, was playing the great power game. The participants decided to defer the question. (At Yalta a compromise of three Soviet votes in the Assembly was struck.) The President declared that 90 percent of the issues at Dumbarton Oaks had been resolved: "Well, that is what we used to call in the old days a darn good batting average."[155]

During the Dumbarton Oaks Conference, Republican presidential candidate Thomas Dewey scored the meeting for subjecting "the nations of the world, great and small, permanently to the coercive power" of the Big Four.[156] Secretary Hull angrily disagreed and managed to dissuade Dewey from further political attacks on the fledgling United Nations Organization. That nonpartisanship, and the inclusion of senators in the Dumbarton Oaks delegation, helped the Roosevelt Administration build its case for the UN with the American people. There would be no Wilsonian League of Nations fiasco this time. Still, some critics wondered how cohesive the new institution would be. One compared the members to marbles in a dish: "put your toe on the dish and the marbles will scatter, each to its own corner."[157] A sign that the advocates, not the critics, would dominate the subsequent debate over American membership in the United Nations came on January 10, 1945, in the Senate. Influential Arthur H. Vandenberg of Michigan, an arch prewar isolationist who was expected to insist on reservations much as Lodge had a generation earlier, delivered a stunning speech urging resuscitation of the Atlantic Charter and American participation in collective security as a curb on aggression—presumably he meant the Soviet variety. Furthermore, he advised the major Allies to sign a security treaty to keep the Axis nations permanently demilitarized; he hoped thereby to allay Soviet fears of a revived Germany and hence render Soviet expansion unnecessary. Vandenberg could accept American membership in the United Nations Organization, because "this is anything but a wild-eyed internationalist dream of a world State. . . . I am deeply impressed (and surprised) to find Hull so carefully guarding our American veto in his scheme of things."[158]

Roosevelt rewarded the vain Vandenberg for his support by naming him a delegate to the San Francisco Conference of April 25–June 26, 1945. Before that meeting, Russia had soured on the new international organization—in part because the provisional pro-Communist government of Poland had not been invited. Just before Roosevelt died on April 12, he appealed to Stalin to send Commissar Molotov to the San Francisco conference as a sign of Soviet seriousness. When Stalin expressed his sadness over the President's death, he also indicated that Molotov would travel to San Francisco. However, the new President, short-tempered Harry S Truman, who had become angry over Soviet manipulation in Poland, exploded that "if the Russians did not wish to join us they could go to hell."[159]

The new secretary of state after Hull's retirement on November 27, 1944, Edward R. Stettinius, Jr., managed the conference in the elegant setting of the San Francisco Opera House. "The Conference opens today—with Russian clouds in every sky," Vandenberg noted in his diary. "I don't know whether this is Frisco or Munich."[160] The 282 delegates did not make decisions without prior approval of the representatives of the big powers, who met each evening in Stettinius' penthouse at the Fairmont Hotel. Still, controversy marred the lofty mood of the conference. The United States again refused to admit Poland, because its government had not been reorganized as required by Yalta. But then the American delegation shocked the conferees by asking for participation by Argentina, which had only declared war against Germany in March. Molotov considered the government in Buenos Aires fascist and thought it "incomprehensible" that Poland

United Nations Symbol. A sign for a postwar peace yet unrealized. (United Nations)

would be refused entry and Argentina admitted.[161] The United States, believing that the Latin American republics would not vote for three Soviet seats in the Assembly unless Argentina were included, would not relent. By the lopsided vote of 32 to 4, with 10 abstentions, Argentina was seated.

Journalist Walter Lippmann detected an American "steamroller" at San Francisco.[162] So did Russia, which objected in blunt language. And so did smaller states, which protested their isolation from key decisions and their impotence in the new United Nations Organization. Fifteen nations abstained, for example, in the vote on the veto formula. The UN Charter, as finally adopted, included the Economic and Social Council and the Trusteeship Council. The latter looked to the eventual independence of colonial areas, but left the British and French empires intact and permitted the United States to absorb former Japanese-dominated islands in the Pacific (Marianas, Carolines, and Marshalls). *Time* magazine aptly termed the United Nations "a charter for a world of power."[163] Indeed, that characterization was evident not only in the veto provision, but in Article 51, which permitted regional alliances such as that the United States and Latin America outlined in the Act of Chapultepec in March. The United States, as War Department official John J. McCloy observed, would "have our cake and eat it too"— freedom of action in the western hemisphere and an international organization to curb aggression in Europe.[164] Amidst memories of 1919, the Senate debated the UN Charter. Senator Tom Connally of Texas, a delegate at San Francisco, thundered: "They know that the League of Nations was slaughtered here in this chamber. Can't you see the blood?—there it is on the wall."[165] The Senate approved the charter on July 28, 1945, by a vote of 89 to 2.

While these plans for the victors unfolded, American officials debated plans for the defeated. The debate over Germany centered on a "constructive" policy (rehabilitation, economic unity, and integration into the European economy) or a "corrective" policy (strict reduction in industry, large reparations, and a decentralized economy).[166] At the center of the controversy stood Secretary of the

"Uncle Sam Pulls the Lever at the UN." Many foreign commentators believed that the United States dominated the new United Nations Organization. (*Ta Kung Pao* of Shanghai–Hong Kong in *United Nations World,* 1951)

Treasury Henry Morgenthau, Jr. As in the case of the refugee problem, Morgenthau stepped outside normal jurisdictional boundaries and proposed a "corrective" plan designed to despoil Germany of industries having potential military value. In early September, 1944 he had informed Roosevelt that the coal- and iron-rich Ruhr area, "the heart of German industrial power," should be stripped of industry.[167] The President introduced this idea at the Quebec Conference of September 12–16, 1944, where he gained Churchill's reluctant signature to a memorandum: "This programme for eliminating the war-making industries in the Ruhr and in the Saar is looking forward to converting Germany into a country primarily agricultural and pastoral in its character."[168] Apparently a bargain was struck at Quebec, wherein Churchill approved the Morgenthau scheme in exchange for the promise of a postwar American loan.

Back in Washington, however, critics lambasted the "Morgenthau Plan." Secretaries Hull and Stimson opposed a harsh economic peace because Germany was the vital center to a revived Western European economy. "Sound thinking teaches that prosperity in one part of the world helps to create prosperity in other parts of the world," Stimson advised Roosevelt. "It also teaches that poverty in one part of the world induces poverty in other parts."[169] Germany had to be revived to encourage postwar prosperity. Using his special access to the President, Morgenthau persuaded Roosevelt in late September to approve an interim Joint Chiefs of Staff directive (JSC/1067), the final version of which came in April, 1945. JCS/1067 ordered programs of denazification and demilitarization, the dismantling of iron, steel, and chemical industries, a controlled economy, and limited rehabilitation. The new President, Harry S Truman, however, thought "Morgenthau didn't know sh— from apple butter" and began a gradual retreat from the Morgenthau Plan and JCS/1067, especially after easing Morgenthau out of office in July of 1945.[170] By the end of the war, then, American plans for postwar Germany remained unsettled.

The Yalta Conference

Near the end of the European war Churchill, Roosevelt, and Stalin met once again, this time at the Livadia Palace near Yalta in the Crimea. The Prime Minister penned a ditty: "No more let us falter! From Malta to Yalta! Let nobody alter!"[171] Meeting from February 4 to 11, 1945, the Big Three, after considerable compromise, made important decisions for the war against the Axis and for the postwar configuration of international affairs, the Yalta "system." After the conclave, Yalta aroused heated controversy akin to the Munich Conference. To later critics, Yalta symbolized a "sell-out" to—or appeasement of—the Soviets, an example of Roosevelt's coddling of the Communist menace. Roosevelt was tired, worn low by the illness that would take his life two months later. His physical weakness and his propensity for personal diplomacy, argued detractors, subjected him to the temptations of a guileful Stalin. But Roosevelt's poor health did not decide the outcome at Yalta. Nor did the presence of Alger Hiss. Later convicted of perjury and denounced by right-wing anti-Communists as a spy for Moscow, Hiss seemed to them an insidious agent of the Communist conspiracy, who undermined American interests. Although at Yalta Hiss was an adviser on questions of international organization, no evidence exists that he influenced Roosevelt or the results of the conference. Other critics have complained that Roosevelt ignored the rights of weak nations like China and Poland, went into sessions unprepared, and failed to use superior American economic and military might to force Soviet concessions. Many of the agreements, furthermore, were secret at the time. Above all else, Yalta became a topic of acrimony because the agreements, cast in vague language, ultimately broke down.

The Big Three entered the conference with different goals. Britain sought a zone in Germany for France, a curb on Soviet expansion into Poland, and protection of the British Empire. Russia wanted reparations to rebuild the devastated Soviet economy, possessions in Asia, a Soviet-influenced Poland, and a Germany so weakened that it could never again march eastward. The United States wanted the United Nations as an institution for postwar world order and American influence, a Russian declaration of war against Japan, a reduction of the Communist presence in Poland, and elevation of China to big power status. Each participant suspected the others' intentions. But, "although the Great Powers differed in their initial viewpoints," historian Diane Shaver Clemens has noted, "a high incidence of consensus was reached at the Conference."[172]

The "consensus" at Yalta was determined not only by a willingness to reconcile differences, but also by the military and diplomatic realities of the moment. Anglo-American troops were bogged down in the Battle of the Bulge in Belgium from mid-December to mid-January, 1945. Churchill had appealed to Stalin to take pressure off the Western Front by stepping up the Russian winter offensive in the east. Russia obliged on January 12. "I am most grateful to you for your thrilling message," a relieved Churchill wrote Stalin.[173] Throughout 1944 the Red Army had cut deeply into German lines on the Eastern Front. Indeed, by the time of the Yalta Conference, Russian soldiers were sweeping westward along a wide front through Poland, Czechoslovakia, and Hungary, with Rumania already freed from German clutches. Thus, the Russians held a formidable bargaining position at Yalta because of their military exploits.

In the Far East also, military realities shaped diplomatic decisions. Japan was fiercely battling American forces in Luzon and the Marianas, and still had a million soldiers in China, two million in the home islands, and another one million in Manchuria and Korea. Americans were taking heavy losses in planes, ships, and men. Iwo Jima, Okinawa, and the atomic bomb still lay in the future. As historian Forrest C. Pogue has concluded, "all in all, the military backdrop for the Yalta negotiations . . . did not yet afford Roosevelt and Churchill the luxury of renouncing or forgoing Soviet military cooperation in Europe and Asia."[174] The point was conspicuous: as close as victory was, Britain and the United States still needed the Russians to win the war.

The setting itself impressed the conferees with the costs of the war. Gutted buildings, abandoned vehicles, and gnarled railways blotted the snow-blanketed countryside around the resort town on the Black Sea. The villas of bygone dukes and tsars still stood grandly, although Nicholas II's Livadia Palace had been badly looted by the retreating Germans. As hosts for the first tripartite conference held on Russian soil, the Soviets strained to make their guests comfortable, with servants and lavish meals. The only complaints were registered against a paucity of toilets and bathtubs and a plethora of bedbugs. The meetings were generally amicable, although Stalin once became ruffled when he misunderstood that Roosevelt's name for him—"Uncle Joe"—was a term of endearment, not ridicule. Molotov wore his customary stone face, but Stalin, Churchill, and Roosevelt

The Yalta Conference. A physically debilitated President confers with the Prime Minister in uniform at the Yalta Conference, February, 1945. Although FDR was ill (he died two months later), he helped write agreements considered at the time a high point of the wartime alliance and a real hope for a peaceful future. (Franklin D. Roosevelt Library)

debated in good humor and frankness, sharing a desire to maintain the Grand Alliance. Stalin especially beamed over Churchill's spirited and belabored defense of the British Empire.

For Churchill, Poland was "the most urgent reason for the Yalta Conference."[175] Seven of the eight plenary sessions grappled with the Polish issue. "We ought to do something," Roosevelt said, "that will come like a breath of fresh air in the murk that exists at the moment on the Polish question."[176] There were actually two Polish governments. The British and Americans recognized the conservative exiled government in London, led by Stanislas Mikolajczyk. Moscow recognized the Communist-led provisional government in Lublin. Stalin was emphatic that any Polish government must be eastward leaning. He reminded his counterparts at the conference that Soviet security was at stake, that the Polish corridor had been the route of deadly German attacks on Russia twice in this century. He insisted not only on Allied support for the Lublin government, but also on Polish boundaries that gave Poland part of Germany (Oder-Neisse line in the west) and Russia part of Poland (Curzon line in the east). Churchill and Roosevelt opposed a Communist Poland but were in no position to bargain effectively, since Soviet troops occupied much of the country. Churchill fumed: "Poland [must] be mistress in her own house and captain of her soul."[177] What he sought was a pro-British Polish regime. Roosevelt said he had several million Polish voters back home who demanded a more representative Polish government. Stalin, castigating the anti-Sovietism of the conservative London Poles, remained adamant.

Compromises were reached. The Curzon line was temporarily set as the eastern boundary. The Yalta agreement read also that a "more broadly based" government would be created in Poland, that the "Provisional Government which is now functioning in Poland should be therefore reorganized on a broader democratic basis with the inclusion of democratic leaders from Poland itself and from Poles abroad," and that "free and unfettered elections" would be held soon.[178] The Communist Lublin group, then, would serve as the nucleus of the postwar Polish state. Much controversy would surround this language later, for the Americans interpreted it to mean that an altogether new government would develop from the reorganization. "Mr. President," said Chief of Staff William D. Leahy, "this is so elastic that the Russians can stretch it all the way from Yalta to Washington without technically breaking it." "I know, Bill—I know it," responded Roosevelt. "But it's the best I can do for Poland at this time."[179] Churchill swallowed the bitter pill, in part because Stalin assured him that the Soviet Union would not intrude in British-dominated Greece, then suffering from civil war. Compromises on other issues also made the Polish settlement tolerable.

Britain, although not keen about dividing Germany, accepted "dismemberment" so long as its ally France received a zone of occupation. Noting that Roosevelt had said that American troops would not long remain in Europe, Churchill cited France as a bulwark against Germany. Stalin protested: France had hardly fought during the war; indeed, the Vichy government had collaborated with the Germans. But Stalin finally accepted a French zone. On reparations, which the Soviets vigorously demanded, Britain and America hedged. They agreed on German reparations "in kind," but refused to set a figure until Germany's ability to pay was determined. The Big Three stated only that they would *discuss* in the future the amount of $20 billion, half of which would go to Russia. Stalin probably assumed that the United States and Britain would henceforth support the $10 billion figure.

Further compromises were struck over the Far East. The American military and the President wanted Soviet participation in the war against Japan. Anticolonialist that he was, Roosevelt also told Stalin privately that he wanted to break up the British Empire, even giving Hong Kong to China, and prevent a French return to Indochina. Although the Yalta accords did not treat these imperial questions, they did include trade-offs between Russia and the United States. Stalin promised to declare war against Japan two or three months after Hitler's defeat, enough time to permit the transfer of his troops to Asia. He agreed to sign a pact of friendship and alliance with Jiang Jieshi's regime, rather than with Mao Zedong's rival Communist group. In return, Russia regained territories and privileges it had lost in 1905: the southern part of Sakhalin, Darien as a free port, Port Arthur as a Soviet naval base, and joint operation of the Chinese Eastern and South Manchurian Railroads. The Kurile Islands were also awarded to the Soviet Union. These agreements, it should be emphasized, were forged without consultation with China, a clear loser at Yalta.

The Allies also compromised on the United Nations Organization. France and China had been added at Dumbarton Oaks as "permanent" members of the Security Council, possessing the veto. Although Churchill had complained earlier that China would vote with the United States, Roosevelt and Stalin knew as well that France was inclined toward British positions. Feeling outnumbered in the Council, Stalin thus asked at Yalta for membership of all sixteen Soviet republics in the General Assembly. He also insisted upon an absolute veto in the Council on all issues, procedural and substantive. Roosevelt agreed to grant the Soviets three seats in the General Assembly and Stalin agreed that the veto could not be cast on procedural questions, such as whether the Council should take up an issue to which the permanent member is a party. The conferees also set April 25 as the date for the organizing meeting of the United Nations in San Francisco.

Besides a restatement of the Atlantic Charter in the "Declaration of Liberated Europe," the establishment of a Reparations Commission, and inconclusive statements on Iran, Yugoslavia, and the Dardanelles, these were the sum of the agreements. Yalta marked a high point of the alliance, the "dawn of the new day," said Harry Hopkins. "We were absolutely certain that we had won the first great victory of the peace—and, by 'we,' I mean *all* of us, the whole civilized human race."[180] But Yalta was not as free of self-interest as Hopkins suggested. The sovereignty of weak nations had been violated. As Churchill told his colleagues: "The eagle should permit the small birds to sing and care not wherefore they sang."[181] France and China had been excluded from the negotiations. Spheres of influence had, in essence, been recognized. Although tough questions had been postponed, each power went home with something from this conference of traditional diplomatic give-and-take that reflected diplomatic and military needs and realities. Roosevelt had played the great power game as deftly as Stalin and Churchill.

Later, when the Yalta agreements collapsed, critics ignored the advantages the United States carried away from the conference—broadening of the Polish government, Russian promise to fight Japan, Russian recognition of Chiang's government, a voting formula in the United Nations, postponement of the reparations question—and charged that Roosevelt had given away too much. But he had little to give away. The United States might have used its economic power in the form of reconstruction aid as a diplomatic weapon, but that would have spoiled the spirit of compromise at Yalta, which served American interests. Nor did Stalin play one of his trump cards: the capture of Berlin during the conference. From Yalta Stalin ordered Marshall G. K. Zhukov to halt the Berlin offensive. His generals were not sure why, but contemporaries and historians have suggested that Stalin wanted to avoid a dramatic conquest, which might have created suspicions and destroyed cooperation at Yalta. Sir Alexander Cadogan thought, for example, that Stalin showed "no bluster: [military] success, instead of going to his head, seemed to have given him the added assurance enabling him to take broad views and to be unafraid of making concessions."[182] Churchill recognized the necessity of compromise: "What would have happened if we had quarrelled with Russia while the Germans still had three or four hundred divisions on the fighting front?"[183] Averell Harriman, although angry that the Yalta accords did not hold up, later offered a sobering perspective on the significance of the conference: "If we hadn't had the Yalta agreement *we* would have been blamed for all the postwar tensions."[184]

To Each His Own: Allied Divergence and Spheres of Influence

At Yalta and throughout the diplomacy of World War II, the Allies attempted to protect and, if possible, extend their spheres of influence. Churchill's spirited defense of the British Empire, from Argentia through Yalta, was an ever present characteristic of wartime diplomacy. "If the Americans want to take Japanese islands which they have conquered," he informed his Foreign Secretary Anthony Eden, "let them do so with our blessing and any form of words that may be agreeable to them. But 'Hands Off the British Empire' is our maxim."[185] With vital interests in the Mediterranean and Persian Gulf, as well as the Far East, Britain resisted any machinery for postwar United Nations-mandated trusteeships. "I will not have one scrap of British Territory flung into that area," Churchill boomed.[186] Some Americans suspected that Churchill's constant postponement of the second front and his strategies for North Africa and Italy aimed at protecting imperial lifelines from either Germany or Russia. His advice to American military leaders, near the war's end, that they drive quickly to Berlin, and if possible even farther into Eastern Europe, to beat the Russians, provided further evidence for this suspicion.

The Churchill-Stalin percentage agreement of October, 1944 illustrated well the movement toward spheres of influence. In early 1944 Churchill concluded that "we are approaching a showdown with the Russians" in the Balkans. It was time for a frank settlement. Roosevelt warned against "any post-war spheres of influence," but agreed to a trial division of authority.[187] The "showdown" could be measured

Pacific Fleet Carriers. A major reason for United States victories in the Pacific theater and for a substantial American role in postwar Asian affairs was the air superiority provided by these *Essex*-class ships (27,000 tons each). The U.S.S. *Essex* leads this flotilla in 1943. (Navy Department, National Archives)

in Rumania, where Soviet troops dominated, Yugoslavia, where independent Communist Josip Tito and his Partisans were emerging, Bulgaria, where an indigenous Communist movement grew with Soviet influence, and Greece, a British-dominated area in the throes of a burgeoning civil war. At a conference with Stalin in Moscow in October, Churchill scribbled some percentages on a piece of paper. In Rumania, Russia would get 90 percent of the power and Britain 10 percent, in Greece Britain would enjoy 90 percent and Russia 10 percent, in Yugoslavia and Hungary a 50–50 split, and in Bulgaria 75 percent would go to Russia and 25 percent to "others." As Churchill recalled, he "pushed this across to Stalin," who "took his blue pencil and made a large tick upon it." Churchill, fearful that posterity would think such important issues had been disposed of in an "offhand manner," suggested that the paper be burned. "No, you keep it," said Stalin.[188] Roosevelt did not remonstrate over the bargain. Always following the path of least resistance, Roosevelt probably "had come to agree with Churchill that some such arrangement as the one reported was advisable, if not essential."[189] The percentage bargain did not last, in large part because local conditions denied the maintenance of artificial percentages of influence. But the agreement probably reinforced Stalin's view that his developing sphere had tacit Western approval.

If Britain was trying to save its sphere of influence, especially in Greece, Russia was attempting to expand its in Eastern Europe. Soviet support for the Lublin Polish government, demands for Polish and Rumanian territory, efforts to exclude the United States and Britain from the joint control commissions in Eastern Europe, and seizure of German-operated property (including Standard Oil equipment in Rumania) alerted American officials to the growing power of Russia vis-à-vis its neighbors. The Soviet handling of the Warsaw uprising of July 31, 1944 alarmed Western observers, convincing many that Soviet callousness had few limits. With Soviet armies some twelve miles from Warsaw, the Polish underground gambled and attacked German forces, believing that the Soviet troops would dash to their aid. But the Soviet Army stopped. For two months the Germans pummeled the Polish fighters, who owed their allegiance to the exiled government in London. The Germans killed 166,000 Poles and leveled half the city. Churchill persuaded Stalin in September to drop supplies to the besieged city, but the Russian leader called the Warsaw uprising a reckless, futile undertaking. He begged off from further support, pointing out that his troops were meeting heavy German resistance. To requests that American planes be permitted to land at Russian airfields after carrying supplies to Warsaw, Stalin first said *"nyet,"* and then permitted landings in mid-September. Whatever the military realities, many charged that Stalin abetted the slaughter of the Warsaw Poles. Churchill spoke of the Soviet "tale of villainy and horror," and British Air Marshall John Slessor later wrote: "How, after the fall of Warsaw, any responsible statesman could trust any Russian Communist further than he could kick him, passes the comprehension of ordinary men."[190] The liberation of Poland by Soviet forces in 1944 ultimately fixed a Communist regime in Warsaw—one that Roosevelt's compromises at Yalta essentially recognized.

The United States itself was expanding and building spheres of influence during the war, although it disapproved of spheres for others. Having already drawn most of the Latin American states into a defense community at the Lima Conference (1938) and in the Declaration of Panama (1939), the United States moved to drive

"Gone with the Wind . . ." In this critical Argentine cartoon of 1940, Uncle Sam, his pledges of neutrality and isolationism discarded, tends the armaments he uses to seduce Latin America. (Antonio Arias Bernal, The Swann Collection of Caricature and Cartoon)

German investments and influence from the western hemisphere. The Export-Import Bank loaned $130 million to twelve Latin American nations in 1939–1941 to help them oust German businesses, cut trade with the Axis, stabilize their economies, and bring them into alignment with American foreign policy. During the war, the United States increased its stake in Bolivian tin, helped build Brazilian warships, expanded holdings in Venezuelan oil, acquired bases in Panama and Guatemala, and nourished the dictatorship of Rafael Trujillo in the Dominican Republic. The American military also began to coordinate armaments and military training with Latin American forces. During the war Latin America shipped 50 percent of its exports, largely much needed raw materials, to the United States. At the Rio de Janeiro Conference (January 15–28, 1942), all but Chile and Argentina voted to break diplomatic relations with the Axis nations. In March of 1945, in the Act of Chapultepec, the United States and Latin America took another step toward a regional defense alliance. Furthermore, American officials recognized that Latin Americans would vote with the United States at the new United Nations. An unwitting and embarrassing statement of February, 1945 by Secretary Stettinius in Mexico City, reminded many that the United States still considered its southern neighbors subservient: "The United States looks upon Mexico as a good neighbor, a strong upholder of democratic traditions in this hemisphere, and *a country we are proud to call our own.*"[191]

American leaders also sought to direct events in postwar Italy and Asia. They essentially excluded the Soviets from the Italian surrender agreement in 1943 and denied them a role in the control commission. Some American officials recognized that Italy, where predominant power rested in American hands, set a precedent for later Soviet predominance in Rumania and Hungary. American officials also insisted on holding the conquered Japanese islands in the Pacific and in unilaterally governing Japan itself. "You're dead right in believing that after this war's over the sentiment of the people will be in favor of having what the government thinks will be enough to maintain our power in the Pacific," Secretary of War Henry L. Stimson told a congressman.[192] Washington also anticipated Jiang's China as an ally in this area of enlarged American influence.

In the Middle East the United States also expanded. In 1939 the Arabian-American Oil Company (Aramco) began to tap their 440,000-square mile concession in Saudi Arabia's rich oil fields. By 1944 American corporations controlled 42 percent of the proved oil reserves of the Middle East, a nineteenfold increase since 1936. In 1944, American companies, with Washington's encouragement, applied for an oil concession in Iran, then occupied by British and Soviet troops and used as a corridor for Lend-Lease shipments to Russia. This request touched off a three-cornered competition for influence in the heretofore British-dominated country. When Roosevelt informed Churchill in 1944 that the United States did not intend to deprive the British of their traditional stakes in the Middle East, the Prime Minister tartly replied: "Thank you very much for your assurances about no sheeps' eyes at our oil fields in Iran and Iraq. Let me reciprocate by giving you fullest assurance that we have no thought of trying to horn in upon your interests or property in Saudi Arabia."[193]

On a global scale, then, the Big Three jockeyed for power and influence. "Spheres of influence do in fact exist," concluded the State Department in early 1945, "and will probably continue to do so for some time to come. . . . In view of the actual Eastern European sphere and the Western Hemispheric bloc (Act of Chapultepec), we are hardly in a position to frown upon the establishment of measures designed to strengthen the security of nations in other areas of the world." Unfortunately, "such measures represent power politics pure and simple."[194] The Atlantic Charter had not restrained the Allies from reaching for postwar spheres of influence in their wartime diplomacy. Therein lay growing fissures in Big Three relations.

With Germany's surrender on May 8, 1945 the Third Reich collapsed in the rubble of bombed-out Berlin. President Truman quickly ended Lend-Lease aid to Russia (he soon partially restarted it), thereby stirring up a "hornets nest" in Moscow, which interpreted the abrupt cutback as diplomatic pressure.[195] With this issue and the Polish question troubling Soviet-American relations, the President sent Harry Hopkins to see Stalin in May, to "use diplomatic language or a baseball bat," as Truman later recalled.[196] The Russians, said the President, "were like people from across the tracks whose manners were very bad."[197] Hopkins chose diplomatic language when he met an irate Stalin. The Marshal told the special envoy that the sudden Lend-Lease cessation had been "brutal": "If the refusal to continue Lend-Lease was designed as pressure on the Russians in order to soften them up," lectured Stalin, "then it was a fundamental mistake."[198] Hopkins denied that the United States practiced economic coercion, and warned that Americans were growing restive about Russia's failure to carry out the Yalta agreement on Poland—a symbol of Soviet-American trust. Stalin frankly explained why he could not permit the anti-Soviet London group, who would probably have won free elections, to govern postwar Poland:[199]

> In the course of twenty-five years the Germans had twice invaded Russia via Poland. Neither the British nor American people had experienced such German invasions which were a horrible thing to endure and the results of which were not easily forgotten. . . . Poland has served as a corridor for the German attacks on Russia. . . . It is therefore in Russia's vital interest that Poland should be both strong and friendly.

Ambassador Harriman reported to Truman that Stalin could not "understand why we should want to interfere with Soviet policy in a country like Poland, which he considers so important to Russia's security, unless we have some ulterior motive."[200] Hopkins got the Marshal to budge a little. Stalin agreed that a handful of ministries should rest in the hands of non-Lublin Poles. He also promised Hopkins, as at Yalta, that Russia would enter the war against Japan and respect Jiang's government in China. Overall, Truman was pleased that Russia had attempted to conciliate American wishes, but he desired to break up the developing Soviet sphere of influence and to consolidate American interests.

Triumph and Tragedy: Potsdam and the Legacy of World War II

When the Big Three gathered in Berlin for the Potsdam Conference (July 16–August 2, 1945), the war in Asia was nearing an end, and the reconstruction of Germany was an immediate reality. Sir Alexander Cadogan described the Berlin environs as a "staggering sight. . . . I don't think it could ever be rebuilt."[201] During the conference, Truman wrote his family that "you never saw such pig-headed people as are the Russians."[202] As for Stalin, "I thought he was an S.O.B.," Truman said after the meeting. "But, of course, I guess he thinks I'm one, too."[203] Gone indeed was the special personal relationship between Roosevelt and Stalin. Truman had come to make final decisions, and, like his advisers, he grew impatient with the Russians. Admiral Leahy thought Stalin "a liar and a crook," and Harriman called the Russians "those barbarians."[204] Churchill, who would leave the conference after the defeat of his Conservative party in British elections (Clement Attlee replaced him), fiddled with his cigars and grunted throughout the sessions. But he took a liking to the new President, whom he described as a "man of exceptional character and ability with . . . simple and direct methods of speech, and a great deal of self-confidence and resolution."[205] Some of that resolution at Potsdam derived from the news Truman learned on the second day of the conference: the successful explosion of an atomic device on July 16 in New Mexico.

By the time of Potsdam, American policy toward postwar Germany had moved a good distance from the Morgenthau Plan and JCS/1067, toward a policy of reconstruction. Germany was now seen by many American officials as a vital link in the economic recovery of Western Europe. Thus, when Germany came up for discussion, Truman resisted dismemberment and large reparations. The final Potsdam accord stated that Germany was to be managed by military governors in each of the four zones, treated as "a single economic unit," and permitted a standard of living higher than its low level of 1945.[206] Transportation, coal, agriculture, housing, and utilities industries were to be rehabilitated. As for reparations, desired by Russia for both revenge and the recovery of its hobbled economy, the United States refused to set a firm figure until Germany's ability to pay was determined. In defense of the American position, Truman recalled the post-World War I reparations tangle. Stalin protested, but all he could get was an agreement that each nation should take reparations from its own zone and that Russia would get some reparations in industrial equipment from the Western zones. In return for the latter Russia would send food to the other three zones. The reparations issue, postponed once at Yalta, was essentially postponed again. The result was, as diplomat George F. Kennan put it, "catch as catch can."[207]

The conferees tangled over Poland. Every time Churchill complained about the absence of free elections in Poland, Stalin mentioned the British domination of Greece. They did agree, however, to set the Oder-Neisse line as Poland's temporary western boundary, thereby granting Poland large chunks of German territory. The Soviet Union agreed to accept Italy as a member of the United Nations. The big powers also established the Council of Foreign Ministers to continue discussion on issues not resolved at Potsdam: peace treaties for the former German satellites; the withdrawal of Allied troops from Iran; postwar control of the Dardanelles; internationalization of inland waterways; and the disposition of Italian colonies. Stalin promised again to enter the war against Japan, although American leaders were less eager about that with the atomic bomb looming as a major weapon. Finally Britain and the United States issued the "Potsdam Declaration" to Japan, demanding unconditional surrender and threatening it with destruction.

The seemingly minor issue of waterways illustrated the tension at Potsdam and became for Truman a test of Soviet intentions. At the conference he pushed for an international authority to govern the eighteen-hundred-mile long Danube River, which wound its way through several countries, including Russia, to the Black Sea. Essentially a combination of two traditional American principles—free navigation and the Open Door—the proposal antagonized the Russians. They countered with a commission limited to riparian states. For Russia the Danube was analogous to America's Panama Canal and Britain's Suez Canal. When Churchill backed Truman on the question, Molotov pressed: "If it was such a good rule why not apply it to the Suez?"[208] Churchill evaded the comparison, and Truman fumed when his personal appeal to Stalin for acceptance of an internationalized Danube was rebuffed. In his *Memoirs* the President drew an exaggerated conclusion. Stalin's attitude on waterways "showed how his mind worked and what he was after. . . . The Russians were planning world conquest."[209] Former State Department official and historian Herbert Feis has written: "History hints that what is done during the first few months after a great war ends is likely to determine the fate of the next generation."[210] The Potsdam Conference demonstrated that.

Potsdam, aptly code-named TERMINAL, left the world much as it had found it—divided and devastated. World War II officially ended on August 14, 1945. Japanese officials surrendered aboard the battleship *Missouri* on September 2. But peace remained elusive, in large part because of the troubling legacy of the war: the vast social, economic, and political dislocations in Europe and Asia. Thirty-five million Europeans had died during the conflict, between fifteen and twenty million of them Russians. The Soviet government's bold machinations in Poland, and call for heavy German reparations, could be partly explained by that tragedy. A generation of young European people in their twenties and thirties had been virtually eliminated. Millions of displaced persons were sadly separated from their homelands. Transportation systems and communications networks were destroyed. Factories were bombed out. Cities were reduced to ashes, including the German city of Dresden, which Allied planes had punished in February, 1945, in a merciless attack of questionable necessity. Parts of Asia also lay in ruins. Tokyo had been fire-bombed, leaving 100,000 dead. China was badly mauled, and faced a civil war. These wrenching effects of the war confronted postwar diplomats with incomparable reconstruction problems, and leftist politicians challenged discredited, but still entrenched, elites.

With the imperial powers in disarray, their colonies, long yearning for the moment and in Asia encouraged by Japan during the waning days of the war, became rebellious. Unable to apply the necessary resources and manpower to curb the nationalist revolutions, the European empires began to crumble. The Dutch battled their Indonesian subjects; France fought the Vietnamese in French Indochina; Britain reluctantly began its exit from Burma, India, and Ceylon.

The rise of Soviet Russia as a major international player was another result of World War II. The "greatest crime of Hitler," said Ambassador Harriman, was that his defeat opened parts of Europe to Russian influence.[211] Russia insisted on being treated as an equal and resented any intimation that it should not have an

Bombed-out French Town, 1944. Europe lay in ruins at the end of the war and American help seemed essential to the reconstruction effort. (U.S. Office of War Information, National Archives)

influential voice in postwar questions. Reeling from its heavy wartime losses and facing massive reconstruction tasks, Russia asked for much and grabbed what it could before the war ended. "You know we have never been accepted in European councils on a basis of equality," Maxim Litvinov complained. "We were always outsiders."[212] Never again.

Russia rose, Britain fell, China floundered, and the United States galloped. Its economy, the "arsenal of democracy," untouched by enemy bombers or marauding armies, was in high gear at war's end. The American gross national product jumped from $88.6 billion in 1939 to $198.7 billion five years later. Observers spoke of an American "production miracle."[213] One Englishman resentfully penned a poem:[214]

> In Washington Lord Halifax
> Once whispered to Lord Keynes:
> "It's true *they* have the money bags
> But *we* have all the brains."

A British Foreign Office diplomat complained that "we shall have to suffer from American arrogance."[215] As the unsurpassed economic leader of the world, alone in a position to provide the capital and goods for recovery abroad, Washington was flushed with power. Imbibing lessons from the 1930s about the need to avoid Munichs, Americans looked forward to shaping a world of peace and prosperity. With greatly increased power, the United States seemed capable of creating the stable world order that had eluded it between the two world wars. State Department official Dean Acheson observed that the "great difference in our second attempt to establish a peaceful world is the wide recognition that peace is possible only if countries work together and prosper together. That is why the economic aspects are no less important than the political aspects of the peace."[216] Through the war years the United States had constructed institutions—UNRRA, World Bank, International Monetary Fund, United Nations—to insure that peace. Despite this attraction to international organizations, the United States pursued its traditional unilateralism as well, especially in Latin America.

The war also wrought changes in the foreign affairs decisionmaking process in the United States. As Richard Barnet has put it, the United States underwent a "bureaucratic revolution."[217] Agencies in the government handling national security matters ballooned in size. The defense establishment became more active in making diplomatic choices. In comparison, the State Department, so frequently bypassed by President Roosevelt, slipped in power. The war spawned a large espionage establishment, beginning with the Office of Strategic Services (OSS) in 1941 and culminating in the Central Intelligence Agency (CIA) six years later. The President as Commander-in-Chief centralized decisionmaking in the White House, while Congress gave up its foreign affairs prerogatives in the constitutional system and applauded bipartisanship. "War had accustomed those in charge of foreign policy to a complacent faith in the superior intelligence and disinterestedness of the executive branch," historian Arthur M. Schlesinger, Jr. has noted.[218] Another consequence of the war was the enlargement of what came to be called the "military-industrial complex," a partnership between businessmen eager for lucrative defense contracts and military men eager for increased budgets. A bureaucratic momentum of defense spending grew from this relationship. Universities, which had been recruited during the war, were not left untouched by it.

Professors of the sciences had developed the atomic bomb at the universities of Chicago and California, Berkeley. "The universities transformed themselves into vast weapons development laboratories," the editor of *Scientific American* concluded.[219] Postwar federal subsidies flowed to colleges not only for arms development, but also for research on Russian studies and intelligence gathering. These lasting changes wrought by the experiences of World War II were not easily identifiable in 1945; their impact would be measured in the immediate future as the Allies struggled to transform their military victory into a stable peace.

Further Reading for the Period 1939–1945

For general accounts of American foreign policy and Allied relations during World War II, see Winston S. Churchill, *Second World War* (1948–1953); R. D. Cuff and J. L. Granatstein, *Canadian-American Relations in Wartime: From the Great War to the Cold War* (1975); Robert Dallek, *Franklin D. Roosevelt and American Foreign Policy, 1933–1945* (1979); Robert A. Divine, *Roosevelt and World War II* (1969); Jean-Baptiste Duroselle, *France and the United States* (1978); Herbert Feis, *Churchill, Roosevelt, Stalin* (1957); Victor Israelian, *The Anti-Hitler Coalition* (1971); Gabriel Kolko, *The Politics of War* (1968); Ralph B. Levering, *American Opinion and the Russian Alliance* (1976); William H. McNeill, *America, Britain, and Russia* (1953); William L. Neumann, *After Victory* (1967); Robert E. Sherwood, *Roosevelt and Hopkins* (1948); Gaddis Smith, *American Diplomacy During the Second World War* (1965); John L. Snell, *Illusion and Necessity* (1963); and Richard W. Steele, "Franklin D. Roosevelt and His Foreign Policy Critics," *Political Science Quarterly* (1979).

Among the biographical studies are Michael Beschloss, *Kennedy and Roosevelt* (1980); John M. Blum, ed., *From the Morgenthau Diaries* (1959–1972), and *The Price of Vision: The Diary of Henry A. Wallace, 1942–1946* (1973); James M. Burns, *Roosevelt: The Soldier of Freedom* (1970); Waldo H. Heinrichs, *American Ambassador* (1966) (on Joseph C. Grew); Warren Kimball, "Churchill and Roosevelt: The Personal Equation," *Prologue* (1974); Joseph P. Lash, *Roosevelt and Churchill, 1939–1941* (1976); Elting E. Morison, *Turmoil and Tradition: The Life and Times of Henry L. Stimson* (1960); Forrest C. Pogue, *George C. Marshall* (1963–1973); and Edward R. Stettinius, Jr., *Roosevelt and the Russians* (1949).

American diplomacy toward Europe, 1939–1941, is treated in Patrick Abbazia, *Mr. Roosevelt's Navy: The Private War of the Atlantic Fleet, 1939–1942* (1975); Thomas A. Bailey and Paul B. Ryan, *Hitler vs. Roosevelt: The Undeclared Naval War* (1979); Mark Chadwin, *The Hawks of World War II* (1968); Wayne S. Cole, *America First: The Battle Against Intervention* (1953); James V. Compton, *The Swastika and the Eagle* (1967); R. H. Dawson, *The Decision to Aid Russia, 1941* (1959); Robert A. Divine, *The Reluctant Belligerent* (1979); Saul Friedlander, *Prelude to Downfall: Hitler and the United States, 1939–1941* (1967); Travis B. Jacobs, *America and the Winter War, 1939–1940* (1981); Warren F. Kimball, *The Most Unsordid Act: Lend-Lease, 1939–1941* (1969); William L. Langer and S. Everett Gleason, *The Challenge to Isolation, 1937–1940* (1952); Richard A. Lauderbaugh, *American Steel Makers and the Coming of the Second World War* (1980); James R. Leutze, *Bargaining for Supremacy: Anglo-American Naval Collaboration, 1937–1941* (1977); Arnold A. Offner, *The Origins of the Second World War* (1975); David Reynolds, *The Creation of the Anglo-American Alliance, 1937–1941* (1982); and Theodore A. Wilson, *The First Summit: Roosevelt and Churchill at Placentia Bay, 1941* (1969).

For the advent of war with Japan, see the books by Borg and Okamoto, Burns and Bennett, Feis, and Neu cited in "Further Reading" for Chapter 10; Robert J. C. Butow, *Tojo and the Coming of the War* (1961) and *The John Doe Associates: Backdoor Diplomacy for Peace, 1941* (1974); Peter Lowe, *Great Britain and the Origins of the Pacific War* (1977); Martin V. Melosi, *The Shadow of Pearl Harbor* (1977); Samuel Eliot Morison, *The Rising Sun in the Pacific* (1973); James Morley, ed., *The Fateful Choice: Japan's Advance into Southeast Asia, 1939–1941* (1980); Gordon W. Prange, *At Dawn We Slept: The Untold Story of Pearl Harbor* (1981); Bruce M. Russett, *No Clear and Present Danger: A Skeptical View of the U.S. Entry into World War II*

(1972); Paul W. Schroeder, *The Axis Alliance and Japanese–American Relations, 1941* (1958); Charles C. Tansill, *Back Door to War* (1952); and Roberta Wohlstetter, *Pearl Harbor: Warning and Decision* (1962).

Wartime diplomacy, Allied strategy, and plans for the postwar world are discussed in Stephen Ambrose, *The Supreme Commander* (1970); Robert Beitzell, *The Uneasy Alliance: America, Britain, and Russia, 1941–1943* (1972); A. Russell Buchanan, *The United States and World War II* (1964); Thomas M. Campbell, *Masquerade Peace: America's UN Policy, 1944–1945* (1973); Diane Shaver Clemens, *Yalta* (1970); R. D. Cuff and J. L. Granatstein, *Canadian-American Relations in Wartime* (1975); Robert A. Divine, *Second Chance: The Triumph of Internationalism in America During World War II* (1967); Walter S. Dunn, Jr., *Second Front Now, 1943* (1980); Herbert Feis, *Between War and Peace: The Potsdam Conference* (1960); Kent R. Greenfield, *American Strategy in World War II* (1963); George C. Herring, Jr., *Aid to Russia, 1941–1946* (1973); William Langer, *Our Vichy Gamble* (1947); William R. Louis, *Imperialism at Bay: The United States and the Decolonization of the British Empire* (1978); David MacIsaac, *Strategic Bombing in World War Two* (1976); Vojtech Mastny, *Russia's Road to the Cold War* (1979); Samuel Eliot Morison, *Strategy and Compromise* (1958); Raymond G. O'Connor, *Diplomacy for Victory: FDR and Unconditional Surrender* (1971); Arthur L. Smith, Jr., *Churchill's German Army: Wartime Strategy and Cold War Politics, 1943–1947* (1977); John L. Snell, ed., *The Meaning of Yalta* (1956); Richard W. Steele, *The First Offensive, 1942* (1973); Mark A. Stoler, *The Politics of the Second Front* (1977); Piotr S. Wandycz, *The United States and Poland* (1980); Russell F. Weigley, *Eisenhower's Lieutenants: The Campaign of France and Germany, 1944–1945* (1981); and Llewellyn Woodward, *British Foreign Policy in the Second World War* (1970–1971).

For wartime Asian questions and China, see David D. Barrett, *Dixie Mission* (1970); Russell D. Buhite, *Patrick J. Hurley and American Foreign Policy* (1973); Warren I. Cohen, *America's Response to China* (1980); Herbert Feis, *The China Tangle* (1953); Suburō Ienaga, *The Pacific War: World War II and the Japanese, 1931–1945* (1978); Akira Iriye, *Power and Culture: The Japanese–American War, 1941–1945* (1981); E. J. Kahn, Jr., *The China Hands* (1975); Michael Schaller, *The U.S. Crusade in China, 1938–1945* (1978); Mark A. Stoler, "The 'Pacific First' Alternative in American World War II Strategy," *International History Review* (1980); Christopher Thorne, *Allies of a Kind* (1977); Tang Tsou, *America's Failure in China, 1941–1950* (1963); and Barbara Tuchman, *Stilwell and the American Experience in China, 1911–1945* (1971).

For United States wartime relations with Latin America, see some of the works cited in "Further Reading" for Chapter 10, and Michael J. Francis, *The Limits of Hegemony* (1977) (Argentina and Chile); Frank D. McCann, Jr., *The Brazilian–American Alliance, 1937–1945* (1973); Stanley Hilton, *Hitler's Secret War in South America, 1939–1945* (1981); and Randall B. Woods, *The Roosevelt Foreign-Policy Establishment and the "Good Neighbor"* (1980) (Argentina).

For United States interest in the Middle East and oil, consult Irvine H. Anderson, *Aramco, the United States, and Saudi Arabia* (1981); Philip J. Baram, *The Department of State in the Middle East, 1919–1945* (1978); Aaron D. Miller, *Search for Security: Saudi Arabian Oil and American Foreign Policy, 1939–1949* (1980); and Michael B. Stoff, *Oil, War, and American Security: The Search for a National Policy on Foreign Oil, 1941–1947* (1980).

For domestic politics and public opinion, see Richard D. Darilek, *A Loyal Opposition in Time of War* (1976); Robert A. Divine, *Foreign Policy and U.S. Presidential Relations, 1940–1948* (1974); Michael Leigh, *Mobilizing Consent: Public Opinion and American Foreign Policy, 1937–1947* (1976); and David L. Porter, *The Seventy-Sixth Congress and World War II, 1939–1940* (1979). For American wartime planning for postwar defense, see Michael S. Sherry, *Preparing for the Next War* (1977).

The sad chronicle of the refugee problem and the Allied response is recounted in Yehuda Bauer, *American Jewry and the Holocaust* (1981); Henry L. Feingold, *Politics of Rescue* (1970); Saul S. Friedman, *No Haven for the Oppressed* (1973); Martin Gilbert, *Auschwitz and the Allies* (1981); Walter Laqueur, *The Terrible Secret* (1981); Arthur D. Morse, *While Six*

Million Died (1968); William E. Nawyn, *American Protestantism's Response to Germany's Jews and Refugees, 1933–1941* (1982); Arnold Offner, *American Appeasement* (1964); Robert W. Ross, *So It Was True: The American Protestant Press and the Nazi Persecution of the Jews* (1980); and David Wyman, *Paper Walls* (1968).

See also the General Bibliography and the following notes.

Notes to Chapter 11

1. Quoted in Theodore A. Wilson, *The First Summit: Roosevelt and Churchill at Placentia Bay, 1941* (Boston: Houghton Mifflin, 1969), p. 109.

2. H. V. Morton quoted *ibid.*, p. 84.

3. Elliott Roosevelt, *As He Saw It* (New York: Duell, Sloan, and Pearce, 1946), p. 33.

4. Winston S. Churchill, *The Grand Alliance* (Boston: Houghton Mifflin, 1950), p. 431.

5. Quoted in Robert E. Sherwood, *Roosevelt and Hopkins* (New York: Harper and Brothers, 1948), p. 236.

6. Francis L. Loewenheim, Harold D. Langley, and Manfred Jonas, eds., *Roosevelt and Churchill: Their Secret Wartime Correspondence* (New York: Saturday Review Press/E. P. Dutton, 1975), p. 155.

7. Harold Nicolson, *Diaries and Letters: The War Years, 1939–1945* (New York: Atheneum, 1966–1968; 3 vols.), II, 385.

8. Quoted in Warren F. Kimball, "Churchill and Roosevelt: The Personal Equation," *Prologue*, VI (Fall, 1974), 179.

9. Quoted in Forrest C. Pogue, *George C. Marshall: Ordeal and Hope, 1939–1942* (New York: Viking Press, 1963–1973; 3 vols.), II, 46.

10. Quoted in Robert A. Divine, *Roosevelt and World War II* (Baltimore: The Johns Hopkins University Press, 1969), p. 44.

11. Quoted in Raymond Esthus, "President Roosevelt's Commitment to Britain to Intervene in a Pacific War," *Mississippi Valley Historical Review*, L (June, 1963), 31.

12. David Dilks, ed., *The Diaries of Sir Alexander Cadogan, 1938–1945* (New York: G. P. Putnam's Sons, 1971), p. 399.

13. Cordell Hull, *Memoirs* (New York: Macmillan, 1948; 2 vols.), II, 975–976.

14. For the Atlantic Charter text, see *Foreign Relations, 1941* (Washington, D.C.: Government Printing Office, 1958), I, 368–369.

15. James MacGregor Burns, *Roosevelt: The Soldier of Freedom* (New York: Harcourt Brace Jovanovich, 1970), p. 550.

16. Quoted *ibid.*, p. 129.

17. Llewellyn Woodward, *British Foreign Policy in the Second World War* (London: Her Majesty's Stationary Office, 1970–1971; 3 vols.), II, 204.

18. *Foreign Relations, 1941*, I, 378.

19. Quoted in William H. McNeill, *America, Britain, & Russia: Their Co-operation and Conflict, 1941–1946* (London: Oxford University Press, 1953), p. 41.

20. Quoted in Anthony Eden, *The Reckoning: Memoirs* (Boston: Houghton Mifflin, 1965), p. 343.

21. Quoted in Burns, *Soldier of Freedom*, p. 609.

22. Quoted in Wilson, *First Summit*, p. 260.

23. Quoted *ibid.*, p. 210.

24. Eden, *The Reckoning*, p. 433.

25. Samuel I. Rosenman, ed., *Public Papers and Addresses of Franklin D. Roosevelt, 1939* (New York: Macmillan, 1938–1950; 13 vols.), VIII, 463.

26. Divine, *Roosevelt and World War II*, p. 37.

27. *Congressional Record*, LXXIV (October 4, 1939), 98.

28. Quoted in John M. Blum, *From the Morgenthau Diaries: Years of Urgency, 1938–1941* (Boston: Houghton Mifflin, 1965), p. 91.

29. Quoted in Patrick Abbazia, *Mr. Roosevelt's Navy: The Private War of the U.S. Atlantic Fleet, 1939–1942* (Annapolis: Naval Institute Press, 1975), p. 142.

30. Rosenman, *Public Papers, 1940*, IX, 263.

31. Quoted in John G. Clifford, "Grenville Clark and the Origins of Selective Service," *Review of Politics*, XXXV (January, 1973), 31–32.

32. Rosenman, *Public Papers, 1940*, IX, 391.

33. Winston S. Churchill, *Their Finest Hour* (Boston: Houghton Mifflin, 1949), p. 404.

34. Quoted in Robert A. Divine, *Foreign Policy and U.S. Presidential Elections, 1940–1948* (New York: New Viewpoints, 1974), pp. 82–83.

35. Loewenheim *et al.*, *Roosevelt and Churchill*, p. 125.

36. Rosenman, *Public Papers, 1940*, IX, 607.

37. *Ibid.*, pp. 640–643.

38. Quoted in George C. Herring, Jr., *Aid to Russia, 1941–1946: Strategy, Diplomacy, and the Origins of the Cold War* (New York: Columbia University Press, 1973), p. 4.

39. Quoted in Warren F. Kimball, *The Most Unsordid Act: Lend-Lease, 1939–1941* (Baltimore: Johns Hopkins Press, 1969), p. 154 and Rosenman, *Public Papers, 1940*, IX, 711–712.

40. Quoted in Kimball, *Most Unsordid Act*, p. 153.

41. *Congressional Record*, LXXVII (March 8, 1941), 2097.

42. Quoted in Herring, *Aid to Russia*, p. 5.

43. Quoted in Blum, *From the Morgenthau Diaries: Years of Urgency*, p. 251.

44. Quoted in Elting E. Morison, *Turmoil and Tradition: A Study of the Life and Times of Henry L. Stimson* (Boston: Houghton Mifflin, 1960), p. 429.

45. *New York Times*, July 24, 1941.

46. Churchill, *Grand Alliance*, p. 370.

47. Quoted in Blum, *From the Morgenthau Diaries: Years of Urgency*, p. 264.

48. August 19, 1941, CAB 65/19, War Cabinet Records 84, Public Record Office, London, England (from the notes of Walter LaFeber).

49. Rosenman, *Public Papers, 1941*, X, 438, 439.

50. Quoted in Wayne S. Cole, *America First: The Battle against Intervention, 1940–1941* (Madison: University of Wisconsin Press, 1953), p. 163.

51. Quoted in William L. Langer and S. Everett Gleason, *The*

Undeclared War, 1940–1941 (New York: Harper and Brothers, 1953), p. 760.

52. Richard W. Steele, *The First Offensive, 1942: Roosevelt, Marshall, and the Making of American Strategy* (Bloomington: Indiana University Press, 1973), p. 47.

53. Sherwood, *Roosevelt and Hopkins*, p. 383.

54. Quoted in Edward M. Bennett, "Joseph C. Grew: The Diplomacy of Pacification," in Richard Dean Burns and Edward M. Bennett, eds., *Diplomats in Crisis: United States-Chinese-Japanese Relations, 1919–1941* (Santa Barbara, Cal.: ABC-CLIO, 1974), p. 78.

55. Herbert Feis, *The Road to Pearl Harbor* (New York: Atheneum, 1967), p. 17.

56. Harold L. Ickes, *The Secret Diary of Harold L. Ickes: The Lowering Clouds* (New York: Simon and Schuster, 1953; 3 vols.), III, 567.

57. Quoted in Waldo H. Heinrichs, *American Ambassador: Joseph C. Grew and the Development of the United States Diplomatic Tradition* (Boston: Little, Brown, 1966), p. 320.

58. Quoted in Charles E. Neu, *The Troubled Encounter: The United States and Japan* (New York: John Wiley and Sons, 1975), p. 168.

59. Barbara Teters, "Yosuke Matsuoka: The Diplomacy of Bluff and Gesture," in Burns and Bennett, eds., *Diplomats in Crisis*, p. 288.

60. Quoted in Asada Sadao, "The Japanese Navy and the United States," in Dorothy Borg and Shumpei Okamoto, eds., *Pearl Harbor as History: Japanese-American Relations, 1931–1941* (New York: Columbia University Press, 1973), p. 248.

61. *Foreign Relations of the United States, 1940* (Washington: Government Printing Office, 1955), IV, 602.

62. Neu, *Troubled Encounter*, p. 175.

63. Quoted in Arnold A. Offner, *The Origins of the Second World War* (New York: Praeger, 1975), p. 193.

64. Quoted in Hilary Conroy, "Nomura Kichisaburo: The Diplomacy of Drama and Desperation," in Burns and Bennett, eds., *Diplomats in Crisis*, pp. 300–301.

65. Robert J. C. Butow, "Backdoor Diplomacy in the Pacific: The Proposal for a Konoye-Roosevelt Meeting in 1941," *Journal of American History*, XXXIX (June, 1972), 59.

66. Quoted in Feis, *Road to Pearl Harbor*, p. 206.

67. *Ibid.*, p. 244.

68. Ickes, *Secret Diary*, III, 346.

69. Quoted in James C. Thomson, Jr., "The Role of the Department of State," in Borg and Okamoto, eds., *Pearl Harbor as History*, p. 101.

70. Quoted in Feis, *Road to Pearl Harbor*, p. 321.

71. Bruce M. Russett, *No Clear and Present Danger: A Skeptical View of the U.S. Entry into World War II* (New York: Harper and Row, 1972), p. 55.

72. Quoted in Neu, *Troubled Encounter*, p. 187.

73. Quoted in Samuel Eliot Morison, *The Rising Sun in the Pacific: 1931–April 1942* (Boston: Little, Brown, 1948), p. 46.

74. Sherwood, *Roosevelt and Hopkins*, p. 434.

75. For example, Charles C. Tansill, *Back Door to War* (Chicago: Henry Regnery, 1952).

76. Roberta Wohlstetter, *Pearl Harbor: Warning and Decision* (Stanford: Stanford University Press, 1962), p. 387.

77. Morison, *Rising Sun*, p. 132.

78. Rosenman, *Public Papers, 1941*, X, 514.

79. Arthur H. Vandenberg, Jr., ed., *The Private Papers of Senator Vandenberg* (Boston: Houghton Mifflin, 1952), p. 1.

80. Samuel E. Morison, *Strategy and Compromise* (Boston: Little, Brown, 1958), p. 25.

81. Memorandum of Conversation with Cordell Hull, September 29, 1944, "Black Notebooks," Box 1, Arthur Krock Papers, Princeton University Library.

82. Charles E. Bohlen, *Witness to History, 1929–1969* (New York: W. W. Norton, 1973), p. 129.

83. Quoted in Geoffrey Perrett, *Days of Sadness, Years of Triumph: The American People, 1939–1945* (Baltimore: Penguin, 1973), p. 197.

84. Saul Friedlander, *Prelude to Downfall: Hitler and the United States, 1939–1941* (New York: Alfred A. Knopf, 1967), p. 161.

85. Quoted in Kimball, "Churchill and Roosevelt," p. 181.

86. Winston S. Churchill, *Triumph and Tragedy* (Boston: Houghton Mifflin, 1953), p. 338.

87. Eden, *The Reckoning*, pp. 336–337.

88. Alfred D. Chandler, *et al.*, eds., *The Papers of Dwight David Eisenhower: The War Years* (Baltimore: The Johns Hopkins Press, 1970; 5 vols.), I, 66.

89. Quoted in Sherwood, *Roosevelt and Hopkins*, p. 563.

90. Quoted in Herbert Feis, *Churchill, Roosevelt, Stalin* (Princeton: Princeton University Press, 1957), p. 42.

91. Quoted in Harry C. Butcher, *My Three Years with Eisenhower* (New York: Simon and Schuster, 1946), p. 29.

92. Quoted in Arthur Bryant, *Triumph in the West, 1943–1946* (London: Collins, 1959), p. 78.

93. Brian L. Villa, "The Atomic Bomb and the Normandy Invasion," *Perspectives in American History*, XI (1978), p. 497.

94. Quoted in Morison, *Strategy and Compromise*, p. 51.

95. *Correspondence between the Chairman of the Council of Ministers of the U.S.S.R. and the Presidents of the U.S.A. and the Prime Ministers of Great Britain during the Great Patriotic War of 1941–1945* (Moscow: Foreign Languages Publishing House, 1957; 2 vols.), II, 70–71.

96. Quoted in Robert Beitzell, *The Uneasy Alliance: America, Britain, and Russia, 1941–1943* (New York: Alfred A. Knopf, 1972), p. 159.

97. Winston S. Churchill, *The Hinge of Fate* (Boston: Houghton Mifflin, 1950), p. 759.

98. Quoted in Raymond G. O'Connor, *Diplomacy for Victory: FDR and Unconditional Surrender* (New York: W. W. Norton, 1971), p. 52.

99. "Memorandum of Conversation with Cordell Hull," November 30, 1943, "Black Notebooks," Box 1, Arthur Krock Papers, Princeton University Library, Princeton, New Jersey.

100. Hull, *Memoirs*, II, 1297.

101. Robert Murphy, *Diplomat Among Warriors* (Garden City: Doubleday, 1964), p. 208.

102. Hull, *Memoirs*, II, 1314–1315.

103. Kimball, "Churchill and Roosevelt," p. 179.

104. Quoted in Roosevelt, *As He Saw It*, p. 176.

105. Henry H. Arnold, *Global Mission* (New York: Harper and Brothers, 1949), p. 465.

106. Quoted in Mark A. Stoler, *The Politics of the Second Front:*

American Military Planning and Diplomacy in Coalition Warfare, 1941-1943 (Westport, Conn.: Greenwood Press, 1977), p. 149.

and Teheran, 1943 (Washington, D.C.: Government Printing Office, 1961), p. 539.

107. Churchill, *Hinge of Fate*, p. 374.

108. Quoted in Pogue, *Marshall: Organizer of Victory, 1943-1945*, III, 313.

109. Quoted in Beitzell, *Uneasy Alliance*, p. 348.

110. *Foreign Relations, Cairo and Teheran*, pp. 594-595.

111. Churchill, *Hinge of Fate*, p. 401.

112. Quoted in Burns, *Roosevelt: Soldier of Freedom*, p. 411.

113. *Foreign Relations, Cairo and Teheran*, pp. 583, 585 and Bohlen, *Witness to History*, p. 149.

114. Rosenman, *Public Papers, 1943*, XII, 558.

115. Churchill, *Hinge of Fate*, p. 133.

116. Warren I. Cohen, *America's Response to China: An Interpretive History of Sino-American Relations* (New York: John Wiley and Sons, 1980; 2nd ed.), p. 157.

117. Quoted in Jonathan Spence, *To Change China: Western Advisers in China, 1620-1960* (Boston: Little, Brown, 1969), p. 236 and in Christopher Thorne, "Indochina and Anglo-American Relations, 1942-1945," *Pacific Historical Review*, XLIV (February, 1976), 76.

118. Theodore H. White, ed., *The Stilwell Papers* (New York: William Sloane Associates, 1948), p. 157.

119. Quoted in Akira Iriye, "The United States as an Asian-Pacific Power," in Gene T. Hsiao, ed., *Sino-American Détente and Its Policy Implications* (New York: Praeger, 1974), p. 12.

120. Quoted in Herbert Feis, *The China Tangle: The American Effort in China from Pearl Harbor to the Marshall Mission* (Princeton: Princeton University Press, 1953), p. 51.

121. Quoted in Burns, *Roosevelt: Soldier of Freedom*, p. 377.

122. Cohen, *America's Response to China*, p. 162.

123. Quoted in Charles F. Romanus and Riley Sunderland, *Stilwell's Mission to China* (Washington, D.C.: Department of the Army, 1953), p. 253.

124. White, ed., *Stilwell Papers*, p. 333.

125. *Foreign Relations of the United States, 1944* (Washington, D.C.: Government Printing Office, 1967), VI, 631-632.

126. David D. Barrett, *Dixie Mission: The United States Army Observer Group in Yenan, 1944* (Berkeley: University of California China Research Monographs, 1970), p. 56.

127. Quoted in John Paton Davies, Jr., *Dragon by the Tail* (New York: W. W. Norton, 1972), p. 381.

128. Quoted in Feis, *China Tangle*, p. 213.

129. Quoted in Russell D. Buhite, *Patrick J. Hurley and American Foreign Policy* (Ithaca: Cornell University Press, 1973), p. 152.

130. Quoted in Barbara W. Tuchman, "If Mao Had Come to Washington: An Essay in Alternatives," *Foreign Affairs*, L (October, 1972), 44.

131. Quoted in Davies, *Dragon by the Tail*, p. 386.

132. Quoted in Feis, *China Tangle*, p. 269.

133. Burns, *Roosevelt: Soldier of Freedom*, p. 545.

134. Quoted in Moshe Gottlieb, "The Berlin Riots and Their Repercussions in America," *American Jewish Historical Quarterly*, LIX (March, 1970), 306.

135. Quoted in Cyrus Adler and Aaron M. Margalith, *With Firmness in the Right: American Diplomatic Action Affecting Jews,* *1840-1945* (New York: American Jewish Committee, 1946), p. 381.

136. Quoted in Saul S. Friedman, *No Haven for the Oppressed: United States Policy Toward Jewish Refugees, 1938-1945* (Detroit: Wayne State University Press, 1973), p. 21.

137. Quoted in Robert A. Divine, *American Immigration Policy, 1924-1952* (New Haven: Yale University Press, 1957), p. 98.

138. Quoted in James MacGregor Burns, *Roosevelt: The Lion and the Fox* (New York: Harcourt, Brace and World, 1956), p. 339.

139. Arnold A. Offner, *American Appeasement: United States Foreign Policy and Germany, 1933-1938* (New York: W. W. Norton, 1976 [c. 1969]), p. 92.

140. Quoted in Henry L. Feingold, *Politics of Rescue: The Roosevelt Administration and the Holocaust, 1938-1945* (New Brunswick, N.J.: Rutgers University Press, 1970), p. 19.

141. Quoted in Friedman, *No Haven*, p. 83.

142. Quoted *ibid.*, p. 103.

143. Quoted in Irwin F. Gellman, "The *St. Louis* Tragedy," *American Jewish Historical Quarterly*, LXI (December, 1971), 156.

144. Quoted in A. J. Sherman, *Island Refuge: Britain and Refugees from the Third Reich, 1933-1939* (Berkeley: University of California Press, 1973), p. 207.

145. Peter Calvocoressi and Guy Wint, *Total War: The Story of World War II* (New York: Pantheon Books, 1972), p. 238.

146. Quoted in Arthur D. Morse, *While Six Million Died: A Chronicle of American Apathy* (New York: Random House, 1968), p. 63.

147. Quoted *ibid.*, pp. 93, 95.

148. Cordell Hull, *Memoirs* (New York: Macmillan, 1948; 2 vols.), II, 1540.

149. Quoted in George Woodbridge *et al.*, *The History of the United Nations Relief and Rehabilitation Administration* (New York: Columbia University Press, 1950; 3 vols.), I, 4.

150. Francis B. Sayre in *Department of State Bulletin*, IX (October 23, 1943), 275.

151. U.S. Department of State, *Treaties and Other International Acts* (Washington, D.C.: Government Printing Office, 1946), series 1501-1502.

152. Quoted in Thomas G. Paterson, *Soviet-American Confrontation: Postwar Reconstruction and the Origins of the Cold War* (Baltimore: The Johns Hopkins University Press, 1973), p. 147.

153. Quoted in Richard N. Gardner, *Sterling-Dollar Diplomacy: The Origins and the Prospects of Our International Economic Order* (New York: McGraw-Hill, 1969; rev. ed.), p. 267.

154. Quoted in Diane Shaver Clemens, *Yalta* (New York: Oxford University Press, 1970), p. 48.

155. Quoted in Robert A. Divine, *Second Chance: The Triumph of Internationalism in America During World War II* (New York: Atheneum, 1967), p. 226.

156. Quoted in Thomas M. Campbell, *Masquerade Peace: America's UN Policy, 1944-1945* (Tallahassee: Florida State University Press, 1973), p. 22.

157. Quoted in Divine, *Second Chance*, p. 229.

158. Diary entry of May 11, 1944 in Gabriel Kolko, *The Politics of War* (New York: Random House, 1968), pp. 270-271.

159. *Foreign Relations of the United States, 1945* (Washington, D.C.: Government Printing Office, 1967), V, 253.

160. Vandenberg, *Private Papers*, p. 176.
161. Quoted in Divine, *Second Chance*, p. 290.
162. Quoted *ibid.*, p. 291.
163. Quoted *ibid.*, p. 297.
164. Quoted in Kolko, *Politics of War*, p. 470.
165. Tom Connally, *My Name Is Tom Connally* (New York: Thomas Y. Crowell, 1954), p. 286.
166. Arnold Wolfers, *United States Policy toward Germany* (New Haven: Yale Institute of International Studies, 1947), p. 3.
167. Quoted in Paterson, *Soviet-American Confrontation*, p. 237.
168. *Foreign Relations, Conference at Quebec, 1944* (Washington, D.C.: Government Printing Office, 1972), p. 467.
169. Henry L. Stimson to the President, September 15, 1944, Box 100, James Forrestal Papers, Princeton University Library.
170. Notebooks, Interview with Harry S. Truman, November 12, 1949, Box 85, Jonathan Daniels Papers, University of North Carolina Library, Chapel Hill, North Carolina.
171. Churchill, *Triumph and Tragedy*, p. 338.
172. Clemens, *Yalta*, p. 287.
173. *Correspondence Between the Chairman . . .*, I, 295.
174. Forrest C. Pogue, "The Struggle for a New Order," in John L. Snell, ed., *The Meaning of Yalta* (Baton Rouge: Louisiana State University Press, 1956), pp. 33–34.
175. Churchill, *Triumph and Tragedy*, p. 366.
176. Quoted *ibid.*, p. 372.
177. Quoted in Vojtech Mastny, *Russia's Road to the Cold War: Diplomacy, Warfare, and the Politics of Communism, 1941–1945* (New York: Columbia University Press, 1979), p. 245.
178. This and subsequent quotations from the accords are from *ibid.*
179. William D. Leahy, *I Was There* (New York: Whittlesey House, 1950), pp. 315–316.
180. Quoted in Sherwood, *Roosevelt and Hopkins*, p. 870.
181. Quoted in Charles E. Bohlen, *Witness to History, 1929–1969* (New York: W. W. Norton, 1973), p. 181.
182. Dilks, *Diaries of Sir Alexander Cadogan*, p. 717.
183. Churchill, *Triumph and Tragedy*, p. 402.
184. Quoted in *New York Times*, February 8, 1970.
185. Quoted in Kolko, *Politics of War*, p. 465.
186. Quoted in Clemens, *Yalta*, p. 241.
187. Quoted in Woodward, *British Foreign Policy in the Second World War*, III, 116–118.
188. Churchill, *Triumph and Tragedy*, pp. 227–228.
189. Feis, *Churchill, Roosevelt, Stalin*, p. 451.
190. Churchill quoted in Louis Fischer, *The Road to Yalta: Soviet Foreign Relations, 1941–1945* (New York: Harper and Row, 1972), p. 179; and Slessor in John Wheeler-Bennett and Anthony Nicholls, *The Semblance of Peace* (New York: W. W. Norton, 1974 [c. 1972]), p. 191.
191. Quoted in Richard L. Walker, *E. R. Stettinius, Jr.* (New York: Cooper Square Publishers, 1965), p. 333. Emphasis added.
192. Quoted in Kolko, *Politics of War*, p. 465.
193. Quoted in Thomas G. Paterson, *On Every Front: The Making of the Cold War* (New York: W. W. Norton, 1979), p. 48.
194. Quoted in Kolko, *Politics of War*, p. 482.
195. Harry S. Truman, *Memoirs* (Garden City, N.Y.: Doubleday, 1955–1956; 2 vols.), I, 228.
196. *Ibid.*, p. 258.
197. Quoted in John Morton Blum, *The Price of Vision: The Diary of Henry A. Wallace, 1942–1946* (Boston: Houghton Mifflin, 1973), p. 451.
198. *Foreign Relations, Berlin*, I, 33.
199. *Ibid.*, I, 39.
200. *Ibid.*, I, 61.
201. Dilks, *Diaries of Sir Alexander Cagodan*, p. 762.
202. Truman, *Memoirs*, I, 402.
203. Quoted in Lisle A. Rose, *After Yalta: America and the Origins of the Cold War* (New York: Charles Scribner's Sons, 1973), p. 51.
204. Journal, August 1, 1945, Box 19, and Memorandum of Conversation with Harriman, July 17, 1945, Box 18, Joseph Davies Papers, Library of Congress.
205. Winston Churchill, "Note of the Prime Minister's Conversation with President Truman at Luncheon, July 18, 1945," Premier 3, 430/8, Prime Minister's Office Records, Public Record Office, London, England.
206. *The Tehran, Yalta & Potsdam Conferences: Documents* (Moscow: Progress Publishers, 1969), p. 323.
207. George F. Kennan, *Memoirs, 1925–1950* (Boston: Little, Brown, 1967), p. 260.
208. *Foreign Relations, Berlin*, II, 365.
209. Truman, *Memoirs*, I, 412.
210. Herbert Feis, *Between War and Peace: The Potsdam Conference* (Princeton: Princeton University Press, 1960), p. 25.
211. Quoted in Walter Millis, ed., *The Forrestal Diaries* (New York: The Viking Press, 1951), p. 79.
212. "Notes on Conversation in Moscow with Maxim Litvinov," by Edgar Snow, December 6, 1944, Box 68, President's Secretary's File, Franklin D. Roosevelt Papers, Franklin D. Roosevelt Library, Hyde Park, New York.
213. Peter F. Drucker, *The Concept of the Corporation* (New York: New American Library, 1964; 2nd ed.), p. xi.
214. Quoted in Gardner, *Sterling-Dollar Diplomacy*, p. xvii.
215. H. D. Clarke in Foreign Office Minutes on the Political Situation in the United States, August 20, 1945, AN2505/4145, Foreign Office Correspondence, Public Record Office.
216. *Department of State Bulletin*, XXII (April 22, 1945), 738.
217. Richard J. Barnet, *Roots of War* (Baltimore: Penguin Books, 1973 [c. 1972]), p. 23.
218. Arthur M. Schlesinger, Jr., *The Imperial Presidency* (New York: Popular Library, 1974), p. 128.
219. Quoted in Barnet, *Roots of War*, p. 42.

Atomic Blast. The second atomic bomb fell on Nagasaki, August 9, 1945, killing at least 60,000. (U.S. Air Force)

12 The Origins of the Cold War, 1945–1950

Diplomatic Crossroad: "The Greatest Thing in History" at Hiroshima, 1945

The crewmen of the B-29 group scrawled rude and poignant anti-Japanese graffiti on the "Little Boy." A major, thinking about his son in the states and a quick end to the war, scratched "No white cross for Stevie" on the 10,000-pound orange and black bomb.[1] The 509th Bombardment Group had been training on the Mariana Island of Tinian since May. At last, it seemed that the United States secret atomic development program ("the Manhattan Project") was nearing fruition. In the evening of August 5, 1945 Colonel Paul "Old Bull" Tibbets informed his men for the first time that their rare cargo was "atomic." He did not explain the scientific process in which two pieces of uranium (U-235), placed at opposite ends of a cylinder, smashed into one another to create tremendous energy. They knew what the equivalent of 20,000 tons of TNT meant, however. At midnight they settled down to a preflight meal, played poker, and waited.

At 1:37 A.M. on August 6 three weather planes took off in the darkness for the urban targets of Hiroshima, Kokura, and Niigata. At 2:45, after photo snapping and well wishing, Tibbets' heavily laden ship, the *Enola Gay*, named after his mother, lifted ponderously off the Tinian runway. The six-hour flight was uneventful, marked by the dodging of cumulus clouds and the nerve-wracking final assembly of the bomb's inner components. Followed by two observation planes stocked with cameras and scientists, the *Enola Gay* spotted the Japanese coast at 7:30 A.M. The weather plane assigned to Hiroshima, the primary target, reported clear skies. Tibbets headed for that city.

"This is history," he intoned over the intercom, "so watch your language."[2] But in those anxious moments someone actually forgot to switch on the tape recorder. At 31,600 feet and 328 miles per hour the *Enola Gay* began its run on Hiroshima. Crew members fastened on welder's goggles. Bombardier Thomas Ferebee prepared to cross the hairs in his bombsight. At 8:15 A.M. he shouted "bombs away." The *Enola Gay* swerved quickly to escape. The hefty "Little Boy"

Enola Gay. On August 6, 1945, just before takeoff, Colonel Paul Tibbets waved from the cockpit of his aircraft *Enola Gay*. Tibbets hailed from Miami and was a veteran of the European theater. For commanding the atomic mission, Tibbets was awarded the Distinguished Service Cross. (U.S. Air Force)

"**Little Boy.**" The nuclear weapon detonated over Hiroshima was 120 inches long and 28 inches in diameter, and weighed about 10,000 pounds. (Los Alamos Scientific Laboratory, courtesy of the Harry S Truman Library)

fell for fifty seconds and then exploded about 2,000 feet above ground, a near perfect hit at hypo-center. A brilliant flash of light temporarily blinded the fliers. The ship trembled, hit by a wave of sound like a baseball bat hitting an ash can. Crew members looked back. "My God," sighed co-pilot Captain Robert Lewis, as he watched the huge, purplish cloud of smoke, dust, and debris rise 40,000 feet into the atmosphere. "Even though we had expected something terrific," he remembered, "what we saw made us feel that we were Buck Rogers twenty-fifth century warriors."[3]

Hiroshima was Japan's eighth largest city, with 250,000 people. Manhattan Project director Lieutenant General Leslie Groves, with the President's approval, had ranked it first on the target list because it housed regional military headquarters, but it was largely a residential and commercial city. On the cloudless, warm morning of August 6, 1945, Hiroshima's inhabitants heard the bombing alert siren. An "all clear" sounded when it was discovered that only a weather plane had passed over. Everything seemed routine, for Hiroshima had largely been spared from American bombs during the war. Forty-five minutes later, at 8:15 A.M., people labored at their jobs or moved fearlessly in the streets. Few heard the *Enola Gay* overhead. Suddenly a streak of light raced through the sky. A blast of lacerating heat traveling at the speed of light rocked the city. The temperature soared to suffocating levels. Trees were stripped of their leaves. Buildings blew apart like firecrackers. Debris shot through the air like bullets. Permanent shadows were etched into concrete. The sky grew dark, lighted only by the choking fires that erupted everywhere. Winds swirled violently and raindrops intermittently struck the cluttered ground. Some victims thought the Americans were now unleashing gasoline drops to feed the spreading fires. It seemed as though a huge scythe had leveled Hiroshima.

As the giant mushroom cloud churned above, dazed survivors stumbled about like scarecrows, their arms raised to avoid the painful rubbing of burned flesh. The victims' condition was gruesome: skin peeling off like ribbons; gaping wounds; vomiting and diarrhea; intense thirst. A badly wounded Dr. Michihiko Machiya noted that "no one talked, and the ominous silence was relieved only by a subdued rustle among so many people, restless, in pain, anxious, and afraid, waiting for something else to happen."[4] The nightmare was later recorded in statistics: about 130,000 dead, as many wounded, and 81 percent of the city's buildings destroyed. About 20 American prisoners of war also perished there.

President Harry S Truman thought the successful mission against Hiroshima the "greatest thing in history."[5] American aircraft continued their destructive conventional bombing of other Japanese cities. On August 9, a second atomic bomb smashed Nagasaki, killing at least 60,000. The Japanese surrendered five days later. Presidential aide Admiral William D. Leahy was less euphoric than some over victory, for he thought that "in being the first to use it, we had adopted the ethical standard common to the barbarians of the Dark Ages. I was not taught to make war in that fashion, and wars cannot be won by destroying women and children."[6]

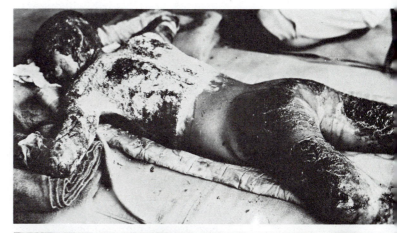

Victims at Hiroshima. Flash-burned victims shortly after the destruction of Hiroshima. Estimates are that in the five years after Hiroshima and Nagasaki another 130,000 people died. (Photographs courtesy of Dr. A. A. Liebow, Army Institute of Pathology)

As Leahy's comment attests, the decision to use the atomic bomb against an urban center met criticism within the small circle of government officials and scientists who were privy to the Manhattan Project. Although Truman always claimed that he never lost a night's sleep over his momentous decision, several advisers and physicists were restless. They presented what they thought were viable alternatives to dropping the bomb on a civilian population: (1) follow up Japanese peace feelers; (2) blockade and bomb Japan conventionally; (3) have Russia declare war on Japan; (4) warn Tokyo about the bomb and threaten its use; (5) demonstrate the bomb on an unpopulated island or area with international observers, including Japanese; (6) conduct a military landing on the outlying Japanese island of Kyushu. The overriding themes were that use of the bomb would constitute a moral blot on the American record, that it would jeopardize the chances of postwar international control of the awesome weapon, and that it was unnecessary because Japan was near military defeat anyway.

The general thrust of those who, like Truman himself, chose to drop the atomic bomb on a populated target was that the war should be ended as quickly as possible to save American lives. That simple reason helps to explain the decision, but decisions seldom derive from single factors and this one is no exception. Three primary and intertwined motives induced policymakers to inflict atomic horror upon the citizens of Japan. Together, the three suggest the central point: Truman found no compelling reasons against dropping atom bombs on Hiroshima and Nagasaki and important advantages in doing so.

The first motive—emotion—dated from December 7, 1941, when the Japanese bombed Pearl Harbor without warning. Vengeful Americans never forgot or forgave that disaster. The Japanese, as Truman said time and time again, could not be trusted. Revenge was the order of the day; they had to be repaid in kind. This popular attitude was strengthened by the racist American image of the Japanese, which drew upon a long tradition of anti-Oriental prejudice. The Japanese were stereotyped as crafty and sadistic. Hollywood movies portrayed suicidal, mad, grinning Nipponese pilots bearing down upon American aircraft with bloodthirsty delight. The *kamikaze* attacks fed such images in 1945. Americans hated the Japanese—the "slant-eyes"—more than the Germans, and 13 percent in a Gallup poll of December, 1944 recommended the extermination of all Japanese. Others advised sterilization. "We are drowning and burning the bestial apes all over the Pacific," Admiral William Halsey boasted on a newsreel, "and it is just as much pleasure to burn them as to drown them."[7] This irrational emotion was influential. Truman himself said on August 11, 1945: "When you have to deal with a beast you have to treat him as a beast."[8]

The second motive—military momentum—merged with the first and dated from the establishment of the Manhattan Project in August, 1942. This program began after European scientists, through a letter from Albert Einstein to President Franklin D. Roosevelt, warned that Germany might develop a nuclear device for military purposes. From the start, the assumption underlying the two-billion-dollar secret American project was that once a bomb was developed it would be used to end the war. Truman inherited this assumption from the Roosevelt Administration. His decision was not so much a decision to drop the bomb, but rather a decision *not* to reject that assumption, not to break the momentum. Furthermore, the large-scale bombing of civilian populations, such as those of Dresden and Tokyo, was an accepted practice by 1945. By August, 1945, however, this compel-

Hiroshima. The ruins of Japan's eighth largest city bespoke the birth of the atomic age. (U.S. Air Force)

ling momentum had taken on an irrational quality, for the Germans had been knocked out of the war and Japan faced certain defeat.

The third factor that helped persuade Truman to unleash the atomic bomb was the diplomatic advantage that might accrue to the United States. The diplomatic bonus materialized when American leaders, while at the Potsdam Conference, learned about the successful test explosion at Alamogordo, New Mexico on July 16, 1945. Throughout the war, Churchill and Roosevelt had kept the secret of the bomb from Russia, in part to use it for diplomatic leverage in the postwar period. Some scientists and advisers protested that excluding Russia, an ally, from any knowledge, would jeopardize or kill opportunities for successful postwar negotiations. At the Potsdam meeting, Truman did casually and cryptically inform Stalin that the United States had "a new weapon of unusual destructive force."[9] Stalin muttered that he hoped America would use it against the Japanese. It is likely that the Soviet dictator already knew from his intelligence network about the existence of the joint Anglo-American atomic development program, although he probably did not know the magnitude of the bomb and certainly did not know how soon or whether it would be used.

Churchill learned about the test in New Mexico directly from the American delegation at Potsdam. "Now I know what happened to Truman yesterday," the Prime Minister noted. "When he got to the meeting after having read this report [on the New Mexico success] he was a changed man. He told the Russians just where they got on and off and generally bossed the whole meeting."[10] Two diplomatic advantages suggested themselves. First, the bomb might gain diplomatic concessions by strengthening the United States' negotiating position vis-à-vis the Soviets. Russia might be intimidated to make concessions on Eastern European questions if the bomb revealed its destructive power on a Japanese city. Second, the use of the bomb might end the war in the Pacific before the Russians could declare war against Japan; such a circumstance would deny Russia any part in the postwar control of Japan and perhaps forestall Russian military entry into Manchuria. Until the explosion at Alamogordo the United States had desired Soviet military action against Japan; the bomb's triumph in the sands of New Mexico expunged that desire.

All three factors—emotion, military momentum, and diplomatic advantage—explain the tragedies at Hiroshima and Nagasaki. The diplomatic aspect was added as a late bonus; the bomb would have been dropped whether such a consideration existed or not. To have decided against dropping the atomic bomb, Truman would have had to deny the passion and momentum which had built up by midsummer, 1945. Pearl Harbor could be avenged, the war ended quickly, American lives

James F. Byrnes (1879–1972) and Harry S Truman (1884–1972). Both the secretary of state and the President, here on their way back from the Potsdam Conference, anticipated that the atomic bomb would serve as a diplomatic bargaining weapon in the postwar period. South Carolinian Byrnes served as secretary of state for 1945–1947. (U.S. Navy, courtesy of the Harry S Truman Library)

saved, and the American diplomatic position shored up—the advantages far outweighed the disadvantages in the American mind. Still, the costs were not inconsequential. Some of the alternatives, or a combination of them, might have terminated the war without the heavy death toll and the grotesque suffering of the survivors. The failure to discuss atomic development and control with the Russians during the war bequeathed to the postwar generation both division and fear. The United States never directly threatened to use the weapon in the early Cold War to gain Soviet concessions; the threat was *implied* only. Yet "the bomb" fixed itself as a corrosive feature of the Soviet-American confrontation.

Soviet-American Confrontation

If Hiroshima symbolized the destructive power possessed by the United States in 1945, a war-wracked Europe, resembling a rubble heap, constituted one of the United States' major postwar problems. It is awesome indeed to realize that 35 million people died in Europe during the Second World War. Those Europeans who survived were homeless and hungry, and the contrast with prosperous Americans, untouched by enemy bombers or soldiers, was stark. Then, too, the French, British, and Dutch, weakened by the war, were no longer able to manage their rebellious colonial domains, particularly in Asia, and began to pull back. Britain, for example, granted independence to India in 1947 and Burma in 1948, and the Dutch left Indonesia a year later. Throughout the postwar period, the decolonization process begun by World War II continued, presenting challenges to the United States.

The United States also faced a major new power bent upon asserting its authority in international relations. Soviet Russia assumed a demanding postwar position and its pushy behavior, its suspicion, and its blunt language antagonized Americans. Diplomat Dean Acheson said the Soviets were not housebroken, and Truman complained that they negotiated "with a boorishness worthy of stable boys."[11] At the end of the war, the Soviet Union had troops in most of the Eastern European countries and Germany. It lacked an effective navy or air force and did not possess the atomic bomb, but it had become a strong regional power by virtue of its military exploits. Motivated by traditional Russian nationalism, a fervent Communist ideology, a craving for security against a revived Germany, and the huge task of reconstruction, the leaders of the Kremlin determined to make the most of the limited power they held. Often rude and abusive, yet cautious and realistic, Josef Stalin determined never again to see his country invaded through Eastern Europe. The image of "Uncle Joe" soon dissipated. Nevertheless, compared to the United States, as chargé d'affaires George F. Kennan reported from Moscow, Russia was still the "weaker force."[12]

The United States emerged from World War II a global power for the first time in its history. American diplomats were self-conscious about their supreme power and attempted to use it to shape an American-oriented postwar world. With troops in Asia and Europe, the world's largest navy and air force, a monopoly of the atomic bomb, and a high-gear economy, the United States demanded first rank in world affairs. As one scholar has put it, the United States held the "prime weapon of *de*struction—the atomic bomb—and the prime weapon of *recon*struction—such wealth as no nation hitherto had possessed."[13] President Truman heralded America as the "giant of the economic world," and British Ambassador Lord Halifax

Josef Stalin (1879–1953). The ruthless leader of Russia since the 1920s, Stalin ran an authoritarian state and conducted a foreign policy marked by suspiciousness and bluntness. His daughter recalled that "he saw enemies everywhere" and Lenin once remarked that Stalin was "too rude." (*The Reporter,* 1952. Copyright 1952 by Fortnightly Publishing Co., Inc.)

reported that "by contrast with the exhausted and devastated countries of western Europe, the United States sees itself, as a result of the war, endowed with colossal productive and fighting capacity."[14] While public pressure compelled Truman to demobilize the armed forces faster than he wished, the Soviet Union itself demobilized, although it still retained a large standing army.

Washington was encouraged to exercise its power by the fundamental factors of ideology and the economic requirements of the nation. American ideology integrated political and economic tenets in a "peace and prosperity" philosophy. Simply stated, this ideology held that world peace and order depended upon the existence of prosperity and political democracy. Poverty and economic depression, on the other hand, bred totalitarianism, revolution, communism, the disruption of world trade through economic competition, and war. Prosperity became the handmaiden of stability, political freedom, unrestricted trade, and peaceful international relations. This thinking was not new to the postwar era, for Americans had long believed that they were prosperous because they were democratic and democratic because they were prosperous.

American leaders determined that *this time,* unlike after World War I, the United States would seize the opportunity to fulfill its ideological premises. As historian Gaddis Smith has described diplomat Dean Acheson's historical understanding, "only the United States had the power to grab hold of history and make it conform."[15] The lessons of the 1920s and 1930s tugged at the leaders of the 1940s, and there was a good deal of arrogance in both American ideology and behavior nurtured by this desire to throw off the mistakes of the past. The British complained about America's "irritating cockahoop moods."[16] On the simplest level

Makers of American Foreign Policy from 1945 to 1950

Presidents	Secretaries of State
Harry S Truman, 1945–1953	Edward R. Stettinius, Jr., 1944–1945
	James F. Byrnes, 1945–1947
	George C. Marshall, 1947–1949
	Dean G. Acheson, 1949–1953

Americans believed themselves a successful people, with admirable institutions and ideals worthy of universal adoption. The postwar period seemed an opportune time to install America's concept of "peace and prosperity" as the world's way—a time to express traditional American expansionism.

Postwar expansionism was also stimulated by another factor of a fundamental character: the vital needs or requirements of the American economy. Truman and other leaders frankly stated the facts: the United States *had* to export American goods and *had* to import strategic raw materials. By 1947 United States exports accounted for one-third of total world exports and were valued at $14 billion a year. Pivotal industries, such as automobiles, trucks, machine tools, steel, and farm machinery relied heavily upon foreign trade for their well-being. Farmers exported about half of their wheat. Many Americans, remembering the Great Depression, predicted economic catastrophe unless American foreign trade continued and

"**What Next?**" Jack Lambert's 1946 cartoon of Truman captured the feeling of many Americans that the President, new at his job, was overwhelmed by postwar problems. (Jack Lambert, *Chicago Sun Times*)

expanded. Although less than 10 percent of the GNP, exports exceeded in volume such elements of the GNP as consumers' expenditures on durable goods, total expenditures by state and local governments, and private construction. Further-more, imports of manganese, tungsten, and chromite, to name a few, were essential to America's industrial system. Foreign trade, however, was threatened by the sickness of America's best customer, Europe, which lacked the resources to purchase American products, and by nationalists in former colonial areas, who controlled raw materials sources for both Europe and America. To protect its interests and to fulfill its ideology the United States undertook foreign aid pro-grams that eventually became global in scale.

President Harry S Truman felt the flush of American power, shared the ideol-ogy, and knew well the economic needs of the country. A self-confident party regular from the Pendergast machine in Kansas City, Truman had long experi-enced the rough-and-tumble of politics. Whereas Roosevelt had been charming and often evasive, Missouri-bred Truman was blunt and straightforward. "The buck stops here" read a sign on his desk. He prided himself on simple, direct language and quick decisions. Critics said he frequently shot before he thought. "Give 'em hell Harry," the crowds shouted. Truman had the "steady energy of a commission salesman, the aplomb and brashness of a riverboat gambler," and the "sass" of a bantam rooster, wrote one biographer.[17] With his intense eyes peering through thick lenses, Truman relished the verbal brawl. His hurried simplification of issues, his amateurish application of lessons from the past, and his quick-tempered style spawned jokes that often fit the truth. Why did the President arrive late for a press conference? "He got up this morning a little stiff in the joints and had trouble putting his foot in his mouth." Somebody rewrote a proverb: "To err is Truman."

A statesman's style may reveal his nation's bargaining position. In April, 1945, Soviet Foreign Minister V. M. Molotov visited the White House and President Truman gave him a vigorous tongue-lashing. Stubborn Molotov stormed out of the office, stung by language more suitable for a ward politician in Missouri who had not delivered enough votes to the machine. After the encounter, the first meeting between the new President and a high-ranking Soviet official, Truman gloated to a friend: "I gave it to him straight 'one-two to the jaw.' I let him have it straight."[18] Truman's confident style drew strength from actual American power. He could "get tough," as the saying went at the time, because the United States was in fact powerful. Truman told Ambassador to Russia W. Averell Harriman that he was not afraid of the Soviets, because they "needed us more than we needed them." He did not expect to win 100 percent of the American case, but "we should be able to get 85 percent."[19] Overall, United States foreign policy after World War II was neither accidental nor aimless, but rather self-conscious and forceful.

The confrontation between the United States and Russia, the "Cold War," had its origins in the different postwar needs, ideology, style, and power of the two rivals and drew upon an historical legacy of distrust. Each saw the other, in mirror image, as the world's bully. Each charged the other with assuming Hitler's ag-gressive mantle. Americans compared Nazism and Communism, Hitler and Stalin, and coined the phrase "Red Fascism." The international structure or balance was in a shambles. Putting it back into some kind of order would automatically generate tension. Conflict was inevitable, but perhaps the Cold War was not. Here is where American style and tactics counted. The heated American rhetoric,

"Red Fascism." This popular notion among Americans suggested that German nazism and Russian communism were really one and the same and that the 1940s would see totalitarian aggression like that of the 1930s. Such thinking aroused fears of another "Munich" and "appeasement" and thereby hindered negotiations. (*The Reporter,* 1950. Copyright 1950 by Fortnightly Publishing Co. Inc.)

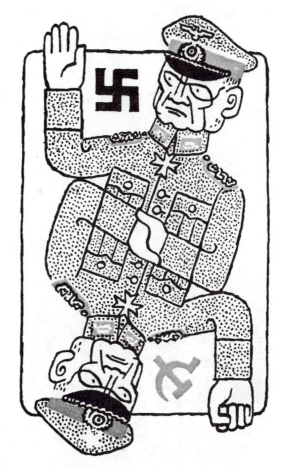

constant alarms, "get tough" style, unilateral decisions, manipulation of international agencies, rejection of reasonable alternative policies, uncompromising stances, use of foreign aid as a diplomatic weapon—all helped bring on the Cold War.

Diplomatic Battleground in Eastern Europe

By the end of the war Eastern Europe had become a Soviet sphere of influence. It was the one area of the world largely closed off to American influence, where the Soviet Union stood most powerful. Although some observers considered Eastern Europe an impenetrable and solid Soviet bloc, the region looked more like a patchwork quilt. The Soviet presence in Eastern Europe before 1947–1948 was neither uniform nor consistent. Russia had no imperial blueprint for its neighbors. Poland, with its Communist Lublin government in control, was firmly within the Soviet grasp. Rumania, an anti-Soviet German satellite during the war, suffered under a Soviet-imposed government. The Soviet Union gained territory at the expense of Poland, Finland, and Rumania after postwar boundary settlements. Bulgaria had a large indigenous Communist movement, which gained control through elections without much help from Moscow.

Changes in Europe After World War II

Territorial Changes After World War II

Notes: — The United States, British, and French Zones
of Germany merged in 1949 as the Federal
Republic of Germany.
— The Russian Zone of Germany became the
German Democratic Republic in 1949.
— The four zones of Austria merged in 1955
to become the Federal Republic of Austria.

Hungary and other nations developed differently. The conservative Hungarian Smallholders' party of Ferenc Nagy won national elections in November, 1945 by routing the Communists, who managed to get only 17 percent of the vote. The Nagy government remained in office until a Communist coup in the spring of 1947. In Finland, to demonstrate the political complexity in Eastern Europe further, non-Communist leaders recognized their precarious position with respect to neighboring Russia and adopted a neutral position vis-à-vis the Soviet-American confrontation. Finland thus retained its independence and in 1948 even ousted from its Cabinet the lone Communist member. Yugoslavia, although a Communist state, established its independence from Moscow under the leadership of Josip Broz Tito. The growing schism became public in 1948 when Belgrade and Moscow bitterly split. Finally, there was the tragic case of Czechoslovakia, an independent socialist country with a democratic political process and ties with the West. Czech officials recognized the advisability of a middle course. A coalition government under non-Communist President Eduard Beneš and Foreign Minister Jan Masaryk assumed office after free elections in May, 1946. Communists held membership in the government, with 9 of 26 top-level positions and 114 of 300 National Assembly seats, but the Soviet Union for a time refrained from meddling directly in Czech affairs. Not until February, 1948, after the Cold War was well advanced, did the Communists seize control of Czechoslovakia during a domestic crisis.

The Soviet presence in Eastern Europe before 1948, then, was conspicuous and often repressive, but not absolute. Communists were active, sometimes gaining control of repressive ministries of interior (police). Stalin seemed hesitant and uncertain, having a different policy for each Eastern European country. The Russian leader said he wanted "friendly governments," not satellites. In early 1945, in stating his case regarding Poland, Stalin emphasized security: "Throughout history Poland has been the corridor for attack on Russia. We have to mention that during the last thirty years Germany twice has passed through this corridor. The reason for this was that Poland was weak. Russia wants a strong, independent, and democratic Poland. . . . It is not only a question of honor for Russia, but one of life and death."[20] Still bitter over the *cordon sanitaire* the Western powers constructed around Russia after World War I, staggering from the loss of 15–20 million Russian dead during the recent war, and fearing that some day Germany might march again, Soviet leaders demanded security through influence among their neighbors. They also believed that the 1944 Moscow percentage bargain, armistice agreements, and Yalta accords acknowledged their primary position in Eastern Europe. Thus the Soviets began building their own *cordon sanitaire*.

United States goals for the area clashed with those of the Soviet Union. Washington sought "free elections" and the "Open Door" for trade, both traditional principles calculated in part to reduce Soviet influence. The Soviets signed bilateral trade treaties with many of the Eastern European states, which established favors anathema to America's Open Door policy and multilateral approach to trade. Although Americans had minimal commercial ties with Eastern Europe, American diplomats preached the Open Door as a way of driving a wedge into the area. The application of the principle of "free elections" also proved difficult in Eastern Europe. There was little tradition of democracy, except in Czechoslovakia, and free elections in most of those nations would have meant strongly anti-Soviet governments threatening Soviet security (such as the London Poles). The question of elections in Hungary demonstrates the complexity of the question. During late

1946 it was the *non-Communist* Nagy who delayed elections, because he knew the Communists would lose badly and that result might trigger an intrusive Soviet response. What both the United States and the Soviet Union wanted in Eastern Europe was not democratic, but friendly governments. After all, critics asked, if "free elections" were the ultimate and universal goal of American diplomacy, why was the principle not applied to the United States sphere of influence in Latin America, where Washington recognized a host of military dictators?

The Soviets hence charged the United States with a double standard. When American leaders consciously excluded Russia from participation in the postwar reconstruction of Italy and Japan, the Soviets cited the Italian example as a precedent for their machinations in Eastern Europe. Secretary of War Henry L. Stimson was alive to the problem in 1945: "Some Americans are anxious to hang on to exaggerated views of the Monroe Doctrine and at the same time butt into every question that comes up in Central Europe."[21] Furthermore, V. M. Molotov dipped into the 1946 edition of the *World Almanac* to illustrate how economically strong the United States was compared to the war-weakened states. He contended that an Open Door in Eastern Europe would actually mean ultimate American economic domination, because the United States had no real economic competitors. In short, the Soviet Union looked upon American goals in Eastern Europe as guises for United States expansion in an area of vital importance to its own security. The Americans, in rebuttal, pointed out that the Russians had emasculated the Declaration of Liberated Europe agreed to at Yalta.

At the Yalta and Potsdam conferences, at the Foreign Ministers conferences in London (September–October, 1945) and Moscow (December 1945), at the Paris Peace Conference (April–October, 1946), and in numerous diplomatic notes, the United States sought influence in Eastern Europe to counter the Soviets. It tried nonrecognition of the pro-Soviet governments, but abandoned that after slight Soviet concessions, such as the addition of a handful of non-Communists to the Polish government. Some American leaders thought the continued United States monopoly of the atomic bomb would force Soviet concessions. Stimson recorded in his diary that Byrnes "looks to having the presence of the bomb in his pocket" at the London Conference.[22] A telling incident occurred at that conference. Molotov, as if he had been reading Stimson's diary, asked Byrnes if he had "an atomic bomb in his side pocket." "You don't know Southerners," Byrnes replied. "We carry our artillery in our pocket. If you don't cut out all this stalling and let us get down to work, I am going to pull an atomic bomb out of my hip pocket and let you have it."[23] Molotov apparently laughed, but his suspicious mind must have fixed on the implications of the answer to his light question. Still, the implied threat of the bomb did not budge the Soviets from Eastern Europe, and the United States never practiced a conscious "atomic diplomacy" of direct threat.

Stimson opposed the use of the bomb as a diplomatic weapon in September, 1945. He had earlier embraced the thought of forcing Soviet concessions, but reversed himself when he told the President that the United States should share the secret of the bomb to spur postwar cooperative relations. "For if we fail to approach them now and merely continue to negotiate with them, having this weapon rather ostentatiously on our hip, their suspicions and their distrust of our purposes and motives will increase." Stimson, then seventy-eight, and a former Cabinet officer under William Howard Taft, Herbert Hoover, and Franklin Roosevelt, offered Truman some sage advice: "The chief lesson I have learned in a long life is the only way you can make a man trustworthy is to trust him; and the surest way you can make a man untrustworthy is to distrust him and show your distrust."[24] Stimson gained the support of Secretary of Commerce Henry Wallace, but Secretary of the Navy James V. Forrestal rejected any effort to "buy [Russian] understanding and sympathy. We tried that once with Hitler."[25] Truman sided with Forrestal.

The United States also used foreign aid as a diplomatic weapon in Eastern Europe. Byrnes stated the policy in 1946: "We must help our friends in every way and refrain from assisting those who either through helplessness or for other reasons are opposing the principles for which we stand."[26] In short, no loans or aid for Eastern Europe. This policy backfired, for it left those countries dependent upon Soviet aid and drove them deeper into the Soviet orbit. In Czechoslovakia, for example, the United States in 1946 abruptly severed an Export-Import bank loan to press Beneš to remove the Communists from his government. As non-Communist Foreign Trade Minister Hubert Ripka complained bitterly in late 1947 about American behavior, "these idiots started the usual blackmail: 'Okay, you can have 200,000 or 300,000 or even 500,000 tons of wheat, but on one condition only—that you throw the Communists out of the Czechoslovak Government.'" The result: "And now these idiots in Washington have driven us straight into the Stalinist camp."[27]

The United States, through such pressure tactics on the Soviet sphere of influence, helped intensify the Cold War. That is, during 1947–1948 the Russians read American policies, including American encouragement to dissident anti-Soviet political groups, as threats to their security and so tightened their grip. George F. Kennan has suggested, for example, that the Czech coup was the Soviet

"I Can't Give You All Up For One Angel Of Peace." The burly Russian savors the attention of the Eastern Europeans in this critical Turkish cartoon. (*ULUS,* Ankara, in *United Nations World,* 1947)

response to the Marshall Plan, a major American aid program that the Soviets considered a challenge to their tenuous position in Eastern Europe. Overall, Washington exaggerated the extent of Soviet control in Eastern Europe and pressed the peoples of that region to align with the West. Yet the Eastern Europeans, so close to Russian power, could not and would not affront the Soviet Union. Washington treated only Finland and Yugoslavia as exceptions, forwarding some aid to them. American policymakers showed little understanding of the difference between an independent country (like Czechoslovakia) influenced by the Soviet Union and a subjugated country (like Poland). To Americans all were Soviet satellites, and because the Soviets were uncompromising in their heavy-handedness in manipulating governments, they deserved utter condemnation. Yet, as contemporary critics asked, would the Eastern Europeans have retained some of their independence and been better off had Washington cooled its rhetoric, meddled less, recognized what it ultimately could not change, and maintained economic and political ties through foreign aid? Perhaps. What we do know is that Russian behavior did not happen in a vacuum. American pressure aroused Soviet fears and hence countermeasures damaging to the Eastern Europeans.

Getting Tough with the Russians, 1946

The question of Eastern Europe broke up the London Conference of Foreign Ministers (September–October, 1945). Byrnes demanded representative governments in Bulgaria and Rumania before he would sign any peace treaties with the former German satellites. Molotov countered with questions about British-dominated Greece and American-dominated Japan. The conferees left London unable to agree even on a public communiqué. Byrnes became convinced that the Soviets had welshed on the Yalta Declaration on Liberated Europe and that they could not be trusted. At the Moscow Conference in December, 1945, the secretary of state tempered his tough stand somewhat and got Stalin to accept a token broadening of the Rumanian and Bulgarian regimes. The Russians also accepted Byrnes's ideas for a general peace conference to be held in Paris in 1946 and a United Nations Atomic Energy Commission to prepare plans for international control.

Yet Truman grew impatient. Byrnes had not kept the President informed about the Moscow proceedings. More important, Truman had decided upon a firmer line against the Soviet Union. As he put it in January of 1946, "I'm tired of babying the Russians."[28] The new "get tough" policy developed through the early months of 1946. Republican leaders like Senator Arthur Vandenberg of Michigan helped shape it with their denunciations of "appeasement," recalling the horrors of the 1930s and warning against new Munichs. The news of a Canadian spy ring that had sent atomic secrets to Russia broke in February, about the same time that Stalin gave a cocky pre-election speech that convinced some Americans that Russia was arming for war. From Moscow, on February 22, chargé d'affaires George F. Kennan wrote an alarmist and influential cable which declared that "we have here a political force committed fanatically to the belief that with [the] US there can be no permanent modus vivendi."[29] The "long telegram" was widely circulated in Washington and devoured with relish by those who believed there could be no compromise with Russia. Kennan later apologized that the cable read like a primer published by "the Daughters of the American Revolution, designed to arouse the citizenry to the dangers of the Communist conspiracy."[30]

On March 5, Winston Churchill, no longer prime minister, spoke in Fulton, Missouri. President Truman sat prominently on the platform and heard the eloquent orator declare that the United States "stands at this time at the pinnacle of world power." Churchill then lashed out at the Soviets: "From Stettin in the Baltic to Trieste in the Adriatic, an iron curtain has descended across the continent."[31] Most Americans applauded his stiff anti-Russian tone, but they warmed much less to his call for an Anglo-American alliance outside the fledgling United Nations Organization. "Don't be a ninny for imperialist Winnie," pickets later chanted in New York City.[32] Truman was pleased with Churchill's forceful language. Secretary Wallace, however, a dissenter from the "get tough" approach, feared that the Anglo-Americans were trying to "strut around the world and tell people where to get off."[33] An angry Stalin asserted that nations were not willing to exchange the "lordship of Hitler for the lordship of Churchill."[34] The war of words escalated.

The Iranian crisis peaked in early 1946 just as the Truman Administration was deciding to throw its power into making the Soviet Union more cooperative. The crisis began quietly in 1944 when British and American oil companies applied for Iranian concessions, and it became a classic example of competition for spheres of influence. Unwilling to be excluded from a bordering country, Russia soon applied for an oil concession too. The British, who had long dominated Iran, were no longer powerful enough to sustain their position. Reluctantly London looked to Washington for backing, and was pleased to find that the wartime and postwar American quest for petroleum in the Middle East served as a counterweight against the Soviets. By 1944 American corporations controlled 42 percent of the "proved" oil reserves of the Middle East, a nineteen-fold increase in American holdings there since 1936.

A 1942 treaty with Iran allowed the British and Soviets to occupy the country and required them to leave six months after the end of the war. American supply units and soldiers were also there, largely shipping Lend-Lease goods to Russia. In mid-1945 an indigenous rebellion in northern Iran (Azerbaijan) was encouraged by the Soviets. In January, 1946, working with American officials, Iran took the question of Soviet meddling to the United Nations Organization. The Soviets were irate, pointing out that British troops remained. Iran and Russia entered direct negotiations, but they did not reach an accord by March 2 when all foreign troops, by treaty, had to depart. American soldiers had withdrawn in January, but, very important, left military advisers behind; British troops departed in early March. The Russians thus stood alone in defiance of the treaty and aroused considerable international protest. In April, however, Moscow and Teheran concluded an agreement and Soviet forces left. In exchange for this withdrawal, Iran agreed to establish a joint Iranian-Soviet oil company, subject to approval by its parliament. After this agreement, the Iranian Prime Minister took a strong stand against Russia and the rebels in Azerbaijan, often following the advice of American Ambassador George V. Allen. In late 1946, Iranian armed forces, advised by Major General Robert W. Grow of the United States Army, squelched the insurrection in northern Iran. Russia took no steps to defend its Azerbaijani friends. Not until October, 1947, did the legislature consider the joint oil company; it rejected the agreement by a convincing vote of 102 to 2.

The Soviets exploded in anger. They had been eased from Iran while Britain and the United States had driven in stakes. Arthur C. Millspaugh, former United States

V. M. Molotov (1890—). Popularly known as "stone ass," the Soviet foreign minister was a tough-minded negotiator who cleared most decisions with Stalin. When he became angry, a bump appeared on his forehead, a sure signal to American diplomats that something dramatic was about to break out. He organized a "Molotov Plan" to counter the "Marshall Plan." (*The Reporter,* 1956. Copyright 1956 by The Reporter Magazine Co.)

financial adviser to the Iranian government, pinpointed the issue when he commented that "Iran's geographic relation to the Soviet Union is roughly comparable to the relation of Mexico or Canada to the United States."[35] It was as if Mexico City or Ottawa had become allied with Moscow—a spheres-of-influence and security question. The Russians wanted what the British and Americans already had: oil and influence. Moscow feared the foreign penetration of a neighboring state. Years later, Truman embellished the Iranian story by claiming that he had sent the Russians an ultimatum to get out of Iran or face American troops. He may have contemplated sending one, but the State Department has denied the existence of such a message. Yet this myth is indicative of the simple lesson Americans drew from the conflict: "Get tough" and the Russians will give way. Secretary Henry A. Wallace saw it differently and told a Madison Square Garden audience in September, 1946: "'Getting tough' never brought anything real and lasting—whether for schoolyard bullies or businessmen or world powers. The tougher we get, the tougher the Russians will get."[36] For this speech and Wallace's criticism of American foreign policy, Truman fired him from the Cabinet. "The Reds, phonies and 'parlor pinks' seem to be banded together and are becoming a national danger. I am afraid they are a sabotage front for Uncle Joe Stalin," concluded the President with tortured exaggeration.[37]

A Multitude of Disputes: Loans, Atomic Bombs, and Germany

Three other issues, which flared in 1946 and continued beyond, illustrated Truman's new "get tough" policy: an abortive loan to Russia, the Baruch Plan for atomic control, and Germany. The loan issue began during the war when the Soviet Union requested a reconstruction loan of one billion dollars, later raised to six billion. Some American leaders, like Wallace and Secretary of the Treasury Henry Morgenthau, Jr., thought such a loan would stimulate trade with Russia as well as contribute to amicable relations. Ambassador Harriman and Truman reasoned, on the other hand, that the Russian need for economic help should be exploited for diplomatic leverage. Economic assistance was "one of the most

W. Averell Harriman (1891–). Graduate of Yale, heir to the Harriman railroad empire, investment banker of Brown Brothers, and diplomat, Harriman has been one of America's busiest public servants in the twentieth century. As an architect of the "get tough" policy toward Russia, he advocated using foreign aid in diplomatic bargaining. He served as ambassador to Russia (1943–1946), ambassador to Great Britain (1946), secretary of commerce (1946–1948), and U.S. representative in Europe for the Marshall Plan. Later he became a foreign affairs adviser and negotiator for Presidents John F. Kennedy and Lyndon B. Johnson. (*The Reporter,* 1950. Copyright 1950 by Fortnightly Publishing Co. Inc.)

effective weapons at our disposal" to influence events in Europe, Harriman informed Washington in 1944.[38] Truman "felt we held all the cards and that the Russians had to come to us," and he intended to "play them as American cards."[39]

The "cards" were foreign aid. In early 1946, after months of silence on the issue, the United States reopened the loan question by requesting concurrent discussion on Eastern Europe and Soviet participation in the World Bank. The Soviets hesitated in various diplomatic notes, hardly interested in opening talks designed to weaken their position in Eastern Europe. Nor did they wish to join the American-dominated World Bank. In May, however, they vaguely agreed to discuss Eastern Europe in a *preliminary* fashion. Washington was actually baffled, for it no longer expected Soviet concessions and it did not have enough money left in the Export-Import Bank to grant a large loan. So the State Department responded that it could not accept merely a preliminary exchange of views. The loan issue died with that message, although the general question of foreign aid for Russia would arise again when the Marshall Plan began. Would a loan have eased the increasingly bitter Soviet-American relations? We cannot be sure, but we know that the Soviets faced a major reconstruction problem, that the assistance was badly needed, and that Moscow had made a concession, however vague. Some observers concluded that the Soviet demand for German reparations hardened because of the loan failure, and Harriman suggested that American loan policy "may have contributed to their avaricious policies" in Eastern Europe.[40] The diplomatic use of economic power, by any nation possessing it, is to be expected and may be helpful in achieving mutually beneficial negotiations. Yet the Truman Administration chose to brandish the loan as a diplomatic weapon before negotiations, rather than to utilize it as a bargaining tool at the conference table, thereby producing further schism. In contrast, the United States negotiated with the British and granted a $3.75 billion loan in mid-1946, using aid as a tool to convince London to alter the preferential trading behavior of its Sterling Bloc.

The Baruch Plan was presented to the United Nations Atomic Energy Commission in July, 1946, and it also divided the two powers. The plan emerged from months of intra-administration talks, but its final touches were those of Bernard Baruch, the uncompromising American negotiator. He outlined the proposal for control of atomic weapons: (1) the creation of an international authority; (2) the international control of fissionable raw materials by this authority; (3) inspections to prevent violations; (4) no Security Council vetoes of control or inspections; (5) global distribution of atomic plants for peaceful purposes; (6) cessation of the manufacture of atomic bombs; (7) destruction of existing bombs; (8) these procedures to be taken in stages, with the last stage being the abandonment of the American atomic bomb monopoly.

Not until the last stage, after the Russians had given up atomic bomb development and fissionable materials within their country, and submitted to inspections, would the United States relinquish its monopoly. Furthermore, the United States would control a majority of the members of an international authority, and most of the plants would be in areas friendly to the United States. The Soviets thought they would have to jeopardize their security during these various stages. "In other words," Wallace wrote the President, "we are telling the Russians that if they are 'good boys' we may eventually turn over our knowledge of atomic energy to them."[41] Moscow rejected the Baruch Plan, and the stalemate persisted until 1949, when the Russians successfully exploded their first atomic device. The issue

Berlin Airlift. Citizens of Berlin watch an American cargo plane fly in supplies as part of "Operation Vittles" to circumvent the Soviet blockade of the beleaguered city. (Official U.S. Air Force photo)

seemed insoluble. The Russians obviously could not accept the American plan, and the United States could not be expected to surrender its atomic advantage in such a turbulent world seemingly threatened by a large Red Army. Truman, Byrnes, and Baruch, however, drew the exaggerated conclusion that the Soviet rejection of their plan was further evidence that Moscow intended to obstruct peaceful international relations.

The issue of Germany—zones, reparations, central administration, demilitarization, and the dismantling of war-oriented factories—deepened the schism between the former Allies. France, Britain, the USSR, and the United States each had a zone in defeated Germany and in Berlin, and each did what it liked. The vengeful French proved to be the most obstructionist, refusing to permit any centralized German agencies and arguing for permanent dismemberment. The Soviets tried with mixed success to grab reparations, thereby weakening the entire German economy. The British tried to bestow socialism on their district, but generally wanted a strong Germany to which they could sell goods and from which they could receive coal. The United States sought, according to the Potsdam accords, to treat Germany as one economic unit to speed reconstruction. Americans were not about to pour dollars into Germany for its recovery only to see those dollars flow out as reparations. By 1946 the Morgenthau Plan was near death. Steel- and coal-rich Germany was the vital center of the European economy and had to be reconstructed.

The dismantling of industrial plants slowed down, and in May of 1946, American Military Governor Lucius Clay halted all reparations shipments from the American zone. No more reparations, he told the Russians, until they contributed to German economic unity. As Secretary Forrestal rhetorically asked, "Are we going to try to keep Germany a running boil with the pus exuding over the rest of Europe, or are you going to try to bring it back into inner society?"[42] In December, 1946, the British and Americans combined their zones into "Bizonia." The Federal Republic of Germany (West Germany), a consolidation of "Bizonia" with the French zone, was created in May, 1949. The Soviets, on the other hand, economically exhausted their zone and retaliated in October, 1949 with the establishment of their puppet German Democratic Republic (East Germany).

The Soviets initiated the Berlin blockade (June, 1948–May, 1949) to impede the unilateral Western issuance of a new German currency, which they read as another sign of a unified nation tied to the West. They sealed off land access to Berlin, perhaps hoping to prompt negotiations. One American general urged that an armored column proceed down the East German access road and another advised the bombing of Soviet troops. Truman chose a less provocative airlift. American planes soon swept into the city with food, fuel, and other supplies. He also ordered B-29 bombers to England, concealing the fact that they went without atomic bombs. This deliberate ruse, and his comment that he would use "the bomb" if necessary, chilled people everywhere. For their part, the Soviets never shot down an American cargo plane. Moscow lifted the blockade, but only after suffering worldwide reproach and the creation of the West Germany it had so wanted to prevent. Americans were quick to draw another Cold War lesson: to win, never flinch in the face of Communist aggression.

The Truman Doctrine and Containment

On March 12, 1947 President Harry S Truman spoke dramatically to a special joint session of Congress. Greece and Turkey, he said, were gravely threatened. Unless the United States offered help, "we may endanger the peace of the world—and we shall surely endanger the welfare of this Nation." History seemed to be repeating itself. The Greek-Turkish crisis, the President suggested, was Hitler and World War II all over again. Truman invoked the peace and prosperity idiom when he declared that the "seeds of totalitarian regimes are nurtured by misery and want." The most famous words became known as the Truman Doctrine, the commanding guide to American foreign policy in the Cold War: "I believe that it must be the policy of the United States to support free peoples who are resisting attempted subjugation by armed minorities or by outside pressures."[43] Truman asked for $400 million to insure this policy's success. The President's moving address was short on analysis of the civil war in Greece and the Soviet-Turkish controversy over the strategic Dardanelles, but long on clichés, alarmist language, and panacea. He played on the words "free" and "democratic," leaving the mistaken impression that they fit the Greek and Turkish governments. Truman, however, was not interested in educating people, but in persuading them. The drafters of the speech thought it was the "most important thing that had happened since Pearl Harbor."[44] Unlike Roosevelt's "quarantine" speech, Truman's warning would be followed by action.

The immediate catalysts for the Truman Doctrine were a British request for help in Greece and a lingering squabble over who governed the Dardanelles. When the

Germans withdrew from hobbled Greece in 1944, much of the countryside was controlled by Communist and other leftist Greek nationalist resistance fighters, the ELAS, or National Popular Liberation Army and their political arm the EAM, or National Liberation Front. To re-establish Greek subservience to London, the British soon installed a government in Athens. Violence between the competing factions erupted in December, 1944. British troops, transported to Greece on American ships, joined by rightist sympathizers, and spurred by Churchill's pledge of "no peace without victory," engaged the leftists in vicious warfare.[45] The rebels, in control of most of the nation and thinking themselves within reach of political power through elections, signed a peace treaty in February, 1945 and laid down their arms.

From then until March, 1946, when the civil war flared again, the British-sponsored Athens regime, corrupt, inefficient, and ruthless, set about to eliminate its political foes. The United States sent warships to Greek ports and offered aid through the Export-Import Bank. In September, 1946, Secretary Forrestal announced that the United States would maintain a permanent fleet in the Mediterranean. Although Washington was uneasy about the harsh methods of the Athens government and its close alliance with Britain, still, a friendly regime was better than a leftist or Communist one. Greece limped along, staggered by war-wrought devastation, poor leadership, and civil turmoil. Britain, suffering its imperial death throes, could no longer pay the Greek bill. On February 21, 1947, the British informed Washington that they were pulling out. American officials responded to the British appeal with uncommon alacrity with Truman's special message.

Many congressmen resented Truman's having handed them a fait accompli on March 12, 1947. Critics argued that Truman was bypassing the United Nations in giving direct aid to Greece and Turkey, that the Greek regime was venal, that the program would cost too much, that economic—not military—aid was preferred, that Russia would be antagonized, and that the United States was entering an ill-defined global crusade. To win its case the Truman Administration enlisted the support of Republican Senator Vandenberg in a prime example of bipartisan foreign policy. Truman had scared people with his speech. "Washington," editorialized the *New Republic*, "was smothered under gusts of apprehension."[46] Vandenberg, who often warned against another Munich, predicted a "Communist chain reaction from the Dardanelles to the China Sea and westward to the rim of the Atlantic."[47] Most leaders accepted what would later be called the "domino theory." On April 22 the Senate passed the bill for aid to Greece and Turkey by a 67 to 23 vote; the House followed on May 15 with a positive voice vote. Truman signed the act on May 22.

Critics had pressed the Administration on its contention that Greece and Turkey were threatened by Soviet aggression, but received lame answers. It became clear why. The EAM, although Communist-led, had minimal ties with Russia. Churchill more than once said that Stalin had kept the bargain he made at their 1944 Moscow conference to stay out of the Greek imbroglio. In fact, Stalin disliked the Greek Communists because they were nationalists and they admired the independent-minded Yugoslav leader Tito, who gave them aid. Yet Truman simplified the question, enamored as he and many other Americans were with the notion that all Communists took their orders from Moscow.

The issue over the Dardanelles was also more complex than Truman portrayed it. The United States urged international control over the straits. The Soviets saw the issue quite differently, for they had witnessed Turkish behavior during World War II that permitted German warships to drive through the straits into the Black Sea. Soviet security was at stake. Stalin insisted at Yalta that Russia could no longer "accept a situation in which Turkey had a hand on Russia's throat."[48] For its part, Turkey refused any form of joint control with the Soviets. The Soviets grew angry, verbally blasting the Turks and threatening to take action. Turkey, stated one State Department report, "constitutes the stopper in the neck of the bottle through which Soviet political and military influence could most effectively flow into the eastern Mediterranean and Middle East."[49] Stalin, on the other hand, asked: "What would Great Britain do if Spain or Egypt were given this [Turkish] right to close the Suez Canal, or what would the United States Government say if some South American Republic had the right to close the Panama Canal?"[50] The Truman Administration presented the delicate, and perhaps insoluble, issue in the simplest way: the Soviets wanted to subjugate Turkey. The Soviets probably would have liked to, but there was little evidence that they were trying to.

The Dardanelles issue became a perennial Cold War subject, whereas the Greek civil war came to a conclusion when the rebels capitulated in October, 1949. American aid and advisers had flowed to Greece after 1947. American diplomats intervened in Greek politics. Over 350 American officers accompanied the Greek army in its campaign against the EAM in 1947–1949. Lieutenant General James A. Van Fleet advised the Greek general staff. By 1952 the United States had spent $500 million to build up Greek forces. Understandably Greece became dependent upon American assistance. Truman claimed another Cold War victory, but it was not that simple: the Greek insurgents lost not only because of American intervention, but because the Soviet Union refused to help them and Tito decided to seal off the Yugoslav border to deny Greek leftists a sanctuary. Americans nevertheless drew another lesson from this experience: Moscow-inspired communism could be stopped. Soothing and distorting simplicity had overcome complexity in American thinking. As one student of America's response to revolutions has concluded: "The fifth-column analogy from World War II dominated official thinking. The possibility that men had taken to the hills for reasons of their own and not as agents of a foreign power was never seriously considered."[51]

Another statement of what came to be called "containment" flowed gracefully from the gifted pen of George F. Kennan, director of the State Department's Policy

George F. Kennan (1904—). Graduate of Princeton, Pulitzer Prize-winning historian, career diplomat, and recognized "expert" on Soviet affairs, Kennan was Mr. "X" in 1947 when he articulated the containment doctrine. This brilliant man served W. Averell Harriman in Moscow and then returned home to head the State Department's Policy Planning Staff (1947–1949). Later he became ambassador to Russia (1952) and Yugoslavia (1961–1963). In his memoirs he argued that he had not meant that containment should be implemented militarily or universally. (The Institute for Advanced Study, Princeton, New Jersey)

Planning Staff. The July, 1947 issue of the prestigious journal *Foreign Affairs* carried an article titled "The Sources of Soviet Conduct," written by a mysterious Mr. "X", soon revealed as Kennan. The United States must adopt a "policy of firm containment," he wrote, "designed to confront the Russians with unalterable counterforce at every point where they show signs of encroaching upon the interests of a peaceful and stable world." Such pressure might force the "mellowing" of Soviet power. Kennan sketched a picture of an aggressive, uncompromising Russia driven by ideology. Mechanistic Soviet power, he wrote, "moves inexorably along a prescribed path, like a persistent toy automobile wound up and headed in a given direction, stopping only when it meets some unanswerable force."[52] Kennan was vague on whether economic or military means should be used to implement containment—a key question thereafter.

One of the most vocal critics of containment, journalist Walter Lippmann, predicted trouble. In a series of articles published as *The Cold War* (1947), Lippmann called containment a "strategic monstrosity," because it did not discriminate geographically—did not distinguish vital from peripheral areas. Containment would test American resources and patience without limit. What if Congress should decide, as was its constitutional prerogative, not to fund some presidential ventures in "counter-force?" Lippmann also prophetically observed that the "policy can be implemented only by recruiting, subsidizing and supporting a heterogeneous array of satellites, clients, dependents and puppets." He argued that the answer to world tension was not a seemingly limitless global crusade, but a primary effort to remove foreign troops from all of Europe. He denied the popular notion that the Soviet Union's military force was poised for an attack on Western Europe, a point on which he and Kennan agreed. Finally, Lippmann sadly concluded that Truman and Mr. "X" in their major statements had abandoned their essential responsibility—diplomacy. "For a diplomat to think that rival and unfriendly powers cannot be brought to a settlement is to forget what diplomacy is about."[53]

The Marshall Plan

By 1947 the United States had granted or loaned about nine billion dollars to Europe to help reconstruct its broken economy, to relieve hunger, to encourage trade with America, to avert contagious depression, and to stem radicalism. Despite assistance through the United Nations Relief and Rehabilitation Administration, the World Bank, and the International Monetary Fund, plus the loan to Britain and expenditures for the military occupation of Germany, Washington had failed to secure peace and prosperity. Europe remained prostrate, and Americans predicted that Communists, especially in France and Italy, would exploit the economic chaos. Furthermore, Europe's multibillion dollar deficit posed a real danger to the American economy—Europeans could not buy American products unless they received dollars from the United States. A comprehensive, coordinated program was required, and Secretary of State George C. Marshall called for one when he addressed a Harvard University commencement audience on June 5, 1947. Marshall was a halting, quiet orator, but his message of only 1500 words was lucid. A distraught Europe had to have help to face "economic, social and political deterioration of a very grave character."[54] He vaguely called upon the European nations to initiate a collective plan. British Foreign Minister Ernest Bevin contacted

The Marshall Plan Team. Truman, Secretary of State George C. Marshall (1947–1949), Paul Hoffman, and W. Averell Harriman discuss the European Recovery Program in 1948. Hoffman, president of Studebaker Corporation, served as administrator. (U.S. Information Agency, National Archives)

French Foreign Minister Georges Bidault. They met in Paris in mid-June and reluctantly invited Molotov to join them.

The seemingly open Marshall invitation and the Bevin-Bidault request must have stimulated intense discussion among Kremlin leaders. They sniffed a capitalist trap. The Soviets had hardly completed their diatribes against the Truman Doctrine. *Pravda* first commented that Marshall's plan was designed "for political pressure with the help of dollars, a plan for interference in the domestic affairs of other countries."[55] Yet the Soviets convened in Paris with England and France in late June and early July. Molotov thought Bevin and Bidault had plotted something behind his back. Bidault suspected that Molotov's economic advisers were really spies working with the French Communist party. Bevin did not want Russia in a European recovery program at all—a point the scowling Molotov got quickly. The Paris conferees reached a stalemate. Russia could not accept a program dominated by the United States; it sought instead a loosely structured system to protect individual national sovereignties. That was unacceptable to the United States, and hence to Britain and France. Molotov abruptly left town. "East" and "West," as in Germany, were going their own ways.

The United States had never wanted Soviet participation in the Marshall Plan or European Recovery Program (ERP). Throughout the 1947 discussions, diplomats stated that the United States had to run the plan very tightly. The American strategy was to invite all European nations to join, without mentioning any by name, and to keep firm control over the program. If Russia did not accept American terms, the propaganda value would be immense, for it would appear that Russia had rejected a generous American offer and so further divided the world. Yet it is understandable why the Soviets snubbed the Marshall Plan. The open invitation came at a time when the anti-Soviet Truman Doctrine was only a few months old, and furthermore, Eastern Europe was expected to ship raw materials to industrial Western Europe. Thus the postwar effort of the Eastern Europeans and Russians to industrialize, to become less dependent on Western Europe for manufactured goods, was being challenged. And anyway Russia wanted those raw materials. Also, since Soviet influence in Eastern Europe in 1947 was not comprehensive, from Moscow's perspective, a massive influx of American dollars into the region would have represented a real threat to Russia.

The invitation was probably disingenuous in the first place. It would have been illogical and contradictory for Congress to approve funds for Russia so shortly after it had been persuaded to fund the anti-Soviet Truman Doctrine. The invitation amounted to a diplomatic gesture. It worked, because Americans—participants and historians—could say that Russia made the negative decision, or in more general language, that Russia caused the Cold War. Russia formed a feeble Molotov Plan to counter the Marshall Plan's Organization of European Economic Cooperation and revitalized the old Comintern into a new propaganda agency called Cominform. Moscow forced some Eastern European nations to reject the Marshall Plan; others remained outside, not willing to antagonize the Soviet Union by taking the American side in the Cold War. The already existing but weak Economic Commission for Europe was bypassed, and economically vital West Germany was integrated into the ERP.

After months of discussion about how much to spend and after a huge administration advertising campaign, Congress in March, 1948 passed the Economic Cooperation Act. The coup in Czechoslovakia, scheduled elections in Italy (would they go Communist?), and the growing crisis over Germany, together with a March 17 Truman war scare speech to a joint session of Congress (which revived memories of 1939), garnered the Marshall Plan a vote of 69 to 17 in the Senate and 329

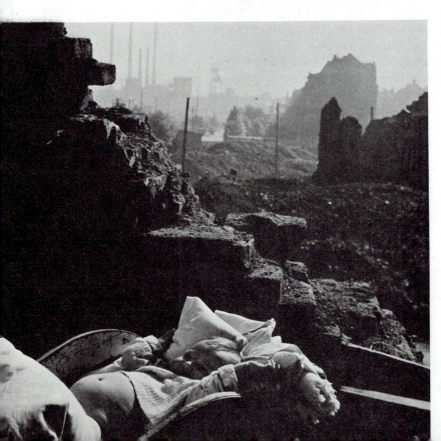

Essen, Germany. In the rubble of this German city rested a new citizen, who because of American reconstruction aid, enjoyed a full stomach. (Harry S Truman Library)

to 74 in the House. Four billion dollars were approved for its first year. Before it ended in 1952, the Marshall Plan, under the Economic Cooperation Administration, sent over thirteen billion dollars into the needy European economy. People went back to work as factories and mines reopened. Although agricultural production recovered slowly, industrial production improved. The European Recovery Program, said Bevin, was "like a lifeline to sinking men."[56]

The generous Marshall Plan stimulated recovery for people in dire need. Americans believed that peace depended upon prosperity, and they knew that the American economy required exports to European markets. Many of the Marshall Plan billions came home to purchase American products. The Marshall Plan, then, was a matter of serious national interest for the United States as well as a humanitarian effort. It had shortcomings too. Europe became dependent upon American aid, less able to make its own choices. Some American funds were used to continue European domination over colonial areas. The program bypassed the United Nations and the Economic Commission for Europe, where, some critics suggested, it might have been carried out with less divisiveness. The Marshall Plan created a deeper rift between the two rivals. It encouraged restrictions on East-West trade, and helped revive West Germany, thereby arousing Moscow's fears of its nemesis. A European Recovery Program was sorely needed, but how it was presented and shaped by the United States had something to do with why it became a divisive element. Finally, the Marshall Plan gave way increasingly to military aid. In 1951 the Economic Cooperation Administration was submerged in the Mutual Security Administration and by 1952 80 percent of American aid to Western Europe was military in nature.

NATO and the Militarization of the Cold War

The military dimension had always been present in American foreign policy. Much of Greek-Turkish aid, for example, was military. In July, 1947, Congress passed the National Security Act, which streamlined the military establishment. It created the Department of Defense, the National Security Council (NSC) to advise the President, and the Central Intelligence Agency (CIA) to gather and collate information through spying and other unspecified functions, which were later interpreted to mean covert activities against foreign governments or citizens. In Europe in March, 1948, Britain, France, and the three Benelux nations, with American encouragement, signed the Brussels Treaty for collective defense. In June the Senate passed (64 to 4) Senator Vandenberg's resolution applauding that effort and suggesting American participation.

After his victory in the election of 1948, Truman summarized American foreign policy in his Inaugural Address of January 20, 1949. Articulating simple juxtapositions of "communism" and "democracy," the President listed four central points. First, he endorsed the United Nations. Second, he applauded the European Recovery Program. Third, he announced that the United States was planning a North Atlantic defense pact. And fourth, "we must embark on a bold new program" of technical assistance for "underdeveloped areas," a reference to the Point Four Program, to be launched in 1950.[57] Dean Acheson became secretary of state that month and guided complicated negotiations on the defense pact. On April 4, 1949 the North Atlantic Treaty was signed in Washington by the five

Dean Acheson (1893–1971). Graduate of Yale and Harvard, wealthy lawyer, and government administrator, this man, as he put it, "was always a conservative." Polished if not stuffy, self-confident if not cocky, Acheson called his critics "primitives." He served as secretary of state for 1949–1953 and helped design NATO. (Portrait by Gardner Cox, National Portrait Gallery, Smithsonian Institution, Gift of Covington and Burling)

Brussels Treaty countries of Britain, France, Belgium, the Netherlands, and Luxembourg, as well as by Denmark, Iceland, Italy, Norway, Portugal, Canada, and the United States (Greece and Turkey joined in 1952 and West Germany in 1954). Article 5 provided "that an armed attack against one or more . . . shall be considered an attack against them all."[58]

Acheson anticipated heated debate at home. After all, the United States had not participated in a European alliance since the days of George Washington, and by 1949 an entangling alliance for some Americans was the equivalent of, if not worse than, original sin. Furthermore, no Russian military attack seemed imminent. Article 5, said critics, meant that the United States was creating a Pearl Harbor in every NATO country, drawing America into a war even if it did not want to go. "Mr. Republican" Senator Robert Taft of Ohio recoiled from NATO, considering it a threat to Russia, a provocative act that would eventually force the United States to send military aid to Europe, and a stimulant to an arms race. Taft noted that the President could commit American troops almost at will without constitutional restraint. Some dissenters thought that the Truman Administration skirted questions on the precise nature of the Soviet threat: was it military, political, or ideological? Other critics from both the left and right thought that the United States was overextending itself, draining its resources—in short, weakening rather than strengthening its position.

The critics made little impact. Fear was rampant and the urge to join the crusade compelling. The times were unusual; tradition had to give way. The outcome in the Senate was a foregone conclusion. James Reston of the *New York Times* reported that "there seems to be ignorance about specific parts of the treaty, indifference or a certain fatalistic approach to the future, combined with an acceptance of the idea of 'doing something' about the Russians."[59] Vandenberg endorsed NATO as a healthy reversal of the Neutrality Acts, which, he said, had encouraged Hitler. When asked in Senate hearings whether the United States planned to send substantial numbers of American troops to Europe to stand in the way of a potential Soviet attack, Secretary Acheson replied "no." It was not clear, then, what difference NATO meant in actual military terms. Soviet divisions far outnumbered those of Western Europe, and the United States possessed the atomic bomb. If Washington did not plan to dispatch troops to Europe, then the military balance remained the same. Basically NATO was a question of giving Europe not arms, but the will to resist, the confidence to thwart internal subversion. Such confidence would also encourage economic recovery under the Marshall Plan. "People could not go ahead and make investments for the future," Harriman recalled, "without some sense of security."[60] NATO also stood as a warning, a deterrent, to the Soviets after the Czech coup. It would serve as a "trip wire." NATO was created for other reasons as well. Acheson wanted to rearm West Germany, and NATO would permit the United States to undertake that revival of German power while reassuring Western Europeans. NATO was also a way of knitting the Western nations more tightly into an American sphere of influence, heading off any tendencies toward neutralism or appeasement in the Western camp, as Harriman put it.

On July 21, 1949 the Senate ratified the NATO Treaty by a handsome 82 to 13 margin. Truman, who had had an enduring respect for the military ever since his own Battery "D" days in World War I, signed the treaty two days later. That day he also sent the Mutual Defense Assistance Bill to Congress bearing a request for a one-year appropriation of $1.5 billion for European military aid. Critics complained that that amount was hardly sufficient to build European forces up to adequate defensive strength, but enough to start an arms race by alarming Russia. The Truman Administration admitted that this request was just a first step in a long-term military program. Containment had taken a distinct turn to military means. The stakes became bigger. In January, 1950, after the Soviets exploded an atomic device, Truman ordered speedier development of a hydrogen bomb, and began serious thinking about integrating West German units into a large European army.

On January 30, 1950 the President asked the State and Defense departments to review American defense policy. Eventually tagged National Security Council Paper Number 68 (NSC-68), the April report predicted prolonged global tension, Soviet military expansion, and relentless Communist aggression (Mao's recent triumph in China was read as an example of an international conspiracy). The United States could thwart the Communist design for world domination largely through a huge military build-up. The American people would have to be persuaded to support larger defense budgets and hence higher taxes. The secret report, most historians now agree, glossed over complexities. It treated communism as a monolith, ignoring differences within the Communist community. It spoke of the "free world," overlooking the many nations allied with the United States that had undemocratic governments. It postulated that communism orchestrated the world's troubles, neglecting to discuss the profound, indigenous nationalist movements that challenged the imperial powers. It made sweeping assumptions about Soviet motives and capabilities without presenting adequate evidence. The report, in short, exaggerated the "threat." Lippmann's warnings against indiscriminate globalism went unheeded; the United States was in fact prepared to become the world's policeman. But how could Americans be convinced to support the report's prescriptions? "We were sweating over it, and then—with regard to NSC-68—thank God Korea came along," recalled an Acheson aide.[61] In September, 1950, a few months after the outbreak of the Korean War, Truman ordered NSC-68's implementation.

American Answers for Asia: The Restoration of Japan and the Chinese Civil War

At the end of World War II Asia entered a major process of reconstitution. In Indochina, Burma, and Indonesia the old imperial system was crumbling. Japan was defeated and occupied. Korea, formerly dominated by Japan, was divided along the thirty-eighth parallel by Russia and the United States. China was still rocked by its long civil war. The colonial powers, recognizing their diminished position, looked to the United States to help them salvage what they could. The Pacific Ocean, they agreed quite reluctantly, would become an American sphere of influence. The ingredients for tremendous Asian conflict existed in substantial quantities: nationalists, retreating imperialists, civil war, occupied countries, and a new and enlarged American and Soviet presence. Who came out best in the reconstruction of Asia depended upon who had the most power.

If the Soviets ran some of the Eastern European countries, the Supreme Commander for the Allied Powers, General Douglas MacArthur, ran Japan. Unlike Germany, Japan was not divided into zones. Depite the establishment of a Far

Eastern Advisory Commission with Soviet membership, the United States made its supremacy stick and rejected Soviet requests for shared power. The United States also assumed power over Micronesia (the Marianas, Marshalls, and Carolines), Okinawa, Iwo Jima, and more then a hundred other Pacific outposts. As if to demonstrate the point, on July 7, 1946, an atomic bomb was tested on the Marshall Island of Bikini. To avoid the charge of imperial land grabbing, the United States had the United Nations place Micronesia under an American trusteeship. In 1949 MacArthur declared that "now the Pacific had become an Anglo-Saxon lake and our line of defense runs through the chain of islands fringing the coast of Asia."[62]

Although occupation officials planned at first to "reform" Japan, they gradually shifted to a revitalization program as the Cold War progressed and it appeared evident that Communist Mao Zedong would win in China. Japan would become a pro-American bastion. During 1947–1950 labor unions were restricted, the reparations program curtailed, production controls in war-related industries relaxed, the antitrust program suspended, Communists barred from government and university positions, and former Japanese leaders reinstated. George F. Kennan helped tailor the rebuilding program in early 1948. Japan and Germany, Kennan later recalled, were "two of our most important pawns on the chessboard of world politics."[63]

The restoration of Japan carried international ramifications. Russia constantly complained, through the ineffective Far Eastern Advisory Commission, about American unilateralism. Finally, in April, 1950, after years of Soviet objection and Defense Department foot-dragging, the United States proceeded without Soviet participation to negotiate a peace treaty with Japan. At that time John Foster Dulles, chief Republican adviser on foreign policy and a skillful negotiator, joined the State Department with the assignment to arrange a settlement with Tokyo. In September, 1951, the United States and fifty other nations signed Dulles' Japanese peace treaty, which restored Japanese sovereignty, gave the United States a base on Okinawa, and permitted the retention of foreign troops in Japan. The Soviet Union refused to sign. A separate Japanese-American security pact was also effected, insuring the presence of American troops and planes on Japanese soil. When the Senate ratified Dulles' handiwork in 1952, the occupation officially terminated. Japan, which a decade earlier bombed Pearl Harbor and earned American opprobrium as a "beast," had become a pivotal element in the postwar American sphere of influence and culturally quite "Americanized."

Americans wanted China within their sphere of influence too. For decades they had preached the Open Door, dreamed of vast Chinese markets and Christian havens, considered China a special friend, if not client, of the United States, and, during World War II, anticipated the elevation of China to great power status. Americans held postwar dreams for a pro-American China, but the Chinese themselves would have it otherwise. Washington underestimated the depth of the Chinese civil war and overestimated the political viability of Generalissimo Jiang Jieshi, who fell from power in 1949. The United States for the period 1945–1949 became a counterrevolutionary force in a revolutionary country. Something had gone wrong in America's dream. Critics began to point the finger. How could the powerful United States "lose" China? they asked. Unwilling to acknowledge that the problem of China was *Chinese*, they searched for answers in the United States. Vicious recriminations helped launch a domestic search for *American* villains who had "sold out" China.

American postwar goals, at least as understood in Washington, were a united non-Communist country under Jiang, trade with the United States, China as a keeper of the balance of power in Asia, and an American ally. At the end of the war, to fulfill these hopes, American troops took positions in northern China, including Beijing and Tianjin. They transported Jiang's soldiers to Manchuria in a race to beat the Communists there. Hundreds of American military officers advised the Nationalist armed forces. The Soviets, following their pledge at Yalta, signed a treaty of friendship with Jiang's regime in August, 1945. Moscow seemed to be abandoning the Chinese Communists of Mao Zedong and Zhou Enlai. The Soviets preferred a divided, weak China that would pose no threat along the 4,150 miles of the Sino-Soviet border. Mao was too independent-minded, too "Titoist" for the Soviet taste. Stalin said the "Chinese Communists are not real Commu-

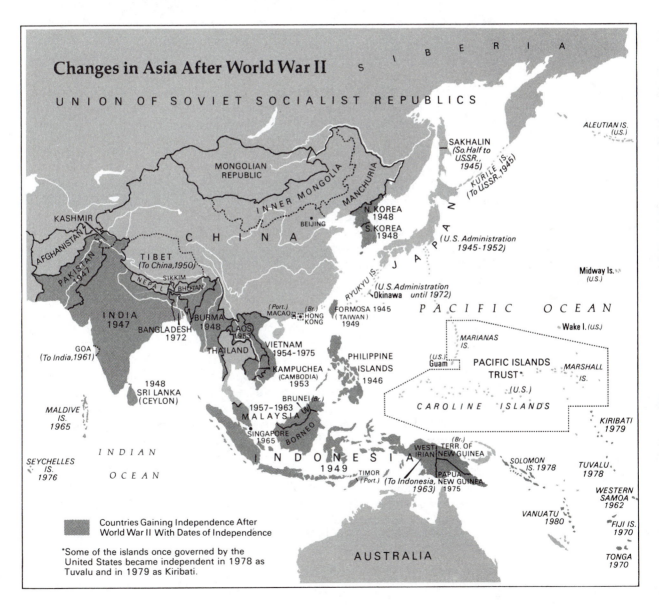

Changes in Asia After World War II

nists. They are 'margarine' Communists."[64] American Foreign Service Officers like John Paton Davies and John S. Service reported from China that relations between Moscow and Mao were tenuous and that the Communists would probably defeat Jiang without much help from Russia, despite the presence of Soviet troops in Manchuria.

American Ambassador Patrick J. Hurley, who, it was said, could strut sitting down, saw an opportunity. If Russia was jilting the Chinese Communists, Hurley reasoned, then Jiang might be able to defeat Mao. The swashbuckling ambassador managed to bring Mao and Jiang together for talks in the fall of 1945, but Jiang proved to be an obstructionist, unwilling to make any concessions, confident that the United States was backing him, and the talks failed. In November Hurley, with his typical blast-furnace approach, resigned and charged that Foreign Service officers had subverted his efforts by favoring Mao and Zhou, or "Mouse Dung" and "Joe N. Lie" as he called them.[65] Hurley's vituperative attack on the professional diplomats satisfied the conspiracy-minded who needed scapegoats for the American frustration over China. The "China experts" had not preferred Mao; they had simply reported the truth about Jiang—that he was corrupt, reactionary, and unlikely to gain the allegiance of the Chinese people, and that the Communists would thus gain support. The experts would pay for their accuracy; in the early 1950s many of them were ousted from the State Department under pressure from red-baiting Senator Joseph McCarthy. If only the Foreign Service Officers had supported Jiang, bellowed Hurley and McCarthy, then he would have won. History knows few more masterful distortions of reality.

After the Hurley debacle, in December, 1945, Truman sent the "Marshall Mission" to China. Headed by highly respected General George C. Marshall, it sought to unite the factions under a non-Communist government. The basic fallacy, again, was that such a task could be accomplished. It testified to a shallow understanding of the Chinese civil war. Yet Marshall arranged a cease-fire in January, 1946. The Communists, apparently trying to avoid a bloody confrontation, saw a coalition government as a nonviolent route to power. About the same time, the Soviets pulled out of Manchuria, after having seized and exported great quantities of equipment as war booty, leaving the area to superior Communist forces. By the end of April, 1946, 90 percent of Manchuria rested in Communist hands. Jiang's headstrong effort, against American advice, to storm into Manchuria to challenge Mao, spelled the end of Marshall's cease-fire. Marshall and the 1,000 American military and naval personnel who advised Jiang's forces could not restrain the overconfident Generalissimo, while Chinese Communists protested that they were being killed by American arms. A chagrined Marshall returned to the United States in January, 1947, to become secretary of state.

Uncertain about what to do next, but hopeful of preventing a Communist victory, Truman dispatched a new delegation. The "Wedemeyer Mission" went to China in July, 1947. General Albert C. Wedemeyer criticized the disarray of the Nationalists, but concluded that China, like Greece, needed an aid program to end the Communist menace. He also suggested that a United Nations commission govern Manchuria. Secretary Marshall vetoed both proposals. China was simply not worth a war of undetermined length or large-scale American military involvement. And a United Nations role in China might prompt the Soviets to suggest one for Greece, where the United States preferred to act alone.

Still not knowing what to do, and unwilling to concede that the Communists might be satisfying Chinese needs, Marshall intervened further by releasing undelivered Lend-Lease goods to Jiang. In the autumn of 1947 he offered the Nationalists arms and ammunition and authorized the Army Advisory Group to train Chinese combat troops on Formosa. In part to answer critics who asked why Greece should be saved from communism but not China—who, in short, insisted that the Truman Administration follow the logic of its own containment doctrine—the White House asked Congress in early 1948 for $570 million in China aid. Under the China Aid Act of April, China was provided with $400 million— enough to anger Mao further, but far too little to save Jiang. Many congressmen saw it as a futile gesture to a dying regime, a Truman tactic to deflect criticism that the Administration had not tried to save Jiang. "China aid," Vandenberg remarked, "is like sticking your finger in the lake and looking for the hole."[66]

Despite about three billion dollars in aid since V-J Day, military advisers, and diplomatic missions, Washington failed to stop Mao's ascent. Jiang let inflation run rampant, neglected tax and land reforms, launched risky military expeditions, tolerated corruption, and rejected talks with Mao. Dispirited soldiers defected from his army. American military equipment fell into Communist hands; ironically, in this way, Mao's troops got more aid from America than from Russia. "We picked a bad horse," the President lamented.[67]

Communist China and American Nonrecognition

In June, 1949, Mao Zedong stated that he was leaning to the side of socialism (Russia) against that "one great imperialist power" (America).[68] Official Washington was not surprised, because since 1945 it had intervened in the Chinese civil war because it believed a Sino-Soviet link already existed. For many Americans, Mao's strident address simply confirmed Moscow's creation of another puppet state, this time in Asia. Even though there was little evidence to demonstrate Soviet direction or supply of the Chinese Communists and contrary facts that suggested an actual Sino-Soviet schism, Americans preferred the words of Secretary of State Dean Acheson, in the famous *China White Paper* of August, 1949, that "the Communist regime serves not [Chinese] interests but those of Soviet Russia."[69] This bald assumption has not enhanced Acheson's reputation, but it was typical of the era. As historian Akira Iriye has written: "Since the documents in the *White Paper* did not warrant the assertion that the Soviet Union had systematically sought to extend its power and influence in China, Acheson must have come to such a sweeping conclusion through the medium of Cold-War visions."[70] The documents in fact showed that there was little the United States could have done, because there was little that Jiang was willing to do. In January, 1949 he sent China's gold supplies to the island of Formosa (Taiwan); in December, the Nationalist government followed. Mao's People's Republic, established on October 1, assumed power.

The Truman Administration had a difficult time explaining the "fall" of China. Critics like publisher Henry R. Luce of *Time* magazine, Republican congressmen, and missionaries charged that Truman had "lost" China, as if it had once "belonged" to the United States. Senator Styles Bridges and Congressman Walter Judd headed an informal, noisy, and influential "China Lobby," which for years had advocated American military involvement in the Chinese civil war. They asked: If the essence of American foreign policy was the containment of communism

"The Open Door." The Communists, led by Mao Zedong defeated the crumbling forces of Jiang Jieshi in 1949, opening a door that the United States had tried to keep closed. (*The Reporter,* 1950. Copyright 1950 by Fortnightly Publishing Co., Inc.)

without geographical limit, as stated in the Truman Doctrine and the "X" article, why did not the United States intervene in China? If Greece, why not China? Truman and his advisers never gave a systematic answer, although at different times they said that China was too large, that a land war in Asia was unthinkable, that Jiang, unlike the Greek government, was unmanageable, that the Greek question was an immediate crisis, that there was no evidence of foreign influence in China, and that the monetary costs were prohibitive. The Truman Administration conceded that the containment doctrine was sound, but argued that the Administration had done the best it could to apply containment in China to stem the Communists. Not good enough, the critics easily shot back.

The United States' failure in China was not due to insufficient aid or lack of concern; rather, more fundamental, American leaders never understood the dynamic force of a peasant society ripe for change and the real appeal the land-reforming Communists had among the Chinese people. Americans never marshaled the courage to admit their mistake in clinging to Jiang. The United States' backing of the unpopular Jiang proved foolhardy because, as historian Barbara Tuchman has noted, "there is little virtue in a client being anti-Communist if he is at the same time rotting from within."[71]

After Mao's victory over Jiang, the United States refused to recognize the People's Republic of China. Behind the nonrecognition policy lay mounting Sino-American animosities. In June of 1949 Communist leaders asked American Ambassador J. Leighton Stuart to meet with them. The Truman Administration vetoed contact. Not only did Truman fear howling protest from the pro-Jiang "China Lobby," but he also resented Chinese Communist behavior. They rudely reminded Americans of their imperialist past, including military participation in the Boxer Rebellion, support for Japan's seizure of Shandong in 1919, and naval gunboat patrols on Chinese rivers in the 1920s and 1930s. They confiscated American property and harassed Americans. American Consul General at Mukden Angus Ward was kept under house arrest from November, 1947, to October, 1949, when he was formally tried, convicted of spying, and expelled from China.

From December of 1949 through February of 1950, Mao negotiated with the Soviets in Moscow and signed a treaty of friendship and alliance. Fearful of a revived Japan and of the American presence in Asia, Mao needed an ally. Stalin was hesitant, wary of a Chinese Tito and a strong China. Although the talks were often acrimonious, because the Soviets wanted to retain their spoils won at Yalta, the United States looked upon the result as evidence that communism was a cohesive monolith. The treaty provided for the withdrawal of Soviet troops from Port Arthur, the transfer of Soviet interests in railroads to China, Soviet commercial rights in Xinjiang (Sinkiang) and Russian control of Outer Mongolia. What is striking is the inconsequential foreign aid Russia promised and the clash of traditional Russian-Chinese national interests. Yet Americans largely ignored the schism, stressed Sino-Soviet ideological affinity, and denounced the treaty as further evidence of the Soviet conquest of China. State Department officer Louis J. Halle later wrote that some American diplomats were quite cognizant of the "long record of conflict between Mao and Moscow. They were, however, intimidated into silence, or if they tried to speak out their careers and reputations were ruined by accusations of treason."[72] The "Chi Commies," as State Department telegrams tagged the new Chinese leaders, would not be recognized. The nonrecognition policy was born in failure, misinterpretation, and exaggeration, for it set the United States firmly against the largest (650 million people) and ultimately most influential nation in Asia. Assistant Secretary of State Dean Rusk facilely summarized the rigid American position in early 1951: "The Peiping regime may be a colonial Russian government—a Slavic Manchukuo on a larger scale. It is not the Government of China. It does not pass the first test. It is not Chinese."[73]

Legacies of the Early Cold War

"We thought we could do anything," noted an American writer who recalled the end of the Second World War. "We were heirs to a smiling and victorious confidence."[74] Indeed, Americans in 1945 were flushed with a sense of power; the British, the Russians, and many other foreign observers noted it with some apprehension. This confidence contributed to America's zealous pursuit of its goals in the postwar period, as did American ideology and economic needs. Shorn of their ignoble "isolationism," impatient to throw off the failures of the depression decade, and committed to a world of peace and prosperity on their terms, Americans were outraged when the Soviet Union, nursing its own sense of growth, challenged the American mission and opportunity. In their frustration to explain how the grand ideals of the Allies had deteriorated to the bickering of the Cold War, Americans—leaders and common folk alike—often adopted superficial assumptions and a diplomatic style befitting the bully on a streetcorner.

"After World War II," Senator J. William Fulbright remembered, "we were sold on the idea that Stalin was out to dominate the world. I didn't have the knowledge or the foresight to make a judgment at that time. . . . Henry Wallace sensed it, he had a feeling about it, but he was ridiculed for being a visionary, an appeaser, unrealistic."[75] As Fulbright suggested, a popular, largely untested idea captivated many Americans in the early Cold War: the Soviet Union had launched a crusade to communize the world. Certainly there were appearances to feed such a notion. Austere, intransigent, and ruthless, Stalin became in American eyes an obstructionist. Soviet diplomatic machinations were alarming, and simple-minded Communist ideology and propaganda offended the ear. The Soviet diplomatic style was rude, with threats as common as compromises.

But the hard evidence for assuming that the Soviets pursued global aggression

"Uncle Sam's World Wide Umbrella." As the donor of large amounts of foreign aid, as the chief partner in military alliances, and as the professor of the containment doctrine, the United States undertook new global responsibilities after World War II. (*The Reporter,* 1950. Copyright 1950 by Fortnightly Publishing Co. Inc.)

did not exist. Nonetheless, Americans thought that revolutions were Moscow-directed. They thus backed the restoration of French imperialism in Vietnam (see pp. 526–527). Exaggerating the Communist threat, Americans embraced soothing simplicity rather than sophisticated analysis. They saw blacks and whites where greys abounded. They articulated what later was called a "domino theory"—if one country falls to communism, others will be tipped in the same direction, like a row of dominoes. They did not believe that Soviet behavior could be explained in part as a response to external factors, such as American behavior; influenced by Kennan's arguments, they posited a mechanistic view that an internal imperative, the need to maintain the totalitarian system and Communist ideology, compelled nasty Soviet actions. Americans reacted; the Soviets acted. Americans defended; the Soviets aggressed. The Soviets certainly practiced an uncooperative diplomacy, but the Truman Administration too often cast a very complex international environment as a simple contest between "good guys" and "bad guys." Analysts would later identify such thinking as the Cold War mentality. George F. Kennan himself later concluded that Americans, especially military planners, exaggerated Soviet behavior and created "the image of the totally inhuman and totally malevolent adversary" and "reconjured [it] daily, week after week, month after month, year after year, until it takes on every feature of flesh and blood and becomes the daily companion of those who cultivate it, so that any attempt on anyone's part to deny its reality appears as an act of treason or frivolity."[76]

American diplomats in the early Cold War years pursued a self-conscious, expansionist, often unilateral, foreign policy. In a world recently ravaged by war, American businessmen and government officials cooperated to expand American foreign trade. By 1947 the United States accounted for one-third of the world's exports. The Americans exploited opportunities such as Middle Eastern oil and tapped the raw materials of the so-called Third World, importing manganese ore from Brazil and India, for example. The United States continued to preach the Open Door policy to help spur this trade and facilitate the investment of $12 billion abroad by 1950, but other nations complained that they could not compete and that therefore the Open Door was really an invitation to American domination. Stalin thought the "Open Door policy as dangerous to a nation as foreign military invasion."[77] The foreign aid program of the postwar years was designed in part to keep trade and investments flowing; American products could not be purchased unless foreigners had dollars to spend on them. One of the chief legacies of the Truman period, then, was the establishment of foreign aid as a major tool of American diplomacy—a way of curbing revolution, thwarting communism, and stimulating the American economy. Americans got in the habit of thinking that dollars could buy diplomatic friends and economic security.

The containment doctrine became the commanding principle of American Cold War foreign policy. When Americans were in doubt, the containment doctrine told them what to do. There were enough successes, enough "lessons," that it became fixed as a cure-all. "Like medieval theologians," Fulbright has noted, "we had a philosophy that explained everything to us in advance, and everything that did not fit could be readily identified as a fraud or a lie or an illusion. . . . The perniciousness of the anti-Communist ideology of the Truman Doctrine arises not from any patent falsehood but from its distortion and simplification of reality, from its universalization and its elevation to the status of a revealed truth."[78] Throughout the 1950s, 1960s, and well into the 1970s, Americans applied the historical lessons of the 1940s, and thereby failed to define precisely the "threat," placed few geographical limits on containment, and increasingly adopted military methods.

Another legacy of the early Cold War affected the American political process. The Truman Administration, sometimes using scare tactics, shaped the thinking of the "foreign policy public." Most foreign policy debates centered on how much to spend, not whether to spend. Congress sometimes proved obstinate, but on the whole Truman got what he wanted. It seemed the contest with the Communists was too important to leave to the people, because, as historian Thomas A. Bailey reasoned, "the masses are notoriously short-sighted and generally cannot see danger until it is at their throats." A President may have to deceive them. Concluded Bailey, in an unabashed endorsement of the practice in 1948: "Deception of the people may in fact become increasingly necessary, unless we are willing to give our leaders in Washington a free hand. . . . [T]he yielding of some of our democratic control of foreign affairs is the price that we may have to pay for greater physical security."[79]

Bipartisanship also helped the President control the making of foreign policy. Americans had to speak with unity. As bipartisan leader Vandenberg proudly concluded, "our Government did not splinter. It did not default. It was strong in the presence of its adversaries."[80] Unfortunately bipartisanship meant too often that legislation was superficially analyzed, that debate was pro forma, that alternative policies were lightly dismissed, and that Congress permitted the President considerable freedom in foreign policy, abdicating its own responsibilities. Acheson bluntly remarked: "Bipartisan foreign policy is the ideal for the executive because you cannot run this damned country any other way except by fixing the whole organization so it doesn't work the way it is supposed to work. Now the way to do that is to say politics stops at the seaboard—and anyone who denies that postulate is a son-of-a-bitch and a crook and not a true patriot. Now if people will swallow that, then you're off to the races."[81]

People swallowed it. Debate—the testing of assumptions—became shallow. Critics were isolated as enemies of the state, appeasers, Communist sympathizers, or just muddleheaded idealists. During the 1948 presidential campaign, in a choice example of "red-baiting," Truman deliberately attempted to link Wallace and the Communists in the American mind. Timid congressmen, afraid of recrimination if they did not join the crusade, and constantly handed alarmist faits accomplis by the President, fell into line. Critics ventured forth in fear with their questions and sometimes at great cost to political careers. Although McCarthyism was just around the corner, it was the Truman Administration that, in 1947, instituted a federal employee loyalty program to identify and ferret out suspected subversives. Definitions of disloyalty were imprecise, and too often criticism was taken for subversion. The lifeblood of a democratic system—debate, free inquiry, tolerance of dissenting views—deteriorated during the Cold War.

Finally, one of the significant legacies of the early Cold War for the United States was Washington's disdain for diplomacy as a means of solving disputes and avoiding confrontations. Walter Lippmann sensed this attitude when he pointed out the shortcoming of the containment doctrine in 1947. There seemed to be little faith in negotiations with the Soviet Union. Truman and Stalin never met again after Potsdam. Each side in the Cold War glared angrily at the other over the barricades, mental and physical, that they constructed after World War II. Both sides became convinced of their absolute rightness, and missed opportunities for diplomatic give-and-take.

Dollar and Atomic Diplomacy. In this Soviet view of American foreign policy Truman wields the atomic bomb and the money bag. Note Winston S. Churchill on the right. (*Krokodil,* U.S.S.R.)

Further Reading for the Period 1945–1950

For general studies of the Cold War, relevant to this chapter and others that follow, see: Stephen Ambrose, *Rise to Globalism* (1980); Richard Barnet, *Roots of War* (1972); Barry M. Blechman and Stephen S. Kaplan, *Force without War: U.S. Armed Forces as a Political Instrument* (1978); Dan Caldwell, *American–Soviet Relations* (1981); A. W. Deporte, *Europe Between the Superpowers* (1979); John L. Gaddis, *Russia, the Soviet Union, and the United States* (1978); Alexander L. George and Richard Smoke, *Deterrence in American Foreign Policy* (1974); Louis Halle, *The Cold War as History* (1967); Stephen S. Kaplan et al., *Diplomacy of Power: Soviet Armed Forces as a Political Instrument* (1981); Richard Kirkendall, ed., *The Truman Period as a Research Field* (1974); Gabriel and Joyce Kolko, *The Limits of Power* (1972); Walter LaFeber, *America, Russia, and the Cold War* (1980); Ralph Levering, *The Cold War, 1945–1972* (1982); Ernest R. May, *"Lessons" of the Past* (1973); Philip Mosely, *The Kremlin and World Politics* (1960); Thomas G. Paterson, ed., *Containment and the Cold War* (1973); Ronald Pruessen and Lynn Miller, eds., *Reflections on the Cold War* (1974); Arthur M. Schlesinger, Jr., *The Imperial Presidency* (1973); Marshall D. Shulman, *Stalin's Foreign Policy Reappraised* (1963); Nikolai V. Sivachev and Nikolai N. Yakovlev, *Russia and the United States* (1979); Ronald Steel, *Pax Americana* (1967); Kenneth W. Thompson, *Cold War Theories* (1981); Robert Tucker, *The Radical Left and American Foreign Policy* (1971); Adam Ulam, *The Rivals* (1971) and *Expansion and Coexistence: The History of Soviet Foreign Policy, 1917–1973* (1974); and Thomas W. Wolfe, *Soviet Power and Europe: 1945–1970* (1970).

Biographical studies include John Blum, ed., *The Price of Vision: The Diary of Henry A. Wallace* (1973); Isaac Deutscher, *Stalin* (1967); Milovan Djilas, *Conversations with Stalin* (1962); Robert H. Ferrell, *George C. Marshall* (1966); the essays on Truman, Acheson, and Kennan by John L. Gaddis, Robert H. Ferrell and David McLellan, and Thomas G. Paterson, in Frank Merli and Theodore A. Wilson, eds., *Makers of American Diplomacy* (1974); W. Averell Harriman and Elie Abel, *Special Envoy to Churchill and Stalin, 1941–1946* (1975); David McLellan, *Dean Acheson* (1976); Gaddis Smith, *Dean Acheson* (1972); Robert Underhill, *The Truman Persuasion* (1981); and Richard Walton, *Henry Wallace, Harry Truman and the Cold War* (1976).

For the origins of the Cold War, including the contest over Eastern Europe, consult Terry H. Anderson, *The United States, Great Britain, and the Cold War, 1944–1947* (1981); Barton J. Bernstein, ed., *Politics and Policies of the Truman Administration* (1970); Thomas Campbell, *Masquerade Peace: America's UN Policy* (1973); Lynn E. Davis, *The Cold War Begins* (1974); Hugh DeSantis, *The Diplomacy of Silence: The American Foreign Service, the Soviet Union, and the Cold War, 1933–1947* (1980); Robert J. Donovan, *Conflict and Crisis: The Presidency of Harry S. Truman, 1945–1948* (1977); Herbert Feis, *From Trust to Terror* (1970); John L. Gaddis, *The United States and the Origins of the Cold War* (1972); Lloyd Gardner, *Architects of Illusion* (1970); Harold F. Gosnell, *Truman's Crises* (1980); Robert M. Hathaway, *Ambiguous Partnership: Britain and America, 1944–1947* (1981); Gabriel Kolko, *The Politics of War* (1968); Geir Lundestad, *The American Non-Policy Towards Eastern Europe, 1943–1947* (1975) and *America, Scandinavia, and the Cold War, 1945–1949* (1980); George T. Mazuzan, *Warren R. Austin at the U.N., 1946–1953* (1977); Robert L. Messer, *The End of an Alliance: James F. Byrnes, Roosevelt, Truman, and the Origins of the Cold War* (1982); Frank A. Ninkovich, *The Diplomacy of Ideas: U.S. Foreign Policy and Cultural Relations, 1938–1950* (1981); Thomas G. Paterson, *On Every Front: The Making of the Cold War* (1979) and ed., *Cold War Critics* (1971); William Taubman, *Stalin's American Policy: From Entente to Détente to Cold War* (1982); Walter Ullmann, *The United States in Prague, 1945–1948* (1978); Piotr S. Wandycz, *The United States and Poland* (1980); Patricia D. Ward, *The Threat of Peace* (1979); and Daniel Yergin, *Shattered Peace* (1977).

The atomic bomb and its impact on diplomacy are discussed in Gar Alperovitz, *Atomic Diplomacy* (1965); Barton J. Bernstein, ed., *The Atomic Bomb* (1975); Robert J. C. Butow, *Japan's Decision to Surrender* (1954); Committee for the Compilation of Materials on Damage Caused by the Atomic Bombs in Hiroshima and Nagasaki, *Hiroshima and Nagasaki* (1981); Herbert Feis, *The Atomic Bomb and the End of World War II* (1966); Gregg Herken,

The Winning Weapon (1981); Richard Hewlett and Oscar Anderson, *The New World* (1962); Lisle Rose, *After Yalta* (1973); and Martin Sherwin, *A World Destroyed* (1975). The H-bomb decision is treated in Herbert F. York, *The Advisors: Oppenheimer, Teller, and the Superbomb* (1975).

For economic diplomacy, postwar reconstruction, and the Marshall Plan, see Irvine H. Anderson, *Aramco, the United States, and Saudi Arabia* (1981); Alfred E. Eckes, Jr., *A Search for Solvency* (1975) (on Bretton Woods) and *The United States and the Global Struggle for Minerals* (1979); Richard Gardner, *Sterling-Dollar Diplomacy* (1969); George Herring, *Aid to Russia, 1941-1946* (1973); Richard Mayne, *Recovery of Europe* (1973); Aaron D. Miller, *Search for Security* (1980) (on Saudi Arabian oil); Thomas G. Paterson, *Soviet-American Confrontation: Postwar Reconstruction and the Origins of the Cold War* (1973); Harry Price, *The Marshall Plan and Its Meaning* (1955); Michael B. Stoff, *Oil, War, and American Security: The Search for a National Policy on Foreign Oil, 1941-1947* (1980); and Theodore A. Wilson, *The Marshall Plan, 1947-1951* (Foreign Policy Association, *Headline Series*, 1977).

For postwar Germany, see Stephen Ambrose, *Eisenhower and Berlin, 1945* (1967); John Gimbel, *The American Occupation of Germany* (1968) and *The Origins of the Marshall Plan* (1976); Warren Kimball, *Swords or Ploughshares? The Morgenthau Plan for Defeated Nazi Germany, 1943-1946* (1976); Bruce Kuklick, *American Policy and the Division of Germany* (1972); Edward N. Peterson, *The American Occupation of Germany* (1978); and Jean Smith, *The Defense of Berlin* (1963).

For Greece, Turkey, the Truman Doctrine, and containment, consult Richard Barnet, *Intervention and Revolution* (1972); Richard Freeland, *The Truman Doctrine and the Origins of McCarthyism* (1971); John L. Gaddis, *Strategies of Containment* (1981); Charles Gati, ed., *Caging the Bear* (1977); John O. Iatrides, *Revolt in Athens* (1972) and ed., *Greece in the 1940s* (1981); Bruce R. Kuniholm, *The Origins of the Cold War in the Near East* (1980); Lawrence S. Wittner, *American Intervention in Greece, 1943-1949* (1982); C. Ben Wright, "Mr. 'X' and Containment," *Slavic Review* (1976); and Stephen Xydis, *Greece and the Great Powers* (1963).

The creation and workings of NATO can be studied in Timothy P. Ireland, *Creating the Entangling Alliance* (1981); Lawrence S. Kaplan, *A Community of Interests: NATO and the Military Assistance Program, 1948-1951* (1980); Robert Osgood, *NATO: The Entangling Alliance* (1962); and Escott Reid, *Time of Fear and Hope: The Making of the North Atlantic Treaty* (1977). See also Samuel F. Wells, Jr., "Sounding the Tocsin: NSC-68 and the Soviet Threat," *International Security* (1979), and Harry R. Borowski, *A Hollow Threat: Strategic Air Power and Containment Before Korea* (1982).

Diplomatic questions in Asia, including decolonization, are treated in Russell Buhite, *Soviet-American Relations in Asia, 1945-1954* (1982); Charles Dobbs, *The Unwanted Symbol* (1981) (on the U.S. and Korea); Herbert Feis, *Contest Over Japan* (1967); Edward Friedman and Mark Selden, eds., *America's Asia* (1971); Gary Hess, *America Encounters India, 1941-1947* (1971); Akira Iriye, *The Cold War in Asia* (1974); Robert J. McMahon, *Colonialism and Cold War: The United States and the Struggle for Indonesian Independence, 1945-49* (1981); Yōnosuke Nagai and Akira Iriye, eds., *The Origins of the Cold War in Asia* (1977); Philip R. Piccigallo, *The Japanese on Trial: Allied War Crimes Operations in the East, 1945-1951* (1979); and William W. Stueck, Jr., *The Road to Confrontation: American Policy toward China and Korea, 1947-1950* (1981).

For American involvement in the Chinese civil war and reaction to Mao's victory, see Dorothy Borg and Waldo Heinrichs, eds., *Uncertain Years: Chinese-American Relations, 1947-1950* (1980); Russell Buhite, *Patrick J. Hurley and American Foreign Policy* (1973); Warren Cohen, *America's Response to China* (1980); Herbert Feis, *The China Tangle* (1953); Ross Koen, *The China Lobby in American Politics* (1974); Gary May, *China Scapegoat: The Diplomatic Ordeal of John Carter Vincent* (1979); James Reardon-Anderson, *Yenan and the Great Powers* (1979); Tang Tsou, *America's Failure in China, 1941-1950* (1963); and Paul Varg, *The Closing of the Door: Sino-American Relations, 1936-1947* (1973).

For the new state of Israel, see Kenneth R. Bain, *The March to Zion: United States Policy and the Founding of Israel* (1979); Ian J. Bickerton, "President Truman's Recognition of Israel," *American Jewish Historical Quarterly* (1968); Leonard Dinnerstein, *America and the*

Survivors of the Holocaust (1982); Zvi Ganin, *Truman, American Jewry, and Israel, 1945–1948* (1979); and John Snetsinger, *Truman, the Jewish Vote, and the Creation of Israel* (1974); Allen Weinstein and Moshe Ma'oz, eds., *Truman and the American Commitment to Israel* (1981); and Evan M. Wilson, *Decision on Palestine* (1979). See also works on the Middle East cited in following chapters.

For domestic politics, anticommunism, interest groups, and public opinion in the early Cold War period, see Robert Divine, *Foreign Policy and U.S. Presidential Elections, 1940–1960* (1974); Justus Doenecke, *Not to the Swift: The Old Isolationists in the Cold War Era* (1979); Robert Griffith and Athan Theoharis, eds., *The Specter: Original Essays on the Cold War and McCarthyism* (1974); Alonzo Hamby, *Beyond the New Deal* (1973); Earl Latham, *The Communist Controversy in Washington* (1966); Richard Neustadt, *Presidential Power* (1980); Ronald Radosh, *American Labor and U.S. Foreign Policy* (1969); Jane Sanders, *Cold War on the Campus: Academic Freedom at the University of Washington, 1946–1964* (1979); Athan Theoharis, *Seeds of Repression* (1971); *The Yalta Myths* (1970); and ed., *Beyond the Hiss Case: The FBI, Congress, and the Cold War* (1982); H. Bradford Westerfield, *Foreign Policy and Party Politics* (1955); and Lawrence Wittner, *Rebels Against War: The American Peace Movement, 1941–1960* (1974). For works on McCarthyism, see Chapter 13, "Further Reading."

For representative essays, see Thomas G. Paterson, ed., *The Origins of the Cold War* (1974). See also the General Bibliography and the following notes.

Notes to Chapter 12

1. Quoted in Hanson W. Baldwin, "Hiroshima Decision," in New York Times, *Hiroshima Plus 20* (New York: Delacorte Press, 1965), p. 41.
2. Quoted in John Toland, *The Rising Sun* (New York: Random House, 1970), p. 780.
3. Quoted in William L. Laurence, *Dawn Over Zero: The Story of the Atomic Bomb* (New York: Alfred A. Knopf, 1946), pp. 219, 221.
4. Michihiko Hachiya, *Hiroshima Diary* (Chapel Hill: University of North Carolina Press, 1955; trans. by Warner Wells), p. 6.
5. Harry S Truman, *Memoirs* (Garden City, N.Y.: Doubleday, 1955–56; 2 vols.), I, 421.
6. William D. Leahy, *I Was There* (New York: Whittlesey House, McGraw-Hill, 1950), p. 441.
7. Quoted in Richard Barnet, *Roots of War* (Baltimore: Penguin Books, 1973), p. 46.
8. Quoted in Barton J. Bernstein, "Roosevelt, Truman and the Atomic Bomb, 1941–1945: A Reinterpretation," *Political Science Quarterly*, XC (Spring, 1975), 61.
9. Truman, *Memoirs*, I, 416.
10. Quoted in Martin J. Sherwin, *A World Destroyed: The Atomic Bomb and the Grand Alliance* (New York: Alfred A. Knopf, 1975), p. 224.
11. Harry S Truman to Eleanor Roosevelt, December 12, 1948, Box 4560, Eleanor Roosevelt Papers, Franklin D. Roosevelt Library, Hyde Park, New York.
12. U.S. Department of State, *Foreign Relations of the United States, 1946, VI* (Washington: Government Printing Office, 1969), 707.
13. Jeanette P. Nichols, "Dollar Strength as a Liability in United States Diplomacy," *Proceedings of the American Philosophical Society, III* (February 17, 1967), 47.

14. Truman quoted in Thomas G. Paterson, *Soviet-American Confrontation: Postwar Reconstruction and the Origins of the Cold War* (Baltimore: The Johns Hopkins University Press, 1973), p. ix; Earl of Halifax to Mr. Bevin, August 9, 1945, AN2560/22/45, Foreign Office Correspondence, Public Record Office, London, England.
15. Gaddis Smith, *Dean Acheson* (New York: Cooper Square Publishers, 1972), p. 416.
16. Minutes on the Political Situation in the United States, August 20–21, 1945, AN2505/4/45, Foreign Office Correspondence, Public Record Office.
17. Bert Cochran, *Harry Truman and the Crisis Presidency* (New York: Funk and Wagnalls, 1973), p. 232.
18. Quoted in John L. Gaddis, *The United States and the Origins of the Cold War* (New York: Columbia University Press, 1972), p. 205.
19. Quoted in John L. Gaddis, "Harry S Truman and the Origins of Containment," in Frank Merli and Theodore Wilson, eds., *Makers of American Diplomacy* (New York: Charles Scribner's Sons, 1974), p. 500.
20. U.S. Department of State, *Foreign Relations of the United States, Yalta* (Washington, D.C.: Government Printing Office, 1955), p. 669.
21. Quoted in Lloyd C. Gardner, *Economic Aspects of New Deal Diplomacy* (Madison: University of Wisconsin Press, 1964), p. 308.
22. Quoted in Barton J. Bernstein, "American Foreign Policy and the Origins of the Cold War," in Bernstein, ed., *Politics and Policies of the Truman Administration* (Chicago: Quadrangle Books, 1970), p. 36.
23. Quoted in Gregg Herken, *The Winning Weapon* (New York: Alfred A. Knopf, 1980), p. 48.

24. Henry L. Stimson and McGeorge Bundy, *On Active Service in Peace and War* (New York: Harper & Brothers, 1948), p. 644.

25. Walter Millis, ed., *The Forrestal Diaries* (New York: The Viking Press, 1951), p. 96.

26. U.S. Department of State, *Foreign Relations, 1946* (Washington, D.C.: Government Printing Office, 1969), *VII*, 223.

27. Quoted in Paterson, *Soviet-American Confrontation*, pp. 129–130.

28. Truman, *Memoirs*, I, 552.

29. *Foreign Relations, 1946, VI* (Washington, D.C.: Government Printing Office, 1969), 706.

30. George F. Kennan, *Memoirs, 1925–1950* (Boston: Little, Brown, 1967), p. 294.

31. *Congressional Record*, 79th Cong., 2nd sess., XCII, A1145–1146.

32. Quoted in Gaddis, *United States and Origins of the Cold War*, p. 309.

33. *Ibid.*, p. 315.

34. *New York Times*, March 14, 1946 (*Pravda* interview).

35. Quoted in Paterson, *Soviet-American Confrontation*, p. 182.

36. *Vital Speeches, XII* (October 1, 1946), 738–741.

37. Quoted in William Hillman, *Mr. President* (New York: Farrar, Straus and Young, 1952), p. 128.

38. *Foreign Relations, 1944, IV*, 951.

39. Paraphrase by Colonel Bernard Bernstein of the President's meeting with him, in U.S. Congress, Senate, Judiciary Committee, 90th Cong., 1st sess., *Morgenthau Diary (Germany)* (Washington, D.C.: Government Printing Office, 1967; 2 vols.), II, 1555.

40. W. Averell Harriman, "Certain Factors Underlying Our Relations with the Soviet Union," November 14, 1945, W. Averell Harriman Papers (in his possession).

41. Quoted in Thomas G. Paterson, ed., *The Origins of the Cold War* (Lexington, Mass.: D. C. Heath, 1974; 2nd ed.), p. 34.

42. Quoted in Paterson, *Soviet-American Confrontation*, p. 235.

43. *Public Papers of the Presidents, Truman, 1947* (Washington, D.C.: Government Printing Office, 1963), pp. 176–180.

44. Joseph Jones, "Memorandum for the File," March 12, 1947, Box 1, Joseph Jones Papers, Harry S Truman Library, Independence, Missouri.

45. Quoted in John O. Iatrides, *Revolt in Athens* (Princeton: Princeton University Press, 1972), p. 208.

46. "The Truman Doctrine," *New Republic, CXVI* (March 24, 1947), 5.

47. *Congressional Record, XCIII* (April 22, 1947), 3772–3773.

48. *Foreign Relations, Yalta*, p. 903.

49. *Ibid., 1946, VII*, 895.

50. "Record of Meeting at the Kremlin, Moscow, 9th October, 1944, at 10 P.M.," Premier 3, 434/4, Prime Minister's Office Records, Public Record Office.

51. Richard Barnet, *Intervention and Revolution* (New York: New American Library, 1968), p. 121.

52. "X," "The Sources of Soviet Conduct," *Foreign Affairs, XXV* (July, 1947), reprinted in Thomas G. Paterson, ed., *Containment and the Cold War* (Reading, Mass.: Addison-Wesley, 1973), pp. 18–33.

53. Lippmann quoted *ibid.*, pp. 41–51.

54. *Department of State Bulletin, XVI* (July 15, 1947), 1159–1160.

55. Quoted in Paterson, *Soviet-American Confrontation*, p. 214.

56. Quoted in Richard D. McKinzie and Theodore A. Wilson, "The Marshall Plan in Historical Perspective" (unpublished paper delivered at annual meeting of the American Historical Association, 1972), p. 8.

57. *Public Papers of the President, Truman, 1949* (Washington: Government Printing Office, 1964), p. 114.

58. *Department of State Bulletin, XX* (March 20, 1949), 340.

59. *New York Times*, May 19, 1949.

60. W. Averell Harriman in "Princeton Seminar," October 10–11, 1953, Box 65, Dean Acheson Papers, Harry S Truman Library.

61. Edward W. Barrett, *ibid.*

62. Quoted in John W. Dower, "Occupied Japan and the American Lake, 1945–1950," in Edward Friedman and Mark Selden, eds., *America's Asia* (New York: Vintage Books, 1971), pp. 146, 170.

63. Kennan, *Memoirs, 1925–1950*, p. 369.

64. Quoted in Herbert Feis, *The China Tangle* (New York: Atheneum, 1965), p. 140.

65. Quoted in Robert A. Hart, *The Eccentric Tradition: American Diplomacy in the Far East* (New York: Charles Scribner's Sons, 1976), p. 156.

66. Quoted in Norman Graebner, *The New Isolationism* (New York: Ronald Press, 1956), p. 14.

67. Quoted in Thomas G. Paterson, "If Europe, Why Not China? The Containment Doctrine, 1947–49," *Prologue, XIII* (Spring, 1981), 37.

68. Quoted in William Stueck, *The Road to Confrontation* (Chapel Hill: University of North Carolina Press, 1981), p. 124.

69. U.S. Department of State, *United States Relations with China* (Washington, D.C.: Department of State, 1949), p. xvii.

70. Akira Iriye, *The Cold War in Asia* (Englewood Cliffs, N.J.: Prentice Hall, 1974), p. 170.

71. Barbara Tuchman, "The United States and China," *Colorado Quarterly, XXI* (Summer, 1972), 12.

72. Louis J. Halle, "After Vietnam—Another Witch Hunt?" *New York Times Magazine*, June 6, 1971, p. 44.

73. *Department of State Bulletin, XXIV* (May 28, 1951), 847.

74. L. E. Sissman, "Missing the Forties," *Atlantic Monthly, CCXXXII* (October, 1973), 35.

75. Quoted in Daniel Yergin, "Fulbright's Last Frustration," *New York Times Magazine*, November 24, 1974, p. 87.

76. George F. Kennan, "The United States and the Soviet Union, 1917–1976," *Foreign Affairs, LIV* (July, 1976), 682.

77. Quoted in W. Averell Harriman and Elie Abel, *Special Envoy to Churchill and Stalin, 1941–1946* (New York: Random House, 1975), p. 528.

78. J. William Fulbright, "Reflections: In Thrall to Fear," *The New Yorker, XLVII* (January 8, 1972), 43.

79. Thomas A. Bailey, *The Man in the Street: The Impact of American Public Opinion on Foreign Policy* (New York: Macmillan, 1948), p. 13.

80. Arthur H. Vandenberg, Jr., ed., *The Private Papers of Senator Vandenberg* (Boston: Houghton Mifflin, 1952), pp. 550–551.

81. Quoted in Theodore A. Wilson and Richard D. McKinzie, "White House versus Congress: Conflict or Collusion? The Marshall Plan as a Case Study" (unpublished paper delivered to the annual meeting of the Organization of American Historians, 1973), p. 2.

Blair House Meeting. Attorney General J. Howard McGrath, President Harry S Truman, and Secretary of Defense Louis Johnson break for lunch on June 27, 1950, after discussing the Korean crisis at Blair House, across the street from the White House. (Harry S Truman Library)

13 Something Old, Something New: Global Confrontations, 1950–1961

Diplomatic Crossroad: American Troops to Korea, 1950

American Ambassador to South Korea John J. Muccio was awakened by a telephone call at 8:00 A.M. "Brace yourself for a shock," his chief deputy said, "the Communists are hitting all along the front!"[1] Muccio dressed hurriedly and rushed out to check the alarming reports. United Press correspondent Jack James, also in Seoul, alertly did the same and earned himself a rare scoop. At 9:50 A.M. he cabled the UP in the United States that North Korean troops had crossed the thirty-eighth parallel. About the same time Muccio cabled Washington about "an all-out offensive."[2]

At 4 A.M. that rainy Sunday morning of June 25, 1950, some 75,000 troops of the Democratic People's Republic of Korea (North Korea) bolted across the thirty-eighth parallel, the boundary drawn after World War II by the United States and Russia which cut Korea into North and South. North Korean units attacked along a 150-mile front with heavy artillery and a spearhead of well-armored tanks that followed the valley roads into the South. The Russian-made tanks rumbled along, seemingly invulnerable to South Korean resistance. South Korean forces quickly collapsed in a rout. General Douglas MacArthur remembered that the North Korean army "struck like a cobra."[3]

James's cable beat Muccio's to the United States, over 7,000 miles away, by a few minutes. It was a hot, humid Saturday evening (June 24) in Washington, D.C., thirteen hours behind Seoul time. The UP called the Department of State to verify James's report. Dumbfounded officers had no information. They phoned Assistant Secretary of State Dean Rusk, then dining with journalist Joseph Alsop in the Georgetown section of Washington. Rusk left the Alsop party about the same time that Muccio's cable reached the State Department. It was decoded. The time was now after 10:00 P.M. Secretary of State Dean Acheson, resting at his Maryland farm just outside the capital, had begun reading himself to sleep when his official phone rang. He got the bad news. A burst of calls soon ricocheted around the Washington area, as official after official was roused. General

J. Lawton Collins, the army chief of staff, heard early morning pounding on the door of his Chesapeake Bay cottage, and immediately recalled a similar incident years before when an aide suddenly awakened him to announce the attack on Pearl Harbor. He was soon racing toward Washington.

Acheson and State Department officials agreed that the United Nations Organization should be notified and an emergency session of the Security Council convened. It was a natural first step, for the United States dominated that body, Korean issues had been handled there before, the principle of collective security in the face of aggression seemed at issue, and they did not know what else to do. At 11:20 P.M. Acheson rang up the President, at home in Independence, Missouri, with his family. "Mr. President, I have very serious news."[4] Acheson told Truman that there was little to do at this point, so he should remain in Missouri, get a good night's sleep, and come to Washington the next day, Sunday, June 25. State Department personnel worked through the night drafting a Security Council resolution that charged North Korea with a "breach of the peace."[5] Meetings in the Pentagon and the State Department debated courses of action. An evacuation of Americans in Seoul was ordered.

President Truman boarded his plane early Sunday afternoon for the trip to the capital. An aide told one reporter: "The boss is going to hit those fellows [Communists] hard."[6] The President stood low in the opinion polls at the time, in large part because he was being charged by Senator Joseph McCarthy of Wisconsin with softness toward communism. Former State Department official Alger Hiss, to right-wing critics the epitome of the "sell-out" spy, had been convicted of perjury in January, and China had "fallen" just a few months before. Bold action now would disarm the President's critics. As Truman sat alone in the airplane *Independence,* he pondered history. He frequently drew lessons from the past and they usually came easily to him. Korea was the American Rhineland, he thought. It was the 1930s all over again. "Communism was acting in Korea just as Hitler, Mussolini, and the Japanese had acted ten, fifteen, and twenty years earlier."[7] There would be no appeasement this time. While he was thinking in flight over the country, the Security Council passed America's resolution of condemnation of North Korea. Except for Yugoslavia's abstention, all the members present voted "yes." The Soviet delegation, which could have cast a veto to kill the measure, was surprisingly absent, still boycotting the United Nations over its refusal to seat the new Communist government in China.

A stern, short-tempered Truman, familiar bow tie firmly in place, deplaned in Washington and headed for a dinner meeting of top officials at Blair House, that elegant federal style building on Pennsylvania Avenue, then being used as a residence during the renovation of the White House. After a chicken dinner the conferees began the weighty task of meeting the Korean crisis. Nobody doubted that Russia had engineered the attack, using its North Korean stooges to probe for a soft spot in the American containment shield. The relationship between Russia and North Korea, an assistant secretary of state remarked, was "the same as that between Walt Disney and Donald Duck."[8] Here was a test of American will and power. Worse still, they speculated, the thrust into South Korea might be only one component of a worldwide Communist assault. Would Tito's Yugoslavia be next? Then Iran? Formosa? French Indochina? The Philippines? Japan? And Germany? The State Department cabled overseas posts to be vigilant. The conferees' memories of World War II helped shape military decisions in this new crisis. Aggression had to be halted. Truman ordered General MacArthur in Japan to send arms and equipment to the South Koreans and to use American war planes to attack the North Korean spearhead. Further, he sent the Seventh Fleet into the waters between the Chinese mainland and Formosa to forestall conflict between the two Chinas.

The nation stirred Monday morning, June 26, with the news of the Korean crisis. In the White House a resolute Truman pointed a finger at Korea on the globe: "This is the Greece of the Far East. If we are tough enough now there won't be any next step."[9] He told a senator that "I'm not going to tremble like a psychopath before the Russians."[10] Although Truman received widespread bipartisan support for his decisions, some conservative Republicans seized the moment to indulge in McCarthyite recriminations. Senator William E. Jenner of Indiana, one of the emotional, cliché-ridden, anti-Communist tramplers of civil liberties in the postwar period, waxed splenetic: "The front paging of the present plight of Korea is a grim reminder that the Russian bear is sprawled across the Eurasian continent, biding its time, digesting its prey, and digging itself in for a long and cruel international winter. The Korean debacle also reminds us that the same sell-out-to-Stalin statesmen, who turned Russia loose, are still in the saddle, riding herd on the American people."[11]

By Monday evening South Korea was clearly sinking, with Seoul about to fall. At 9:00 P.M. another Blair House conference convened. Truman learned that a North Korean plane had been shot down and remarked that he "hoped it was not the last."[12] Again, recollections of the 1930s punctuated the discussion, as diplomats and military leaders vowed to avoid the mistakes of the past by drawing the line against perceived aggression. They believed, too, that the reputation of the United States was at stake. If it did not back its word—its principle of containment—its image would be tarnished and its power diminished. As Acheson put it later: "To back away from this challenge, in view of our capacity for meeting it, would be highly destructive of the power and prestige of the United States. By prestige I mean the shadow cast by power, which is of great deterrent importance."[13] Korea, then, was a supreme test, a symbol, part of a larger whole, a link in a Cold War chain of events. To falter was to forfeit world leadership. American leaders decided to take firm action: United States aircraft and vessels were ordered into full-scale action below the thirty-eighth parallel; Formosa was declared off limits to the mainland Chinese; and military aid was to be sent to Indochina and the Philippines.

Truman did not ask Congress for a declaration of war or a resolution of support. He simply informed key congressmen about the choices he had made as Commander-in-Chief and justified them bluntly: "We've got to stop [the] USSR now."[14] This was war by the executive branch. Critics would soon label it "Mr. Truman's War." On Tuesday, June 27, Americans applauded Truman's response with a sense of relief reminiscent of the day after Pearl Harbor. The United Nations passed another United States-sponsored resolution urging members to aid South Korea. Thus the United Nations approved actions the United States had already taken. Nevertheless, Seoul fell as the American embassy staff burned secret documents in a farewell bonfire. Truman recalled his thinking that day: "If . . . the threat to South Korea was met firmly and successfully, it would add to our successes in Iran, Berlin, and Greece a fourth success in opposition to the aggressive moves of the Communists."[15]

The news of the continued North Korean push into the South sparked talk on June 28 and 29 of sending American troops. Presidential supporters cited historical precedent to counter criticism that Truman had bypassed the congressional right to declare wars: Jefferson had ordered action against the Barbary pirates and McKinley had sent troops into China during the Boxer Rebellion without prior congressional sanction. On the twenty-ninth, Truman ordered American pilots to attack above the thirty-eighth parallel. On Friday, June 30, after visiting the war front, MacArthur asked Truman to send American soldiers to Korea. The President soon gave the order. The risk of global war was great, but American leaders

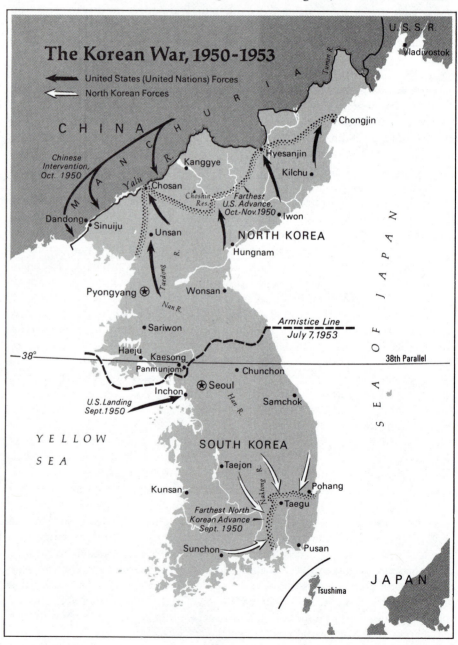

The Korean War, 1950–1953

believed that Russia would not directly enter the fray. Amid reports that the North Korean surge was pushing the South Koreans into a small area at the bottom of the peninsula, the Pusan perimeter, Truman left Washington for a weekend yacht cruise on the Chesapeake. He had made his tough decisions, and, as was characteristic of him, he would not brood over them. The nation mobilized, readying itself for an undeclared but initially popular war against communism. Truman tagged it a "police action." The decision to send American troops to Korea, Truman said in his "Farewell Address" in 1953, "was the most important in my time as President of the United States."[16]

The Korean War and the Cold War

The Korean War lasted thirty-seven months. What began as an American attempt to contain the North Korean onslaught soon became an effort to "liberate" the North from the Communist camp. Until September 15, 1950, the war went badly for the United States, South Korea, and the small numbers of troops offered by allies, all functioning nominally under United Nations auspices. On that day, General MacArthur launched a brilliant amphibious assault at Inchon, several hundred miles behind the North Korean lines. American troops quickly cut through to Seoul. Farther south the American Eighth Army broke out of the Pusan bridgehead. Trapped North Korean soldiers were cut off from supplies. The Inchon victory, General Maxwell Taylor recalled, had an "intoxicating effect" on American leaders.[17] The Truman Administration, envisioning a major Cold War victory, decided to unite the two Koreas by crossing the thirty-eighth parallel in force.

Once Truman decided to push beyond the parallel to the Chinese and Russian borders to wipe out North Korea, the war aims and the consequences of American intervention in Korea were drastically altered. The Chinese had been surprised by the outbreak of the Korean War in June, and the American push to the Yalu River posed a direct threat to their security. Mao Zedong and Zhou Enlai, in noisy public speeches and quiet warnings passed through India, fumed that Beijing would not permit Americans to touch the Chinese border. American officials believed, without adequate intelligence, that China would not enter the war, if only because Russia would restrain its "puppet" regime and because Chinese forces were small and poorly organized. MacArthur told Truman on October 15, "We are no longer fearful of their [Chinese] intervention. . . . They have no air force . . . [and] if the Chinese tried to get down to Pyongyang there would be the greatest slaughter."[18] It was a grand miscalculation. "The advance to the Yalu," scholar David McLellan has written, "is a prime example of an American propensity to take the righteousness of its actions for granted and to ignore the objective reality which its behavior represents to others."[19]

In October, American forces crossed the thirty-eighth parallel and cut deep into the North. On October 26, Chinese "volunteers" hit back. After fierce fighting, however, they retreated—perhaps China's signal that full-scale war could be avoided if the Americans halted their drive. The signal was ignored. On November 8, B-29 bombers struck bridges across the Yalu. These vital links between China and North Korea were attacked almost daily during the month. Then, on November 24, MacArthur's troops jumped off on a major northward offensive. Victory appeared near. Two days later, Chinese forces, at least 200,000 in number, swept down upon MacArthur's unsuspecting armies. Within

Douglas MacArthur (1880–1964). Familiar corn-cob pipe between set teeth, the West Point graduate commanded American forces in Asia during the Second World War, directed the postwar occupation of Japan, and headed the "United Nations" effort in Korea until he was dramatically relieved of duty by the President in April, 1951. Truman once called the general "Mr. Prima Donna." (Library of Congress)

weeks Chinese and North Korean soldiers engulfed the North. MacArthur asked Washington, without success, to approve a massive air strike against China. The United Nations soon branded China an "aggressor." Truman hinted at a news conference that the United States might use the atomic bomb, whereupon the agitated British Prime Minister Clement Attlee quickly flew to Washington to protest that the United States should seek negotiations, not a dangerously expanded war.

By March of 1951 MacArthur had managed to shove Communist forces back across the thirty-eighth parallel. The fighting stabilized at roughly the prewar boundary. Truman thought of negotiations at this point, but MacArthur grew restless, hell-bent on reversing earlier defeats and slashing the North on behalf of the crusade against international communism. He also grew reckless, accustomed as he was to independent decisionmaking. Truman would not let him attack China proper or use Nationalist Chinese forces in Korea, so the general with the Napoleonic ego began to make public statements suggesting that his Commander-in-Chief was an appeaser. To Congressman Joseph Martin, he wrote, in a letter made public in April, 1951: "There is no substitute for victory."[20] Asia, not Europe, argued the general, was the key to defeating Communist aggression. Later he would say that the President had lost his nerve in Korea. On April 11 Truman, backed strongly by the Joint Chiefs of Staff, fired MacArthur for insubordination and for sabotaging chances for a ceasefire by crossing the thirty-eighth parallel again.

The vain general, who had so badly miscalculated Chinese reactions, returned home to ticker-tape parades. In a televised address that left many in tears, he told Congress on April 19 that the war had to be expanded. He closed with the now famous words: "Old soldiers never die; they just fade away."[21] Congressional hearings featuring the old hero revealed that many Americans shared MacArthur's frustrations over military restraint. Americans were used to winning wars; Truman was now talking about something alien—a "limited war," localized and without atomic weapons. One critical soldier wrote home: "We need somebody who will . . . give Russia an ultimatum, slap down a few dissenters . . . , jump into the driver's seat, put the gas to the floor and a hand on the horn, and let her roll so that everyone will see we mean business. Certainly we'll scrape a few fenders, may even lose one or two, but it won't stop us."[22] Senator McCarthy spewed his venom, too. The President, he declared on the Senate floor, "is a rather sinister monster of many heads and many tentacles, a monster conceived in the Kremlin, and then given birth to by Acheson . . . , and then nurtured into Frankenstein proportions by the Hiss crowd, who still run the State Department."[23]

Truman and Acheson replied to the charges of appeasement, and talk of impeachment, by pointing to the risk of world war. Acheson compared MacArthur and other opponents to the farmer who "goes out every morning and pulls up all his crops to see how they have been doing during the night."[24] The Chairman of the Joint Chiefs of Staff, General Omar Bradley, answered critics of the Administration. As much an anti-Communist as the next man, he pointed out that an enlargement of the war would by no means guarantee victory, that it might bring Russia in, and that the United States would lose angry allies in other parts of the world. He rejected the idea of a "showdown" with Soviet communism in Korea, for it would be "the wrong war, at the wrong place, at the wrong time, and with the wrong enemy."[25] In short, Russia was still enemy number one and Europe the primary strategic area. MacArthur faded away, but Truman and the Democrats suffered politically under their tarnished image.

Peace talks began at Panmunjom in July of 1951. They made little headway and

Battle in the United Nations. Dean Acheson squares off with Soviet diplomat Andrei Vishinsky in the arena of the United Nations over the Korean War and a multitude of other squabbles. Vishinsky was famous for his jabs and Acheson for his eloquent and stubborn defenses. (*United Nations World,* 1952)

the fighting continued. In June, 1952, American aircraft blasted the large hydro-electric plants along the Yalu. During the 1952 presidential campaign, Republican candidate Dwight D. Eisenhower pledged, if elected, to go to Korea to find a way to end the conflict. He was elected, in good part because of American frustration with the inconclusive nature of the war. And he went to Korea, but found no easy solution. The most serious difference between Chinese and American negotiators was the disposition of prisoners of war (POWs). Thousands of Chinese and North Korean soldiers, encouraged by a "re-education" program in the South, refused repatriation. A few hundred captives in the North, having undergone Communist "brainwashing," elected to remain above the thirty-eighth parallel. The usual international practice was to return all prisoners, but Truman and Eisenhower wanted to liberate their POWs from Communist rule by keeping them in the South.

In early 1953 Eisenhower put pressure on the Chinese to settle the question. He threatened to widen the war. Secretary of State John Foster Dulles hinted that atomic weapons might be employed in Korea. And Washington "unleashed" Jiang Jieshi to attack the mainland; Nationalist bombing raids in fact followed. The March death of Stalin, combined with these actions, probably helped bring the peace talks to a conclusion. New Soviet policies were more flexible, and Moscow urged Beijing to settle the prisoner question.

On July 27, 1953, the adversaries signed an armistice. They agreed to turn over the POW issue to a committee of neutral nations (ultimately the POWs stayed where they chose—including twenty-one Americans in North Korea). The conferees drew a new boundary line close to the thirty-eighth parallel, which gained South Korea 1,500 square miles of territory. The agreement also provided for a demilitarized zone between the two Koreas. The "Korean Conflict," as it was tagged in the document, thus ended with at least one million South Koreans and over a million North Koreans and Chinese dead. The United States lost 33,000 dead and 105,000 wounded, and spent about twenty billion dollars. The United States supplied over 80 percent of the naval power and over 90 percent of the air support, as well as half the combat troops, in this "United Nations" effort. There were no victors—no dancing, cheering crowds in Times Square. The Cold War persisted. "We have won an armistice on a single battleground—not peace in the world," said Eisenhower. "We may not now relax our guard nor cease our quest."[26]

The Korean War has left many questions, most of which cannot be answered definitively until that distant day when Chinese and Soviet government archives are opened to historians. Speculations abound. Did Russia launch the Korean War? We just do not know for sure. There are plausible reasons why Moscow might have induced its client North Korean government to attack. Since Secretary Acheson had indicated in a speech before the National Press Club on January 12, 1950, that, although South Korea was an area of vital concern to the United States, it lay outside the American defense perimeter, perhaps Stalin thought the United States would not defend the South. The joint chiefs of staff had earlier decided that South Korea was strategically unimportant and indefensible. American economic and military aid to South Korea before the war was comparatively small. Maybe Stalin gambled on a quick victory.

The "gamble thesis" raises a more fundamental question: What did Russia hope to gain? Perhaps Moscow could reaffirm its leadership of the Communist world,

Dean Acheson (1893–1971). He, like the President, assumed that Russia had initiated the Korean War and urged resolute American reaction. The new crisis, coming after his National Press Club speech of January 12, 1950, and other foreign policy woes such as Mao's recent victory in China, emboldened some of his critics to ask once again for his resignation. (*The Reporter,* 1952. Copyright 1952 by Fortnightly Publishing Co. Inc.)

then being challenged by the new Chinese regime. Also, Russia could perhaps block the movement toward a separate Japanese peace treaty, which it saw as a long-term threat to Soviet security. Third, it could unite Korea and gain strength in Asia. Other questions, however, leave doubts about Soviet intentions. Why was the Soviet delegate absent from the United Nations at such a crucial time, especially if the Soviets were planning an attack? More important, why did Russia give such inadequate aid to the North Koreans and Chinese during the war, and especially fail to give an added push when the North Koreans could have defeated the South Koreans and Americans at Pusan, before the success at Inchon? Why, when it had launched a European movement for peaceful coexistence, would Moscow torpedo that effort by provoking war in Asia? Some scholars suggest that the North Koreans, armed heavily by the Soviets, took matters in their own hands in June and launched an attack that surprised the Russians almost as much as the Americans.

This hypothesis derives plausibility from the long-standing civil war between the Northern Communists led by Kim Il-sung and the politicians in the South grouped around Syngman Rhee. Both leaders sought national unification and both looked to foreign sources for material aid. Kim drew large amounts from the Soviet Union; Rhee tapped the United States. In February of 1950, the American Congress authorized $60 million in economic aid for Seoul; in March it voted $10,970,000 in military assistance; and on June 5 it granted another $100 million in economic aid. (An American Military Advisory Group remained active in the South, although American troops departed in July, 1949.) North Korea, fearing a military build-up below the thirty-eighth parallel, may have decided to attack the South before all of this aid could take effect. Also, in May elections, Rhee lost control of the South Korean National Assembly. Kim may have thought he had to strike before Rhee could stabilize his precarious position through his usual repressive measures. For months before June, skirmishes along the border were common as units of both sides crossed the parallel. Some scholars speculate that Rhee himself may have provoked the Northern assault by attacking, on the morning of June 25, the town of Haeju, five miles inside North Korea. As historian Edmund S. Wehrle has suggested, perhaps "both the United States and Russia may merely have found themselves suddenly committed to support the abrupt actions of unruly satellites."[27]

If we do not know for certain how the war began, or why, we *can* measure its consequences. At home in the United States, it meant the repudiation of the Democrats in 1952 and the election of a Republican administration, both made possible by popular exasperation with the stalemate in Korea. It wounded bipartisanship and fueled McCarthyism. It helped set off a "great debate" in the early 1950s over whether Europe or Asia was more important in the campaign against communism and whether the United States was overcommitted around the globe. Truman's handling of the American response to the Korean War also confirmed presidential supremacy in foreign policy; he neither consulted Congress nor asked for a declaration of war. Acheson did not wish to invite hearings which might produce that "one more question in cross-examination which destroys you, as a lawyer. We had complete acceptance of the President's policy by everybody on both sides of both houses of Congress." He did not wish to answer "ponderous questions" that might have "muddled up" Truman's policy.[28] As historian Arthur Schlesinger, Jr. has concluded, Truman "dramatically and dangerously enlarged the power of future Presidents to take the nation into major war." Furthermore, the "Constitution could not easily sustain the weight of the indiscriminate globalism to which the Korean War gave birth."[29]

Indeed, the United States thereafter placed itself against nationalist movements, interpreted as components of an international Communist plot: it gave aid to the French in Indochina, and intervened in the Chinese civil war by aiding Jiang on Formosa. Between 1953 and 1972 South Korea itself received $5.5 billion in foreign aid from the United States. The Korean War also poisoned Sino-American relations. Washington continued to refuse to recognize Mao's government, and China, which had ignobly forced United States troops to retreat and had denied them a victory, became a chief villain in the Cold War melodrama written by Americans. At the same time, the United States became the principal foreign devil for Beijing. The Korean War also demonstrated how easily the United States could influence the United Nations Organization, which dutifully passed American resolutions, and it further strengthened the simple notions of a Communist monolith and suggested that limited wars could alter Communist behavior. Exaggerations became legion. President Truman proclaimed on October 4, 1952, that "We are fighting in Korea so we won't have to fight in Wichita, or in Chicago, or in New Orleans, or on San Francisco Bay."[30]

The Truman Administration utilized the Korean War to fulfill other goals as well. As Acheson noted, the dispatch of troops to Korea "removed the recommendations of NSC-68 from the realm of theory and made them immediate budget for fiscal year 1953 reached $52.6 billion, up from $17.7 billion in 1950. American military expansion was impressive: a much enlarged army; development of tactical nuclear weapons; four more Army divisions for Europe, making a total of six there; the 1952 maiden flight of a new jet bomber, the B-52; the explosion of a thermonuclear device in October, 1952, leading to the 1954 testing of the hydrogen bomb—the "Super." The United States also expanded its military ties abroad. It acquired bases in Saudi Arabia and Morocco, began successful talks with fascist Spain for an air base, and initiated plans for the rearmament of West Germany. In 1951 the United States, Australia, and New Zealand formed the ANZUS Pact. CIA covert operations intensified and strategies for psychological warfare were designed. George F. Kennan, for one, worried that American foreign policy was coming to rest on a dangerously militarized footing. He opposed the decision to develop the H-bomb, for example, because he feared that "we would come to think of our security as embraced solely in the mathematics of whatever power of destruction we could evolve" and forget the fundamental role of diplomacy.[32]

The Foreign Policy of Dwight D. Eisenhower

The stalemated Korean War and the "loss" of China provided Republicans with considerable political ammunition in the 1952 presidential campaign. Bipartisanship was shelved, because the political stakes—removing the Democratic party from its twenty-year hold on the White House—were high. Although Republican candidate General Dwight D. Eisenhower conducted a smiling, moderate campaign, his party's right wing attacked vehemently. The Truman Administration, which had launched containment, gotten "tough" with the Soviets, and established an internal security system, now somehow had become soft on communism.

Richard M. Nixon (1913—). Before he was elected vice-president in 1952, Nixon graduated from Whittier College, took a law degree from Duke University, served in Congress (1946–1951), and represented California as senator (1951–1953). An anti-Communist alarmist who often used excessive language to score debating points, Nixon was, said Adlai Stevenson, ''McCarthy in a white collar.'' Nixon lost a bid for the presidency in 1960, but miraculously returned in 1968 and served in the White House until 1974 when, plagued by the ''Watergate'' political corruption he had spawned, he became the first President to resign. (*The Reporter,* 1960. Copyright 1960 by The Reporter Magazine Co.)

Vice-presidential candidate Richard M. Nixon, already famous for his anti-Communist zeal as a senator, charged that Democratic candidate Adlai E. Stevenson was a graduate of "Dean Acheson's cowardly College of Communist Containment."[33] The Republican party platform, written by John Foster Dulles, loaded invective on the Truman Administration for ineptly squandering American power and for practicing "appeasement."

The containment doctrine became a target of abuse. Republicans called it "negative, futile, and immoral."[34] It had failed because it was too defensive. Dulles proposed "liberation" as a replacement. By that he meant lifting the Communist yoke from Eastern Europe. He was never precise about how to do this; he often merely advocated a propaganda program to arouse Eastern Europeans against their Soviet masters. Democrats retorted that meddling in Eastern Europe would do those people little good because the Soviets would crush them—an assumption the Democrats themselves had rejected during the first years of the Cold War.

"Liberation" did not decide the election of 1952, but the political rhyme "I like Ike" may have. Eisenhower was a sincere, modest, wholesome, and honest person, whose simple rhetoric and homespun illustrations made him attractive to millions. He was also a professional military man and, since the Cold War seemed to be increasingly a military matter, he seemed better qualified for the job than Adlai Stevenson. Although no less a Cold Warrior than Eisenhower, the Democratic governor of Illinois was tainted by his association with the unpopular Truman Administration. Stevenson became the scapegoat for America's Cold War frustrations. Eisenhower's "I shall go to Korea" statement of October 24 helped insure his election with 55 percent of the popular vote.[35]

Makers of American Foreign Policy from 1950 to 1961

Presidents	Secretaries of State
Harry S Truman, 1945–1953	Dean G. Acheson, 1949–1953
Dwight D. Eisenhower, 1953–1961	John Foster Dulles, 1953–1959
	Christian A. Herter, 1959–1961

The lean, happy Ike, arms often raised high forming a large "V" for victory, was a skillful politician. The first Republican President since Hoover, Eisenhower appeared, but was not, simple-minded. His language was so commonplace that reporters listening to his speeches ridiculed his "five-star generalities"; one remarked that "he just crossed the thirty-eighth platitude."[36] He certainly lacked a surefootedness for grammar. His utterances often displayed mangled syntax and Eisenhowerese colloquialisms that produced dizziness in his listeners. How this idiosyncratic style affected foreign diplomats and negotiations is not clear, but it may have fed popular ideas and Democratic grumblings that Eisenhower lacked a grasp of tough realities.

Born in Texas and raised in Abilene, Kansas, Eisenhower graduated from West Point and led an obscure military life until appointed the supreme allied commander in Europe during the Second World War. After the war he served as president of Columbia University and as NATO commander. He liked fishing and golfing, and most of his companions in sport were members of the business elite. Eisenhower admired business leaders and their financial success, and even more than Truman, he appointed a great number to high office in agencies shaping foreign policy. Representatives of business, finance, and law held 76 percent of such posts under Eisenhower, whereas the figure for Truman had been 43 percent. These businessmen tended to look upon the world as something to be managed. They were conservative advocates of "private enterprise" in a world increasingly turning toward revolution and socialism.

Eisenhower and his advisers saw capitalist development as a deterrent to communism, and like the "peace and prosperity" ideologues of Truman days, they venerated foreign trade. As Eisenhower told his Cabinet, there was "no instrument in diplomacy quite as powerful as trade."[37] Eisenhower appointed a Commission on Foreign Economic Policy in 1953, and it urged a more liberal trade policy through tariff reduction. To achieve this goal he extended the reciprocal trade agreements program, expanded the lending authority of the Export-Import Bank, and relaxed controls on trade with Eastern European nations. Total American exports expanded from $15 billion in 1952 to $30 billion in 1960. At first Eisenhower favored trade over aid as a means to combat Communist exploitation of foreign economic woes. But by the mid-1950s he had shifted to a policy of trade and aid to help developing nations. He also emphasized military aid. This emphasis carried benefits for a President interested in balancing the budget. Military aid constituted sound economics, said the President, because it cost less to maintain a Greek soldier than an American one. Throughout the 1950s the United States spent over three billion dollars a year in military assistance overseas under the Mutual Security program. Eisenhower also added a new program in 1954, later called "Food for Peace," wherein the United States disposed of its agricultural surplus overseas. In ten years this program accounted for $12.2 billion in farm exports. And in 1959, after years of ignoring ardent Latin American requests, the United States established the Inter-American Development Bank to spur hemispheric economic projects.

Unlike Truman and Acheson, Eisenhower at least seemed willing to negotiate with the Soviets. Stalin's death in March, 1953 removed one of the original Cold War villains, and in April Eisenhower seized the opportunity to deliver a stirring address titled "The Chance for Peace." The President berated the Soviets for disrupting the postwar world, but he also invited more friendly relations, noted that "an era ended with the death of Joseph Stalin," and revealed his discomfort with militarism. "Every gun that is made, every warship launched, every rocket fired signifies, in the final sense, a theft from those who hunger and are not fed. . . . The cost of one modern heavy bomber is this: a modern brick school in more than 30 cities."[38] Thereafter he often urged disarmament and a reduction in the military methods used to implement the containment doctrine. In 1954 he vetoed the suggestion of Dulles and Nixon that the United States send troops to Indochina to forestall a Vietnamese victory over the French. In 1955 and after, Eisenhower negotiated with the Soviets at summit meetings, reestablishing a practice abandoned by Truman. When asked during the Berlin crisis of 1959 if he would use nuclear weapons, he said "destruction is not a good police force. You don't throw hand grenades around streets to police the streets so that people won't be molested by thugs."[39] And in his "Farewell Address" of 1961 Eisenhower

Dwight D. Eisenhower (1890–1969). Graduate of the United States Military Academy, Supreme Commander in Europe during World War II, and President of Columbia University (1948–1951), smiling "Ike" touched the American imagination in the 1950s—"the bland leading the bland," quipped one humorist. (Dwight D. Eisenhower Library)

warned against a "military-industrial complex"—the powerful lobby of the military establishment and the defense industry—which threatened peace, American liberties, and democratic processes. Eisenhower was an uneasy Cold Warrior, a military man uncomfortable with militarism.

Ike's peace initiatives fizzled and his antimilitarist sentiments were seldom acted upon. Eisenhower ended up espousing and applying the containment doctrine, acting under the lessons learned in the 1940s. He sent troops to Lebanon and helped organize native military units to invade Guatemala and Cuba; his Central Intelligence Agency tried, but failed, to overthrow the Indonesian government in 1958. By 1959 one million Americans were stationed overseas in forty-two countries. By 1960 the Defense Department controlled 35 million acres of land at home and abroad. Defense budgets reached $35–40 million each year, although Eisenhower kept restrictions on them because he feared the United States would spend itself into weakness. Defense expenditures ate up one-half of the 1960 United States budget. New alliances—the Southeast Asia Treaty Organization and Baghdad pact—were formed, revealing in part the American penchant for thinking that an international Communist conspiracy existed. Eisenhower may have wanted to relax tensions with the Soviets and the Chinese, but his foreign policy ultimately did little to achieve relaxation.

Secretary John Foster Dulles and McCarthyism

Secretary of State John Foster Dulles (1953–1959) was a more inflexible Cold Warrior than Eisenhower, but the President, dominating their relationship, tempered some of the secretary's militance. Dulles seemed groomed for the post. His grandfather, John W. Foster, had served as secretary of state in 1892–1893 and the grandson had more than once trooped behind him in foreign capitals. Tutelage from a father who was a Presbyterian minister, education at Princeton and George Washington Law School, service as a negotiator on reparations at the Paris Peace Conference at Versailles, membership in the prestigious Wall Street firm of Sullivan and Cromwell, and worldwide activity on behalf of the Federal Council of Churches gave Dulles a varied, cosmopolitan experience before World War II. After the war he helped promote bipartisanship. In 1952 he vigorously assailed the very policies of the Truman Administration he had helped to shape, but he later admitted that his desire to elect Eisenhower had promoted this political gambit.

Dulles was forceful, ambitious, sharp, self-righteous—a mixture of moral idealism and hard-nosed realism. Indeed, he pursued ideals through the exercise of power. As he told a journalist, the United States "is almost the only country strong enough and powerful enough to be moral."[40] Because he was a dull, flat speaker, he preferred "personal diplomacy"—face-to-face negotiations with foreign diplomats. He despised compromise. Like Acheson, who called Soviet peace initiatives "Trojan doves," Dulles would rather lecture to than negotiate with Communists. He read Soviet initiatives for a reduction of tension as Communist traps. Scholar

John Foster Dulles (1888–1959). Although the President sincerely admired his secretary of state, Eisenhower did question Dulles's "practice of becoming a sort of international prosecuting attorney." The President added that "with strangers his personality may not always be winning, but with his friends he is charming and delightful." (*The Reporter,* 1956. Copyright 1956 by the Reporter Magazine Co. Inc.)

Adam Ulam has mused: "If Moscow proposed a joint declaration in favor of motherhood, this would have called forth position papers from the State Department's Policy Planning Council, somber warnings from Senator [William] Knowland, and eventually a declaration that while the United States welcomed this recognition of the sanctity of family life on the part of the Russians, it would require clear indication that the USSR did not mean to derogate the status of fatherhood."[41] Winston Churchill once remarked that Dulles was the only bull he knew who carried his own china shop with him. Others said, with some exaggeration, that he was a card-carrying Christian who pictured the Cold War as a Biblical contest between good and evil, between atheistic communism and Western Christianity. Dulles thought with much more sophistication and for him moral pronouncements served to counter simplistic Soviet ideological appeals. Still, foreigners thought his incantations were rigid and hardly conducive to fruitful diplomacy. One European newspaper depicted Dulles as the "conscience and straightjacket of the free world."[42] The Soviets respected Dulles as a formidable negotiator but they probably also remembered an old Russian proverb: "A bellowing cow gives little milk."[43] Dulles was not, however, a rigid ideologue. He was a practitioner of power who employed a variety of tools: moral appeals, foreign aid, trade, military training of foreign armies, overseas bases, a ballistic missile program, subversion of governments, and alliances. At least, as Soviet Premier Nikita S. Khrushchev later commented, Dulles "knew how far he could push us, and he never pushed us too far."[44]

The Eisenhower-Dulles team gave catchy phrases to its foreign policy. "Liberation" was one. Another was "massive retaliation," apparently meaning that a Communist aggressor could expect to be bombed with atomic weapons if it stepped across the line. Massive retaliation was designed to distinguish the new administration from Truman's and to convince the Pentagon to accept cuts in the defense budget for conventional forces. So, too, the "new look" for the military: emphasis on atomic armaments and the Air Force. Another catchphrase was "brinkmanship": not backing down in a crisis, even if it meant going to the brink of war. In 1954 Eisenhower uttered the "falling domino principle": "You have a row of dominoes set up, you knock over the first one, and what will happen to the last one is the certainty that it will go over very quickly."[45] The President was explaining that if one country in Asia fell to the Communists, others would fall in rapid succession. The 1957 "Eisenhower Doctrine" read that the United States would intervene in the Middle East if any government threatened by a Communist takeover requested aid. This was another containment "stop" sign; indeed most of these policies or concepts were actually Truman reruns or elaborations of policies set earlier.

Eisenhower once said that "sometimes Foster is just too worried about being accused of sounding like Truman and Acheson."[46] Dulles had watched the harassment of Acheson by Republican right-wingers in endless congressional hearings. They boldly charged Acheson with softness toward communism. Dulles decided to avoid a similar fate by striking his anti-Communist colors early and by permitting McCarthyites to intimidate and demoralize professional Foreign Service Officers in the State Department, an institution that Senator Joseph McCarthy believed harbored Communists or their sympathizers. Dulles demanded "positive loyalty," by which he apparently meant correct thinking, from State Department personnel and appointed an ex-FBI man and McCarthy henchman, Scott McLeod,

Joseph McCarthy (1909–1957). The notorious senator from Wisconsin used the "big lie" as a tool for advancing his political career. He charged without evidence that the State Department was infested with communists. He castigated former secretaries Marshall and Acheson. Graduate of Marquette University, judge, Marine, and Republican, the demagogic senator was once known as the "Pepsi-Cola Kid" for protecting the interests of that company. The Senate "condemned" him in December, 1954. (*The Reporter,* 1951. Copyright 1951 by Fortnightly Publishing Co., Inc.)

the chief security officer. McLeod's distaste for Democrats and "New Dealers" soon manifested itself in witch-hunting tactics that confused criticism with treason. "The quiet reign of terror," Townsend Hoopes has written, "burned its deadly way through the State Department for nearly two years, immolating along the way the careers of several hundred officers and employees."[47] It included the equivalent of book burning, for in early 1953 Dulles ordered books authored by "Communists, fellow travellers, et cetera" to be removed from the libraries of American overseas information centers.[48] Who was an "et cetera"? Bureaucrats gave the broadest interpretation and tossed out the books of such people as Bert Andrews (Washington bureau chief of the *New York Herald Tribune*), Joseph Davies (former ambassador to Russia), Walter White (deceased former head of the NAACP), and historian Foster Rhea Dulles, the secretary of state's own cousin.

One of the more prominent and tragic cases was that of Foreign Service Officer John Carter Vincent, an independent-minded "China hand" who during World War II reported from China that Jiang Jieshi was destined to lose.

McCarthyites took this to mean that Vincent plotted to defeat Jiang. A State Department Loyalty Board cleared Vincent, but the Civil Service Loyalty Review Board declared by a vote of 3 to 2 that his loyalty to the United States was in doubt. Dulles at first rejected that decision. But, seeking to satiate the extreme anti-Communists, he forced Vincent out by questioning his "standards" as an officer. Dulles once asked Vincent if he had read Stalin's *Problems of Leninism.* Vincent said he had not and Dulles replied that Vincent would not have advocated the China policies he did if he had read it. Ross Terrill has commented that "since Stalin failed in China no less than Truman, one may wonder whether Stalin read his own book."[49] Another China specialist, John Paton Davies, was fired even though nine security reviews cleared him. By 1961, State Department Asian specialist James C. Thomson, Jr. has concluded, the purged Bureau of Far Eastern Affairs "was notorious for its rigidity and its resistance to policy change" and "dominated by Cold Warriors and staffed largely by the cowed."[50] President Eisenhower never halted Dulles' disembowelment of the State Department.

"I Hear There's Something Wrong With Your Morale." Secretary Dulles launched a costly purge of Foreign Service Officers to satisfy the right wing of the Republican party. (*Herblock's Here and Now,* Simon & Schuster, 1955)

U.S. FOREIGN SERVICE

After Stalin's death, Eisenhower tried to encourage changes in Soviet foreign policy through his "Chance for Peace" speech, wherein he asked "what is the Soviet Union ready to do?"[51] The early signs for improved Soviet-American relations seemed auspicious. Moscow helped end the deadlock over Korea, opened diplomatic relations with Yugoslavia and Greece, abandoned territorial claims against Turkey, toned down its anti-American rhetoric, and launched a "peace offensive." Although the Soviet crushing of an East Berlin riot in June reminded Americans of the past, the freeing of Stalinist victims from forced labor camps conversely suggested that Stalin's heirs were not replicas of their long-time master.

Soviet leaders scrambled for position in the succession crisis. Gradually Nikita S. Khrushchev, son of a farmer, and for years the Communist party boss of the Ukraine, climbed to the top of the Kremlin hierarchy and eased out Stalin's apparent favorite Georgi Malenkov. By September, 1953, Khrushchev was first secretary of the Central Committee of the party; five years later he took the title "Premier." Portly and amiable, Khrushchev was an impulsive, competitive person of coarse speech. Eisenhower did not care for the man. Khrushchev, the President concluded, was not a statesman, "but rather a powerful, skillful, ruthless, and highly ambitious politician." Worse, he was "blinded by his dedication to the Marxist theory of world revolution and Communist domination."[52] Vice-President Nixon described the Soviet leader as a "bare knuckle slugger who had gouged, kneed, and kicked."[53] On his part, Khrushchev thought Eisenhower "a good man, but he wasn't very tough."[54]

Both Eisenhower and Khrushchev concentrated their attention on Europe, still troubled by large armies, hostile blocs, Germany, and divided Berlin—all reminders of the unresolved problems bequeathed by World War II. Because of European squabbles the United States and the Soviet Union were spending billions for large military systems. The Soviets stressed the development of ballistic missiles, while Americans emphasized intercontinental bombers under the concept of "massive retaliation." By 1955, American bombers capable of dropping atomic devices on Russia numbered 1,350; the Soviets had 350 in the same category. Soviet ground forces outnumbered their American counterparts by a 2–1 margin. An expert on Soviet affairs, Zbigniew Brzezinski, has written that the United States "now seemed to have both the capacity to inflict very heavy damage on the Soviet Union and to significantly impede any Soviet effort to seize Western Europe."[55] In one attempt to expand this capacity, Dulles sponsored the European Defense Community (EDC) as a plan to integrate European forces, including West German units. When the French balked, he warned them that the United States would undertake an "agonizing reappraisal." Paris called his bluff and rejected EDC. The secretary had to settle for an enlarged Western European Union in late 1954 and West German membership in NATO in May, 1955. Nineteen fifty-five was a banner year for ringing Communist nations with military alliances: SEATO went into effect, the American defense treaty with Nationalist China became active, the Baghdad Treaty was signed, and West Germany joined NATO. To counter an expanded NATO in 1955, the Soviets formed their own military organization, the Warsaw Pact of Eastern European nations.

The two giants, then, continued their military posturing. But they seemed more willing to reach accommodations, however minimal. The Cold War cost too many dollars and rubles, so both sides wanted to trim their military expenditures. Diplomacy returned to Soviet-American relations. On May 15, 1955 Russia and the United States signed an accord to end their ten-year joint occupation of Austria and to create an independent, neutral Austria. Although Dulles soon bragged that the Austrian State Treaty symbolized a Soviet retreat, a victory for his "liberation" policy, he did not drop his guard. He suspected Soviet trickery and warned about new dangers: "the wolf has put on a new set of sheep's clothing, and while it is better to have a sheep's clothing on than a bear's clothing on, because sheep don't have claws, I think the policy remains the same."[56]

Throughout 1954–1955, from several corners of the globe, came calls for a summit meeting of the great powers. Winston Churchill made an eloquent plea and Democrats in Congress urged negotiations. Eisenhower was cautious in the face of Dulles' long list of reasons why Americans should not meet with the Soviets: a summit conference would permit them to use propaganda on a grand scale; it would let them appear equal to Americans; a summit might encourage neutralism, for other countries would fear less and align less; it would be best to wait until the West German military was larger; the Soviets would not bargain seriously because totalitarianism depended upon an outside enemy. Eisenhower overruled him, for the President thought that one could not speak of Soviet intentions without testing them in discussions. Making the best of this setback, Dulles advised the President to avoid social settings where he might be photographed with Soviet officials. If that was difficult, Eisenhower should maintain "an austere countenance on occasions where photographing together is inevitable."[57]

Russia, the United States, Britain, and France met in Geneva from July 18 to 23, 1955. Just before leaving for that beautiful city where diplomats historically seek international peace, Eisenhower and Dulles assured congressmen that "Geneva was not going to be another Yalta."[58] The reference was timely, for early in 1955 Dulles had engineered the publication of the secret *Yalta Papers* in an abortive attempt to embarrass the Democrats. Geneva was certainly no Yalta, because the Big Four struck no concrete agreements. Everybody was trying to impress, to score points for prestige. Even evangelist Billy Graham journeyed to the city of John Calvin and preached to a throng of 35,000. Reporters and photographers flocked around smiling dignitaries. Eisenhower ignored Dulles' advice and behaved in his usual amiable manner. The Russians were sensitive to appearances; Khrushchev,

Nikita S. Khrushchev (1894–1971). The short, stocky Soviet Premier who succeeded Stalin could wear either memorable smiles or scowls. He denounced the former dictator in a "de-Stalinization" speech in 1956 and contributed to a short-lived thaw in the Cold War during the decade. He fell from power in 1964. (*The Reporter,* 1956. Copyright 1956 by the Reporter Magazine Co.)

for example, was embarrassed because the Russians flew into Geneva in a two-engine plane, whereas Eisenhower and Dulles disembarked from a more imposing four-motor aircraft. Khrushchev, the peasant of little schooling, was also aware that he was being tested by graduates of West Point, Eton, Oxford, and the Sorbonne. "Would we be able to represent our country competently?" Khrushchev thought before Geneva. His answer afterward: "We had established ourselves as able to hold our own in the international arena."[59]

American officials believed before Geneva that they would have the upper hand in bargaining. As Ike told a press conference, the United States was approaching negotiations "from a greater position of strength than we ever had before."[60] Dulles said before Geneva that the Russians were economically weak and on the verge of collapse. That drew a heated rebuttal from Khrushchev. At the conference itself, East and West split over the issues of German reunification, European security, and arms control. Correspondent James Reston reported, the conferees "disagreed so nicely."[61] Each side wanted to unite Germany but to set the terms. Americans sought a unified Germany which could join NATO. Both sides favored arms control, but parted over methods. Eisenhower dramatically presented his "open skies" proposal, wherein Russia and the United States would exchange maps and submit their military installations to aerial inspection to insure compliance with control agreements. On this American propaganda ploy designed to counter pre-Geneva Soviet appeals for disarmament, Eisenhower later remarked: "We knew the Soviets wouldn't accept it. We were sure of that, but we took a look and thought it was a good move."[62] Indeed, secrecy was one of Russia's deterrents, keeping Americans guessing on whether the inferior Soviets were catching up in airborne striking power. That secrecy ended in 1956 when the United States unilaterally instituted a version of the "open skies" proposal: reconnaisance flights of high altitude U-2 planes over the Soviet Union.

When Eisenhower returned home, he applauded a "new spirit of conciliation and cooperation" and assured Americans that he had not penned any secret agreements.[63] Geneva was largely a ceremonial affair. Russia did recognize West Germany in 1955, and that fall Khrushchev indicated he endorsed "détente." Yet, he went on: "if anybody thinks that for this reason we shall forget about Marx, Engels, and Lenin, he is mistaken. This will happen when shrimps learn to whistle."[64] About all that came out of the summit were cultural exchanges. One "cultural" consequence of Geneva was Vice-President Nixon's 1959 trip to Russia, where at a display of American products in a Moscow exhibition, he engaged Khrushchev in the "kitchen debate" on the disputed merits of capitalism. And journalist I. F. Stone wrote in 1955 about the visits of Communists to the Kiwanis Club of Des Moines, Iowa, and about the excursions of American farmers to the fields of Kharkov: "Nothing is more deadly for the war spirit than the discovery that the enemy, too, is human."[65]

Disillusionment followed Geneva because differences remained great. Russia still wanted Germany removed from NATO and NATO expunged from Europe. The United States still wanted Russia excluded from Eastern Europe and the indefinite perpetuation of American nuclear superiority. "Well, I think," said Dulles on the last day of the conference, "it is a little premature to talk about the 'era of good feelings.'"[66] Former diplomat W. Averell Harriman, a partisan Democrat, charged that the "free world was psychologically disarmed" by the "spirit of Geneva," which was actually a Soviet "smokescreen" for further aggres-

Preparation for the "Kitchen Debate." Khrushchev and Vice-President Richard M. Nixon sip Pepsi-Cola at the American National Exhibition in Moscow in July, 1959, just before their "kitchen debate" over the comparative virtues of capitalism and socialism. (PepsiCo, Inc.)

sion.[67] Harriman's extreme conclusion underestimated the degree to which Dulles was perpetuating the Cold War diplomacy that Harriman himself had helped launch in the 1940s.

The Cold War thaw of 1955 marked a brief interlude in the Soviet-American confrontation in Europe. It did signal that neither Moscow nor Washington had the power to force significant changes in European alignments. Nobody liked this seeming permanence of Cold War lines in Europe, but neither side wanted to risk war to alter the status quo. After Geneva, Eisenhower appeared bored with his job and contemplated not seeking re-election in 1956. That possibility almost became reality when he was felled in September, 1955 by a coronary thrombosis after playing twenty-seven holes of golf. But within months he recovered and won a substantial victory over Democratic candidate Adlai Stevenson, who had charged that the Eisenhower Administration was losing the Cold War to the Soviets.

In February, 1956, Khrushchev, once the loyal follower of Stalin and supporter of the bloody purges of the 1930s, delivered a momentous speech to the Twentieth Party Congress. He denounced Stalin for domestic crimes, initiated a "de-Staliniazation" program, endorsed "peaceful coexistence," and suggested that the Kremlin would now recognize different brands of communism. In the Communist nations of Eastern Europe, this apparent acceptance of Titoism emboldened erstwhile victims of Stalinism to challenge Stalinist politicians in office. "Polycentrism" in the Communist world became an irresistible force: ideological affinity, yes, but Moscow's domination, no. The abolition of the Cominform in April seemed to demonstrate Moscow's new tolerance for diversity. Young people and intellectuals soon insisted on self-determination. In Poland, for example, a labor dispute in mid-1956 ballooned into national resistance to Soviet tutelage. After using force to put down riots, Russia compromised with Polish nationalism by reluctantly accepting as the Polish Communist party chairman Wladyslaw Gomulka, heretofore denied influence because Stalin thought him too "Titoist". The United States, which had been giving aid to Tito himself for years, soon offered Poland economic assistance. Any crack in the Communist edifice was encouraged by the Eisenhower Administration. "Our hearts go out" to the Poles, the President declared.[68] Also the Central Intelligence Agency began to train, in West Germany, para-military units composed of East Europeans who might intervene in uprisings in Poland, Rumania, and Hungary.

Revolt erupted next in Hungary. Young revolutionaries marched and fought in the streets of Budapest. A new government, backed by local revolutionary councils throughout Hungary, took a drastic step when it announced that Hungary was pulling out of the Warsaw Pact and thereby becoming neutral in the Cold War. Khrushchev looked upon neutrals in Eastern Europe much as Dulles looked upon them elsewhere—with utter disdain. Russia began to move troops into Hungary and on November 4 crushed the resistance with brute force. The courageous hand-to-tank combat of underarmed students and workers in the streets of Budapest stirred global sympathy. The West would have scored some propaganda points against Russia had not British, French, and Israeli troops invaded Egypt shortly before the Soviets smashed the Hungarian Revolution. The West now had to share the moral revulsion against aggression. The simultaneous Suez and Hungarian crises demonstrated how much the Cold War antagonists feared losing their spheres of influence.

The Polish and Hungarian rebellions seemed to satisfy Dulles' dream of "liberation." The Eisenhower Administration had been encouraging discontent in Eastern Europe through the Voice of America and the CIA-financed Radio Free

"I'll be Glad to Restore Peace to the Middle East, Too." The ugly Soviet suppression of the Hungarian rebellion of 1956 prompted this telling cartoon by Herblock. (*Herblock's Special for Today,* Simon & Schuster, 1958)

Propaganda Balloons for Eastern Europe. Although the United States did not send troops or military supplies to Hungary during the 1956 uprising there, in the 1950s the Free Europe Committee floated message-filled balloons across the "iron curtain" from West Germany to stir up unrest with Soviet rule. (Franklin D. Roosevelt Library)

Europe, which beamed anti-Soviet propaganda broadcasts into the Soviet sphere. Dulles hinted that nations which split from the Soviet orbit would receive American foreign aid. In 1953, Congress had passed the first annual Captive Peoples' Resolution as a spur to self-determination in Eastern Europe. Three years later the secretary of state hailed the Hungarian tumult as evidence of the "weakness of Soviet imperialism. . . . The captive peoples should never have reason to doubt that they have in us a sincere and dedicated friend who shares their aspirations."[69] In the midst of the crisis, on November 2, Dulles suffered severe abdominal pains from the cancer that would eventually kill him in 1959. Following surgery he was incapacitated for weeks and did not manage the American response to the Hungarian Revolution. Even had he been healthy, however, it is doubtful American policy would have been different. Although Hungarian dissidents appealed for some kind of American intervention and expected it, Washington was "boxed," as one official put it.[70]

The United States simply lacked the means to direct or influence events in the Soviet sphere, short of full-scale war. "Poor fellows, poor fellows," Eisenhower told a journalist. "I think about them all the time. I wish there were some way of helping them."[71] "Liberation" was exposed for the hollow and misleading generality it had always been. The Eisenhower Administration lowered immigration barriers to permit over 20,000 Hungarian refugees to enter the United States and introduced a resolution condemning Soviet force in the General Assembly of the United Nations. That was all Americans could do. Still, Eastern Europeans themselves had succeeded in forcing the Soviets to make some compromises with nationalism, thereby reducing Soviet authority in the region, the brutal crushing of the Hungarian uprising notwithstanding.

From *Sputnik* to U-2

In 1956–57, the United States seemed on the defensive and the Soviets on the offensive. Washington's adjustment to this appearance took the now familiar military course. The United States hastened to patch up its crumbling European alliance, rocked by American disapproval of British-French military actions in the Middle East. Thus NATO was reinvigorated and American intermediate range ballistic missiles were placed in Britain. Still, the French became bogged down in a colonial war in Algeria and had to transfer many of their NATO contingents to Africa. An economic recession in the United States in 1957 further sapped Western vitality. The United States and its allies were by no means weak or insecure, but their unity and confidence were waning.

Communists grew pompous in the face of the apparent Western malaise. "The East Wind Prevails Over the West Wind," asserted Mao Zedong. [72] On October 4, 1957 it appeared so. That day the Russians launched into outer space the world's first man-made satellite, *Sputnik*. Two months earlier the Soviets had fired the first intercontinental ballistic missile (ICBM). These achievements in rocketry shocked Americans into the realization that the Soviets had surpassed them in missile development. Never comfortable in second place, Americans chastised Eisenhower for apparently letting American power and prestige slip; the Democrats in particular sensed political advantage and publicly attacked the Administration. "The idea of *them* [Democrats] charging *me* with not being interested in *defense!*" General Eisenhower snapped. "Damn it, I've spent my whole life being concerned with defense of our country." [73] Although the "United States still had a substantial lead in strategic weapons," as historian Stephen Ambrose has noted, prominent Americans began to speak of a "bomber gap" and "missile gap." [74] A Ford Foundation Commission study, the "Gaither Report," fed popular fears about the same time that the Soviets were outstripping the United States both militarily and economically. Like NSC-68 in 1950, the "Gaither Report" in 1957 urged a large American military buildup. The Eisenhower Administration knew that *Sputnik* had not undermined American security, because since 1956 American U-2 spy planes, flying at high altitude with sensitive instruments, had been gathering intelligence data on Soviet military capabilities. Yet, as the British ambassador reported, *Sputnik* stunned official Washington: "The Russian success in launching the satellite has been something equivalent to Pearl Harbor. The American cocksureness is shaken." [75]

Presidential Assistant Sherman Adams bantered that the United States was not interested in scoring in an outer-space basketball game. When in November another *Sputnik* circled the globe, this time with a dog aboard, someone quipped that next the Russians would orbit cows—hence: the herd shot 'round the world. The Eisenhower Administration, of course, took the missile matter seriously. The President accelerated the American ballistic missile program. He ordered the dispersal of Strategic Air Command bombers and continued U-2 flights. In

January, 1958, rocket scientists, many of them former Germans like Werner von Braun brought to the United States at the end of World War II, successfully launched an American satellite named Explorer I. In July, the National Aeronautics and Space Administration (NASA) was created; its expensive operations culminated in 1969 in the landing of Americans on the moon. America's educational system was given a jolt by *Sputnik,* too. Why wasn't "Johnny" keeping up with "Ivan"? Many answered that Russian schools offered superior instruction in mathematics and science. The National Defense Education Act (NDEA), passed in September, 1958, provided for federal aid to finance new educational programs in the sciences, mathematics, and foreign languages. Soviet-American competition helped make education a Cold War phenomenon. One university president declared in the 1960s that the nation's colleges and universities had become "bastions of our defense, as essential as . . . supersonic bombers."[76]

The continued militarization of the Cold War and the new emphasis on missile development alarmed George F. Kennan, an earlier architect of the containment doctrine. In November and December of 1957 Kennan delivered the "Reith Lectures" in London, vaguely calling for the "disengagement" of foreign troops from Eastern Europe and Germany, restrictions on nuclear weapons in that area, and a unified, nonaligned Germany. The ideas were neither his alone, nor new. Earlier in the year, for example, Polish Foreign Minister Adam Rapacki advocated a "denuclearized zone" in Central and Eastern Europe.[77] The "Rapacki Plan" seemed a sensible way to reduce the atomic arms race, but the Eisenhower Administration, despite its own appeals for disarmament, did not pursue the proposal. In the fall of 1957 Kennan tried to keep the idea alive through his

Titan II Missile. Standing ten stories high and packing the explosive power of nine million tons of TNT (equivalent to 700 Hiroshima bombs), this surface-to-surface intercontinental ballistic missile (ICBM) is ready for launching from its underground silo. The decision to develop the Titan I was made in 1955; the Titan booster was successfully tested four years later; and in 1962 the bigger and longer Titan II was launched. Since 1963 this missile has been part of the Strategic Air Command, deployed at bases in Arizona, Kansas, and Arkansas. As of 1980, the United States had fifty-four Titans, each armed with a deadly nuclear warhead. (U.S. Air Force)

eloquent lectures widely broadcast over BBC radio. Also, in order to reduce Moscow's security fears, he wanted to remove Germany from the Cold War and thereby permit a withdrawal of Soviet troops from Eastern Europe. He was critical, too, of the Eisenhower Administration's strengthening of NATO, which he labeled a "military fixation" at a time when diplomacy was needed.[78]

Kennan's suggestions were greeted with unalloyed hostility by leading Americans. Former Secretary of State Dean Acheson spared Eisenhower and Dulles the task of debating "disengagement". "Next to the Lincoln Memorial in moonlight," columnist James Reston wrote, "the sight of Mr. Dean G. Acheson blowing his top is without doubt the most impressive view in the capital."[79] Acheson warned against a new American isolationism. Should Kennan's plan be realized, he scolded, Russia might reintroduce troops into Eastern Europe, threaten Western Europe, and actually sign an anti-American military pact with the new united Germany. The Russians simply could not be trusted. A rearmed West Germany must remain in the American camp. More soberly, German-born Henry A. Kissinger, a Harvard political scientist, argued that a German defense line had to be held against a potentially aggressive Russia. In his *Nuclear Weapons and Foreign Policy* (1957), Kissinger also criticized Dulles' concept of "massive retaliation" and appealed instead for a mobile, tactical missile system tied to flexible fighting units so that conventional wars would not ignite nuclear annihilation. Kennan answered Acheson and Kissinger, both committed to the military Cold War in Europe, that the United States would never know Russia's intentions unless it negotiated. He spoke of new "realities" in Europe which made the 1950s different from the 1940s. Walter Lippmann, who had criticized Kennan's containment in 1947, stood with him in 1957. People like Acheson and Kissinger, Lippman complained, are "like old soldiers trying to relive the battles in which they won their fame and glory. . . . Their preoccupation with their own past history is preventing them from dealing with the new phase of the Cold War."[80]

The "disengagement" debate had hardly subsided before a crisis over Berlin demonstrated the importance of Kennan's suggestions for defusing European issues. West Berlin, 110 miles inside Communist East Germany, was a bone in the Russian throat, as Khrushchev put it. Approximately three million East German defectors, many of them skilled workers, had used West Berlin as an escape route since 1949. For Americans and their allies, including the West German government of Konrad Adenauer, the city was an espionage and propaganda center for activities directed eastward. West Berlin's prosperity, induced by billions of dollars in American aid, glittered next to somber East Berlin. Washington heated Soviet tempers by bragging about economic success in West Berlin and applauding the East German exodus. The United States also insisted that the two Germanies be united under free elections and refused to recognize the East German government. Finally, the continued rearmament of West Germany, including American planes capable of dropping nuclear bombs, alarmed Russia, which had endorsed the Rapacki Plan.

In November of 1958 the Soviet Union boldly issued an ultimatum to solve the German "problem" through negotiations. Within six months, warned Khrushchev, unless East-West talks on Germany had begun, Russia would sign a peace treaty with East Germany, thereby ending the occupation agreements still in effect from World War II and turning East Berlin over to the East German regime. He recommended that Berlin be converted to a "free city" without foreign troops.

"Braggers." In this Japanese cartoon Khrushchev and Eisenhower brag about their missiles during the serious arms race of the 1950s. (Nasu, courtesy of the State Historical Society of Missouri)

Washington was clearly worried, because it did not recognize East Germany and therefore would not negotiate with it. To deal with it would be to accept the Soviet position that there were two Germanies. Such an acceptance would in turn call into question the post-World War II occupation rights and hence the American presence within West Berlin itself. Unwilling to accept anything less than a united Germany tied to NATO, the United States was not eager to negotiate "disengagement" with the Russians. Dulles called the Russians reckless and braced himself for an episode in brinkmanship. Dean Acheson and Army Chief of Staff Maxwell Taylor urged the President to test Soviet intentions by sending American military units through the corridors to West Berlin. Eisenhower rejected such inflammatory advice and stalled. Privately Eisenhower said that "in this gamble, we are not going to be betting white chips, building up the pot gradually and fearfully. Khrushchev should know that when we decide to act, our whole stack will be in the pot."[81] Khrushchev wanted to talk, not fight. He backed away from his ultimatum and agreed to a foreign ministers conference for May, 1959, which proved inconclusive, a trip of September, 1959 to the United States to speak with Eisenhower, and ultimately a Paris summit meeting in May, 1960.

Khrushchev's tour of the United States in September, 1959 was a real spectacle. Eisenhower personally welcomed him, hoping to "soften up the Soviet leader even a little bit. Except for the Austrian peace treaty, we haven't made a chip in the granite in seven years."[82] Dulles had died of cancer in April, so Eisenhower was more in the forefront of diplomacy now. Khrushchev and his party began a national tour. The Premier inspected an IBM plant, fell in love with the city of San Francisco, cuddled babies just like an American politician, and visited a Hollywood movie set where he was offended by the bare legs exposed in a cancan dance—a sign to him of the decadence of Western capitalism. He was annoyed that proper security arrangements could not be made for a trip to Disneyland. He seemed, in brief, altogether human. He plugged "peaceful coexistence" and said that his earlier statement that "we will bury capitalism" should not be taken in a literal or military sense. "I say it again—I've almost worn my tongue thin repeating it—you may live under capitalism and we will live under socialism and build communism. The one whose system proves better will win. We will not bury you, nor will you bury us."[83] Khrushchev reminded Americans that they had sent troops into the Russian civil war during the World War I period, and they reminded him that they had also sent relief aid in the early 1920s. After ten days on the road, the Soviet Premier went to Camp David, that quiet, secluded presidential retreat near the Catoctin Mountains in Maryland. For two days the two leaders exchanged war stories and discussed the question of Berlin in a relaxed atmosphere. Eisenhower would not agree to a new summit meeting until Khrushchev abandoned his Berlin ultimatum. The Premier agreed to do so. Although the President and Premier were no closer to a German settlement, observers identified a "Spirit of Camp David"—a willingness on both sides to talk their way to détente.

In 1959–1960 Eisenhower himself made a number of foreign trips in a deliberate effort to conduct "personal diplomacy." His new vigor and determination to ease tensions suggested that Ike had been previously restrained by Dulles' intransigence. Just before Khrushchev's visit to the United States, the President had flown to London, Paris, and Bonn for talks with European leaders. In December he traveled 22,000 miles to eleven nations in Europe, Asia, and North Africa. Among his hosts were Pope John XXIII, neutralist Prime Minister Jawaharlal Nehru of India, where a million people in New Delhi hailed Eisenhower as the "Prince of Peace," and Francisco Franco, the dictator who had authorized American air bases on Spanish soil. It was a "goodwill" tour that the engaging President relished. In February, 1960, he toured Latin America for two weeks and encountered a mixed

Camp David, 1959. Eisenhower and Khrushchev discussed Berlin in a relaxed manner at the Maryland presidential retreat, but the "Spirit of Camp David" soon evaporated. (Dwight D. Eisenhower Library)

reception. And then he departed for the Paris summit meeting in May. There the "goodwill" ended.

Two weeks before that summit meeting, on May 1, 1960, an American airplane carrying high-powered cameras and other reconnaisance instruments was shot down over Sverdlovsk in the Ural Mountains, 1,200 miles within the Soviet Union. The U-2 intelligence plane was part of a CIA operation and was flying from a base in Turkey to one in Norway. Although such flights had been conducted for four years and the Soviets had learned about them, this was the first time that Soviet firepower had been able to reach the high altitude craft. Evidently pilot Francis Gary Powers' U-2 had engine trouble and dropped several thousand feet before being shot down. He parachuted and was captured immediately, unable or unwilling to use his CIA-issued poison needle. CIA officials in the United States knew only that a plane was missing. NASA, used as "cover," announced routinely on May 3 that a "research airplane" studying weather patterns over Turkey had apparently crashed. Two days later Khrushchev cryptically announced that an American airplane had been shot down over Russia after it had violated Soviet air space. Thereafter, the Eisenhower Administration bungled badly. The State Department issued a fabricated statement that a weather plane piloted by a "civilian" had probably strayed over Russian territory by mistake. On May 6 Premier Khrushchev exploded that story by displaying photographs of the uninjured pilot, his spy equipment, and his pictures of Soviet military installations. Then the State Department lamely admitted that the plane was "probably" on an intelligence operation. No longer able to keep the truth hidden, Eisenhower decided to speak out. "I felt anything but apologetic," he recalled.[84] The President took responsibility for the U-2 reconnaisance flights and said they were necessary to avoid another Pearl Harbor. With such logic, Emmet John Hughes has noted, the Administration transformed "an unthinkable falsehood into a sovereign right."[85] This was the dramatic background to the summit meeting of May, which was supposed to deal with Berlin. At Paris Khrushchev denounced American aggression, demanded an apology for the U-2 flights, and stalked out of the conference. Soviet-American hostility, despite years of "personal diplomacy" and "thaws," was as intense as ever in 1960.

The Containment of China

The Chinese Communists were not unhappy with this deterioration in Soviet-American relations. From the mid-1950s onward, Beijing openly condemned Moscow's concept of "peaceful coexistence" and any movement toward a Soviet-American rapprochement. China opposed summit meetings and criticized Khrushchev's timidity in not sending troops to Lebanon in 1958 to drive out American soldiers. The *People's Daily* chastised Khrushchev for "yielding to evil" and "coddling wrong."[86] Beijing believed that the Soviets refused Chinese requests for assistance in nuclear development because of this "coddling" of the capitalist adversary. Some Western observers have suggested that Khrushchev seized upon the U-2 incident to wreck the Paris summit so as to demonstrate that Moscow could still be uncompromising with the capitalist West and to deflate Chinese criticism of Russian "appeasement." In any case, a Communist détente with the United States in the 1950s was anathema to Chinese leaders, who recognized the deep roots of the Sino-American antagonism: American aid before 1949 to Jiang;

**Mao Zedong (1893–
1976).** Chief of the Communist party in "Red
China," father of the successful Communist Revo-
lution, and radical philoso-
pher-poet, Mao vigorously
criticized United States
"imperialism." Yet he
helped launch Sino-Ameri-
can détente before his
death. (*The Reporter,*
1956. Copyright 1956
by The Reporter Maga-
zine Co.)

Chinese harassment of Americans; Washington's nonrecognition policy; bitter
Chinese denunciations of American "imperialism"; the Sino-Soviet Treaty of 1950;
American blockage of Chinese membership in the United Nations; continuing
American support for Jiang on Formosa; and the Chinese-American military
confrontation in Korea.

In early 1953, President Eisenhower "unleashed" Jiang Jieshi by announcing
that the Seventh Fleet would no longer block his attempts to attack the mainland.
Jiang actually lacked the resources for a major fight, but the decision alarmed
Beijing, especially after Nationalist bombing raids began to hit coastal regions.
Throughout the 1950s Jiang pledged a return to China. He received an annual
average of over $250 million in American economic and military assistance. The
Seventh Fleet remained in the Formosa Straits, prompting the Communists to
protest that it was as if China stationed vessels between Hawaii and the United
States. By the late 1950s, as well, China was ringed by American bases and armed
forces stretching from Japan to South Korea. In 1954 the United States had created
SEATO, an alliance of the United States, France, Britain, Australia, New Zealand,
Thailand, Pakistan, and the Philippines, pledged to assist one another when their
"peace and safety" were threatened. The new pact was essentially aimed at "Red
China" and Beijing's support, on behalf of international communism, of nationalist revolution in Indochina. In December, 1954, Taiwan and the United States
signed a mutual defense treaty. The following year Congress, by an overwhelming
vote of 83–3 in the Senate and 410–3 in the House, gave the President authority in
the "Formosa Resolution" to use American troops if necessary to defend Taiwan
and adjoining islands. The United States in 1957 placed on Taiwan missiles capable of firing nuclear warheads.

Washington also resisted cultural or economic contacts with China. American
officials forbade American journalists to accept China's 1956 invitation to visit the
mainland. The State Department even banned the shipment of a panda bear to the
United States, because the animal had been born in China. At the 1954 Geneva
Conference on Indochina (see next chapter), Chinese and American diplomats
barely mixed. At one point Foreign Minister Zhou Enlai approached Secretary of
State John Foster Dulles intending to shake hands, but Dulles, afraid that photographers would record this contaminating event, brusquely shunned Zhou's out-
stretched hand by turning his back. The United States also imposed a trade
embargo on China, hoping that that would weaken the Beijing government.

In 1954–1955 a major dispute brought the two nations to the brink. In early 1955
Dulles advised the President, "there is at least an even chance that the United
States will have to go to war."[87] Two tiny islands triggered the confrontation.
Quemoy and Matsu, only a few miles off the Chinese mainland, were heavily
fortified islands occupied by about 60,000 Nationalist troops. They served as bases
for Nationalist commando raids against China as well as defensive posts for
Formosa. In mid-1954 China announced its intention to "liberate" Formosa, not a
serious threat because the People's Republic lacked the amphibious equipment
required for such a venture. But in September its shore batteries began to bombard
Quemoy and Matsu. Eisenhower elected to defend the islands, not because they
were important to United States security (they were not) or because they were
important to Formosa's security (it is doubtful they were), but because they stood
as symbols of American toughness in the face of the Communist menace.

China had the legal case for possession on its side, but that did not matter.

According to Vice-President Richard Nixon, American policy "was formulated on the principle that we should stand ready to call international Communism's bluff on any pot, large or small. If we let them know that we will defend freedom when the stakes are small, the Soviets are not encouraged to threaten freedom where the stakes are higher." Indeed, "that is why the two small islands . . . are so important in the poker game of world politics."[88] Congress gave Eisenhower a blank check in the "Formosa Resolution" and waited anxiously. Lacking nuclear weapons and any guarantees of support from Russia, China defused the crisis by offering to open discussions. Beginning in 1955 at Geneva, and after 1958 in Warsaw, Chinese and American officials quietly talked at the ambassadorial level about Taiwan, trade, and other topics. These limited discussions constituted the only sensible, civil element in Chinese-American relations.

In 1958, Quemoy and Matsu again became a flash point when more shells from the mainland hit the fortified islands, where Jiang had built up his forces, reaching 100,000 by 1958. During the new crisis Eisenhower ordered American airlifts to these troops and Seventh Fleet escorts for Nationalist supply ships. He stated in a televised address in September that abandoning the offshore islands would constitute a "Western Pacific Munich." "If history teaches us anything, appeasement would make it more likely that we would have to fight a major war."[89] Critics retorted that the islands were not worth American blood or the risk of nuclear war. America's European allies protested against a wastage of American resources over Quemoy and Matsu. Beijing was unabashed: "Supported by the United States, the Chiang Kai-shek clique has for long been using coastal islands such as Quemoy . . . and Matsu . . . as advance bases for conducting all sorts of harassing and disruptive activities. . . . The Chinese Government has every right to deal resolute blows and take necessary military action against Chiang Kai-shek's troops entrenched on the coastal island[s]."[90] Eisenhower and Dulles stepped back from the brink, as did the People's Republic. After Dulles and Jiang signed an agreement in October that the Formosan leader would not use force to "free" the mainland, Jiang withdrew some of his troops from Quemoy and Matsu and the United States suspended the escorting of Nationalist vessels. On its part, Beijing relaxed its bombardment of the islands. "Who would have thought when we fired a few shots at Quemoy and Matsu," Mao asked, "that it would stir up such an earth-shattering storm?"[91] The mutual de-escalation calmed the storm, but Sino-American relations remained embittered.

The New Challenge: Nationalism and the Third World

In the period 1946–1960, thirty-seven new nations emerged from colonial status in Asia, Africa, and the Middle East. In 1958, twenty-eight prolonged guerrilla insurgencies were under way. Eighteen countries became independent in 1960 alone. Revolutions and the collapse of empires thus claimed a central place in international affairs. These great changes occurred in the "Third World"—the "underdeveloped" or "developing" countries that were largely nonwhite, located in the southern half of the globe, and mostly nonindustrialized. In a somewhat derogatory term, the industrialized West called them "backward" nations. Once the Cold War lines were fairly firm in Europe, the Soviet-American confrontation shifted to the Third World. The stakes were high. These countries were rich in raw materials and had for decades served the needs of the industrial nations. In 1959

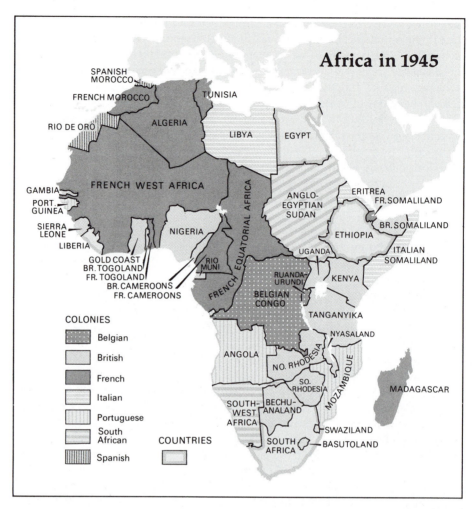

COLONIES

Belgian

British

French

Italian

Portuguese

South African

Spanish

COUNTRIES

over one-third of American direct private investments abroad were in the Third World. Underdeveloped nations also bought manufactured goods and provided strategic sites for air and naval bases.

The volatile conditions in these "emerging" nations did not permit easy management by outsiders. Many of their leaders were anticolonial revolutionaries who established leftist, undemocratic regimes. Long exploited, they were poor countries, eager for economic improvement without foreign ownership. Nationalism was intense, politics unstable. Many of these developing nations declared themselves "uncommitted" or "neutral" in the Cold War, and both Washington and Moscow faced strong odds against trying to bring upstarts into their respective camps. However, in longer-established Third World nations, particularly in Latin America, in an effort to beat back rebel challenges, the United States continued to support governments controlled by military, political, or economic elites.

The Eisenhower Administration and its successors fared poorly. American leaders did not deal with the new nationalism as a force in itself, but as part of the Cold War struggle. They confused "nationalism" and "neutralism" with "communism" and assumed that much of the trouble in the Third World was inspired by Moscow. "Yet to blame the danger of these [explosions] on the presence of

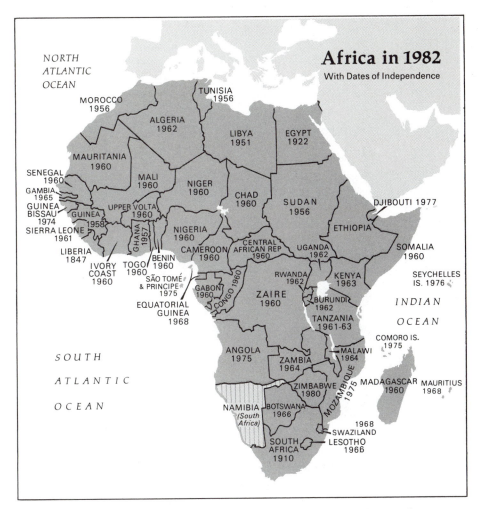

Africa in 1982
With Dates of Independence

Communists," one scholar has written, "is like blaming the inherent danger in a huge mass of exposed combustible materials on the possible presence of arsonists."[92] The Eisenhower-Dulles team tried to apply the venerable containment doctrine to these regions in a futile effort to curb the new challenge.

America's great wealth proved a handicap. Americans were known as the "People of Plenty," to borrow the title of a 1954 book by historian David M. Potter. Foreigners both envied and resented America's unmatched abundance; many wanted to be like Americans, and grew indignant over the difficulty of becoming so. The image of the "Ugly American" exacerbated foreign resentment. In 1958 William J. Lederer and Eugene Burdick wrote a novel with that title to underscore the reasons why the United States had a tarnished reputation in the Third World. They noted, among other problems, that Americans abroad flaunted their wealth and that American diplomats often isolated themselves from the poor countryside by living lavishly in a "Golden Ghetto."[93] The authors appealed for Foreign Service Officers who spoke the language of the host country and would live, without accustomed comfort, among the "people." In this way, they argued rather superficially, the United States would win the struggle against communism.

American racism, symbolized by Jim Crow practices, also handicapped the

Anti-Imperialist Protest. During his tour of Asia in 1953, Vice-President Nixon was greeted with this nationalist sign of disapproval. (Department of State, National Archives)

The sign reads:

PAX VOBISCUM.

Peace and arm'ment are incompatible;
Nixon, make not yourself contemptible,
By urging milit'rist Jap to re-arm,
To stage yet another March-hare's run.
Mark well! The rise of the Glorious East
Tolls death-knell to Imperialists' Feast.

United States. In December, 1952, when the attorney general asked the Supreme Court to strike down segregation in public schools, his brief read that "it is in the context of the present world struggle between freedom and tyranny that the problem of racial discrimination must be viewed." American segregation, in short, "furnished grist for the Communist propaganda mills."[94] He was right. In 1955 the Indian ambassador was refused service in an airport restaurant in Texas because of his dark skin. In 1957, on Route 40 leading into Washington, the finance minister of Ghana was denied food at a Howard Johnson's. President Eisenhower tried to assuage the insult by inviting him to breakfast at the White House. In the same year, when Eisenhower sent federal troops to Little Rock, Arkansas to escort black children to school in the midst of ugly white protest, the President criticized that state for a "tremendous disservice . . . to the nation in the eyes of the world."[95] With Soviet propaganda in the Third World mocking the blatant contradiction between America's professed principles and actual practice, the Voice of America and the State Department struggled to create a more favorable image.

Americans professed a revolutionary tradition ("the Spirit of '76") and often said they identified with the revolutionary aspirations of others. "We ourselves are the first colony in modern times to have won independence," Dulles proclaimed in 1954. "We have a natural sympathy with those everywhere who would follow our example."[96] But something was out of kilter between that tradition and American foreign policy in the post-World War II period. Professor K. E. Boulding suggested that the American attitude toward revolution "is a compound feeling of both love and hate, affectionate regard for the infants toddling in our early footsteps and unresolved guilt about our own breakaway."[97] Basically, Americans had become satiated, propertied representatives of the status quo. Revolution was no longer in America's national interest because it challenged an established order that guaranteed Americans both a prominent position in international relations and an affluent society. Mr. Dooley had remarked at the start of the century: "A riv'lution can't be bound be th' rules iv th' game because it's again' the rules iv th' game."[98] Americans at mid-century adhered to the "rules."

The American Revolution itself had been a rebellion of limited social change—nothing like the wrenching social revolutions of the twentieth century. "The men who pushed the American Revolution were not nationalists compelled to spend years in the jails of the colonial power," historian Carl N. Degler has written, "but political leaders seeking only to continue their free governments as they knew them all their lives."[99] Many Americans had been soured by the bloody excesses of the French Revolution. In the 1830s Alexis de Tocqueville observed that "in no other country in the world is the love of property more active and more anxious than in the United States; nowhere does the majority display less inclination for those principles which threaten to alter, in whatever manner, the laws of property."[100] To Americans in the nineteenth century, a "proper" revolution was a limited one like their own. As early twentieth-century revolutions, like those in Mexico, China, and Russia, rocked international equilibrium, the United States increasingly found itself a target rather than a model of revolution. One government report put the problem frankly in 1945: "The United States leans toward propertied classes who place a premium on order and trade."[101] So it was during the Eisenhower years. In late 1960, when forty-three Afro-Asian states, led by India, sponsored a United Nations resolution proclaiming irresistible and necessary the process of liberation from colonialism, the United States abstained from voting, not wishing to offend colonial nations and Cold War friends like Portugal.

The Soviets, with their own brand of revolutionary past, had their troubles in the Third World, too. On the ideological level, both Marxism and the professed anticolonialism of the Soviet Union enjoyed wide appeal. In the mid-1950s Khrushchev toured India, Burma, and Afghanistan; and Russia, however inexpertly, launched a foreign aid offensive. It agreed, for example, to build a $91 million steel plant in India and the Aswan Dam in Egypt. Between 1954 and 1959 Indonesia received the equivalent of a quarter-billion dollars in Soviet aid. At the Bandung Conference of 1955, where twenty-nine "nonaligned" states representing about one-quarter of the world's population met to applaud "neutralism" and Russia's call for "peaceful coexistence," it became evident that the "free world" was less popular than the "Communist world" in the Third World. Yet the Soviet Union came up against nationalism, too, and gained few allies. Egypt's Gamal Abdal Nasser and India's Jawaharlal Nehru would not become Soviet clients. Khrushchev, during a 1955 trip in India, vehemently denounced the West, and the neutralist Indians resented this blatant effort to bring the Cold War into their country. Then, too, Arab nationalism, not Soviet communism, dominated the Middle East. And in Latin America, between 1945 and 1955, sixteen nations outlawed the Communist party. As historian Donald Dozer wrote in 1959, "Latin Americans can be depended upon to adopt a solidary opposition to Soviet and every other imperialism . . . in defense of their independence and their institutions."[102] The Soviets, like the Americans, could not tolerate or exploit independent nationalism. Nor did they have the economic resources to make good on many of their foreign aid promises. Finally, they could not explain away the giant contradiction between their rhetoric on self-determination and their brutal suppression of Eastern European countries.

American officials remained fearful, however, that Soviet-directed communism would exploit nationalistic sentiment and poverty in the Third World. Foreign aid was the primary United States tool for combating the perceived threat, although the Central Intelligence Agency took on increasing importance as a manipulator of Third World events, with the secretary of state's brother Allen W. Dulles as its director, 1953–1961. Whereas during the 1949–1952 period over three-quarters of total American economic assistance went to Europe, in the years 1953–1957 three-quarters flowed to developing countries. By 1961 over 90 percent of United States aid went to the Third World. But to Washington's distress, many of the recipients refused to choose sides in the Cold War. As Nasser asserted: "We will not be subjected—either by West or East."[103] Such nonalignment naturally drew fire from Americans seeking political returns from foreign aid. To Dulles, it seemed, neutralism was but a deceitful stage on the way to communism. So he declared it an "immoral and shortsighted conception."[104] With such negative statements the United States faced the prevalent nationalist currents and earned itself the title of the New Rome—a counterrevolutionary in a revolutionary world.

Tests in the Middle East and Latin America

America's troubles with the Third World are illustrated by two complex crises in the Middle East and Latin America. In 1952 Nasser led young Egyptian army officers against King Farouk, their vulgar, pro-Western ruler, who fled to Europe with his harem and his wealth. As head of state, Nasser initiated land reform and pledged to eliminate British control of the Suez Canal. A 1954 agreement, reluctantly signed by London, provided for a phased withdrawal. To maintain western influence in the Middle East, the United States tried in 1955 to rally nations to its side by promoting the Baghdad Pact, a military alliance of Britain, Turkey, Iran, Iraq, and Pakistan. Iran had been won over in 1953 when the United States, through the intervention of the CIA and a cut-off of foreign aid, helped overthrow Iranian nationalist Mohammed Mossadegh, who had attempted to nationalize foreign oil interests. American companies produced about 50 percent of the region's oil. Israel, the Jewish state Truman had quickly recognized after its creation in May, 1948, was drawn closer to the United States by foreign aid totaling $374 million from 1952 to 1961. Yet bitter Arab-Israeli conflict thwarted American hopes for order in the Middle East. After the Israelis raided the Gaza Strip in 1955 and exposed Egypt's military weakness, Cairo signed an arms agreement with Czechoslovakia. Heretofore Western nations had monopolized arms sales in the Middle East.

Despite his dislike for Nasser's independent spirit, Dulles decided to employ foreign aid to draw him toward the West. In December, 1955, the secretary offered to fund Nasser's dream of the Aswan Dam on the Nile, a potential source of electrical power and irrigation. During the next year the World Bank worked out the details of the $1.3 billion project, involving British, American, and World Bank monies. About the same time Egypt joined an anti-Israeli military alliance with

Saudi Arabia, Syria, and Yemen. Anger from vocal Jewish-Americans swept down on Washington and southern congressmen asked why the United States should support a project that would permit Egypt to produce competitive cotton. Eisenhower and Dulles, who disapproved of Nasser's neutralism and who may have thought that the Czech arms deal signified Egyptian alignment with the Soviets, grew less interested in the dam. Cairo had, not long before, recognized the People's Republic of China, and this also annoyed Washington. Part of the Eisenhower Administration's thinking can be gleaned from a rhetorical question Dulles asked: "Do nations which play both sides get better treatment than nations which are stalwart and work with us?"[105] Some American officials actually thought the arms deal was a bluff because the Soviets lacked adequate military supplies to fulfill it. Dulles' abrupt withdrawal of the Aswan Dam offer in July, 1956 thus afforded an opportunity not only to punish neutralism but to expose Soviet feet of clay.

Gamal Abdal Nasser (1918–1970). The bold Egyptian leader and advocate of Arab nationalism evicted the British from his country, but when he seized the Suez Canal, the British, joined by the French and Israelis, returned in arms. (*The Reporter,* 1956. Copyright 1956 by The Reporter Magazine Co.)

But American economic pressure backfired. Nasser quickly seized the Suez Canal, intent upon using its $25 million annual profit to help build the Aswan Dam. Without consulting Washington, the British and French huddled with Israel and planned a military operation. In late October and early November, 1956, British, French, and Israeli forces invaded Egypt and nearly captured the canal. Eisenhower was boiling mad, especially furious that his wartime friend Anthony Eden, now Prime Minister, would proceed without informing him. To make matters worse, Dulles had just entered the hospital for treatment of his cancer. Eisenhower publicly upbraided the British and French for taking military action that might draw the Soviets into the Middle East and that took the spotlight off simultaneous Soviet brutalities in Hungary. To force the European and Israeli offenders out, American officials introduced a United Nations resolution calling for withdrawal and a cutback of oil shipments to the invaders. By late December the troops departed, leaving a United Nations peacekeeping unit, which returned the canal, now clogged with sunken ships, to Egypt.

The Suez crisis produced mixed results for America. Although the United States retained its oil holdings and Middle Eastern friends, it alienated the leading Arab nation, Egypt. By withdrawing the Aswan Dam offer, Washington opened the Middle Eastern door to Soviet influence, the very opposite of what the United States wanted; the Russians eventually built the dam. Relations with Britain and France were fractured. Although the United States stood against this abortive return of Victorian imperialism, it simultaneously snubbed nationalism and neutralism, and thereafter the United States became further ensnarled in the tumultuous politics of the Middle East. In 1957, for example, Saudi Arabia let the United States keep its air base at Dhahran in exchange for American military aid and a promise not to station Jewish-Americans at the base. That year Washington also issued the "Eisenhower Doctrine" and in 1958 sent 14,000 troops to Lebanon to head off a threatened coup by pro-Nasser Arabs. In the American ledger this was another Cold War "victory," but the phrase rang hollow.

Nationalism also tightened its grip on the United States' own sphere of influence, Latin America. Through the Rio Pact (a defensive military alliance formed in 1947), the Organization of American States (launched the following year but formally established in 1951 to help settle inter-American disputes), investments of $8.2 billion by 1959, economic assistance totaling $835 million for the period 1952–1961, and support to military dictators like Fulgencio Batista in Cuba, the United States perpetuated its hegemony over neighbors to the south. But many

Latin Americans were restless, and their nationalism, which had already challenged the United States in Mexico, became strident. Latin American poverty was stark; illiteracy rates were high; health care was inadequate; a population explosion was under way; productivity showed miniscule growth; profits from raw materials like sugar and oil flowed through American companies to the United States; and Washington had taken the region for granted. However, as the Cold War shifted to the Third World, Washington grew wary of Latin American discontent. American anticommunists joined long-standing economic interests to revitalize United States attention to its client states. Dulles told a congressional committee in 1953 that "if we don't look out, we will wake up some morning and read in the newspapers that there happened in South America the same kind of thing that happened in China in 1949."[106] To prevent such a debacle in Latin America, the United States was willing to use force, the Good Neighbor policy notwithstanding.

Guatemala became a test case. In 1950, leftist Jacobo Arbenz Guzman was elected President. He set land reform as a central goal, because 2 percent of the population owned 70 percent of the land. The influential United Fruit Company, a huge banana exporter and the nation's largest landowner, became a target. Under the agrarian reform law of 1952, Guatemala expropriated about 400,000 of United Fruit's idle acres. Arbenz offered to compensate the firm in government bonds, using the value of the land as previously declared by the company itself for tax purposes (about $2 million). United Fruit quickly demanded over $15 million. The State Department backed the claim. Hiring lobbyists to exploit American anticommunism, the company launched a major propaganda program in the United States. The message: communism, working through Arbenz, was creating a beachhead in Central America. Although Arbenz did appoint some communists to governmental posts, there were none in his cabinet. Moreover, those communists and the Arbenz government had quite minimal contacts with the Soviet Union. Scholars have concluded that the Eisenhower Administration's depiction of the Arbenz regime as communist-dominated is not supported by the evidence. Nonetheless, as Ambassador John Peurifoy reported, Arbenz "thought like a Communist and talked like a Communist, and if not actually one, would do until one came along."[107]

Sometime in 1953 Eisenhower approved a CIA plan to overthrow the Arbenz government. Using a headquarters base in Florida and $5–7 million, the CIA began to hire mercenary soldiers from the ranks of Guatemalan exiles. Training camps in Nicaragua and Honduras prepared them for an invasion. Colonel Carlos Castillo Armas, a graduate of the Army staff school at Fort Leavenworth, Kansas, was picked to become the new President. In early 1954 the United States prodded the Organization of American States to declare, by a 17–1 vote, that the domination of any American state by the "international communist movement" would constitute a threat to the hemisphere.[108] The Guatemalan foreign minister protested the action as "the internationalization of McCarthyism."[109] Washington also cut off technical assistance funds to Guatemala. Aware that the United States intended to topple him and unable to buy arms from non-Communist sources, Arbenz turned to Communist nations for help. In May, 1954, a Swedish ship sailed to Guatemala with weapons made in Czechoslovakia. This arms shipment served as the immediate catalyst for launching the last stage of the CIA operation.

On June 18, after the CIA bribed Guatemalans, planted fictitious news stories about Arbenz's submission to the Soviets, and dropped supplies at United Fruit facilities, Castillo Armas's small force attacked from Honduras. American planes bombed Guatemala City. Gripped by fear and abandoned by his military, Arbenz fled into exile.

Castillo Armas soon returned United Fruit lands and jailed his detractors. In 1957 he fell to assassination, but the new regime remained a staunch United States ally. In fact, it provided training sites for Cuban exiles being readied by the CIA to overthrow another Latin American nationalist, Fidel Castro (see pp. 539–542). Although encouraged by their successful covert operation in Guatemala to stage coups elsewhere, United States officials had to endure loud protest. British Prime Minister Clement Attlee, for one, blasted Washington for a "plain act of aggression, and one cannot take one line on aggression in Asia and another line on aggression in Central America."[110] Many Latin Americans also grew angry, as became evident in April–May, 1958, when Vice-President Nixon went south on a goodwill tour.

In Montevideo, Uruguay, anti-Yankee pickets mingled with the cheering crowds when Nixon motored through the city. Determined to counter what he considered Communist agitation, Nixon stopped at the University of the Republic and engaged students in an emotional debate on American foreign policy. Nixon claimed a rhetorical "victory" over the Communists, and went on to Peru, where

Rioters Stone Nixon in Venezuela. His car surrounded by hostile Venezuelan protesters, Vice-President Nixon experienced a grueling outbreak of anti-Americanism in May, 1958. He was forced to leave Caracas ahead of schedule, his experience highlighting problems in Latin America for the United States. (United Press International)

anti-American sentiment welled up at San Marcos University. Nixon pondered whether to visit the institution. American Ambassador Theodore Achilles urged him to go: "One characteristic common throughout this hemisphere is that people admire courage. They have contempt for fear. That is why the bullfight is a favorite sport here." Nixon decided not to run from a "bunch of Communist thugs."[111] He was stoned and spat upon. He then headed for Caracas.

In Venezuela all hell broke loose. Earlier in 1958 the ruthless dictatorship of Marcos Perez Jimenez ("P.J.") had been overthrown by a military junta. "P.J." had been a special friend of the United States during his seven-year rule. In 1954 the United States had decorated him with the Legion of Merit. In 1955 Dulles had told a Senate committee that Venezuela "has adopted the kind of policies which we think that other countries of South America should adopt. Namely, they have adopted policies which provide in Venezuela a climate which is attractive to foreign capital to come in."[112] When Jimenez was driven from Caracas and the Eisenhower Administration provided asylum for him and his hated chief of police, Venezuelan bitterness toward the United States deepened. Into this volatile environment stepped Nixon, emboldened by his earlier ventures among shouting students. His motorcade in Caracas was halted by hostile crowds and blockades; demonstrators stoned his car, shattering windows. They smashed fenders, rocked the automobile, and threatened the vice-president's life. A Secret Service agent drew his pistol: "Let's get some of these sons-of-bitches."[113] Before shooting broke out, however, Nixon's car somehow sped away. Eisenhower dispatched two airborne infantry companies to the Caribbean, but Nixon left Venezuela without further trouble. His toughness under stress gained him public admiration in the United States. "A national defeat," noted one chagrined journalist, "has been parlayed into a personal political triumph."[114]

After Nixon's trip, Washington stuck to its policy of hegemony but began to spend more money below the border. Nixon's recommendations to the President largely stressed the ways in which the United States might better influence its southern neighbors. For example, he suggested that American officials "must do a more effective job of reaching the opinion-makers of Latin America." Next, in what reads like a contradiction: "We must develop an economic program for Latin America which is distinctively its own." He further advised that the United States "should not appear to give dictators, of either the right or the left, the same moral approval that we gave to leaders who were trying to build free and democratic institutions."[115] He urged more military aid to Latin America to halt communism, more United States courage in the face of adversity, and more sensitivity about ways of providing aid so as not to offend Latin American pride. Nixon essentially advocated a change in public relations, not in policy. The shallowness of his proposals helped reveal why the United States was troubled in its response to Third World nationalism. Third World leaders were calling for self-determination, equality among nations, and ownership of their own raw materials. New United States "Madison Avenue" techniques, critics argued, would not alter those goals. The one positive program to emerge from the rethinking generated by Nixon's proposals was the Inter-American Development Bank, to which the United States subscribed about $500 million in 1959. That year, however, students and other vocal nationalists in Panama rioted against the United States. They resented American control of the Canal Zone and tried to plant Panamanian flags there. Zone police and United States infantry beat them back. Over 120 were wounded.

Space-Age Toy Shop. Children at a Christmas-decorated window marvel at toy models of military weaponry and destructive gadgetry created to wage the cold war in the 1950s. Adults played with the real things. (A. Kovarsky, Swann Collection of Caricature and Cartoon)

Holding the Line, 1950–1961

When the Eisenhower Administration gave way to the Democratic Administration of John F. Kennedy in January, 1961, it was holding the line—against nationalism, against revolution, against neutralism, against communism, against Soviet Russia, against China. Despite the catchy phrases of the Eisenhower-Dulles years, there had been no new departures in foreign policy. "Liberation" was "containment" by different means. The "Eisenhower Doctrine" was an extension of the "Truman Doctrine." Dulles' strictures against neutralism sounded very much like Truman's declaration that all nations must choose between two ways of life. The "domino theory" in Asia differed little from the Truman Administration's alarmist predictions that if Greece fell, the Middle East would fall and then Europe would be undermined. Eisenhower and Dulles reinforced the Truman-Acheson hostility to "Red China." Both administrations intervened, with different methods, in the Middle East. Both took Latin America for granted. Both had Berlin crises accentuate their determination to draw West Germany into Western Europe. Indeed, the continuity in American foreign policy from Truman through Eisenhower is conspicuous. America's Cold War institutions, its high defense budgets, its large and intransigent foreign affairs bureaucracy, its assumptions from the past—all ground on, largely resistant to change, perpetuating a momentum begun by Truman.

But the world had changed. In 1945 the United States sat atop the hierarchical structure of international relations. There were few restraints upon the exercise of its power. Americans confidently placed restraints on others. A bipolar world developed with lines fairly well drawn between the two camps. But as the Soviet Union and the United States built their economies and military forces toward a stalemate, particularly in Europe, the bonds of stability loosened elsewhere. Throughout the 1950s new nations claimed independence and threw off the shackles of colonialism. These new nations of the Third World did not wish to join sides in the Cold War. Even more troubling for the superpowers were the rebellions in their own spheres of influence. Latin America became less responsive to United States tutelage, and political turmoil and anti-Yankeeism ran rampant. The 1959 victory of nationalists in the Cuban Revolution symbolized the new challenge (see next chapter). Anti-American Japanese rioters forced Eisenhower to cancel a trip to Japan in 1960, and Europeans like Charles de Gaulle of France sought restrictions on United States influence. For the Soviets there were the Hungarian Revolution, growing discontent in Eastern Europe, and a challenge from China for leadership in the Communist camp. The crude display in November, 1960 of Khrushchev banging his shoe at the United Nations suggested to some that in their desperation the Soviets were going mad.

The bipolar world was becoming multipolar. Neither Russia nor America, tied to rigid policies and military programs basically defending the status quo, adjusted

Khrushchev at the United Nations, 1960. The Soviet Premier's temper flared into childish outbursts that rudely interrupted speakers. At one point, a devilish smirk on his face, he took off his shoe and banged it on the table. (United Nations)

A Saddened "Ike." The end of Eisenhower's administration included cancellation of a trip to Japan because of anti-American riots, the U-2 crisis, and the breakup of the Paris Conference. Just before leaving office, the still popular general warned Americans against a military-industrial complex. (*The Reporter*, 1960. Copyright 1960 by The Reporter Magazine Co.)

well to the new complexity. Although both professed an understanding of Third World needs and aspirations, both sought to place curbs on nationalism. After all, notwithstanding their propaganda, they wanted friends or allies, not a fulfillment of the principle of self-determination. The two antagonists, in their drive to accumulate friends through foreign aid and subversion, became vulnerable to cries for economic assistance from newly independent small nations. Washington often paid the dollars but gained few friends. Its basic antipathy toward revolutionary nationalism, socialism, the nationalization of land and industry, and neutralism created a formidable barrier between the United States and the Third World. Nor did military alliances like SEATO and CENTO, CIA activities in Iran and Guatemala, the training of counterrevolutionaries in South Vietnam (see next chapter), and the sending of troops to Lebanon reveal an American understanding of the new challenge.

If, as critics said, the Eisenhower Administration was unimaginative in dealing with the Third World, it also evinced little innovation in its relations with the Soviet Union or China. The arms race continued, evolving into a space race and missile race. Washington seemed only minimally interested in considering ideas for reducing tension in Central Europe and Germany, quickly rejecting the Rapacki Plan and "disengagement" proposals. Surely the Soviet Union did not make accommodation easy on these issues, but as Kennan pointed out, diplomacy was hardly given a chance. For China there was nonrecognition, a tired policy that simply isolated the United States from one of the world's most important nations. Holding the line with Jiang Jieshi on Formosa became an absurdity when many other Western nations recognized the Peking government and traded with it. By 1961 nonrecognition did not make sense, but it was fixed.

Perhaps the Eisenhower Administration could not easily break free from old policies and habits because of domestic political restrictions. McCarthyism did compel a blind anticommunism and did inhibit sophisticated analysis. But McCarthyism as a political force had begun to peter out by 1954. One of its offshoots in that year was the Bricker Amendment, a proposed addition to the

Constitution limiting the President's authority to make executive agreements (as distinct from treaties) in foreign affairs. Senator John Bricker of Ohio said he wanted to prevent another Yalta; others recalled Truman's decision to send troops to Korea without congressional sanction. The Administration, joined by Cold Warriors from the Truman years, defeated this thrust against executive power, but by a narrow margin in a congressional vote. Eisenhower henceforth faced few domestic restraints on his foreign policy. The President remained a popular hero and Congress usually granted his requests. The "Formosa Resolution" of 1955, for example, passed 83–3 in the upper chamber and 410–3 in the lower body. The "Eisenhower Doctrine" of 1958 earned a 72–19 vote from the Senate and a 350–60 count in the House. The Cold War consensus shaped in the 1940s was still pervasive, not merely the property of McCarthyites. The Eisenhower Administration failed to devise new policies for new realities and to undertake negotiations with its myriad adversaries, not only because of the emotional restraints of such forces as Joe McCarthy and the China Lobby, but because of its own assumptions.

In the election of 1960, the Democrats charged not that the Cold War should be abandoned, but rather that it should be won. They differed from Eisenhower in the methods with which to continue the old fight and to reverse the United States' declining position in the Third World. "Indeed, although their accents and rhythms were different," Townsend Hoopes has concluded, "the fervent anti-Communist absolutes of John Foster Dulles were embedded in the very bone structure of John Fitzgerald Kennedy's inaugural address."[116]

In studying the Eisenhower-Dulles record, it is tempting to balance each negative with a positive. But that attempt would be misleading. Eisenhower did negotiate with the Soviets and did warn Americans against a "military-industrial complex." The Austrian State Treaty was effected. Eisenhower kept more militant types like Dulles and Nixon in check and tried to limit military spending. He did avoid a full-scale intervention in Indochina in 1954 (see next chapter). He was forced to deal with a world posing many perceived threats to American power. The Soviets were often intransigent, and comparative American power was bound to slip as Russia recovered from World War II. And with the rise of new nations, power was bound to disperse. Yet whatever its positive intentions, the Eisenhower Administration's achievements in diplomacy were few. The "Spirit of Camp David" evaporated. In the end, Eisenhower settled "for the half-solace of a series of truces."[117] Holding the line defensively and unimaginatively against ever growing challenges, Washington did not consider whether the line might be partially erased to accommodate new configurations.

Further Reading for the Period 1950–1961

For general studies of the Cold War that cover this period, see the works cited in the first paragraph of the "Further Reading" section in Chapter 12.

The Korean War is discussed in Frank Baldwin, ed., *Without Parallel* (1975); Ronald J. Caridi, *The Korean War and American Politics* (1969); Bruce Cummings, *The Origins of the Korean War* (1981); Francis H. Heller, ed., *The Korean War* (1977); Glenn D. Paige, *The Korean Decision* (1968); David Rees, *Korea: The Limited War* (1964); Robert R. Simmons, *The Strained Alliance* (1975); John W. Spanier, *The Truman-MacArthur Controversy* (1959); and Allen Whiting, *China Crosses the Yalu* (1960).

For Eisenhower, Dulles, and their foreign policy, see Charles Alexander, *Holding the Line*

(1975); Stephen E. Ambrose, *Ike's Spies: Eisenhower and the Espionage Establishment* (1981); Blanche W. Cook, *The Declassified Eisenhower* (1981); Robert A. Divine, *Eisenhower and the Cold War* (1981); Louis Gerson, *John Foster Dulles* (1968); Richard Goold-Adams, *The Time of Power: A Reappraisal of John Foster Dulles* (1962); Norman Graebner, *The New Isolationism* (1956); Fred I. Greenstein, "Eisenhower as an Activist President," *Political Science Quarterly* (1979–1980); Michael Guhin, *John Foster Dulles* (1972); Townsend Hoopes, *The Devil and John Foster Dulles* (1973); Emmet J. Hughes, *The Ordeal of Power* (1963); Burton I. Kaufman, *Trade and Aid: Eisenhower's Foreign Economic Policy* (1982); George F. Kennan, *Russia, the Atom, and the West* (1958); Peter Lyon, *Eisenhower: Portrait of the Hero* (1974); G. Bernard Noble, *Christian A. Herter* (1970); Herbert S. Parmet, "Power and Reality: John Foster Dulles and Political Diplomacy," in Frank Merli and Theodore Wilson, eds., *Makers of American Diplomacy* (1975) and *Eisenhower and the American Crusades* (1972); James Patterson, *Mr. Republican* (1972) (on Robert A. Taft); Ronald W. Pruessen, *John Foster Dulles: The Road to Power* (1982); and Kenneth T. Young, *Negotiating with the Chinese Communists: The United States Experience, 1953–1967* (1968).

For Soviet policies and European questions, consult John C. Campbell, *Successful Negotiation: Trieste 1954* (1976); Edward Crankshaw, *Khrushchev* (1966); Michael P. Gehlen, *The Politics of Coexistence: Soviet Methods and Motives* (1967); Alfred Grosser, *The Western Alliance* (1975); Michael M. Harrison, *The Reluctant Ally: France and Atlantic Security* (1981); Jack M. Schick, *The Berlin Crisis* (1971); Jean Smith, *The Defense of Berlin* (1963); Michel Tatu, *Power in the Kremlin* (1969); and William Zimmerman, *Soviet Perspectives on International Relations, 1956–1967* (1969).

The nuclear arms race and missile development are treated in Edmund Beard, *Developing the ICBM* (1976); Barbara B. Clowse, *Brainpower for the Cold War: The Sputnik Crisis and the National Defense Education Act of 1958* (1981); Robert A. Divine, *Blowing on the Wind: The Nuclear Test Ban Debate, 1954–1960* (1978); Jerome H. Kahan, *Security in the Nuclear Age* (1975); Michael Mandelbaum, *The Nuclear Question* (1979); George H. Quester, *Nuclear Diplomacy: The First Twenty-Five Years* (1970); Chalmers M. Roberts, *The Nuclear Years: The Arms Race and Arms Control, 1945–1970* (1970); and Ernest J. Yanarella, *The Missile Defense Controversy* (1977).

For the rise of the Third World and Middle Eastern issues, see Chester L. Cooper, *The Lion's Last Roar: Suez, 1956* (1978); Melvin Gurtov, *The United States Against the Third World* (1974); J. C. Hurewitz, *Soviet-American Rivalry in the Middle East* (1969); George Lenczowski, *The Middle East in World Affairs* (1980); Gail E. Meyer, *Egypt and the United States* (1980); Donald Neff, *Warriors at Suez* (1981); Barry Rubin, *The Arab States and the Palestine Conflict* (1981); Nadav Safran, *From War to War: The Arab-Israeli Confrontation, 1948–1967* (1969); L. S. Stavrianos, *Global Rift: The Third World Comes of Age* (1981); Edmund Stillman and William Pfaff, *The New Politics* (1961); Robert W. Stookey, *America and the Arab States* (1975); and Hugh Thomas, *The Suez Affair* (1966).

Latin American–United States relations are the subject of Samuel L. Baily, *The United States and the Development of South America, 1945–1975* (1976); Cole Blasier, *The Hovering Giant: U.S. Responses to Revolutionary Change in Latin America* (1976); Richard Immerman, *The CIA in Guatemala: The Foreign Policy of Intervention* (1982); Stephen Kinzer and Stephen Schlesinger, *Bitter Fruit* (1982) (on Guatemala); and Ramon Ruiz, *Cuba: Making of a Revolution* (1968).

For the impact of McCarthyism, consult some of the works cited in "Further Reading" in Chapter 12, and Stanley D. Bachrack, *The Committee of One Million: "China Lobby" Politics, 1953–1971* (1976); Edwin R. Bayley, *Joe McCarthy and the Press* (1981); Michal R. Belknap, *Cold War Political Justice: The Smith Act, the Communist Party, and American Civil Liberties* (1977); Robert Griffith, *The Politics of Fear: Joseph R. McCarthy and the Senate* (1970); and Mary S. McAuliffe, *Crisis on the Left: Cold War Politics and American Liberals, 1947–1954* (1978). Also see Frances FitzGerald, *America Revised* (1979) for a study of how history schoolbooks handled the Cold War and foreign policy in the 1950s–1960s.

See also the General Bibliography and the following notes.

Notes to Chapter 13

1. Quoted in Glenn D. Paige, *The Korean Decision* (New York: The Free Press, 1968), p. 82.
2. Glenn D. Paige, ed., *1950: Truman's Decision* (New York: Chelsea House Publishers, 1970), p. 49.
3. Quoted in David Rees, *Korea: The Limited War* (London: Macmillan, 1964), p. 36.
4. Harry S. Truman, *Memoirs* (Garden City: Doubleday, 1955–1956; 2 vols.), II, 332.
5. Paige, *1950*, p. 63.
6. Quoted in Paige, *Korean Decision*, p. 114.
7. Truman, *Memoirs*, II, 333.
8. Quoted in *New York Times*, June 26, 1950.
9. Quoted in Beverly Smith, "The White House Story: Why We Went to War in Korea," *Saturday Evening Post, CCXXIV* (November 10, 1951), 80.
10. Quoted in Paige, *Korean Decision*, p. 149.
11. *Congressional Record, XCVI* (June 26, 1950), 9188.
12. Memorandum of Conversation, "Korean Situation," June 26, 1950, Department of State Records (Decimal File), Washington, D.C.
13. Dean Acheson, *Present at the Creation* (New York: W. W. Norton, 1969), p. 405.
14. "Meeting with Congressional Leaders," notes of George Elsey, June 27, 1950, Box 71, George Elsey Papers, Harry S. Truman Library, Independence, Missouri.
15. Truman, *Memoirs*, II, 340.
16. *Public Papers of the Presidents, Harry S. Truman, 1952–1953* (Washington, D.C.: Government Printing Office, 1966), p. 1200.
17. Maxwell Taylor, *Swords and Plowshares* (New York: W.W. Norton, 1972), p. 134.
18. Quoted in Martin Lichterman, "To the Yalu and Back," in Harold Stein, ed., *American Civil-Military Decisions* (Birmingham: University of Alabama Press, 1963), p. 598.
19. David S. McLellan, "Dean Acheson and the Korean War," *Political Science Quarterly, LXXXIII* (March, 1968), 39.
20. United States Senate, Committee on Armed Services and Committee on Foreign Relations, *Military Situation in the Far East* (Hearings), 82nd Cong., 1st Sess. (Washington, D.C.: Government Printing Office, 1951; 5 parts), Part 5, p. 3182 (letter of March 20, 1951).
21. *Congressional Record, XCVII* (April 19, 1951), 4125.
22. Senate, *Military Situation*, Part 4, p. 3089 (letter of May 24, 1951).
23. *Congressional Record, XCVII* (April 24, 1951), 4261.
24. *Department of State Bulletin, XXIII* (November 27, 1950), 839.
25. Senate, *Military Situation*, Part 2, p. 732.
26. *Public Papers of the Presidents, Dwight D. Eisenhower, 1953* (Washington, D.C.: Government Printing Office, 1960), p. 147.
27. Edmund S. Wehrle and Donald F. Lach, *International Politics in East Asia Since World War II* (New York: Praeger Publishers, 1975), p. 90.
28. "Princeton Seminar," February 13–14, 1954, Box 66, Dean Acheson Papers, Harry S. Truman Library.
29. Arthur M. Schlesinger, Jr., *The Imperial Presidency* (New York: Popular Library, 1973), pp. 138, 168.
30. *Public Papers, Truman, 1952–1953*, p. 708.
31. Acheson, *Present at the Creation*, p. 420.
32. Quoted in Lloyd Gardner, *Architects of Illusion* (Chicago: Quadrangle Books, 1970), p. 230.
33. Quoted in Barton J. Bernstein, "Election of 1952," in Arthur M. Schlesinger, Jr. and Fred L. Israel, eds., *History of American Presidential Elections* (New York: Chelsea House Publishers, 1971; 4 vols.), IV, 3246.
34. *Ibid.*, p. 3284.
35. Quoted in Robert A. Divine, *Foreign Policy and U.S. Presidential Elections: 1952–1960* (New York: New Viewpoints, 1974), p. 74.
36. Quoted *ibid.*, p. 28 and in Bernstein, "Election of 1952," p. 3241.
37. Notes of Sherman Adams on Cabinet meeting of January 12, 1953, Box 7, Sherman Adams Papers, Dartmouth College Library.
38. *Public Papers of the Presidents, Dwight D. Eisenhower, 1953* (Washington: Government Printing Office, 1960), pp. 182–183.
39. *Ibid., 1959* (Washington: Government Printing Office, 1960), p. 252.
40. Quoted in Herbert S. Parmet, "Power and Reality: John Foster Dulles and Political Diplomacy," in Frank Merli and Theodore Wilson, eds., *Makers of American Diplomacy* (New York: Charles Scribner's Sons, 1974), p. 593.
41. Adam Ulam, *The Rivals* (New York: Viking Press, 1971), p. 230.
42. Quoted in Townsend Hoopes, *The Devil and John Foster Dulles* (Boston: Atlantic, Little, Brown, 1973), p. 492.
43. Quoted in Adam Ulam, *Expansion and Coexistence* (New York: Frederick A. Praeger Publishers, 1974; 2nd ed.), p. 545.
44. Nikita S. Khrushchev, *Khrushchev Remembers* (New York: Bantam Books, 1971; trans. by Strobe Talbott), p. 435.
45. *Public Papers of the Presidents, Eisenhower, 1954* (Washington: Government Printing Office, 1960), p. 383.
46. Quoted in Emmett John Hughes, *The Ordeal of Power* (New York: Dell, 1964 [c. 1962]), p. 98.
47. Hoopes, *Devil and John Foster Dulles*, p. 158.
48. Quoted in Earl Latham, *The Communist Controversy in Washington* (New York: Atheneum, 1969), p. 338.
49. Ross Terrill, "When America 'Lost' China: The Case of John Carter Vincent," *Atlantic Monthly, CCXXIV* (November, 1969), 79.
50. James C. Thomson, Jr., "On the Making of U.S. China Policy, 1961–9: A Study in Bureaucratic Politics," *China Quarterly*, No. 50 (April–June, 1972), p. 222.
51. *Public Papers, Eisenhower, 1953*, p. 187.
52. Dwight D. Eisenhower, *The White House Years: Mandate for Change, 1953–1956* (Garden City, New York: Doubleday, 1963), p. 522.
53. Richard M. Nixon, *Six Crises* (Garden City, New York: Doubleday, 1962), p. 258.
54. Khrushchev, *Khrushchev Remembers*, p. 434.
55. Zbigniew Brzezinski, "The Competitive Relationship," in Charles Gati, ed., *Caging the Bear* (Indianapolis: Bobbs-Merrill, 1974), p. 168.

56. Quoted in Walter LaFeber, *America, Russia, and the Cold War, 1945–1980* (New York: John Wiley and Sons, 1980; 4th ed.), p. 183.

57. Quoted in Hoopes, *Devil and John Foster Dulles*, p. 295.

58. Sherman Adams, *Firsthand Report* (New York: Popular Library, 1962 [1961]), p. 177.

59. Khrushchev, *Khrushchev Remembers*, pp. 430, 438.

60. *Public Papers of the Presidents, Eisenhower, 1955* (Washington: Government Printing Office, 1959), p. 507.

61. *New York Times*, July 24, 1955.

62. Quoted in Herbert S. Parmet, *Eisenhower and the American Crusades* (New York: Macmillan, 1972), p. 406.

63. *Public Papers, Eisenhower, 1955*, p. 730.

64. Quoted in Denis Healey, "'When Shrimps Learn to Whistle': Thoughts After Geneva," *International Affairs*, XXXII (January, 1956), 2.

65. I. F. Stone, *The Haunted Fifties* (New York: Random House, 1963), p. 104.

66. Quoted in Hoopes, *Devil and John Foster Dulles*, p. 300.

67. Averell Harriman, "The Soviet Challenge and the American Policy," *Atlantic Monthly*, CXCVII (April, 1956), 45.

68. Dwight D. Eisenhower, *The White House Years: Waging Peace, 1956–1961* (Garden City, New York: Doubleday, 1965), p. 60.

69. *Department of State Bulletin*, XXV (November 5, 1956), 697.

70. Robert Murphy quoted in LaFeber, *America, Russia, and the Cold War*, p. 192.

71. Quoted in Charles C. Alexander, *Holding the Line: The Eisenhower Era, 1952–1961* (Bloomington, Indiana: Indiana University Press, 1975), p. 180.

72. Quoted in Brzezinski, "The Competitive Relationship," p. 171.

73. Quoted in Hughes, *Ordeal of Power*, p. 216.

74. Stephen Ambrose, *Rise to Globalism* (Baltimore: Penguin Books, 1980; 2nd ed.), p. 229.

75. Quoted in Harold Macmillan, *Riding the Storm, 1956–1959* (New York: Harper & Row, 1971), p. 320.

76. Quoted in Richard Barnet, *Roots of War* (Baltimore: Penguin Books, 1973 [c. 1972]), p. 43.

77. Noble Frankland and Royal Institute of International Affairs, *Documents on International Affairs, 1957* (London: Oxford University Press, 1960), p. 157.

78. Quoted in Thomas G. Paterson, ed., *Containment and the Cold War* (Reading, Mass.: Addison-Wesley, 1973), p. 114.

79. *New York Times Book Review*, March 2, 1958, p. 26.

80. Quoted in Paterson, *Containment and the Cold War*, p. 116.

81. Quoted in Hoopes, *Devil and John Foster Dulles*, p. 470.

82. Eisenhower, *Waging Peace*, p. 432.

83. *Khrushchev in America* (New York: Crosscurrents Press, 1960), p. 120.

84. Eisenhower, *Waging Peace*, p. 550.

85. Hughes, *Ordeal of Power*, p. 261.

86. Quoted in Edward Crankshaw, *The New Cold War: Moscow v. Peking* (Baltimore: Penguin Books, 1965 [c. 1963]), p. 81.

87. Quoted in Eisenhower, *Mandate for Change*, p. 477.

88. Nixon, *Six Crises*, p. 273.

89. *Public Papers, Eisenhower, 1958* (Washington, D.C.: Government Printing Office, 1959), p. 697.

90. Quoted in Melvin Gurtov, "The Taiwan Strait Crisis Revisited: Politics and Foreign Policy in Chinese Motives," *Modern China*, II (January, 1976), 79.

91. Quoted in John Gittings, "New Light on Mao: His View of the World," *China Quarterly*, No. 60 (December, 1974), p. 755.

92. Robert L. Heilbroner, "Making a Rational Foreign Policy Now," *Harper's Magazine*, CCXXXVII (September, 1968), 65.

93. William J. Lederer and Eugene Burdick, *The Ugly American* (New York: Fawcett Publications, 1958), p. 234.

94. C. Vann Woodward, *The Strange Career of Jim Crow* (New York: Oxford University Press, 1974; 3rd ed.), p. 132.

95. *Public Papers, Eisenhower, 1957* (Washington, D.C.: Government Printing Office, 1957), p. 694.

96. *Department of State Bulletin*, XXX (June 21, 1954), 936.

97. Kenneth E. Boulding, "The U.S. and Revolution," in *The U.S. and Revolution* (Santa Barbara, California: Center for the Study of Democratic Institutions, 1961), p. 4.

98. Finley Peter Dunne, *Dissertations of Mr. Dooley* (New York: Harper and Brothers, 1906), p. 130.

99. Carl N. Degler, "The American Past: An Unsuspected Obstacle in Foreign Affairs," *American Scholar*, XXXII (Spring, 1963), 194.

100. Alexis de Tocqueville, *Democracy in America*, edited by Richard D. Heffner (New York: New American Library, 1956), p. 267.

101. State, War, and Navy Coordinating Committee, "Political and Military Problems in the Far East; the Policy of the United States with Respect to the Soviet Union in the Far East," November 29, 1945, James F. Byrnes Papers, Clemson University Library (from the notes of James Gormly).

102. Donald Dozer, *Are We Good Neighbors?* (Gainesville: University of Florida Press, 1959), p. 353.

103. Quoted in Edmund Stillman and William Pfaff, *The New Politics* (New York: Harper and Row, Publishers, 1961), p. 127.

104. *Department of State Bulletin*, XXXIV (June 18, 1956), 1000.

105. Quoted in Hoopes, *Devil and John Foster Dulles*, p. 337.

106. Quoted in LaFeber, *America, Russia, and the Cold War*, p. 159.

107. Quoted in Eisenhower, *White House Years: Mandate for Change*, p. 422.

108. Quoted in Dozer, *Are We Good Neighbors?*, p. 340.

109. Quoted in Philip B. Taylor, "The Guatemalan Affair: A Critique of U.S. Foreign Policy," *American Political Science Review*, L (September, 1956), 791.

110. *Ibid.*, p. 804.

111. Nixon, *Six Crises*, pp. 198–199.

112. U.S. Senate, Committee on Finance, *Trade Agreements Extension* (Hearings), 84th Cong., 1st Sess. (1955), Part 4, p. 2049.

113. Quoted in Nixon, *Six Crises*, p. 219.

114. James Reston quoted in J. Fred Rippy, "The Hazards of Dale Carnegie Diplomacy," *Inter-American Economic Affairs*, XII (Summer, 1958), 35.

115. Quoted in Nixon, *Six Crises*, pp. 229–230.

116. Hoopes, *Devil and John Foster Dulles*, p. 505.

117. Hughes, *Ordeal of Power*, p. 299.

The United States Embassy in Saigon. American soldiers inspect the outer wall of the embassy compound, blasted open by Viet Cong commandos in one of the first attacks of the Tet offensive of early 1968. (Richard Swanson, *Life* Magazine, © Time, Inc.)

14 Bearing the Burden: The Vietnam Years, 1961–1969

Diplomatic Crossroad: The Tet Offensive in Vietnam, 1968

"They're coming in! They're coming in! VC in the compound," the young MP shouted into his radio.[1] Seconds later he and another guard were gunned down by attacking Viet Cong commandos. Moments before, about 3:00 A.M. that January 30, 1968, the compound of the American Embassy in Saigon, South Vietnam, was quiet, the only noise coming from the whirring air conditioners and the fireworks exploding nearby in celebration of the Lunar New Year, or Tet. Only a few Americans were guarding the grounds. Completed in 1967 at a cost of $2.6 million, the six-story embassy building was protected by shatterproof Plexiglas windows, a concrete sun shield covering the entire structure, and an eight-foot high, thick outer wall. Topped by a helicopter pad, the fortified building was an imposing reminder of the American presence in Southeast Asia. One critical Vietnamese thought it "the symbol of America's power to stay, to destroy, to change a whole way of life, to propose and dispose at will."[2]

At 2:45 A.M. a Renault taxi cab and Peugeot truck moved without lights into the early morning darkness from a repair shop a few blocks from the embassy. About fifteen Viet Cong passengers leaped from their vehicles and fired at two embassy MP's. The stunned Americans fired back and hastily bolted the heavy steel gate to the compound. Soon a huge explosion blew a three-foot hole in the wall. The VC scrambled through, firing automatic rifles at the two MP's, who managed to radio for help before they died. The invaders then unleashed their antitank guns and rockets, transported into Saigon weeks before under shipments of tomatoes and firewood. The thick teakwood embassy doors took a direct hit, sending the United States seal crashing to the ground. Inside, a skeleton crew of Central Intelligence Agency and Foreign Service officials felt it was "like being in a telephone booth in the *Titanic* while the ship was going down."[3] A few blocks away, Ambassador Ellsworth Bunker was awakened and whisked away to a secret hiding place for protection. The news of the attack spread quickly across

"What the Hell's Ho Chi Minh Doing Answering Our Saigon Embassy Phone . . . ?" Paul Conrad's cartoon expressed well the startled American response to the attack upon the United States Embassy in South Vietnam, in January, 1968. President Lyndon Johnson had earlier reported that most of the Asian country was "secure" against the Viet Cong and North Vietnamese. (© 1968, Los Angeles Times. Reprinted with permission Los Angeles Times Syndicate)

Saigon. Flash bulletins reached the United States. In Washington, where it was afternoon, presidential adviser Walt W. Rostow immediately labeled the Viet Cong assault on the embassy a "grandstand" play.[4] Few American leaders could believe that "Bunker's bunker" had been invaded. After all, on January 17, in his State of the Union message, President Lyndon B. Johnson himself had said that most of South Vietnam was "secure," and the embassy seemed the most secure of any site.

In Saigon's dim morning light, American soldiers counterattacked. MPs used a jeep to knock down the steel gate and paratroopers landed by helicopter on the roof. By 9:15 A.M. the compound was "secure" and General William "Westy" Westmoreland arrived to survey the littered yard. He counted nineteen dead Vietnamese (four were friendly embassy employees), five dead Americans, and two Viet Cong prisoners, and thereupon, to the disbelief of those around him, declared an American victory. One reporter mumbled that the compound looked like a "butcher shop in Eden," and another mournfully described the "bodies twisted over the ornamental shrubbery and their blood pooling in the white gravel rocks of the embassy garden."[5]

The bold sally against the embassy was but one part of the well-coordinated, massive Tet offensive. Apparently conceived in Communist North Vietnam by General Vo Nguyen Giap, famous for his defeat of the French at Dienbienphu in 1954, the offensive was launched on January 30–31, 1968 by Viet Cong and North Vietnamese soldiers. "The map of South Vietnam," scholar Peter Poole has written, "was lit up like a pinball machine by separate enemy attacks."[6] The forays struck thirty-six of the forty-four provincial capitals, over a hundred other villages, the gigantic Tan Son Nhut airbase, and numerous sites in Saigon. The Communist forces attacked when about half of the South Vietnamese Army (ARVN) was on leave for the Tet holiday, for in the past each side had observed a truce during the New Year celebrations. The VC and North Vietnamese hoped to seize the cities, foment a general sympathetic uprising, force ARVN and American forces to move to the cities—leaving a vacuum in the countryside, and disrupt the governmental bureaucracy. The Viet Cong Order of the Day prophesized "the greatest battle ever fought throughout the history of our country. It will bring forth worldwide changes, but will also require many sacrifices."[7] Secretary of State Dean Rusk remarked shortly after the assaults that the Tet offensive "may well be the climactic period of the struggle in Southeast Asia."[8] General Westmoreland somberly compared it to Pearl Harbor.

After Tet the "mighty U.S. suddenly seemed as impotent as a beached whale."[9] Yet the ARVN and American armies struck back "with the fury of a blinded giant," according to Pulitzer Prize-winning journalist Frances Fitzgerald. "Forced to fight in the cities, they bombed, shelled, and strafed the most populous districts as if they saw no distinction between them and the jungle."[10] Americans at home watched the counterattacks every night on color television and many were appalled by the bloodshed. To dislodge the VC from Hué, South Vietnam's old imperial capital and third largest city, American and ARVN forces used everything from nausea gas to rockets. "Nothing I had seen during the Second World War in the Pacific [and] during the Korean War" matched the "destruction and despair" in Hué, recalled a journalist.[11] After three weeks of vicious warfare, the Communists fled, 100,000 people had become refugees, thousands lay dead, and American bombings had reduced a once-beautiful city to rubble. Communist ruthlessness was sadly discovered in the mass graves of over 2,000 civilians executed by the Viet Cong.

In the northwest corner of South Vietnam several thousand American soldiers bravely resisted a siege of their two-square-mile hillside at Khe Sanh, which, according to Westmoreland, "served to lure North Vietnamese to their deaths."[12] Hundreds of Americans died during the first months of 1968, as enemy rockets zeroed in on the strategic but vulnerable base. American B-52s countered by dropping tons of bombs on the surrounding area. By the end of March, remembered a colonel, "the jungle had become literally a desert—vast stretches of scarred, bare earth with hardly a tree standing, a landscape of splinters and bomb craters."[13] Some observers predicted an American Dienbienphu, but American soldiers held their ground and the Communist troops never launched a major assault at Khe Sanh. Still, to many Americans, the sight of pinned-down GIs represented a new defensive posture for the United States in Vietnam.

The provincial capital of Ben Tre symbolized the costs of the Tet offensive. To ferret out the VC, American and ARVN forces leveled Ben Tre, killing a thousand civilians. In unforgettable words, an American officer declared that "it became necessary to destroy the town to save it."[14] That statement joined one newsreel to sear American memory. The NBC *Huntley-Brinkley News* program of February 1 showed a brief film clip of the national police chief of South Vietnam pointing a pistol at the head of a suspected VC. As reporter John Chancellor narrated "rough justice on a Saigon street," General Nguyen Ngoc pulled the trigger and blasted the young man. The 52 seconds of footage, said an NBC producer, was the "rawest, roughest film anyone had ever seen."[15]

The Johnson Administration, having said that the war was showing steady progress for the South Vietnamese and that a Communist offensive had been expected, suffered an ever-growing "credibility gap" with the American people. January was a bad month for Lyndon B. Johnson. On the twenty-third the North Koreans captured the American spy ship *Pueblo* and its entire crew off the Korean coast. The international balance of payments for the United States, Johnson learned, was running at an adverse annual rate of seven billion dollars. A B-52 with four H-bombs aboard was lost in Greenland. And Senator Eugene McCarthy, a "dove" on Vietnam, was gaining political stature as a challenger to Johnson's renomination to the presidency. Johnson quickly labeled the Tet attacks a "complete failure," thereby setting off a national debate about the consequences of the offensive.[16]

Some critics pointed to the wrenching costs of Tet. By mid-March one-eighth of the South Vietnamese people were embittered refugees in their own country. Over forty thousand Viet Cong were killed. Over a thousand American and two thousand ARVN forces died. The Communists had gone "for broke," thought Westmoreland.[17] One critic, Senator Robert Kennedy, soon also to declare himself a candidate against Johnson for the Democratic presidential nomination, said "it is as if James Madison [had claimed] victory in 1812 because the British only burned Washington instead of annexing it to the British Empire."[18] "Victory" and "defeat" seemed hollow words to describe the Vietnamese carnage. "Perhaps failure," wrote a columnist in the *Wall Street Journal*, "is anything short of total success."[19] Most agreed that the losers were the Vietnamese civilians. Questions were raised, too, about what the United States would do next, especially in light of official public statements that the Tet offensive was only a minor setback, if one at all. "What will we do with the initiative when we regain it?" asked the *Washington Post*.[20] Senator Stuart Symington quizzed Secretary Rusk: "It is clear what we are losing, but what do we win if we win?"[21] On the televised program *Face the Nation*, after Secretary of Defense Robert McNamara recited the Tet figures for dead VC, a reporter asked him: "Isn't there something Orwellian about it, that the more we kill, the stronger they get?"[22]

As a Texan who often remembered the Alamo, President Johnson decried the

Rough Justice on a Saigon Street.
The South Vietnamese national police chief executes a suspected Viet Cong guerrilla in the street during the early tense days of the Tet offensive, 1968. Associated Press photographer Eddie Adams caught the moment of impact in this shocking picture, as did an NBC television crewman. (Wide World Photos)

"chorus of defeatism."[23] He authorized 10,500 more troops for Vietnam, gave hawkish speeches against quitting under fire, and flamboyantly toured some American military bases. He aroused his defenders. "Don't be discouraged by the croakers," advised historian Allan Nevins.[24] Columnist Joseph Alsop told him to call up the military reserves; the President would be "feckless, foolish, and derelict in his duty" if he did not.[25] Journalist William Shannon, remembering the 1944 Battle of the Bulge, told his readers that "we must be patient and stoical, not fluttering foolishly with every enemy thrust and parry."[26] The President was nevertheless worried. He conceded that the Viet Cong had scored a "psychological victory," and privately Westmoreland admitted that the VC had dealt South Vietnam a "severe blow."[27] Although the VC had not generated a national rebellion, had failed to hold the cities, and had suffered huge casualties, they had freed thousands of prisoners, disrupted the South Vietnamese governmental structure, crippled the American "pacification" program in the countryside, gained more influence in rural areas, heaped monstrous refugee and reconstruction problems on the Saigon regime, and proved that they were capable of massive assaults—in short, that it was difficult for either side to assume it could "win."

In late February Johnson ordered the new Secretary of Defense, Clark Clifford, a former Truman adviser, to undertake a major review of Vietnam policy, after General Westmoreland suggested that 206,000 more American troops join the more than 500,000 already there. The generals, including Joint Chiefs of Staff Chairman Earle G. Wheeler, one student of Tet has written, "hoped that Clifford would be a *tabula rasa* on which they could write their plan."[28] They planned a major new ARVN-American offensive. Within the Pentagon, formerly timid dissenters began to gain Clifford's ear, as they pleaded for de-escalation of the violence. Vietnam could not be saved by destroying it, advisers like Under Secretary of the Air Force Townsend Hoopes and Deputy Secretary of Defense Paul Nitze counseled. Furthermore, Vietnam was draining America's resources from its more serious confrontation with the key enemy, the Soviet Union. Priorities had to be put straight. In early March, too, Rusk began to speak with the President about halting the bombing of North Vietnam as an inducement to peace talks. In the New Hampshire Democratic primary on March 12, McCarthy made a surprisingly strong showing against the President, by polling 42 percent of the vote to Johnson's 49 percent. Johnson also talked with the quintessential Cold Warrior about Vietnam. Dean Acheson, as usual, was blunt: "With all due respect, the Joint Chiefs of Staff don't know what they're talking about."[29] Clifford found that out when he fired a series of questions at the generals. He was dismayed that they did not know how long the fighting would continue or how many more men would be required. "All I had was the statement, given with too little self-assurance to be comforting," Clifford recalled, "that if we persisted for an indeterminate length of time, the enemy would choose not to go on."[30] Clifford's review committee, the *Ad Hoc* Task Force on Vietnam, recommended in early March a step-up in bombing North Vietnam and the deployment of 20,000 additional American troops, but Clifford expressed private doubts to the President. Later in the month, another advisory body, the "Wise Men," or Senior Informal Advisory Group on Vietnam made up of several Truman era diplomats and generals, among others, told the President that victory was impossible. "The President was visibly shocked by the magnitude of the defection," Hoopes later noted.[31] Indeed, he began to dream he was Woodrow Wilson paralyzed from the neck down.

Lyndon B. Johnson (1908–1973). A tired President confers with Generals Creighton Abrams and Earl Wheeler at the National Security Council meeting of March 27, 1968. A few days later, having made his decisions about the Vietnam War, Johnson removed himself as a candidate in the presidential race, ending a political career of unusual energy and influence. (Courtesy of The Lyndon B. Johnson Library)

On March 31 Johnson spoke on prime time television. "We are prepared to move immediately toward peace through negotiations," he announced. Although the United States was sending another 13,500 men to South Vietnam and more military aid to ARVN, he reported that American airplanes would halt their bombing of a major portion of North Vietnam. "Even this limited bombing of the North could come to an early end—if our restraint is matched in Hanoi [the North Vietnamese capital]."[32] The President spoke again about the alarming disparity in the American balance of payments, and he asked Congress to pass a higher tax bill to pay for a proposed increase in aid to South Vietnam of $5.1 billion over the next two years. His conciliatory message appealed for peace talks. Then, to the amazement of viewers and even some of his advisers, Johnson said he would not seek re-election. Tet had claimed a political casualty. On April 3 the North Vietnamese agreed to bargain at the conference table. Discussions began on May 14. The fighting and talking—and dying—would go on for several ghastly years more, but there would never again be anything to match the horror of Tet, 1968. Out of the sacrifices of Hué, Saigon, Khe Sanh, and Ben Tre had come a belated and grudging willingness to try diplomacy.

Indochina: War and Diplomacy Before 1961

The tragic Tet offensive was a conspicuous but not an unusual experience in Vietnamese history. Before the 1960s that history was marked by centuries of resistance to foreigners—Chinese, French, Japanese, and Americans. In 1867 France colonized Vietnam and soon began to exploit the country's raw materials, as well as those of Laos and Cambodia, which became protectorates in 1883 and part of French Indochina in the 1890s. Rice, rubber, tin, and tungsten were taken from the Indochinese Peninsula to European markets. France constructed a haughty and repressive imperial government and monopolized land holdings, while over

Ho Chi Minh (1890–1971). The Vietnamese nationalist and Communist led his nation's battle against foreigners for decades. Secretary of Defense Robert McNamara thought him a "tough old S.O.B. And he won't quit no matter how much bombing we do." (*The Reporter,* 1950. Copyright 1950 by Fortnightly Publishing Co., Inc.)

80 percent of the Vietnamese people existed as poor, rural peasants. From 1867 onward the embittered Vietnamese, in varying degrees of intensity, battled their French overlords.

The most famous nationalist leader in the twentieth century was Ho Chi Minh, born in 1890 to a low-level government employee. Later described as a "small man, with a face the color of tea, a beard the color of rice, a piercing look beneath a forehead crowned by a somewhat absurd lock of hair," Ho traveled to Europe and at the time of World War I took up with other Vietnamese to plead for independence.[33] In Paris, Ho sent a memorandum to the Big Four leaders at the Versailles Conference, but his upstart anticolonial ideas, despite their deliberate reference to Woodrow Wilson's principle of self-determination, went unnoticed by the conferees. Because the Communists seemed to be the only political force vigorously denouncing colonialism, Ho and other nationalists joined the Communist party and throughout the twenties and thirties lived and agitated in China and Russia. In 1930–1931 the French brutally suppressed a Vietnamese peasant rebellion, killing 10,000 and deporting another 50,000. "It is safe to say," scholar Joseph Buttinger has concluded, "that if the French had chosen a less disastrous approach to the land question and employed all available means for eliminating rural poverty, the Communist movement in Vietnam would never have gained its extraordinary strength."[34]

In 1940–41 the rampaging Japanese took over Vietnam, but left collaborating French officials in charge. Vietnamese nationalists, including Ho's Communists, went underground, used China as a base, and in 1941 organized the Viet Minh, a coalition of nationalist groups led by the Communist party. In the final days of World War II, Viet Minh guerrillas tangled with Japanese troops, liberated some northern provinces, and worked with the United States Office of Strategic Services (OSS). An OSS interpreter recalled that Ho "would talk about American ideals and how he was sure America would be on his side" in the postwar period.[35] Ho sent formal messages to Washington, depicted himself as the George Washington of his country, and often mentioned the American Declaration of Independence and the Atlantic Charter. In late August, 1945, Ho's Viet Minh organized the Democratic Republic of Vietnam in Hanoi. On September 2, he proclaimed Vietnam's independence, borrowing phrases from America's document of July 4, 1776.

During the Second World War, the United States warily watched events in Vietnam, but hardly considered them of great significance. In the fall of 1944 State Department officials told the President that Indochina and Southeast Asia were "potentially important markets for American exports. They lie athwart the southwestern approaches to the Pacific Ocean and have important bearing on our security and the security of the Philippines."[36] Roosevelt, eager to break up the despised French empire, spoke vaguely about placing Indochina under international trusteeship. The British, protective of their own empire, protested that such a policy would mark a bad precedent. State Department officials, often out of touch with the President, wanted to restore French power in Indochina as a counterweight against potential Russian influence. Ambassador to Russia W. Averell Harriman predicted that the Soviet Union would become a "world bully" and "reach into China and the Pacific."[37]

Roosevelt never formulated precise plans for Indochina. A combination of British, United States State Department, and French pressures undermined the trusteeship idea, and the President only faintly objected. At Yalta he decided not to discuss Indochina with an aroused Winston Churchill. The President thought it "better to keep quiet just now."[38] "Above all," historian Walter LaFeber has written, "American officials, including Roosevelt, wanted an orderly, nonrevolutionary Southeast Asia open to Western interests."[39] Such an objective, once the trusteeship notion was discarded, could not be achieved through a Viet Minh government. So the French, with British military help and American tolerance, returned to Vietnam. They were not welcomed. Abandoned by the United States, receiving no support from Russia, and now facing French forces, the Viet Minh accepted a compromise with France in March, 1946: DRV status as a "free state" in the French Union and French military occupation of northern Vietnam. It soon became clear that Paris intended to re-establish its former grip. Viet Minh and French soldiers clashed in December. One French bombardment of Haiphong killed several thousand civilians. The Viet Minh responded with guerrilla terror. For the next eight years Vietnam was wracked by bloody combat, with the French holding the cities and the Viet Minh the countryside.

Indochina, Truman Administration adviser Clark Clifford later recalled, was seen at first as a "French problem."[40] To win Paris' favor for its postwar policies in Europe, Washington acquiesced in the re-establishment of French colonialism in Vietnam. Although in the early postwar months Ho Chi Minh had sent a number of letters to Washington requesting economic assistance and support for independence, he never received replies. As the Cold War heated up in 1946–1947, Ho's Moscow "training" became a topic of American discussion. By late 1946 the Department of State considered him an "agent of international communism," although some State Department officers dissented and pointed out that Vietnamese leaders were nationalists, not servants of Moscow. Some commentators saw Ho as an Asian Tito. It did not matter, because Secretary Dean Acheson settled the question in 1949: Ho was an "outright Commie."[41] That year the French installed Bao Dai, who had served the Japanese in World War II, as their Vietnamese leader. In February, 1950, Washington recognized this French puppet.

Mao's victory in China and the outbreak of the Korean War stirred considerable American interest in Indochina. Seeing that area as another Cold War battleground, rather than as a localized, indigenous nationalist rebellion against European imperialism, the Truman Administration extended foreign aid to help the beleaguered French. In 1950 Washington sent $150 million in aid and a contingent of military advisers to Vietnam. In the period 1945–1954 the United States gave over two billion of the five billion dollars that Paris spent to keep Vietnam within the French empire. In 1954 United States aid covered 78 percent of the cost of the war, and over three hundred Americans were assigned to Vietnam as part of the Military Assistance Advisory Group—all to no avail. In the spring of 1954, at Dienbienphu, a fortress where the besieged French had chosen to stand or fall, Viet Minh forces moved toward a major, symbolic victory. The Eisenhower Administration was divided on a response. Vice-President Richard M. Nixon and Secretary of State John Foster Dulles urged the despatch of American troops and bombers; Army Chief of Staff Matthew Ridgway opposed large-scale intervention. In April President Dwight D. Eisenhower uttered the "falling domino" theory to explain American interest in Southeast Asia and sounded out the Congress and Britain about an American, or joint, military operation. The replies were timid; Vietnam could not be saved for France by military action. When the French forces at Dienbienphu surrendered on May 7, Washington was leaning against military intervention.

A few days earlier, on April 26, 1954, representatives from France, Russia, Britain, China, the United States, Bao Dai's Vietnam, the DRV, Laos, and Cambodia met in Geneva to discuss the morass in Vietnam. If war would not work, thought the Western powers, perhaps diplomacy would halt the deterioration of the once-glorious French stature in Asia. But the French themselves upset American hopes. A new government, led by Pierre Mendès-France, pledged to end the war quickly. With Ho's Viet Minh in control of two-thirds of Vietnam, the conferees signed the Geneva Accords in July. The Viet Minh, now assured that their military successes had led to political victory, accepted the accords: temporary partition of Vietnam at the seventeenth parallel; French withdrawal to below that latitude; neither North nor South Vietnam to sign military alliances or permit foreign bases on Vietnamese soil; national elections to be held in 1956; unification of the country after elections; and elections also in neighboring strife-torn Laos and Cambodia, the other territories in French Indochina. The United States, however, refused to sign the agreements. The National Security Council found the Geneva settlement a "disaster" that represented a "major forward stride of Communism which may lead to the loss of Southeast Asia."[42] Quite an exaggeration, but apparently the United States believed that Communist China, which had sent some aid to the Viet Minh, would use Vietnam as a base for expansion. As French reporter Bernard Fall, longtime Vietnam watcher, has noted, the "struggle now began to rebuild a truncated land into a viable non-Communist Vietnamese state."[43]

In October a smiling Ho Chi Minh returned to Hanoi, still the "frail, stooped wisp of a man whose classic endurance of body and soul were almost visible aspects of his being."[44] In early 1955 he warned his followers in language quite different from that of a decade before that "we must be vigilant . . . against the plans of the imperialistic Americans who are seeking to intervene in Indochina, to incite their lackeys, to sabotage the armistice accords, and to cause war."[45] He could not have known, of course, that much of this would in fact occur; at that very time Washington was designing its strategy to establish a new regime in South Vietnam. Not about to "mourn the past," as Dulles remarked, the United States moved deliberately.[46] It created the Southeast Asia Treaty Organization in September, 1954 to protect Cambodia and Laos from Communist aggression and South Vietnam from the Viet Minh. SEATO violated the spirit of the Geneva Accords by specifying protection over the southern half of Vietnam—now treated, it seemed, as a separate state. After the creation of SEATO the seventeenth parallel seemed less a provisional and more a permanent line.

In the South, the United States backed the new government of Prime Minister Ngo Dinh Diem, a non-Communist Vietnamese nationalist and Catholic who had spent a number of years in the United States before the Geneva Conference and who had gradually undermined the authority of Bao Dai. An enlarged group of American advisers, in violation of Geneva, began to train a South Vietnamese army, and millions in American military and economic assistance flowed to Diem's government. In mid-1955 the government in the North invited preliminary talks to plan the national election scheduled by Geneva for 1956. Diem refused, and the Eisenhower Administration, convinced that Ho would win an election, publicly endorsed the cancellation of the electoral provisions of the Geneva Accords, thereby dealing a setback to unification. In 1955 Diem held his own referendum in the South. That blatant fraud gave him 98.2 percent of the vote. In Saigon, his backers vigorously stuffed the ballot boxes so that 605,000 votes emerged from 450,000 registered voters.

The two Vietnams went their separate ways, with the North receiving aid from both Russia and China, but cautiously avoiding dependence on either by deftly shifting intimacy from one to the other. Diem received American aid of about $300

Eisenhower, Ngo Dinh Diem (1901–1963), and Dulles. The South Vietnamese nationalist Diem, from a mandarin and Catholic family, spent time in exile in the United States before returning to his country as Premier (1954–1963). His police state rule did not seem to upset President Eisenhower or Secretary Dulles in May, 1957 when they met with Diem in Washington. (Dwight D. Eisenhower Library)

million a year, but true to the Vietnamese tradition of resisting foreign influence, he ignored American advice on the need for political and economic reforms. He also placed family members in profitable positions, tolerating corruption. Americans supported Diem's suppression of those Viet Minh remaining in the South, but not his crude methods. In 1956 he jailed 20,000 to 30,000 suspected Communists in "re-education" camps. Angry Southern rebels, ignoring Hanoi's advice to practice restraint, desperately retaliated by killing village teachers, policemen, and government officials in a reign of terror. Exploiting widespread rural support and general anti-Diem dissent, the Viet Minh organized the National Liberation Front in December, 1960. Hanoi, for the first time since Geneva playing a direct but timid role in the South, encouraged this Communist-dominated political group. Diem labeled the front the "Viet Cong," meaning Vietnamese Communists, to discredit it.

Although Washington and Saigon would later claim that the new Vietnamese war was initiated by aggression from the North, most scholars agree that the Viet Cong sprang from the peculiar, repressive environment of the South, at first received more spiritual than material help from the North, and engaged Diem in a *civil war*. Because of Cold War conditioning and an awareness of the economic and strategic value of the Indochinese Peninsula, however, American officials did not view the new conflict as a *Vietnamese* question. Rather, they depicted it as a great power confrontation between Russia or China and the United States. Senator John F. Kennedy said in 1956 that Diem's Vietnam was the "cornerstone of the Free World in Southeast Asia, the keystone to the arch, the finger in the dike."[47] In 1961 Kennedy became President of the United States.

"Action Intellectuals" and the Foreign Policy of John F. Kennedy

The 1960 presidential election was a contest between two Cold Warriors with distinctively different styles. Republican Richard M. Nixon seemed bland and tied to the shopworn phrases of the 1950s. Democratic candidate John F. Kennedy, who beat Nixon by a narrow margin, aroused support through the slogan: "I think it's time America started moving again."[48] Both Nixon and Kennedy were part of the "containment generation" of people who matured politically in the 1940s and imbibed the popular lessons of World War II and the Cold War. Historian Robert Divine has concluded that Kennedy "sincerely believed in the cold war shibboleths that men like Dean Acheson and John Foster Dulles had been voicing for a decade and a half."[49] Both Nixon and Kennedy had been elected to Congress in 1946 and heard President Truman enunciate the "Truman Doctrine" the following year. In 1960, Kennedy charged that the Eisenhower-Nixon Administration had failed to enter the new battleground of the Cold War, the Third World, thus consigning it to communism without a fight. With the U-2 affair, the noisy demise of the Paris summit meeting, an adverse balance of payments, cancellation of a presidential visit to Japan, and crises in Cuba, the Congo, and Indochina all as the immediate backdrop, Kennedy and many Americans believed that Russia (or communism) was winning the Cold War. "I think there is a danger that history will make a judgment," Kennedy stated in August of 1960, "that these were the days when the tide began to run out for the United States. These were the times when the communist tide began to pour in."[50] The next month his words smacked of John

John F. Kennedy (1917–1963). Before becoming President, JFK represented Massachusetts in the House (1947–1953) and the Senate (1953–1961). His book *Profiles in Courage* (1957), ghostwritten by historian Jules Davids and aide Theodore Sorensen, won a Pulitzer Prize. One of the President's under-publicized achievements was the Trade Expansion Act of 1962 and the subsequent "Kennedy Round" of trade negotiations, which reduced tariffs. (*The Reporter,* 1962. Copyright 1962 by The Reporter Magazine Co.)

Foster Dulles himself when he described the Cold War as a "struggle for supremacy between two conflicting ideologies: Freedom under God versus ruthless, godless tyranny."[51] Kennedy pledged to move the Cold War from stalemate and potential Communist victory to American triumph.

Kennedy said he did not mind being called Truman with a Harvard accent. Born in 1917 to wealthy, Catholic, politically active parents, John Fitzgerald Kennedy graduated from Harvard College and served with honor in World War II. In 1940, at the time his father was ambassador to Great Britain, his senior thesis was published as *Why England Slept,* with the theme that England should have demonstrated a willingness to use force in resisting Nazi aggression, rather than embracing weakness. For Kennedy's generation, the Munich agreement became the "Munich syndrome" or appeasement lesson. During the Cuban Missile Crisis, Kennedy tapped that historical legacy for a policy rationale: "The 1930s taught us a clear lesson: aggressive conduct, if allowed to go unchecked and unchallenged, ultimately leads to war."[52] He also remembered the experience of the 1940s. As presidential assistant and grand theorist Walt Whitman Rostow reported, the "first charge of the Kennedy Administration in 1961—somewhat like the challenge faced by the Truman Administration in 1947— was to turn back the Communist offensive."[53] History both tugged at the Kennedy advisers and pushed them.

So did the distinctive style and personality of the young President. "All at once you had something exciting," recalled a student campaigner in comparing the Eisenhower and Kennedy days. "You had a young guy who had kids, and who liked to play football on his front lawn. He was a real human being. He was talking about pumping some new life into the country . . . just giving the whole country a real shakedown and a new image. . . . Everything they did showed that America was alive and active. . . . To run a country it takes more than just mechanics. It takes a psychology."[54] Call it psychology, charisma, charm, image, mystique, or cult, Kennedy had it. Photogenic and quick-witted, he became a television star. Observers marveled at his speed-reading abilities. Decrying softness in the American people, he challenged their egoes by launching a physical fitness program. Handsome, articulate, ingratiating, dynamic, energetic, competitive, athletic, cultured, bright, self-confident, cool, analytical, mathematical, zealous— these were the traits universally ascribed to the President. People often listened not to what he said, but to how he said it, and he usually said it with verve and conviction. He simply overwhelmed. Dean Rusk remembered him as an "incandescent man. He was on fire, and he set people around him on fire."[55] For historian-politician and presidential assistant Arthur M. Schlesinger, Jr., JFK had "enormous confidence in his own luck," and "everyone around him thought he had the Midas touch and could not lose."[56]

Style and personality are usually important to the conduct of diplomacy; how we behave obviously affects how others read us and respond to us, and our personal characteristics and needs generate measurable behavior. Many of his friends have commented that John F. Kennedy was driven by a desire for power, because power ensured winning. Furthermore, he personalized issues, converting them into tests of will. Diplomacy became a matter of crises and races. His father, Joseph P. Kennedy, demanded excellence. As political scientist James Barber has pointed out, old Joe "pressed his children hard to compete, never to be satisfied with anything but first place. The point was not just to try; the point was to win."[57] John developed a thirst for victory and a self-image as the vigorous man. Aroused in the

Arthur M. Schlesinger, Jr. (1917—) and Kennedy. The distinguished historian-politician became a special assistant to the President in 1961 and helped plan policies for Latin America. His partisan defense of JFK, *A Thousand Days* (1965), won a Pulitzer Prize. (John F. Kennedy Library)

campaign of 1960 by the stings of anti-Catholic bias, by misplaced right-wing charges that he was soft on communism, and by his narrow victory over Nixon, Kennedy, once in office, seemed eager to prove his toughness. He took up challenges with zest and soon Americans watched for box scores on the missile race, the arms race, and the space race. Kennedy and his advisers, it seems, thought that Premier Nikita Khrushchev and the Russians were testing them as men. In early 1961, when they discussed the possibility of a summit meeting with Khrushchev, Kennedy asserted that "I have to show him that we can be as tough as he is. . . . I'll have to sit down with him, and let him see who he's dealing with."[58] John F. Kennedy and his aides feared to be thought fearful.

With these psychic needs and with their high intellectual talents, the Kennedy officials came to Washington, "swashbuckling" and suffering from "auto-intoxication," commented one observer.[59] Cocky, thinking themselves the "right" people, they were, as skeptical Under Secretary of State Chester Bowles later

Robert Strange McNamara (1916—). Kennedy's mathematically minded secretary of defense was infatuated with charts. Graduate of the University of California, Berkeley and a Ford Motor executive, McNamara applied dollar-saving efficiency methods to his department and served as war minister for the Vietnamese conflict. In 1968 he became president of the World Bank. (*The Reporter,* 1967. Copyright 1967 by The Reporter Magazine Co.)

complained, "sort of looking for a chance to prove their muscle." They were "full of belligerence."[60] Schlesinger captured the mood: "Euphoria reigned; we thought for a moment that the world was plastic and the future unlimited."[61] Kennedy's alarmist Inaugural Address reflected the new spirit. Its swollen Cold War language was matched only by its pompous phrasing: "the torch has been passed to a new generation." He paid homage to historical memories when he noted that his generation had been "tempered by war" and "disciplined by a hard and bitter peace." Then came those moving, but in hindsight rather frightening words: "Let every nation know that we shall pay any price, bear any burden, meet any hardship, support any friend, oppose any foe to assure the survival and the success of liberty."[62] No halfway measures here. Kennedy and his assistants, impatient and tough, thought they could lick anything—or anyone.

The Kennedy people considered themselves "can-do" types, who with rationality and careful calculation could revive an ailing nation and world. Theodore H. White tagged them "the Action Intellectuals."[63] "Management" became one of the catchwords of the time. With adequate data, and they had an inordinate faith in data, they were certain they could succeed. When an heretical White House assistant attempted to persuade Secretary of Defense Robert McNamara, the "whiz kid" from the Ford Motor Company, that the Vietnam venture was doomed, the efficiency-minded McNamara shot back: "Where is your data? Give me something I can put in the computer. Don't give me your poetry."[64] There were dangers in a heavy reliance on quantified information. "Ah, *les statistiques,*" said a Vietnamese general to an American official. "We Vietnamese can give him [McNamara] all he wants. If you want them to go up, they will go up. If you want them to go down, they will go down."[65] Nonetheless, with its faith in formulas and the computer, the Kennedy "can-do" team brought a freshness to American foreign policy, if not in

Makers of American Foreign Policy from 1961 to 1969

Presidents	*Secretaries of State*
John F. Kennedy, 1961–1963 Lyndon B. Johnson, 1963–1969	Dean Rusk, 1961–1969

substance, at least in slogans: "The Grand Design" for Europe; the "New Africa" policy; "Flexible Response" for the military; the "Alliance for Progress" for Latin America; and the "New Frontier" at home.

Kennedy's Secretary of State, Dean Rusk, was somewhat uneasy with the crusading "action intellectuals," but he was a loyal member of the team. A Rhodes Scholar, Rusk had been a military intelligence officer in Asia during World War II, a political science instructor, an assistant secretary of state under Truman, and in the 1950s president of the Rockefeller Foundation. Truman warhorses Robert Lovett and Dean Acheson enthusiastically recommended Rusk to Kennedy, who liked Rusk's quiet, modest, and unflappable manner. The President wanted to design his own foreign policy and did not desire a secretary of state who was too independent-minded or outspoken. The relatively unknown Rusk fit the bill. "The gentle, gracious Rusk," presidential assistant Theodore C. Sorenson later noted, "deferred almost too amiably to White House initiatives and interference."[66] A native of Georgia and the son of a Presbyterian minister, Rusk formed his world view in the 1930s and 1940s. The containment doctrine especially guided him. Somebody scratched graffiti in a State Department telephone booth: "Dean Rusk is a recorded announcement."[67] He often compared Ho Chi Minh and Mao Zedong to Hitler, Vietnam to Greece in 1947, and peace protesters to the appeasers of Nazi Germany; he warned against Asian Munichs. In his eight years as secretary, Rusk agonized over Vietnam, opposing a military Americanization of the war, but refusing to withdraw until a non-Communist government was secure. So he ended up backing escalation. Lyndon Johnson appreciated his loyalty: "He has the compassion of a preacher and the courage of a Georgia cracker. When you're going in with the Marines, he's the kind you want at your side."[68]

Dean Rusk (1909–). A graduate of Davidson College and a former Rhodes Scholar at Oxford, Rusk served Kennedy and Johnson as a loyal secretary of state. Vietnam consumed his secretaryship. "Personally, I made two mistakes," he recalled. "I underestimated the tenacity of the North Vietnamese and overestimated the patience of the American people." (Lyndon B. Johnson Library)

U.S.S. *Sam Rayburn.* Laid down in 1962 and launched the next year, this Polaris submarine with sixteen missile tubes and a missile range of 2,875 miles became part of a large Kennedy-inspired military buildup. The first Polaris submarine was commissioned in 1959. (U.S. Navy, Naval Photographic Center)

Building Arms and Nations Under Kennedy

One of the Kennedy Administration's top priorities was military expansion. During the presidential campaign of 1960 Kennedy charged that the Eisenhower Administration was losing the Cold War by tolerating a "missile gap" favorable to Russia. The charge was part politics, part exaggeration by the military establishment, part frustrating symbol of the post-Sputnik shock, and part guesswork based upon conflicting sets of intelligence estimates. Democrats, led by Senator Stuart Symington, declared that the Soviets would have a 3–1 edge in Intercontinental Ballistic Missiles (ICBMs) by 1962. Eisenhower, who had warned in 1959 against the "feverish building of vast armaments to meet glibly predicted moments of so-called 'maximum peril,'" knew the charge was nonsense;[69] U-2 intelligence flights revealed that the Soviets were not undertaking a massive missile program. The United States was in fact immensely superior.

Once in office, Kennedy and McNamara learned how wrong they were, but, worried by Soviet belligerence and Third World insurgencies and determined to negotiate from strength, they began a mighty expansion of the military and soon bragged about American nuclear supremacy. They called their defense strategy "flexible response," providing a method for every conceivable kind of war.

The Special Forces or Green Berets would conduct counterinsurgency against wars of national liberation; conventional forces would handle limited wars; more and better missiles would deter war or serve as primary weapons in nuclear war; at home, bomb or fallout shelters would protect Americans under a civil defense plan; and, when required, the United States would participate in collective security arrangements through the United Nations. In 1961 Kennedy increased the defense budget by 15 percent. Obviously not paying attention to Eisenhower's Farewell Address, he enlarged the Army, Air Force, Navy, and missile arsenal. By 1963 the United States had 275 major bases in 31 nations; 65 countries were "hosting" United States forces, and the American military was training soldiers in 72 countries. Also, one and a quarter million military-related American personnel were stationed overseas. In 1961, the United States had 63 ICBM's; by 1963 that figure had jumped to 424. During 1961–1963, NATO's nuclear firing power increased 60 percent. This tremendous military spurt goaded the Soviets, who alarmed Americans in September, 1961, by resuming atmospheric nuclear testing and by exploding a monster bomb of 50 megatons the next month. The irony of the arms race was that the more missiles Americans acquired, the more vulnerable they became, as the Russians tried to keep up by also building more. Although Kennedy established the United States Arms Control and Disarmament Agency, his heavy military emphasis tended to discourage disarmament and to play down diplomatic solutions to crises. His one diplomatic achievement in this area was the Nuclear Test Ban Treaty of 1963, in which the United States and Russia agreed to halt atmospheric but not underground tests.

Kennedy met with Khrushchev at Vienna in June, 1961, to discuss a test ban treaty, Berlin, and Laos. Khrushchev's style, Kennedy was warned, ranged from "cherubic to choleric."[70] Kennedy sought to prove his toughness at Vienna, to show the Russians that they "must not crowd him too much."[71] At the conference Khrushchev began a war of nerves by insisting that Berlin become a "free city," thereby ending Western occupation; if the United States did not negotiate the question, he threatened, Russia would sign a separate treaty with East Germany. "If Khrushchev wants to rub my nose in the dirt, it's all over," snapped Kennedy. "That son of a bitch won't pay any attention to words. He has to see you move."[72]

"The Purpose of the Meeting Is to Take Measurements." Nikita S. Khrushchev and John F. Kennedy convened at the summit in Vienna in June, 1961 and sized one another up. (Parrish, Chicago Tribune–New York News Syndicate, Inc.)

Still, some presidential advisers told Kennedy that he probably had not rebutted the Premier vigorously enough at Vienna and that Khrushchev may have left the meeting thinking that he had out-dueled the young President. Kennedy vowed it would never happen again.

Eschewing negotiations over Berlin, the President decided to force the issue. Some of his assistants thought he should try diplomacy, but Kennedy listened to Dean Acheson. That ardent Cold Warrior seemed to welcome a confrontation by daring the Russians. Echoing Acheson's sentiments, Kennedy announced on July 25 that Berlin was "the great testing place of Western courage and will." He asked Congress for a $3.2 billion addition to the regular defense budget and authority to call up military reservists. He frightened Americans by also requesting $207 million to begin a civil defense, fall-out shelter program—"in the event of an attack."[73] His exaggerated, alarmist language helped turn a Soviet-American issue into a major crisis. On August 13 the Soviets suddenly put up a barbed wire barricade, followed by an ugly concrete block barrier, between the two Berlins. The Berlin Wall became a tragic symbol of Soviet repression, and finally shut off the exodus of immigrants that Khrushchev had so often protested. Washington could not knock the wall down, so it sent a contingent of troops along the access road through East Germany to West Berlin without incident. In September Kennedy finally invited Soviet-American talks. The crisis passed, and critics asked if it had been necessary. Yet Berlin remained a Soviet-American tension point. Kennedy traveled there in June of 1963 to underscore the American will to stay, and electrified a mass rally with emotional words: *Ich bin ein Berliner* (I am a Berliner)."[74]

The Berlin Wall. East German soldiers replace barbed wire with concrete slabs at the ugly Berlin Wall erected by the Soviets in 1961 to stop the flow of refugees to West Berlin. (United Press International)

"Could You Point Out the Ground You've Taken? We're Here to Secure and Develop it Economically." A "nation-building" team cooperates with a counterinsurgency team in this parody of the "modernization" efforts of Americans overseas. (Editorial cartoon by Pat Oliphant, © 1976, Los Angeles Times. Reprinted with permission of Universal Press Syndicate)

As Kennedy dealt with the old sores of the Cold War, he also attended to events in the Third World, the region he thought most vulnerable to revolution and communism and at the same time most susceptible to American influence. His governing concept was "nation building." The Kennedy team understood the force of nationalism in the Third World; rather than flatly oppose it, the "action intellectuals" sought to use or channel it. Through "modernization," or what the Kennedy team called "peaceful revolution" or "middle-class revolution," Third World nations would be helped through the stormy times of economic infancy to economic and hence political maturity.[75] The hope was that evolutionary, controlled, economic development would insure non-Communist political stability. "Modern societies must be built," one of the chief theoreticians of the concept, Walt W. Rostow, declared, "and we are prepared to help build them."[76] Kennedy liked to quote Mao's statement that "guerrillas are like fish, and the people are the water in which fish swim. If the temperature of the water is right, the fish will thrive and multiply."[77] Kennedy sought to affect the temperature of the water through modernization, and counterinsurgency became his means. Whether or not Khrushchev had given his January, 1961 proclamation that Russia would support movements of national liberation, the Kennedy team would probably have undertaken counterinsurgency operations to defeat the destabilizing insurgencies. These movements might permit Communist exploitation and check traditional United States economic expansion. Counterinsurgency took several forms, all reflecting the "can-do" philosophy: the training of native police forces and bureaucrats, flood control, transportation and communications, and community action projects. Most dramatic were the American Special Forces units, or Green Berets. Kennedy personally elevated their status in the military and supervised their choice of equipment. It was assumed, for example, that they would apply America's finest technology in Vietnam to succeed where the French had failed.

Besides enlarging counterinsurgency forces and continuing and extending foreign aid, the Kennedy Administration created the Peace Corps to assist in "nation building." Established by executive order in 1961, this volunteer group of mostly young Americans numbered 5,000 by early 1963 and 10,000 a year later. They went into developing nations as teachers, agricultural advisers, and technicians. The Peace Corps, although certainly a self-interested arm of American foreign policy, blunted some of the sharper edges of poverty and hardship. Hundreds of dedicated individuals worked to improve living conditions, in stark contrast to the destructive presence of the United States military in Indochina at the same time. Peace Corps monuments—irrigation systems, water pumps, larger crops—arose throughout Latin America and Africa, but the corps's humanitarian

AN ANSWER TO THE LIBERAL ARTS GRADUATE WHO ASKS:

What Can I Do in the Peace Corps?

Peace Corps Pamphlet. One of the instruments of "nation building," and Kennedy's pet project, the Peace Corps attracted young graduates of American universities for service in developing countries. Thousands of humane individuals, including some middle-aged and elderly Americans, took up the call. (The Peace Corps)

efforts fell far short of resolving the Third World's profound squalor or winning many friends to American foreign policy.

The Kennedy Administration also embarked upon the "Alliance for Progress" in Latin America to head off revolution. Launched at the Punta del Este meeting of the Organization of American States in August, 1961, the alliance envisioned spending $20 billion in funds from the United States and international organizations. In return, the Latin Americans promised land and tax reforms, housing projects, and health improvements. Initiated with great fanfare, the alliance soon sputtered. American businessmen did not invest as expected; the State Department dragged its feet in bureaucratic lethargy; Latin American nationalists disliked United States control; elites resisted reforms and pocketed American money; the gap between rich and poor widened; middle-class Latin Americans, whom Washington counted upon, proved to be selfish; and the United States abandoned its requirement that political democracy accompany economic change. In Colombia dams were built but needed land reforms were ignored. When the United States cut off aid to Haiti and Peru because of their repressive regimes, some Latin American governments protested American "intervention." What the alliance produced, complained critics, was a better grade of dictator. One of the architects of the alliance, Arthur M. Schlesinger, Jr., had told the President in early 1961 that Latin America was "set for miracles."[78] The "miracles" never materialized, and for all its sincere intentions to improve living conditions, the *Alianza para el Progreso* became in the last analysis another form of interference to maintain United States hegemony in the hemisphere. By the mid-1960s, under the leadership of staunchly conservative diplomat Thomas Mann, the alliance had turned its resources to military purposes, such as internal security forces. Cuba's Fidel Castro thought the alliance "a politically wise concept put forth to hold back the tide of revolution." It did not work, he pointed out, "because those in charge of seeing that the agrarian reform was implemented in Latin America were the very owners of the lands."[79]

The difficulties of "nation building" were also revealed dramatically in the Congo (now called Zaire), which was granted hurried independence from Belgium in mid-1960. Civil war quickly erupted. Backed by American and European cobalt and copper interests, Moise Tshombe tried to detach Katanga Province from the new central government headed by Patrice Lumumba. The United States, fearing Communist penetration of the volatile former colony, helped a United Nations mission quell the Katanga insurrection. Secretary Rusk prophetically worried about the consequences of the United States intervention. "What are the prudent and practical limitations on our traditional view of colonialism?" he asked privately. "One or two more Congo's—and we've had it."[80] Although Lumumba died in 1961, by early 1963 the central Congolese government had defeated Tshombe. About a year later, however, a major leftist revolt supported by Russia, Communist China, and Ghana, broke out. With the United Nations forces gone, the CIA soon bolstered former enemy Tshombe as the new leader of the central government, and with direct American aid, including military advisers, he recruited white mercenaries. The rebels responded by terrorizing white foreigners. In November of 1964, a small force of Belgian paratroopers dropped from American aircraft into the Congo to rescue Belgian and American citizens. Although there had never been a serious "Communist threat" in the Congo, the Kennedy Administration was reading Cold War lessons and thus thrust itself into the shaky politics of Africa. American Ambassador to Guinea William Attwood noted that leading African nationalists felt humiliated by the American and foreign intervention in the Congo, because "the white man with a gun, the old plunderer who had enslaved his ancestors, was back again, doing what he pleased, when he pleased, where he pleased. And there wasn't a damn thing Africa could do about it, except yell rape."[81] Attwood exaggerated, but he did identify the chief source of resistance to American "nation building"—nationalism itself.

Cuba and the Bay of Pigs

Africa counted as a sideshow compared to Latin America, formerly a secure American sphere of influence. Cuba claimed center stage. On July 26, 1953, a young lawyer and Cuban nationalist, Fidel Castro, attempted to overthrow the harsh American-backed regime of Fulgencio Batista. Beaten back, Castro fled to Mexico; he returned to Cuba in 1956 but failed again. This time he escaped into the mountains, where for three years he augmented his guerrilla forces and sporadically fought Batista's American-supplied army. In early 1959 the cigar-smoking, bearded rebel seized Havana and initiated social and economic programs designed to reduce the extensive United States interests that had developed since 1898 and had come to dominate Cuba's sugar, mining, and utilities industries. The new Havana government confiscated American property, and, knowing that he alienated the United States by this action, Castro began to look to Russia for help. Cuba and Russia struck a trade agreement in early 1960, and Castro increasingly used simplistic Communist language to explain the Cuban revolution. Historians debate when this authoritarian nationalist committed himself to "communism," but two elements in his thought seem consistent: socialism and nationalistic anti-Americanism. Often citing the abhorred Platt Amendment, which Cubans

Fidel Castro (1926–).
The Cuban dictator's bitter anti-Americanism and uncompromising call for socialist revolutions throughout the hemisphere were matched by Washington's angry anti-Castroism and firm resolve to knock him from his perch, especially after the signing of the Soviet-Cuban trade agreement of February, 1960. In the early 1960s, under "Operation Mongoose," the CIA tried several times to kill Castro with poison. (*The Reporter,* 1962. Copyright 1962 by The Reporter Magazine Co.)

called a yoke of colonialism, Castro determined that the only path to liberation from United States economic exploitation was public, rather than private, ownership of productive facilities. "This revolution may be like a watermelon," one American businessman remarked. "The more they slice it, the redder it gets."[82]

Castro's angry mixture of nationalism and communism and strong-arm tactics, including execution without fair trial, antagonized Washington, which had hesitantly supported Batista almost to the last. When the American Society of Newspaper Editors invited Castro to the United States for a speech in April, 1959, President Eisenhower refused to meet with him. Instead he departed for Augusta, Georgia to play golf on his favorite course. One conclusion seemed clear in Washington: Castro had to be squashed. In March, 1960, Eisenhower ordered the CIA to train Cuban exiles in Guatemala for a potential invasion of their former homeland. And in July the United States drastically reduced imports of Cuban sugar, hoping thereby to stagger the Cuban economy. Castro replied by seizing American-owned sugar mills. The Russians, meanwhile, were declaring the Monroe Doctrine dead. Eisenhower began to protest this seeming attempt by "international communism to intervene in the affairs of the Western Hemisphere."[83] Just before leaving office Eisenhower broke off diplomatic relations with Cuba. To Castro, courtship with Moscow seemed to provide protection against hostile "Yanquis." Anti-Castro American Ambassador to Cuba Philip W. Bonsal frankly admitted that Castro's "thrust in 1959 was radically and exclusively nationalistic; it became oriented toward dependence on the Soviet Union only when the United States, by its actions in the spring of 1960, gave the Russians no choice other than to come to Castro's rescue."[84] When Eisenhower undertook a "goodwill" tour of Latin America in early 1960 he was disconcerted to read a placard in a Rio de Janeiro crowd: "We like Ike; We like Fidel too."[85]

During the 1960 presidential campaign, candidate Kennedy hammered on the issue of Cuba. He called Castro a "source of maximum danger" and lambasted Eisenhower and Nixon for permitting a "communist satellite" to spring up on "our very doorstep." Kennedy called for a "serious offensive" against Cuba: "we do not intend to be pushed around any longer and in particular do not intend to be pushed out of our naval base at Guantánamo, or denied fair compensation for American property he has seized."[86] Critics complained that he was inviting an American Hungary in the western hemisphere. Just before leaving office in January, 1961, Eisenhower advised the incoming President to accelerate the exile training program. Kennedy seemed a willing recipient of such counsel.

Cuba was hardly a puppet of Russia or a threat to American security in 1961. "The Castro regime is a thorn in the flesh," Senator J. William Fulbright argued, "but it is not a dagger in the heart."[87] Still, ignoring America's own contribution to Castro's anti-Americanism, Kennedy defined it as a test of will, a new Cold War battleground, and he decided to remove the Cuban irritation. The CIA assured him that it could deliver another Guatemala, just like 1954—or even better. The CIA predicted that the Cuban people would rise up against their Communist masters. CIA agents pinpointed Cochinos Bay, the "Bay of Pigs," as the invasion site and organized a Cuban Revolutionary Council to take office after the successful expedition. Uneasy with the plan, Kennedy disapproved any direct American military involvement. But the now-or-never aura of the operation, CIA assurances, and concern that the trained exiles would embarrass him politically if he scotched the venture, convinced Kennedy to proceed. He anticipated criticism. Thus

Kennedy put Arthur M. Schlesinger, Jr. to work writing a justification or "White Paper." The Kennedy Administration never attempted to open talks with the Castro government, and it never consulted Congress on what amounted to war with Cuba.

In mid-April, 1961, 1,400 CIA-trained commandos departed from Guatemala for Cuba. They met early resistance from Castro's militia, no sympathetic insurrection occurred, and within two days the invasion had become a fiasco. Like his brother John, Attorney General Robert Kennedy found defeat difficult to accept. "We just could not sit and take it"; Moscow might think Americans "paper tigers." Walt Rostow, sensitive to Kennedy *machismo,* reassured him that "we would have ample opportunity to prove we were not paper tigers in Berlin, Southeast Asia, and elsewhere."[88] After the disaster President Kennedy, who had vetoed American air support for the invasion, blamed the CIA and joint chiefs of staff for faulty intelligence and sloppy execution. He never questioned his policy of attempting to overthrow a sovereign government, only the methods for doing it. Little sobered by the Bay of Pigs setback, Kennedy announced the lesson learned: "let the record show that our restraint is not inexhaustible." He vowed a "relentless struggle in every corner of the globe" with communism.[89] During the next several years, the United States imposed an economic blockade on Cuba, ousted the island nation from the Organization of American States, refused to recognize Castro, directed United States Information Agency propaganda at the Havana regime, continued aid to anti-Castro forces in Miami, Florida, and even sponsored assassination plots on Castro's life. For their part, the Cubans attempted to stimulate revolution and anti-Americanism in other nations through such daring rebels as Ché Guevara, who finally died at the hands of CIA-directed Bolivian soldiers in 1967. The Bay of

"Cuban Fiasco." After the failure at the Bay of Pigs, recriminations rocketed around Washington. JFK chastised the CIA for a host of errors, including selecting a beachhead that Castro knew very well because it was his favorite fishing spot. CIA officials grumbled that the President should have salvaged the operation by committing American forces. The Cuban exiles felt they had been double-crossed, for they had expected direct United States military support. Kennedy recognized that he had "handed his critics a stick with which they would forever beat him." (Roy Justus, *Minneapolis Star*)

Pigs, or "Battle of Giron Beach," was etched like the Platt Amendment on the Cuban mind. An official Cuban tourist map of the 1970s described Giron Beach as the site of "the first defeat of imperialism in America."[90]

The Cuban Missile Crisis

The Kennedy Administration's preoccupation with Castro's Cuba helped precipitate one of the Cold War's momentous crises. The Cuban Missile Crisis of October, 1962, as Nikita Khrushchev remarked, was a time when "the smell of burning hung in the air."[91] "A Hard Rain's A-Gonna Fall," wrote folksinger Bob Dylan. On October 14, a U-2 reconnaissance plane photographed medium-range (1,100-mile) missile sites under construction in Cuba. After gathering more data, American officials informed the President on October 16 that the Soviet Union had indeed placed missiles in Cuba. Kennedy created an Executive Committee of the National Security Council (Ex Comm), consisting of his "action intellectuals" and experienced diplomats from the Truman years. Besides McNamara, brother Robert, McGeorge Bundy, Maxwell Taylor, and Theodore Sorenson, there were Dean Acheson, Paul Nitze, and Robert Lovett, among others. Dean Rusk participated little in the exhausting, sometimes panicky, always vigorous, marathon meetings of Ex Comm. Kennedy had instructed them to find a way to remove the missiles. Something had to be done.

The Soviet installation of missiles was a reckless decision. Moscow's motivation is not altogether clear, although Khrushchev probably did not want a nuclear confrontation. Khrushchev himself has written that after the Bay of Pigs invasion the Soviets and Cubans predicted that the United States would strike again, an act that had to be prevented. "If the United States had not been bent on liquidating the Cuban revolution," Fidel Castro has said, "there would not have been an October crisis."[92] Russia was already committed, through large shipments of arms, to the maintenance of Cuban sovereignty and did not wish to "lose" Cuba. "We had to think up some way of confronting America with more than words," Khrushchev recalled. Then, too, the Russian leader, noting the presence of threatening American missiles in Turkey, reasoned that missiles in Cuba would teach Americans "just what it feels like to have enemy missiles pointing at you; we'd be doing nothing more than giving them a little of their own medicine."[93] Analysts have also suggested that Moscow was actually trying to force negotiations over Berlin and removal of the missiles from Turkey. Another explanation derives from debate within the Kremlin, wherein some Russian hawks disapproved Khrushchev's "peaceful coexistence" and worried about the Chinese challenge to Soviet pre-eminence among Communists. Khrushchev may have thought he needed a Cold War triumph to disarm his Kremlin critics and to demonstrate to Peking and other Communist capitals that Russia would take serious measures to defend an ally. Maybe he wanted what some observers called a nuclear "quick-fix"—the appearance of nuclear parity. It is difficult to believe that the Russians thought they could have installed the missiles without being detected. Ship after ship, loaded with components and technicians, conspicuously docked in Cuba. When the U-2 flights spotted the missiles, some sat uncamouflaged at their sites, thereby easily photographed. Khrushchev certainly knew about U-2s. Maybe he expected detection and then an offer from Kennedy to negotiate their removal, in conjunction with other issues like Berlin and Turkey. If so, Khrushchev grossly miscalculated and helped initiate a frightening crisis.

Kennedy and the Ex Comm initially gave little attention to negotiations to remove the missiles, and hardly probed for Soviet motivation. They feared that prolonged diplomacy would give Russian technicians enough time to make the missiles operational. Ex Comm discussions centered on questions of a military response. Several alternatives were discussed and rejected. Dean Acheson, among others, favored an air strike. Robert Kennedy listened and passed a note to his brother: "I now know how Tojo felt when he was planning Pearl Harbor."[94] Bobby said that he did not want his brother to become a Tojo. Anyway, Air Force officials reported they could not guarantee one hundred percent success; some missiles might remain in place for firing against the United States. Russians might also be killed. The joint chiefs of staff recommended a full-scale military invasion, a successful Bay of Pigs with American soldiers, thus getting rid of both the missiles and Castro. Although alluring, such a scheme could mean a prolonged war with Cuba, heavy American casualties, and a Soviet retaliatory attack upon Berlin. A private overture to Castro was ruled out, as was the suggestion that the issue be given to the United Nations. Ambassador to the United Nations Adlai Stevenson's proposal that the United States offer to trade the missiles in Turkey for those in Cuba met open derision. The Ex Comm members, tired and irritable, finally decided upon a naval blockade or "quarantine" of arms shipments to Cuba. Some members warned that such an action might prompt the Soviets to blockade Berlin and that the main problem, the removal of the missiles, would remain unsolved.

Soviet Missile Site at San Cristobal, Cuba. This low-level photograph was taken in October, 1962, when Soviet technicians were busily trying to assemble the various components of medium-range missiles. (U.S. Air Force)

The "quarantine," pushed ardently by McNamara, constituted a compromise between armed warfare and doing nothing and left open options for further escalation.

Kennedy, recalling the lessons of the 1930s and refusing to approach Moscow for talks, went on national television on October 22 and set off a war of nerves with Moscow. He announced a blockade, soon endorsed by a compliant Organization of American States, and insisted that Khrushchev "halt and eliminate this clandestine, reckless and provocative threat to world peace."[95] Over 180 American ships patrolled the Caribbean, and the American naval base on Cuba, Guantánamo, was reinforced. A B-52 bomber force loaded with nuclear bombs took to the skies. On October 24, Soviet vessels sailed toward the blockade. "It looks really mean, doesn't it," remarked the President as he awaited a collision.[96] But the Russian ships stopped. Secretary General of the United Nations U Thant urged talks; Khrushchev quickly called for a summit meeting. Kennedy replied that the missiles had to be removed first. The hours passed without a flare-up, but the tension was electric. On October 26 a Soviet agent contacted correspondent John Scali of the American Broadcasting Company and offered to disengage the missiles if the United States promised publicly not to invade Cuba in the future. Later Dean Rusk told Scali, "remember when you report this—that eyeball to eyeball, they blinked first."[97] Then came a long letter from Khrushchev stating much the same offer, but still insisting that the missiles were defensive, not offensive.

The next day, October 27, the crisis accelerated. FBI agents learned that Soviet officials in New York City were burning documents, perhaps a sign that war loomed. A U-2 plane was shot down over Cuba. Work continued with greater speed at the Cuban missile sites to make them operational. Also, another Khrushchev letter arrived in Washington on the 27th. The Premier raised the stakes: Russia would withdraw the missiles from Cuba if the United States removed its missiles from Turkey. Kennedy exploded at his advisers, because he had ordered the removal of the strategically vulnerable and obsolete Jupiter missiles from Turkey some months before. Nothing had been done, but Kennedy was not now interested in a swap. Robert Kennedy suggested that the President ignore the last letter and answer the first. JFK thereupon endorsed Khrushchev's first proposal: removal of the missiles in Cuba in exchange for a public American pledge to respect Cuba's territorial integrity. On the 28th Khrushchev agreed to these terms. Kennedy had thrown down the gauntlet and Khrushchev, fortunately, had not picked it up. The crisis was over. "Khrushchev, that complex, humane gambler-bandit," Walt Rostow later concluded, "did not stop until he felt the knife on his skin."[98]

Although congressmen and popular opinion applauded Kennedy's "finest hour," critics asked if the crisis was necessary. They questioned Kennedy's willingness to risk nuclear war, his disdain for private negotiations, and his resort to public confrontation. Ex Comm advisers and former ambassadors to Russia Charles Bohlen and Llewellyn Thompson urged private talks upon the President. Walter Lippmann on October 25 wrote a widely read column asking why, when the President met privately in the White House with Soviet Foreign Minister Andrei Gromyko on October 18, Kennedy did not show the Russian diplomat the U-2 photographs and seek a diplomatic solution then and there. The President could have warned him that the United States would go public with its demand for removal if the Soviets did not act posthaste. Public statements on television were not calculated to defuse a serious crisis. Yet Kennedy issued a public ultimatum, leaving Khrushchev little chance to repudiate his mistake or to save face, usually the very stuff of effective diplomacy. Kennedy risked the lives of millions of Americans and Russians in a scary gamble that the Soviets would back down. The members of the Ex Comm were bright and dedicated, Robert Kennedy recalled, but "if six of them had been President of the U.S., I think that the world might have been blown up."[99] "We were in luck," John Kenneth Galbraith later commented, "but success in a lottery is no argument for lotteries."[100]

Why Kennedy chose to ignore the possibilities of negotiations remains a topic of considerable debate. As most Ex Comm members noted, it does not appear that the Soviet missiles in Cuba, forty-two in number, altered the strategic balance of power. The medium-range weapons did not diminish America's overwhelming nuclear superiority. It would have been suicidal for the Russians to use the missiles in Cuba. Yet, as Sorenson concluded, the balance would have been "altered *in appearance;* and in matters of national will and world leadership, as the President said later, such appearances contribute to reality."[101] Regardless of strategic importance, then, the Kennedy people thought the very placement of missiles a diminution of American credibility and a direct challenge to American hegemony in Latin America. It was a matter of prestige, another test of will. Most observers have agreed that something had to be done to remove the weapons. But why a public confrontation? Put another way, American security was not threatened, but the Administration of John F. Kennedy may have been. Congressional elections were scheduled for early November and the Republicans were harping, before the missile crisis, about Kennedy's failure at the Bay of Pigs and his seeming irresolution over Cuba. Public toughness against the Soviets over the Cuban missiles would disarm his critics and protect his Administration's foreign policy from a hostile Congress. Perhaps politics demanded a bold stance. Then, too, there was the style and psyche of the "action intellectuals" who craved a victory, especially after the Bay of Pigs, the Vienna summit experience, and the Berlin Wall. Adolf A. Berle, one of Kennedy's leading advisers on Latin America, recorded in his diary: "This [Cuban Missile Crisis] is reprise on the Bay of Pigs business and this time there will be no charges that somebody weakened at the crucial moment."[102]

No weakness indeed—but an alarming example of brinkmanship. Afterward Kennedy seemed more willing to avoid crises and to entertain ideas of arms control. The 1963 Test Ban Treaty was one result, as was the installation of the "hot line," a direct telephone link between the White House and Kremlin. Yet, as scholar James Nathan has argued, "force and toughness became enshrined as instruments of policy." Some of the lessons the Kennedy advisers drew from the crisis encouraged military solutions to diplomatic problems because of their belief, Nathan has written, "that success in international crisis was largely a matter of national guts; that the opponent would yield to superior force; that presidential control of forces can be 'suitable' . . . , and that crisis management and execution are too dangerous and events move too rapidly for anything but the tightest secrecy."[103] The Russians read different lessons. They had been humiliated publicly. They had been shown to be inferior in nuclear power. The Chinese rubbed salt in the wound and exacerbated the bitter Sino-Soviet split by demeaning the Russians for having capitulated. Khrushchev would fall from power in 1964, but even before his ouster, Moscow determined to enter the nuclear arms race on a massive scale. As one Soviet leader remarked: "Never will we be caught like this again."[104]

The Green Berets. President Kennedy helped select equipment for Special Forces units like this one at Fort Bragg. The Green Berets were trained in counterguerrilla methods and sent into the jungles of Vietnam, among other places. (U.S. Army)

The Kennedyites prided themselves on their success as managers, but the legacy of the Cuban Missile Crisis meant an intensified arms race with the Soviets, alienation of America's allies (especially France), and an arrogant belief in the efficacy of American answers to world problems through the exercise of United States power.

Indochina Still: The Kennedy Escalation and Legacy, 1961–1963

Continued unrest in Laos and Vietnam placed those Asian trouble spots high on the "action intellectuals'" list for the remedial magic of counterinsurgency and nation building. Rostow saw an opportunity to use "our unexploited counter-guerrilla assets"—helicopters and Special Forces units. "In Knute Rockne's old phrase," he told President Kennedy, "we are not saving them for the Junior Prom."[105] The landlocked agricultural nation of Laos, wracked by civil war, seemed to provide a testing ground. Granted independence at Geneva in 1954, Laos chose neutralism in the Cold War when nationalist leader Souvanna Phouma organized a coalition government of neutralists and the pro-Communist Pathet Lao in 1957. The Eisenhower Administration opposed the neutralist government and initiated a major military aid program to build up the rightist and corrupt Laotian army; by 1961, $300 million had been spent. The money helped only slightly to improve the army's desire or ability to fight, but it did disrupt the Laotian economy through inflation and graft. In 1958 CIA-funded rightists helped displace Souvanna and shape a pro-American government without Pathet Lao participation. Washington soon dispatched military advisers to the new but shaky regime.

Souvanna Phouma returned to power after a coup in August, 1960, but the United States undermined him by again equipping rightist forces. Seeking a counterweight to American influence, Souvanna received assistance from Moscow and North Vietnam. But in December he fled his country. "The Americans say I am a Communist," he sighed. "All this is heartbreaking. How can they think I am a Communist? I am looking for a way to keep Laos non-Communist."[106] Unwilling to accept neutralism, the United States had helped convert a civil war into a big power confrontation. For Eisenhower the problem was simple: "the fall of Laos to Communism would mean the subsequent fall—like a tumbling row of dominoes—of its still-free neighbors, Cambodia and South Vietnam and, in all probability, Thailand and Burma. Such a chain of events would open the way to Communist seizure of all Southeast Asia."[107] The neutralists and the Pathet Lao, it appeared to Eisenhower, were simply part of a global Communist conspiracy.

The incoming Kennedy Administration did not perceive the Laotian problem much differently, although Kennedy was miffed over having to deal with it. In a rephrasing of the "domino theory," adviser Arthur M. Schlesinger, Jr. later explained that "If Laos was not precisely a dagger pointed at the heart of Kansas, it was very plainly a gateway to Southeast Asia."[108] In March Kennedy blotched the historical record by blaming the Pathet Lao for preventing the creation of a neutral Laos. As conspicuous Soviet aid flowed to the Pathet Lao, Kennedy determined to halt the imminent collapse of the pro-American government. He ordered the Seventh Fleet into the South China Sea, alerted American forces in Okinawa, and moved 500 Marines with helicopters into Thailand a short distance from the Laotian capital. Then the Bay of Pigs disaster struck. Fearing to appear weak with one arm tied down in Cuba, Kennedy flexed the other in Laos. The President instructed the several hundred American military advisers in Laos, heretofore involved in covert operations, to discard their civilian clothes and dress in more ostentatious military uniforms as a symbol of American resolve. The Soviets wanted no fight in Laos. In April, 1961 they endorsed Kennedy's appeal for a cease-fire. But the Soviets were unable to control the independent-minded Pathet Lao, who battled on. Kennedy asked the joint chiefs of staff if an American military expedition could succeed. The military experts demurred. However, "if we are given the right to use nuclear weapons," remarked JCS Chairman General Lyman L. Lemnitzer, "we can guarantee victory."[109] Somebody in the room incredulously suggested the President ask the general what he meant by "victory." Kennedy adjourned the meeting, wondering what to do.

The answer came in Geneva, where a conference on Laos began in May, 1961. Although it took deft diplomatic pressure from W. Averell Harriman, continued bloodshed in Laos, and hard bargaining lasting until June, 1962, the major powers did sign a Laotian agreement. Laos would be neutral; it could not enter military alliances or permit foreign military bases on its soil. Souvanna Phouma headed the new government. Bernard Fall, veteran observer of Southeast Asia, measured the results of the United States involvement in Laos by looking at the difference between the neutralist government of the 1950s that the United States had subverted and that of 1962: "Instead of two communists in Cabinet positions, there would be four now; instead of having to deal with 1,500 poorly armed Pathet Lao fighters, there were close to 10,000 now well-armed with new Soviet weapons."[110] Still, peace did not come to that ravaged land. In late 1962, in clear violation of the agreement it had just signed, Washington secretly began arms shipments to Souvanna's government, which increasingly turned to the right. The pretext was the presence of small numbers of North Vietnamese soldiers in the north, but it seems evident that Washington had not given up its goal of building a sturdy pro-American outpost in Indochina. Unbeknownst to the American people, the United States began in 1964 secret bombing raids against Pathet Lao forces, after a right-wing coup had diminished Souvanna's authority. By then Laos' major problem was that it lay too close to Vietnam, where American intervention had also escalated under Kennedy.

"This is the worst one we've got, isn't it," Kennedy asked Rostow. "You know, Eisenhower never mentioned it. He talked at length about Laos, but never uttered the word Vietnam."[111] For the next decade Vietnam would indeed become America's "worst one." Some Kennedy watchers have suggested that his intervention in Vietnam and his bold action in the Cuban missile crisis stemmed from his reaction to the criticism of the joint chiefs of staff and such hawks as columnist Joseph Alsop that he had weakened over Laos, and that, in turn, his success in the missile episode further emboldened him in Vietnam. Whatever the relationship of events, Kennedy shared America's antirevolutionary and expansionist attitudes. Early in his Administration he decided to apply counterinsurgency methods in Vietnam to gain a triumph over communism. Washington soon kept a "box score" on counterinsurgency efforts. Vietnam was beset by a nasty civil war between the National Liberation Front and the Diem regime. The Kennedy advisers considered the conservative, vain Premier Ngo Dinh Diem a liability, but as Vice-President Lyndon B. Johnson put it privately—after having publicly annointed Diem the Winston Churchill of Asia—"Sh--, man, he's the only boy we got out there."[112]

Kennedy was cautious about Vietnam, hardly wanting to tie American fate to a faltering Diem or to tread the disastrous path already traveled by the French. He said he did not want to launch a white man's war in Asia and that Asians had to fight their own battles. But because he accepted the "domino theory," interpreted all Communists as part of an international conspiracy, thought that China lay behind the Vietnamese turmoil, and believed that "nation building" promised success, he expanded the American presence. "We have a very simple policy in Vietnam," Kennedy told a news conference in September, 1963. "We want the war to be won, the Communists to be contained, and the Americans to go home."[113] Asked that year if he would reduce aid to South Vietnam, the President replied that he would not. "Strongly in our mind is what happened in the case of China at the end of World War II, where China was lost. . . . We don't want that."[114] In January, 1961, Kennedy authorized $28.4 million to enlarge the South Vietnamese army and another $12.7 million to improve the civil guard. In May he sent Vice-President Johnson to Saigon. That veteran Texas politician stated the problem in extreme terms: either "help these countries . . . or throw in the towel in the area and pull back our defenses to San Francisco and a 'Fortress America.'"[115] That month Kennedy also ordered 400 Special Forces soldiers and another 100 military "advisers" to South Vietnam. Meanwhile the Viet Cong captured more territory and accelerated the violence through a bloody campaign of assassinations of village chiefs. In October a United States intelligence report indicated that 80–90 percent of the 17,000 Viet Cong in South Vietnam were recruited in the South, and hence were not from North Vietnam, and that most of their supplies were also Southern. Although this estimate exploded the theory of advisers like Walt Rostow that the Vietnamese crisis was a case of aggression by North Vietnam, the report apparently made only a slight impact on Kennedy.

The President was, however, troubled by conflicting viewpoints, so in October he dispatched two hawks, General Maxwell Taylor and Walt Rostow, to South Vietnam to study the war firsthand. Diem naturally asked for more American military aid, and when Taylor returned to Washington he urged the President to send American combat troops. Rusk questioned such advice, arguing that Diem must first reform his conservative government; and the intelligence agencies suggested that sending such military assistance would likely arouse a North Vietnamese counterresponse. McNamara and the joint chiefs of staff supported Taylor and Rostow. Conscious that his decision violated the Geneva Accords but unwilling to say so publicly, Kennedy authorized in November a large increase in American forces or "advisers" in South Vietnam. By the end of 1961 there were 3,205; at the start of the year the figure had been about 900. During 1962 the figure jumped to 9,000, and at the time of Kennedy's death in November, 1963 the number had reached 16,700. American troops, helicopter units, minesweepers, and air reconnaisance aircraft went into action. In 1962, 109 Americans died and in 1963, 489. A "strategic hamlet" program was initiated to fortify villages and isolate them from Viet Cong influence. This population control through barbed wire, however, proved disruptive and unpopular with villagers and permitted the Viet Cong to appear as Robin Hoods. Then, too, many of the American weapons actually ended up in Viet Cong hands. From New Delhi, a doubting Ambassador John Kenneth Galbraith asked the President a telling question: "Incidentally, who is the man in your administration who decides what countries are strategic? I would like to have his name and address and ask him what is so important about this real estate in the space age. What strength do we gain from alliance with an incompetent government and a people who are largely indifferent to their own salvation?"[116] To allay such questioning, the Administration issued optimistic statements. In February of 1963 Rusk announced that the "momentum of the Communist drive has been stopped."[117]

In May, 1963 the difficulties of "nation building" were exposed when South Vietnamese troops attacked protesting and unarmed Buddhists in Hué, massacring nine. The incident erupted after Diem, a Catholic, had banned the flying of

A Suicide in Protest, Saigon. Quang Duc, a Buddhist monk aged seventy-three, set his gasoline-drenched yellow robes afire in June, 1963, at a main intersection in Saigon to protest Diem's restrictions on Buddhists. (Wide World Photos)

Buddhist flags. Vietnam was a nominally Buddhist country governed by Catholics; the remnants of French colonialism were evidenced in various privileges, including education, for Catholics. Although the Buddhist demonstrations were a vehicle for the expression of long-standing nationalist sentiments, Diem soon equated Buddhism with communism. The Viet Cong were actually as surprised as Diem with the Buddhist uprising. On June 10 a Buddhist monk sat in a Saigon street, poured fuel over his body, and immolated himself. The appalling sight led Diem's callous sister-in-law Madame Nhu to chortle about "Buddhist barbecues." During the late summer and fall the protest spread; so did Diem's military tactics, including an attack upon Hué's pagoda. Also, thousands of students were arrested, including the children of many of Diem's own civil and military officers. Kennedy publicly chastised Diem and exerted pressure by reducing aid. Senior South Vietnamese generals, now aware that Diem was no longer in American favor, asked American officials how they would respond to a coup d'état. The new Ambassador, Henry Cabot Lodge, unsuccessful Republican vice-presidential candidate in 1960, was ready to dump Diem in order to get on with the war, but officials in Washington were divided. McNamara sent a new study mission. Marine General Victor H. Krulak and State Department officer Joseph Mendenhall took a hurried tour; Krulak reported that the war was going well despite the Buddhist squabble, and Mendenhall argued that the Vietnamese were more displeased with Diem than with the Viet Cong. A puzzled Kennedy asked: "You two did visit the same country, didn't you?"[118]

Washington continued cool relations with Diem, who proved more and more resistant to American advice. In early October the Vietnamese generals informed the CIA that they were going to overthrow the recalcitrant premier. Lodge did not discourage them from the undertaking, a signal the generals fully appreciated. The White House was less eager than Lodge for the coup, fearing a failure. On November 1 the generals surrounded the Saigon palace with troops, took Diem prisoner, and murdered him. The assassination shocked Kennedy. "I had not seen him so depressed since the Bay of Pigs," Schlesinger recalled.[119] A few weeks later, on November 22, Kennedy himself was assassinated in Dallas. Some observers have suggested that after the presidential election of 1964, when he no longer suffered political vulnerability and was less fearful of right-wing charges of softness on communism, Kennedy would have withdrawn from Vietnam. We can never know for sure. We know only what he *did* for his 1,000 days in office.

The Kennedy legacy defies easy analysis. The "ifs" persist. Kennedy's apologists have asked historians to judge him not so much by his accomplishments, admittedly less than sterling, but rather by his intentions, for, they have argued, had he not been removed from his appointed journey so tragically in 1963, his good intentions would have reached fruition. Others have recommended that students ignore Kennedy's inflated and monolithic Cold War rhetoric, because it was mere political verbiage. Also, there were ambiguities in his actions. He sent soldiers to Vietnam to wage war and Peace Corps volunteers to Latin America to grow food; he combined a compassionate idealism with traditional anti-Communist fervor; he had serious doubts about the escalation of the Cold War and military intervention in the Third World, yet he escalated and intervened. In June, 1963, in a high-minded speech at American University, the President expressed his uneasiness with large weapons expenditures, called for a re-examination of American Cold War attitudes, suggested that conflict with Russia was not inevitable, and appealed

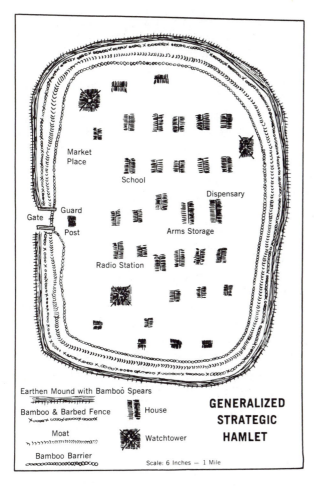

Strategic Hamlet, South Vietnam. Introduced by the Diem regime in 1962, inspired by British counterinsurgency expert Sir Robert Thompson (based upon his experience in Malaya and the Philippines), and funded by the United States, the strategic hamlet program was designed to separate the Viet Cong from their support among the South Vietnamese people. Peasants were moved from ancestral lands, issued identification cards, and required to live in guarded quarters surrounded by barbed wire and bamboo spears. Actually, many of the 6,000 hamlets were poorly managed and defended, alienating the very people the Saigon government was trying to win over. (Courtesy of M. W. Dow, from M. W. Dow, *Nation Building in Southeast Asia.* Boulder, Colorado: Pruett Press, 1966; rev. ed.)

for disarmament. Still, as George F. Kennan has noted, "one speech is not enough."[120] Nor was Kennedy willing to reverse the nonrecognition policy toward China or restore the standing of the "China hands" so maligned by Dulles and McCarthy in the early 1950s. The Sino-Soviet split did not impress him: "A dispute over how to bury the West is no ground for Western rejoicing."[121]

The ambitious "nation-building" thrust proved faulty, in large part because it was so interventionist in the affairs of other peoples. In trying to be the "world's social worker," wrote critic John McDermott, the United States practiced "welfare imperialism."[122] The nation-building concept did not pay proper attention to complexities—the multitude of indigenous forces, the varied traditions of other cultures, the entrenched position of native elites, and the persuasive appeals of the insurgent left. Americans discovered in the 1960s that economic growth and democracy did not necessarily go hand in hand, that a middle class could be selfish (if one existed at all), that some nations had no tradition of liberal politics, that not all insurgencies are Communist, and that rebels, closer to their nation's pulse, believe deeply in their cause. The nation-building concept also overestimated America's power to shape other nations. It assumed that soldiers from Connecticut, Iowa, North Carolina, and California could manage "natives" abroad, much as they had done in the Philippines or in Latin America through much of the twentieth century. Unable to force reform on others, Americans often violated their principles by supporting the elite or military or by trying to topple regimes. The concept assumed too that the United States had an obligation to cope with insurgencies everywhere. It made few distinctions between key and peripheral areas. It did not define the "threat" carefully. It tried to do too much; it was globalism gone rampant. The concept, furthermore, possessed a procapitalist, private-enterprise bias, while in the Third World, "private" development was traditionally identified with imperialist exploitation and hence was unpopular.

The Kennedy foreign policy did not assess the strain that would be placed on America's resources and endurance in its long-term global role as policeman, teacher, and social worker. In other words, the Kennedy team tended to take for granted the American people and the constitutional system, including congressional prerogatives in policymaking, as they centralized foreign policy in the White House. Overall, then, the revered, clinical concepts of the Kennedy Administration came up against a host of realities at home and abroad. The Administration often neglected diplomacy, sometimes turning to it only after inflaming crises through military responses. The Kennedy team was reluctant to do little or nothing, or to get out of the way of the profound, even inexorable, movement toward national liberation in the Third World. Several years after Kennedy's death, the *Wall Street Journal* reflected on the diplomatic record of the Kennedy years: "too much vigor and too little restraint, too much grace and too little earthiness, too much eloquence and too little thoughtfulness . . . , too much flexibility and too little patience, too much brilliance and too little common sense."[123]

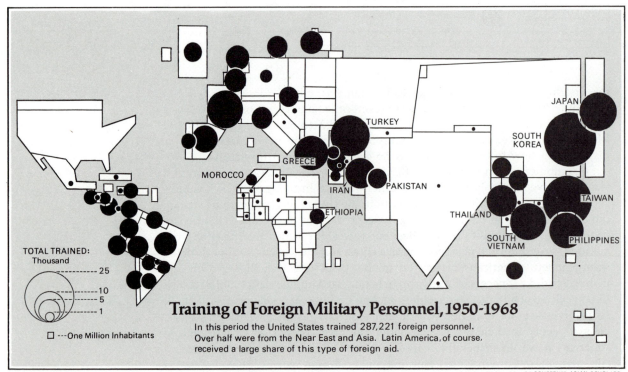

Training of Foreign Military Personnel, 1950-1968

In this period the United States trained 287,221 foreign personnel.
Over half were from the Near East and Asia. Latin America, of course,
received a large share of this type of foreign aid.

TOTAL TRAINED:
Thousand
25
10
5
1

□ ---One Million Inhabitants

Lyndon B. Johnson (1908–1973) and Hubert H. Humphrey (1911–1978). Vice-President Hubert H. Humphrey of Minnesota does as the Texan does on the LBJ Ranch, 1964. Elected to the Senate in 1949, Humphrey was noted for civil rights and social reform legislation before he joined Johnson on the 1964 Democratic ticket. In 1968, troubled by the tragedy in Vietnam, he ran for the presidency against Richard M. Nixon, but lost a close election. (Lyndon B. Johnson Library. Photo by Staughton)

No More Munichs, No More Cubas: The Foreign Policy of Lyndon B. Johnson

The presidential transition from John F. Kennedy to Lyndon B. Johnson (LBJ) was smooth. Johnson kept on many of Kennedy's foreign policy advisers. McNamara stayed until early 1968; Rusk remained until the end; when McGeorge Bundy stepped down in 1966 as adviser on national security affairs, Walt Rostow left the State Department to take on that assignment and to become one of LBJ's most ardent supporters. Others resigned. If Johnson lacked Kennedy's zeal for "nation building," he had his own brand of international reform, derived from a sensitivity to the ugliness of poverty. Influenced by his New Deal reform years, he talked about building Tennessee Valley Authorities abroad. "I want to leave the footprints of America there [Vietnam]. I want them to say, 'This is what the Americans left—schools and hospitals and dams. . . .' We can turn the Mekong [River area] into a Tennessee Valley."[124] He shared the Cold War assumptions of most Americans, repeatedly citing the "lessons" of Munich, Greece, China, and Korea, and adding some Texas history of his own. "Just like the Alamo," Johnson remarked about Vietnam, "somebody damn well needed to go to their aid."[125]

Johnson was a political maestro from the poor, dusty hill territory of Texas between Fort Worth and San Antonio. "It is unrelenting country," his gracious and well-respected wife Lady Bird commented, "and Lyndon is unrelenting, too."[126] In explaining his energy, an aide said Johnson had "extra glands."[127] He gulped his meals and drove his Lincoln Continental at breakneck speed over his Texas ranch, wildly dodging cattle. An incessant talker, he usually talked about himself and his triumphs. He was cocky, moody, and persuasive. "When you got the Johnson treatment," remarked Benjamin Bradlee of the *Washington Post,* "you really felt as if a St. Bernard had licked your face for an hour, had pawed you all over."[128] LBJ raged and exaggerated. Critics became "rattlebrains" and "Nervous Nellies" and Vietnam a "raggedy-ass fourth-rate country."[129] And: "[If] we don't stop the Reds in South Vietnam, tomorrow they will be in Hawaii, and next they will be in San Francisco."[130] And he once said about the Organization of American States: "It couldn't pour piss out of a boot if the instructions were written on the heel."[131] A "credibility gap" dogged his Administration, not so much because he told barefaced lies, but because he embellished the actual record with exaggerations and trite analogies in a drawl that sometimes made him appear to be stupid. He was not. His mind was quick and retentive, although very much a captive of the past. "He is purely and aggressively American"—a British journalist claimed— "the first uninhibited product of the American frontier to take over since Andrew Jackson."[132]

Johnson's foreign policy was marked by military responses, hurried decisions, spread-eagle patriotism, hyperbolic rhetoric, overreaction, stubbornness, and intolerance for dissenting views. He seemed to thrive on crises, those times when, as he put it, he was "like a jackrabbit hunkered up in a storm."[133] The many crises were not due solely to the Texan's style or personality, however. A general international phenomenon that caused a slippage of American authority—the diffusion of world power—helps explain the tumult of the 1960s. That is, in that decade blocs were breaking up, NATO members were demanding more independence from Washington, and the Third World, on the rise since the decade before, commanded more autonomy in world affairs. In responding to these changes, the United States clung to the past, still thinking that Uncle Sam could direct events through the exertion of arms and aid. The articulate Chairman of the Senate Foreign Relations Committee, J. William Fulbright of Arkansas, thought Americans suffered under an "arrogance of power" that left the United States by the end of the 1960s a "crippled giant."[134]

During Johnson's five years in office Vietnam consumed his energies, his ambitions, his reputation. He left relations with Russia and China much as he had found them—calmer after the Cuban Missile Crisis, but still strained and based upon military competition. He met with Soviet Premier Aleksei Kosygin in Glassboro, New Jersey in 1967, but the proclaimed "spirit of Glassboro" proved superficial. That year the Johnson Administration asked Congress for the construction of a controversial antiballistic missile system (ABM), a new set of "defensive" weapons to maintain a posture of massive retaliation or deterrence, not just against Russia but against the nuclear-armed Chinese as well. The Soviets already had a limited ABM system and American generals wanted one too. They argued that the United States would not be able to knock Soviet missiles out in wartime, leaving Americans vulnerable to attack; and, because by the late 1960s the Soviets had achieved near nuclear parity with the United States, the Pentagon called again for nuclear superiority. The heated debate over further enlargement of the arms race via the ABM was still fuming when Johnson left office (see Chapter 15). Steps toward arms control were timid, although Russia, America, and over fifty other nations signed a nuclear nonproliferation treaty in 1968 (ratified in 1969), a pledge not to spread nuclear weapons to other nations. Unfortunately neither France nor China agreed, and the menacing nuclear weapons still stood in the United States, Great Britain, and Russia. Nonsigner India joined the elite nuclear weapons circle in 1974, demonstrating again the diffusion of power.

In Latin America, smoldering nationalism, the frequency of military coups, and Castro's irritating survival helped define Johnson's policies, which smacked of Roosevelt's Big Stick. Johnson put Assistant Secretary of State Thomas C. Mann in charge of the Alliance for Progress and it soon withered away from neglect. Mann also issued his "Mann Doctrine," a simple declaration that the United States was more interested in supporting anti-Communist governments through economic assistance than in opposing military regimes—a negation of Kennedy's fading hope that democracy would accompany economic growth. In 1964 Washington supported a right-wing military takeover in Brazil, and when Panamanians rioted against American control of the Canal Zone, Johnson employed strong language in telling the President of Panama that the United States would not tolerate insults to the American flag. In 1965, fearing another Cuba, Johnson sent more than 20,000 American soldiers into the Dominican Republic. The trouble had started when, in late 1962, after the assassination of dictator Rafael Trujillo the year before, radical reformer Juan Bosch was elected President of the economically depressed Caribbean country. Ten months later a military coup ousted him. But in April, 1965, pro-Bosch rebels launched a new civil war against the military regime. Johnson and his advisers, with trigger-finger quickness and with very fragmentary evidence, assumed that the revolt was Communist or "Castroite" or nearly so. They ordered an American invasion. "This was a democratic revolution smashed by the leading democracy of the world," a chagrined Bosch declared.[135]

The President also took the opportunity to declare the "Johnson Doctrine." Henceforth, he announced, the United States would unilaterally prevent any Communist government from taking office in the hemisphere, would insist on peaceful change, and would defend "free" nations. Thus, while the United States positioned troops around the globe to prevent others from establishing spheres of influence, it attempted to maintain its own traditional sphere in Latin America. (In 1968, after the Soviets had ruthlessly invaded rebellious Czechoslovakia, the Kremlin issued rationalizations which sounded much like those of Johnson in 1965.) The American inability to distinguish between nationalism and communism, critics noted, meant that the United States was forfeiting the support of leftist reformers in the Third World. As Senator Fulbright, who opposed the Dominican venture, complained: "we have made ourselves the prisoners of the Latin American oligarchs who are engaged in a vain attempt to preserve the status quo—reactionaries who habitually use the term communist very loosely, in part . . . in a calculated effort to scare the United States into supporting their selfish and discredited aims."[136] As for the exaggerated Communist threat in Latin America, the words of a familiar verse seemed to fit:

> As I was going up the stair,
> I met a man who wasn't there.
> He wasn't there again today.
> I wish to God he'd go away!

"Now I am the most denounced man in the world," Johnson stated publicly after the Dominican intervention.[137] An abundance of anti-Americanism, with the President singled out as an impulsive Texan, did flash across the world. But the criticism was directed more against American actions in Vietnam than against those in Latin America. Soon after Diem's death, the National Liberation Front, Secretary General U Thant of the United Nations, France, and many concerned Americans called for a coalition government in Saigon and neutralism or neutralization. It seemed a propitious time for negotiations. Yet President Johnson announced in December, 1963, that the United States sought "victory," because the "neutralization of South Vietnam would only be another name for a Communist take-over."[138] In February, 1964, the American-advised South Vietnamese began covert commando raids and sabotage missions into North Vietnam. Air strikes hit Laos, through which some supplies flowed south. Still, the war did not go well for the American-backed Saigon regime. By April the Viet Cong controlled 42 percent of the villages, compared with 34 percent for the Saigon government; 24 percent were classified "neutral." During the 1964 presidential campaign, Republican candidate Barry Goldwater urged an attack upon Ho Chi Minh's North Vietnam to reverse the trend, an idea already expressed in Saigon by Prime Minister (and General) Nguyen Khanh and endorsed by Walt Rostow and General Maxwell Taylor inside Washington. Johnson, however, chided Goldwater for dangerous warmongering and pledged he would not send American boys to fight in Vietnam.

On August 4, 1964, in the dark of evening, the United States destroyers *Maddox* and *C. Turner Joy* apparently tangled with some North Vietnamese torpedo boats in the Gulf of Tonkin. Although the alleged offenders fled and neither American ship endured damage, the Johnson Administration exploited the issue to enlarge the war. That very night, the President went on television to announce retaliatory air strikes against North Vietnamese targets, including a major oil depot near Vinh. "The challenge that we face in Southeast Asia today is the same challenge that we have faced with courage and that we have met with strength in Greece and Turkey, in Berlin and Korea, in Lebanon and in Cuba," Johnson said the next day when he sent a resolution to Congress.[139] The "Tonkin Gulf Resolution" passed on August 7 without much debate and by huge margins, 466–0 in the House and 88–2 in the Senate. Only Senators Ernest Gruening of Alaska and Wayne Morse of Oregon dissented. The resolution authorized the President to "take all necessary measures to repel any armed attack against the forces of the United States and to prevent further aggression."[140] This open-ended language placed considerable warmaking power in the hands of the President. For Johnson, the resolution "was like Grandma's nightshirt—it covered everything."[141] Belatedly regretting in 1970 this concession to the "imperial presidency," the Senate repealed it.[142]

Controversy surrounds the Tonkin Gulf incident. For example, North Vietnam admitted attacking the *Maddox* on August 2, but not 4, in retaliation for the *Maddox*'s participation in offensive actions against North Vietnam. The *Maddox* itself may or may not have been directly involved in these forays, but it plied waters recently frequented by South Vietnamese raiders attacking North Vietnamese islands. At one point the *Maddox* had ventured within four miles of the targeted islands. The August 2 attack on the *Maddox* was a serious one in which two torpedoes were fired at the American ship. Hanoi claimed there was no attack whatsoever two days later. The best that can be gleaned from the contradictory evidence is that the captain of the *Maddox* thought he had been attacked that cloudy night of August 4. Uncertainty or not, Johnson reacted quickly. The war in Vietnam was on its way to becoming Americanized.

After the Tonkin Gulf affair, American officials drew up plans for bombing raids on North Vietnam, and after Johnson's overwhelming victory in the November elections, those plans took on importance. In early December Johnson approved in principle bombing raids against North Vietnam and stepped-up bombing of Laos. The American people were not informed of this critical shift in warmaking, but they did watch with growing apprehension the political instability in Saigon, where generals vied for political power and the Buddhists marched for a negotiated peace and neutralism. On February 7, 1965, after a Viet Cong attack upon the American airfield at Pleiku in which nine Americans died, Johnson ordered retaliatory air strikes against North Vietnam. Within hours of the decision of February 7, forty-nine carrier-based American jets dropped bombs above the seventeenth parallel. By March the United States had undertaken a sustained bombing program—"Operation Rolling Thunder." Johnson argued that escalated violence was necessary to protect the American soldiers already there. The very American presence, it now seemed, justified a larger American presence. Uncle Sam, charged some critics, was moving step by step into a quagmire. Johnson had never gone to Congress for a declaration of war, but the President had no doubts about the containment of international communism dating from the 1940s: "Let no one think for a moment that retreat from Viet-Nam would bring an end to conflict. The battle would be renewed in one country and then another. . . . We must say in Southeast Asia—as we did in Europe—in the words of the Bible: 'Hitherto shalt thou come, but no further.'"[143]

With the argument that he had to provide security for Americans in South Vietnam, Johnson also moved more and more ground troops into that troubled land, sending them first to Da Nang, a large American air base. By the end of 1965, United States forces in South Vietnam numbered 184,314; a year later they totaled 385,000. "I don't want to save my face, I just want to save my ass," Johnson was reported to have said as proof of his desire to avoid a large Asian war. A doubter asked: "Does he conceive of that portion of himself as extending all the way to Southeast Asia?"[144] In 1966 American bombers hit oil depots in the North, and by midyear 70 percent of the North's storage capacity had been destroyed. Predictably, Hanoi increased its flow of arms and men into the South, the heavy bombing apparently having had little impact in undercutting either the Viet Cong and North Vietnamese commitment or their ability to resist. During 1965–1968 the United States lost six billion dollars worth of aircraft, or 800 planes, over North Vietnam. General William Westmoreland kept asking for more troops, and Johnson grew restless about the escalation. "When we add divisions, can't the enemy add divisions?" he asked in April, 1967. "If so, where does it all end?"[145] Yet the President approved more. By the start of 1968 American forces totaled 535,000. The peak level of 542,000 was reached in February, 1969. "I deeply believe we *are* quarantining aggressors over there," Johnson remarked, "just like the smallpox." Citing simple historical precedent, he went on: "Just like FDR and Hitler, just like Wilson and the Kaiser. . . . What I learned as a boy in my teens and in college about World War I was that it was our lack of strength and failure to show stamina

Wayne L. Morse (1900–1974). An independent-minded maverick politician from Oregon, Morse was one of only two senators to vote against the Tonkin Gulf Resolution of 1964. An early critic of American intervention in Vietnam and an impassioned orator, Senator Morse was never afraid to ask a bold question or to state pro-vocative opinions. He served in the Senate from 1945 to 1969 and sat on the Foreign Relations Committee. (*The Reporter,* 1956. Copyright 1956 by The Reporter Magazine Co.)

Flight to Safety in South Vietnam.
With bombs about to rain from American aircraft on their village of Qui Nhon, which apparently harbored Viet Cong snipers, this family flees across a river. Kyoichi Sawada won a Pulitzer Prize for this photograph of 1965. (United Press International, photo by Kyoichi Sawada)

that got us into that war." For Johnson, history was repeating itself; once again "aggression" would be stopped.[146]

In this period of escalation, 1965–1968, the bloodshed and dislocation were awesome. In "search and destroy" missions under a strategy of "attrition," American and South Vietnamese forces bombed and destroyed villages that harbored suspected Viet Cong, the "Charlie." Tens of thousands of civilians died, many from fiery napalm attacks. "It gets completely impersonal," explained an American air officer. "After you've done it for a while you forget that there are people down there."[147] Refugees grew in number as "pacification" camps became overcrowded. By the end of 1967, as many as four million people, or 25 percent of the population, were refugees. The United States and Saigon, according to two students of the Vietnamese war, "were building up large islands of hostile peasants," some of whom turned sympathetically toward the Viet Cong.[148] To deny the enemy food and to expose hideouts, American defoliation teams sprayed millions of pounds of chemicals like Agent Orange on crops and forests, denuding the landscape and inadvertently exposing nearby GIs to the poison. In Saigon, the regimes of General Nguyen Cao Ky and Nguyen Van Thieu had jailed 20,000 political critics by 1968. Americans alone did not inflict this nightmare upon South Vietnam, for the Viet Cong and North Vietnamese were shooting back, but it was the overwhelming American fire power and clearing operations that inflicted this horror,

Viet Cong Tunnel. One of the reasons for the frustration of American efforts to defeat the elusive Viet Cong is illustrated in this United States Army depiction of a "typical" VC tunnel. Living off the land and under it, the black-clad guerrillas defied superior American military power. (U.S. Army)

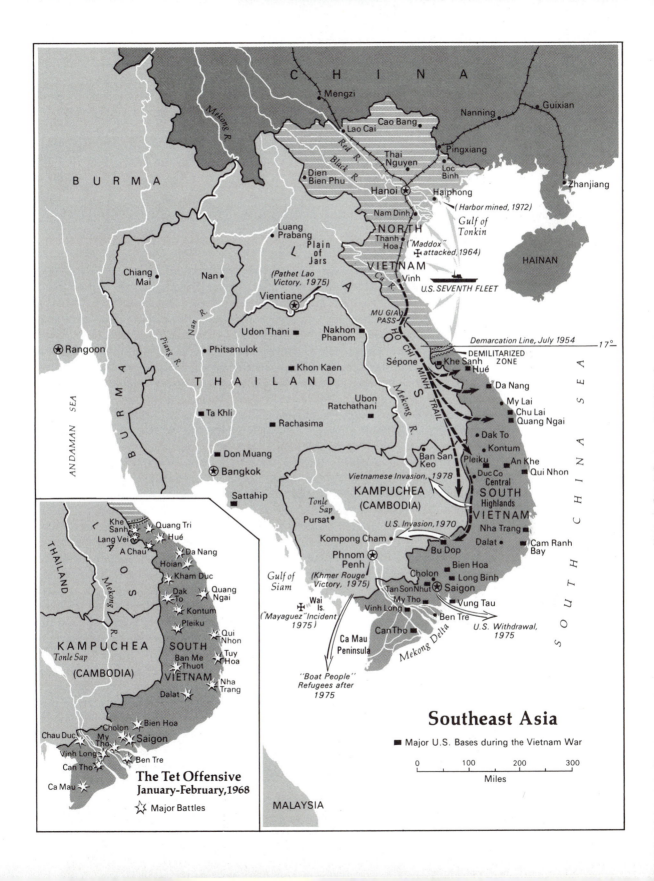

CHINA

Mengzi

Nanning
Guixian

Cao Bang

Lao Cai

Thai
Nguyen

Pingxiang

Loc
Binh

Dien
Bien Phu

Hanoi ✪

Haiphong

Zhanjiang

Red R.

Black R.

Nam Dinh

(Harbor mined, 1972)

BURMA

Luang
Prabang

Plain
of
Jars

NORTH

Thanh
Hoa

Gulf of
Tonkin

"Maddox"
✝ attacked, 1964)

HAINAN

Chiang
Mai

Nan

(Pathet Lao
Victory, 1975)

Vientiane ✪

VIETNAM

Ca R.

Vinh

U.S. SEVENTH FLEET

L

Nan R.

Udon Thani

Nakhon
Phanom

MU GIA
PASS

Demarcation Line, July 1954

17°

A

DEMILITARIZED
ZONE

Phitsanulok

Sépone

Khe Sanh

Plang R.

Khon Kaen

THAILAND

Hué

Da Nang

My Lai
Chu Lai
Quang Ngai

H

Ubon
Ratchathani

Ta Khli

Rachasima

O

Mekong R.

C

Dak To
Kontum

H

I

M

Don Muang

Ban San
Keo

Pleiku

An Khe
Qui Nhon

Bangkok ✪

I

N

Duc Co

Central

H

SOUTH

Highlands

Sattahip

Tonle
Sap

Vietnamese Invasion, 1978

KAMPUCHEA
(CAMBODIA)

Pursat

T

R

A

I

L

VIETNAM

Nha Trang

Dalat

Cam Ranh
Bay

ANDAMAN SEA

U.S. Invasion, 1970

Kompong Cham

Bu Dop

Bien Hoa

Long Binh

SOUTH CHINA SEA

Phnom
Penh ✪

(Khmer Rouge
Victory, 1975)

Gulf of
Siam

Cholon

Tan Son Nhut

Saigon ✪

Long Xuyen

Vung Tau

✝ Wai
Is.
("Mayaguez"
Incident
1975)

Vinh Long

My Tho

Ben Tre

U.S. Withdrawal,
1975

Ca Mau
Peninsula

Can Tho

Mekong Delta

"Boat People"
Refugees after
1975

Southeast Asia

■ Major U.S. Bases during the Vietnam War

0   100   200   300
Miles

The Tet Offensive
January-February, 1968

☆ Major Battles

Khe
Sanh

Quang Tri
Hué

Lang Vei

A Chau

Da Nang

Hoian

THAILAND

LAOS

Kham Duc

Quang
Ngai

Dak
To

Kontum

Mekong R.

Pleiku

Qui Nhon

KAMPUCHEA

Tonle Sap

(CAMBODIA)

SOUTH

Ban Me
Thuot

Tuy
Hoa

VIETNAM

Nha
Trang

Dalat

Cholon

Bien Hoa

Chau Duc

My
Tho

Saigon

Vinh Long

Ben Tre

Can Tho

Ca Mau

MALAYSIA

much of it televised into American homes every evening. In the period 1965–1973 American aircraft dropped bombs in Indochina amounting to three times the explosives used in World War II. To many Americans, massacres like that at My Lai on March 16, 1968, where an American Army platoon commanded by Lieutenant William Calley shot to death scores of helpless women and children, or "gooks," represented a depravity unbecoming a civilized nation. As was so often true of the official manipulation of news and the military's coverup of unfavorable reports, the story of the My Lai massacre did not become public until twenty months later.

Political Dissent and Peace Efforts: Shedding the Burden

As the war escalated, critics in the United States became more outspoken. Students and faculty at universities began to hold "teach-ins" in 1965, beginning with the University of Michigan in March. Hundreds refused military draft calls and went to jail or fled to Canada. The protest songs of Bob Dylan and Joan Baez inspired rallies. Many protested the expenditure of billions of dollars in Vietnam when social maladjustments at home begged for attention. Johnson tried a "guns-and-butter" approach in the 1960s, but more and more was spent on guns for Vietnam and his reformist "Great Society" programs suffered. The liberal-minded National Student Association, secretly funded by the CIA, was upstaged by the radical Students for a Democratic Society (SDS). Representatives of major corporations, such as Dow Chemical, a maker of napalm, were beset by sit-ins when they attempted to recruit employees on campus. In early 1967, 300,000 demonstrators marched in New York City and in November 100,000 surrounded the Pentagon. They were often vitriolic and impolite, shouting down prowar speakers or government spokesmen with "Hey, hey, LBJ, how many kids did you kill today?"

More reserved, prominent intellectuals, like linguist Noam Chomsky, political scientist Hans Morgenthau, Jr., and a disaffected Arthur M. Schlesinger, Jr., called for withdrawal from Vietnam. Businessmen, lawyers, and clergymen, too, organized into antiwar groups. Widely watched television commentators like CBS's Walter Cronkite increasingly editorialized the evening news with an antiwar bias. The critics' arguments were multifaceted: the war cost too much and weakened needed reform at home; America's youth was dying—30,000 by 1968; inflation and a worsening balance of payments were weakening the economy; the ghastly bloodshed was immoral; the war damaged relations with allies and foes alike; the war could not be won; the President was usurping power and undermining the constitutional system of checks and balances; and domestic America was being ripped apart by dissension. Widely respected historian Henry Steele Commager placed the Vietnamese revolt in a larger context when he told a Senate committee that the rebellion "is against two or three hundreds of years of exploitation and of imperialism. . . . And by what seems to me a most unfair, but perfectly understandable process, a great many of the antagonisms against the European West are focused on us."[149] America had stepped into a traditional struggle over which it could not exert control. Above all else, the critics argued, the United States had succumbed to a debilitating globalism of anticommunism, overcommitment, and overextension. In short, some critics complained about how the war was being conducted, whereas others, more searching, criticized globalism itself.

Harvard Strike, 1969. The clenched fist and V-shaped fingers became symbols of the antiwar movement. (*Old Mole,* 1969, University of Connecticut Library)

The growing public disaffection with the war encouraged dissenters in the House and Senate. Senator J. William Fulbright and some of his colleagues had had lingering doubts about the Tonkin Gulf Resolution. Fulbright decided in 1965 that America was "losing its perspective on what exactly is within the realm of its power and what is beyond it."[150] In February, 1966 his Senate Foreign Relations Committee conducted publicly televised hearings. Administration spokesmen defended the war, citing the traditional need to contain communism. Critical senators, however, kept asking what it was the United States was containing in Vietnam. The Soviet Union? China? North Vietnam? The Viet Cong? Wars of national liberation? Communism? Revolution? It was a frustrating set of possibilities. Secretary Rusk settled on China as the main culprit, especially after Chinese leader Lin Piao declared in 1965 that China would encourage wars of national liberation in the Third World. American leaders interpreted this, incorrectly, to mean that China would initiate them. "It is on this spot," as Rostow once asserted, "that we have to break the liberation war—Chinese type. If we don't break it here we shall have to face it again in Thailand, Venezuela, elsewhere. Vietnam is a clear testing ground for our policy in the world."[151] Although China was North Vietnam's chief supplier of arms until the mid-1960s, the Soviet Union took over that costly role in an attempt to match American armaments and curry favor in Hanoi. Generally overlooked in the search to find the enemy was the fundamental fact that the conflict in South Vietnam grew from indigenous roots—that it was a civil war. The important Fulbright hearings touched on that fact, but the surprise testimony came from the poised and persuasive figure of George F. Kennan. The father of containment insisted that the containment doctrine, designed for a stable

Antiwar Newsletter. Although college students seemed to predominate in antiwar marches like this one in the 1960s, opinion polls revealed that in the nation as a whole, people under 35 supported the war more than did people over 35. Women more than men of all ages opposed escalation and advocated withdrawal. Not until 1970 did a majority of Americans favor a pullout from Vietnam. (University of Connecticut Library)

European nation-state context in the 1940s, was not applicable in Asia. Facile analogies with the 1940s did not face the new realities of the 1960s. He urged a gradual withdrawal from Vietnam. So did Senator Eugene McCarthy of Minnesota, who declared in late 1967 that he would attempt to unseat President Johnson for the 1968 Democratic nomination.

The Johnson Administration lashed back at this apparent defection from the Cold War consensus, citing polls showing that most Americans would not tolerate a Viet Cong victory. Yet doubters grew within its own ranks. "Increasingly," observed Johnson adviser and Princeton historian Eric F. Goldman, "he was seeing himself as the lonely, traduced figure limned against history resolutely doing right, grimly awaiting the verdict of the future."[152] Rostow tried to reassure Johnson with statistical charts showing the "enemy's" heavy loss of life and property, but overarching reality could not be ignored: the United States, with a gross national product 325 times as great as that of North Vietnam, the United States, the most heavily industrialized, most militarily powerful, richest nation on earth, could not subdue rural Vietnam. Nor could Johnson, the supreme politician, ignore the burgeoning dissent inside and outside his Administration. McNamara's growing disenchantment and 1967 decision to resign both shocked and angered the President. White House national security adviser McGeorge Bundy, Under Secretary of State George Ball, and close political adviser Bill Moyers had departed already. The President took petulant verbal potshots at them for leaving his team and for having questioned his quest for victory in Vietnam with their appeals for a stop to the bombing. In 1967–1968 it was evident that winning was an elusive goal; Johnson seemed determined at least not to lose. He would stick it out, it appeared, like Davy Crockett at the Alamo.

His critics said that opportunities for peaceful negotiations should be seized. Throughout the 1965–1968 escalation period, international groups, including the United Nations and the Vatican, reached for peace. In 1965, through Italy, Hanoi offered a peace plan resembling the 1954 Geneva agreements. For the month of

The Vietnam Hearings, 1966. As Chairman of the Senate Foreign Relations Committee, J. William Fulbright (on the right) held numerous "educational" hearings to ask government officials like Defense Secretary Robert McNamara (on the left) to explain why the United States fought in Vietnam. Here the two adversaries ham it up nose to nose. Earlier Harry S Truman ridiculed the Rhodes Scholar and former president of the University of Arkansas as "Senator Halfbright." (Wide World Photos, courtesy of University of Arkansas Library)

January, 1966, Johnson halted the bombing of North Vietnam while American diplomats encouraged mediation in foreign capitals. During the bombing pause the United States increased its troop strength in South Vietnam. America's peace offensive hinged on tremendous obstacles to negotiations. The United States would not talk until North Vietnam ceased its "aggression." The National Liberation Front would not be recognized as a political force in the South. Hanoi, increasingly speaking for the Viet Cong, would not negotiate until a permanent bombing halt was instituted and until the NLF was granted political status. Assistant Secretary of Defense John McNaughton, another "hawk" rapidly becoming a "dove," concluded that the United States was in essence demanding "capitulation by a Communist force that is far from beaten."[153] A promising start toward a negotiated settlement through a Polish representative, in December, 1966, was tragically crippled when American bombers stepped up air strikes around Hanoi to pressure the "enemy" to come to the conference table on American terms. Hanoi thereupon scuttled the Polish peace initiative. Another bombing pause came in February, 1967, in part induced by McNamara's argument that the bombing was not seriously impeding the flow of arms and soldiers into the South, much of it on bicycles over narrow, jungle paths (the "Ho Chi Minh Trail"), or undermining Northern morale. Former State Department official and critic George Ball commented that the United States "is using a hammer to kill a mosquito."[154] Johnson in his "San Antonio formula" of 1967, insisted on an end to "infiltration" before suspending bombing or beginning to negotiate. But, as Clark Clifford wrote two years later, "the North Vietnamese had more than 100,000 men in the South. It was totally unrealistic to expect them to abandon their men by not replacing casualties, and by failing to provide them with clothing, food, munitions, and other supplies. We could never expect them to accept an offer of negotiations on those conditions."[155] After each pause, the bombing was intensified.

And then the Tet offensive of early 1968 wrought its havoc; the trend of military escalation and Johnson's political career were wrenched out of shape; the bombing was scaled down, and the peace talks finally began in Paris. In November, Richard M. Nixon defeated Vice-President Hubert Humphrey for the presidency. Back in Texas in January, 1969, Lady Bird Johnson remarked that "the coach has turned back into a pumpkin and the mice have all run away."[156] In 1961 John F. Kennedy had asked Americans to "pay any price" and "bear any burden." Many refused. The new Nixon Administration would then be faced with the task of halting the decline of American power and maintaining American interests abroad while at the same time mollifying the evident discontent with globalism. As Americans asked, "How could Vietnam happen?" and received such answers from critics as mindless anticommunism, the domino theory, the momentum of containment, the arrogance of power, presidential hubris, economic expansion and the military-industrial complex, bureaucratic politics, an inadvertent and ignorant walk into a quagmire, racist views of "inferior" Asians, welfare imperialism, right-wing domestic political pressure, insensitivity to morality, and a failure to understand an alien culture, the incoming Administration was asking, "How can the United States get out?"

Antiwar Buttons. Opponents of the Vietnam War demonstrated their protest in a panoply of buttons urging withdrawal and peace. (Division of Political History, Smithsonian Institution)

Further Reading for the Period 1961–1969

Several works cited in Chapters 12 and 13 also treat this period in diplomatic history. Studies that discuss 1960s foreign policy and leaders include Richard J. Barnet, *Intervention and Revolution* (1972); Douglas S. Blaufarb, *The Counterinsurgency Era: U.S. Doctrine and Performance, 1950 to the Present* (1977); Warren I. Cohen, *Dean Rusk* (1980); Charles DeBenedetti, *The Peace Reform in American History* (1980); Alfred Grosser, *The Western Alliance* (1980); Melvin Gurtov, *The United States Against the Third World* (1974); David Halberstam, *The Best and the Brightest* (1972); Jim Heath, *Decade of Disillusionment* (1975); John B. Martin, *Adlai Stevenson and the World* (1977); Robert A. Packenham, *Liberal America and the Third World* (1973); Walt W. Rostow, *Diffusion of Power* (1972); Arthur M. Schlesinger, Jr., *Robert Kennedy and His Times* (1978); and Franz Schurmann, *Logic of World Power* (1974).

John F. Kennedy's record is discussed in Desmond Ball, *Politics and Force Levels: The Strategic Missile Program of the Kennedy Administration* (1981); Curtis Cate, *The Ides of August: The Berlin Wall Crisis, 1961* (1978); Honoré Catudal, *Kennedy and the Berlin Wall Crisis* (1980); Robert A. Divine, "The Education of John F. Kennedy," in Frank Merli and Theodore A. Wilson, eds., *Makers of American Diplomacy* (1974); John W. Evans, *The Kennedy Round in American Trade Policy* (1971); Louise FitzSimons, *The Kennedy Doctrine* (1972); David Nunnerly, *President Kennedy and Britain* (1972); Lewis J. Paper, *The Promise and the Performance* (1975); Thomas G. Paterson, "Bearing the Burden, " *Virginia Quarterly Review* (1978); Jack Schick, *The Berlin Crisis, 1958–1962* (1974); Arthur M. Schlesinger, Jr., *A Thousand Days* (1965); Glenn T. Seaborg and Benjamin S. Loeb, *Kennedy, Khrushchev, and the Test Ban* (1981); Robert M. Slusser, *The Berlin Crisis of 1961* (1973); Richard Walton, *Cold War and Counterrevolution* (1972); Stephen Weissman, *American Foreign Policy in the Congo, 1960–1964* (1974); and Ernest J. Yanarella, *The Missile Defense Controversy* (1977).

For United States relations with Latin America, see Samuel L. Baily, *The United States and the Development of South America, 1945–1975* (1976); Jan K. Black, *United States Penetration of Brazil* (1977); Cole Blasier, *The Hovering Giant: U.S. Responses to Revolutionary Change in Latin America* (1976); Theodore Draper, *The Dominican Revolt* (1968); Piero Gleijeses, *The Dominican Crisis* (1978); Jerome Levinson and Juan de Onís, *The Alliance That Lost Its Way* (1970); Phyllis R. Parker, *Brazil and the Quiet Intervention, 1964* (1979); F. Parkinson, *Latin America, The Cold War, and the World Powers, 1945–1973* (1974); and Daniel A. Sharp, *U.S. Foreign Policy and Peru* (1972).

Studies of Cuban-American relations and the Cuban Missile Crisis include Graham Allison, *Essence of Decision* (1971); David Detzer, *The Brink: Cuban Missile Crisis, 1962* (1979); Herbert Dinerstein, *The Making of a Missile Crisis: October 1962* (1976); James Nathan, "The Missile Crisis, " *World Politics* (1975); and Peter Wyden, *Bay of Pigs* (1979).

Lyndon B. Johnson and his diplomacy are scrutinized in Robert A. Divine, ed., *Exploring the Johnson Years* (1981); Philip Geyelin, *Lyndon B. Johnson and the World* (1966); Eric Goldman, *The Tragedy of Lyndon Johnson* (1968); Doris Kearns, *Lyndon Johnson and the American Dream* (1976); Robert Sellen, "Old Assumptions versus New Realities: Lyndon Johnson and Foreign Policy," *International Journal* (1973); and Sidney Weintraub, ed., *Economic Coercion and U.S. Foreign Policy* (1982).

For the origins of the Vietnamese revolution and Vietnamese politics, consult Joseph Buttinger, *Vietnam: A Political History* (1970); Bernard Fall, *The Two Vietnams* (1967); James P. Harrison, *The Endless War* (1982); Ronald E. Irving, *The First Indochina War: French and American Policy, 1945–1954* (1975); David Marr, *Vietnamese Anti-Colonialism, 1885–1925* (1971) and *Vietnamese Tradition on Trial, 1920–1945* (1981); John T. McAlister, Jr., *Vietnam: The Origins of Revolution* (1971); Douglas Pike, *History of Vietnamese Communism* (1978) and *Viet Cong* (1972).

Studies of the United States in Southeast Asia and the Vietnam War include Peter Braestrup, *Big Story: How the American Press and Television Reported . . . Tet* (1977); Michael

Charlton and Anthony Moncrieff, eds., *Many Reasons Why: The American Involvement in Vietnam* (1978); Chester Cooper, *The Lost Crusade* (1970); Russell H. Fifield, *Americans in Southeast Asia* (1973); Frances FitzGerald, *Fire in the Lake* (1972); Stephen A. Garrett, *Ideals and Reality: An Analysis of the Debate Over Vietnam* (1978); Leslie H. Gelb and Richard K. Betts, *The Irony of Vietnam* (1979); Joseph Goldstein et al., *The My Lai Massacre and Its Cover-up* (1976); Allan E. Goodman, *The Lost Peace: America's Search for a Negotiated Settlement of the Vietnam War* (1978); George C. Herring, *America's Longest War* (1979); Townsend Hoopes, *The Limits of Intervention* (1969); George M. Kahin and John W. Lewis, *The United States in Vietnam* (1969); Paul M. Kattenburg, *The Vietnam Trauma in American Foreign Policy, 1945–1975* (1980); Michael Maclear, *The Ten Thousand Day War, Vietnam: 1945–1975* (1981); New York Times, *Pentagon Papers* (1971); Archimedes L. A. Patti, *Why Viet Nam?* (1980); Peter Poole, *The United States and Indochina from FDR to Nixon* (1973); Herbert Y. Schandler, *The Unmaking of a President: Lyndon Johnson and Vietnam* (1977); Robert Shaplen, *Time Out of Hand: Revolution and Reaction in Southeast Asia* (1970); Wallace J. Thies, *When Governments Collide: Coercion and Diplomacy in the Vietnam Conflict, 1964–1968* (1980).

Military decisions and operations in the Vietnam War are the subject of Robert L. Gallucci, *Neither Peace Nor Honor* (1975); Douglas Kinnard, *The War Managers* (1977); Guenter Lewy, *America in Vietnam* (1978); Edgar O'Ballance, *The Wars in Vietnam, 1954–1973* (1975); Jeffrey Race, *War Comes to Long An* (1972); and James C. Thompson, *Rolling Thunder* (1980).

See also the General Bibliography and the following notes.

Notes to Chapter 14

1. Quoted in Joseph L. Dees, "The Viet Cong Attack that Failed," *Department of State News Letter*, No. 85 (May, 1968), p. 22.

2. Tran-van Dinh, "Six Hours that Changed the Vietnam Situation: The New Year Siege of the Saigon Embassy," *Christian Century*, LXXXV (March 6, 1968), 289.

3. Don Oberdorfer, *Tet!* (Garden City, New York: Doubleday, 1971), p. 25.

4. Quoted *ibid.*, p. 18.

5. Quoted *ibid.*, p. 33, and in Frances FitzGerald, *Fire in the Lake: The Vietnamese and the Americans in Vietnam* (New York: Vintage Books, 1972), p. 518.

6. Peter A. Poole, *The United States and Indochina from FDR to Nixon* (Hinsdale, Ill.: The Dryden Press, 1973), p. 177.

7. Quoted in Robert Shaplen, *Time Out of Hand: Revolution and Reaction in Southeast Asia* (New York: Harper Colophon Books, 1970; rev. ed.), p. 408.

8. *Department of State Bulletin*, LVIII (March 4, 1968), 304.

9. *Time*, XLI (February 9, 1968), 15.

10. FitzGerald, *Fire in the Lake*, p. 524.

11. Shaplen, *Time Out of Hand*, p. 416.

12. William C. Westmoreland, *A Soldier Reports* (Garden City, N.Y.: Doubleday, 1976), p. 348.

13. Quoted in Townsend Hoopes, *The Limits of Intervention* (New York: David McKay, 1969), p. 213.

14. Quoted in George McTurnan Kahin and John W. Lewis, *The United States in Vietnam* (New York: Dell, 1969; rev. ed.), p. 373.

15. Quoted in George A. Bailey and Lawrence W. Lichty, "Rough Justice on a Saigon Street: A Gatekeeper Study of NBC's Tet Execution Film," *Journalism Quarterly*, XLIX (Summer, 1972), 222.

16. *Public Papers of the Presidents: Lyndon B. Johnson, 1968* (Washington: Government Printing Office, 1970), p. 152.

17. Westmoreland, *A Soldier Reports*, p. 311.

18. Quoted in *Newsweek*, LXXI (February 19, 1968), 24.

19. Ward Just, "That Long Night at the U.S. Embassy," *Wall Street Journal*, February 19, 1968, p. 20.

20. *Washington Post*, March 6, 1968.

21. U.S. Senate, Foreign Relations Committee, *Foreign Assistance Act of 1968—Part 1—Vietnam* (Washington: Government Printing Office, 1968), p. 100.

22. *Department of State Bulletin*, LVIII (February 26, 1968), 261.

23. Lyndon B. Johnson, *The Vantage Point: Perspectives of the Presidency, 1963–1969* (New York: Holt, Rinehart and Winston, 1971), p. 384.

24. Quoted in *Public Papers, Johnson, 1968*, p. 287.

25. Quoted in Hoopes, *Limits of Intervention*, p. 149.

26. William V. Shannon, "Viet Cong Escalation," *Commonweal*, LXXXVII (February 23, 1968), 613.

27. Quoted in Marvin Kalb and Elie Abel, *Roots of Involvement* (New York: W. W. Norton, 1971), p. 211.

28. John B. Henry II, "February, 1968," *Foreign Policy*, No. 4 (Fall, 1971), p. 19.

29. Quoted in Kalb and Abel, *Roots of Involvement*, p. 235.

30. Clark M. Clifford, "A Viet Nam Reappraisal," *Foreign Affairs*, XLVII (July, 1969), 612.

31. Hoopes, *Limits of Intervention*, p. 217.

32. *Public Papers, Johnson, 1968*, p. 470.

33. Jean Lacouture, *Ho Chi Minh: A Political Biography* (New York: Vintage Books, [1967], 1968), p. 3.

34. Joseph Buttinger, *Vietnam: A Dragon Embattled* (New York: Frederick A. Praeger, 1967; 2 vols.), I, 174–175.

35. Quoted in U.S. Senate, Committee on Foreign Relations, *The United States and Vietnam: 1944–1947* (Washington: Government Printing Office, 1972), p. 3.

36. Quoted in Christopher Thorne, "Indochina and Anglo-American Relations, 1942–1945," *Pacific Historical Review*, XLIV (February, 1976), 93.

37. Quoted in Walter LaFeber, "Roosevelt, Churchill, and Indochina: 1942–45," *American Historical Review*, LXXX (December, 1975), 1289.

38. Quoted in Gary R. Hess, "Franklin Roosevelt and Indochina," *Journal of American History*, LIX (September, 1972), 364.

39. LaFeber, "Roosevelt, Churchill, and Indochina," p. 1295.

40. Clifford, "Viet Nam Reappraisal," p. 603.

41. Quoted in U.S. Senate, *United States and Vietnam: 1944–1947*, pp. 18, 21.

42. Quoted in New York Times, *The Pentagon Papers* (New York: Bantam Books, 1971), p. 14.

43. Bernard Fall, *The Two Viet-Nams* (New York: Frederick A. Praeger, 1967; 2nd ed.), p. 233.

44. Robert Shaplen, *The Lost Revolution* (New York: Harper and Row, 1965), p. 98.

45. Quoted *ibid.*

46. Quoted in Kahin and Lewis, *United States in Vietnam*, p. 61.

47. Quoted in Robert A. Divine, "The Education of John F. Kennedy," in Frank Merli and Theodore Wilson, eds., *Makers of American Diplomacy* (New York: Charles Scribner's Sons, 1974), p. 623.

48. Quoted in Theodore C. Sorensen, *Kennedy* (New York: Harper and Row, 1965), p. 199.

49. Divine, "Education of John F. Kennedy," p. 621.

50. *New York Times*, August 25, 1960.

51. Quoted in Richard J. Walton, *Cold War and Counterrevolution: The Foreign Policy of John F. Kennedy* (Baltimore: Penguin Books, [1972], 1973, p. 9.

52. *Public Papers, John F. Kennedy, 1962* (Washington: Government Printing Office, 1963), p. 807.

53. Walt W. Rostow, "The Third Round," *Foreign Affairs*, XLII (October, 1963), 5–6.

54. Don Ferguson in Peter Joseph, *Good Times: An Oral History of America in the Nineteen Sixties* (New York: William Morrow, 1974), p. 4.

55. *Ibid.*, p. 54.

56. Arthur M. Schlesinger, Jr., *A Thousand Days: John F. Kennedy in the White House* (Boston: Houghton Mifflin, 1965), p. 259.

57. James Barber, *The Presidential Character* (Englewood Cliffs, N.J.: Prentice-Hall, 1972), p. 298.

58. Quoted in Kenneth P. O'Donnell and David F. Powers, *"Johnny, We Hardly Knew Ye": Memoirs of John Fitzgerald Kennedy* (Boston: Little, Brown, 1972), p. 287.

59. Midge Decter, "Kennedyism," *Commentary*, XLIX (January, 1970), 21.

60. Oral History Interview by Chester Bowles, pp. 49, 90, John F. Kennedy Library, Massachusetts.

61. Schlesinger, *A Thousand Days*, p. 217.

62. *Public Papers, Kennedy, 1961* (Washington: Government Printing Office, 1962), pp. 1–3.

63. Theodore H. White, "The Action Intellectuals," *Life*, LXII (June, 1967), 43.

64. Quoted in David Halberstam, "The Programming of Robert McNamara," *Harper's Magazine*, CCXLII (February, 1971), 62.

65. Quoted in Roger Hilsman, *To Move a Nation: The Politics of Foreign Policy in the Administration of John F. Kennedy* (Garden City, N.Y.: Doubleday, 1967), p. 523.

66. Sorensen, *Kennedy*, p. 270.

67. Quoted in David Halberstam, *The Best and the Brightest* (Greenwich, Conn.: Fawcett Publications, 1973), p. 770.

68. "Memorandum of Conversation with President Johnson," by Max Frankel, July 8, 1965, Box 1, "Black Notebooks," Arthur Krock Papers, Princeton University Library, Princeton, New Jersey.

69. *Public Papers, Dwight D. Eisenhower, 1959* (Washington: Government Printing Office, 1960), p. 8.

70. "Biographic Briefing Book," June, 1961, Box 126, President's Office File, John F. Kennedy Papers, Kennedy Library.

71. Schlesinger, *A Thousand Days*, p. 348.

72. Quoted *ibid.*, p. 391.

73. *Public Papers, Kennedy, 1961*, pp. 534, 536.

74. *Ibid., 1963* (Washington: Government Printing Office, 1964), p. 524.

75. Memorandum by Arthur M. Schlesinger, Jr., [1961], Box 121, President's Office File, John F. Kennedy Papers, Kennedy Library.

76. Marcus G. Raskin and Bernard B. Fall, eds., *The Viet-Nam Reader* (New York: Vintage Books, 1967; rev. ed.), p. 113.

77. Quoted in Seyom Brown, *The Faces of Power* (New York: Columbia University Press, 1968), p. 164.

78. Memorandum by Arthur M. Schlesinger, Jr., [1961], Box 121, President's Office File, John F. Kennedy Papers, Kennedy Library.

79. Quoted in Frank Mankiewicz and Kirby Jones, *With Fidel: A Portrait of Castro and Cuba* (New York: Ballantine Books, 1975), p. 175.

80. Dean Rusk to G. Mennen Williams, January 8, 1962, Box 29, Records of G. Mennen Williams, Department of State Records, National Archives, Washington, D.C.

81. William Attwood, *The Reds and the Blacks: A Personal Adventure* (New York: Harper & Row, 1967), p. 219.

82. Quoted in Walter LaFeber, ed., *America in the Cold War* (New York: Wiley, 1969), p. 139.

83. *Public Papers, Eisenhower, 1960–61* (Washington: Government Printing Office, 1961), p. 567.

84. Philip W. Bonsal, *Cuba, Castro, and the United States* (Pittsburgh: University of Pittsburgh Press, 1971), p. 67.

85. Dwight D. Eisenhower, *The White House Years: Waging Peace, 1956–1961* (Garden City, N.Y.: Doubleday, 1965), p. 527.

86. Quoted in Walton, *Cold War and Counterrevolution*, pp. 36–37.

87. Quoted in Schlesinger, *A Thousand Days*, p. 251.

88. Walt W. Rostow, *The Diffusion of Power* (New York: Macmillan, 1972), pp. 210–211.

89. *Public Papers, Kennedy, 1961*, pp. 304–306.

90. Quoted in Stanley Meisler, "Reports and Comment: Cuba," *Atlantic Monthly*, CCXXXVI (September, 1975), 4.

91. Quoted in Hilsman, *To Move a Nation*, p. 157.
92. Quoted in Mankiewicz and Jones, *With Fidel*, p. 150.
93. Nikita S. Khrushchev, *Khrushchev Remembers* (New York: Bantam Books, 1971; trans. by Strobe Talbott), pp. 546–547.
94. Robert F. Kennedy, *Thirteen Days: A Memoir of the Cuban Missile Crisis* (New York: W. W. Norton, 1969), p. 31.
95. *Public Papers, Kennedy, 1962*, p. 808.
96. Quoted in Kennedy, *Thirteen Days*, p. 67.
97. Quoted in Hilsman, *To Move a Nation*, p. 219.
98. Rostow, *Diffusion of Power*, p. 297.
99. Quoted in Ronald Steel, "Endgame," *New York Review of Books*, March 13, 1969, p. 22.
100. John Kenneth Galbraith, "The Plain Lessons of a Bad Decade," *Foreign Policy*, No. 1 (Winter, 1970–71), 32.
101. Sorensen, *Kennedy*, p. 678.
102. Adolf A. Berle, *Navigating the Rapids, 1918–1971: From the Papers of Adolf A. Berle* (New York: Harcourt Brace Jovanovich, 1973), p. 774.
103. James A. Nathan, "The Missile Crisis: His Finest Hour Now," *World Politics*, XXVII (January, 1975), 269, 280–281.
104. Quoted *ibid.*, p. 274.
105. Memorandum for the President by Walt W. Rostow, March 29, 1961, Box 193, National Security Files, Kennedy Papers, Kennedy Library.
106. Quoted in Schlesinger, *A Thousand Days*, p. 330.
107. Eisenhower, *White House Years: Waging Peace*, p. 607.
108. Schlesinger, *A Thousand Days*, p. 324.
109. Quoted *ibid.*, p. 338.
110. Bernard Fall, *Anatomy of a Crisis: The Laotian Crisis of 1960–1961* (Garden City, N. Y.: Doubleday, 1969), p. 229.
111. Quoted in Rostow, *Diffusion of Power*, p. 265.
112. Quoted in Halberstam, *Best and the Brightest*, p. 167.
113. *Public Papers, Kennedy, 1963*, p. 673.
114. *Ibid.*, p. 659.
115. New York Times, *Pentagon Papers*, p. 129.
116. John Kenneth Galbraith, *Ambassador's Journal: A Personal Account of the Kennedy Years* (Boston: Houghton Mifflin, 1969), p. 311 (March 2, 1962).
117. U.S. Senate, *Foreign Assistance Act of 1968—Part I—Vietnam*, p. 218.
118. Quoted in George C. Herring, *America's Longest War* (New York: Wiley, 1979), p. 101.
119. Schlesinger, *A Thousand Days*, p. 997.
120. Quoted in Louise FitzSimons, *The Kennedy Doctrine* (New York: Random House, 1972), p. 15.
121. Quoted in Jim F. Heath, *Decade of Disillusionment: The Kennedy-Johnson Years* (Bloomington: Indiana University Press, 1975), p. 137.
122. John McDermott, "Welfare Imperialism in Vietnam," *The Nation*, CCIII (July 25, 1966), 85.
123. *Wall Street Journal*, January 21, 1971.
124. Quoted in Heath, *Decade*, p. 186.
125. Quoted in Barber, *Presidential Character*, pp. 51–52.
126. Quoted in Robert W. Sellen, "Old Assumptions versus New Realities: Lyndon Johnson and Foreign Policy," *International Journal*, XXVIII (Spring, 1973), 206.
127. Quoted in Hugh Sidey, *A Very Personal Presidency* (New York: Atheneum, 1968), p. 187.
128. Quoted in *Boston Globe*, September 15, 1980.
129. Quoted in Eric F. Goldman, *The Tragedy of Lyndon Johnson* (New York: Alfred A. Knopf, 1969), pp. 484, 499; Halberstam, "Programming of Robert McNamara," p. 64.
130. Quoted in Philip Geyelin, *Lyndon B. Johnson and the World* (New York: Frederick A. Praeger, 1966), p. 20.
131. Quoted in Goldman, *Tragedy*, p. 382.
132. Quoted in Geyelin, *Lyndon B. Johnson*, p. 22.
133. Quoted in Barber, *Presidential Character*, p. 87.
134. J. William Fulbright, *The Arrogance of Power* (New York: Vintage Books, 1966) and *The Crippled Giant* (New York: Vintage Books, 1972).
135. Quoted in *Newsweek*, LXV (May 17, 1965), 52.
136. Fulbright, *Arrogance of Power*, pp. 91–92.
137. *Public Papers, Lyndon B. Johnson, 1965* (Washington: Government Printing Office, 1966; 2 vols.), I, 480.
138. Quoted in Kahin and Lewis, *United States and Vietnam*, p. 152.
139. *Public Papers, Lyndon Johnson, 1963–1964* (Washington: Government Printing Office, 1965; 2 vols.), II, 930.
140. *Congressional Record*, CX (August 7, 1964), 18471.
141. Quoted in Robert A. Divine, *Since 1945: Politics and Diplomacy in Recent American History* (New York: Wiley, 1975), p. 148. 1975), p. 148.
142. Arthur M. Schlesinger, *The Imperial Presidency* (New York: Popular Library, 1973).
143. *Department of State Bulletin*, LII (April 26, 1965), 607.
144. Quoted in Robert L. Beisner, "1898 and 1968: The Anti-Imperialists and the Doves," *Political Science Quarterly*, LXXXV (June, 1970), 197–198.
145. Quoted in New York Times, *Pentagon Papers*, p. 567.
146. Quoted in Doris Kearns, *Lyndon Johnson and the American Dream* (New York: Harper and Row, Publishers, 1976), p. 329.
147. Quoted in Jonathan Mirsky, "The Root of Resistance," *The Nation*, CCVII (August 5, 1968), 90.
148. Kahin and Lewis, *United States and Vietnam*, p. 370.
149. U.S. Senate, Committee on Foreign Relations, *Changing American Attitudes Toward Foreign Policy* (hearings), 90th Cong., 1st Sess. (February 20, 1967), p. 25.
150. Quoted in Heath, *Decade*, p. 249.
151. Quoted in Stephen Ambrose, *Rise to Globalism* (Baltimore: Penguin Books, 1980; 2nd ed.), p. 287.
152. Goldman, *Tragedy*, p. 511.
153. Quoted in Donald F. Lach and Edmund S. Wehrle, *International Politics in East Asia Since World War II* (New York: Praeger Publishers, 1975), p. 338.
154. George W. Ball, *The Discipline of Power* (Boston: Little Brown, 1968), p. 321.
155. Clifford, "Viet Nam Reappraisal," p. 608.
156. Quoted in Johnson, *Vantage Point*, p. 568.

At the Great Wall, 1972.
President Richard M.
Nixon and Patricia Nixon
visited the Great Wall during their momentous trip
to China in February.
There the President ut-
tered a memorable banal-
ity: ''I think that you
would have to conclude
that this is a great
wall. . . . As we look at
this wall, we do not want
walls of any kind between
peoples.'' (White House)

15 The Perils of a Grand Design, 1969–1977

Diplomatic Crossroad: Richard M. Nixon's Trip to China, 1972

The President's chief security officer aboard the aircraft radioed an American agent at the Beijing airport below: "What about the crowd?" The answer came back: "There is no crowd." The disbelieving officer asked: "Did you say, 'No crowd'?"[1] Indeed, when President Richard M. Nixon's blue and silver jet, the *Spirit of '76*, touched down on the Chinese runway that wintry morning of February 21, 1972, the reception was decidedly restrained and spartan. Apparently the Chinese wanted observers to think the United States was more eager than the People's Republic of China (PRC) for this dramatic meeting. Usually the Chinese greeted visiting dignitaries at the Capital Airport with cheering schoolchildren waving flags, but only "a vast silence" welcomed Nixon.[2] When the President emerged from the plane he awkwardly kept his arms at his sides, difficult for one who habitually waved his hands when departing an aircraft.

At the foot of the stairs stood trim seventy-three-year-old Premier Zhou Enlai, a veteran Communist who had served Chairman Mao Zedong as key administrator since the success of the Chinese Revolution in 1949. Nixon and Zhou formally shook hands—the very gesture that Secretary John Foster Dulles had spurned at Geneva in 1954. The Premier noticed Henry A. Kissinger and purred, "Ah, old friend."[3] The television cameras whirred, sending back to the United States, via satellite, picture postcards of the historic encounter. The ceremony was brief, with no speeches. The visitors could not miss a large banner: "Make trouble, fail; make trouble again, fail again; make trouble until doom: that is the logic of the imperialists and reactionaries."[4] Zhou and Nixon sped toward Beijing, passing a grey landscape of communes, their caretakers indoors to escape the freezing temperatures. Portraits of Mao and political signs hung everywhere. The Chinese had painted over one poster which read: "We Must Defeat the U.S. Aggressors and All Their Running Dogs Wherever They May Be."[5]

Nixon's "journey for peace" contrasted sharply with the previous quarter century in which formal diplomatic relations had not existed between the two countries.[6] For years they had blasted each other as aggressors and had gone to war against one another in Korea. The United States maintained close ties with the PRC's archenemy Jiang Jieshi in Taiwan, while China aided America's foe in Vietnam. This history of hostility and confrontation was not forgotten by Nixon and Zhou on February 21, 1972. But each was now convinced that cooperation best served his own country's interests.

In 1969, newly inaugurated President Nixon had asked his assistant for national security affairs, Henry A. Kissinger, to review relations with China. At first Kissinger did not think reconciliation possible with the "fanatic" Chinese Communists.[7] But the Nixon Administration soon sent private and public signals to Beijing. United States Seventh Fleet operations were scaled back in the Taiwan Straits, and American restrictions on trade with China were relaxed. China picked up the signals. Early in 1970 PRC diplomats once again began meeting with American officials in Warsaw—talks that China had suspended two years earlier as a protest against American warfare in Vietnam. After the Chinese recommended that the Sino-American discussions be moved to Beijing, Nixon responded by lifting restrictions against Americans wanting to travel to the People's Republic. Suddenly, in April of 1971, an American table tennis team competing in Japan received and accepted an invitation to visit China. Quips about "ping-pong diplomacy" did not detract from the symbolic significance of the trip.

Using Pakistan as an intermediary, Kissinger made plans to go to China himself. In Islamabad, the Pakistani capital, Kissinger feigned illness and dropped from public view. On July 9, 1971, he secretly boarded a plane for Beijing. He soon reported to the President that "the process we have now started will send enormous shock waves around the world. . . ."[8] A few days later, on July 15, President Nixon captured headlines with the dramatic announcement that he would go to China to "seek the normalization of relations."[9]

Renewed Sino-American relations seemed to promise a number of advantages. Because of the gaping Sino-Soviet split, American recognition of the People's Republic would keep Moscow wondering what Washington intended. Conceivably the United States might be able to pit the antagonistic Communist nations against one another. As one journalist put it, "The President is in the position of the lovely maiden courted by two ardent swains [China and Russia], each of whom is aware of the other but each of whom is uncertain of what happens when the young lady is alone with his rival."[10] And with the American economy sagging, the legendary China market once again loomed large in American imaginations. Another motive lay in China's possession of nuclear weapons. Beijing had not accepted international atomic antiproliferation controls. Without Chinese adherence, nuclear arms control agreements were ultimately feeble. Then, too, American recognition of China might encourage Beijing to reduce its aid to North Vietnam and to urge upon Hanoi a political settlement of the Vietnam War.

The China trip also promised Nixon political profits at home. Antiwar Democratic Senator George McGovern had launched a conspicuous campaign against the Nixon Administration's continued intervention in Vietnam, and in March, New Hampshire would hold the first presidential primary of 1972. "Look," Kissinger frankly remarked, "it wasn't just a matter of this summit—[Nixon's] political ass was on the line."[11] Liberal-left Americans had been calling for relations

Marco Polo. Political cartoonist Ray Osrin portrayed two reasons for the Nixon journey to China, 1972. Kissinger's secret 1971 trip to China was code named "Polo." (Ray Osrin in *The Cleveland Plain Dealer*)

with China for years, and Democrats soon applauded the Nixon journey. At the same time, the right wing of the Republican party could hardly charge that Nixon, the proven anti-Communist, had turned soft on Communism. Dominating all was the importance of the China journey to the general Nixon-Kissinger policy of "détente"—the relaxation of international tensions with Communist nations to protect American interests. As Kissinger put it: "We needed China to enhance the flexibility of our diplomacy."[12]

The Chinese had their own reasons for inviting Nixon. From their vantage point the United States no longer ranked as their number one threat, for Sino-Soviet relations had seriously deteriorated. Military skirmishes in 1969 on the shared 4,150 mile border caused many Chinese, recalling the brutal Russian invasion of Czechoslovakia in 1968, to fear a Soviet attack. The Soviet Union constructed an air base in Mongolia; the Chinese dug bomb shelters and tunnel networks. Resuming Sino-American ties, then, might deter the Soviets. "The principle of using barbarians to control barbarians," Asian specialist James C. Thomson, Jr. noted, "is hardly new to Chinese geopolitics."[13] China also feared a revived Japan, and a Sino-American rapprochement might unsettle Japan, keeping Tokyo off-guard and cautious. Or it might, as actually happened, lead to the opening of Sino-Japanese relations, thereby also strengthening China against Russia. Finally, China was interested in attracting American trade and reducing the United States commitment to Taiwan.

On the flight to China, Nixon, Kissinger, and their aides studied black notebooks about Chinese politics, culture, and diplomacy. Included were CIA analyses of Mao and Zhou and "talking points" that Nixon committed to memory. The planes were "air-borne universities."[14] Joining the presidential party of thirty-seven—which included Secretary of State William Rogers, upstaged as always by Kissinger—was a press corps of eighty-seven, heavy with television news personalities. Americans carried specially printed souvenir matchbooks and wore flags in their lapels. All in all, the Nixon journey was a carefully staged diplomatic performance aimed at prime-time evening television screens back home.

The President had no sooner arrived at his guesthouse when he was invited to meet with Chairman Mao. Soon seated in overstuffed chairs, Nixon, Kissinger, Mao, and Zhou talked warmly for about an hour. Tang Wensheng, a Brooklyn-born Radcliffe graduate who had become a Chinese citizen, served as interpreter. Seventy-eight-year-old Mao, although ill, remained an imposing figure, esteemed by the Chinese as the leader of the Long March and father of the People's Republic. "He has the quality of being at the center wherever he stood," remarked Kissinger. "It moved with him wherever he moved."[15] During the conversation, Mao smiled and bantered. "Our common old friend Generalissimo Chiang Kai-shek [Jiang Jieshi] doesn't approve of this," he teased.[16] Zhou Enlai also impressed the Americans. Always gracious, the crew-cut, bushy-browed leader seemed tireless. Born into a well-to-do Mandarin family, he spoke English, Russian, French, and Japanese as well as Chinese. A skillful negotiator with a sharp memory, he handled the day-to-day diplomatic chores and never sought the limelight. American diplomats contrasted his quiet, patient style with the blunt, haggling manner of Soviet diplomats. And, as Zhou liked to tell his American counterparts, "*our* word counts."[17]

That evening, in the Great Hall of the People, Zhou hosted a massive banquet for 800 guests. Sipping glasses of *mao tai,* a potent 150 proof rice liquor, Nixon and Zhou, Americans and Chinese, generously toasted one another. As a Chinese military band somewhat stiltedly played "Home on the Range," the President remarked: "Never have I heard American music played better in a foreign land." Then, tearing a page from Chinese Communist history, he called for a "long march together." And he even quoted Mao himself: "Seize the day, seize the hour. This is the hour," proclaimed the President.[18]

On February 22 Nixon and Zhou conferred for much of the afternoon, while journalists filed reports on the Chinese life-style—clean streets, gauze masks to prevent infectious diseases, acupuncture techniques for surgery, anti-imperialist banners, expertise in table tennis, regimented schools, puritanical social habits, irrigation systems, improved nutrition and health since 1949, Mao's photographs plastered on village walls, bicycles on the streets, the monotony of blue dress, the pioneering and diligent character of the Chinese, and so much more. Conservative and fervent anti-Communist William Buckley did not appreciate the comments of a Nixon aide who found the journalist in a souvenir shop: "Doing a little trading with the enemy, Bill?"[19] Although Buckley resisted new attitudes, images began to change quickly. After years of thinking the Chinese a bestial enemy, Americans now considered them human—loving and suffering like the rest of mankind. Whereas in the 1960s Americans used words like "ignorant, warlike, treacherous, and sly" to describe the "Red Chinese," after the 1972 trip they described them as "hard-working, intelligent, progressive, artistic, and practical."[20] As for Chinese images of Americans, the *Peking Daily* of February 22, in what analysts thought was a unique issue, carried pictures of Nixon's meeting with Mao. No longer was the American President the demonic traducer. Any friend of Mao's became a friend of China's.

Every night after the social events, an exhausted Kissinger sat down with the Vice-Foreign Minister to fashion language for a joint communiqué. On February 27, after much bickering, the document was issued. It suggested that the Chinese and Americans had agreed to disagree. For their part, the Americans stated their

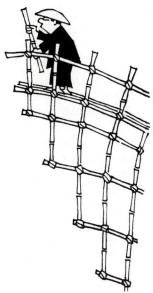

**"A Brick, A Bamboo, A
Brick, A Bamboo . . ."**
A French cartoonist's view
of the delicate process of
building Sino-American
relations in the late 1960s
and early 1970s. (Pierre,
Aux Ecoutes)

opposition to "outside pressure or intervention" in Asia—meaning Vietnam. They reaffirmed their friendly relations with South Korea and Japan. The Chinese, on the other hand, declared that they would continue to support "the struggles of all oppressed people" against large nations which attempt to "bully" the small. All foreign troops should be withdrawn from Asia, especially Vietnam. On the "murderously tough problem"[21] of Taiwan, which the United States still recognized as the offical government of China, the Chinese part of the communiqué admonished the United States to withdraw its military forces from the island. There was only one China. The American response was equivocal, calling for a "peaceful settlement of the Taiwan question by the Chinese themselves." Both parties agreed, however, that "neither should seek hegemony in the Asia-Pacific region and each is opposed to efforts by any other country or group of countries to establish such hegemony"—a thinly veiled slap at Russia. Finally, both sides appealed for increased cultural and commercial contacts.[22]

Diplomacy done, on the seventh day of his trip, February 28, the President bade farewell at Shanghai to his hosts and proclaimed that "this was the week that changed the world."[23] Typically, Nixon had rushed to judgment.

Nixon, Kissinger, and a Grand Design

The two leaders who orchestrated this surprising turnabout in Sino-American relations, Nixon and Kissinger, were quite different individuals who shared the same assumptions about American foreign policy. Richard Milhous Nixon, the grocer's son from Whittier, California, relished the "big play" in politics and preferred to be known as a man who would "turn like a cobra" on anyone who crossed him.[24] He apparently wanted the Russians and others to think him irrational and unpredictable. This self-professed "madman theory" would supposedly deter adversaries or cause them to settle on American terms.[25] A secretive, suspicious man, Nixon privately said about Kissinger, "I don't trust Henry, but I can use him."[26] The President did not trust many people. He complained that the CIA was too liberal, staffed by Ivy Leaguers; he had little confidence in the State Department; he thought the news media was out to "get" him; he scorned intellectuals and protesters. His administration guarded itself against these "enemies" through secrecy and through a variety of executive crimes and corrupt political practices later known collectively as Watergate. In part because he did not trust his aides, and in part because he wanted a complete record of his administration, Nixon secretly taped conversations in the White House. When made public by court order, the tapes inspired an impeachment process that Nixon himself, caught in bare-faced lies, terminated by resigning from the presidency on August 8, 1974, thereby elevating Gerald Ford to the White House. The Watergate scandal included the wiretapping of foreign policy advisers and journalists. The uncovering of this illegal behavior weakened the executive branch in its ongoing struggle with Congress over policymaking and stripped the sacred garb from the phrase "national security," which Nixon had invoked for months to keep the tapes from public exposure.

After Nixon's ignoble departure Henry A. Kissinger stayed on. Presidential assistant for national security affairs (1969–1976) and secretary of state (1973–1977), Kissinger thought Nixon an "egomaniac" apparently "obsessed by the fear that he was not receiving adequate credit" for foreign policy triumphs like the change in China policy.[27] An ambitious political scientist of German-Jewish ancestry, with an Old World accent, Kissinger had escaped from Nazism in 1938. He spent much of his academic life advising government officials and politicians like Nelson A. Rockefeller. In his widely-read book *Nuclear Weapons and Foreign Policy* (1957), Kissinger criticized "massive retaliation" for limiting American choices and rejected George F. Kennan's "disengagement" proposals. He also wrote an earlier book on European relations after the 1815 Congress of Vienna, extolling

"Some Chicken, Some Egg." Henry A. Kissinger (1923–) received his doctorate in 1954 from Harvard, where he taught until Nixon appointed him national security affairs adviser in 1969. An architect of détente, the German-born political scientist also undertook extensive travel to trouble spots like the Middle East and Africa to conduct personal negotiations. Critics on the left compared him to "Dr. Strangelove," the slightly deranged fictional character in the movie by that name who perpetrated a nuclear holocaust. Critics on the right thought Kissinger too conciliatory to the dreaded Communists. (*The Economist,* London, 1975)

Makers of American Foreign Policy from 1969 to 1977

Presidents	Secretaries of State
Richard M. Nixon, 1969–1974	William P. Rogers, 1969–1973
Gerald Ford, 1974–1977	Henry A. Kissinger, 1973–1977

the conservative balance-of-power techniques Austria's Prince Metternich had used to curb revolution.

Reflective, charming, witty, seldom rattled, energetic, persistent, and vain, "Henry the Navigator" was one of the most traveled diplomats in American history. He reveled in personal diplomacy—one-to-one conversations wherein he could exercise his demonstrated skills to create an atmosphere of trust with foreign leaders. He thrived on the give-and-take, the head-to-head contest, the battle of words, the manipulation of power and people. His "devilish nimbleness" and evident rapport with people of different cultures brought him negotiating successes.[28] As the nation's unrivaled diplomatic leader in the 1969–1977 period, Kissinger managed an impressive number of roles: theorist, policymaker, negotiator, presidential adviser, bureaucratic infighter, and public spokesman. He and Nixon agreed early that policy would be made in the White House; the State Department and other parts of the foreign affairs bureaucracy would be sidestepped, even kept in the dark. Kissinger used private, secret "back channels" to communicate with foreign governments, thereby undermining the official negotiators of the State Department and creating a serious problem of morale in the Foreign Service. William P. Rogers served as a loyal secretary of state until 1973, but Nixon granted him little authority. Nor did Congressmen enter the circle of White House decisionmakers. In good part because it had so often been bypassed, the Congress responded with the War Powers Act (1973), wherein the President could commit American troops abroad for no more than sixty days, and after that period would need congressional approval. Congress also vexed Kissinger by cutting foreign aid to Turkey, Cambodia, South Vietnam, and Angola. If there had been no Watergate scandal and no interference from Congress, Kissinger lamented, he could have accomplished so much more.

Despite the intragovernmental tussles and complaints against his "one-man authoritarianism," Kissinger remained a popular figure.[29] He charmed journalists and occasionally leaked secret information to them to generate favorable newspaper stories. He joked about himself in a way that amused detractors and well-wishers alike. To an admirer who once approached him and declared, "Dr. Kissinger, I want to thank you for saving the world," the secretary replied, "You're welcome."[30] Kissinger also cultivated a "swinger" image until his 1974 marriage. He visited nightclubs arm-in-arm with attractive women, including movie star Jill St. John, and seemed to enjoy the twittering about his smiling approval of a belly-dancer, a moment captured by a photographer. "I've always acted alone," he told an interviewer. "Americans admire the cowboy leading the caravan alone astride his horse. . . . This romantic, surprising character suits me." In negotiations, "my playboy reputation has been and still is useful, because it has helped and helps to reassure people, to show them I'm not a museum piece."[31]

Kissinger's domestic critics rarely underestimated him. They questioned the secrecy that surrounded presidential domination of diplomacy. When academicians, businessmen, and lawyers, many of whom frequented the Council on Foreign Relations or wrote for its prestigious journal *Foreign Affairs*, became disenchanted with his leadership, Kissinger exploded: "What the hell is an Establishment for, if it's not to support the President?"[32] Critics argued that Kissinger was following the ruthless maxim that the ends justify the means: he wiretapped aides and journalists because unauthorized leaks were breaking his seal of secrecy; he defended the President in the lowest days of Watergate; he relied recklessly on huge arms sales; he sponsored CIA plots abroad that held America up to ridicule for advocating democracy but undermining it; and he endorsed the murderous bombing of the people of Southeast Asia. Nonetheless, he was awarded the Nobel Peace Prize in 1973 for his negotiation of a Vietnamese settlement permitting American withdrawal.

Kissinger and Nixon prided themselves on being pragmatists rather than ideologues. "[Woodrow] Wilson had the greatest vision of America's world role," the President once remarked. "But he wasn't practical enough."[33] Kissinger sought to purge "sentimentality" from American foreign policy.[34] The phrase that most generally described the thrust of the Nixon-Kissinger diplomacy was "détente." It meant limited cooperation with the Soviet Union and the People's Republic of China within a general environment of rivalry. Détente was a means, a process, a climate in which to reduce international tensions and sustain United States leadership in world politics. Détente was supposed to produce a geopolitical balance of power, or "equilibrium," by containing the Soviet Union and China and curbing radical revolution.[35] To Nixon and Kissinger, the world divided into roughly five power centers: Russia, America, China, Japan, and the Common Market nations of Western Europe. Under détente, each great center had the responsibility to keep order among smaller states and clients in its region and to refrain from intervening in another's sphere. Because the "five great economic superpowers will determine the economic future," Nixon explained, "and, because economic power will be the key to other kinds of power, [they will determine] the future of the world. . . ."[36]

The Nixon-Kissinger team, like those before it, saw Soviet-American competition as the primary element in world affairs. But the Nixon administration recognized 1970s realities and sought to exploit them to American advantage. It recognized that by 1970 the Soviet Union had achieved nuclear parity or equality with the United States, that the Soviets were suffering severe internal economic problems and needed outside help, that the Sino-Soviet split was profound, and that world power (capital and weaponry) had become diffused as nations had recovered from the Second World War and colonies had broken away from empires. These conditions placed limits on American activity, but they also provided opportunities to shape new relationships. America, said Nixon, was moving from containment through confrontation to containment through negotiation.

Détente and SALT

The Nixon Administration emphasized the triangular relationship among Russia, China, and the United States—that is, it attempted to play the two Communist states off against one another, to keep one worrying about what the United States was doing with the other; thus the two could contain one another. For the Soviets there would be both incentives (such as capital and trade) to encourage restraint, and penalties (such as large arms sales to Soviet adversaries or closer ties to China) to punish expansionist behavior. Washington believed, moreover, that the Soviets could be tamed by making them economically reliant upon the United States. "If we can create a situation in which the use of military force would jeopardize a mutually profitable relationship," explained Secretary of Commerce Peter G. Peterson, "I think it can be argued that our security will have been enhanced."[37]

The new approach to the major Communist countries seemed to make common sense to Kissinger and Nixon. Moscow and Beijing might help the United States extricate itself from war in Vietnam. The Cold War was costing too much; détente supposedly offered a cheaper way of pursuing the containment doctrine by reducing the necessity for interventions, spiraling military expenditures, and new nuclear weapons systems. Thus the Nixon Administration reduced the armed forces from 3.5 million in 1968 to 2.3 million in 1973, ended the draft, and in 1972 negotiated a strategic arms limitation treaty (see p. 581). At a time when American foreign trade needed a boost to eliminate a billion-dollar deficit in the balance of payments, détente conjured up images of expanded markets. Thus massive grain shipments flowed to Russia—in 1972, 25 percent of the American wheat crop—and American corporations like Pepsi-Cola and Chase Manhattan Bank started operations in the U.S.S.R. American exports to Russia reached $2.3 billion in 1976. Businessmen also flocked to Asia in a revival of the great China market dream.

Détente seemed to promise much, but it ran into numerous obstacles. The Nixon-Kissinger grand strategy rested on some questionable assumptions. It overestimated the importance of the triangular relationship, especially the usefulness of China as a check on the Soviets. It assumed wrongly that the Russians could manage their "friends" in North Vietnam or India or the Middle East and that Third World troubles derived from, and could be calmed by, great power decisions. The Nixon Administration still saw small states as proxies of the great powers and thus interpreted events largely through a Cold War perspective. In other words, the grand strategy paid too little attention to the local sources of disputes and the fierce independence of nationalist and neutralist governments. Kissinger spent much of his time trying to keep détente glued together against the backdrop of violent conflicts in Asia, Africa, and the Middle East, and economic challenges from the Organization of Petroleum Exporting Countries (OPEC). Even America's friends caused difficulty: Iran insisted on huge arms shipments but raised oil prices, threatening the American economy; Saudi Arabia demanded sophisticated weaponry but refused to help resolve the explosive Arab-Israeli conflict.

Détente also attracted a wide array of domestic protesters. Jews in the United States denounced Soviet-American agreements that did not assure the right of Russian Jews to emigrate. Americans of Eastern European descent called détente a sellout of their Communist-dominated homelands. Liberals criticized Kissinger's arrogant presumption of superpower domination and his support for authoritarian regimes that trampled on human rights. Not only did morality seem absent; the Nixon and Ford Administrations also seemed to contradict themselves. For example, they appealed for arms control while they broke records for arms sales abroad ($10 billion in 1976 alone). Hard-line anti-Communists labeled Kissinger an appeaser who conceded the Communists too much and who abandoned America's status as the number one nation. By 1976 the secretary of state had concluded that "the principal danger we face is our own domestic divisions."[38]

Nonetheless, the Nixon Administration claimed a number of diplomatic triumphs. The opening of China was one. Although Nixon exaggerated the effects of Sino-American rapprochement, the turnaround did serve the national interest. It helped thwart reconciliation between the two Communist giants. It tied down several Soviet military divisions in Asia—away from NATO. It spawned new ties between Japan and China that contributed to Asian stability. And it nurtured a promising trading partnership. In 1973 large companies like Boeing, Radio Corporation of America, and Monsanto Chemical signed contracts with the Chinese. Chinese-American trade began to climb, reaching $700 million in 1973. Also, cultural exchanges and travel between the once-distant nations reduced mutual ignorance. In 1973 Washington and Beijing exchanged "Liaison Offices" or mini-embassies. Formal diplomatic relations would wait until 1979, after Watergate, Nixon's resignation, the 1976 presidential election, the deaths of Mao and Zhou, and new political alignments within China.

The improvement in Sino-American relations did have some tragic side effects. In 1971 the Bengalis of East Pakistan rebelled against the military dictatorship of West Pakistan and declared the independent nation of Bangladesh. The Pakistani government attempted to crush the eastern revolution and carried out a slaughter

Beijing Ball Park. This American magazine advertisement, titled "Yankees come here," appeared after Nixon's trip. It read: "The way things are going in China, hot dogs will be sold right along with egg rolls." Mao, of course, never donned a baseball uniform nor blasted a home run over the Great Wall, but Sino-American détente inspired exaggerations like this. (Lucy Gould, *Parade*. Courtesy of Frankfurt Communications, Inc., New York)

that American officials at the scene called genocide. The Indians, who had just signed a treaty of friendship with the Soviet Union, intervened in the civil war on behalf of the rebels. The White House, against considerable State Department objection, ordered a "tilt" in favor of Pakistan.[39] American weapons flowed to Pakistan, foreign aid to India stopped, and a naval task force steamed into the Bay of Bengal. "We can't allow a friend of ours and China's [Pakistan] to get screwed in a conflict with a friend of Russia's [India]," Kissinger explained.[40] Indeed, the White House took a global rather than regional view of the crisis and concluded that India was doing Russia's work. Moscow replied that India was no puppet of the Soviet Union. In the end, Indian-American relations deteriorated, and the United States found itself on the side of the losers. But the Administration thought it had prevented a potentially devastating Indian attack upon West Pakistan, a valued American ally.

Although Washington and Moscow put the hot line into use and swapped blunt words during the Indo-Pakistani conflict, détente remained American policy. The President and his national security affairs adviser traveled to the Soviet capital in May of 1972 for a productive summit meeting. Nixon told President Leonid Brezhnev that "I know that my reputation is one of being a very hard-line, cold-war-oriented, anti-communist." But now he believed capitalism and communism could "live together and work together."[41] They struck agreements on cooperation in space exploration (a joint space venture was launched in 1975) and trade (large grain sales soon followed). The leaders also discussed Vietnam and concluded that small nations should not interfere with détente. Only a few weeks earlier, when Nixon had escalated the bombing of North Vietnam, he feared that an angry Moscow might cancel the summit. The Russians did not; to them détente came first.

The summit conferees concentrated on the Strategic Arms Limitation Talks (SALT) agreements. When the Nixon Administration entered office, it inherited a legacy of doctrines and missiles that defined United States nuclear strategy. (See "The Nuclear Arms Race: A Glossary," p. 580.) In the 1960s, the doctrine of "massive retaliation" evolved into the concept of "mutual assured destruction" or MAD. That is, it was assumed that each adversary was capable of inflicting such heavy losses on the other's industry and population that neither would launch a nuclear attack upon the other. MAD's viability depended upon each side's "second-strike capability": the capacity to absorb a first strike and still destroy the attacker with a retaliatory or second strike. By 1969 American strategists sought a superiority of forces through what was called the triad: land-based intercontinental ballistic missiles (ICBMs), long-range B-52 bombers, and submarine-launched ballistic missiles (SLBMs), all armed with nuclear weapons. To help guarantee superiority, the United States had also begun to flight-test the "multiple independently targetable reentry vehicle" (MIRV), a vehicle equipped with a warhead and mounted with similar vehicles on one missile for delivery against widely separated targets. Finally, President Nixon inherited initial planning for an "antiballistic missile" (ABM) system to defend cities and ICBMs thought vulnerable to Soviet attack. ABMs were designed to intercept and neutralize incoming warheads. Because ABMs theoretically (their efficiency was questionable) protected offensive weapons from attack, critics feared that the other side would be encouraged to build more missiles to overcome the ABM protection, thus further stimulating an already accelerated nuclear arms race.

The Nuclear Arms Race: A Glossary

Anti-ballistic missile (ABM): A defensive missile designed to destroy an incoming enemy ballistic missile before its warhead reaches its target.

Ballistic missile: A rocket-propelled missile that leaves the atmosphere and returns to earth in a free fall.

Cruise missile: A guided missile that flies to its target within the earth's atmosphere, close to the surface. The cruise missile can carry a nuclear warhead and can be launched from the air, land, or sea.

Delivery vehicle: A missile or strategic bomber that delivers a warhead to its target.

Deployment: Installing weapons, making them ready for action.

First strike: An initial nuclear attack by one country to knock out an adversary's strategic nuclear forces.

Intercontinental ballistic missile (ICBM): A land-based vehicle capable of traveling over 3,000 nautical miles to deliver one or more warheads.

Launcher: The equipment that launches a strategic weapon. For example, an ICBM in-ground silo, a submarine missile tube, or a strategic bomber.

Missile experimental (MX): An advanced American intercontinental ballistic missile capable of carrying up to ten MIRVs.

Multiple independently-targetable reentry vehicle (MIRV): A vehicle loaded with a warhead and mounted, along with several similar vehicles, on one ballistic missile. Once separated from the missile, each MIRV can be directed against a different target.

Mutual assured destruction (MAD): The ability of both the United States and the Soviet Union to inflict damage so severe that neither is willing to initiate a nuclear attack.

Neutron bomb: Called an "enhanced radiation weapon," this nuclear bomb is designed primarily to kill people and to inflict less damage on buildings and landscape than other nuclear bombs.

Second strike capability: The ability to launch a retaliatory nuclear attack after being hit by an opponent's first strike.

Strategic weapon or arms: A long-range weapon capable of hitting an adversary's territory. ICBMs, SLBMs, and strategic bombers are so classified.

Submarine-launched ballistic missile (SLBM): A ballistic missile carried in and launched from a submarine. American SLBMs have included the Polaris, Poseidon, and Trident.

Surface-to-air missile (SAM): A missile launched from the earth's surface for the purpose of knocking down an adversary's airplanes.

Tactical nuclear weapons: Short-to-medium-range, low-yield nuclear weapons for battlefield use. Deployed mainly by NATO forces.

Theater nuclear forces (TNF): Intermediate-range nuclear weapons systems, notably NATO's Pershing-IIs targeted on the Soviet Union, and the Soviet SS-20s and Backfire bombers targeted on Western Europe.

Triad: The three-part structure of American strategic forces (ICBMs, SLBMs, and strategic bombers).

Warhead: That part of a missile which contains the nuclear explosive intended to inflict damage.

By 1968 the United States had deployed 1054 ICBMs to the Soviets' 858; the United States led in SLBMs, 656 to 121 and in long-range bombers 545 to 155. The United States also stood superior in total nuclear warheads, about 4200 to 1100, and in the accuracy of its weapons systems. Yet American officials knew that the Soviets were constructing new missiles, submarines, and bombers at a faster pace. In a few years these new weapons would give the Soviets nuclear parity with the United States. When Nixon and Kissinger began to direct American foreign policy, the two great nuclear powers had become "fencers on a tightrope: each facing the other, weapon in hand, balancing precariously; neither willing to drop his weapon and give way to the other; each fearing to thrust decisively because such a thrust would topple them both, attacker and victim, to mutual disaster."[42]

President Nixon soon abandoned the no longer tenable doctrine of superiority and accepted "sufficiency," or parity of forces with the Soviet Union.[43] Still, he decided to phase in the ABM system, for which Congress, after heated debate and a close vote, provided funds. Nixon also ordered the installation of MIRVs. Thus the United States could enter the SALT talks, he said, from a position of strength.

The first SALT talks began in Helsinki in November, 1969, and alternated between that city and Vienna until 1972. SALT-I culminated on May 26, 1972 at the Moscow summit with the signing of two agreements. The first, a treaty, limited the deployment of ABMs for each nation to two sites only. In essence the accord satisfied the MAD doctrine, because it left urban centers in both countries vulnerable. The other accord, an interim agreement on strategic offensive arms, froze the existing number of ICBMs already deployed or in construction. At the time, the Soviet Union led 1607 to 1054. The interim agreement also froze SLBMs at 740 for the U.S.S.R. and 656 for the United States, although the two nations were permitted to raise these numbers to 950 and 710 respectively if they dismantled one ICBM for every SLBM added. SALT-I did not limit the hydra-headed MIRVs, thus leaving the United States superior in deliverable warheads, 5700 to 2500. Nor did the agreement restrict long-range bombers, in which the United States ranked first with about 450, compared to about 200 for the Soviets. Finally, SALT-I did not prohibit the development of new weapons. The United States, for example, moved ahead on the Trident submarine (eventually to replace the Polaris-Poseidon fleet), the B-1 bomber (to replace the B-52), and the cruise missile (a highly accurate, low-flying guided missile). Indeed, as Kissinger told the defense secretary, "The way to use this freeze is for us to catch up."[44] Hearing that kind of reasoning and witnessing persistently high defense budgets, some analysts, like Herbert Scoville, Jr., former deputy director of the CIA, concluded that "arms control negotiations are rapidly becoming the best excuse for escalation rather than toning down the arms race."[45] Still, SALT-I marked an unprecedented step in advancing frank strategic arms talks and in placing limits on specified nuclear weapons. In August, 1972, the Senate passed the ABM treaty by an 88–2 vote; a joint congressional resolution later endorsed the interim agreement. Détente's reputation soared. Conservative critics charged, however, that even though the American arsenal of nuclear warheads was vastly greater than the Soviets', the United States still lagged behind the Soviet Union in delivery vehicles (ICBMs, SLBMs, and strategic bombers). Numerical equality in all categories, then, was the only way to avoid the public perception of American inferiority.

Negotiations on SALT-II opened in late 1972, but progress was slow. At Vladivostok, U.S.S.R. in November, 1974, Presidents Ford and Brezhnev initialed a set of principles to guide the talks. They agreed, first, to place a ceiling of 2,400 on the total number of delivery vehicles permitted each side. They agreed, second, that each side could equip no more than 1,320 missiles with MIRVs. Critics who thought the United States was dodging real arms control complained that the numerical ceilings were actually higher than the levels either side had reached. Thus Vladivostok, even if only a statement of principles, legitimized the arms race. "Using the Vladivostok agreement to slow the arms race," one analyst has written, "is analogous to attempting to dam a wide stream by dropping one large rock in its middle."[46]

After 1974 the SALT-II talks bogged down over which types of weapons should be included in the 2,400 ceiling. The United States insisted that the new Soviet bomber, the Backfire, be included, and the Soviets demanded inclusion of the American cruise missile. Americans thought the U.S.S.R. was seeking superiority; Russians thought the same about the United States. Neither side yielded before 1977, the year the SALT-I agreements expired. By then the United States wielded 8,500 warheads, compared to 5,700 in 1972; comparable Soviet figures were 4,000 and 2,500. Total strategic delivery vehicles by January, 1978, numbered 2,059 for the United States and 2,440 for the Soviet Union. Détente obviously had not checked the nuclear arms race, but it had provided a negotiating environment that at least permitted the heavily-armed adversaries to sit face-to-face, month-after-month, year-after-year, searching for ways to reduce the chances for nuclear holocaust.

In Europe détente also worked to ease tensions. Willy Brandt, the West German Chancellor, pursued a policy of *Ostpolitik* to remove the two Germanies from great power competition. A West German–Soviet treaty of August, 1970 identified détente as the goal of both countries and recognized the existence of two Germanies. A few months later Brandt signed an agreement with Poland that confirmed the latter's postwar absorption of German territory to the Oder-Neisse line. Then, in June, 1972, the four powers occupying Berlin signed an agreement wherein Russia guaranteed Western access to the city and relaxed restrictions on travel between the two Berlins. Finally, in December, 1972, the two Germanies themselves initialed a treaty that provided for the exchange of diplomatic representatives and membership in the United Nations for both (effected in 1973). The Berlin Wall still stood as a reminder of a bitter Cold War past, but it had been hurdled.

The Last Washington Painting. Alan Sonneman's oil painting reflected the alarm that some Americans felt over the ever-expanding nuclear arms race. The Department of Defense reported that, in a massive nuclear exchange, as many as 165 million Americans and 100 million Russians would be killed. (Courtesy of Alan Sonneman, © 1979–1980)

At the Conference on Security and Cooperation in Helsinki, Finland, in the summer of 1975, thirty-five nations, including Canada, the United States, and all of Europe (save Albania) came together in what has been described as the peace conference that officially ended the Second World War. That is, the delegates accepted the permanence of existing European boundaries, including adjustments made in Germany and Eastern Europe at the end of the war three decades earlier. The conferees pledged themselves to détente and endorsed a list of human rights for all Europeans. This last accord met with skepticism. It seemed unlikely that the Soviets would honor this human rights provision, for it would require serious liberalization of their authoritarian system. Indeed, when Soviet dissident intellectuals, citing Helsinki, demanded freedom of speech, the Kremlin had them arrested. Nor did the United States let human rights issues upset détente. In mid-1974, after his arrest and deportation from the Soviet Union, dissident writer Aleksandr Solzhenitsyn, whose *The Gulag Archipelago* (1974) described and condemned Soviet oppression, asked to visit with President Ford. Ford turned the expatriate down, fearing that, if he did not, Moscow might halt progress toward SALT-II.

War and Peace in the Middle East

The Nixon Doctrine, announced in July, 1969, declared that henceforth the United States would supply military and economic assistance but not manpower to help nations defend themselves. "We must avoid that kind of policy that will make countries in Asia so dependent upon us that we are dragged into conflicts such as the one that we have in Vietnam."[47] This meant, apparently, that the United States was retiring its badge as the world's policeman. It was not that simple. Third World countries held a place in the Nixon-Kissinger scheme for equilibrium because of their vulnerability to disruptive radicalism and hence to pernicious Soviet influence. Kissinger cited Moscow's endorsement of national liberation movements to argue, therefore, that the internal politics of developing nations were intertwined with the "international struggle."[48] When troubles arose in the Third World, the first impulse of Nixon, Ford, and Kissinger was to interpret them as moves in the game of great power politics.

Problems in the Middle East were interpreted in that way, and the tensions there sorely tested détente. Basic American goals since the Second World War were to contain or neutralize Soviet influence in the oil-rich region and to ensure the flow of petroleum to the West. After the 1956 Suez crisis, Soviet Russia and the United States armed Egypt and Israel respectively. In June, 1967, after years of growing friction and months of threats and counterthreats, Israel attacked Egypt and Syria, which had merged temporarily as the United Arab Republic. In the Six-Day War, the Israelis, using American-supplied weapons, scored a devastating victory by capturing the ancient city of Jerusalem from Jordan, the Golan Heights from Syria, and the entire Sinai Peninsula, including the eastern bank of the Suez Canal, from Egypt. Half of the Arab states broke diplomatic relations with Washington. Soviet vessels were permitted access to Arab ports. With pressure from American Jews, the United States sold fifty F-4 Phantom jets to Israel in December of 1968.

By the time Nixon and Kissinger entered office in early 1969, the Middle East, said the President, had become a "powder keg."[49] The Nixon Administration

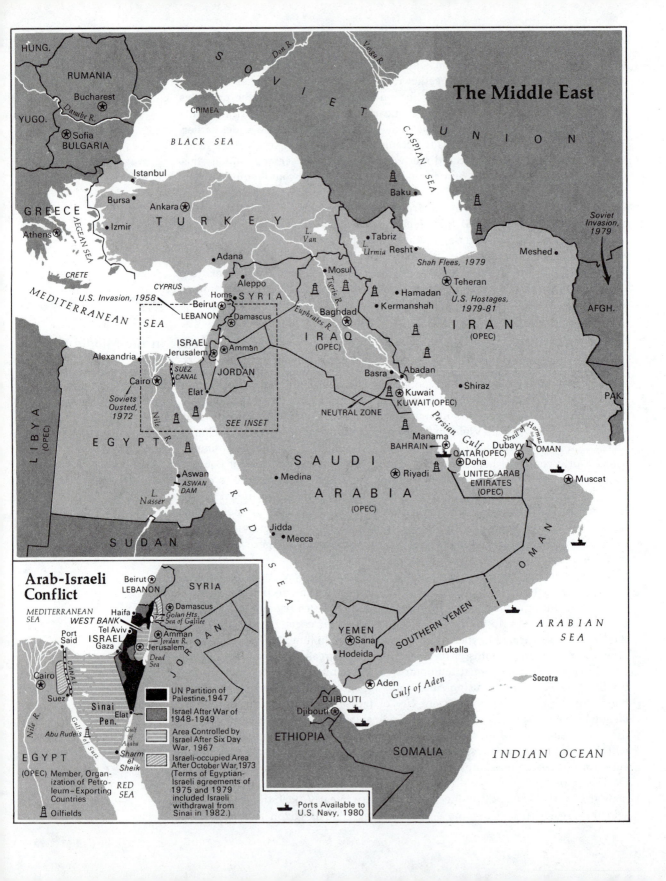

The Middle East

HUNG.
RUMANIA
Bucharest
YUGO.
Danube R.
Sofia
BULGARIA
BLACK SEA
CRIMEA
Don R.
Volga R.
SOVIET UNION
CASPIAN SEA
Baku
Soviet Invasion, 1979

GREECE
Athens
AEGEAN SEA
Istanbul
Bursa
Izmir
Ankara
TURKEY
Adana
L. Van
L. Urmia
Tabriz
Resht
Meshed
AFGH.
Shah Flees, 1979
Teheran
U.S. Hostages, 1979-81
Hamadan
Kermanshah
IRAN (OPEC)

MEDITERRANEAN SEA
CRETE
CYPRUS
U.S. Invasion, 1958
Aleppo
Homs
SYRIA
Beirut
LEBANON
Damascus
Mosul
Tigris R.
Euphrates R.
Baghdad
IRAQ (OPEC)
Basra
Abadan
Shiraz

ISRAEL
Jerusalem
Amman
JORDAN
Alexandria
Cairo
SUEZ CANAL
Elat
NEUTRAL ZONE
Kuwait
KUWAIT (OPEC)
Persian Gulf
Strait of Hormuz

Soviets Ousted, 1972
Nile R.
SEE INSET
EGYPT
LIBYA (OPEC)
Aswan
ASWAN DAM
L. Nasser
SUDAN

SAUDI ARABIA (OPEC)
Medina
Riyadi
Manama
BAHRAIN
QATAR (OPEC)
Doha
Dubayy
UNITED ARAB EMIRATES (OPEC)
OMAN
Muscat

Jidda
Mecca
RED SEA
OMAN
YEMEN
Sana
Hodeida
SOUTHERN YEMEN
Mukalla
ARABIAN SEA
Socotra
Aden
Gulf of Aden
DJIBOUTI
Djibouti
ETHIOPIA
SOMALIA
INDIAN OCEAN

PAK.

Arab-Israeli Conflict

MEDITERRANEAN SEA
Beirut
LEBANON
SYRIA
Haifa
WEST BANK
Tel Aviv
ISRAEL
Gaza
Port Said
CANAL
Cairo
Suez
Nile R.
Sinai Pen.
Abu Rudeis
EGYPT
(OPEC)
Sharm el Sheik
Gulf of Aqaba
Gulf of Suez
Elat
RED SEA
Damascus
Golan Hts.
Sea of Galilee
Amman
Jordan R.
Jerusalem
Dead Sea
JORDAN

■ UN Partition of Palestine, 1947
▨ Israel After War of 1948-1949
▦ Area Controlled by Israel After Six Day War, 1967
▩ Israeli-occupied Area After October War, 1973 (Terms of Egyptian-Israeli agreements of 1975 and 1979 included Israeli withdrawal from Sinai in 1982.)

(OPEC) Member, Organization of Petroleum-Exporting Countries
⚓ Oilfields

⚓ Ports Available to U.S. Navy, 1980

worried that the persistent Arab-Israeli conflict would give the Soviets an avenue into the Middle East. In the spirit of détente, Washington and Moscow began talks on the Middle East that proved futile. Egypt insisted on Israeli withdrawal from occupied territory; Israel, nonetheless, steadfastly refused to "be sacrificed by any power or interpower policy and will reject any attempt to impose a forced solution on her. . . ."[50] As American Phantom jets began to arrive in Israel, as Washington wrestled with a new Israeli request for many more aircraft and tanks, and as the Israelis conducted bombing raids deep into Egypt in January of 1970, the Soviets began their own military escalation. In the spring of 1970, Soviet surface-to-air missiles (SAMs) were shipped to Egypt to provide a defense system against Phantom attacks. Thousands of Soviet troops, advisers, and pilots answered Egypt's call for assistance. Washington growled at Moscow and gave Israel more F-4s and electronic equipment to improve Israeli accuracy against Egypt's missile sites. "Was this the stuff of détente?" people asked.

Meanwhile, Palestinian Arabs, many of them refugees ousted from their lands in 1948 when Israel was created as a nation, grew more frustrated. The Palestine Liberation Organization (PLO), formed in 1964 by several guerrilla groups, came under the aggressive leadership of Yasir Arafat four years later. Many Arab leaders backed the organization in its demand for the elimination of the Jewish state and for the creation of a Palestinian homeland. In 1970 a radical wing of the PLO hijacked airliners and temporarily seized passengers, including Americans, as hostages. The same year, PLO troops with Syrian help battled King Hussein's armies in Jordan. Palestinian terrorists murdered Israeli athletes at the 1972 Olympic Games in Munich. The Israelis retaliated, assassinating PLO figures abroad.

Soviet relations with the PLO and Egypt grew rocky in the early 1970s, as Moscow tried to restrain both of them out of fear that Washington would scuttle détente if Middle East tensions continued. For its part, the Nixon Administration from 1970 to 1973 followed a "standstill diplomacy."[51] It assumed that the Middle East had been stabilized by the sustained arming of Israel ($1.2 billion in American military credits, 1971–1973), Soviet restraint, and the emergence of a seemingly more moderate Egyptian government under Anwar al-Sadat (after Nasser died in September, 1970). Actually, Sadat was plotting a new war against Israel. He asked the Soviets for more weapons, but received few. In the summer of 1972 he abruptly expelled several thousand Soviet technicians and military advisers. Then, on October 6, 1973, Egyptian and Syrian forces struck Israel. The attack took Israel and the United States by surprise. At first the Israelis suffered heavy losses and the Arabs regained land lost in 1967. Tel Aviv pressed Washington for stepped-up military aid. On October 9 Nixon promised more Phantoms. "We will not let Israel go down the tubes," he said.[52] Moscow responded by transporting military equipment to Syria.

In the midst of the crisis, the shadow of Watergate lengthened over the Nixon Administration. On October 10, Vice President Spiro Agnew resigned after evidence surfaced that he had accepted payoffs as governor of Maryland years before. Ten days later Nixon fired the special Watergate prosecutor for getting too close to damaging evidence. The coincidence of domestic and foreign crises frayed nerves. The White House staff feared that Moscow might think the government was weak or incapacitated.

Golda Meir (1898–1978), Nixon, and Kissinger. In 1973, the Prime Minister of Israel got a pointer from the President in Washington, as the secretary of state prepared for his "shuttle diplomacy" in the Middle East. (Department of State *Newsletter*)

On October 13 Nixon ordered a massive airlift of military materiel to Israel. The "Middle East may become in time what the Balkans were in Europe before 1914," a tired Kissinger commented.[53] Soviet Premier Aleksei Kosygin flew to Cairo in the hope of persuading Sadat to accept a ceasefire. Suspicious, Kissinger advised that the Soviets be "run into the ground" by delivery of more American equipment to Israel than the U.S.S.R. could match.[54] Kissinger himself flew to Moscow on October 20, learning en route that the Saudis had embargoed oil shipments to the United States. By October 21 most of the Arab members of the Organization of Petroleum Exporting Countries (OPEC) had joined the embargo. Kissinger and the Soviets finally arranged a ceasefire in the Mideast War on October 22. But the Israelis, who were now winning, violated the truce lines. Moscow then angrily threatened intervention, and both Washington and Moscow put their forces on alert. Kissinger admonished the Israelis to honor the ceasefire. This time they did, and a new ceasefire held.

The Arab-Israeli contest threatened the American economy. Arab states like Saudi Arabia, which for three decades had supplied Western nations with inexpensive petroleum, were now using their black riches as a weapon: they placed an embargo on petroleum shipments to the United States and quadrupled the price of crude oil for Western Europe and Japan. The United States, importing between 10 and 15 percent of its oil from the Middle East, endured an energy crisis. Gasoline prices at the pumps spun upward and anxious drivers lined up, sometimes for hours, hoping to fuel their automobiles. The embargo was lifted in March, 1974, but prices remained high and America's vulnerability had been exposed.

Kissinger launched "shuttle diplomacy" to prevent another Mideast blow-up. With impressive stamina and patience, he bargained in Cairo and Tel Aviv intermittently for two years. President Sadat was soon saying, "Dr. Henry, you are my favorite magician."[55] Washington also pressed Israel. At one point, in March of 1974, Kissinger thought he had failed because of Israeli intransigence. "It's tragic to see people dooming themselves to a course of unbelievable peril," he told top Israeli officials.[56] Yet, finally, on September 1, 1975, Egypt and Israel initialed an historic, Kissinger-designed agreement that provided for an eventual Israeli pullback from part of the Sinai, created a United Nations-patrolled buffer zone, and placed American technicians in "early warning" stations to detect military activities. Washington also tendered promises of substantial foreign aid to both Egypt and Israel.

Thorny problems remained in the Middle East. The Palestinian Arabs still lived in refugee camps and demanded a homeland, while Israelis entrenched themselves in occupied territories, building industries, farms, and houses. Jordan still demanded the return of the West Bank, and Syrian-Israeli hostility persisted as the Golan Heights remained in Israel's hands. Moreover, a bloody civil war broke out in Lebanon, which prompted Syria to send in troops in 1976. Sophisticated American weapons continued to be shipped to both the Arabs and Israelis after the October war, and Sadat warned that military conflict could erupt again. Egypt's economy remained unstable, fanning political unrest. In March, 1976, Sadat, who needed American technology and mediation, denounced Russia, say-

"You're Like a Bunch of . . . of . . . of . . . CAPITALISTS!!" The oil embargo by the OPEC nations in 1974 produced anger among Americans who found that gasoline stations ran out of the vital fuel or that what they could buy had been drastically raised in price. Venezuela and the Arab nations replied that they were only doing what the developed nations had done to them for decades. (Dennis Renault, *Sacramento Bee*)

ing that "99 percent of the cards in the game are in America's hands whether the Soviet Union likes it or not."[57] Once Cairo turned so emphatically toward the United States, American policy in the Middle East looked more like old-fashioned containment than détente. Critics surmised that Kissinger's failure to include the Soviets (and the Palestinians) in Middle Eastern diplomacy ensured that a full Arab-Israeli settlement could never be achieved. One ominous sign was Soviet support for Libya's President Muammar al-Qaddafi, a radical anti-American, pan-Arabist who came to power in 1969 and thereafter denounced all peace efforts.

As a counterweight to "Soviet intrusion and radical momentum" in the Middle East, the Nixon and Ford Administrations fashioned a closer alliance with the Shah of Iran.[58] Nixon and Kissinger visited Teheran in 1972 and promised the Shah all the nonnuclear weapons he wanted and American technicians to help Iranians operate the sophisticated hardware. The Iranian military gorged itself on huge amounts of modern American arms that the police-state monarch bought, thanks to galloping oil revenues ("petro-dollars"). American corporate executives rushed to Iran to display their submarines, fighter aircraft, assault helicopters, and missiles. The Shah bought generously. In 1977 his nation ranked as the largest foreign buyer of American-made arms, spending $5.7 billion that year alone. For 1973–1978 the bill was $19 billion. His armed forces became the most powerful in the region. But doubters in the shahdom thought such excessive military spending foolhardy when the Iranian per capita income was only $350 and such funds could be better applied to alleviating the nation's economic woes. Also, the Shah's CIA-trained secret service jailed or killed critics with a ruthlessness that drew protest from many Americans. To improve his image in the United States he hired a New York advertising agency and lavishly bestowed gifts on prominent Americans. Official Washington regarded Iran as a pillar of stability in the turbulent Middle East, but critics argued that the huge infusion of weapons actually caused instability.

Confrontations in Latin America and Africa

Compared to the Middle East, Latin America seemed quiet and manageable. Thousands of Latin American military officers still trained in the United States, some at the Inter-American Defense College in Washington, D.C., where they learned urban counterinsurgency and jungle warfare techniques. The amount of United States trade with the Western Hemisphere remained large. In the early 1970s about one-third of Latin American exports went to the United States and about two-fifths of the region's imports came from the United States. In 1976, Latin American countries supplied 34 percent of the United States' petroleum imports, 68 percent of its coffee, 57 percent of its sugar, 47 percent of its copper, and 98 percent of its bauxite. In that year United States direct investments in its southern neighbors totaled about $17 billion. Despite these strong ties, Latin American governments increasingly flung challenges at Washington. Soon after taking office, Nixon sent Governor Nelson Rockefeller on a "fact-finding" mission to Latin America. Demonstrations erupted across South America, and parts of his trip had to be canceled. The governor reported to the President in August, 1969, that the United States caused deep resentment through its "paternalistic attitude" and arrogant attempts to "direct the internal affairs of other nations to an unseemly degree."[59]

Mexico was especially sensitive. It refused to honor the economic blockade of Cuba, strongly criticized the 1965 Dominican intervention, and, in its 1972 Charter of Economic Rights and Duties of Nations, boldly proclaimed the economic independence of small states and their right to expropriate foreign enterprises. The charter further urged that developed nations share their wealth with poorer countries. In 1974 the United Nations approved the Charter 120 to 6, with the United States voting "no." The United States also engaged Peru and Ecuador in a "tuna war," after those nations declared a 200-mile territorial limit and began seizing American fishing vessels in coastal waters. After 1968, a new, radical (non-Communist), military government in Peru deliberately set out to break the country's economic dependence on the United States by nationalizing an Exxon oil subsidiary and other American-owned properties. Venezuela also searched for ways to reduce its economic reliance on the United States. A founding member of OPEC in 1960, Caracas joined the Arabs in drastically raising petroleum prices in the 1970s, and in 1976 it too nationalized American-owned oil companies.

In the eyes of the Nixon Administration, Chile posed the gravest threat to United States dominance, for in September, 1970, it elected as President Salvador Allende, an unabashed Marxist, a physician by profession, and a founder of Chile's Socialist party. Thinking that the Soviets and Cubans lurked behind Allende's political campaign, Washington had used the CIA to send hundreds of thousands of dollars in bribe and propaganda money into Chile to thwart his electoral victory. The CIA also cooperated with the International Telephone and Telegraph Company's covert effort to back a right-wing candidate. "I don't see why we have to let a country go Marxist just because its people are irresponsible," Kissinger said at the time he endorsed the secret spoiling operations.[60] Having failed to prevent Allende's election, Nixon ordered the CIA to stimulate a military coup before the Chilean Congress confirmed Allende's triumph. When that tactic also failed, the CIA undertook an elaborate and expensive project to undermine the Allende government. Following presidential advice to "make the economy scream" in Chile in order to unsettle Allende's policies, which included the nationalization of American-owned copper corporations (Kennecott and Anaconda), the CIA cooperated with American companies to block credit and the shipment of spare parts.[61] Economic aid to Chile was cut off and Export-Import Bank loans were denied, but military assistance continued as the CIA conspired with Chilean army officers. The United States government also covertly spent six million dollars to subsidize newspapers and political parties opposed to Allende. This foreign pressure, combined with internal political resistance to Allende's economic decisions, threw Chile into turmoil.

In 1973 Allende was overthrown by a military junta and killed. The new government returned companies to private hands, suspended freedom of speech and press, jailed dissenters, and gained notoriety for torturing and murdering political opponents. In the end, the Nixon Administration had obtained what it wanted— in essence, a successful Bay of Pigs operation. But critics protested United States intervention in the internal politics of a sovereign state. The covert operations, which cost many Chileans their lives, were incompatible with American principles and ideals. Republican Senator Richard Schweiker sadly observed, "The

Frank Church (1924–). Graduate of Stanford University and Democratic senator from Idaho (1957–1981), Church became a major figure on the Foreign Relations Committee, serving as its chairman, 1979–1981. A thoughtful critic of the Vietnam War who believed that containment was inapplicable to Southeast Asia, Church also headed a special Senate committee which revealed United States complicity in the overthrow of Chile's elected President Salvador Allende. (The Historical Office, United States Senate)

Communists argue that we capitalists will never give Communists a chance to get elected through democratic means, and Socialists can never succeed . . . because we would never let them." Schweiker never believed such charges—until Chile. "We have proved Castro and the Communists right by our inept and stupid blundering in Chile. . . ."[62] Others judged the sordid affair an overreaction stemming from an exaggeration of a Soviet/Communist threat.

The Nixon and Ford Administrations also thought it wise to keep Cuba isolated. Under Fidel Castro, Cuba was a Communist state and close ally of Russia. "There'll be no change toward that bastard while I'm President," snapped Nixon early in his administration.[63] In the fall of 1970, at the time of Allende's election, Nixon concluded from sketchy evidence that the Soviets were building a nuclear submarine base at Cienfuegos, Cuba in violation of their agreement after the 1962 missile crisis to refrain from placing offensive weapons on the island. The President and Kissinger decided "to face the Soviets down."[64] They privately warned Ambassador Dobrynin that détente was endangered. Dobrynin assured Kissinger that the Russians were not building a naval facility. Some commentators have speculated that Kissinger deliberately exaggerated the issue in order to justify his anti-Allende policy; that is, he wanted Americans to think that Chile too could become a Soviet military base. In any case, the episode quickly passed. The Nixon Administration claimed a victory over the Soviets through quiet but firm diplomacy. It is not clear what Castro thought about this great-power confrontation over his territory. In 1972 the Cuban leader signed an anti-hijacking treaty with the United States to discourage terrorism on the airways. Three years later the Organization of American States, against United States opposition, lifted its economic blockade of Cuba. But these positive steps were reversed when Cuban troops in Africa helped Angolan radicals come to power. Any further normalization of relations with Cuba seemed impossible until those Cuban troops departed.

Until the mid-1970s Africa stood low on the Nixon-Ford-Kissinger list of diplomatic priorities. Administration policy sought to expand American material interests, strengthen ties with white minority regimes in Portuguese Angola, Rhodesia, and South Africa, and yet encourage progress toward racial harmony. The National Security Council explained in a memorandum (NSSM 39) that "the whites are here to stay and the only way that constructive change can come about is through them."[65] Washington believed that the black majorities feared white military superiority and would therefore refrain from major violent confrontation. In February, 1970, Nixon told Kissinger, then preparing a general presidential message to Congress on foreign policy, to "make sure there's something in it for the jigs, Henry."[66] This crude, condescending remark about black Africans reflected the attitude underlying Administration policy. The Nixon Administration relaxed the arms embargo to white South Africa; Congress in 1971 passed the Byrd Amendment permitting the United States to buy chromium from Rhodesia despite a United Nations-declared economic boycott of Ian Smith's white minority government. Black Africans would protest, CIA Director Richard Helms confidently told a National Security Council meeting, but "they need us."[67] He may have been referring to the more than $2 billion invested in black Africa and to American purchases of cobalt, oil, manganese, and platinum.

Events in Angola eventually shattered American complacency and forced a shift in policy. Since the early 1960s black rebel groups had battled the Portuguese in Angola. Playing a double game in that decade, the CIA channeled funds to a faction of freedom fighters while Washington officially backed Portugal and sold it military equipment to quell the nationalist rebellion. The Soviets began to support one of the guerrilla groups, the Popular Movement for the Liberation of Angola (MPLA). As Portugal floundered in 1974–1975, the independence movement gained momentum. Secretary Kissinger decided that the outcome in Angola held global implications, that America had to take another stand against Russian expansionism by confronting the MPLA. In 1975 the CIA spent $32 million on covert operations involving propaganda, shipments of arms and communications gear, the hiring of white mercenaries, and payments to anti-MPLA political figures. The State Department official in charge of African affairs, Nathaniel Davis, vigorously opposed this secret military intervention, arguing that a commitment of American prestige and resources would not succeed because the United States simply could not control the revolution or local events in Africa. American involvement would merely stimulate increased Soviet activity. Davis urged that the United States appeal to African leaders in Tanzania and Zambia to negotiate a diplomatic solution. "If we are to have a test of strength with the Soviets," he advised Kissinger, "we should find a more advantageous place."[68] When President Ford nevertheless decided on covert aid and a military solution, Davis resigned.

In November, 1975 Portugal granted independence to Angola. The insurgent factions then fought one another in a civil war, with the American clients doing poorly despite support from the United States and China. South Africa also dispatched troops to support an American-backed group. The Soviets and Cubans substantially increased their aid to the MPLA in late 1975, flying advisers and troops into Angola in the thousands. Although the timing is confused, many analysts have concluded that the large Soviet-Cuban build-up came after that of the United States and South Africa.

In the fall of 1975, Davis's resignation and leaks about the secret intervention moved the story into the headlines. Congress stirred. Another Vietnam? Actually, a select number of congressmen and senators had been briefed earlier in the year and had acquiesced in the covert operations. But doubts multiplied after the escalation of warfare, major foreign intervention, and the steady gains of the MPLA. The Administration was preparing to spend another $25 million for arms. "That's when Congress pulled the plug," President Ford later wrote.[69] In December the Senate voted to stop military expenditures for action in Angola; the House followed suit in January of 1976. Kissinger complained that Americans were traumatized by Vietnam; he upbraided Congress for missing a strategic opportunity to confront the Soviets. Congress had "lost their guts," said Ford.[70]

Opponents replied that the United States should never have meddled in an African civil war. The MPLA was not a Soviet puppet, they argued, and given MPLA's successes, the United States would end up on the losing side, thereby discrediting itself. Further, they suggested that discussions with the MPLA—preventive diplomacy—should have been initiated to reduce the violence. "You may be right in African terms, but I'm thinking globally," Kissinger retorted.[71] That kind of thinking, replied one African specialist, "betrays an obsessional, self-defeating preoccupation with superpower global antics reminiscent of the grimmest days of the cold war."[72] When in early 1976 the MPLA won the civil war, the Administration sharply denounced the Soviets and stopped using the word détente.

The Angolan experience prompted reconsideration of American policy toward Africa. So did the outbreak of racial violence in South Africa, where the white government in 1976 crushed a black rebellion in the township of Soweto. America's desire for bountiful Nigerian oil also recommended a change of course. The United States, reasoned Kissinger, was in danger of being isolated from the continent, with black radicals, Russians, and Cubans denying Americans economic links and naval facilities. The United States must do something to "avoid a race war," to contain foreign intervention, and to "prevent the radicalization of Africa," Kissinger belatedly concluded.[73] Arms shipments went to Kenya and Zaire. Economic ties were strengthened through investments by companies like Bethlehem Steel and Kaiser Aluminum, in pursuit of titanium and bauxite respectively. The secretary of state began to disengage the United States from white regimes in Rhodesia and South Africa, urging the latter to abandon its segregationist policy of *apartheid.* "Africa's problems," Kissinger said, "must be for Africans to solve."[74] Such changed language could not disguise the fact that Africa had become an expanded arena for the Cold War combatants.

Economic Foreign Policy: Hard Times

"History has shown that international political stability requires international economic stability," Kissinger said in 1975.[75] He had conspicuous cause for worry, for the 1970s marked a disturbing watershed in the history of the world economy. The international economic order created in the wake of the Second World War foundered. The Bretton Woods monetary mechanism (see pp. 405–406) faltered; the dollar skidded; famines starved millions of people at a time when grain stocks fell to record postwar lows; dwindling natural resources spawned political tensions; and the former colonies of the Third World challenged the industrial nations to share decisionmaking power. Crisis after crisis jolted the international system. The worldwide recession of the early 1970s was the worst since the 1930s. Inflation raised the cost of industrial goods for developing countries. Dramatically climbing OPEC oil prices hit poor and rich nations alike, while the price of some other commodities, like copper, slumped, causing economic downturns in nations dependent upon the export of one product. Economists coined the term "Fourth World"—poor, less-developed countries (LDCs) that lacked profitmaking raw materials, relied heavily upon imports of food, and built up large debts owed to governments and private banks. Nations began raising protectionist barriers, further impeding world trade. The Soviet Union and the People's Republic of China engaged in world trade as never before, in quest of agricultural products and high technology, and enlarged East-West trade became a headline issue. So did the questions of how to avoid a fierce race among nations to exploit the mineral riches on the ocean's floor and how to deal with the powerful multinational corporations that operated around the globe. Few diplomats knew where the new economic paths led.

"America's prosperity," Kissinger noted, "could not continue in a chaotic world economy."[76] The United States produced about one-third of all the world's goods and services. It remained the world's largest trading nation. In 1970 United States exports stood at $27.5 billion; by 1977 they had climbed to $121.2 billion. Large firms, like Coca-Cola, Gillette, and IBM, earned over half of their profits abroad.

Many American jobs depended upon a healthy foreign trade. In 1976, for example, one out of every nine manufacturing workers produced goods for export. Exports accounted for one out of every four dollars of agricultural sales in 1977. American industry also relied on imports of raw materials: 75 percent of the tin, 91 percent of the chrome, 99 percent of the manganese, and 64 percent of the zinc consumed by Americans in 1975 came from foreign sources. In 1977 the nation imported over 40 percent of the petroleum it used. These import needs had become conspicuous in 1971 when, for the first time since the depression decade of the 1930s, the United States suffered a trade deficit, importing more than it exported. Six years later, the trade imbalance reached $26.5 billion, due in large part

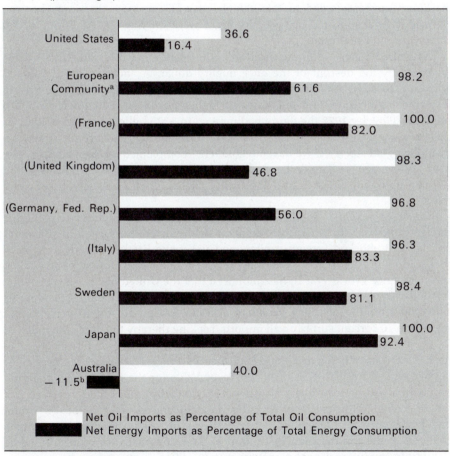

Dependence of Developed Countries on Imported Energy, 1973*
(percentages)

United States — 36.6 / 16.4
European Community[a] — 98.2 / 61.6
(France) — 100.0 / 82.0
(United Kingdom) — 98.3 / 46.8
(Germany, Fed. Rep.) — 96.8 / 56.0
(Italy) — 96.3 / 83.3
Sweden — 98.4 / 81.1
Japan — 100.0 / 92.4
Australia — 40.0 / −11.5[b]

☐ Net Oil Imports as Percentage of Total Oil Consumption
■ Net Energy Imports as Percentage of Total Energy Consumption

**Source:* Roger D. Hansen and the staff of the Overseas Development Council, *The U.S. and World Development: Agenda for Action, 1976* (New York: Praeger Publishers, Inc., 1976), p. B-11. Quoted from Committee for Economic Development, Research and Policy Committee, *International Economic Consequences of High-Priced Energy: A Statement on National Policy,* September 1975 (New York), p. 77.

[a]Belgium, Denmark, France, Fed. Rep. of Germany, Ireland, Italy, Luxembourg, Netherlands, and United Kingdom.
· [b]Net energy exporter.

to imported energy sources. American direct investments abroad—about half the world's total of foreign direct investments—equaled $75.5 billion in 1970 and $149.8 billion in 1977, thus further defining the United States as a pivot of the international economy. Although the greatest part of these American investments remained in developed countries (73 percent in 1975), those investments in developing nations were frequently threatened by political unrest, terrorist acts, and nationalization.

Overall in the world economy, the United States seemed to be losing its competitive edge, and foreigners had less confidence in the once-vaunted American ability to sustain a global economic order. Japan and West Germany, strategic allies but commercial rivals, rose as economic giants to challenge America in the international marketplace. In fact, Japanese automobiles, televisions, and electronic equipment seized a large share of markets within the United States. Once dominant, American producers of computers, high technology, and aerospace machinery now struggled to retain high rank. Then, too, Americans became alarmed when it appeared that wealthy Arabs were "buying up" American banks, companies, and real estate.

The United States' declining position in the economic world was further demonstrated by the descent of the once mighty dollar. A "dollar glut" developed abroad, induced by American foreign aid programs, military expenditures, private investments, inflation, and purchases of higher-priced oil. Foreigners held $78 billion in 1969; by 1977 the figure had jumped to $373 billion. Foreign holders of dollars wanted to exchange them for gold, thus putting pressure on America's dwindling gold stock. "If we have no gold left," complained a Nixon adviser, "we have no leverage."[77] The dollar declined in value against such currencies as the German mark and Swiss franc. The United States faced a balance-of-payments crisis.

In its first two years, the Nixon Administration paid scant attention to economic foreign policy. Then, when the President finally acted, he turned to unilateral policies that shocked foreign capitals and upset the Bretton Woods system of cooperation. In August, 1971 after the dollar had fallen to its lowest point against the mark since World War II, he announced that the United States was devaluing the dollar (by increasing the dollar price of an ounce of gold) and suspending its convertibility into gold. The President also cut foreign aid by 10 percent, and imposed a 10 percent surtax on all imports, seeking thereby to reduce the influx of Japanese and European goods and to put diplomatic pressure on other nations to heed American calls for revaluations of their currencies to make them less competitive with the dollar. Kissinger, less responsible for the new policies than the President and Secretary of the Treasury John Connally, later called this "declaration of economic war on the other industrial democracies" an example of "brutal unilateralism."[78] In December, representatives of ten leading trading nations gathered at the Smithsonian Institution in Washington to try to restore some stability to the international monetary system. After stormy sessions, America's economic competitors agreed to revalue their currencies to bring them more into line with the dollar. The United States then lifted its import surcharge and once more made the dollar exchangeable for gold. But the Smithsonian agreement did not work for long; in early 1973 the United States again devalued the dollar. The United States also withdrew the dollar from a fixed rate system and let it "float," its value determined no longer by agreement, but by supply and demand in the monetary marketplace. Efforts by the International Monetary Fund to restore an orderly system fell short.

America's international money problems were intertwined with foreign trade problems. Not only were American goods priced too high to compete with Japanese or European products, but also the European Economic Community (Common Market) engaged in preferential trade arrangements and export subsidies that hurt American sales abroad. Japan remained highly protectionist at home, yet its products penetrated worldwide markets. In reaction, protectionists in the Congress, wanting to limit imports of textiles, steel, and shoes, introduced a bill in 1970 to impose import quotas and thus reverse America's liberal trade policy. This bill never came to a vote, but it denoted a trend toward protectionism, as had the 1971 10 percent surcharge on imports. Nixon himself sent a strong signal to Tokyo that year when he threatened quotas on textile imports. The angry Japanese thereupon agreed voluntarily to limit their textile exports to the United States.

From 1967, when the Trade Expansion Act of 1962 expired, to 1975, when a new trade act became law, the President had no authority to conclude trade agreements. Nonetheless, multilateral trade negotiations, under the auspices of the long-working General Agreement on Tariffs and Trade (1947), began in Tokyo in 1974. Five years later the "Tokyo Round" of negotiations finally produced accords, largely liberal in character. Overall, tariffs were reduced about 30 percent. The signatories, including the United States, also wrote codes to regulate other practices such as subsidies and dumping. Yet they failed to liberalize trade in agriculture. Many protectionist practices continued, prompting the chief American negotiator in 1980 to remark that "the free flow of world trade remains largely an ideal."[79]

Economic relations with Third World nations were also troubled. Kissinger warned, "The division of the planet between rich and poor could become as grim as the darkest days of the Cold War."[80] In 1972, though the developing world had 74 percent of the world's population, it represented only 17 percent of the world's combined Gross National Product (GNP). In 1976, GNP per capita stood at $6,414 in the industrialized world, but only at $538 in the developing nations (excluding the oil-rich countries). From the perspective of the developing nations (the "South"), it seemed imperative that the wealthy nations (the "North") reduce their profits by charging less for manufactured goods and technology, offer foreign assistance and loans at low rates, reduce tariff barriers, pay more for imported raw materials through commodity price agreements, and refrain from interference when foreign-owned corporations were nationalized or restricted. Developing countries also insisted on a greater voice in international institutions such as the World Bank. Behind these economic demands lay political purpose: economic improvement would supposedly decrease dependency on foreigners, enhance political autonomy, and redress the balance of international power.

The economic demands were first articulated in 1964 by the Group of 77—a coalition of developing nations. Numbering more than a hundred countries by the 1970s, these countries used the United Nations as a forum. They dominated the General Assembly, and in 1974 that body endorsed a New International Economic Order encompassing their demands. The United States, Japan, and Western European nations agreed to talk, some compromises were struck, but by the early 1980s a stalemate existed.

The Rich and Poor Countries: A Comparison, 1960 and 1972*
(percentages)

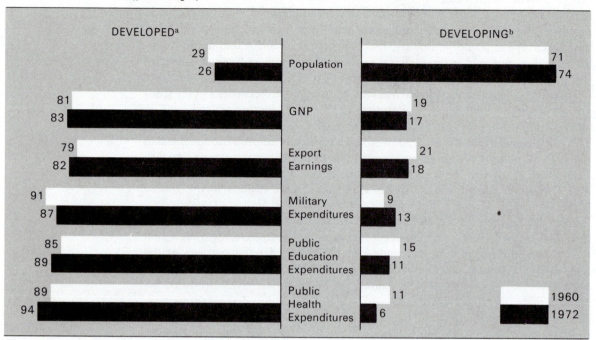

DEVELOPED[a]   DEVELOPING[b]

	DEVELOPED		DEVELOPING	
Population	29		71	
	26		74	
GNP	81		19	
	83		17	
Export Earnings	79		21	
	82		18	
Military Expenditures	91		9	
	87		13	
Public Education Expenditures	85		15	
	89		11	
Public Health Expenditures	89		11	
	94		6	

☐ 1960   ■ 1972

* *Source:* Roger D. Hansen and the staff of the Overseas Development Council, *The U.S. and World Development: Agenda for Action, 1976* (New York: Praeger Publishers, Inc., 1976), p. A-9. Based on Ruth Leger Sivard, *World Military and Social Expenditures, 1974,* published under the auspices of the Institute for World Order (New York), pp. 6 and 17; export figures from *International Trade, 1973–74* (Geneva: General Agreement on Tariffs and Trade, 1974), Publication Sales No. GATT/1974-4, Table E.

[a]Includes North America, USSR, most European countries, Oceania, Israel, Japan, and South Africa.
[b]Includes Latin America, a few southern European countries, Asia (except Israel and Japan), and Africa (except South Africa).

Many in the First World complained that the Third World countries hurt themselves by allocating their resources unwisely. They spent more on military weaponry than on research to combat diseases that afflicted millions. India, fearing Chinese and Pakistani nuclear capabilities, allotted billions to produce a nuclear bomb in 1974 instead of devoting those funds to fertilizers and agricultural research to overcome severe food shortages. Political instability or dictatorships (such as the ruthless regime of Idi Amin, who ordered the murder of thousands in Uganda) interrupted development plans, wasted foreign assistance, and produced tragic human suffering. The developing world, critics argued, should put its own house in order before demanding that rich nations share their wealth.

North-South leaders also made little headway toward solving the problem of food shortages. Insufficient fertilizer, inadequate farm acreage, environmental pollution, droughts, and shrinking fish supplies due to overharvesting condemned perhaps one-quarter of mankind to hunger. The drought that swept Africa in the early 1970s caused at least 10,000 deaths a day. A high birth rate and falling death rate put severe pressure on available food supplies. In 1975 the world population passed 4 billion; demographers predicted that it would top 6 billion in just twenty-five years. Nutritionists estimated that between a half billion and one billion people were already eating less than the number of calories required to sustain ordinary physical activity.

At the 1974 World Food Conference in Rome, the United States voted to help finance an International Fund for Agricultural Development to expand food production in developing countries. But the United States continued to market surplus food for profit, most notably in large grain sales to the dollar-paying Russians. And food aid, always political, became more so; in 1973–1974 over half of American food assistance went to clients South Vietnam, Cambodia, and South Korea. At the same time, because of the OPEC oil embargo and rising petroleum costs, the United States reduced its exports of petroleum-derived fertilizers, thus contributing to a deficiency of fertilizer in the developing world. The shortage meant that 15 million fewer tons of grain were produced worldwide in 1974. As the CIA noted, "in bad years . . . Washington would acquire virtual life-and-death power over the fate of the multitudes of the needy."[81] The 1970s were bad years.

Although American foreign aid strategy in the early 1970s aimed to assist especially the most impoverished people through projects to improve nutrition, family planning, health, and education, and the production of food, developing nations complained that the United States was cutting back when the need was greatest. Although total foreign aid (economic and military) had increased from $6.6 billion

Famine in Chad, Africa. Drought-stricken Chad was only one of many poor nations that suffered in the world hunger crisis of the 1970s, wherein millions died. (CARE, New York)

in 1970 to $7.8 billion in 1977, the proportion of the United States GNP devoted to development assistance actually decreased. Because of fast-paced inflation, moreover, the aid dollars bought less. In 1977 Americans spent about four times as much on tobacco products as their government expended on development aid. Kissinger attempted to meet some of the South's demands; however, he reflected a growing American impatience with the "confrontational" manner in which the developing nations pressed their case and their assumption that growth was "a quick fix requiring only that the world's wealth be properly redistributed through tests of strength instead of a process of self-help over generations."[82] American popular sentiment for foreign aid gradually eroded.

Another contentious issue in North-South relations was the international law of the sea. Water covers 70 percent of the earth's surface. Disputes over navigation and fishing rights had divided nations for generations, but in the 1960s a new question became urgent: who owned the rights to the gas, petroleum, and minerals like manganese and nickel that rested in the deep seabed? Offshore oil drilling was well advanced, but the exploitation of the ocean's mineral riches was just beginning. American companies like Kennecott Copper and United States Steel began to invest large sums in new technology to explore the ocean floor. From the perspective of developing nations, the seabed resources should be shared by all nations as a "common heritage of mankind."[83] The United States endorsed this general principle in 1970, but at the United Nations-sponsored Law of the Sea Conference, which opened in 1973 and continued into the early 1980s, American officials rejected the South's call for a powerful international seabed agency with exclusive rights over the mining of ocean resources. Because the new authority would be governed on a one-nation, one-vote basis, the United States and other industrial nations would become the minority and lose their competitive advantage. Washington insisted on the right of private commercial exploitation, with no limits on profits or access to sites. But in 1976–1977 the United States compromised, now recommending a dual system: private development and an international authority, the latter to be assigned exclusive exploitation of certain mining sites. Still, until agreement was reached on a law of the sea, Kissinger insisted, "the United States can and will proceed to explore and mine on its own."[84]

The South and North also debated controls on multinational corporations, the South seeking tighter controls and a larger proportion of the giant companies' profits earned from operations in developing nations. Ten of the top twelve multinationals in the mid-1970s were American, including General Motors, Exxon, and Ford Motor. As economic powers, they ranked above most of the world's nations. They sometimes intervened in the politics of other nations or bribed foreign leaders to gain contracts. Investigations revealed that Lockheed Aircraft and Exxon, among others, spent millions to bribe overseas politicians—a practice Congress tried to halt through the 1977 Foreign Corrupt Practices Act. The multinationals' economic decisions—where to locate a plant, for example—held real importance for developing nations who welcomed multinational investments but resented outside control. The South also protested that the multinationals employed too few "locals" in high positions and exploited natural resources without adequate compensation. Critics also charged that the multinationals had become global mini-empires, beyond the reach of national laws, thus undermining the traditional nation-state. Business executives and American government officials responded that multinational enterprises brought benefits to developing nations in higher wages, tax revenues, and technology transfers. Whether beneficial or detrimental, multinational corporations by the early 1970s had become major actors in the international system. Washington was reluctant to restrain them because they brought profits home, but the South vowed to restrict them—one of the many economic issues that challenged the Nixon-Kissinger grand design.

Vietnam: From a Wider War to Withdrawal

"What we are doing now with China is so great, so historic, the word 'Vietnam' will be only a footnote when it is written in history," Kissinger declared in 1971.[85] With superpower relations paramount in the Nixon-Kissinger diplomacy, Vietnam became, in the words of a senior White House official, simply a "cruel side show."[86] It was cruel, but it was not a side show. America's longest war continued to claim central attention until 1975. The Nixon Administration worried that the persisting war could damage the President at home and spoil détente. At the same time, the Administration hoped that through détente, the United States might be able to enlist the support of Moscow and Beijing to pressure North Vietnam into concessions at the on-again, off-again Paris peace talks. "I'm not going to end up like LBJ," Nixon early assured his advisers. "I'm going to stop that war. Fast."[87] The troubling question was under what terms the United States could withdraw and still achieve a "peace with honor," to quote Nixon's constant refrain. During the 1968 presidential campaign Nixon stated vaguely that he had a plan for ending the war. He avoided further details and simply recalled that President Eisenhower had brought the Korean War to a close shortly after taking office. Nixon also mentioned that Ike had threatened the use of nuclear weapons.

At the outset, Nixon weighed his options. He could simply pull out of the war, "lock, stock and barrel," as Senate Majority Leader Mike Mansfield advised.[88] But Nixon vetoed that suggestion, for one of his war goals was the maintenance of a non-Communist government in South Vietnam. He would not sacrifice an ally. As played out over the next four years, the new Nixon strategy had several related components—all pointing to a desire to end the war but not lose it. First, Washington capitalized on détente, trying to convince China and Russia, large-scale suppliers of the Vietnamese Communists, to force Hanoi to compromise. Second, the United States itself, through military escalation, signaled Ho Chi Minh that Nixon was willing to punish the "enemy" harshly where Johnson had not. Kissinger believed that North Vietnam must have a "breaking point."[89] Third, Nixon exploited his "madman" image to keep Hanoi wondering if he might be crazy enough to order an atomic attack on the North Vietnamese capital. Fourth, the President sought to strengthen South Vietnam through huge infusions of foreign aid and the training of a larger South Vietnamese army. This "Vietnamization" dovetailed with the emphasis of the Nixon Doctrine on self-help. It meant, Ambassador Bunker remarked, "changing the color of the bodies."[90] And last, to pacify the American people while the Administration drove toward an acceptable peace, Nixon gradually withdrew American troops from Vietnam and issued tough-tongued speeches to counteract the doves. The President and Kissinger had decided, as Nixon explained the troop withdrawal decision, "to drop a bombshell on the gathering spring storm of antiwar protest."[91]

The multifaceted scheme did not work. There is little evidence that either Moscow or Beijing pressed their ally to meet American terms. Indeed, they continued to supply North Vietnam. Ho Chi Minh and the Viet Cong leaders did not bow to foreign wishes, Communist or otherwise. It remained, after all, a *Vietnamese* revolution and war. Ho's legions had outlasted the Japanese and French, and they were not about to abandon their goals, especially when it appeared that the Americans, after the Tet offensive, were in retreat. As for Nixon's attempts to quiet dissent at home, every new escalation swelled the ranks of the critics and finally prompted Congress to limit the President's ability to enlarge the war. By the summer of 1971, according to one survey, only 31 percent of the American people approved of Vietnam policies. Nor did Vietnamization convert South Vietnam into a powerful military state. Although American ships, planes, helicopters, rifles, and millions of dollars poured into South Vietnam, the detrimental effects outweighed the positive. South Vietnam became dependent upon continued American aid to keep its gorged army in the field, thus undermining the ultimate objective of getting South Vietnam to stand on its own feet. America's aid nourished the notoriously corrupt regime of General Nguyen Van Thieu, a government bloated with self-serving officials and a top-heavy bureaucracy. Thieu's regime was "a network of cliques held together by American subsidies," unpopular and ultimately incapable of conducting a winning effort.[92] Finally, because dependency breeds contempt, Vietnamese of different persuasions came to regard the Americans as new colonialists.

In early 1969 the Paris peace negotiations stalled over the basic issues of troop withdrawals (Nixon wanted North Vietnam's forces to pull out of the South) and the survival of the Thieu government. The Communists continued to advance on the ground in Vietnam. Administration officials talked privately of "one very savage punch" through air strikes at the North, but Nixon worried about public disapproval and instead decided to bomb Communist sanctuaries in Cambodia—but to do it secretly so that neither Congress nor the American people knew about it.[93] Code-named MENU, the secret bombing of Cambodia began in March, 1969 with punishing B-52 sorties. But leaks soon brought the story into the newspapers. Nixon and Kissinger then secretly ordered the Federal Bureau of Investigation to wiretap at least four journalists and thirteen White House, State, and Defense Department aides in an unsuccessful effort to discover the source of these leaks.

As Vietnamization proceeded, Nixon grew impatient with the enemy for insisting on complete victory. Kissinger, in August, 1969, began a series of secret meetings with North Vietnamese representatives that lasted into 1973. In the first encounter in Paris, Kissinger warned that North Vietnam must change its rigid stance or face "measures of the greatest consequences."[94] Meanwhile, American soldiers were being brought home, so that by the end of 1971 the troop level had dropped to 139,000. Protest against the war continued nonetheless. On October 15, 1969, a quarter of a million people peacefully marched in Washington, calling for a moratorium on the war. "Don't get rattled—don't waver—don't react," Nixon told himself.[95] The President asked the "great silent majority of my fellow Americans" to help him in his effort to "win the peace" and urged Vice President Spiro Agnew to attack the news media.[96] Public support for the President momentarily climbed because he seemed to be winding down the war.

Events in Cambodia actually prompted the Nixon Administration to expand the war. In March, 1970, the neutralist government of Prince Norodom Sihanouk was overthrown by a pro-American general, Lon Nol. Nixon saw new opportunities:

"We Demand: Strike!" The thrust into Cambodia in 1970 prompted a new wave of domestic protests, including a demand from the radical Boston paper *Old Mole* that students go on strike. Many universities temporarily suspended classes to discuss the costly war. (*Old Mole,* 1970, University of Connecticut Library)

25¢ NUMBER 19   A RADICAL BI-WEEKLY   BOSTON, MASSACHUSETTS   MAY 15 - MAY 28

OLD MOLE

WE DEMAND:

1 That the United States government end its systematic oppression of political dissidents and release all political prisoners, such as Bobby Seale and other members of the Black Panther Party.

2 That the United States government cease the Vietnam War that it unilaterally and its escalation of into Cambodia and Laos; immediately withdraw all forces from Southeast Asia.

3 That the universities end their complicity with the United States war machine by the immediate end to defense research, ROTC, counterinsurgency research, and all other such programs.

STRIKE!

aid Lon Nol against the Khmer Rouge (Cambodian Communists) and the North Vietnamese, who used Cambodian territory for supplies and as a staging area to attack South Vietnam; step up the attack on the North Vietnamese in Cambodia, already being hit by American bombing raids; send unmistakable signals to Hanoi that it had better relent; and show his Senate critics "who's tough."[97] Since Lon Nol might not cling to power for very long unless the United States helped him, Nixon decided to "go for broke."[98] Despite considerable opposition from the State and Defense Departments, the President ordered American troops to invade Cambodia in late April. "You have to electrify people with bold decisions. Bold decisions make history," the President insisted.[99] A cascade of history-making protest rolled across America. Antiwar demonstrations rocked college campuses. As Nixon called the protestors "bums," students at Kent State University in Ohio and Jackson State College in Mississippi were driven back by rifle fire—some were shot to death. The sight of unarmed students lying dead on their campuses horrified the nation. Press and television reporters expressed frank criticism. Members of Henry Kissinger's staff resigned in protest. In June the Senate voted to terminate the Tonkin Gulf Resolution of 1964 and passed the Cooper-Church Amendment cutting off funds for military operations in Cambodia. Although the House failed to pass the latter measure, it was clear that Nixon faced domestic trouble. He reacted by lengthening his enemies list. A "seige mentality" began to grip the White House.[100]

Nixon declared the Cambodian incursion a complete success. Communist arms, equipment, and food were captured and hundreds of enemy troops killed. Although Americans did not find or destroy the "headquarters" that Nixon cited as a major objective, the invasion probably slowed the Communist momentum and bought time for Vietnamization. The bold venture also widened the war, caused the sanctuaries to spread out, and further bloodied Cambodia. North Vietnam substantially increased its aid to the Khmer Rouge insurgents, who gained many new recruits radicalized by the American invasion. Lon Nol became another besieged Asian leader dependent upon United States assistance. South Vietnamese units, which entered Cambodia with American troops, stayed there to sustain Lon Nol's army after the Americans withdrew on June 30, thus stretching South Vietnam's resources to another front.

North Vietnam and the Viet Cong answered the sally into Cambodia by boycotting the Paris peace negotiations. The war dragged on. Through 1970 and 1971 Nixon refused to alter course, except to increase the military activity. He ordered "protective reaction strikes" against North Vietnam after American reconnaissance planes were shot down. These raids hurt, but the North Vietnamese remained intransigent. North Vietnam was "a sovereign independent country," declared Defense Minister Vo Nguyen Giap, "and no sovereign independent country will allow its enemy to spy freely upon it."[101] In early 1971, Nixon approved a South Vietnamese invasion of Laos, where Giap's forces met the invaders head-on in some of the fiercest fighting of the war. Losses on both sides were high, and the South Vietnamese were forced to make a hasty retreat.

At home the bigger war wrought more turmoil. After a court-martial in March, 1971 found First Lieutenant William Calley guilty of murdering unresisting children, women, and old men at My Lai in 1968, Nixon stepped in and said he would review the case before the sentencing—until that time Calley was placed under house arrest only. (Calley won parole in November, 1974). The uproar over Nixon's display of moral obtuseness in the Calley case had hardly subsided when, in June, 1971, the *New York Times* began to print the *Pentagon Papers*, a long, secret Defense Department history of American intervention in Vietnam, complete with classified documents. Leaked by a former Pentagon official, Daniel Ellsberg, the papers fortified critics in their argument that American Presidents consistently had tried to win a military victory, and had frequently withheld the facts from the American public. More and more Americans believed their highest officials had lied and that the United States should never have become involved in Southeast Asia in the first place. The White House raged against Ellsberg. After the Supreme Court failed to halt publication of the documents, Nixon set up a "plumbers" group to stop such leaks and to find ways to discredit Ellsberg. "Watergate" soon followed.

The year 1972 brought the presidential trip to China and SALT-I—and even greater escalation of the war in Vietnam. In Paris, Kissinger continued to meet intermittently in secret with North Vietnamese representatives, always rejecting the Communist plea that the United States withdraw its support from Thieu. But the North Vietnamese claimed that Thieu would rig any postwar election, as he had rigged the one that elected him president in 1972. When the talks again faltered, North Vietnam sent its own message to Washington in March of that year by way of a major invasion of the South. The surprise onslaught struck deep into South Vietnam and threw the Saigon government into disarray. Nixon vowed to give Hanoi a "bloody nose."[102] Soon American B-52 bombers unloaded tons of explosives on fuel depots around Hanoi and Haiphong, where four Soviet merchant ships were sunk by accident. Kissinger warned the Soviets that détente was threatened unless the offensive ceased. "Why are you turning against *us* when it is Hanoi that has challenged you?" asked Dobrynin.[103] In May the President announced the mining of Haiphong harbor, a naval blockade of the North, and more massive bombing raids code named LINEBACKER-I. "The bastards have never been bombed like they're going to be bombed this time," he vowed.[104] During the seven months of LINEBACKER-I, American aircraft flew 41,653 sorties and dropped over 155,000 tons of bombs on North Vietnamese storage facilities, air bases, power plants, bridges, tunnels, and by mistake, hospitals. The flow of supplies to the South slowed, but the North Vietnamese troops still encamped there, angrier than before.

In fall of 1972, Kissinger and Le Duc Tho, chief North Vietnamese negotiator, talked intensely in Paris. Nixon again tried diplomacy. He was up for re-election and his Democratic opponent, Senator George McGovern, a confirmed dove, berated the President daily for pursuing a military solution. In early October, Kissinger and Tho came to an agreement that provided for American withdrawal sixty days after a ceasefire, the return of American prisoners of war, and a political arrangement in the South that ultimately included elections. In short, both sides made concessions—North Vietnam gave up its demand that Thieu resign, and the United States dropped its insistence that North Vietnamese troops pull out of the South. Kissinger was enthusiastic, but when he traveled to Saigon, Thieu balked, resenting not having been consulted beforehand. He rejected the peace plan, refusing to accept the presence of North Vietnamese forces in the South during the ceasefire period. Nixon worried that Thieu might propagandize a sellout to the Communists just days before the presidential election, and thus sent Kissinger back to the negotiating table. The Communists, suspecting trickery, published the agreement that they had crafted with Kissinger. And they made new demands. Still, on October 31, Kissinger told the press "peace is at hand."[105] It was not.

Back in Paris, on November 20, Kissinger and Le Duc Tho resumed their meetings. In early December, after heated exchanges, they reached terms very much like those Thieu and Nixon had torpedoed in October. But a final agreement faltered over the status of the Demilitarized Zone (DMZ). Kissinger suspected the Communists of deliberately holding up a peace settlement, perhaps counting on an unconditional military victory. He thereupon broke off the talks. "Tawdry, filthy sh——s," Kissinger said of his adversaries.[106] Nixon promised Thieu tons of new military equipment and backing if the North broke a peace settlement.

The carrot for Saigon, the stick for Hanoi. Nixon ordered the bombing of North Vietnam above the 20th parallel—"jugular diplomacy," Kissinger called it.[107] From December 18 to 20, LINEBACKER-II planes pounded North Vietnam hour-upon-hour in saturation bombing that a Kissinger aide called "calculated barbarism."[108] Everything from factories to water supplies were hit in the so-called "Christmas bombing." Fifty-foot bomb craters gaped in Hanoi and Haiphong. North Vietnam's largest hospital was destroyed in error—"by bombs escaping the normal bomb train."[109] At least 2,000 civilians perished. One journalist tried to explain why Americans had become infatuated with bombing: "We seek prestige. We seek credibility. We seek honor. *That* is why. And in the course of all this seeking, all this bombing, our souls have withered. Day by day we are turning into monsters. For a hundred reasons, and for no reason whatever, we are blowing men, women, and children to bits with our bombs, and we can't feel a thing."[110] Nixon privately commented that he was once again playing his "madman" role to scare the Communists into concessions.[111]

On December 22 Washington informed Hanoi that the bombing would stop if the North Vietnamese would re-enter negotiations. The talks resumed, and on January 27, 1973, Kissinger and Tho at last signed an agreement. The United States promised to withdraw its remaining troops within sixty days; both sides would exchange prisoners; an international commission would oversee the cease-

"Une Grande, une Immense Majorité Silencieuse." President Nixon said that he was devising his policies to suit the majority of Americans who remained silent during the vocal protests of the 1960s and early 1970s. In this harsh sketch, Vazquez de Sola translated Nixon's "silent majority" into war dead. (Swann Collection of Caricature and Cartoon)

fire; and a coalition council would conduct elections in the South. The issue of the DMZ was settled with some new language. Although the Viet Cong accepted the terms, Thieu as before stood aloof. American officials dealt bluntly with him this time: accept or suffer a cut-off of American aid. Thieu bitterly capitulated. "Ah, these great powers who divide the world among themselves!" he remarked. "They have an open market everywhere and what does it matter if this market costs the life of a small country?"[112] American critics noted that in the four years of the Nixon-Kissinger war, more than 20,000 Americans and countless Vietnamese had died for peace terms that most likely could have been achieved in 1969.

Nixon believed the Christmas bombings had succeeded—had forced a more pliable enemy to the bargaining table. But for several reasons commentators have been skeptical. The United States took heavy losses in those twelve days. The Pentagon admitted losing 26 planes over North Vietnam, fifteen of them expensive B-52s, the backbone of the strategic bomber force. How much longer could the United States waste its powerful air force? Moreover, the final agreement was much like that reached in October, before the bombing. The North Vietnamese did not agree to anything important that they had not already accepted, and the United States position did not improve. Kissinger has asked if the changes in the peace terms were "significant enough to justify the anguish and bitterness of those last months of the war?" His answer: "Probably not for us; almost surely for Saigon" because its acquiescence came only after the bombings.[113] Finally, the popular outcry in the United States against the President grew deafening, and Nixon could not ignore it. Congress was about to reconvene, and many returning legislators were in a mood to eliminate funds for the bombing. Perhaps through North Vietnam's willingness to resume negotiations, "Nixon got himself off the hook," as historian George C. Herring has written.[114]

The ceasefire broke down quickly as each side moved to strengthen itself militarily. The United States maintained military and CIA "advisers" in Vietnam and transferred millions of dollars worth of equipment and bases to the Saigon regime. One peace term called for the United States to provide Hanoi with substantial reconstruction funds. But when the ceasefire collapsed, that agreement was shelved. American warships still cruised off the Southeast Asian coasts, and the bombing of Cambodia continued. Congress began to move again, this time against a President weakened by Watergate revelations, voting in June, 1973 to require the President to cease military actions in any part of Indochina. Nixon vetoed the measure, but accepted a compromise deadline of August 15. In November came the War Powers Act. In 1974 Congress rejected Kissinger's appeal for $1.5 billion in military aid for Thieu's faltering government, voting $700 million instead.

Cut loose from the American umbilical cord, pressed by North Vietnamese and Viet Cong advances, and plagued by thousands of desertions, Thieu and his coterie seemed paralyzed by early 1975. Then, in violation of the ceasefire, the Communists launched an offensive whose swift success surprised even them. The Army of the Republic of Vietnam (ARVN) quickly disintegrated as a fighting force. Many ARVN troops were captured or killed. Refugees clogged the highways; the turmoil in the countryside and cities left some civilians near starvation. Vast amounts of American-made military hardware were abandoned.

On April 30, 1975 both the war for Vietnamese independence and the civil war in the South abruptly ended. On that tumultuous day the victorious Viet Cong

Uncle Sam. Cartoonist Bill Mauldin depicted a bedraggled and bruised Uncle Sam after the hasty withdrawal from Vietnam that spelled defeat in America's longest war. (Copyright 1975, *Chicago Sun-Times*. Reproduced by courtesy of Bill Mauldin)

and North Vietnamese streamed into Saigon and renamed it Ho Chi Minh City in honor of the nationalist leader who had died in 1969. It was an ugly ending for the losers. For days, frantic Vietnamese had surged toward the Tan Son Nhut airbase where American planes loaded with evacuees were departing. But there were not enough airplanes, people blocked the runways, and enemy rockets smashed into the frightened crowds. Thousands of people engulfed the American embassy, whose roof served as a landing pad for helicopters from offshore ships. American servicemen and officials fought back the scrambling, crying Vietnamese. Thieu, the generals, other high-ranking officials, and those who had the money to bribe their passage, had managed to escape earlier, but thousands of panic-stricken Vietnamese who had been "compromised" by their years of cooperation with United States agencies were left behind. Some were sent to Communist "reeducation camps." Others escaped as "boat people," and sailed away in unseaworthy craft with inadequate water and food. Some were picked up and saved; a great many starved or drowned. Human tragedy also struck Cambodia and Laos, where, in 1975, the Communist insurgents also triumphed. In Cambodia the Khmer Rouge imposed a brutal regime that brought death to tens of thousands.

The Americans thus exited from their longest war without victory. The costs were large. Over 57,000 Americans died in Vietnam. The number of Vietnamese dead is incalculable, but estimates suggest that in the period 1965–1974 between 300,000 and 430,000 civilians in South Vietnam were killed. Another quarter-million South Vietnamese soldiers died. In a country of only 17 million people, hundreds of thousands of people were maimed, and 5 to 8 million South Vietnamese became refugees. Communist military losses have been estimated at over half a million. Civilian death statistics in North Vietnam have not been published. Civilian deaths in Cambodia, before and after 1975, also numbered in the thousands. Since 1950 the United States had spent at least $155 billion in Southeast Asia. Perhaps another $200 billion would be paid to American veterans of the war in the future. The war fueled inflation and political instability at home. Nixon's trampling upon civil liberties and the Watergate abuses were perpetrated in large part because of the strains the war placed on the White House and because of frustrations over leaks. The war produced serious political trouble for two presidents—Johnson and Nixon—temporarily, at least, weakening the office of president. Believing that their highest officials had too often lied and deceived, Americans' trust in their government was seriously eroded. The prolonged Vietnam War alienated American allies and undermined whatever goodwill the United States had accumulated in the Third World. Finally, the war and its tragic ending further weakened an already troubled détente. Not accustomed to defeat, some Americans wondered along with an American official who asked "how so many with so much could achieve so little for so long against so few."[115]

The Lessons of Vietnam Debated

Americans only reluctantly searched for lessons after the Vietnam debacle, and what debate there was took place largely among the intellectual and governmental elite. Most citizens were more relieved that it was over than inquisitive about consequences. They switched it off like a TV set. Mention of Vietnam, for example, was rare in the 1976 presidential campaign. "Coming back to America," recalled a Vietnam veteran, "I was shocked . . . that no one even talked about it."[116]

Hawkish leaders who talked about it feared that defeat in Vietnam had weakened America's credibility, inviting the nation's "enemies" to exploit Washington's setback. Although these critics believed the United States needed to demonstrate its supremacy once again, they bemoaned a "Vietnam syndrome" that allegedly prevented America's taking the role of world leader. Nixon's Secretary of Defense James Schlesinger regretted that the military had operated with too many restraints during the war. Next time, he advised, the United States should bomb earlier the enemy's cities, the heart of its military power. Generals Maxwell Taylor and William Westmoreland lamented that they could have gained victory if only the American people had not suffered a failure of will during the Tet offensive. Just let the military do its job next time, unencumbered by public or congressional pressure. The mistake was in not applying massive military force adequately or early enough. To other hawks, Vietnam was the wrong terrain on which to battle communism; the United States should choose the next site with strategic advantages on its side and use aerial and naval power rather than troops. Or the United States should change its strategy to emphasize limited or theater nuclear warfare. And America should find more reliable allies. Henry Kissinger said the lesson of Vietnam was that "outside effort can only supplement, but not create, local efforts and local will to resist."[117] A former architect of American intervention in Indochina, McGeorge Bundy, joined others in insisting that the Vietnam War was unique and therefore should not govern responses to future crises. The "lesson," then, was to draw no lessons. The historian and former Kennedy adviser, Arthur M. Schlesinger, Jr., argued that the United States had stepped inadvertently deeper and deeper into a quagmire without really knowing what it was getting into. The war, then, was basically an accident, a mistake.

Some political scientists, with Harvard's Graham Allison as a leading spokesman, used what they called a "bureaucratic model" to interpret events. They suggested that it is difficult to blame individuals, because of the way the impersonal, oversized bureaucracy resists change, follows standard operating proce-

Vietnam Refrain. Presidents Eisenhower through Ford kept talking about ultimate victory in Vietnam but kept losing the war. In 1975, Ford made a last-ditch effort to gain a small victory in the tragic *Mayaguez* affair. (Mike Peters, *Dayton Daily News,* 1975)

dure, and becomes rutted in traditional channels. According to this view, the bureaucracy in Washington took on a momentum of its own that no one seemed able to control. This bureaucracy, then, had to be reformed by encouraging more dissent and debate within "the system" and by eschewing fixed doctrines and knee-jerk anti-communism. Still other observers blamed the Vietnam disaster on strong presidents like Johnson, who actually controlled the bureaucracy through appointments, an overpowering personality, and a pervasive ideology. This viewpoint implied that a future change in presidents would bring about a diplomatic reformation. Some commentators noted that the Vietnam War's causes and consequences exposed the "imperial presidency" and executive abuses in the constitutional system. They optimistically concluded that, in the future, Congress, with larger committee staffs, would command a more competitive position in the making of foreign policy and place restraints on headstrong presidents.

Other opinions differed radically. Vietnam was not unique, inadvertent, accidental, presidential, or bureaucratic, but rather a prime example of American global expansionism and arrogance, encouraged by a zealous belief that the United States, through superior power and ideals, could and should manage events almost everywhere. Thus the United States was likely to persist in overseas interventionism, if only to restore its prestige. The *Mayaguez* incident of May, 1975 seemed to suggest as much. At a time when the United States was in retreat from Southeast Asia, some Cambodian naval patrol boats seized the American merchant ship *Mayaguez* off the coast of Cambodia. Washington responded with a show of force. The United States, claimed President Ford, had to demonstrate its "resolve" in the face of charges that it had become a helpless giant after the failure in Vietnam.[118] American Marines landed on islands off the Cambodian coast, American warships attacked and sank Cambodian gunboats, and American bombers struck an air base and a petroleum depot. The *Mayaguez* was recaptured, but forty-one Americans died in the mission. Americans applauded the hurried, bold response. "It's good to win one for a change," declared a congressman.[119] But critics claimed the public boasts about clobbering a much weaker nation suggested that Americans had learned too little from Vietnam.

The Vietnam War, said other critics, revealed the shortcomings of the containment doctrine, which had failed to make distinctions between peripheral and vital areas, which applied military force to political problems, and which, according to poet and former policymaker Archibald MacLeish, "put us in bed with every anti-Communist we could find."[120] Analyst Edmund Stillman wrote: "Freedom *is* divisible. Some places are worthy of defense. Some are not. Some are capable of being defended. Some are not. And some places are not free, were not free, and quite possibly never will be free."[121] Ronald Steel, an eloquent critic of *Pax Americana*, likewise commented that the "elementary rule of playing power politics is that you win some and lose some, but that you should never confuse knights and bishops with pawns."[122]

In one of the most searching evaluations, Richard J. Barnet of the Institute for Policy Studies in Washington, D.C. wrote in *Roots of War* (1972) that the "Vietnam War was certainly a mistake. But it was not an accident. . . . The Vietnam War has had a unique result not because American policy has been fundamentally different from what it was when the American military effort smashed the Greek guerrilla movement in 1949 or suppressed the Dominican revolution in 1965 but because the Vietnamese exacted a price for American victory that the United States was unwilling to pay." He predicted more Vietnams unless the American people examined "those drives within our society that impel us toward destruction": the concentration of power in the national security bureaucracy; the capitalist economy and its business creed, which has sought influence abroad to maintain the American standard of living; and the vulnerability of the public to manipulation by national security managers.[123]

Historian Henry Steele Commager, sickened by the use of napalm and evidence of atrocities, wondered why "we find it so hard to accept this elementary lesson of history, that some wars are so deeply immoral that they must be lost, that the war in Vietnam was one of these wars, and that those who resist it are the truest patriots."[124] To some, then, defeat became a victory for humane values. Yet skeptics pointed out that the American people as a whole and probably many leaders had not really understood what their exercise of power meant for others abroad. They still clung to notions of superiority and self-righteousness that rationalized their own destructive behavior. They protested outrageous sabotage by Arab terrorists, but supported the American destruction of villages in Vietnam. They complained bitterly when Third World nations took control of their own natural resources, yet forgot that the United States had exploited those resources for decades. Americans still practiced the double standard, and still believed themselves somehow exceptional.

Some commentators urged "neo-isolationism" as the appropriate posture after Vietnam. "Compared to people who thought they could run the universe," remarked Walter Lippmann, "I *am* a neo-isolationist and proud of it."[125] Never again should the United States practice unrestrained global interventionism. Neo-isolationism, then, would be a healthy check on presidential ambitions for foreign ventures and undeclared wars. Yet neo-isolationism seemed short-lived. Political scientist Robert Tucker, for example, wrote a book in 1972 entitled *A New*

Isolationism, defending the new thinking. But after the OPEC oil embargo and heightened Middle Eastern tensions, he advocated a rejuvenated containment: the creation of permanent American military bases in the Middle East, and military intervention if necessary, to provide "countervailing power" against either Soviet or Arab threats to the oil fields that sustained the Western allies and Japan. "Radical movements and radical regimes must be defeated," he declared, to protect American vital interests.[126]

By the late 1970s there was growing public discussion of the Vietnam experience and its consequences. Some of the 2.8 million Vietnam veterans demanded better benefits and recognition of their sacrifices, arguing that they should not be blamed for the failure of a policy. Public attention was aroused as well by films like *Coming Home* (1978), *The Deer Hunter* (1978), and *Apocalypse Now* (1979), memoirs like C. D. B. Bryan's *Friendly Fire* (1976), Philip Caputo's *A Rumor of War* (1977), and Michael Herr's *Dispatches* (1977), oral histories like Al Santoli's *Everything We had* (1981) and Mark Baker's *Nam* (1981), and novels like James Webb's *Fields of Fire* (1978).

As the 1980s opened, the debate centered largely on the major issue of whether the United States could have won the Vietnam War. A significant body of conservative opinion held that the war could have been won had dissenters not impeded the war effort and had civilian officials not restrained the generals. In the 1980 presidential campaign, for example, Republican candidate Ronald Reagan claimed that "ours was, in truth, a noble cause."[127] Then as President Reagan he declared that American troops "were denied permission to win."[128] Defeat was self-inflicted, he insisted. America could have been victorious.

On the other hand, those who doubted that the United States could have won the Vietnam War raised several questions. Since the bombing of North Vietnam did not significantly impede the flow of materiel and men to the South, only an

History, Reagan, and Vietnam. In the late 1970s and early 1980s, as Americans pondered their Vietnam experience, Republican candidate and President Ronald Reagan said that the lost war should be put out of mind, forgotten. Yet he also repeatedly reminded Americans that they could have won the war and that they should draw from the tragedy the lesson that the United States should enlarge its military power and apply it without restraint in the future. (Bob Englehart, *Hartford Courant*)

American invasion of the North would have sufficed to defeat the enemy. This strategy would have entailed heavy American casualties and a long occupation of a hostile population that had demonstrated its tenacity against foreigners through decades of warfare. Would the American people support a prolonged, expensive, and bloody occupation while fighting continued in the South? Would Americans accept the killing of tens of thousands of people by bombing the irrigation dikes of the North? Would Americans willingly be drafted into a cause with such an uncertain end? Such an invasion of the North, moreover, would have risked war with both Russia and China. Russia might have been dissuaded by détente from rescuing the North, but China had promised publicly that it would intervene as it had in Korea in 1950 if the United States moved north. Could the United States have won if the Vietnam War turned into a conflagration of the great powers?

To have won, suggested some, the United States would also have had to destroy what it was trying to save. That is, using more military power would have produced more deaths and more refugees. What would be left after "victory"? Perhaps at best an internally-divided, economically-feeble nation needing huge infusions of American aid, but still vulnerable to collapse. Even if the military had been unleashed—and given the amount of firepower and bombs displayed in Southeast Asia some critics doubted that it had ever been much restrained—it would still have faced intractable problems: an inhospitable terrain and climate; jungle, leeches, malaria, and enemy booby traps; an elusive adversary deeply committed to its cause, battle-tested, and able to live off the land (*its* land); and a South Vietnamese people who often sheltered Communist soldiers. Doubters of the "win" thesis have noted further that the United States received very little help from its allies. In fact most of its European allies urged Washington to stop wasting its resources on a secondary and fruitless venture. Of America's forty allies by treaty, only Australia, New Zealand, South Korea, and Thailand sent combat troops. The United States fought virtually alone.

The United States could not have won, others have argued, because there was no political base upon which to build. The South Vietnamese governments were corrupt, unstable, and unpopular. Coups and attempted coups too frequently rocked Saigon. "The political foundations of the military effort need to be strong," political scientist Stanley Hoffmann has noted. "If they are rotten, the likelihood that one will build them up with a war in progress is quite low."[129] The South Vietnamese desertion rate was high. "I served as an adviser to three separate ARVN battalions," recalled one veteran Marine officer, "every one of which, every time we were in combat, split."[130] The South Vietnamese people did not seem to want to fight. The "war of attrition" alienated many South Vietnamese, as did the unsettling strategic hamlet program, disruptive "search and destroy" missions, burning of villages, requiring of identity cards, bombings of innocents, and the flourishing of bars and houses of prostitution. Growing numbers of "friends" in the South actually became hostile, resenting the dependency of their devastated land. In sum, the containment policy could not be successful because local political conditions were so unfavorable.

Problems in the military itself, others have concluded, reduced the chances for victory. Because officers wanted to reassure superiors that they were turning back the enemy, some suppressed intelligence information and many submitted false reports on the numbers killed. One colonel recalled one exaggerated "scorecard": when two different reports of four Viet Cong and two Viet Cong killed were sent to headquarters, personnel there joined the figures to read forty-two killed.[131] "If he's dead and Vietnamese, he's VC [Viet Cong]" was the prevailing assumption in the field.[132] Decisionmakers in Washington were thus misled on how badly the war was going. The military also suffered from corruption and mismanagement—in some cases a black market for equipment developed. Drug usage among American troops became a serious problem. Perhaps as many as ten percent took heroin; many more smoked cheap marijuana. Racial tension between whites and blacks and "fragging"—the murder of officers by enlisted men by means of a hand grenade or other weapon—further reduced combat effectiveness. What amounted to a "kill and destroy" strategy proved counterproductive, sending disaffected South Vietnamese into the arms of the Communists. In other words, to have improved its performance in Vietnam at all, the United States would have had to replace its military leaders and reform its army—an impossible undertaking in wartime—that would still have been insufficient for victory.

For all of these reasons, then, some observers seriously questioned the thesis that victory was attainable had it not been for domestic opposition and a loss of will. Whatever the answer, it was certain that succeeding administrations would have to operate in a domestic political setting of uncertainty and anxiety about the post-Vietnam direction of American foreign policy. Conservative defenders of the war stood ready to criticize any policy that smacked of retrenchment or "another Munich." Liberals and radicals stood alert to attack any policy that seemed to offer "another Vietnam." And in this highly-charged environment, the unfulfilled Nixon-Kissinger grand design disintegrated further.

Further Reading for the Period 1969–1977

Richard M. Nixon, Henry A. Kissinger, and 1970s diplomatic issues are discussed in Coral Bell, *The Diplomacy of Detente: The Kissinger Era* (1977); Henry Brandon, *The Retreat of American Power* (1973); Seyom Brown, *The Crises of Power* (1979); Warren I. Cohen, *America's Response to China* (1980); Thomas M. Franck and Edward Weisband, *Foreign Policy by Congress* (1979); John L. Gaddis, *Russia, the Soviet Union, and the United States* (1978); Lloyd C. Gardner, ed., *The Great Nixon Turnaround* (1973); Stephen Graubard, *Kissinger: Portrait of a Mind* (1973); Michael M. Harrison, *The Reluctant Ally: France and Atlantic Security* (1981); Stanley Hoffmann, *Primacy or World Order* (1978) and "The Case of Dr. Kissinger," *New York Review of Books* (December 6, 1979); Gene T. Hsiao, ed., *Sino-American Détente and Its Policy Implications* (1974); Robert C. Johansen, *The National Interest and the Human Interest* (1980); Alan M. Jones, Jr., *U.S. Foreign Policy in a Changing World* (1973); Bernard and Marvin Kalb, *Kissinger* (1974); Morton A. Kaplan and Kinhide Mushakoji, eds., *Japan, America, and the Future World Order* (1976); Walter LaFeber, *America, Russia, and the Cold War* (1980); Anthony Lake, *The "Tar Baby" Option: American Policy Toward Southern Rhodesia* (1976); David Landau, *Kissinger: Uses of Power* (1972); Roger Morris, *Uncertain Greatness* (1977) (Kissinger); Robert E. Osgood et al., *Retreat from Empire* (1973); Jonathan Schell, *The Time of Illusion* (1976); Arthur M. Schlesinger, Jr., *The Imperial Presidency* (1973); John Spanier and Joseph Nogee, eds., *Congress, the Presidency and American Foreign Policy* (1981); Laurence Stern, *The Wrong Horse* (1977) (on Cyprus, Greece, and Turkey); John Stoessinger, *Henry Kissinger: The Anguish of Power* (1976); Tad Szulc, *The Illusion of Peace* (1978); Jennifer S. Whitaker, *Conflict in Southern Africa* (Foreign Policy Association, *Headline Series*, 1978); and Garry Wills, *Nixon Agonistes* (1970).

For Soviet-American relations, détente, and SALT, see Richard J. Barnet, *The Giants: Russia and America* (1977); Robert F. Byrnes, *Soviet-American Academic Exchanges, 1958–1975* (1976); Marshall I. Goldman, *Détente and Dollars: Doing Business with the Soviets* (1975); Roger Kanet, ed., *The Soviet Union and the Developing Nations* (1976); Thomas B. Larson, *Soviet-American Rivalry* (1978); Michael Mandelbaum, *The Nuclear Question* (1979); John Newhouse, *Cold Dawn: The Story of SALT* (1973); Morton Schwartz, *Soviet Perceptions of the United States* (1978); and Paula Stern, *Water's Edge* (1979) (on the Jackson Amendment).

The Vietnam War, its end, and its lessons are the subject of Leslie H. Gelb and Richard K. Betts, *The Irony of Vietnam: The System Worked* (1979); Allan E. Goodman, *The Lost Peace: America's Search for a Negotiated Settlement of the Vietnam War* (1978); George C. Herring, *America's Longest War* (1979); Anthony Lake, ed., *The Vietnam Legacy* (1976); Gareth Porter, *A Peace Denied: The United States, Vietnam, and the Paris Agreement* (1975); Earl C. Ravenal, *Never Again: Learning from America's Foreign Policy Failures* (1978); William Shawcross, *Sideshow: Kissinger, Nixon and the Destruction of Cambodia* (1979); and W. Scott Thompson and Donaldson D. Frizzill, eds., *The Lessons of Vietnam* (1977). See also works listed in the "Further Reading" section for Chapter 14.

For the many international economic issues, see George W. Ball, ed., *Global Companies* (1975); Richard J. Barnet, *The Lean Years* (1980); Richard J. Barnet and Ronald Müller, *The Global Reach: The Power of the Multinational Corporations* (1974); I. M. Destler, *Making Foreign Economic Policy* (1980); I. M. Destler, Haruhiro Fukui, and Hideo Sato, *The Textile Wrangle: Conflict in Japanese-American Relations, 1969–1971* (1979); Alfred E. Eckes, *The United States and the Global Struggle for Minerals* (1977); Ann L. Hollick, *U.S. Foreign Policy and the Law of the Sea* (1981); Raymond F. Hopkins and Donald J. Puchala, *Global Food Interdependence* (1980); Stephen Krasner, *Defending the National Interest: Raw Materials and U.S. Foreign Policy* (1978); David Morawetz, *Twenty-Five Years of Economic Development, 1950–1975* (1977); Robert K. Olson, *U.S. Foreign Policy and the New International Economic Order* (1981); William and Paul Paddock, *Time of Famines: America and the World Food Crisis* (1976); Robert A. Pastor, *Congress and the Politics of U.S. Foreign Economic Policy, 1929–1976* (1980); Joan E. Spero, *The Politics of International Economic Relations* (1981); and Mitchel B. Wallerstein, *Food for War—Food for Peace* (1980). See also several primers in the Foreign Policy Association's *Headline Series*: Charles P. Kindleberger, *America in the World Economy* (1977); Lloyd N. Cutler, *Global Interdependence and the Multinational Firm* (1978); Phyllis T. Piotrow, *World Population* (1980); and Sol M. Linowitz, *World Hunger* (1980).

For the Middle East and the Arab-Israeli conflict, see Trevor N. Dupuy, *Elusive Victory: The Arab-Israeli Wars, 1947–1974* (1978); Robert O. Freedman, *Soviet Policy toward the Middle East Since 1970* (1978); Jon D. Glassman, *Arms for the Arabs: The Soviet Union and War in the Middle East* (1975); George Lenczowski, *The Middle East in World Affairs* (1980); William B. Quandt, *Decade of Decisions: American Policy Toward the Arab-Israeli Conflict, 1967–1976* (1977); Bernard Reich, *Quest for Peace: United States–Israel Relations and the Arab-Israeli Conflict* (1977); Barry Rubin, *Paved with Good Intentions* (1977) (Iran); Jeffrey Z. Rubin, ed., *Dynamics of Third-Party Intervention: Kissinger in the Middle East* (1981); Edward R. F. Sheehan, *The Arabs, Israelis, and Kissinger* (1976); Benjamin Shwadran, *Middle East Oil: Issues and Problems* (1977); and Robert W. Stookey, *America and the Arab States* (1975).

Latin American–United States relations, including Chile, are treated in Robert J. Alexander, *The Tragedy of Chile* (1978); Samuel L. Baily, *The United States and the Development of South America, 1945–1975* (1976); Richard R. Fagen, ed., *Capitalism and the State in U.S.–Latin American Relations* (1979); T. H. Moran, *Multinational Corporations and the Politics of Dependence: Copper in Chile* (1974); James Petras and Morris Morely, *The United States and Chile* (1975); Stephen G. Rabe, *The Road to OPEC: United States Relations with Venezuela* (1982); Paul E. Sigmund, *The Overthrow of Allende and the Politics of Chile, 1964–1976* (1977); and Arthur P. Whitaker, *The United States and the Southern Core: Argentina, Chile, and Uruguay* (1976).

See also the General Bibliography and the following notes.

1. Quoted in Marvin Kalb and Bernard Kalb, *Kissinger* (Boston: Little, Brown, 1974), p. 266.
2. Hugh Sidey in *Life*, LXXII (March 3, 1972), 12.
3. Quoted in Kalb and Kalb, *Kissinger*, p. 267.
4. Joseph Kraft, *The Chinese Difference* (New York: Saturday Review Press, 1973), p. 19.
5. *Newsweek*, LXXIX (February 28, 1972), 13.
6. *Department of State Bulletin*, LXVI (March 6, 1972), 290.
7. Henry Kissinger, *White House Years* (Boston: Little, Brown, 1979), p. 163.
8. *Ibid.*, p. 754.
9. *Public Papers of the Presidents, Richard M. Nixon, 1971* (Washington, D.C.: Government Printing Office, 1972), p. 819.
10. Harry Schwartz, "The Asian Triangle," *New York Times*, February 21, 1972.
11. Quoted in William L. Safire, *Before the Fall: An Inside View of the Pre-Watergate White House* (Garden City, N.Y.: Doubleday, 1975), p. 452.
12. Kissinger, *White House Years*, p. 1049.
13. James C. Thomson, Jr., "China's New Diplomacy: A Symposium (II)," *Problems of Communism*, XXI (January-February, 1972), 49.
14. *New York Times*, February 21, 1972.
15. Quoted in Henry Brandon, *The Retreat of American Power* (New York: Dell, 1972), p. 190.
16. Quoted in Richard Nixon, *RN: The Memoirs of Richard Nixon* (New York: Grosset & Dunlap, 1978), p. 561.
17. Quoted in Kissinger, *White House Years*, p. 1056.
18. *Department of State Bulletin*, LXVI (March 20, 1972), 421.
19. Quoted in Safire, *Before the Fall*, p. 12.
20. George Gallup, "U.S. Image of Red China Shows Favorable Change," *Hartford Courant*, March 12, 1972.
21. Kissinger quoted in Theodore H. White, *The Making of the President, 1972* (New York: Atheneum, 1973), p. X.
22. The communiqué is printed in *Department of State Bulletin*, LXVI (March 20, 1972), 435–438.
23. Nixon, *RN*, p. 580.
24. Quoted in Safire, *Before the Fall*, p. 102 and Nixon, *RN*, p. 529.
25. H. R. Haldeman, *The Ends of Power* (New York: Times Books, 1978), p. 98.
26. Quoted in Roger Morris, *Uncertain Greatness: Henry Kissinger and American Foreign Policy* (New York: Harper & Row, 1977), p. 3.
27. Quoted in Richard Valeriani, *Travels with Henry* (New York: Berkley Books, [1979], 1980), p. 123; Kissinger, *White House Years*, p. 1094.
28. Stanley Hoffmann, *Primacy or World Order* (New York: McGraw-Hill, 1978), p. 33.
29. Unnamed Senator quoted in Leslie H. Gelb, "Kissinger and Congress," *New York Times*, February 22, 1975.
30. Quoted in Kalb and Kalb, *Kissinger*, p. 13.
31. "An Interview with Oriana Fallaci: Kissinger," *New Republic*, CLXVII (December 16, 1972), 21–22.
32. Quoted in J. Garry Clifford, "Change and Continuity in American Foreign Policy Since 1930," in James T. Patter-son, ed., *Paths to the Present* (Minneapolis: Burgess, 1975), p. 137.
33. Quoted in Garry Wills, *Nixon Agonistes: The Crisis of the Self-Made Man* (Boston: Houghton Mifflin, 1970), p. 20.
34. Kissinger, *White House Years*, p. 191.
35. *Ibid.*, p. 55.
36. *Public Papers, Nixon, 1971*, p. 806.
37. Quoted in John L. Gaddis, *Russia, the Soviet Union, and the United States* (New York: Wiley, 1978), p. 262.
38. Quoted in Elaine P. Adam and Richard P. Stebbins, eds., *American Foreign Relations, 1976: A Documentary Record* (New York: New York University Press, 1978), p. 13.
39. Quoted in Tad Szulc, *The Illusion of Peace: Foreign Policy in the Nixon Years* (New York: Viking, 1978), p. 442.
40. Quoted in Nixon, *RN*, p. 527.
41. *Ibid.*, p. 611.
42. Michael Mandelbaum, *The Nuclear Question: The United States & Nuclear Weapons, 1946–1976* (Cambridge, England: Cambridge University Press, 1979), p. 218.
43. *Public Papers, Nixon, 1969*, p. 19.
44. Kissinger, *White House Years*, p. 1245n.
45. Quoted in Richard J. Barnet, *The Giants: Russia and America* (New York: Simon and Schuster, 1977), p. 102.
46. Robert C. Johansen, *The National Interest and the Human Interest* (Princeton, N.J.: Princeton University Press, 1980), p. 55.
47. *Public Papers, Nixon, 1969*, p. 548.
48. Kissinger, *White House Years*, p. 117.
49. Quoted in Robert W. Stookey, *America and the Arab States* (New York: Wiley, 1975), p. 221.
50. Quoted in William B. Quandt, *Decade of Decisions: American Policy Toward the Arab-Israeli Conflict, 1967–1976* (Berkeley: University of California Press, 1977), p. 91.
51. *Ibid.*, p. 127.
52. Nixon, *RN*, p. 924.
53. Quoted in Kalb and Kalb, *Kissinger*, p. 473.
54. Quoted in Quandt, *Decade of Decisions*, p. 188.
55. Quoted in Edward R. F. Sheehan, "How Kissinger Did It: Step by Step in the Middle East," *Foreign Policy*, No. 22 (Spring, 1976), p. 48.
56. Quoted in Edward R. F. Sheehan, *The Arabs, Israelis, and Kissinger* (New York: Reader's Digest Press, 1976), p. 162.
57. Quoted in *New York Times*, March 15, 1976.
58. Kissinger, *White House Years*, p. 1264.
59. Quoted in Samuel L. Baily, *The United States and the Development of South America, 1945–1975* (New York: New Viewpoints, 1976), p. 118.
60. Kissinger, *White House Years*, p. 673.
61. Quoted in U.S. Senate, Staff Report of Select Committee to Study Governmental Operations with Respect to Intelligence Activities, *Covert Action in Chile, 1963–1973* (Washington, D.C.: Government Printing Office, 1975), p. 33.
62. U.S. Senate, Select Committee to Study Governmental Operations with Respect to Intelligence Activities, *Intelligence Activities*, vol. 7, *Covert Action* (hearings) (Washington, D.C.: Government Printing Office, 1976), p. 45.
63. Quoted in Morris, *Uncertain Greatness*, p. 106.

64. Kissinger, *White House Years*, p. 645.

65. Quoted in Stephen R. Weissman, "CIA Covert Action in Zaire and Angola: Patterns and Consequences," *Political Science Quarterly*, XCIV (Summer, 1979), 281.

66. Quoted in Morris, *Uncertain Greatness*, p. 131.

67. Quoted in *ibid.*, p. 117.

68. Nathaniel Davis, "The Angola Decision of 1975: A Personal Memoir," *Foreign Affairs*, LVII (Fall, 1978), 114.

69. Gerald R. Ford, *A Time to Heal: The Autobiography of Gerald R. Ford* (New York: Harper & Row, 1979), p. 345.

70. Quoted in Thomas M. Franck and Edward Weisband, *Foreign Policy By Congress* (New York: Oxford University Press, 1979), p. 46.

71. Quoted in Tom Wicker, "How Not to Think Globally," *New York Times*, March 14, 1976.

72. John A. Marcum, "Lessons of Angola," *Foreign Affairs*, LIV (April, 1976), 418.

73. *Department of State Bulletin*, LXXV (July 12, 1976), 46.

74. *Ibid.*, LXXIV (June 7, 1976), 714.

75. *Ibid.*, LXXII (June 2, 1975), 713.

76. *Ibid.*

77. Quoted in Szulc, *Illusion of Peace*, p. 454.

78. Kissinger, *White House Years*, pp. 955, 962.

79. Reuben Askew quoted in Charles W. Kegley, Jr. and Eugene R. Wittkopf, *World Politics: Trend and Transformation* (New York: St. Martin's Press, 1981), p. 181.

80. *Department of State Bulletin*, LXXIII (September 22, 1975), 425.

81. Quoted in Johansen, *National Interest and the Human Interest*, p. 13.

82. Quoted in Adam, *American Foreign Relations, 1976*, p. 478.

83. United Nations, General Assembly, *Official Records*, 22nd Session, August 18, 1967, Agenda Item 92, Annexes, Document A/6695, Memorandum by Permanent Mission of Malta, p. 1.

84. *Department of State Bulletin*, LXXIV (April 26, 1976), 535.

85. Quoted in Michael Roskin, "An American Metternich: Henry A. Kissinger and the Global Balance of Power," in Frank J. Merli and Theodore A. Wilson, eds., *Makers of American Diplomacy* (New York: Charles Scribner's, 1974), p. 698.

86. Quoted in Tad Szulc, "How Kissinger Did It: Behind the Vietnam Cease-Fire Agreement," *Foreign Policy*, No. 15 (Summer, 1974), p. 35.

87. Quoted in Haldeman, *Ends of Power*, p. 81.

88. Quoted in Stanley Millet, ed., *South Vietnam: U.S.–Communist Confrontation in Southeast Asia, 1969* (New York: Facts on File, 1973–1974; 7 vols.), IV, 64.

89. Quoted in Morris, *Uncertain Greatness*, p. 164.

90. Quoted in James A. Nathan, "Commitments in Search of a Roost: The Foreign Policy of the Nixon Administration," *Virginia Quarterly Review*, L (Summer, 1974), 337.

91. Nixon, *RN*, p. 448.

92. Frances FitzGerald, *Fire in the Lake: The Vietnamese and the Americans in Vietnam* (New York: Vintage Books, 1972), p. 544.

93. Quoted in Szulc, *Illusion of Peace*, p. 153.

94. Nixon, *RN*, p. 396.

95. *Ibid.*, p. 403.

96. *Public Papers, Nixon, 1969*, p. 909.

97. Nixon quoted in Morris, *Uncertain Greatness*, p. 175.

98. Nixon, *RN*, p. 450.

99. Quoted in William Shawcross, *Sideshow: Kissinger, Nixon and the Destruction of Cambodia* (New York: Pocket Books, 1979), p. 152.

100. Charles Colson quoted in George C. Herring, *America's Longest War: The United States and Vietnam, 1950–1975* (New York: Wiley, 1979), p. 233.

101. Quoted in Millet, *South Vietnam, 1970*, V, 107.

102. Quoted in Herring, *America's Longest War*, p. 240.

103. Quoted in Nixon, *RN*, p. 605.

104. Quoted in Herring, *America's Longest War*, p. 241.

105. Kissinger, *White House Years*, p. 1399.

106. Quoted in Nixon, *RN*, pp. 733.

107. Quoted in Herring, *America's Longest War*, p. 247.

108. Morris, *Uncertain Greatness*, p. 190.

109. Guenter Lewy, *America in Vietnam* (New York: Oxford University Press, 1978), p. 414.

110. "The Talk of the Town," *The New Yorker*, XLVIII (September 23, 1972), 27.

111. Quoted in Thomas L. Hughes, "Foreign Policy: Men or Measures?" *The Atlantic*, CCXXXIV (October, 1974), 56.

112. Quoted in Oriana Fallaci, *Interview with History* (Boston: Houghton Mifflin, 1976), p. 56.

113. Kissinger, *White House Years*, p. 1467.

114. Herring, *America's Longest War*, p. 249.

115. Robert Komer in W. Scott Thompson and Donaldson D. Frizzell, eds., *The Lessons of Vietnam* (New York: Crane, Russak, 1977), p. 211.

116. Quoted in Mark Baker, *Nam: The Vietnam War in the Words of the Men and Women Who Fought There* (New York: William Morrow, 1981), p. 314.

117. *Department of State Bulletin*, LXXIII (July 7, 1975), 3.

118. Ford, *A Time to Heal*, p. 275.

119. Carroll Hubbard, Jr., quoted in *ibid.*, p. 284.

120. Archibald MacLeish, "Now Let Us Address the Main Question: Bicentennial of What?" *New York Times*, July 3, 1976.

121. Edmund Stillman, in "America Now: A Failure of Nerve?" *Commentary*, LX (July, 1975), 83.

122. Ronald Steel in *ibid.*, p. 79.

123. Richard J. Barnet, *Roots of War* (Baltimore: Penguin Books, 1972), pp. 7–8, 9.

124. Henry Steele Commager, "The Defeat of America," *New York Review of Books*, October 5, 1972, p. 13.

125. Quoted in Ronald Steel, *Walter Lippmann and the American Century* (Boston: Little, Brown, 1980), p. 586.

126. Robert W. Tucker, *The Purposes of American Power* (New York: Praeger, 1981), pp. 113, 178.

127. Quoted in *New York Times*, August 19, 1980.

128. Quoted in George C. Herring, "The 'Vietnam Syndrome' and American Foreign Policy," *Virginia Quarterly Review*, LVII (Fall, 1981), 595.

129. Stanley Hoffmann in "Vietnam Reappraisal," *International Security*, VI (Summer, 1981), 4.

130. Robert Müller in "After Vietnam: How We Lost a Generation," *Washington Post*, May 25, 1980, p. B4.

131. John B. Keeley in *ibid.*, July 6, 1981.

132. Quoted in Philip Caputo, *A Rumor of War* (New York: Ballentine Books, 1977), p. 69.

Iranian Protestors, 1979. After seizing the American embassy in Teheran in early November, 1979, young Iranians marched in the streets, taunting President Jimmy Carter, and daring the United States to do something about the American personnel held hostage. Coming in the aftermath of American defeat in Vietnam, the Iranian crisis added to the growing fear among Americans that their power no longer commanded respect or results. (Wide World Photos)

16 Reviving America in a World of Diffused Power: Foreign Policy Since 1977

Diplomatic Crossroad: The Iranian Hostage Crisis, 1979–1981

"Everybody downstairs! There's a break-in," shouted a Marine guard at the United States Embassy in Teheran, Iran.[1] Just moments earlier, on the morning of November 4, 1979, radical Islamic student demonstrators had been chanting "Death to the Shah" and "Death to America" in nearby streets. Then they quickly stormed the embassy that their religious leader Ayatollah Ruhallah Khomeini had branded a "nest of spies."[2] After snipping the gate chains with bolt-cutters, they swarmed over the compound. Marine guards retreated into buildings, using only tear gas to hold back the mob. The attackers were "lowing for death," recalled one American trapped inside.[3] In the chancery, American officials, including CIA officers operating under "cover" as foreign service personnel, hurried to burn documents and codebooks and smash communications equipment. The armed militants entered room after room, grabbing terrified Americans. "We're paying you back for Vietnam," snarled one to a blindfolded captive.[4] All told, sixty-six Americans were captured. Their captors called them "hostages" and insisted that they would be freed only after Mohammad Reza Shah Pahlavi was returned to Iran for trial.

What had set off this angry outpouring of anti-Americanism? Why were Iranian revolutionaries "blind drunk with their hatred" for the United States?[5] The immediate catalyst for seizing the embassy was the exiled Shah's admission to a New York hospital on October 22. But Iranian hostility had been mounting since the 1950s. The Shah had come to power in 1941, replacing his father, who had claimed the throne by force in the 1920s. The young Shah increasingly relied upon American advice and assistance. This dependence was demonstrated most emphatically in 1953 when he had to flee Iran after nationalists, led by Prime Minister Mohammad Mossadegh, gained control of the government and nationalized the Anglo-Iranian Oil Company. The CIA, in operation AJAX, successfully plotted with royalist Iranians and British officials to restore the

Shah to the Peacock Throne and drive Mossadegh from the country. In 1957, with CIA help, he organized SAVAK, a secret police organization that suppressed dissent and terrorized the population. The Shah became a staunch anti-Communist ally, a pillar of American influence in the Middle East.

In the 1970s many Iranians turned against the Shah, called by some that "corrupt germ."[6] Muslim fundamentalists resented Western influences, which included movies and rights for women. Intellectuals and students protested the suppression of civil liberties. Social democrats who fled with Mossadegh in the 1950s demanded a constitutional government. For different reasons, merchants, young workers, and feudal landholders felt aggrieved by the Shah's "white revolution" or modernization of the Iranian economy. Inflation, unemployment, inadequate housing for the millions who moved from village to city, and preferential jobs for skilled foreigners also created unrest. Ethnic separatists in Kurdistan continued their fight for autonomy. SAVAK, which became the symbol of the Shah's police state, committed brutalities that ultimately helped to unite disparate groups against the monarch and the United States. SAVAK practiced systematic terror; its agents destroyed property, raped prisoners, performed unspeakable tortures, and summarily executed dissidents.

Iranians also objected to purchases of arms from the United States. In the period 1973–1978, the Shah spent $19 billion of the nation's oil wealth on American weapons. He bought helicopters, fighter aircraft, destroyers, and missiles. Iran possessed the mightiest military in all of the Middle East, but thousands of Iranians thought the Shah was wasting the nation's resources. "It was the arms-sale program, more than any other aspect of the alliance between the United States and Iran," scholar Barry Rubin has written, "that compromised the Shah's image with Iranians and led them to believe that he was America's 'man.'"[7]

Just before Jimmy Carter became President in 1977, Iranian-American relations had begun to show signs of real strain. The Shah was complaining that America looked like a crippled giant after defeat in Vietnam and that the Pentagon was too closely scrutinizing his arms purchases. He threatened to trade elsewhere, and when his request for a nuclear reactor was turned down in Washington, he bought one in France. In 1976 the United States sold the Shah 160 F-16 fighter aircraft for $3.4 billion, but congressional criticism of the deal resounded all the way to the Shah's palace. Also, Americans were upset with the Iranian leader for his role in pushing up OPEC oil prices.

In late 1977, President Carter, in Teheran, toasted the Shah for making Iran "an island of stability" and for earning "the respect and admiration and love which your people give to you."[8] The President was most likely paying polite deference to an American ally, but it seems, too, that his intelligence sources were faulty, dependent as they seemed to be upon SAVAK and accustomed to thinking that the Shah acted as a stable element in the chaotic Middle East. Nor had American intelligence learned that the Shah was dying of cancer, perhaps making him fatalistic and lethargic, less able to cope with the revolution that swept over him.

In 1978, demonstrations, riots, strikes, and general public protest shook Iran. The Shah declared martial law and turned his military against the protesters. "No one realized the dedication of his opponents, how much the man was hated, and how much he had lost touch. . . ," remarked one State Department officer.[9] At first, guided by his adviser for national security affairs, Zbigniew Brzezinski,

Carter publicly backed the besieged Shah, praising him for his "progressive administration."[10] The President then ordered shipments of tear gas cannisters, police batons, and other riot control equipment to Iran's military. As the crisis accelerated in late 1978, American officials began to advise the Shah to compromise with his growing opposition by transforming his government into a constitutional monarchy. The Shah refused to give up any authority. Americans in Iran found that their President's public praise for the monarch endangered their lives. "I am identified, however wrongly, with the repression imposed by Teheran," said an American teacher.[11]

In late December, as Iranian demonstrators yelled "Carter gives the guns, the Shah kills the people," American officials took another look and urged the Shah to leave his country.[12] Washington despatched General Robert Huyser to Teheran to try to arrange a government in which the military would have a substantial voice. Brzezinski asked American Ambassador William H. Sullivan if a military coup could be staged. "I regret that the reply I made is unprintable," Sullivan later wrote.[13] Sullivan was furious because, despite his advice, officials in Washington had made no effort to meet with Khomeini, the evident leader of the rebellion, who was in exile in Paris. A civilian government appointed by the Shah, who left Iran on January 16, was endorsed by the United States, but rejected by the Ayatollah. The eighty-one-year-old Khomeini returned triumphantly to Iran on January 31 and immediately lectured the United States to stay out of Iran's affairs.

After departing Teheran, the Shah moved from country to country, for few wanted to house a repudiated despot and risk cutbacks of oil shipments by anti-Shah Arabs. Earlier in the crisis, Washington had informed the Shah that he was welcome in the United States. But as Americans learned that "our problem in Iran is us," Carter decided to rescind the offer.[14] Secretary of State Cyrus Vance supported the decision to withdraw the invitation, but Brzezinski did not. Nor did David Rockefeller of the Chase Manhattan Bank, whose financial ties to Iran were apparently substantial, or former Secretary of State Henry A. Kissinger. Both petitioned the White House to remain loyal to a longtime ally who needed help, to stop treating the Shah like "a flying Dutchman" in search of a safe place to land.[15] Carter listened to Kissinger's appeal, in part because he wanted the influential diplomat's public support for the then-pending SALT-II treaty. In October, 1979, Carter learned that the Shah, then in Mexico, was very ill and that he would die unless he received medical attention in the United States. The President then agreed to admit the Shah to a New York hospital, despite a warning from the American embassy staff in Teheran that such a move could ignite Iranian protest and endanger American lives. With Carter's decision, one hostage commented later, "we threw a burning branch into a bucket full of kerosene."[16] The Iranian foreign minister explained his country's anger: "It is as if Franco's Spain had offered to treat Hitler for cancer immediately after the Second World War."[17] Two weeks later, the Iranian students seized the embassy.

The taking of the hostages was more than an act to force the Shah's return. First, it was Iran's way of preventing the Shah from launching a counterrevolution from the United States. No plan of American intervention seems to have existed, yet Iranians thought Washington would surely try to return the Shah to his throne. They remembered 1953. Second, it helped Iran break diplomatic relations with the United States. To the new leaders, the United States was simply an aggressor

that would always seek to dominate Iran, and thus it was best to end the relationship altogether. Finally, the hostage drama permitted Khomeini to use heated anti-Americanism as an instrument to overwhelm civilian moderates who bitterly competed with him and his clerics for control of the revolution. Given these apparent intentions, analysts asked if there was anything Carter could do.

The Carter Administration, putting the safety of the hostages first, adopted a policy approximating "restrained anger."[18] The President felt "the same kind of impotence that a powerful person feels when his child is kidnapped."[19] Carter rejected several offers of advice: he would not return the Shah to certain death, apologize for past American behavior, or take military action. The latter might spark the killing of the hostages, prompt Muslims throughout the Middle East to attack American property, or set off a war that might entice the Soviets to intervene.

Carter instead chose to apply gradually increasing counterpressure. He announced that the visas of some 50,000 Iranian students in the United States would be reviewed; those not studying would be deported. This effort proved ineffective because the government had a hard time locating the Iranians, and the cases moved slowly through the courts. On November 14 the President froze Iranian assets in the United States valued at about $8 billion. American officials secretly asked Palestine Liberation Organization leader Yasir Arafat to help. He did, persuading the revolutionary government to release thirteen hostages (most of the women and blacks). Washington also enlisted the help of other foreign governments and private emissaries. The United Nations and the International Court of Justice called for the unconditional release of the hostages. But the hostages languished in captivity—they were not mutilated or sexually abused, but they endured mock executions, solitary confinement, beatings, and daily harassment.

At home Americans debated who had "lost" Iran—echoes of an earlier debate over who had "lost" China. Kissinger upbraided the Carter Administration for "self-abasement" and appealed for a "reassertion of American will."[20] Veteran diplomat George Ball retorted that it was "fatuous" for Kissinger to claim that he would never have let the Shah fall in the first place. "What would Mr. Kissinger have done [against the internal revolt]? Sent the Sixth Fleet steaming up the Gulf?"[21] American officials grew frustrated under the pressure of Iranian taunts, confusion and indecision within the Teheran government, and domestic political sniping. As hopes rose and fell with each attempt to negotiate, many assumed that the Iranian leaders simply could not be trusted. On April 7, 1980, the United States broke off diplomatic relations with Iran and imposed an economic embargo. Despite Secretary of State Cyrus R. Vance's opposition, Carter also ordered the Joint Chiefs of Staff to carry out a complicated rescue plan—to "lance the boil" of American frustration, as Brzezinski put it.[22]

On April 24, eight large helicopters lifted off the deck of the carrier U.S.S. *Nimitz* in the Arabian Sea. At the same time six C-130 Hercules transports took to the skies from a base somewhere in the Middle East, possibly Egypt. All headed for a rendezvous in the Iranian desert; from there, rescue teams planned to infiltrate Teheran and the American Embassy to free the hostages. But two of the helicopters malfunctioned before reaching the desert; another lost a hydraulic line at the rendezvous point. Carter then personally aborted the mission. In the hasty and dusty exit, a helicopter and a C-130 collided, killing eight crew members. After a weary President Carter reported the tragedy, Secretary Vance, who had

Jimmy Carter's World. Trouble after trouble beset the President. The Iranian crisis joined domestic economic turmoil and other divisive foreign policy issues to raise doubts about Carter's leadership abilities. The American people turned him out of office in 1981. (Cartoon by Tony Auth. Reprinted with permission from *Foreign Policy* magazine, no. 31, Summer, 1978. Copyright 1978 by the Carnegie Endowment for International Peace) opposed the risky venture from the start and who had earlier submitted his resignation, quietly left the administration. Carter endured much criticism for undertaking a project that risked the lives of some hostages. His political opponents complained that he had endorsed the mission to improve his sagging political fortunes. Others wondered if the American military, in post-Vietnam doldrums, was capable of anything other than bureaucratic squabbling within the walls of the Pentagon.

After the rescue attempt, American leaders seemed resigned to a prolongation of the hostage crisis. The Iranian issue receded from daily news headlines, but Americans did not forget the hostages. Many displayed yellow ribbons to symbolize their prayers for the safe return of the captives. Four major events finally facilitated a resolution. First, the Shah died in Egypt in July, 1980. Second, Khomeini's Islamic clerics won control of the parliament; they no longer needed the hostages for their political purposes. Third, in September, Iraq and Iran went to war, and Iran found that it had few friends or funds. Iran's oil exports, a major source of government revenue, had virtually stopped due to lack of spare parts and the sabotage of a pipeline by Khuzistan separatists. And fourth, Ronald Reagan, who promised a tougher posture, was elected President. Behind the scenes, American and Iranian diplomats met with Algerian mediators. On the day before Reagan took office, an agreement was struck: freedom for the hostages in exchange for the unfreezing of Iranian assets. On the 20th day of January, 1981—inauguration day—the hostages were released. After 444 days of imprisonment, they returned home to a relieved nation.

"It was rather strange that there were so few questions when it ended," wrote a *New York Times* editor.[23] Indeed, Americans seemed to push this embarrassing episode out of mind, to return to the domestic economic crisis and the new Administration's formulas for solving it. There was some second-guessing, of course. Should Carter have played up the hostage issue so much, thereby signaling to the

The Hostages Return. After 444 days in captivity, the fifty-two Americans held prisoner in Iran came home to celebrations and warm embraces. This hand-made placard awarded final victory to the United States. (U.S. Department of State, Audio-Visual Service Division. Photograph by Robert Kaiser)

Iranians that they had in fact done something that stung and would continue to sting Americans? But with the Iranians jeering Washington day-after-day, with Kissinger harping on America's weakness, with the extensive television coverage, with this gross violation of diplomatic immunity, with Carter's compassion for other human beings, could the President have moved the issue from the limelight?

What did it all mean? The United States lost an ally that had a large army, huge quantities of oil, and intelligence posts that provided American agents with data on Soviet missile tests—an ally that had spent billions of dollars in the United States on arms. American pride and prestige were diminished by the long crisis. Self-doubt about the American leadership role in the world, already prevalent after Vietnam, deepened. Still, America's loss was not automatically Russia's gain. The Iranians remained ardently anti-Soviet. As for American politics, the hostage crisis helped cost Carter the 1980 presidential election. The winner, Ronald Reagan, drew the lesson that the United States should build a larger military establishment to deter terrorists in the future. Other Americans pointed out that the United States, because of its conservative worldwide presence, could expect to be the target of revolutionaries again and again. It would be better, therefore, to disassociate from regimes considered to be American creations. Some commentators argued that the Iranian crisis reinforced the lesson of Vietnam: large infusions of American aid and weaponry, such as had flowed to the Shah, could not guarantee the survival of an unpopular and corrupt regime. As the Iranian revolution descended into tyrannical rule, executions of Khomeini foes, and renewed civil war, it seemed that self-destruction, not American intervention, would relieve the world of revolutionary menaces.

The outpouring of emotional patriotism that greeted the returning hostages suggested that the nation needed heroes—"the national hungering for a moment of pride."[24] But anger coexisted with joy. "There seems to be a craving in the national psyche to bash someone around," commented radical journalist I. F. Stone.[25] A Nashville, Tennessee woman complained about the loss of "American superiority," and an Oklahoma man thought Carter had been too timid. "I agree with Teddy Roosevelt. Walk softly and carry a big stick," the Oklahoman said. "And club the hell out of them if you need to."[26]

Jimmy Carter and the World

Teddy Roosevelt's "big stick" was exactly what Jimmy Carter found wrong with American foreign policy when he came to office in 1977—too much bluster, too much military, and too much insensitivity toward the peoples of the Third World. During the campaign of 1976, Carter joined critics of the Nixon-Ford-Kissinger years in demanding "no more Vietnams" and "no more Chiles." He promised to reduce military budgets, bring some of America's overseas forces home, trim arms sales abroad, and slow nuclear proliferation. He berated the Republicans for tarnishing America's moral integrity through support for dictatorial regimes. Yet at times Carter sounded more like an inveterate Cold Warrior than a peacemaker. He blamed Ford and Kissinger for permitting a decline of American power: "Our country is not strong anymore; we're not respected anymore." He mocked détente: "The Soviet Union knows what they want in détente, and they're getting

Makers of American Foreign Policy since 1977

Presidents	Secretaries of State
Jimmy Carter, 1977–1981	Cyrus R. Vance, 1977–1980
	Edmund Muskie, 1980–1981
Ronald Reagan, 1981–	Alexander M. Haig, Jr., 1981–1982
	George P. Shultz, 1982–

it. We have not known what we've wanted and we've been out-traded in almost every instance." [27] He criticized the White House for accepting the Soviet domination of Eastern Europe and for authorizing huge grain sales to Russia. President Gerald Ford thought Carter was playing politics—attracting the hawks by bemoaning the descent of American power and wooing the doves by advocating cuts in defense spending. "He wavers, he wanders, he wiggles, and he waffles," Ford complained. [28] Carter retorted that America's strength derived not simply from armaments but also from its image as a practitioner of its own declared principles.

"Are you proud of our nation?" asked Carter just minutes after he won the 1976 election. His jubilant followers shouted a resounding "yes." [29] This upbeat moment, after the downbeat years of Watergate, Vietnam, CIA abuses, corporate bribes of foreign leaders, and soaring OPEC oil prices, was inspired by a wealthy peanut farmer with a toothy smile. Carter entered politics as a Georgia state senator in the 1960s and, in 1970, was elected governor. After a four-year gubernatorial term, this relatively obscure Democrat set out to win the presidency. He astounded the professionals by doing so. Energetic, ambitious, self-confident, and meticulous about details, Jimmy Carter cherished the traditional values of hard work and family responsibility. A devout Baptist, he became a "born again" Christian, awakened to a religious revival by his evangelical sister Ruth, a faith-healer.

People did not know what to expect of Carter at the beginning of his administration. His foreign affairs experience was limited to membership on the Trilateral Commission, organized by Columbia University political scientist Zbigniew Brzezinski and banker David Rockefeller. The commission brought together business, political, and academic notables for discussions of global problems bedeviling industrial Western Europe, Japan, and North America—especially North-South issues. The new President's secretary of state was Cyrus Vance, a wealthy West Virginia-born lawyer who was widely respected as a selfless public servant. By the late 1970s Vance had come to believe that military interventionism was counterproductive. He said that he had learned from the Vietnam War that the United States cannot "prop up a series of regimes that lacked popular support" [30] and that with world power diffused, "there can be no going back to a time when we thought there could be American solutions to every problem." [31] When Vance quietly resigned in April, 1980, he had become disenchanted because Carter seemed to be embracing military means and listening increasingly to Brzezinski, whom the President had named his assistant for national security

Cyrus R. Vance (1917–).
Yale graduate and former
deputy secretary of de-
fense, "Cy" Vance
brought extensive diplo-
matic experience to his
post as secretary of state.
Vance won plaudits for his
role in negotiating the
Panama Canal treaties and
SALT-II. His resignation in
1980 was the first such
act made in protest by a
secretary of state since the
resignation of William
Jennings Bryan in 1915.
(Carter White House Photo
Office Collection. Carter
Presidential Materials Project. National Archives and
Records Service)

affairs. Brzezinski was known as an unreconstructed Cold Warrior, and State
Department officials often bristled over the manner in which he competed for
presidential favor. "While Mr. Vance played by Marquis of Queensbury rules,"
said one, "Mr. Brzezinski was more of a street fighter."[32] Another compared the
presidential adviser to a rat-terrier constantly nipping at Vance's ankles.

Despite personal and bureaucratic tussles, the Carter Administration sought
ambitious, basically traditional goals. "U.S. foreign policy is like an aircraft carrier," remarked Brzezinski. "You simply don't send it into a 180-degree turn; at
most you move it a few degrees to port or starboard."[33] One general goal was the
projection of American influence and ideals abroad. Brzezinski explained that the
United States wanted "to make the world congenial to ourselves" and "to prevent
America from being lonely."[34] The Carter Administration believed that emphasizing North-South relations more than the East-West contest would build up
America's diminished standing in the Third World. The United States would have
to make some concessions to nationalism—economic and political—and would
have to accept the reality of leftist governments in Africa and Latin America. The
President declared that the "intellectual and moral poverty" of military interventionism had been demonstrated in Vietnam.[35] Carter argued further that Third
World problems grew not from Communist plots or the superpower duel, but

Zbigniew Brzezinski (1928–). This Warsaw-born son of a Polish diplomat emigrated to America in 1953. Before becoming Carter's assistant in 1977, he was a Columbia University political scientist who wrote many works on Soviet affairs, pressing for a hard line in East-West relations. According to a fellow White House adviser, Brzezinski relished his role as "the first Pole in 300 years in a position to really stick it to the Russians." (*Hartford Courant*)

from deep-seated, indigenous economic, social, racial, and political problems. One symbol of his sympathetic approach to the developing world was Carter's appointment of Andrew Young as Ambassador to the United Nations. A black, former civil-rights activist and congressman, Young gradually improved the American dialogue with suspicious Third World diplomats. But in 1979, Young was forced out of office after he made unauthorized contact with representatives of the Palestine Liberation Organization, a group the United States did not recognize.

The "soul" of American foreign policy, Carter insisted, was the defense and extension of human rights for foreign peoples.[36] The President held this his personal contribution to world affairs. Through the internationalization of the Bill of Rights, America could recover its prestige and pride, and add moral force to the nation's arsenal. Drawing upon Woodrow Wilson's ideas, the 1948 United Nations Universal Declaration of Human Rights, and his own religious commitment, Carter vowed to win for all peoples the freedom to work, vote, worship, travel, speak, assemble, and get a fair trial. Slavery, genocide, torture, forced labor, arbitrary arrest, rigged elections, and suspensions of civil liberties were anathema. Dictators were warned to respect human rights—free political prisoners, for example—or face cutbacks in American foreign aid.

Carter said Americans had to put their "inordinate fear of Communism" behind them, but the containment, if not rollback, of Soviet Russia remained a basic objective of American foreign policy.[37] Containment would be pursued through new weapons systems and streamlined conventional forces. The Soviet Union would also be checked by encouragement of pluralism and nationalism in Eastern Europe, Voice of America broadcasts beamed at Russia (Carter increased them by 25 percent), closer relations with the People's Republic of China (the so-called "China card"), continued strategic arms limitations talks, the cultivation of nationalist governments in the Third World, and public denunciations of Soviet violations of human rights. In 1980 the President also proclaimed the Carter Doctrine: the containment of Soviet expansionism in the Middle East.

The Carter Administration rejected the options of "Fortress America" (isolationism) and "Atlas America" (global policeman) in favor of "Participant America."[38] That meant an emphasis on worldwide diplomatic activism or preventive diplomacy: advancing the peace process in the Middle East; normalizing relations with China; improving ties with ally and economic competitor Japan; mediation of conflict in the Third World; negotiating improvements in human rights abroad; and creating economic stability through talks on the law of the sea and other economic issues. The United States seemed to some ready to pursue "leadership without hegemony."[39]

Compromises in Latin America

Although the Iranian hostage crisis and the bipolar rivalry with the Soviet Union came to dominate the President's foreign policy, Carter launched early an active diplomacy toward Latin America, the Middle East, and Africa. In Latin America, Carter championed human rights and worked to accommodate the United States to the inexorable force of nationalism. More than ever before, the Latin American governments were claiming an independent role in world politics, ignoring United States advice, buying and selling in the world market, and purchasing arms in Europe. Brazil, Mexico, and Cuba were emerging as influential nations. United States supremacy in Latin America was no longer a given. Poverty, rapid population growth, and natural disasters beset the area. To help relieve these conditions, Latin Americans petitioned for lower United States tariffs, support for higher commodity prices, less diplomatic backing of American corporations locked in disputes with Latin American governments, and the transfer of technology on convenient terms. The Carter Administration listened because much was at stake: $59 billion in trade (1979); American investments of $24.4 billion (1979); imports of petroleum, copper, and tin from the south; and Latin America's thirty votes in the United Nations. Foreign aid ($726 million in 1977–1978) was one means of influence, but Carter also sought to reduce hostility toward the United States by abandoning the hectoring that, in the past, had too often alienated Latin Americans from the "colossus of the North."

Most Latin Americans took it as a good sign that the United States would negotiate to return the Canal Zone to Panama. Panamanians had long resented the 1903 treaty granting the United States a ten-mile wide, 500 square mile slice of territory, cutting their nation in half. "What nation of the world can withstand the humiliation of a foreign flag piercing its own heart?" asked Panamanian President

Omar Torrijos.[40] After violent anti-American riots in 1964 revealed the depth of Panamanian feeling, President Johnson initiated negotiations. The talks moved very slowly.

When Carter entered office he made it a priority to bring the negotiations to fruition, and results came quickly. Two treaties were signed in 1977 and ratified the following year. One treaty, abrogating the 1903 document, provided for the integration of the Canal Zone into Panama. The United States would relinquish control over the Zone and the canal in the year 2000. The United States also agreed to increase Panama's percentage of the canal's revenues to boost its sick economy. The other treaty stated that the United States had the right to defend the "neutrality" of the canal forever. In a national referendum Panamanians approved the treaties by a 2-1 margin. The President of Colombia applauded Carter for a "policy that is more human and less big stick."[41]

A heated debate soon erupted in the United States. Conservative critics hoisted the flag of patriotism and denounced the treaties as diabolical instruments of appeasement, isolationism, and surrender. "Is America really going the way of Rome?" lamented one senator.[42] To many Americans the United States "owned" the canal. Ronald Reagan, running hard for the Republican presidential nomination, mangled the historical record by declaring that the Zone "is sovereign United States territory just the same as Alaska . . . and the states that were carved out of the Louisiana Purchase."[43] Others complained: American defense would be weakened by giving up a key waterway; the United States would be broadcasting to allies and enemies alike that it was retreating from world power; and American withdrawal from Panama would create a vacuum that Cuba and Russia might fill. The American Legion and other veterans groups lined up against the treaties and the Conservative Caucus launched a letter-writing campaign that flooded senatorial offices with anti-treaty mail. Many people were "still riding up the hill with Teddy Roosevelt," observed Gale McGee of Wyoming, a treaty supporter.[44]

The Carter Administration rebutted its critics through a massive propaganda campaign. The Committee of Americans for the Canal Treaties enlisted veteran diplomat W. Averell Harriman, former CIA Director William Colby, labor leader George Meany, and General Maxwell Taylor, among others. Former President Gerald Ford and former Secretary of State Henry A. Kissinger worked for approval. Executives of the National Association of Manufacturers and multinational corporations holding large investments in Latin America endorsed the agreements. The case for the treaties stressed the goodwill the United States would gain after retiring the imperialistic document of 1903. If the United States insisted on staying in Panama, it might invite a protracted guerrilla war; a few well-placed sticks of dynamite could render the canal altogether useless to the United States. Some argued that the strategic value of the canal had declined because aircraft carriers were too big to move through the waterway. Others pointed out that its economic worth had also dwindled because less than 10 percent of United States foreign trade went through the canal, and the new, large cargo ships and supertankers could not squeeze through the locks.

As the debate drew to a close in early 1978, the Administration increasingly used arguments that alarmed Panamanians. That is, Carter emphasized the considerable power the United States could exercise in Panama for years to come. Indeed, a "memorandum of understanding," signed by Torrijos and Carter and later added to the neutrality treaty by the Senate, provided for United States intervention after 2000 to thwart "any aggression or threat directed against the Canal or against the peaceful transit of vessels through the Canal." The memorandum also read that in times of crisis American ships could go to the head of the line.[45]

On March 16, 1978 the Senate approved the neutrality treaty 68–32; the other treaty was passed on April 18 by a similar count—in both cases only one vote more than the two-thirds tally mandated by the Constitution. But the treaties did not pass without amendments. One was the handiwork of a freshman senator from Arizona, Dennis DeConcini, who worried about future revolution in Panama. His "condition," which Torrijos accepted after a personal plea from Carter, stated that if canal operations were ever interrupted, the United States would have the unilateral right to intervene, "including the use of military force *in* the Republic of Panama."[46] A Panamanian lawyer thought it a humiliation: "It says the U.S. can treat Panama the way the Russians treat the Hungarians and Czechs."[47] Carter judged that he would face defeat on the vote unless he accepted this interventionist provision. Nonetheless, it dulled the gloss of "the single most positive action to be undertaken in recent years in our relations with Latin America."[48]

Nationalist stirrings in Nicaragua also vexed the Carter Administration. Since 1936, that Central American state had been ruled by the Somoza family. Dictatorial, brutal, and corrupt, the Somoza dynasty nevertheless had gained United States support as a stable, reliable anti-Communist ally and had received military aid, which it used to suppress critics. Nicaragua had served as a staging area for CIA operations against Guatemala (1954) and Cuba (1961), and Nicaraguan troops had joined American Marines during the occupation of the Dominican Republic (1965). All the while, Nicaraguans suffered high rates of poverty, malnutrition, and illiteracy, and the Somozas amassed huge wealth, coming to own much of the country's land and industry. A long-smoldering popular rebellion exploded in 1978, led by the leftist Sandinista National Liberation Front (FSLN). The FSLN was founded in 1962 and named for insurgent César Augusto Sandino, who had fought American occupation in the 1920s and 1930s. As the insurgency gained momentum, businessmen, Catholic clergymen, and intellectuals joined what was considered as much a popular war of national liberation from both the Somozas and the United States as a class war. General Anastasio Somoza Debayle, a graduate of West Point (1946), answered with torture, executions, and the bombing of the civilian population.

Wanting to support neither Somoza nor the revolutionary Sandinistas, the Carter Administration at first urged mediation. Then, in late 1978 and early 1979, Carter aides tried to form a new government that would ensure Somoza's departure and restrict the influence of the Sandinistas. Somoza balked and the effort failed. In mid-1979 the FSLN opened its final offensive. At that point Washington tried to contain the revolution's radicalism by encouraging the National Guard—Somoza's hated personal army—to "preserve order."[49] When attempts to set up the Guard as the successor government to Somoza failed, American diplomats pressed the new, broadly-based provisional government to share power with more nonradicals, or be denied reconstruction assistance. "The only way to characterize this is blackmail," complained the Reverend Miguel D'Escoto, the foreign minister-designate. "They're trying to bargain with the blood of our people."[50]

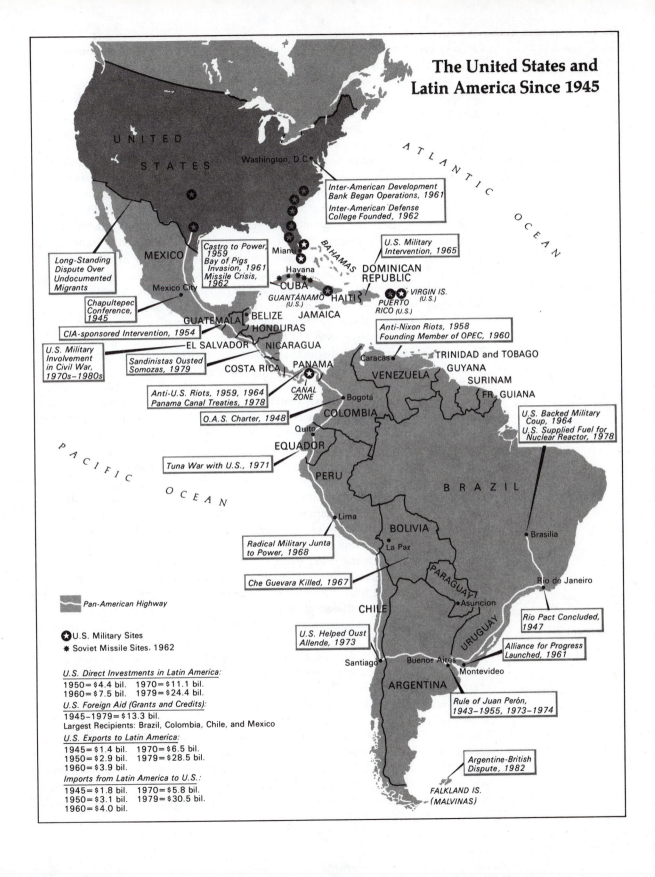

The United States and Latin America Since 1945

Washington, D.C.

Inter-American Development Bank Began Operations, 1961

Inter-American Defense College Founded, 1962

Long-Standing Dispute Over Undocumented Migrants

MEXICO

Mexico City

Castro to Power, 1959 Bay of Pigs Invasion, 1961 Missile Crisis, 1962

Miami

BAHAMAS

U.S. Military Intervention, 1965

DOMINICAN REPUBLIC

Havana

CUBA

GUANTÁNAMO (U.S.)

HAITI

JAMAICA

VIRGIN IS. (U.S.)

PUERTO RICO (U.S.)

Chapultepec Conference, 1945

GUATEMALA

BELIZE

HONDURAS

CIA-sponsored Intervention, 1954

EL SALVADOR

NICARAGUA

Anti-Nixon Riots, 1958 Founding Member of OPEC, 1960

U.S. Military Involvement in Civil War, 1970s–1980s

Sandinistas Ousted Somozas, 1979

COSTA RICA

PANAMA

Caracas

TRINIDAD and TOBAGO

GUYANA

VENEZUELA

SURINAM

FR. GUIANA

Anti-U.S. Riots, 1959, 1964 Panama Canal Treaties, 1978

CANAL ZONE

Bogotá

COLOMBIA

O.A.S. Charter, 1948

Quito

U.S. Backed Military Coup, 1964

U.S. Supplied Fuel for Nuclear Reactor, 1978

EQUADOR

Tuna War with U.S., 1971

PERU

B R A Z I L

Lima

BOLIVIA

Radical Military Junta to Power, 1968

La Paz

Brasília

Che Guevara Killed, 1967

PARAGUAY

Rio de Janeiro

Asuncion

Rio Pact Concluded, 1947

CHILE

URUGUAY

U.S. Helped Oust Allende, 1973

Alliance for Progress Launched, 1961

Santiago

Buenos Aires

Montevideo

ARGENTINA

Rule of Juan Perón, 1943–1955, 1973–1974

Argentine-British Dispute, 1982

FALKLAND IS. (MALVINAS)

ATLANTIC OCEAN

PACIFIC OCEAN

Pan-American Highway

⭐ U.S. Military Sites

✳ Soviet Missile Sites, 1962

U.S. Direct Investments in Latin America:
1950 = $4.4 bil.   1970 = $11.1 bil.
1960 = $7.5 bil.   1979 = $24.4 bil.

U.S. Foreign Aid (Grants and Credits):
1945–1979 = $13.3 bil.
Largest Recipients: Brazil, Colombia, Chile, and Mexico

U.S. Exports to Latin America:
1945 = $1.4 bil.   1970 = $6.5 bil.
1950 = $2.9 bil.   1979 = $28.5 bil.
1960 = $3.9 bil.

Imports from Latin America to U.S.:
1945 = $1.8 bil.   1970 = $5.8 bil.
1950 = $3.1 bil.   1979 = $30.5 bil.
1960 = $4.0 bil.

On July 17, 1979, Somoza and his entourage fled the battle-scarred country; he was later assassinated in Paraguay.

Carter had abandoned a client state supported by seven previous United States administrations. After the new government promised a mixed economy and pluralist politics, and only after Mexico, Venezuela, and others offered loans, Carter asked Congress for $75 million in economic assistance to Nicaragua. "We cannot guarantee that democracy will take hold there," remarked Vance. "But if we turn our backs on Nicaragua, we can almost guarantee that democracy will fail."[51] Congress waited until July, 1980 to appropriate the funds because conservatives delayed the bill with emotional charges that the Nicaraguan government was communist. Carter rejected that accusation and seemed to move toward nourishing the independent Nicaraguan socialism he had earlier failed to tame. Many Nicaraguans naturally resented the United States' long-time ties with Somoza, the initial tampering with their revolution, and then the long delay in extending foreign aid. Tension between Managua and Washington ran high, especially when the United States suspended economic aid in early 1981 on the grounds that the Sandinistas were aiding anti-American rebels in El Salvador.

Mexico strongly backed the new Sandinista government—just one more sign that Mexican nationalism and United States policy were once again colliding. Three issues particularly disturbed Mexican-American relations: immigration, trade and investment, and the pricing of oil and natural gas. Mexico and the United States have shared a 2,000 mile border since the 1840s. Goods and people have moved across it with ease, benefiting both economies. Hundreds of thousands of Mexicans in the 1970s entered the United States without immigration papers. These illegal immigrants or undocumented aliens numbered about 2–4 million by 1980. In 1978 alone, American border patrols captured one million Mexicans trying to cross the international boundary; perhaps as many as 500,000 migrants passed unnoticed that year. Most were young males trying to escape the depressed economy of Mexico for employment in the United States; they did not come to settle, but to work temporarily. Great numbers returned to Mexico each year. "It is not a crime to look for work," remarked President López Portillo, especially when American employers were offering jobs.[52]

American critics, on the other hand, contended that these illegal laborers displaced American workers, drove down wages and burdened the taxpayer by ending up on the welfare rolls. Although evidence for these charges was inconclusive, the migrants were nonetheless flouting American law. Yet even here confusion abounded because of a glaring inconsistency: it was illegal for undocumented migrants to take jobs, but legal for employers to hire them.

Carter tackled the *indocumentado* controversy early in his administration. In August, 1977, he asked Congress for new legislation: "amnesty" for those illegal migrants already in the United States; tighter border controls; and fines for employers who hired undocumented workers. The Mexican government angrily criticized Carter's initiative, not because of the specific proposals, but because Carter had not consulted Mexico City before unilaterally issuing his reform package. Congress backed away and created a commission to study general immigration policy, chaired by the Reverend Theodore M. Hesburgh, president of the University of Notre Dame. In March, 1981, the commission urged stricter border controls, an automated system of tracking aliens in the United States to verify their departure, deportation of undocumented migrants, legislation to make it illegal to hire undocumented aliens, and the legalization of residence for illegal aliens already living in the United States. President Ronald Reagan recommended many of these proposals to Congress in July, adding a plan to seize vessels with illegal migrants aboard and a program to permit up to 50,000 Mexican laborers to work in the United States for designated periods.

Economic questions also troubled Mexican-American relations. By 1980 Mexico ranked as the United States third most important trading partner, after Canada and Japan. The United States took about three-quarters of Mexico's exports, valued at $12.5 billion, and provided about 70 percent of Mexico's imports, valued at $15.1 billion. The United States share of total foreign investment in Mexico was 69 percent, or over $5 billion. Some Mexican nationalists complained of dependency on their northern neighbor; others asked for lower American tariffs or tighter regulation of foreign investments. As a symbol of independence from the United States, Mexico looked to more diversified foreign trade and investment.

The Mexicans appeared to gain some leverage in the late 1970s, when vast quantities of oil and natural gas were discovered in Mexico. Energy-hungry Americans greeted the discovery with optimism, anticipating that Mexico, not a member of OPEC, would sell at bargain prices. Mexico did sell most of its petroleum to the United States, but at a price actually higher than that charged by Saudi Arabia. Americans grumbled. Mexicans asked why they should bail the United States out of its energy crisis at the expense of Mexico's economic development, especially when the United States would not help relieve Mexico's economic distress by opening its doors to Mexican workers. Natural gas aroused similar questions. American companies signed agreements with Mexico to purchase large amounts, and in 1977 Mexico began to build an expensive pipeline to ship the gas northward. But when the American secretary of energy refused to

Uncle Sam and Mexican Oil. Mexico's development of its petroleum resources attracted the oil-hungry United States. But it also gave the Mexicans a sense of bargaining strength in relations with their powerful northern neighbor. (© Margulies/Rothco)

accept the Mexican price, the deal fell through. Mexican leaders fumed—especially when the secretary commented that Mexico would "sooner or later" have to sell to the United States.[53] A new agreement was struck in September, 1979. "We received much less gas at a much higher price at a much later date," complained a former ambassador to Mexico, and the "adverse political fallout was being felt long after the event."[54] Still, in 1980, oil and natural gas accounted for 50 percent of American imports from Mexico.

The "political fallout" from the 1959 Cuban Revolution continued as well. The Carter Administration initially sought to reduce tensions. In March, 1977, American and Cuban negotiators met for the first time in sixteen years. In September of that year, Cuba and the United States each established Interests Sections in the other's country. Carter also lifted the ban on travel to Cuba. Fidel Castro seemed to indicate support for the President's human rights policy by releasing 3,600 political prisoners in late 1978. These positive developments, however, were diminished by other issues. The Soviet Union was pouring about $3 million a day into Cuba to sustain the island's fragile economy. Americans argued that Cuba had become a puppet of Moscow and pointed to the continued Soviet military presence on the island as evidence. Moreover, Washington protested Cuban "adventurism" in Angola and Ethiopia, where Cuban troops served as mercenary surrogates for the Soviets. Castro insisted that he was pursuing *Cuba's* commitment to Third World revolution, noting, for example, that the Cubans were in Angola as early as the 1960s, independent of the Soviets. To Washington, Cuban and Soviet policy were indistinguishable. Secret, high-level talks in 1978–1980 failed to normalize relations or relax the trade embargo.

An unusual crisis erupted in the spring of 1980 that further soured relations. Castro announced that Cubans wishing to leave the country could use Peruvian visas if they could get them. Thousands jammed into the Peruvian embassy grounds. Carter thereupon announced that the United States would take in some of the "refugees." Castro soon declared that any Cuban who wanted to emigrate could do so by boat from the port of Mariel. Before long all makes and shapes of watercraft shuttled between Cuba and the United States in a "freedom flotilla" that brought about 100,000 Cubans to American processing centers. Problems arose immediately, because Castro had emptied his jails of "undesirables" and sent them to the United States. "Fidel has flushed his toilet on us," the mayor of Miami bitterly charged.[55] Many of the new arrivals languished in detention centers in the United States, where some rioted. Americans felt tricked, their humanitarian effort soiled. Some blamed Carter for letting in so many new workers at a time of substantial unemployment in the United States.

Elsewhere in Latin America, right-wing governments resisted Carter's efforts to improve human rights, although Haiti, Argentina, and the Dominican Republic did release hundreds of political prisoners. In 1977 Carter suspended military aid to Guatemala when its regime sanctioned the murder and torture of political opponents; two years later he froze American aid to Bolivia after that nation's military seized power. Democratic leaders in Latin America praised Carter's efforts to put distance between the United States and the dictatorships, and they were genuinely saddened by his defeat in the election of 1980. Henry Forde, prime minister of Barbados, remarked that Carter had done much "to correct the image of the United States as an unfeeling giant."[56]

The Middle East emerged as the most tense and dramatically changing area of the world in the Carter years. The Iranian revolution and hostage crisis, continued civil war in Lebanon, the Arab-Israeli conflict, war between the two Yemens, the Iranian-Iraqi war, the Soviet thrust into Afghanistan (see p. 642), and Western reliance on Persian Gulf oil put the region in the headlines day after day. The United States had economic, military, and diplomatic interests, in the Middle East. Saudi Arabia served as America's largest supplier of imported oil. In 1980 Israel and Egypt together received about one-third of *all* American foreign aid to the world. During the period 1971–1981, the United States sold $47.7 billion worth of weaponry to Middle Eastern countries. Arms worth $6.4 billion were sold to the Saudis in 1979 alone; Iran was by far the largest buyer (see p. 618). American weapons became the instruments of war in the Middle East: Israel used American warplanes to attack Palestinian communities in Lebanon; revolutionary Iran used its arms to battle Iraq; and North Yemen used American weapons to fight South Yemen. Syrians, South Yemenis, and Iraqis, on the other hand, brandished Russian armaments. United States officials argued that the massive supply of American weapons contributed to a balance of power and stability in the Middle East, but doubters chided Washington for escalating a Mideast arms race.

Building on Kissinger's earlier efforts, the Carter team concentrated on bringing Egypt and Israel to the peace table. President Anwar al-Sadat of Egypt made this easier. He astonished the world in November, 1977 by journeying to Jerusalem to ask Israel's leaders for peace and an Israeli withdrawal from all occupied lands. In essence Sadat was the first Arab leader to recognize the state of Israel. When the Sadat initiative faltered, Carter intervened in the negotiations. In September, 1978, he brought Israeli Prime Minister Menachem Begin and President Sadat to Camp David. During September 5–17, Carter wooed and cajoled. "Your President is a wonderful man," remarked Israel's minister of foreign affairs. "He is constantly learning. He was constantly taking notes. He was always writing out formulas and revising them. . . . His will not to fail is fantastic."[57]

Carter did not fail. Egypt and Israel signed two agreements. The first was a statement of goals requiring further negotiations: self-government for the West Bank and Gaza and future involvement of Jordanian and Palestinian representatives in the peace process. The second agreement, called a "framework" for peace, provided for Israeli withdrawal from the Sinai, including military installations and oilfields, in exchange for Egyptian diplomatic recognition. But once resumed, the Egyptian-Israeli negotiations stumbled again, and Carter again pressed for compromise. In March, 1979 he flew to the Middle East to meet separately with Begin and Sadat. He flattered and he implored. He made it clear to the Israeli Cabinet at one point that if he went home without an accord he would fix blame on Israeli leaders.

The presidential presence worked. On March 26, 1979, the Egyptian-Israeli Peace Treaty was signed. It provided for the phased withdrawal of Israel from the Sinai, to be completed in 1982; the stationing of United Nations forces along the Egyptian-Israeli boundary to monitor the agreement; American air surveillance; full economic and diplomatic relations between Cairo and Tel Aviv (ambassadors were exchanged in early 1980); and the opening of negotiations on Palestinian

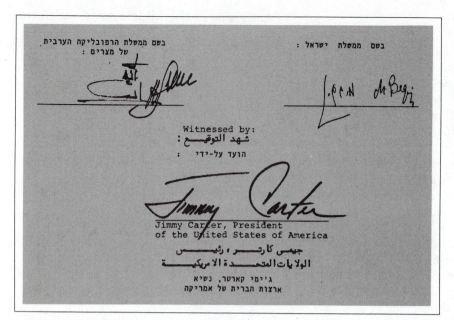

בשם ממשלת הרפובליקה הערבית
של מצרים :

בשם ממשלת ישראל :

Witnessed by:
شهد التوقيــع :
הועד על-ידי :

Jimmy Carter, President
of the United States of America
جيمى كارتــــر ، رئيـــــس
الولايات المتحـــدة الامريكيــة
ג'ימי קארטר, נשיא
ארצות הברית של אמריקה

Signatures on the Egyptian-Israeli Peace Treaty of March 26, 1979. The historic document, hammered out under the patient guidance of the American President, was signed by Egypt's President Anwar al-Sadat, Israeli Prime Minister Menachem Begin, and President Jimmy Carter. (U.S. Department of State)

rights in the occupied West Bank and Gaza. After thirty years of war, peace came to part of the Middle East. Carter frankly recognized that it was "the first step of peace. . . . There now remains the rest of the Arab world. . . ."[58] Yet the rest of the Arab world, especially the PLO, denounced the treaty for not recognizing the right of Palestinians to a homeland. Even Jordan's King Hussein, long considered an Arab moderate, blasted the peace in late 1980 as a "dead horse" because it ignored the homeland question.[59] Still, neither Washington nor Tel Aviv would recognize the PLO. By the end of Carter's administration, Israel and the PLO, the latter with Syrian help, were shooting at one another in Lebanon.

Although African issues did not carry the urgency of Middle Eastern problems, the Carter Administration launched a drive to identify the United States with African nationalism and to end the "last vestiges of colonialism" in Zimbabwe/ Rhodesia and Namibia.[60] Carter's new ambassador to the United Nations, Andrew Young, became the President's chief adviser on African affairs. "African solutions to African problems" was his motto.[61] Young believed that American support of a strong and stable black Africa, through foreign aid and trade, would successfully reduce Soviet influence in the continent. African nationalism, not American interventionism, would contain Russia and protect American interests.

Much seemed at stake in Africa. First, the continent had "political clout"—a third of the membership in the United Nations.[62] Second, Africa possessed a bulging storehouse of valuable raw materials. Zaire ranked as the United States' largest supplier of cobalt; Nigeria was the nation's second largest source of imported oil; Gabon supplied manganese; Namibia had the world's largest uranium mine; and South Africa shipped manganese, platinum, chromium, and antimony to the United States. Third, Africa held great trade and investment potential, because the fifty nations hungered for development capital and modern technology. By 1979 Americans had invested about $4 billion in black Africa and another

$1.6 billion in South Africa. Total trade with Africa passed the $30 billion figure. Fourth, Africa's strategic location aroused interest. Its ports and airfields were coveted because they lay along major sea lanes through the Persian Gulf, Indian Ocean, and Atlantic Ocean. Fifth, because of the region's political instability, it became an arena for great power competition. Sixth, American blacks were descendents of Africans. As a political constituency in the United States, they kept national leaders alert to African issues and accountable for their decisions.

The Carter Administration sought especially to cultivate Nigerian friendship, to convince white South Africa to ease its repression of blacks and to grant independence to Namibia, to move Zimbabwe/Rhodesia to black majority rule, and to blunt Soviet and Cuban influence in Africa. Nigeria, Africa's most populous nation, ranked seventh in the world in oil production and carried weight in continental African politics. Nigeria became independent in 1960, and in 1967 suffered an ugly civil war wherein Biafran rebels were defeated at a cost of over a half million lives. World opinion, including that of the United States, was hostile toward the military regime that perpetrated such a human tragedy. But in the

Andrew Young (1932–). A graduate of Howard University and the Hartford Theological Seminary, the Reverend Young had been Dr. Martin Luther King's right-hand man in the civil rights movement of the 1950s–1960s and a Georgia congressman before Carter named him ambassador to the United Nations. Young was forced to resign in 1979 when he admitted meeting with representatives of the Palestine Liberation Organization, whose participation in negotiations he deemed essential to a lasting Middle East peace. (United Nations. Photograph by Y. Nagata)

United States Dependence on Raw Materials Imports, 1980

SELECTED RAW MATERIALS	PERCENT OF DOMESTIC CONSUMPTION DERIVED FROM IMPORTS	MAJOR FOREIGN SOURCES* AND USES
Columbium	100%	Brazil, Canada, Thailand — Boiler steel, refinery equipment, jet engines, gas turbines
Mica (sheet)	100%	India, Brazil, Madagascar — Electrical and electronic equipment
Strontium	100%	Mexico — Color television picture tubes, pyrotechnics
Graphite	100%	Mexico, South Korea, Madagascar, U.S.S.R. — Steel, refractories, lubricants
Industrial Diamonds	100%	Ireland, South Africa, Belg.-Lux., U.K. — Abrasives, drills, phonograph needles, glass cutters
Manganese	97%	South Africa, Gabon, Brazil, France — Steel, dry cell batteries, chemicals, paints
Tantalum	97%	Thailand, Canada, Malaysia, Brazil — Electronic components, machinery
Bauxite & Alumina	94%	Jamaica, Guinea, Australia, Surinam — Pots and pans, window frames, house siding, abrasives
Cobalt	93%	Zaire, Belg.-Lux., Zambia, Finland — Gas turbine engines, magnetic materials, mining tools
Chromium	91%	South Africa, U.S.S.R., Philippines, Turkey — Metals, chemicals, refractories, jet engines
Platinum—Group Metals	87%	South Africa, U.S.S.R., U.K. — Jewelry, chemicals, fuel cells, electrodes, dental fillings
Fluorspar	84%	Mexico, South Africa, Spain — Chemicals, water fluoridation
Tin	84%	Malaysia, Bolivia, Thailand, Indonesia — Cans, containers, ceramics, pigments
Asbestos	76%	Canada, South Africa — Asbestos-cement pipe, flooring, insulation, gaskets
Nickel	73%	Canada, Norway, New Caledonia, Dom. Rep. — Steel, electroplating, nuclear reactors
Potassium	62%	Canada, Israel — Fertilizers, chemicals, soap
Cadmium	62%	Canada, Australia, Mexico, Belg.-Lux. — Hardware, batteries, pigments, plastics
Zinc	58%	Canada, Spain, Mexico, West Germany — Galvanizing iron and steel, die castings, bleaches, paints
Tungsten	54%	Canada, Bolivia, Thailand, South Korea — Incandescent lamps, jet engines, high pressure equipment
Antimony	53%	South Africa, Mexico, Bolivia, China — Ammunition, flame retardants, batteries, glass
Mercury	49%	Spain, Algeria, Italy, Canada, Yugoslavia — Catalyst for plastics and resins, gauges, thermostats
Titanium (ilmenite)	47%	Australia, Canada, South Africa — Jet engines, missile parts, pigments, battle helmets
Selenium	40%	Canada, Japan, Yugoslavia — Electronic components, photocopiers, glass, chemicals
Barium	38%	Peru, Ireland, Mexico, Morocco — Well-drilling, television picture tubes, optical glass
Gypsum	38%	Canada, Mexico, Jamaica — Plasters, cements
Petroleum	31%	Saudi Arabia, Nigeria, Libya, Mexico — Fuels, asphalt, plastics, synthetic rubber
Gold	28%	Canada, U.S.S.R., Switzerland — Jewelry, electronics, dental fillings, investment bars
Iron Ore	22%	Canada, Venezuela, Brazil, Liberia — Steel, ships, machine tools, razor blades, nuts and bolts
Vanadium	15%	South Africa, Chile — Construction equipment, pipelines, welding rods
Copper	14%	Canada, Chile, Zambia, Peru — Electrical wire, bearings, coins, steel cases

* 1976–1979 data from U.S. Department of the Interior, U.S. Department of Energy, and U.S. Department of the Navy.

1970s, when America endured its energy crisis and Nigeria expanded its oil production, relations improved. Both Carter and Young visited Nigeria early, acknowledging the nation's importance to Africa's future.

Because of its riches, traditional ties to the United States, blatant racism, and white minority government, South Africa also stood at the forefront of African-American relations. Carter chided the South Africans for their segregationist policy of *apartheid*—removals of blacks from homelands, discriminatory wages based on race, denial of voting rights, absence of civil liberties, and arbitrary arrest, among other abuses. During a visit to South Africa, Vice-President Walter Mondale called for one-person, one-vote (85% of South Africa was non-white), not only because he thought it right, but because "perpetuating an unjust system is the surest incentive to increase Soviet influence and even racial war. . . ."[63] South African leaders rejected American meddling and defended their racist policies.

The Carter Administration never used economic sanctions to gain concessions from South Africa, even though American economic links with that country were considerable. Trade climbed to $4 billion in 1979, and the largest concentration of American investment in the continent rested in South Africa. In the mid-1970s, twenty-nine of America's top fifty corporations operated there, with General Motors, Mobil, Exxon, Ford, General Electric, and Firestone at the top of the list. Although American critics argued for disinvestment until South Africa halted *apartheid,* the furthest some American companies would go was to accept the Sullivan Principles. Devised by black Philadelphia minister Leon H. Sullivan, also a member of the General Motors board of directors, the guidelines amounted to a voluntary, general pledge to follow nondiscriminatory employment practices in the Republic of South Africa. By 1979 only 116 of the 300 American firms active there had endorsed the Sullivan Principles, and very few blacks held managerial positions in American-owned companies. Many African leaders favored an American economic boycott and protested the sale of American aircraft to the regime. They were also dismayed by Carter's approval of Export-Import Bank loans (until Congress stopped them). One Nigerian official condemned America's "outright collaboration with South Africa" and pressed Washington to be truer to its rhetoric of human rights.[64] The Carter Administration defended its policies with several arguments: the United States needed certain strategic minerals from South Africa; disinvestment would hurt native blacks by causing unemployment; if American investors pulled out, competitors would simply move in, denying the United States both profits and leverage on the regime; and the impact of divestiture would be minimal, given South Africa's unusual self-sufficiency. Most American analysts agreed, however, that South Africa was heading for certain race war.

If there was no change in South African *apartheid,* there was also little movement on the status of Namibia, a former German colony that had come under South Africa's jurisdiction after the First World War. In 1966 the United Nations revoked South Africa's mandate over Namibia and demanded independence, but South Africa defiantly continued to rule the mineral-rich territory. The radical South West African People's Organization (SWAPO) battled South African armies from sanctuaries in Angola and Zambia and vowed a war of national liberation that American leaders feared might bring the great powers into further conflict in Africa.

In contrast, the bitter civil war between whites and insurgent blacks finally ended in Zimbabwe/Rhodesia. Ian Smith's white government, created in 1965, made token gestures to black majority rule, but Carter insisted on real change. One of the President's first efforts in early 1977 was to persuade Congress to repeal the 1972 Byrd Amendment. This provision had permitted the United States to trade with Zimbabwe/Rhodesia in chromium, despite the United Nations–declared economic boycott of Smith's regime. Carter then refused to accept the results of 1979 elections because they were tilted in favor of whites. Finally, after delicate British-led negotiations, an all-races, nation-wide election in April, 1980, produced a new government led by former black rebel Robert Mugabe. The result provided a rare example of diplomacy resolving a civil war.

By the close of Carter's tenure, United States influence in Africa stood as high as it had ever been—despite Andrew Young's ouster in 1979. Trade with black Africa was improving. The United States gained access to military facilities in Somalia after the Russians had been expelled from that nation in 1977. Carter was pleased, moreover, to find that many African countries joined the United States in a 104–18 vote for a United Nations General Assembly resolution condemning the Soviet invasion of Afghanistan. In fact, Soviet and Cuban influence in Africa was mostly confined to Ethiopia and Angola, and even the latter was reaching out for better relations with Western nations. Nigeria's President Obasanjo reflected widespread African opinion when he warned Moscow and Havana "not to overstay their welcome" in the two countries. Africa, he said, did not desire to subjugate itself to a "new imperial power."[65]

Born Again Cold War: Carter and the Communists

Carter's new approach to the Third World ultimately became overshadowed by the old problem of containing the Soviet Union, especially after the Red Army slashed into Afghanistan in late 1979. From the outset, the Carter Administration was divided by conflicting interpretations of Soviet intentions and capabilities. Some officials believed that North-South relations were more important than the East-West rivalry and that it was inaccurate to explain global problems by always pointing an accusing finger at a Russian bear that looked anything but vigorous, unsettled as it was by domestic troubles and stirrings for liberation in Eastern Europe. "Are the Soviets 5 feet tall or 10 feet tall?" asked Russian studies specialist Marshall Shulman, an aide to Vance.[66] Although Shulman and others in the State Department thought the Soviets were adversaries with whom the United States could negotiate, Brzezinski and his White House staff stressed Soviet expansionism in the Middle East and Africa. Brzezinski called for an American posture that the Soviets would read as "a challenge to their legitimacy and thus to their very existence. . . ."[67] His opponents thought he was advocating destruction of the Soviet system itself.

Buffeted by these competing views, Carter vacillated, apparently uncertain about which way to turn. One time, for example, he asked Vance and Brzezinski to submit separate memoranda for a major speech on Soviet-American relations to be delivered at Annapolis in June, 1978. Two contrasting statements were dispatched to the Oval Office. Essentially stapling the different papers together, the President gave an address marked by a glaring contradiction between toughness and conciliation, between the "mailed fist and the dove's coo."[68] Still, as Vance learned, the President leaned toward Brzezinski's counsel of toughness, even before Afghanistan.

Barely a month in office, the Carter Administration exhorted the Soviet government to permit Dr. Andrei Sakharov, a leading dissident, to speak freely against that government. The Soviets reacted crossly, telling Americans to stop meddling in their domestic affairs. To Moscow, Carter's call for human rights was yet another example of Washington's abandonment of détente. Still smarting from the 1974–1975 controversy over the Jackson-Vanik amendment to the 1974 Trade Act (requiring the Soviets to relax restrictions on Jewish emigration before the United States would grant most-favored-nation tariff treatment), the anti-Soviet tone of the 1976 presidential campaign, and American overtures to Russia's archenemy China, the Kremlin itself was ready to be tough when Carter entered the White House. From the American perspective, the Soviets seemed bent on a military build-up: Cuban troops and Soviet advisers in Angola; modernization of the Soviet navy and Warsaw Pact forces; and an increase in missiles pointed at NATO countries. Moscow officials claimed that they were only trying to match the United States in the arms race; and that, in any case, détente never meant that they would cease their support for leftist Third World nations. In this environment laced with suspicion and hostility, Secretary Vance journeyed to Moscow in March, 1977 to reenergize the SALT process with a sudden, publicized proposal for deep cuts in ICBMs—where the Soviets were strongest. The surprised and angered Soviets quickly sent him home. They also defied Carter's sermons by stepping up harassment of Jews attempting to immigrate to Israel and of dissident intellectuals who criticized the Communist regime.

Soviet-American relations steadily deteriorated. In March, 1978, Carter denounced the Kremlin for conducting a proxy war in Ethiopia, using Cubans to battle Somalia, a new-found American friend that had futilely invaded Ethiopia to seize disputed land. The President's blunt speech was designed, boasted Brzezinski, to "prove we weren't soft."[69] In May, Brzezinski traveled to China with the intention of signaling the Soviets that Sino-American "parallel interests" were something for them to worry about.[70] Hints of United States arms sales to the People's Republic caused one Russian official to complain that the United States was "smuggling" weapons aimed against the U.S.S.R. through the "back door" in Asia.[71] Carter also warned that a Russian military build-up in Eastern Europe would be met by strengthening NATO defenses. "We are not going to let the Soviet Union push us around."[72] To register disapproval of the Soviets' repression of domestic critics, Carter canceled the sale of a $7 million computer to the Soviet news agency Tass. Yet other Russian-American trade was at the same time reaching new highs. Moscow expressed puzzlement over "constant zigzags and inconsistency" in American behavior.[73]

In December, 1978 pro-Soviet Vietnam invaded Kampuchea (Cambodia) to rid that devastated nation of the brutal rule of Pol Pot, the pro-Chinese Communist who had gained power four years earlier. To Americans, this invasion stood as another example of a Soviet war by proxy. Then, on January 1, 1979, playing the "China card" with authority, Carter formally recognized the People's Republic of China. Chinese Deputy Premier Deng Xiaoping soon toured the United States, using his American platform to denounce the Soviet Union as an imperialist bear threatening world peace.

Despite the bitterness enveloping Soviet-American relations, the two super-powers inched their way toward a new strategic arms limitation agreement. The SALT-II talks, which began in November, 1972, produced some guidelines in the form of the 1974 Vladivostok accord, but then sputtered. Meanwhile the giants deployed new missiles and enlarged their arsenals of warheads (see p. 582 and glossary, p. 580). In the SALT-II talks of 1977–1979, the Soviets tried but failed to block American development of the new MX (missile experimental), an improved ICBM designed to carry ten MIRVs; the Trident-II submarine-launched missile, capable of carrying fourteen warheads; and the cruise missile. The Americans sought but failed to block the new Soviet supersonic bomber—the Backfire. Its range of 5,500 miles suggested that it would be used against Western Europe and China, but in a one-way mission it could strike the United States. The prolonged negotiations culminated in the SALT-II treaty, signed at the Vienna summit in June, 1979.

One of the most complex treaties ever negotiated, SALT-II established for the first time numerical equality between the United States and the Soviet Union in total strategic nuclear delivery vehicles: each side was limited to 2,400, to be reduced to 2,250 in 1982. MIRVed launchers, specifically, were limited to 1,200 and the number of warheads that delivery vehicles could carry was also limited. And because "we don't trust the Soviet Union," as the Director of the Arms Control and Disarmament Agency put it, the treaty provided that each side could pursue technical verification of compliance without interference.[74] Whereas the treaty would require the Soviets to dismantle over 250 existing delivery vehicles, the Americans could expand from their current 2,060 to the ceiling of 2,250.

Jimmy Carter (1924–) and Leonid I. Brezhnev (1906–) in Vienna, 1979. Soviet-American relations were strained throughout the Carter years. The adversaries did agree on SALT-II, but the Soviet invasion of Afghanistan prompted Carter to shelve the nuclear arms control agreement. Brezhnev was a formidable opponent. A graduate of a metallurgical institute, an active Communist party worker and officer during the 1940s and 1950s, and later Chairman of the Presidium of the Supreme Soviet (1960–1964; 1970–) and the Communist Party of the Soviet Union (1966–), Brezhnev endorsed détente but still insisted that "the class aims of socialism and capitalism are opposite and irreconcilable." (Carter White House Photo Office Collection. Carter Presidential Materials Project. National Archives and Records Service)

SALT-II soon fell victim to the hostile Soviet-American relations that preceded it. The treaty languished in the Senate. Some Americans argued that progress on nuclear arms control should be linked to Soviet behavior on other issues—such as human rights and the military presence in Angola and Ethiopia. Other critics insisted that any agreement with the Soviets was suspect, because they were so untrustworthy. Just before Carter left for Vienna, Senator Henry Jackson of Washington, who took a "stick-it-to-the-Russians"[75] approach to diplomacy, compared the President to Neville Chamberlain and charged him with "appeasement in its purest form."[76] Jackson and other hawks also believed that the Soviets were pursuing superiority, not equivalence, and hence by the mid-1980s would be able to destroy America's land-based missiles in a first strike. SALT-II therefore endangered American security. Anyway, they charged, accurate verification could not be guaranteed. Dovish critics, on the other hand, found the SALT-II limitations too meager, permitting continued nuclear weapons growth. The most that could be said of the agreement, they averred, was that it codified the arms race.

Admitting that SALT-II was but a small step in a long process toward deep-cut agreements, the Carter Administration concentrated on rebutting conservative critics. Without SALT-II, the State Department explained, the Soviets would enlarge their nuclear forces at a brisker pace. The United States would feel compelled to keep up, and therein lay the makings of an expensive, spiraling arms race. SALT-II, moreover, curbed the Soviets but placed minimal restraints on American nuclear weapons development. As for the alleged vulnerability of American ICBMs, Carter officials pointed out that the Soviets would have to deposit two warheads on every ICBM silo to ensure destruction—and that was highly unlikely. First, in a "single cosmic roll of the dice" the timing must be near-perfect so that one incoming warhead did not explode before the other, destroying it before it could reach its target ("fratricide").[77] Second, missile accuracy was quite problematical: wind speed, changes in atmospheric density, and irregularities in gravitational field could alter a missile's course. Third, the Soviets would have to assume that the President would stand by—even with 20–30 minutes warning—and let American ICBMs be destroyed in their silos. Fourth, even if a Soviet first-strike somehow destroyed the land-based ICBMs, only about 30 percent of America's nuclear forces would be damaged—the rest of the triad, SLBMs and airborne strategic bombers, would remain to annihilate Soviet cities and tens of millions of people. "They [the Soviets] are not supermen; they are not fools either," remarked State Department officer Leslie H. Gelb.[78]

As if to prove both dovish and hawkish critics correct—that SALT-II really did mean a weapons build-up rather than arms control and that United States security was really endangered—Carter soon made decisions that contrasted sharply with his 1976 campaign pledge to reduce military spending. To ensure the survivability of the ICBMs, Carter decided to deploy the MX as a mobile missile in a vast network of tracks and underground shelters. In a giant shell game, 200 missiles would be constantly shuttled through the 9,000-mile system, making them impossible for the Soviets to target. Critics thought the highly accurate MX would stimulate a feverish arms race, because it would provide the United States with a "counterforce" capability, that is, the ability to knock out Soviet ICBMs in a first strike. Skeptics also noted that the MX deployment would not be completed until 1990;

if the ICBMs were truly vulnerable, then the MX was hardly a suitable solution to the immediate problem, whereas arms control negotiations and agreements might be. The cost also alarmed many Americans: estimates ran from $33.8 billion to over $100 billion. Protesting citizens of Utah and Nevada, where the MX network would be constructed, predicted ecological disorder in their region.

If Carter clouded the meaning of SALT-II by injecting the MX issue, he further jeopardized ratification by sparking a "pseudo-crisis" in the fall of 1979.[79] He accused the Soviets of sneaking a combat brigade of about 2,600 troops into Cuba to threaten other Caribbean islands. When the surprised yet conciliatory Soviets replied that the troops had in fact been there for several years, were training Cubans, and would continue in that limited function, Carter retreated from the storm he had stirred up. "I have concluded that the brigade issue is certainly no reason for a return to the Cold War."[80] Asked later why the episode had ever occurred, Under Secretary of State David D. Newsom diplomatically answered: "The White House is naturally conscious of the Presidential image. . . ."[81] Indeed, Carter's need to improve his standing in the public opinion polls by appearing tough apparently lay behind the dispute. In any case, the imbroglio further poisoned the atmosphere for SALT-II by suggesting that the Soviets were once again up to no good and that Carter—the President who signed SALT-II—was inept. Senator Frank Church, chairman of the Foreign Relations Committee, temporarily postponed hearings on SALT-II and said that ratification was unlikely as long as the Soviet combat troops remained in Cuba.

With senatorial ratification of the treaty in doubt in early December, and with the hostage crisis raising fears that the Soviets might meddle in Iran, Carter tried to win votes from the hawks through other decisions. He announced an expensive five-year military expansion program and NATO approval of an American plan to deploy 572 Pershing-II ballistic missiles and ground-launched cruise missiles in Western Europe to counter the Soviet medium-range SS-20 missiles trained on America's allies. To critics who protested that Carter had too soon forgotten the lesson of Vietnam that he himself had drawn—the need for restraints on military action—the President replied that "not every instance of the firm application of power is a potential Vietnam."[82] As 1979 closed, however, Carter still did not have the votes for SALT-II.

The shocking Soviet invasion of Afghanistan in late December killed the treaty's chances for survival and elevated to orthodoxy Brzezinski's hard-line views about a malevolent Soviet Union. Thousands of Red Army troops marched into neighboring Afghanistan to prop up a Soviet-backed regime weakened by Muslim rebels. The Soviet Union imposed a new government, executed political prisoners, and stayed to battle the Afghan rebels. At the start Carter picked up the "hot line" telephone and vented his outrage against Brezhnev. For the President, the invasion marked a "quantum jump in the nature of Soviet behavior" and the most serious threat to peace since the Second World War.[83] Carter worried too because about one-third of America's oil imports came from the Persian Gulf region; for Japan and allies in Western Europe, the figures were three-quarters and two-thirds respectively. Soviet troops, the White House hastened to note, were now only 300 miles from the Strait of Hormuz, through which that precious petroleum was transported. Was the invasion of Afghanistan part of a Soviet master plan to deny America and its allies vital fuel and thereby precipitate a depression worse than that of the 1930s? Would the Soviets take advantage of the chaos in Iran and move against that nation too? The Carter Administration acted as if it feared the worst. "Putting 'a Red thread' through the complexities of the Gulf area seemed to us to be a desirable and justified simplification" to arouse the American people, Brzezinski later explained.[84]

In early 1980 Carter announced a wide range of punishments for the Soviet Union. He withdrew the SALT-II treaty from the Senate. He stopped high technology sales and grain shipments to the U.S.S.R. He proposed a boycott of the Summer Olympic Games scheduled for Moscow, curtailed Soviet fishing privileges in American waters, and imposed a moratorium on the opening of new Soviet consular offices in the United States. He outlined military actions as well: arms assistance for Pakistan, a state bordering the Soviet Union; creation of American naval facilities in Oman, Kenya, Somalia, and Egypt; organization of a rapid deployment force for use in the Middle East; the positioning of two carrier task groups in the region; and a much increased defense budget. The President asked an obliging Congress to enact legislation requiring young men to register for the draft, so that an army could more quickly be mobilized in case of war. The CIA also secretly aided the Afghan rebels. Carter, wrote a former Nixon assistant, was turning to "the hawks for quick fixes."[85] Others cheered that the "Vietnam syndrome" had ended.

In his State of the Union address of January 24, 1980, the President proclaimed the Carter Doctrine: "An attempt by any outside force to gain control of the Persian Gulf region will be regarded as an assault on the vital interests of the United States of America, and such an assault will be repelled by use of any means necessary, including military force."[86] As another statement of containment, it sounded familiar themes. But serious problems impeded its implementation. When Washington offered $400 million to Pakistan, its dictator dismissed the amount as "peanuts" and demanded more.[87] The Saudis refused to let the American military use their facilities, and West Germany and Japan declined to interrupt their lucrative trade with the Soviet Union. West German Chancellor Helmut Schmidt thought Carter unpredictable: "We do not need nervousness, war cries, or excited or provocative speeches."[88] Brazil and Argentina increased their grain shipments to the Russians, diminishing the impact of the American embargo. Many countries rejected the Olympics boycott; Lord Killanin, indignant head of the international committee, boldly deplored the use of athletes "as pawns in political problems that politicians cannot solve themselves."[89]

The Carter Doctrine also stimulated debate at home. Unlike the Truman and Eisenhower Doctrines, it was not offered to Congress for scrutiny or approval, and some congressmen felt slighted. The venerable father of containment, George F. Kennan, scolded Carter for unnecessarily creating a war atmosphere and encouraging militarism. Kennan and others denied that the Soviet attack on Afghanistan was a prelude to further aggression; they emphasized that the U.S.S.R. had invaded a bordering state to save a client government from collapse. A "thundering" Carter was carrying a "small stick," Kennan lamented. Moreover, Carter had played all of his cards at the outset and Russia was still encamped in Afghanistan. "Was this really mature statesmanship on our part?" Kennan asked.[90] Some observers faulted Carter for simplistically pressing the Persian Gulf states to choose between East and West, when instead their nonalignment might be the best de-

Coca-Cola in China. In April, 1981, the Coca-Cola Company opened a bottling plant in China, where the famous soft drink was known as "tasty happiness." Humorist Art Buchwald assayed this product of Sino-American détente: "I don't mind 800 million Chinese drinking a bottle a day, but I don't want them to bring back the empties." (Courtesy, Coca-Cola Company, 1979)

fense against Soviet advances. Others thought Carter had capitulated fully to Cold Warriors like Brzezinski in another diplomatic lurch, going too far, too fast. Some complained that the President adopted the alarmist line to improve his political standing. "I think Carter hyped Afghanistan," snapped Congressman and presidential aspirant John Anderson.[91] An insider, Under Secretary of State David D. Newsom, revealed soon after the crisis that the Carter Doctrine "grew out of last minute pressures for a presidential speech," rather than from a cool calculation of Middle Eastern policy.[92]

As Soviet-American relations plummeted, Sino-American relations continued to improve. After American recognition of China in early 1979, Washington and Beijing began to cooperate on a number of fronts, because they wanted to use each other to contain the Soviet Union. A United States–China trade agreement went into effect in early 1980 and the Export-Import Bank extended credit to China. American companies began to work on a major Chinese hydroelectric project and to explore for oil in the China Sea. Chinese markets beckoned American farmers; in 1977–1980 China ranked fourth in the world as a buyer of United States agricultural exports, taking about half of the nation's cotton exports in 1979 alone. Mineral-short America eyed China's large deposits of tin, chrome, and tungsten. In 1980 American exports to China totaled $4 billion, up from $807 million in 1974. China replaced Russia as the United States' largest Communist trading partner; in 1980 American exports to the Soviet Union stood at a comparatively low $1.5 billion.

Sino-American military and cultural ties expanded as well. Sales agreements were struck for radar gear, helicopters, and transport aircraft. The United States also supplied equipment for spy stations along the tense Sino-Soviet border. China passed intelligence data on Soviet missile tests to the United States. China and America initiated student and scholar exchanges, began to share scientific knowledge in energy physics and earthquakes, among other fields, and welcomed cultural delegations, such as the popular visit of the Boston Symphony to Beijing in early 1979.

The status of Taiwan, however, remained a divisive issue. Although the United States severed formal diplomatic relations with the Republic of China on Taiwan, unilaterally terminated the 1954 mutual defense treaty, and withdrew all American forces and military installations from the island, private Americans maintained strong economic links. The United States government maintained low-level official ties through an "Institute," and actually kept up the flow of military aid. The People's Republic insisted on repossessing Taiwan, but threats of force subsided. On the question of Taiwan, then, China and the United States continued to agree to disagree. There was little disagreement, however, over the need to cooperate to contain the Soviet Union.

Carter's Fall, Reagan's Rise

Just before Americans went to the polls in November, 1980, to decide whether President Jimmy Carter should be replaced by Republican Ronald Reagan, many Americans felt that the nation's power had slipped, that its role as the world's policeman, banker, businessman, and teacher had broken down, and that a meek Carter Administration was doing too little to reverse the negative trend. A Nashville woman lamented, "growing up, we learned in history that America was the best at everything. We had the respect of the whole world. But where can you go today and be respected for being American?"[93] High OPEC prices, huge deficits in the balance of payments, defeat in Vietnam, revolution in Nicaragua, the return of the Canal Zone to Panama, Castro's defiance, Soviet nuclear equivalence and SALT-II, the Iranian hostage crisis, and the Soviet invasion of Afghanistan—all these persuaded worried Americans that the United States looked and acted weak in the face of threats. Carter had failed to convince them that in an interdependent, multipolar world of some 150 nations, a decline in United States power was inevitable. He bluntly told them that the 1970s and 1980s were decades of limits and scarcity. Used to rhetoric from other Presidents about boundless growth, Americans grew angry with the new message and the messenger. Americans, concluded one historian of American diplomacy, were "suffering a serious case of empire shock for the first time in their cultural history."[94]

The Carter Administration and the President were not undeserving of criticism. The Administration's record was mixed and its behavior erratic. Republican Senator Charles Mathias of Maryland described Administration statements as "an antiphonal chorus of hawk and dove."[95] Part of the problem stemmed from the constant feuding between the State Department and Brzezinski's White House staff. Policy appeared confused or unsettled. Also, Carter had seldom been able to give a rousing speech, to pound the bully pulpit. "His written speeches on prime time were soporific, a matter partly of soft tone and curious cadence, partly a reflection of his public personality, which was toned down, 'de-pomped,'" wrote noted specialist on presidential power Richard E. Neustadt.[96] Carter lacked FDR's charm, Eisenhower's popularity, JFK's television presence, LBJ's ability to handle Congress, and Nixon's exploitation of spectaculars.

Carter also made himself vulnerable to criticism by contradicting some of his stated goals. He claimed that he would reduce the American military presence abroad, but there were more military personnel overseas in 1980 (489,000) than in 1976 (460,000). Carter promised to withdraw American forces from South Korea, but then reversed himself. He strongly advocated nuclear nonproliferation, but agreed in 1980 to ship 38 metric tons of enriched uranium fuel to India, even though that nation had refused to permit international inspection against nonpeaceful uses and had snubbed the Non-Proliferation Treaty. He said he would reduce defense spending, but increased the Pentagon's budget, recommending for fiscal year 1982 a 14.5 percent rise over fiscal year 1981. The President vowed to trim arms sales abroad, but foreign military sales actually climbed from $8.3 billion in 1977 to $15.3 billion in 1980, because Carter ultimately deemed them necessary to win support for his diplomacy from such states as Egypt and Saudi Arabia.

Carter's human rights policy also appeared inconsistent. He condemned Soviet mistreatment of dissidents, but muted his criticism of abuse by such allies as Egypt, South Korea, and the Philippines or potential allies like China and Saudi Arabia. Critics complained that the President championed human rights, but then supplied weapons to regimes that suppressed internal dissent. For example, Amnesty International, the London-based, independent organization that monitors the worldwide status of human rights, cited Argentina, Brazil, Guatemala, Indonesia, Iran, Morocco, the Philippines, South Korea, Taiwan, and Thailand for government-approved torture, political terrorism, or arbitrary arrest. In 1976–1980 the United States sent $2.3 billion in military aid to those ten nations and sold them weapons worth $13.7 billion. The arms included anti-riot gear, pistols, and rifles. The United States also trained thousands of foreign officers and police at overseas bases and American military schools. "The United States stands at the supply end of a pipeline of repressive technology" and "will remain a party to any violations of human rights committed in those countries," concluded two students of the subject.[97] Conservative critics thought human rights should never have been a major thrust in the first place. They complained that Carter was behaving like an evangelical preacher in a world of sinners; that he invited revolutions such as the one in Iran by weakening or undermining leaders whom America needed as loyal, strategic partners. Condemning human wrongs was one thing, but attempting to ensure human rights was another. The record showed that Carter's efforts did lead to the freeing of hundreds of political prisoners abroad, but the President's detractors faulted it as either too little or too meddlesome.

The President's defenders attributed his problems and mixed record to domestic politics. Carter may have played politics with the Cuban brigade issue, the rescue attempt in Iran, and the Afghan crisis, they admitted, but he had to because of vigorous right-wing pressure. The Cold Warriors made ill-founded but formidable charges that Carter was an appeaser who had presided over the nation's fall from prominence. The Committee on the Present Danger proved a special thorn in Carter's side. Founded in 1976 and modeled after a similar anti-Soviet organization of the early 1950s, this pressure group included such hawks as former Under Secretary of State Eugene V. Rostow, former Secretary of State Dean Rusk, Harvard historian Oscar Handlin, and Paul Nitze, who had composed NSC-68 in 1950 (see p. 457). It charged that the United States was shamefully retreating before the Soviet threat. The answer: enlarge the military even more and scrap SALT-II. Because he wanted to be re-elected, it has been argued, the President could not ignore this influential voice. Yet, as Vance said shortly after his resignation, "smart politics produce bad policies."[98]

Could Carter's troubles be blamed on Congress? Foreign policy was highly partisan in the Carter years, and Congress was susceptible to special interest lobbyists for Israel and Greece, among others. Moreover, foreign leaders hired American public relations firms to improve their image with American politicians. In fact, South Korean intelligence agents compromised some members of Congress in a scandal dubbed Koreagate. Some Senators, using their own staffs of experts, seemed to think they were secretaries of state. Congress did intrude into policymaking: it stopped certain military shipments, placed stipulations on foreign aid, scrutinized Administration decisions, and tinkered with the Panama Canal treaties. Presidential aides claimed that if the United States appeared inconsistent in its foreign policy, the reason lay in meddling by Congress. Critics replied that Carter, not Congress, made and executed policy on the major issues, and that Congress was an appropriate watchdog over an inept President.

Despite a turbulent world and noisy critics, the Carter Administration believed it had pursued noble goals and achieved diplomatic successes. Carter officials brought the rhetoric, if not always the substance, of morality to American foreign policy in an effort to establish that American power lay not simply in its military capabilities but in its values. They were frank in explaining the limits of American influence in a world of diffused power. Through the work of Andrew Young and others, the Carter team partially restored America's credibility in the Third World and in the United Nations. The Carter Administration made more people conscious of the need to deal with long-range issues, not just immediate crises. Pointing to the Egyptian-Israeli peace, Panama Canal treaties, normalization of relations with China, progress on the law of the sea and the North-South dialogue, an end to civil war in Zimbabwe, nuclear modernization of NATO, creation of a rapid deployment force, and an improved American status in Africa, Professor Brzezinski proudly filled out the Administration's report card as his term ended. The grade: A−/B+.

Republican presidential candidate Ronald Reagan resolutely disagreed. Born in Illinois in 1911, a graduate of Eureka College, a long-time professional actor, and governor of California, from 1967 to 1975, Reagan was nearly seventy years old during the 1980 campaign and had no experience in national government or foreign affairs. Carter quipped that if Reagan ever had to go to a summit meeting with foreign leaders, they would have to wear name tags for his benefit. Many thought Reagan an extremist and an ideologue of the far right. He was noted for reckless statements and factual inaccuracies, and had a penchant for applying military solutions to diplomatic problems. "His is a kind of 1952 world," remarked a former Reagan aide. "He sees the world in black and white terms."[99] Surrounded by pollsters and communications specialists, Reagan proved an astute politician and an effective communicator. His easy-going style, straightforward language, and self-deprecating humor were political assets. Reagan probably drew most strength from Carter's weakness: the President's approval rating in the Gallup Poll of July, 1980, slumped to 21 percent, a figure lower than Harry S Truman's during the Korean War and even lower than Richard M. Nixon's just before his resignation.

Reagan slammed Carter repeatedly with the theme of "America in decline." The Republican candidate called for a huge expansion of the military. "America has never gotten in a war because we were too strong," Reagan said.[100] In a display of raw anti-communism not seen in some years, Reagan charged that an expansionist Soviet Union "underlies all the unrest that is going on. If they weren't engaged in this game of dominoes, there wouldn't be any hot spots in the world."[101] Any residue of détente, such as SALT-II, had to be dumped. Labeling the Republican standard-bearer careless and belligerent, Carter replied that "strength is imperative for peace, but the two must go hand in hand."[102] He argued to no avail. Bothered by domestic economic troubles and attracted to Reagan's promise to "make America great again," the American people turned Carter out by a vote of 43,901,812 to 35,483,820.[103] The Republicans also gained control of the Senate; liberal, dovish Senators Birch Bayh of Indiana, Frank Church of Idaho, John Culver of Iowa, and George McGovern of South Dakota joined Carter in defeat.

America on Its High Horse: Reagan Rides to the Rescue

"The era of self-doubt is over"; "Americans want to be number one"; "we are acting to restore confidence in American leadership through a more robust defense of U.S. ideals and interests"—such early statements signaled the mood of

Ronald Reagan's foreign policy.[104] The new administration explained that its primary assignment was to restrain the Soviet Union, instigator of the world's major problems. Analysts were quick to say that Arab-Israeli rivalry, not Soviet behavior, fostered Mideast tensions; that poverty and authoritarian regimes stirred people to revolt in Central America; and that ethnic differences, economic questions, and the legacy of anti-colonialism lay at the root of African issues. Reagan officials, however, thought in terms of an earlier age of bipolarism, global containment, and confrontation. Soon the Reagan Administration directed unvarnished rhetoric against Russia, began a massive military build-up and downplayed arms-control negotiations, planned for showdowns with Third World countries believed to be Soviet clients or threatened by the Soviets, and pursued anti-Soviet allies worldwide. References to human rights became muted; in fact, Reagan officials made a distinction between communist totalitarian governments and non-communist authoritarian regimes. They pledged to aid the latter as they lined up with the United States against Soviet Russia.

President Reagan appointed General Alexander M. Haig, Jr. secretary of state. "Al Haig is a man who telegraphs his punches and goes straight toward his objectives," reported a White House official.[105] The steely-eyed secretary became famous for mixing his metaphors and indulging in befuddling bureaucratic jargon. Reagan downgraded the office of national security adviser in the hope of avoiding the feuding that bedeviled the Carter Administration. His new assistant for national security affairs was Richard V. Allen, noted for his anti-Communist zeal. A former researcher and business consultant, Allen was one of many members of

Alexander M. Haig, Jr. (1924–). A graduate of West Point, General Haig served in the Nixon White House before leaving Watergate Washington to become NATO's commander in 1974. Five years later he assumed the presidency of United Technologies, a large defense contractor. As secretary of state, Haig became famous for obfuscation. Once, after his comments at a staff meeting were leaked, he remarked that "it couldn't have been me speaking. It was too clear." In June, 1982, he abruptly resigned. (David Humphrey, Department of State)

the Committee on the Present Danger who joined the Reagan Administration: James L. Buckley became Under Secretary of State; Jeane J. Kirkpatrick became Ambassador to the United Nations; William J. Casey became Director of Central Intelligence; and Eugene V. Rostow became Director of the Arms Control and Disarmament Agency. The most famous member of the anti-Soviet organization to go to Washington was Ronald Reagan himself.

In his first year as President, Reagan encountered bickering among subordinates. Haig tangled openly with Secretary of Defense Casper W. Weinberger, while Haig and Allen competed for control of foreign policy. The secretary of state's hair-trigger temper flared publicly; he once snapped that a White House official was waging "guerrilla war" against him.[106] Critics quipped that Haig was seeking "haigemony"; they mocked him with CINCWORLD, an acronym which read as "Commander in Chief of the World." The President tried to end the squabbling. When, in 1982, Allen admitted accepting $1000 from a Japanese newspaper for setting up an interview with Mrs. Nancy Reagan, and when earlier charges that Allen had exploited his contacts with the Nixon Administration for personal gain were repeated, the White House eased him out. The new national security adviser was William P. Clark, Jr., a former California judge and friend of the President who knew little about foreign affairs. Haig, himself, abruptly resigned in June, 1982, after feuding with the President over policy toward Europe and the Middle East. Reagan quickly named George P. Shultz as the new secretary of state. An economist and international business executive with a doctorate from the Massachusetts Institute of Technology, Shultz had served in Nixon's cabinet and was known as a "team player."

The clashes within the Administration did not prevent it from pursuing a simplistic but ardent anti-Soviet foreign policy. Barely settled into the White House, Reagan remarked that the Soviet Union was prepared "to commit any crime, to lie, to cheat" to achieve a one-world Communist state.[107] Secretary Haig soon accused the Russians of being the conscious source for the "training, funding, and equipping" of international terrorists.[108] Presidential aides cautioned Reagan not to ad lib, and intelligence officers quietly reported that there was no evidence to link the Soviets to terrorists like the Red Brigades in Italy or the Red Army in Japan, but there was some information to tie Moscow to the PLO. "Haig was generally correct," explained one official, "but he overstated the case."[109] Such overstatements bothered veteran diplomat George W. Ball, who feared that the spirit of John Foster Dulles had returned to Washington: "So, now once more we shiver in the icy winds of the Cold War. Diplomacy is for sissies. . . ."[110]

To counter the perceived Soviet threat, the Administration developed a five-year $1.5 trillion defense budget, the largest peacetime arms buildup in American history. Reagan approved the construction of 100 B-1 bombers estimated to cost about $3 billion each. He ordered the assembly and stockpiling of the neutron bomb (see glossary p. 580), revived the production of poison gas for chemical warfare, and planned for the deployment of the MX, although not in Carter's track system. The protected MX was necessary, said Reagan, because the United States had to close the "window of vulnerability"—the theoretical vulnerability of American land-based ICBMs to a Soviet first strike.[111] When Moscow denounced Washington's new plans but promised to match them, Reagan remarked: "They're screaming like they're sitting on a sharp nail."[112]

Reagan's swelling of American military power stimulated worldwide debate. To Reagan's claim that the Soviet Union was outspending the United States on defense, analysts noted that American calculations of Soviet expenditures were wrongly based on what it would cost the Soviets to buy weapons and pay an army at American prices. Moreover, the President failed to count the spending of NATO allies on the American side. As for the B-1 bomber, dissenters thought it unnecessary. The superior Stealth bomber, an aircraft much less subject to reading by enemy radar, would be ready in 1989, only three years after the B-1's appearance. The B-1 was thus likely to become the most expensive interim weapon in modern history. Critics also decried development of the cruise missile, because this weapon could not be easily detected or verified. Once such missiles were deployed, diplomats would be unable to negotiate limits on them since verification was impossible. The Soviets would feel compelled to develop similarly concealable weapons, advancing the dangerous arms race another notch.

The debate over weapons reinvigorated the movement to curb nuclear armaments. The Roman Catholic Bishops of Texas, evangelist Billy Graham, the World Council of Churches, and the Union of Concerned Scientists joined peace groups in appeals for restraint. The American Medical Association asked members to inform the President that "there is no adequate medical response to a nuclear

Military Power: The United States vs. the U.S.S.R., 1980–1981

	UNITED STATES	SOVIET UNION
Intercontinental Ballistic Missiles (ICBMs)	1052[a]	1398
Submarine-launched Ballistic Missiles (SLBMs)	576[b]	950
Long-range Strategic Bombers	348[c]	156
Total Delivery Vehicles (ICBMs, SLBMs, Bombers)	1976	2504
Nuclear Warheads	9200	6000
European Nuclear Forces[d]	924	2537
Anti-Ballistic Missile Launchers (ABM)	0	32
Aircraft Carriers	12	1
Armed Forces Personnel	2,050,000 (plus 2,768,000 NATO forces)	4,822,000 (plus 1,122,000 Warsaw Pact forces)
Gross National Product (GNP)	$2,500 billion	$1,375 billion

* Although the United States lagged behind the Soviet Union in certain categories, the U.S. Department of Defense and other government sources explained that the figures revealed a basic equivalence in strategic nuclear power. Moreover, in measuring the fighting abilities of both sides, technological skills, qualities of leadership, and economic strength must be considered. Also, some of the Soviet military power was deployed, not against Western Europe or the United States, but against China.

[a] 52 single-warhead Titan-IIs (2 others were out of commission and not counted); 450 single-warhead Minuteman IIs; and 550 MIRVed Minuteman IIIs.
[b] 80 Polaris; 304 Poseidon; 192 Trident.
[c] B-52s.
[d] Total launchers for Western allies (NATO and France) and Warsaw Pact. Figures represent bombers and missiles. The Soviets disputed the figures (disagreeing on which weapons should be counted) and offered instead: 1,031 for the Western allies and 1,055 for the Warsaw Pact. Under NATO auspices, the United States set 1983 for deployment of 108 Pershing missiles and 464 ground-launched cruise missiles in Europe.

holocaust." One doctor called nuclear war the "final epidemic."[113] If Boston were hit, a half-million people would die, hundreds of thousands would suffer ghastly burns, deep lacerations, radiation poisoning, and multiple fractures, and the hospitals, including the famed Massachusetts General, would be reduced to rubble. George F. Kennan added his voice to the anti-nuclear movement. "Cease this madness," he implored.[114] Complaining that Reagan's views on the U.S.S.R. were "the marks of an intellectual primitivism," Kennan recommended an immediate 50 percent cut in nuclear arsenals on both sides, the denuclearization of much of Europe, a complete ban on nuclear testing, and a freeze on new weapons.[115] In early 1982, 17 senators (one-sixth of the Senate) and 128 House members (30 percent of that body) endorsed the freeze, and towns across America voted for resolutions urging the Reagan Administration to negotiate arms reductions.

Europeans also debated the issue. In the fall of 1981, huge crowds of demonstrators in Bonn, London, Rome, and Amsterdam called for negotiations and a ban on the soon-to-be installed Pershing and cruise missiles. Protestors from all walks of life demanded that both Washington and Moscow sit down to talk and that the NATO countries foreswear the new weapons. American leaders thought the Europeans too jittery, but statements by United States officials caused some of the alarm. For example, the President said that he could foresee a limited nuclear war in Europe, thus sparing the two great powers. Haig started a furor when he remarked that NATO had a contingency plan to fire a nuclear weapon in Europe as a warning, should Soviet conventional forces ever advance westward. Although Defense Secretary Weinberger soon contradicted Haig in public, saying that no such plan existed, Europeans wondered if the escalating rhetoric about nuclear war reflected an American view that a nuclear war could be limited or winnable.

To satisfy Western European leaders who favored missile development but who faced protest, and to quiet the antinuclear movement, Reagan agreed to begin talks in Geneva on limits to theater nuclear forces (TNF) in Europe. In late 1981 the President announced the American proposal for the European negotiations: the United States would cancel its deployment of the new Pershings and cruise missiles in NATO nations if the Soviet Union would dismantle its SS-20, SS-4, and SS-5 missiles pointed at Western Europe. Washington believed this "zero option" would end Soviet nuclear superiority in Europe, but Moscow answered that if British and French nuclear forces and American weapons on ships and aircraft were tallied, the two sides were actually already even. Also, argued the Soviets, the new NATO missiles could reach the U.S.S.R., but the SS-20s could not hit America. As for negotiations on strategic nuclear weapons, the President announced in May, 1982, that SALT was being replaced by START (Strategic Arms Reduction Talks). He said he hoped to reduce significantly the total number of ballistic missile warheads and land-based missiles, especially those on the Soviet side.

While the battle of words and numbers raged, the Reagan Administration in April, 1981, lifted the grain embargo that President Carter had imposed after the Soviet invasion of Afghanistan. Almost simultaneously, Haig designated Moscow "the greatest source of international insecurity today."[116] When asked, Administration officers admitted that the Soviets had made no concessions—such as withdrawal from Afghanistan or restraint in Poland—before the embargo was terminated. What undoubtedly prompted the turnabout was Reagan's decision to fulfill his 1980 campaign promise to American farmers. In October, the United States sold Russia wheat and corn, a deal that enriched American farmers by about $3 billion. Hawkish conservatives blasted the Administration for putting commerce ahead of confrontation with communism.

Confrontation, however, did characterize relations with countries considered Soviet clients and with rebel groups considered instruments of communism. In El Salvador, for example, the Reagan Administration found "a textbook case of indirect armed aggression by Communist powers."[117] Cuba and the Soviet Union were identified as masterminds of the civil war in that Central American state. Embarrassed American officials soon admitted under public questioning that their "White Paper" detailing alleged Communist machinations had been hastily prepared and that it contained numerous errors and much speculation. Nonetheless, El Salvador seemed a place where the United States could "win one for a change," as one senator put it.[118] A presidential assistant explained that "El Salvador itself doesn't matter—we have to establish credibility," and Reagan resurrected the domino theory by saying that "we are the last domino."[119] For Reagan officials, El Salvador stood as a symbol of East-West conflict.

El Salvador was a very poor country haunted by a high infant mortality rate, illiteracy, and violence. The nation had long been ruled by the army and a small landed elite—2 percent of the people owned half of the land. In October, 1979, however, two reform-minded colonels seized power and organized a new government with civilian José Napoleón Duarte as president. The elite responded by organizing death squads to assassinate reformers and radicals alike. Duarte soon found that he could not control government security forces, who also targeted suspected radicals. Roman Catholic clergymen, the Christian Democratic party, labor unionists, students, journalists, and others demanded controls on the military—"one of the most out-of-control, violent, bloodthirsty groups of men in the world," according to Ambassador Robert E. White.[120] A mix of centrist and leftist parties created the Revolutionary Democratic Front to challenge Duarte's regime. Civil war raged. In 1980, at least 13,000 Salvadorans died, largely at the hands of the right-wing death squads and government security forces.

Determined to find a non-Marxist solution to the Salvadoran civil war and to push land reform, the Carter Administration had extended economic aid to Duarte's besieged government. But it also sent military advisers and military assistance. Reagan and Haig, stressing military victory rather than reform, sent American helicopters, trucks, jeeps, and more weapons, and increased the number of advisers. "We have training squads in more than 30 countries today," said the President, "so this isn't an unusual thing that we are doing."[121]

"The White House did not appreciate how rapidly El Salvador would take off in the minds of the press as a Vietnam," a presidential assistant remarked.[122] American and foreign protestors marched against American intervention in the civil war. "It is not at all a question of Communist subversion," French President François Mitterand argued, but "the people's refusal to submit to misery and humiliation."[123] Mexican President López Portillo called Washington's assertion that the internal Salvadoran crisis stemmed from external Cuban and Soviet sources "an insult to our intelligence."[124] The Reagan Administration resisted international appeals for talks between the rebels and Duarte, apparently counting on a military triumph. "They thought it was like rolling a drunk," Ambassador White commented.[125] But as the war against the insurgents persisted, Ameri-

Ronald Reagan (1911–) and José López Portillo (1920–). During a congenial meeting in 1981, the actor-rancher-President and the President of Mexico discussed Central American crises, petroleum and gas, Mexican migration, and international economic issues. A lawyer, professor of political science, and government official for economic and financial affairs, López Portillo became President in 1976 and asserted a central role for Mexico in inter-American affairs. (The White House. Photograph by Michael Evans)

can officials met in early 1982 with Mexican diplomats who offered to mediate an end to the crisis. In May of that year, Salvadoran elections, boycotted by the rebels, removed Duarte in favor of a right-wing government that soon announced it was shelving the program for land reform.

The Reagan Administration blamed much of the Salvadoran trouble on Nicaragua and Cuba. Haig claimed that the Soviets had a "hit list" of Central American countries, with Nicaragua first, followed by El Salvador, Honduras, and Guatemala.[126] To Reaganauts, the Sandinista government in Nicaragua had already fallen under the spell of Cuba, and hence Russia. The Sandinistas had invited hundreds of Cuban advisers and teachers into Nicaragua, built up the military, and leaned toward a one-party state. American officials also identified Nicaragua as a conduit for Cuban arms shipments to the rebels in El Salvador—a charge sharply denied by the Sandinistas.

In 1981 Washington cut off all aid to the Nicaraguan government, only to see France and Mexico offer assistance. In the Florida Everglades, anti-Sandinista exiles trained as a private army and began to filter back into Nicaragua. When Managua protested, a State Department official replied that "as long as they don't hurt anybody and as long as they don't actually conspire to invade in a specific way," the trainees were not breaking American law.[127] In Honduras, the CIA funded anti-Sandinista commandos. Nicaraguan leaders grew alarmed as well over public American musings about military options against their country. "It's bringing back the politics of Taft and Teddy Roosevelt," snapped one Nicaraguan.[128] In early 1982, Haig said the United States would sign a nonaggression pact with Nicaragua and pledge not to assist anti-Sandinista groups if Nicaragua would end the flow of Communist weapons to El Salvador. The Nicaraguans replied that they could not end something they had never begun, but that they welcomed Haig's apparent willingness to talk.

Reagan officials saw Cuba as the wolf at the sheep's throat. They banned tourist and business travel to Cuba, denied Cuban officials visas for travel to the United States, placed restrictions on shipments of Cuban newspapers and magazines to the United States, and initiated "Radio Martí" to broadcast anti-Castro propaganda into Cuba. To counter the perceived Cuban-Soviet threat to the western hemisphere, Washington also sent military advisers to Honduras and expanded the training of Latin American soldiers at the Army School of the Americas in Panama, where in 1981 nearly 11,000 of them studied methods of counterinsurgency. In early 1982 President Reagan announced the "Caribbean Basin Initiative" to stimulate trade and investment in the region. Besides the extension of American economic aid, he promised military assistance, especially to El Salvador, declaring that the United States would do "whatever is prudent and necessary" to defeat "brutal and totalitarian forces" backed by Cuba and the Soviet Union.[129] Although Castro signaled Washington that he was willing to open talks, and an American envoy traveled to Havana to confer with the Cuban leader, both sides believed normalization of relations was improbable for some time.

The Reagan Administration also squared off with Libya. The bellicose Muammar al-Qaddafi openly supported and trained terrorist groups. Reagan officials declared the Libyan leader part of an international terrorist network funded by the Soviet Union, and in May, 1981, ordered Libyan diplomats out of Washington. In August, as United States forces staged maneuvers in the Mediterranean near Libyan shores, U.S.S. *Nimitz*-based fighter planes tangled with Libyan aircraft, shooting down two. In late 1981, American officials announced that Libyan terrorists had entered the United States to assassinate President Reagan. Washington banned travel to Libya and asked Americans to leave Qaddafi's nation. In early 1982, the United States placed an embargo on imports of Libyan oil, which America's European allies refused to join. Critics said that Reagan was noisily overreacting to an ambitious but weak leader of only 2.5 million tribal people. Meanwhile, the Libyan assassins disappeared, and the dramatic story dropped from the news. Federal investigators did disclose, however, that former CIA officials and Green Berets were, in fact, training Libyans in terrorist tactics and supplying them with weapons.

Across the world, the Reagan Administration strove to attract nations to its anti-Sovietism and counterrevolutionary posture. The CIA received permission to accelerate its covert activities. But military compacts and the export of American arms ranked as the Administration's favorite means of cultivating friends and harassing enemies. In his first three months in office, Reagan offered $15 billion in military aid. In mid-1981, the United States and Pakistan struck a $3.2 billion economic and military agreement that included the transfer of sophisticated F-16 jet fighters. When Washington pledged military equipment to the People's Republic of China, Taiwan was angered and soon received assurances that it could expect fighter planes. American officials increased aid to Sudan and dispatched Green Berets to Liberia. Reagan asked Congress to lift its prohibition on aid to insurgents in Angola, where a Marxist government held power. The State Department also fashioned a changed policy for South Africa. "We will support proven

Give War a Chance. During his confirmation hearings in January, 1981, Secretary of State-designate Alexander M. Haig, Jr. said: "There are more important things than peace—there are things which we Americans must be willing to fight for." Such statements alarmed people at home and abroad who thought him too eager to apply military solutions to political problems and too inclined toward confrontation with the Soviet Union and leftist Third World nations. As for El Salvador, where Haig and Reagan thrust the United States into a civil war, the secretary declared: "We are going to succeed and not flounder as we did in Vietnam." (Bob Englehart, *Hartford Courant*)

friends," uttered the assistant secretary of state for African affairs. "It is not our task to choose between black and white."[130] The fifty-nation Organization of African Unity denounced an "unholy alliance between Washington and Pretoria," as African-American relations deteriorated.[131]

The sale of military equipment to Saudi Arabia in 1981 produced the only major congressional debate on Reagan's determination to arm friendly nations. Although most Americans looked on the Saudis as Arab moderates and necessary suppliers of oil, worries grew that the sale of airborne warning and control system (AWACS) aircraft and Sidewinder missiles, among other military items worth $8.5 billion, would endanger America's ally Israel or further feed an already hazardous Middle Eastern arms race. Reagan vowed not to permit Saudi Arabia "to be an Iran," saying, "there's no way that we could stand by and see that [country] taken over by anyone that would shut off that oil."[132] But pro-Israeli groups lined up against the sale, pointing out the Saudis' failure to recognize Israel and endorse the Camp David accords. When Tel Aviv officials bluntly criticized Washington for the weapons sale, Reagan shot back, "It is not the business of other nations to make American foreign policy."[133] Through a personal lobbying effort "as strong as train smoke," as one senator observed, Reagan moved the huge arms sale through the Senate by a 52–48 vote.[134] "The whole dynamic is on the side of the President," remarked Republican Senator Slade Gorton of Washington. "He has the ability to make a deal if a deal is necessary."[135] Gorton knew this firsthand, having voted for the AWACS sale after the White House promised $26 million for a Seattle hospital.

Angry words flared again between Israel and the United States. Premier Begin complained that anti-Semitic tactics had been employed to win approval of the sale. In December, 1981, after Israel abruptly annexed the occupied Syrian territory of the Golan Heights, Washington suspended talks on a strategic agreement. Begin exploded, "Are we a banana republic?" To American protests against the destructive Israeli bombing raids of suspected PLO strongholds in Lebanon, the premier grumbled that he had read the history of the Vietnam War and knew about the loss of civilian life in Southeast Asia—"you don't have a right, from a moral perspective, to preach to us," he said.[136] Meanwhile, Israeli-Egyptian talks on "autonomy" for Palestinians languished, and the assassination of President Sadat by Egyptian rebels further jeopardized the Mideast peace process, as did Israel's bloody ground invasion of Lebanon in June, 1982.

As the Reagan Administration closed out its first year, tragic events in Poland further disrupted Soviet-American relations. The Solidarity labor movement, after earning concessions from the Communist government through strikes and protests, called for a national referendum on the future of that government and a reexamination of Poland's military alliance with the Soviet Union. For months Moscow had warned the Poles against weakening the Communist regime. In December, the Polish military cracked down, imposing martial law and arresting Solidarity leaders. Washington reacted quickly. It suspended a number of economic relationships with Poland and blamed the U.S.S.R. for the "forces of tyranny" unleashed against its neighbor.[137] Reagan cut back Soviet-American trade and banned Soviet airline flights to the United States, but elected to do little more. NATO countries reacted cautiously, in part because they possessed little leverage in Polish affairs and in part because they did not want to interrupt their own lucrative trade with Russia. The one lever the West could apply—insistence that Poland pay its billions of dollars in delinquent debts to Western banks and governments—was not at first activated, even by the United States. Poland seemed doomed to rule by hard-line Communists who feared both the popular workers' revolt and the Kremlin's threats of intervention if Solidarity were not crushed.

Absorbed in the Soviet-American relationship, the Reagan Administration showed minimal interest in sustaining the North-South dialogue. Reagan reversed Carter's sympathetic regard for Third World problems. Snubbing the Third World call for a new international economic order, Secretary Haig declared an end to "sterile debates and unrealistic demands."[138] Washington told the leaders of developing nations to work out their problems through free-market economics, private enterprise, and guidance from a successful North. American officials urged Third World nations to lift controls on foreign investors and, instead, to provide incentives. When nations were finally near agreement on a law of the sea, Reagan insisted upon revisions to protect private American deep-sea mining interests. Third World nations said they would go ahead with a new treaty even if the United States refused to sign. In May, 1981, the United States was the only nation among 119 to vote against a United Nations resolution to limit the marketing of baby formula in developing nations. Extensive medical opinion held that the aggressive sales efforts of formula companies were causing too many nursing mothers to feed their babies the artificial liquid mixed with polluted water rather than the more healthful breast milk. But Reagan officials, true to their creed, rejected any interference in private business.

"A gathering storm" in Canadian-American relations also troubled the Reagan Administration.[139] More than one-fifth of America's exports went to Canada, and one-quarter of the United States' foreign investment had located there. Canada, a NATO ally, usually backed American foreign policy. But these strong ties were sorely tested by "Canadianization"—Canada's drive for economic independence. This process sought to reduce the foreign share of investment in firms operating in Canada and to favor Canadian-owned companies. Especially targeted was the energy industry, where American interests were large; Canada expected that its nationals would own half of the oil and gas industry by 1990. Although both sides uttered familiar words about their common heritage, tension between Ottawa and Washington reached an awkward high. Canadian Prime Minister Pierre Trudeau mused that "living next to you is in some ways like sleeping with an elephant. No matter how friendly and even-tempered is the beast, if I may call it that, one is affected by every twitch and grunt."[140]

In the early 1980s the United States faced a formidable agenda of world issues. Threats of trade wars, an expanding global population with hundreds of millions enduring grinding poverty, pollution of limited clean water supplies, fertilizer and food shortages, the disappearance of the world's forests, and drug trafficking in heroin and other debilitating narcotics—all accentuated human misery and challenged leaders. So did the number of refugees—perhaps 10 million of them—who fled from economic and political calamities in Indochina, Central America, the Caribbean, the Middle East, and the Horn of Africa.

Attempts to settle territorial disputes through force also continued to disturb world affairs and to entangle American foreign policy. In early 1982, for example, Argentina and Britain went to war over the Falkland or Malvinas Islands, whose ownership they had contested since the 1830s. After Argentine troops suddenly seized the British colony, Britain ordered its fleet to retake the islands. Secretary Haig at first tried to mediate between the two United States "friends." But when his diplomatic efforts failed, the United States backed Britain. Some Latin Americans protested Washington's support for colonialism, but others recognized that the Reagan Administration felt compelled to stand with its NATO ally against the Argentine invasion.

Yet another danger to world peace was nuclear proliferation. A growing number of countries bought nuclear reactors from Western companies. Although recipients of nuclear technology and fissionable materials avowed that they intended only to produce electricity, skeptics warned of possible diversions to nuclear weaponry. Israel, which probably possessed a nuclear bomb, set a disturbing precedent in mid-1981 when its planes bombed Iraq's reactor. Would Arab nations then feel it necessary to destroy Israel's nuclear installations? Would other nations attempt similar attacks against adversaries? Libya posed another danger: Qaddafi apparently offered one million dollars to anyone who would deliver an atomic bomb to him. Intelligence reports also revealed that Israel, South Africa, and Taiwan were cooperating to develop atomic arms. South Africa, it appeared, was supplying the other two with weapons-grade uranium.

The problem that seemed least manageable was terrorism—violence calculated to intimidate the politically and economically powerful. Whether the terrorists' goals were leftist, such as those of the Baader-Meinhof gang in West Germany, or rightist, as in the case of the death squads in El Salvador, their methods were similar: bombings, kidnappings, and murders. Some terrorists hijacked airplanes to dramatize their cause. The decade of the 1970s saw over 6,000 terrorist incidents, with more than 3,000 deaths. Terrorists especially threatened diplomats, business executives, military officers, and the property of multinational corporations. The latter paid millions of dollars in ransom to ensure the safe return of kidnapped executives. In 1980 Americans were the primary targets of terrorists; about two-fifths of all terrorist incidents were directed against Americans and their property, especially in Latin America. In 1981, five American military advisers were fired upon in Honduras; United States military installations were at-tacked in West Germany; American General James L. Dozier, a NATO officer, was kidnapped in Italy, but later rescued by police. Americans counted the 1979–1981 holding of hostages in Iran the worst terrorist case of all. The United States itself became an area for terrorism: in 1976 anti-Castro Cubans in alliance with Chile's secret police murdered former Chilean Ambassador Orlando Letelier in Washing-ton, D.C.; before the Shah's fall, SAVAK harassed Iranian students at American colleges; and in 1982 Armenian nationalists murdered a Turkish diplomat in the streets of Los Angeles.

As they entered the 1980s, Americans seemed determined on bold action to reassert United States supremacy in the international community. Great powers have seldom relinquished their domains and commanding positions without re-luctance—witness the Spanish, Dutch, Portuguese, French, and British imperial death throes. Americans, too, have clung to declining power. They have stoutly hurled challenges at their detractors; they have defended their global interests; they have continued to assume that they have answers to others' problems; they have reaffirmed their self-appointed mission to purify an imperfect world; and they have restated their belief in American exceptionalism. Quoting Tom Paine from the days of the American Revolution, Ronald Reagan declared in 1980, "We have it in our power to begin the world over again."[141]

Further Reading for the Period Since 1977

Studies of the Carter-Reagan years include some works mentioned in Chapter 15 and Richard J. Barnet, *Real Security* (1981); Betty Glad, *Jimmy Carter: In Search of the Great White House* (1980); Michael M. Harrison, *The Reluctant Ally: France and Atlantic Security* (1981); Stanley Hoffmann, "Requiem," *Foreign Policy* (1981) (on Carter); Robert C. Johansen, *The National Interest and the Human Interest* (1980); Michael T. Klare and Cynthia Arnson, *Supplying Repression: U.S. Support for Authoritarian Regimes Abroad* (1981); Roger Morris, *Haig: The General's Progress* (1982); A. Glenn Mower, *The United States, the United Nations, and Human Rights* (1979); James A. Nathan and James K. Oliver, *United States Foreign Policy and World Order* (1981); Nancy P. Newell and Richard S. Newell, *The Struggle for Afghanistan* (1981); Robert Olson, *U.S. Foreign Policy and the New International Economic Order* (1981); Kenneth Oye, Donald Rothchild, and Robert Lieber, eds., *Eagle Entangled* (1979); Samuel Payne, Jr., *The Soviet Union and SALT* (1980); Andrew J. Pierre, *The Global Politics of Arms Sales* (1982); Jonathan Schell, *The Fate of the Earth* (1982); Richard H. Solomon, ed., *The China Factor: Sino-American Relations & the Global Scene* (1981); Strobe Talbott, *Endgame: The Inside Story of SALT II* (1979); Sandy Vogelgesang, *American Dream, Global Nightmare: The Dilemma of U.S. Human Rights Policy* (1980); Thomas W. Wolfe, *The SALT Experience* (1979); and Stanley Wolpert, *Roots of Confrontation in South Asia: Afghanistan, Pakistan, India, and the Superpowers* (1982).

The Middle East, Egyptian-Israeli relations, and the Iranian crisis are discussed in Fred Halliday, *Iran: Dictatorship and Development* (1979); J. C. Hurewitz, *The Persian Gulf After Iran's Revolution* (Foreign Policy Association, *Headline Series,* 1979); Paul Jabber, *Not By War Alone: Security and Arms Control in the Middle East* (1981); Michael Ledeen and William Lewis, *Debacle: The American Failure in Iran* (1981); George Lenczowski, *The Middle East in World Affairs* (1980) and ed., *Iran Under the Pahlavis* (1978); Barry Rubin, *Paved with Good Intentions: The American Experience and Iran* (1980); Amin Saikal, *The Rise and Fall of the Shah* (1980); and John D. Stempel, *Inside the Iranian Revolution* (1981).

For Latin America, including Mexican and Central American issues, see Wayne Cornel-ius, *Building the Cactus Curtain* (1980) (on Mexican migration); Bernard Diederich, *Somoza and the Legacy of U.S. Involvement in Central America* (1981); Richard D. Erb and Stanley R. Ross, *United States Relations with Mexico* (1981); Paul R. Ehrlich, et al., *The Golden Door* (1981) (on Mexican migration); Richard R. Fagen, ed., *Capitalism and the State in U.S.-Latin American Relations* (1979); Lars Schoultz, *Human Rights and United States Policy Toward Latin America* (1981); George W. Grayson, *The Politics of Mexican Oil* (1981); Robert H. McBride, ed., *Mexico and the United States* (1981); Susan K. Purcell, ed., *Mexico-United States Relations* (1981); Peter H. Smith, *Mexico: The Quest for a U.S. Policy* (1980); and Thomas W. Walker, *Nicaragua: The Land of Sandino* (1982).

African questions are treated in Arthur Gaushon, *Crisis in Africa* (1981); Rene Lemarchand, ed., *American Policy in Southern Africa* (1978); Robert I. Rotberg, *Suffer the Future: Policy Choices in Southern Africa* (1980); Study Commission on U.S. Policy Toward Southern Africa, *South Africa: Time Running Out* (1981); Jennifer S. Whitaker, *Conflict in Southern Africa* (Foreign Policy Association, *Headline Series*, 1978) and ed., *Africa and the United States* (1978).

See also *Great Decisions* (annual) and *Headline Series*, both publications of the Foreign Policy Association; the *America and the World* series published annually by *Foreign Affairs* magazine; *American Foreign Relations: A Documentary Record* published annually by the Council on Foreign Relations; and publications on current topics by the Institute for Policy Studies, Washington, D.C. and the Institute for World Order, New York.

See also the General Bibliography and the following notes.

Notes to Chapter 16

1. Quoted in "Days of Captivity: The Hostages' Story," *New York Times*, February 4, 1981, p. A9.
2. Quoted in William B. Quandt, "The Middle East Crisis," *Foreign Affairs: America and the World 1979*, LVIII (1980), 544.
3. Moorhead C. Kennedy quoted in "Days of Captivity," p. A9.
4. Quoted in Doyle McManus, *Free at Last!* (New York: New American Library, 1981), p. 16.
5. Journalist William D. Hartley quoted in *U.S. News & World Report*, LXXXVIII (January 28, 1980), 32.
6. Ayatollah Khomeini quoted in "America in Captivity: Points of Decision in the Hostage Crisis," *New York Times Magazine*, May 17, 1981, p. 58.
7. Quoted in Barry Rubin, *Paved with Good Intentions: The American Experience and Iran* (New York: Oxford University Press, 1980), p. 260.
8. *Public Papers of the Presidents, Jimmy Carter, 1977* (Washington, D.C.: Government Printing Office, 1977–1978; 2 vols.), II, 2221.
9. Quoted in Robert Shaplen, "Eye of the Storm-I," *The New Yorker*, LVI (June 2, 1980), 50.
10. Quoted in Rubin, *Paved with Good Intentions*, p. 223.
11. Quoted in *ibid.*, p. 230.
12. *Ibid.*, p. 238.
13. William H. Sullivan, "Dateline Iran: The Road Not Taken," *Foreign Policy*, No. 40 (Fall, 1980), p. 186.
14. Unidentified former Pentagon official quoted in David Schoenbaum, "The United States & Iran's Revolution: Passing the Buck(s)," *ibid.*, No. 34 (Spring, 1979), p. 20.
15. Quoted in *New York Times*, November 18, 1979.
16. Moorhead C. Kennedy quoted in *ibid.*, February 4, 1981.

17. Sadegh Ghotbzadeh quoted in Eric Rouleau, "Khomeini's Iran," *Foreign Affairs*, LIX (Fall, 1980), 10.
18. Attorney General Benjamin Civiletti, "Oral Argument on Iran Presented to the World Court," December 10, 1979, Department of State Current Policy No. 118.
19. Quoted in "America in Captivity," p. 101.
20. Quoted in *ibid.*, p. 83.
21. Quoted in Rubin, *Paved with Good Intentions*, p. 257.
22. Zbigniew Brzezinski, "The Failed Mission," *New York Times Magazine*, April 18, 1982, p. 64.
23. *Ibid.*, p. 33.
24. Journalist Hedrick Smith in *New York Times*, February 1, 1981.
25. Quoted in McManus, *Free at Last*, p. 233.
26. Quoted in Steven V. Roberts, "The Year of the Hostage," *New York Times Magazine*, November 2, 1980, p. 63.
27. Quoted in Jules Witcover, *Marathon: The Pursuit of the Presidency, 1972–1976* (New York: Viking, 1977), p. 596.
28. Quoted in Betty Glad, *Jimmy Carter: In Search of the Great White House* (New York: W. W. Norton, 1980), p. 391.
29. Quoted in *ibid.*, p. 399.
30. Quoted in *Washington Post*, January 12, 1977.
31. Quoted in *New York Times*, May 2, 1979.
32. Leslie H. Gelb in *ibid.*, April 29, 1980.
33. Quoted in *Newsweek*, LXXXVIII (December 27, 1976), 19.
34. Quoted in James A. Nathan and James K. Oliver, *United States Foreign Policy and World Order* (Boston: Little, Brown, 1981; 2nd ed.), p. 413.
35. *Public Papers, Carter, 1977*, I, 956.
36. *Public Papers, Carter, 1978* (Washington, D.C.: Government Printing Office, 1979; 2 vols.), II, 2164.

37. Quoted in John L. Gaddis, *Strategies of Containment* (New York: Oxford University Press, 1982), p. 345.

38. Address by Assistant Secretary of International Organization Affairs Charles W. Maynes, "The World in 1980: America's Basic Options," April, 1980, Department of State Current Policy No. 149.

39. Phrase of Marina V. N. Whitman, "Leadership without Hegemony," *Foreign Policy*, No. 20 (Fall, 1975), p. 138.

40. Quoted in Richard Hudson, "Storm Over the Canal," *New York Times Magazine*, May 16, 1976, p. 24.

41. Quoted in *New York Times*, September 28, 1977.

42. Orrin Hatch quoted in Walter LaFeber, *The Panama Canal: The Crisis in Historical Perspective* (New York: Oxford University Press, 1979; expanded ed.), p. 254.

43. Quoted in *ibid.*, p. 190.

44. Quoted in *ibid.*, p. 213.

45. *Department of State Bulletin*, LXXVIII (May, 1978), 52.

46. *Ibid.*, p. 53. Emphasis added.

47. Quoted in LaFeber, *Panama Canal*, p. 246.

48. Cyrus Vance in U.S. Senate, Committee on Foreign Relations, *Panama Canal Treaties* (hearings; 4 parts), Part 1 (1978), p. 11.

49. White House official quoted in Richard R. Fagen, "Dateline Nicaragua: The End of the Affair," *Foreign Policy*, No. 36 (Fall, 1979), p. 189.

50. Quoted in *ibid.*, p. 188.

51. *Department of State Bulletin*, LXXIX (November, 1979), 15.

52. Quoted in Michael S. Teitelbaum, "Right versus Right: Immigration and the Refugee Policy in the United States," *Foreign Affairs*, LIX (Fall, 1980), 46.

53. James R. Schlesinger quoted in Richard R. Fagen and Henry R. Nau, "Mexican Gas: The Northern Connection," in Richard R. Fagen, ed., *Capitalism and the State in U.S.–Latin American Relations* (Stanford, Cal.: Stanford University Press, 1979), p. 407.

54. Robert H. McBride, "The United States and Mexico: The Shape of the Relationship," in Robert H. McBride, ed., *Mexico and the United States* (Englewood Cliffs, N.J.: Prentice-Hall, 1981), p. 16.

55. Quoted in Saul Landau, "The Bay of Pigs: The Fiasco that Refuses to be Forgotten," *Los Angeles Times*, April 19, 1981.

56. Quoted in *Hartford Courant*, November 20, 1980.

57. Moshe Dayan quoted in *The New Yorker*, LIV (October 2, 1978), 29–30.

58. *Department of State Bulletin*, LXXIX (May, 1979), 1.

59. Quoted in *Hartford Courant*, December 22, 1980.

60. Andrew Young in Elaine P. Adam and Richard P. Stebbins, eds., *American Foreign Relations, 1977: A Documentary Record* (New York: New York University Press for the Council on Foreign Relations, 1979), p. 301.

61. Quoted in Walter LaFeber, *America, Russia, and the Cold War, 1945–1980* (New York: Wiley, 1980; 4th ed.), p. 295.

62. G. Edward Clark, "Sub-Saharan Africa and the United States—Part 2," *Department of State Bulletin*, LXXX (April, 1980), 1.

63. Quoted in Adam and Stebbins, *American Foreign Relations, 1977*, p. 309.

64. General Obasanjo quoted in Donald Rothchild, "U.S. Policy Styles in Africa: From Minimal Engagement to Liberal Internationalism," in Kenneth A. Oye, Donald Rothchild, and Robert J. Lieber, eds., *Eagle Entangled: U.S. Foreign Policy in a Complex World* (New York: Longman, 1979), p. 327.

65. Quoted in Foreign Policy Association, *Great Decisions, '79* (New York: Foreign Policy Association, 1979), p. 60.

66. Quoted in *New York Times*, December 7, 1978.

67. Zbigniew Brzezinski, "From Cold War to Cold Peace," in G. K. Urban, ed., *Détente* (New York: Universe Books, 1976), pp. 264–265.

68. Hodding Carter III, "Life Inside the Carter State Department," *Playboy*, XXVIII (February, 1981), 215.

69. Quoted in Lawrence T. Caldwell and Alexander Dallin, "U.S. Policy Toward the Soviet Union: Intractable Issues," in Oye, Rothchild, and Lieber, eds. *Eagle Entangled*, p. 220.

70. Quoted in *New York Times*, May 29, 1978.

71. George Arbatov quoted in Joseph Kraft, "Letter from Moscow," *The New Yorker*, LIV (October 16, 1978), 122–124.

72. *Public Papers, Carter, 1978*, I, 1160.

73. *Pravda* quoted in George McGovern, "How to Avert a New 'Cold War,'" *The Atlantic Monthly* CCXLV (June, 1980), 52.

74. Paul Warnke, "SALT Two—The Home Stretch," September, 1978, Department of State Current Policy No. 31.

75. Leslie H. Gelb, "A Draw is a Win," *New York Times Book Review*, November 4, 1979.

76. Quoted in Strobe Talbott, *Endgame: The Inside Story of SALT II* (New York: Harper & Row, 1980), p. 5.

77. Secretary of Defense Harold Brown quoted in Christopher A. Kojm and the Editors of the Foreign Policy Association, *The ABC's of Defense* (New York: Foreign Policy Association, Headline Series 254, April, 1981), p. 29.

78. Leslie H. Gelb, "The Facts of SALT II," April, 1979, Department of State Current Policy No. 65.

79. Senate Majority Leader Robert Byrd quoted in Anthony Lewis, "The Cuban Molehill," *New York Times*, October 4, 1979.

80. *Public Papers, Carter, 1979* (Washington, D.C.: Government Printing Office, 1980; 2 vols.), II, 1805.

81. Quoted in Robert Shaplen, "Eye of the Storm-III," *The New Yorker*, LVI (June 16, 1980), 76.

82. Quoted in Robert W. Tucker, *The Purposes of American Power* (New York: Praeger, 1981), p. 26.

83. Quoted in John G. Stoessinger, *Why Nations Go to War* (New York: St. Martin's Press, 1982; 3rd ed.), p. 193.

84. George Urban, "A Long Conversation with Dr. Zbigniew Brzezinski: The Perils of Foreign Policy," *Encounter*, LVI (May, 1981), 18.

85. William Safire, "Bay of Tonkin Time," *New York Times*, January 10, 1980.

86. *Department of State Bulletin*, LXXX (February, 1980), Special B.

87. Quoted in *New York Times*, March 8, 1980.

88. Quoted in *ibid.*, January 22, 1980.

89. Quoted in Glad, *Carter*, pp. 461–462.

90. *New York Times*, February 1, 1980.

91. Quoted in Elizabeth Drew, *Portrait of an Election: The 1980 Presidential Campaign* (New York: Simon and Schuster, 1981), p. 156.

92. David D. Newsom, "America Engulfed," *Foreign Policy*, No. 43 (Summer, 1981), p. 17.

93. Quoted in Roberts, "Year of the Hostage," pp. 60.

94. William A. Williams letter in *The Nation*, CCXXXII (February 14, 1981), 162.

95. Quoted in Daniel P. Moynihan, "Reflections: The SALT Process," *The New Yorker*, LV (November 19, 1979), 177.

96. Richard E. Neustadt, *Presidential Power: The Politics of Leadership From FDR to Carter* (New York: Wiley, 1980), p. 235.

97. Michael T. Klare and Cynthia Arnson, *Supplying Repression: U.S. Support for Authoritarian Regimes Abroad* (Washington, D.C.: Institute for Policy Studies, 1981), p. 7.

98. Quoted in *New York Times*, June 6, 1980.

99. John P. Sears quoted in Hedrick Smith, "Reagan: What Kind of World Leader?" *New York Times Magazine*, November 16, 1980, p. 174.

100. Quoted in Congressional Quarterly, *President Reagan* (Washington, D.C.: Congressional Quarterly, 1981), p. 103.

101. Quoted in Smith, "Reagan," p. 172.

102. Quoted in Congressional Quarterly, *President Reagan*, p. 104.

103. Quoted in Cecil V. Crabb, Jr., "The Reagan Victory: Diplomatic and Strategic Implications," in Ellis Sandoz and Cecil V. Crabb, Jr., eds., *A Tide of Discontent: The 1980 Elections and Their Meaning* (Washington, D.C.: Congressional Quarterly Press, 1981), p. 158.

104. Reagan and Alexander M. Haig, Jr., quoted in *New York Times*, May 28, 1981; Sanford J. Ungar, "Alexander Haig: Pragmatist at State," *The Atlantic Monthly*, CCXLVII (March, 1981), 15; *Department of State Bulletin*, LXXXI (June, 1981), 5.

105. Quoted in *New York Times*, September 14, 1981.

106. Quoted in *ibid*, November 4, 1981.

107. Quoted in William G. Hyland, "U.S.-Soviet Relations: The Long Road Back," *Foreign Affairs: America and the World, 1981*, LX (1982), 525.

108. Quoted in *New York Times*, May 3, 1981.

109. *Ibid*.

110. George W. Ball, "That Old Cold War Obsession," *Washington Post*, July 6, 1981.

111. Quoted in Robert E. Osgood, "The Revitalization of Containment," *Foreign Affairs: America and the World, 1981*, LX (1982), 475.

112. Quoted in *New York Times*, August 16, 1981.

113. Quoted in *ibid*., December 10, 1981.

114. George F. Kennan, "Cease this Madness," *The Atlantic Monthly*, CCXLVII (January, 1981), 25–28.

115. George F. Kennan, "On Nuclear War," *New York Review of Books*, XXVIII (January 21, 1982), 10, 12.

116. Quoted in *New York Times*, April 26, 1981.

117. *Department of State Bulletin*, LXXXI (March, 1981), 7.

118. Quoted in *New York Times*, February 27, 1981.

119. Quoted in William M. LeoGrande, "A Splendid Little War: Drawing the Line in El Salvador," *International Security*, VI (Summer, 1981), 27, 45.

120. Quoted in *New York Times*, March 8, 1981.

121. *Department of State Bulletin*, LXXXI (April, 1981), 12.

122. Quoted in Sidney Blumenthal, "Marketing the President" *New York Times Magazine*, September 13, 1981, p. 112.

123. Quoted in *New York Times*, July 2, 1981.

124. Quoted in Richard E. Feinberg, "Central America: No Easy Answers," *Foreign Affairs*, LIX (Summer, 1981), 1141.

125. Quoted in Marvin E. Gettleman *et al.*, eds., *El Salvador: Central America in the New Cold War* (New York: Grove Press, 1981), p. 355.

126. Quoted in *New York Times*, March 19, 1981.

127. Assistant Secretary of State for Inter-American Affairs Thomas O. Enders quoted in *ibid.*, December 23, 1981.

128. Sergio Ramírez Mercado quoted in *ibid.*, January 14, 1982.

129. "Caribbean Basin Initiative," February 24, 1982, Department of State Current Policy No. 370.

130. Chester Crocker, "Regional Strategy for Southern Africa," August 29, 1981, Department of State Current Policy No. 308.

131. Quoted in *New York Times*, June 28, 1981.

132. Quoted in *ibid.*, October 2, 1981.

133. Quoted in *ibid*.

134. Quoted in *ibid.*, November 1, 1981.

135. Quoted in *ibid.*, October 29, 1981.

136. Quoted in *ibid.*, December 21, 1981.

137. Reagan quoted in *Washington Post*, December 24, 1981.

138. "A New Era of Growth," September 21, 1981, Department of State Current Policy No. 314.

139. United States Ambassador Paul H. Robinson, Jr., quoted in *New York Times*, September 21, 1981.

140. Quoted in Ivo D. Duchacek, *Nations and Men* (Hinsdale, Ill.: Dryden Press, 1975; 3rd ed.), p. 146.

141. Quoted in *New York Times*, July 18, 1980.

Appendix

Makers of American Foreign Policy

Presidents	Secretaries of State	Chairmen of the Senate Foreign Relations Committee
George Washington (1789–1797)	Thomas Jefferson (1790–1794)	
	Edmund Randolph (1794–1795)	
	Timothy Pickering (1795–1800)	
John Adams (1797–1801)	Timothy Pickering (1795–1800)	
	John Marshall (1800–1801)	
Thomas Jefferson (1801–1809)	James Madison (1801–1809)	
James Madison (1809–1817)	Robert Smith (1809–1811)	James Barbour (1816–1818)
	James Monroe (1811–1817)	
James Monroe (1817–1825)	John Quincy Adams (1817–1825)	James Barbour (1816–1818)
		Nathaniel Macon (1818–1819)
		James Brown (1819–1820)
		James Barbour (1820–1821)
		Rufus King (1821–1822)
		James Barbour (1822–1825)
John Quincy Adams (1825–1829)	Henry Clay (1825–1829)	Nathaniel Macon (1825–1826)
		Nathan Sanford (1826–1827)
		Nathaniel Macon (1827–1828)
		Littleton W. Tazewell (1828–1832)
Andrew Jackson (1829–1837)	Martin Van Buren (1829–1831)	Littleton W. Tazewell (1828–1832)
	Edward Livingston (1831–1833)	John Forsyth (1832–1833)
	Louis McLane (1833–1834)	William Wilkins (1833–1834)
	John Forsyth (1834–1841)	Henry Clay (1834–1836)
		James Buchanan (1836–1841)
Martin Van Buren (1837–1841)	John Forsyth (1834–1841)	James Buchanan (1836–1841)
William H. Harrison (1841)	Daniel Webster (1841–1843)	William C. Rives (1841–1842)
John Tyler (1841–1845)	Daniel Webster (1841–1843)	William C. Rives (1841–1842)
	Abel P. Upshur (1843–1844)	William S. Archer (1842–1845)
	John C. Calhoun (1844–1845)	
James K. Polk (1845–1849)	James Buchanan (1845–1849)	William Allen (1845–1846)
		Ambrose H. Sevier (1846–1848)
		Edward A. Hannegan (1848–1849)
		Thomas H. Benton (1849)
Zachary Taylor (1849–1850)	John M. Clayton (1849–1850)	William R. King (1849–1850)
Millard Fillmore (1850–1853)	Daniel Webster (1850–1852)	Henry S. Foote (1850–1851)
	Edward Everett (1852–1853)	James M. Mason (1851–1861)
Franklin Pierce (1853–1857)	William L. Marcy (1853–1857)	James M. Mason (1851–1861)

ii

Makers of American Foreign Policy

Presidents	Secretaries of State	Chairmen of the Senate Foreign Relations Committee
James Buchanan (1857–1861)	Lewis Cass (1857–1860)	James M. Mason (1851–1861)
	Jeremiah S. Black (1860–1861)	
Abraham Lincoln (1861–1865)	William H. Seward (1861–1869)	Charles Sumner (1861–1871)
Andrew Johnson (1865–1869)	William H. Seward (1861–1869)	Charles Sumner (1861–1871)
Ulysses S. Grant (1869–1877)	Elihu B. Washburne (1869)	Charles Sumner (1861–1871)
	Hamilton Fish (1869–1877)	Simon Cameron (1871–1877)
Rutherford B. Hayes (1877–1881)	William M. Evarts (1877–1881)	Hannibal Hamlin (1877–1879)
		William W. Eaton (1879–1881)
James A. Garfield (1881)	James G. Blaine (1881)	Ambrose E. Burnside (1881)
		George F. Edmunds (1881)
Chester A. Arthur (1881–1885)	Frederick T. Frelinghuysen (1881–1885)	William Windom (1881–1883)
		John F. Miller (1883–1887)
Grover Cleveland (1885–1889)	Thomas F. Bayard (1885–1889)	John F. Miller (1883–1887)
		John Sherman (1887–1893)
Benjamin Harrison (1889–1893)	James G. Blaine (1889–1892)	John Sherman (1887–1893)
	John W. Foster (1892–1893)	
Grover Cleveland (1893–1897)	Walter Q. Gresham (1893–1895)	John T. Morgan (1893–1895)
	Richard Olney (1895–1897)	John Sherman (1895–1897)
William McKinley (1897–1901)	John Sherman (1897–1898)	William P. Frye (1897)
	William R. Day (1898)	Cushman K. Davis (1897–1901)
	John Hay (1898–1905)	
Theodore Roosevelt (1901–1909)	John Hay (1898–1905)	William P. Frye (1901)
	Elihu Root (1905–1909)	Shelby M. Cullom (1901–1913)
	Robert Bacon (1909)	
William Howard Taft (1909–1913)	Philander C. Knox (1909–1913)	Shelby M. Cullom (1901–1913)
Woodrow Wilson (1913–1921)	William Jennings Bryan (1913–1915)	Augustus O. Bacon (1913–1915)
	Robert Lansing (1915–1920)	William J. Stone (1915–1919)
	Bainbridge Colby (1920–1921)	Henry Cabot Lodge (1919–1924)
Warren G. Harding (1921–1923)	Charles E. Hughes (1921–1925)	Henry Cabot Lodge (1919–1924)
Calvin Coolidge (1923–1929)	Charles E. Hughes (1921–1925)	Henry Cabot Lodge (1919–1924)
	Frank B. Kellogg (1925–1929)	William E. Borah (1925–1933)
Herbert C. Hoover (1929–1933)	Henry L. Stimson (1929–1933)	William E. Borah (1925–1933)
Franklin D. Roosevelt (1933–1945)	Cordell Hull (1933–1944)	Key Pittman (1933–1941)
	Edward R. Stettinius, Jr. (1944–1945)	Walter F. George (1941)
		Tom Connally (1941–1947)

Makers of American Foreign Policy

Presidents	Secretaries of State	Chairmen of the Senate Foreign Relations Committee	Secretaries of Defense	Assistants to the President for National Security Affairs
Harry S Truman (1945–1953)	Edward R. Stettinius, Jr. (1944–1945) James F. Byrnes (1945–1947) George C. Marshall (1947–1949) Dean G. Acheson (1949–1953)	Tom Connally (1941–1947) Arthur H. Vandenberg (1947–1949) Tom Connally (1949–1953)	James V. Forrestal (1947–1949) Louis A. Johnson (1949–1950) George C. Marshall (1950–1951) Robert A. Lovett (1951–1953)	
Dwight D. Eisenhower (1953–1961)	John F. Dulles (1953–1959) Christian A. Herter (1959–1961)	Alexander Wiley (1953–1955) Walter F. George (1955–1957) Theodore F. Green (1957–1959) J. W. Fulbright (1959–1975)	Charles E. Wilson (1953–1957) Neil H. McElroy (1957–1959) Thomas S. Gates, Jr. (1959–1961)	Robert Cutler (1953–1955; 1957–1958) Dillon Anderson (1955–1956) William H. Jackson (1956) Gordon Gray (1958–1961)
John F. Kennedy (1961–1963)	Dean Rusk (1961–1969)	J. W. Fulbright (1959–1975)	Robert S. McNamara (1961–1968)	McGeorge Bundy (1961–1966)
Lyndon B. Johnson (1963–1969)	Dean Rusk (1961–1969)	J. W. Fulbright (1959–1975)	Robert S. McNamara (1961–1968) Clark M. Clifford (1968–1969)	McGeorge Bundy (1961–1966) Walt W. Rostow (1966–1969)
Richard M. Nixon (1969–1974)	William P. Rogers (1969–1973) Henry A. Kissinger (1973–1977)	J. W. Fulbright (1959–1975)	Melvin R. Laird (1969–1973) Elliot L. Richardson (1973) James R. Schlesinger (1973–1976)	Henry A. Kissinger (1969–1976)
Gerald R. Ford (1974–1977)	Henry A. Kissinger (1973–1977)	J. W. Fulbright (1959–1975) John Sparkman (1975–1979)	James R. Schlesinger (1973–1976) Donald Rumsfeld (1976–1977)	Henry A. Kissinger (1969–1976) Brent Snowcroft (1976–1977)
Jimmy Carter (1977–1981)	Cyrus R. Vance (1977–1980) Edmund Muskie (1980–1981)	John Sparkman (1975–1979) Frank Church (1979–1981)	Harold Brown (1977–1981)	Zbigniew Brzezinski (1977–1981)
Ronald Reagan (1981–)	Alexander M. Haig, Jr. (1981–1982) George P. Shultz (1982–)	Charles Percy (1981–)	Casper Weinberger (1981–)	Richard Allen (1981) William P. Clark, Jr. (1981–)

General Bibliography

Reference Works

Annual Surveys: Amnesty International, *Annual Report* (1961–) (on human rights conditions); Council on Foreign Relations, *American Foreign Relations, 1971–: A Documentary Record* (1976–) and *The United States in World Affairs, 1931–1970* (1932–1972); International Institute for Strategic Studies, *The Military Balance* (1959/60–); London Institute of World Affairs, *The Yearbook of World Affairs* (1947–); Royal Institute of International Affairs, *Survey of International Affairs, 1920–1963* (1972–1977); Ruth L. Sivard, *World Military and Social Expenditures, 1974–* (1974–); *The Statesman's Year Book: Statistical and Historical Annual of the States of the World* (1864–); Stockholm International Peace Research Institute, *SIPRI Yearbook: International Armaments and Disarmament* (1969–); United Nations, *The United Nations Disarmament Yearbook* (1976–).

Atlases: Arthur Banks, *A Military History Atlas of the First World War* (1975) and *A World Atlas of Military History* (1973–1978); Geoffrey Barraclough, *The Times Atlas of World History* (1979); Andrew Boyd, *An Atlas of World Affairs* (1957–1970); Lester J. Cappon, ed., *Atlas of Early American History: The Revolutionary Era, 1760–1790* (1976); Council on Foreign Relations, *Political Handbook and Atlas of the World* (1963–); Edward W. Fox, *Atlas of American History* (1964); Martin Gilbert, *First World War Atlas* (1970); *International Geographic Encyclopedia and Atlas* (1976); Kenneth T. Jackson and James T. Adams, *Atlas of American History* (1978); *Oxford Regional Economic Atlas: The United States and Canada* (1975); William R. Shepherd, *Shepherd's Historical Atlas* (1976); U.S. Department of the Interior, *The National Atlas of the United States of America* (1970); U.S. Military Academy, *The West Point Atlas of American Wars, 1689–1953* (1959); Peter Young, ed., *Atlas of the Second World War* (1973).

Biographies: Samuel F. Bemis and Robert H. Ferrell, eds., *The American Secretaries of State and Their Diplomacy* (1927–); Paolo E. Coletta, Robert G. Albion, and K. Jack Bauer, eds., *American Secretaries of the Navy* (1980); *Concise Dictionary of American Biography* (1928–); *Current Biography* (1940–); *Dictionary of American Biography* (1946–); John A. Garraty, ed., *Encyclopedia of American Biography* (1974); Norman Graebner, ed., *An Uncertain Tradition: American Secretaries of State in the Twentieth Century* (1961); *International Who's Who* (1935–); Frank Merli and Theodore Wilson, eds., *Makers of American Diplomacy* (1974); *National Cyclopedia of American Biography* (1898–); *Political Profiles, Truman Years to . . .* (1978); Robert Sobel, ed., *Biographical Dictionary of the United States Executive Branch, 1774–1977* (1977); U.S. Congress, Senate, *Biographical Directory of the American Congress, 1774–1971* (1971); U.S. Department of State, *The Biographic Register, 1870–* (1870–) and *The Secretaries of State* (1978); Charles Van Doren, ed., *Webster's American Biographies* (1974); *Webster's American Military Biographies* (1978); *Who's Who in America* (1899–); *Who's Who in the World* (1970–).

Chronologies: *Facts on File: A Weekly World News Digest* (1940–); Bernard Grun, *The Timetables of History: A Horizontal Linkage of People and Events* (1975); *Keesing's Contemporary Archives: Weekly Diary of World Events* (1931–).

Encyclopedias and Dictionaries: James T. Adams, *Dictionary of American History* (1942–1961); Mark M. Boatner, III, *Encyclopedia of the American Revolution* (1974); Congressional Quarterly, *Congress and the Nation, 1945–1976* (1965–1977); Alexander DeConde, ed., *Encyclopedia of American Foreign Policy* (1978); *Dictionary of American History* (1976); R. Ernest Dupuy and Trevor N. Dupuy, *The Encyclopedia of Military History* (1977); John E. Findling, *Dictionary of American Diplomatic History* (1980); Robert Goralski, *World War II Almanac, 1931–1945* (1981); Stanley Hochman, *Yesterday and Today: A Dictionary of Recent American History* (1979); *International Encyclopedia of the Social Sciences* (1968–); Howard R. Lamar, ed., *The Reader's Encyclopedia of the American West* (1977); Richard B. Morris, *Encyclopedia of American History* (1982); Richard B. Morris and Graham W. Irwin, eds., *Harper Encyclopedia of the Modern World* (1970); Thomas Parrish, ed., *The Simon and Schuster Encyclopedia of World War II* (1978); Glenn Porter, *Encyclopedia of American Economic History* (1980); Stephen Thernstrom, ed., *Harvard Encyclopedia of American*

Ethnic Groups (1980); C. L. Thompson et al., eds., *The Current History Encyclopedia of Developing Nations* (1981); U.S. Department of the Navy, *Dictionary of American Naval Fighting Ships* (1959–); U.S. Department of State Library, *International Relations Dictionary* (1978); Jack E. Vincent, *A Handbook of International Relations* (1968).

Statistics: Arthur Banks and William Overstreet, eds., *Political Handbook of the World, 1975–* (1975–); George H. Gallup, *The Gallup Poll: Public Opinion, 1935–1977* (1972–1978); *International Year Book and Statesmen's Who's Who, 1953–* (1953–); U.S. Agency for Economic Development, *Economic Assistance Programs* (1970); U.S. Agency for International Development, *United States Overseas Loans and Grants and Assistance from International Organizations, July 1, 1945–Sept. 30, 1980* (1981); U.S. Bureau of the Census, *Historical Statistics of the United States: Colonial Times to 1970* (1975) and *Statistical Abstract of the United States* (1879–); U.S. Central Intelligence Agency, *The World Factbook* (1981–); U.S. Department of State, *Status of the World's Nations* (1963–).

Documents (Collections and Series)

Robert L. Branyan and Lawrence H. Larsen, eds., *The Eisenhower Administration, 1953–1961: A Documentary History* (1971); Council on Foreign Relations, *Documents on American Foreign Relations, 1938/1939–1970* (1939–1973); Francis Deak, ed., *American International Law Cases, 1783–1968* (1971–1978); Leon Friedman, comp., *The Law of War: A Documentary History* (1972); Norman A. Graebner, ed., *Ideas and Diplomacy* (1964); G. H. Hackworth, *Digest of International Law* (1940–1944); D. H. Miller, ed., *Treaties and Other International Acts* (1931–1948); Edgar B. Nixon and Donald B. Schewe, eds., *Franklin D. Roosevelt and Foreign Affairs* (1969–); *The Pentagon Papers* (various editions); *Public Papers of the Presidents* (1961–) (from Truman to the present); Royal Institute of International Affairs, *Documents on International Affairs, 1928–1963* (1929–1973); A. M. Schlesinger, ed., *The Dynamics of a World Power: A Documentary History of U.S. Foreign Policy, 1945–1973* (1973); *Treaties and Alliances of the World* (1974); U.S. Arms Control and Disarmament Agency, *Documents on Disarmament* (1960–); U.S. Congress, *American State Papers* (1832–1859); U.S. Department of State, *American Foreign Policy: Current Documents, 1956–1967* (1956–1969), *Foreign Relations of the United States, 1861–* (1862–), *Press Conferences of the Secretaries of State, 1922–1974* (no date), and *United States Treaties and Other International Agreements, 1950–* (1952–); *Vital Speeches of the Day* (1934–); Marjorie M. Whiteman, *Digest of International Law* (1963–1970); World Peace Foundation, *Documents on American Foreign Relations* (1939–1952).

Bibliographies

American History: Ray A. Billington, ed., *The American Frontier* (1965); Robert E. Burke and Richard Lowitt, eds., *The New Era and the New Deal, 1920–1940* (1981); E. D. Cronon and T. D. Rosenof, eds., *The Second World War and the Atomic Age, 1940–1973* (1975); Don E. Fehrenbacher, ed., *Manifest Destiny and the Coming of the Civil War* (1970); E. James Ferguson, ed., *Confederation, Constitution, and Early National Period, 1781–1815* (1975); Frank Freidel, ed., *Harvard Guide to American History* (1974); Rodman W. Paul, ed.,

The Frontier and the American West (1977); Robert V. Remini and Edwin A. Miles, comps., *The Era of Good Feelings and the Age of Jackson, 1816–1841* (1979); U.S. Senate, Senate Historical Office, *The United States Senate: A Historical Bibliography* (1977).

Diplomatic and International Relations:* Samuel Flagg Bemis and Grace Gardner Griffin, *Guide to the Diplomatic History of the United States, 1775–1921* (1935); John Braeman et al., eds., *Twentieth Century American Foreign Policy* (1971); Richard Dean Burns, ed., *A Guide to American Foreign Relations Since 1700* (1982); Council on Foreign Relations, *Foreign Affairs Bibliography: A Selected and Annotated List of Books on International Relations, 1919–* (1933–); Justus D. Doenecke, ed., *The Literature of Isolationism: A Guide to Non-Interventionist Scholarship, 1930–1972* (1972); Wilton B. Fowler, *American Diplomatic History Since 1890* (1975); Alexander DeConde, *American Diplomatic History in Transformation* (1976); Norman A. Graebner, ed., *American Diplomatic History Before 1900* (1978); Byron Dexter, ed., *The Foreign Affairs 50-Year Bibliography: New Evaluations of Significant Books on International Relations, 1920–1970* (1972); A. J. R. Groom and C. R. Mitchell, eds., *International Relations Theory: A Bibliography* (1978); Gerald K. Haines and J. Samuel Walker, eds., *American Foreign Relations* (1981); Charles S. Maier, "Making Time: The Historiography of International Relations," in Michael Kammen, ed., *The Past Before Us* (1980); Robert L. Pfaltzgraff, Jr., *The Study of International Relations: A Guide to Information Sources* (1977); Elmer Plischke, ed., *U.S. Foreign Relations: A Guide to Information Sources* (1980).

Military, Navy, and Wars: Richard Dean Burns and Milton Leitenberg, *War in Vietnam* (1980); Paolo E. Coletta, ed., *A Bibliography of American Naval History* (1981); Justus Doenecke, "Beyond Polemics: An Historiographical Re-Appraisal of American Entry into World War II," *History Teacher* (1979); A. G. S. Enser, *A Subject Bibliography of the Second World War: Books in English, 1939–1974* (1977); Arthur Gillingham and Barry Roseman, *Cuban Missile Crisis: A Selected Bibliography* (1976); John Greenwood, ed., *American Defense Policy Since 1945: A Preliminary Bibliography* (1973); Robin Higham, ed., *A Guide to the Sources of United States Military History* (1975); Robin Higham and Donald J. Mrozek, eds., *A Guide to the Sources of United States Military History: Supplement I* (1981); John E. Jessup, Jr. and Robert W. Coakley, eds., *A Guide to the Study and Use of Military History* (1979); John R. Lewis, *Uncertain Judgment: A Bibliography of War Crimes Trials* (1979); Myron J. Smith, Jr., *American Naval Bibliography* (1972–1974) and *World War II at Sea* (1976); Norman E. Tutorow, ed., *The Mexican-American War: An Annotated Bibliography* (1981).

Arms Control, Disarmament, and Peace: Richard Dean Burns, *Arms Control and Disarmament: A Bibliography* (1977); Richard Dean Burns and Susan Hoffman, comps., *The SALT Era: A Selected Bibliography* (1977); Bernice A. Carroll et al., *Peace and War: A Guide to Bibliographies* (1981); Blanche Wiesen Cook, *Bibliography on Peace Research in History* (1969); United Nations, *Disarmament: A Selected Bibliography* (1965–).

---

* For the most recent and comprehensive bibliography in diplomatic history, see the work edited by Richard Dean Burns, *A Guide to American Foreign Relations Since 1700.*

Relations with Countries and Regions: Thomas A. Bryson, *United States–Middle East Diplomatic Relations, 1784–1978: An Annotated Bibliography* (1979); Mohamed A. El-Khawas and Francis A. Kornegay, Jr., eds., *American–South African Relations: Bibliographic Essays* (1975); Charles C. Griffin, ed., *Latin America: A Guide to the Historical Literature* (1971); K. C. Liu, *Americans and Chinese* (1963); E. R. May and J. C. Thomson, Jr., *American–East Asian Relations: A Survey* (1972); James M. McCutcheon, comp., *China and America: A Bibliography of Interactions, Foreign and Domestic* (1973); Michael C. Meyer, ed., *Supplement to a Bibliography of United States–Latin American Relations Since 1810* (1979); David F. Trask, Michael C. Meyer, and Roger R. Trask, eds., *A Bibliography of United States–Latin American Relations Since 1810* (1968).

World Affairs Topics: Robert G. Albion, *Naval and Maritime History: An Annotated Bibliography* (1972); Nicole Ball, *World Hunger: A Guide to the Economic and Political Dimensions* (1981); Robert Blackey, ed., *Modern Revolutions and Revolutionists: A Bibliography* (1976); Paul W. Blackstock and Frank L. Schaf, Jr., eds., *Intelligence, Espionage, Counterespionage, and Covert Operations: A Guide to Information Sources* (1978); Ingrid Delupis, ed., *Bibliography of International Law* (1975); Michael Haas, comp., *International Organization: An Interdisciplinary Bibliography* (1971); Wesley L. Gould and Michael Barkun, eds., *Social Science Literature: A Bibliography for International Law* (1972); Augustus R. Norton and Martin H. Greenburg, *International Terrorism: An Annotated Bibliography and Research Guide* (1979); Myron J. Smith, Jr., *The Secret Wars: A Guide to Sources in English* (1980–1981).

Overviews of Relations with Countries and Regions

Afghanistan: Louis Dupree, *Afghanistan* (1973); Nancy P. Newell and Richard S. Newell, *The Struggle for Afghanistan* (1981).

Africa: Edward W. Chester, *Clash of Titans: Africa and U.S. Foreign Policy* (1974); Phillip Curtin, *African History* (1978); Charles F. Gallagher, *The United States and North Africa: Morocco, Algeria, and Tunisia* (1963).

Argentina: Harold F. Peterson, *Argentina and the United States, 1810–1960* (1964); Arthur P. Whitaker, *The United States and Argentina* (1954) and *The United States and the Southern Cone: Argentina, Chile, and Uruguay* (1976).

Australia: C. H. Grattan, *The United States in the Southwest Pacific* (1961); Werner Levi, *American-Australian Relations* (1947); Trevor R. Reese, *Australia, New Zealand, and the United States, A Survey of International Relations, 1941–1968* (1969).

Austria: William B. Bader, *Austria Between East and West, 1945–1955* (1966); Karl S. Stadler, *Austria* (1971).

Bangladesh: See Brown under listing for India.

Belgium: Frank E. Huggett, *Modern Belgium* (1969).

Bolivia: See Pike under listing for Peru.

Brazil: Roger W. Fontaine, *Brazil and the United States* (1974); Lawrence F. Hill, *Diplomatic Relations between the United States and Brazil* (1932); Frank D. McCann, *The Brazilian-American Alliance, 1937–1945* (1973).

Burma: John F. Cady, *The United States and Burma* (1976).

Canada: J. B. Brebner, *North Atlantic Triangle* (1966); Gerald M. Craig, *The United States and Canada* (1968); George P. DeT. Glazebrook, *A History of Canadian External Relations* (1950); H. L. Keenleyside and G. S. Brown, *Canada and the United States* (1952); S. F. Wise and Robert C. Brown, *Canada Views the United States* (1967).

Caribbean: Lester D. Langley, *Struggle for the American Mediterranean: United States–European Rivalry and the Caribbean, 1900–1970* (1976) and *The United States and the Caribbean, 1900–1970* (1980); Dexter Perkins, *The United States and the Caribbean* (1966); Whitney T. Perkins, *Constraint of Empire: The United States and Caribbean Intervention* (1981).

Central America: Ralph L. Woodward, *Central America: A Nation Divided* (1976).

Chile: Frederick B. Pike, *Chile and the United States, 1880–1962* (1963); Arthur P. Whitaker, *The United States and the Southern Cone: Argentina, Chile, and Uruguay* (1976).

China (and Taiwan): Jerome Ch'en, *China and the West* (1979); Warren I. Cohen, *America's Response to China* (1980); John K. Fairbank, *China Perceived: Images and Policies in Chinese-American Relations* (1974) and *The United States and China* (1972); John Gittings, *The World and China, 1922–1972* (1974); Michael Schaller, *The United States and China in the Twentieth Century* (1979).

Colombia: E. Taylor Parks, *Colombia and the United States, 1765–1934* (1935); Stephen J. Randall, *The Diplomacy of Modernization: Colombian-American Relations, 1920–1940* (1977).

Cuba: Philip S. Foner, *A History of Cuba in Its Relations with the United States* (1962–); Lester Langley, *The Cuban Policy of the United States* (1968); Ramon Ruiz, *Cuba: The Making of a Revolution* (1968); Robert F. Smith, *The United States and Cuba* (1960); Hugh Thomas, *Cuba* (1971). See also listing for Caribbean.

Dominican Republic: G. Pope Atkins and Larman C. Wilson, *The United States and the Trujillo Regime* (1972); Ian Bell, *The Dominican Republic* (1981); Rayford W. Logan, *Haiti and the Dominican Republic* (1968). See also listing for Caribbean.

East Asia: Akira Iriye, *Across the Pacific: An Inner History of American-East Asian Relations* (1967); Ernest R. May and James C. Thomson, Jr., eds., *American-East Asian Relations: A Survey* (1972); James C. Thomson, Jr., Peter W. Stanley, and John C. Perry, *Sentimental Imperialists: The American Experience in East Asia* (1981). See also listings for China and Japan.

Ecuador: See Pike under listing for Peru.

Egypt: See listing for Middle East.

El Salvador: Alastair White, *El Salvador* (1973). See also Woodward under listing for Central America.

Finland: Max Jakobson, *Finnish Neutrality* (1969). See also listing for Scandinavia.

France: Henry Blumenthal, *France and the United States: Their Diplomatic Relations, 1789–1914* (1970); Jean-Baptiste Duroselle, *France and the United States: From the Beginnings to the Present* (1978); Marvin R. Zahniser, *Uncertain Friendship* (1975).

Germany: Michael Balfour, *West Germany* (1968); Hans W. Gatzke, *Germany and the United States* (1980); Roger Morgan, *The United States and West Germany 1945–1973* (1974).

Great Britain: Harry C. Allen, *Great Britain and the United States* (1955); Kenneth Bourne, *Britain and the Balance of Power in North America, 1815–1908* (1967); Charles S. Campbell, *From Revolution to Rapprochement: The United States and Great Britain, 1783–1900* (1974); H. G. Nicholas, *The United States and Britain* (1975).

Greece: Theodore A. Couloumbis, *Greek Political Reaction to American and NATO Influences* (1966); Theodore A. Couloumbis and John O. Iatrides, eds., *Greek-American Relations* (1980); D. George Kousoulas, *Modern Greece* (1974).

Guatemala: Richard Immerman, *The CIA in Guatemala: The Foreign Policy of Intervention* (1982). See also listing for Central America.

Haiti: Robert Heinl and Nancy G. Heinl, *Written in Blood* (1978); Rayford W. Logan, *Diplomatic Relations of the United States with Haiti, 1776–1891* (1941) and *Haiti and the Dominican Republic* (1968); Robert I. Rotberg, *Haiti* (1971). See also listing for Caribbean.

India: William J. Barnds, *India, Pakistan, and the Great Powers* (1972); W. Norman Brown, *The United States and India, Pakistan, Bangladesh* (1972); Gary R. Hess, *American Encounters India, 1941–1947* (1971); Harold R. Issacs, *Images of Asia: American Views of China and India* (1958).

Indonesia: Robert J. McMahon, *Colonialism and Cold War* (1981); Franklin B. Weinstein, *Indonesian Foreign Policy and the Dilemma of Dependence* (1976). See also listing for Southeast Asia.

Iran: Peter Avery, *Modern Iran* (1965); Nikki R. Keddie, *Roots of Revolution* (1981); George Lenczowski, *Russia and the West in Iran, 1918–1948* (1949); Rouhollah K. Ramazani, *The Foreign Policy of Iran, 1500–1941* (1966) and *Iran's Foreign Policy, 1941–1973: A Study of Foreign Policy in Modernizing Nations* (1975); Barry Rubin, *Paved with Good Intentions* (1980). See also listing for Middle East.

Ireland: Donald H. Akenson, *The United States and Ireland* (1973); Thomas N. Brown, *Irish-American Nationalism, 1870–1890* (1966).

Israel: Bernard Reich, *Quest for Peace: United States–Israel Relations and the Arab-Israeli Conflict* (1977); Nadav Safran, *Israel: Embattled Ally* (1978) and *The United States and Israel* (1963).

Italy: Alexander DeConde, *Half-Bitter, Half-Sweet* (1971); H. Stuart Hughes, *The United States and Italy* (1979); Norman Kogan, *The Politics of Italian Foreign Policy* (1963).

Japan: Charles E. Neu, *The Troubled Encounter* (1975); William L. Neumann, *America Encounters Japan* (1963); Edwin E. Reischauer, *The United States and Japan* (1965). See also listing for East Asia.

Korea: Frank Baldwin, ed., *Without Parallel: The American-Korean Relationship Since 1945* (1974); U.S. Department of State, *Historical Summary of United States–Korean Relations, 1834–1962* (1962).

Latin America: Samuel Flagg Bemis, *The Latin American Policy of the United States* (1943); Cole Blasier, *The Hovering Giant* (1976); Gordon Connell-Smith, *The United States and Latin America* (1974); Harold E. Davis et al., *Latin American Diplomatic History: An Introduction* (1977) and *Latin American Foreign Policies* (1975); Federico G. Gil, *Latin American–United States Relations* (1971); J. Lloyd Mecham, *The United States and Inter-American Security, 1889–1960* (1961) and *A Survey of United States–Latin American Relations* (1965); Graham H. Stuart and James L. Tyner, *Latin America and the United States* (1975).

Lebanon: P. Edward Haley and Lewis W. Snider, eds., *Lebanon in Crisis* (1979).

Liberia: Charles M. Wilson, *Liberia* (1971). See also listing for Africa.

Malaysia: James W. Gould, *The United States and Malaysia* (1969).

Mexico: Howard F. Cline, *The United States and Mexico* (1963); Karl M. Schmitt, *Mexico and the United States, 1821–1973* (1974).

Middle East: Richard Allen, *Imperialism and Nationalism in the Fertile Crescent* (1974); John A. DeNovo, *American Interests and Policies in the Middle East, 1900–1939* (1963); James A. Field, *America and the Mediterranean World, 1776–1882* (1969); Philip Groisser, *The United States and the Middle East* (1981); George Lenczowski, *The Middle East in World Affairs* (1980); William R. Polk, *The United States and the Arab World* (1975); Benjamin Shwadran, *The Middle East, Oil, and the Great Powers* (1973); Robert W. Stookey, *America and the Arab States* (1975).

Morocco: Luella J. Hall, *The United States and Morocco, 1776–1956* (1971). See also listing for Africa.

New Zealand: See Reese under listing for Australia.

Nicaragua: Richard Millett, *Guardians of the Dynasty* (1977); Thomas W. Walker, *Nicaragua: The Land of Sandino* (1981). See also Woodward under listing for Central America.

Norway: Ronald G. Popperwell, *Norway* (1972); Sigmund Skard, *The United States in Norwegian History* (1976). See also listing for Scandinavia.

Panama: Walter LaFeber, *The Panama Canal* (1978).

Pakistan: See Barnds and Brown under listing for India.

Peru: James C. Carey, *Peru and the United States, 1900–1962* (1964); Frederick B. Pike, *The United States and the Andean Republics: Peru, Bolivia, and Ecuador* (1977).

Philippines: Teodoro A. Agoncillo, *Short History of the Philippines* (1969); Theodore Friend, *Between Two Empires* (1965); Garel A. Grunder and William E. Livezey, *The Philippines and the United States* (1951); Milton W. Meyer, *A Diplomatic History of the Philippine Republic* (1965); Peter W. Stanley, *A Nation in the Making: The Philippines and the United States, 1899–1921* (1974); George E. Taylor, *The Philippines and the United States* (1964).

Poland: Piotr Wandycz, *The United States and Poland* (1980).

Russia (and Soviet Union): John L. Gaddis, *Russia, the Soviet Union, and the United States* (1978); George F. Kennan, *Russia and the West under Lenin and Stalin* (1961); Nikolai Sivachev and Nikolai N. Yakovlev, *Russia and the United States* (1979); Adam B. Ulam, *Expansion and Coexistence* (1973).

Saudi Arabia: Irvine H. Anderson, *Aramco, the United States, and Saudi Arabia* (1981); Aaron D. Miller, *Search for Security: Saudi Arabian Oil and American Foreign Policy, 1939–1949* (1980). See also listing for Middle East.

Scandinavia: Franklin D. Scott, *Scandinavia* (1975) and *The United States and Scandinavia* (1950).

South Africa: Richard W. Hall, *Southern Africa* (1981); Thomas J. Noer, *Briton, Boer, and Yankee: The United States and South Africa, 1870–1914* (1978). See also listing for Africa.

Southeast Asia: Russell H. Fifield, *Americans in Southeast Asia* (1973); Robert Shaplen, *Time Out of Hand* (1970). See also listings for Vietnam and other countries.

Spain: James W. Cortada, *Two Nations over Time: Spain and the United States, 1776–1977* (1978) and ed., *Spain in the Twentieth-Century World* (1980).

Switzerland: Heinz Meier, *Friendship Under Stress: U.S.–Swiss Relations, 1900–1950* (1970) and *The United States and Switzerland in the Nineteenth Century* (1963).

Syria: Tabitha Petran, *Syria* (1972); Patrick Seale, *The Struggle for Syria: A Study in Post-War Arab Politics, 1945–1958* (1965). See also listing for Middle East.

Turkey: George S. Harris, *Troubled Alliance: Turkish-American Problems in Historical Perspective, 1945–1971* (1972); Harry N. Howard, *Turkey, the Straits and U.S. Policy* (1974); L. V. Thomas and R. N. Frye, *The United States and Turkey and Iran* (1951).

Uruguay: See Whitaker under listing for Argentina.

Venezuela: Sheldon B. Liss, *Diplomacy and Independence* (1978); Stephen G. Rabe, *The Road to OPEC: United States Relations with Venezuela, 1919–1976* (1982).

Vietnam: Frances Fitzgerald, *Fire in the Lake* (1972); George C. Herring, *America's Longest War* (1979); George M. Kahin and John W. Lewis, *The United States in Vietnam* (1969). See also listing for Southeast Asia.

Overviews of Subjects

Bureaucracy: Graham Allison, *Essence of Decision* (1971); I. M. Destler, *Presidents, Bureaucrats, and Foreign Policy* (1974); Morton H. Halperin, *Bureaucratic Politics and Foreign Policy* (1974); Morton H. Halperin and Arnold Kanter, eds., *Readings in American Foreign Policy: A Bureaucratic Perspective* (1973); Irving L. Janis, *Victims of Groupthink* (1972); Stephen D. Krasner, "Are Bureaucracies Important?" *Foreign Policy* (1972).

Codes: Ralph E. Weber, *United States Codes and Ciphers, 1775–1938* (1979).

Cold War: Stephen E. Ambrose, *Rise to Globalism* (1980); Zbigniew Brzezinski, "How the Cold War Was Played," *Foreign Affairs* (1972); Louis Halle, *The Cold War as History* (1967); Walter LaFeber, *America, Russia, and the Cold War* (1980); Thomas G. Paterson, *On Every Front* (1979); Adam B. Ulam, *The Rivals* (1971).

Congress: Holbert B. Carroll, *The House of Representatives and Foreign Affairs* (1966); Robert A. Dahl, *Congress and Foreign Policy* (1950); David N. Farnsworth, *The Senate Committee on Foreign Relations* (1961); James A. Robinson, *Congress and Foreign Policy-Making* (1967); Goran Rystad, ed., *Congress and American Foreign Policy* (1981); John Spanier and Joseph Nogee, eds., *Congress, the Presidency, and Foreign Policy* (1980); Francis O. Wilcox, *Congress, the Executive and Foreign Policy* (1971). See also listing for President.

Constitution: Louis Henkin, *Foreign Affairs and the Constitution* (1972).

Containment: Charles Gati, ed., *Caging the Bear* (1974); Thomas G. Paterson, ed., *Containment and the Cold War* (1973); John L. Gaddis, *Strategies of Containment* (1982).

Cultural Relations: Paul J. Braisted, ed., *Cultural Affairs and Foreign Relations* (1968); Philip H. Coombs, *The Fourth Dimension of Foreign Policy: Educational and Cultural Affairs* (1964); Morrell Heald and Lawrence S. Kaplan, *Culture and Diplomacy: The American Experience* (1977); Akira Iriye, "Culture and Power: International Relations as Intercultural Relations," *Diplomatic History* (1979); Frank A. Ninkovich, *The Diplomacy of Ideas: U.S. Foreign Policy and Cultural Relations, 1938–1950* (1981); Charles A. Thomson and Walter H. C. Laves, *Cultural Relations and U.S. Foreign Policy* (1963).

Department of State and Foreign Service: William Barnes and J. H. Morgan, *The Foreign Service of the United States* (1961); Homer L. Calkin, *Women in the Department of State* (1978); Alexander DeConde, *The American Secretary of State* (1962); Warren F. Ilchman, *Professional Diplomacy in the United States, 1779–1939*

(1961); Elmer Pliscke, *United States Diplomats and Their Mission: A Profile of American Diplomatic Emissaries Since 1778* (1979); Robert Schulzinger, *The Making of the Diplomatic Mind: The Training, Outlook and Style of United States Foreign Service Officers, 1908–1931* (1975); Richard H. Werking, *The Master Architects: Building the United States Foreign Service, 1890–1913* (1977).

Deterrence: Alexander L. George and Richard Smoke, *Deterrence in American Foreign Policy* (1974).

Economic Relations: Mira Wilkins, *The Emergence of Multinational Enterprise: American Business Abroad from the Colonial Era to 1914* (1970) and *The Maturing of Multinational Enterprise* (1975); Benjamin H. Williams, *Economic Foreign Policy of the United States* (1929); William Woodruff, *America's Impact on the World: A Study of the United States in the World Economy* (1975).

Foreign Aid: David Baldwin, *Economic Development and American Foreign Policy, 1943–1962* (1966); Library of Congress, *U.S. Foreign Aid* (1959); Robert A. Packenham, *Liberal America and the Third World* (1973).

Ideology: Richard J. Barnet, *Roots of War* (1972); Edward M. Burns, *The American Idea of Mission* (1957); Arthur A. Ekirch, Jr., *Ideas, Ideals, and American Diplomacy* (1966); Robert E. Osgood, *Ideals and Self-Interest in America's Foreign Relations* (1953); David M. Potter, *People of Plenty* (1954); E. L. Tuveson, *Redeemer Nation: The Idea of America's Millennial Role* (1968); William A. Williams, *The Contours of American History* (1966) and *The Tragedy of American Diplomacy* (1962).

Immigration and Ethnic Influence: Marion T. Bennett, *American Immigration Policies* (1963); Robert A. Divine, *American Immigration Policy, 1924–1952* (1957); Louis L. Gerson, *The Hyphenate in Recent American Politics and Diplomacy* (1964); Stephen Thernstrom, ed., *Harvard Encyclopedia of American Ethnic Groups* (1980).

Imperialism: Michael B. Brown, *The Economics of Imperialism* (1974); Benjamin J. Cohen, *The Question of Imperialism: The Political Economy of Dominance and Dependence* (1973); Gabriel Kolko, *The Roots of American Foreign Policy* (1969); Harry Magdoff, *Imperialism: From the Colonial Age to the Present* (1978); Dexter Perkins, *The American Approach to Foreign Policy* (1968); Richard W. Van Alstyne, *The Rising American Empire* (1960).

Interventionism: Richard J. Barnet, *Intervention and Revolution* (1972); Doris A. Graber, *Crisis Diplomacy* (1959); Robin Higham, ed., *Intervention or Abstention* (1975).

Isolationism: Selig Adler, *The Isolationist Impulse* (1957); Norman A. Graebner, *The New Isolationism* (1956); Manfred Jonas, *Isolationism in America, 1935–1941* (1966); Leroy N. Rieselbach, *The Roots of Isolationism* (1960).

Labor: Ronald Radosh, *American Labor and United States Foreign Policy* (1969).

Manifest Destiny: Norman A. Graebner, ed., *Manifest Destiny* (1968); Frederick Merk, *Manifest Destiny and Mission in American History* (1963); Albert K. Weinberg, *Manifest Destiny* (1935).

Military: C. Joseph Bernardo and Eugene H. Bacon, *American Military Policy: Its Development Since 1775* (1955); Walter Millis, *Arms and Men* (1958); Russell F. Weigley, *The American Way of War* (1973).

Monroe Doctrine: Dexter Perkins, *A History of the Monroe Doctrine* (1963).

Navy: William R. Braisted, *The United States Navy in the Pacific, 1897–1909* (1958) and *. . . 1909–1922* (1971); Kenneth J. Hagan, ed., *In Peace and War: Interpretations of American Naval History, 1775–1978* (1978); Robert E. Johnson, *The Far China Station: The U.S. Navy in Asiatic Waters, 1800–1890* (1979) and *Thence Round Cape Horn: The Story of United States Naval Forces on Pacific Station, 1818–1923* (1963); Allan R. Millett, *Sempter Fidelis: The History of the United States Marine Corps* (1980); Elmer B. Potter, ed., *Sea Power* (1981); Harold and Margaret Sprout, *The Rise of American Naval Power, 1776–1918* (1966); William N. Still, *American Sea Power in the Old World: The United States Navy in European and Near Eastern Waters, 1865–1917* (1980).

Neutral Rights: Philip C. Jessup, ed., *Neutrality* (1935–1936); Carlton Savage, *Policy of the United States Toward Maritime Commerce in War* (1934).

Nuclear Arms Race and Control: William F. Bader, *The U.S. and the Spread of Nuclear Weapons* (1968); Richard G. Hewlett and Francis Duncan, *Nuclear Navy, 1946–1962* (1974); Jerome H. Kahan, *Security in the Nuclear Age* (1975); Michael Mandelbaum, *The Nuclear Question: The United States & Nuclear Weapons, 1946–1976* (1979); George Quester, *Nuclear Diplomacy* (1970).

Pan-Americanism: J. Lloyd Mecham, *The United States and Inter-American Security, 1889–1960* (1961); Arthur P. Whitaker, *The Western Hemisphere Idea* (1954).

Peace Movements: Peter Brock, *Pacifism in the United States from the Colonial Era to the First World War* (1968) and *Twentieth-Century Pacifism* (1970); Charles Chatfield, *For Peace and Justice: Pacifism in America, 1914–1941* (1971); Merle Curti, *Peace or War* (1936); Charles DeBenedetti, *The Peace Reform in American History* (1980); David Patterson, *Toward a Warless World* (1976); Lawrence S. Wittner, *Rebels Against War: The American Peace Movement, 1941–1960* (1969).

Philanthropy: Merle Curti, *American Philanthropy Abroad* (1963); Robert L. Daniel, *American Philanthropy in the Near East, 1820–1960* (1970).

President: E. S. Corwin, *The President* (1957); Robert A. Divine, *Foreign Policy and U.S. Presidential Elections, 1940–1960* (1974); Erwin C. Hargrove, *The Power of the Modern Presidency* (1974); Manfred Landecker, *The President and Public Opinion* (1968); John E. Mueller,

War, Presidents, and Public Opinion (1973); Richard E. Neustadt, *Presidential Power* (1980); W. Taylor Revely, *War Powers of the President and Congress* (1981); Arthur M. Schlesinger, Jr., *The Imperial Presidency* (1973). See also listings for President and Bureaucracy.

Press: Bernard C. Cohen, *The Press and Foreign Policy* (1963); James Reston, *The Artillery of the Press: Its Influence on American Foreign Policy* (1967).

Propaganda: Leo Bogart, *Premises for Propaganda: The United States Information Agency's Operating Assumptions in the Cold War* (1976); Robert E. Elder, *The Information Machine* (1968); John W. Henderson, *The United States Information Agency* (1969); Ronald I. Rubin, *The Objectives of the U.S. Information Agency: Controversies and Analysis* (1968); Thomas C. Sorensen, *The Word War: The Story of American Propaganda* (1968).

Public Opinion: Gabriel Almond, *The American People and Foreign Policy* (1950); Bernard C. Cohen, *The Public's Impact on Foreign Policy* (1973); Ralph B. Levering, *The Public and American Foreign Policy, 1918–1978* (1978); James Rosenau, *Public Opinion and Foreign Policy* (1961) and ed., *Domestic Sources of Foreign Policy* (1967). See also listing for President.

Race: George W. Shepherd, Jr., ed., *Racial Influence on American Foreign Policy* (1971); Rubin F. Weston, *Racism in U.S. Imperialism: The Influence of Racial Assumptions on American Foreign Policy, 1893–1946* (1972).

Summit Conferences: Keith Eubank, *The Summit Conference, 1919–1960* (1966); Elmer Plischke, *Summit Diplomacy* (1958).

Tariff: Sidney Ratner, *The Tariff in American History* (1972); Frank W. Taussig, *Tariff History of the United States* (1931); Tom E. Terrill, *The Tariff, Politics, and American Foreign Policy, 1874–1901* (1974).

United Nations: Lincoln P. Bloomfield, *The United Nations and U.S. Foreign Policy* (1967); D. S. Cheever and H. F. Haviland, Jr., *Organizing for Peace: International Organization in World Affairs* (1954); Clark M. Eichelberger, *UN: The First Twenty-Five Years* (1970); John G. Stoessinger, *The United Nations and the Superpowers* (1973).

Index

discussion here, it hardly matters. Public libraries, however much we librarians as concerned citizens might wish it, don't drive the demographic changes in this nation. However, if we hope to be the public's library, rather than the librarians' library, or the Trustees' library, or the city government's employment program, or the newspaper editor's sentimental wishful thinking about "culture," we must respond to the demographic and social changes that do drive the actual *use* of public libraries. If we wish to be effective, if we wish to continue to be an educational and cost-sharing public information utility, dedicated to improving the quality of life of the middle-class citizen—our public—we must *Give 'Em What They Want.*

Give 'Em What They Want

Having said that, we know that, based on personal experience, we're in trouble with many readers. Let us explain just what we mean when we say *Give 'Em What They Want.* And, along the way, express our puzzlement with the apparent willingness, even enthusiasm, of many public librarians who seemingly insist on the policy *Give 'Em What They **Don't** Want.* Or, perhaps, *Give 'Em What They **Should** Want.* True, librarians in academic and school libraries have the guiding responsibility to support the teaching mission of their parent institutions, and are, then, fundamentally committed to instruction, to making sure that students learn what they are supposed to learn to qualify for graduation. Along the way, these librarians try to provide the resources to qualify the faculty to teach and to do research (which muddies the waters here a bit, because research often has little or nothing to do with teaching).

Librarians in public libraries have no teaching responsibilities (except, perhaps, for preschool children) and cannot and should not compete with the research function of universities and colleges. Public libraries make information and recreation (it is almost always difficult to separate those two functions) affordable to the general public through sharing. Like water distribution, or sewers, or highways. They provide educational services in the broadest sense to the broadest cross section of the public, but they are not an academic institution, and an attempt to make a public library into an academic institution, or to serve as yet another academic institution in the community, kills its effectiveness as the public's library—the only library the public has access to.

Libraries in Core Cities

And yet that is just exactly what many public libraries try to do, especially those in the old center cities, cities where the decline in their economic and social viability has coincided with the movement of the middle class to the *edge cities*, along with business and industry. The public libraries in these core cities, instead of redefining their roles to serve a new clientele, those of lower income and less education, those who have not been traditionally library users, have attempted to turn themselves into so-

called public *research libraries*—institutions, however, with no research clientele. As warehouses housing millions of unneeded,
unwanted, out-of-date collections of books, they have been designated by state libraries as *libraries of last recourse* or *state resource
centers,* at ruinous cost and extremely little use by those who
provide the tax funds to support them.

Why? The answer, at least to some, is extraordinarily simple:
they have become totally preoccupied with their preservation as
institutions, although they are not institutions without a mission, without a clientele, without a reason to exist except as public monuments to public sentimentality and public pride in an
illustrious past—a past which is irretrievable. There may be
some hope that they can redefine themselves through using
modern technology for communication and adoption of a very
different mission. This mission cannot maintain the traditional
role of public libraries or mirror that of an academic or research
library for the scholar. Few scholars exist outside of a university
setting or in high-technology industry, which maintains its own
type of information facility. The mission of the past no longer is
viable. The mission of the future is not yet clearly defined.

To be fair to library administrators and trustees, it takes extraordinary leadership, political consciousness, and time to redefine and modernize public library services to and insure
relevancy to modern lifestyles and demands, whether the library
is located in a core city or suburb or town. The public itself,
which seldom thinks about public library service to the extent
that they think about public education, for example, supports
with its money (granted, very little of it) and sentiment and nostalgia (lots and lots of it), the vision of public libraries of 1938,
whether small and cozy or large and imposing. An example:
when governmental revenues, both state and city, reached a dip-
ping point in 1991, the Enoch Pratt Free Library of Baltimore, a
shell of its former importance to the ordinary library user of the
thirties through the fifties, in a city which had, over the years,
lost 30 percent of its population and much of its middle class,
tried to reduce its branches from 28 to 20. The newspapers ran
repeated stories about the terrible educational and social consequences of the closings, nearly all of the columnists of the Baltimore *Sun* told nostalgic stories of the favorite literary heroes or
heroines of their childhoods (never, interestingly, of their current use, or nonuse, of the Pratt Library), and pickets appeared
outside the branches scheduled to be closed. The trustees and
management, in an attempt to maintain some vestige of quality
library service by downsizing the branch system to match the
drop in population and change in use, had tried closings before,
only to have minimal infusions of funds prevent the closings.
The decline in government revenues continued, however, and
this time it looked (in 1991) as if the reduction in facilities to meet
the reduction in demand might succeed. It didn't: two months

later, a few dollars were found that kept the hardly used branches open until the end of the fiscal year. The vision of 1938 lives on, kept barely alive by heroic measures in the face of economic and demographic doom.

Whether, of course, it might have been much better management to close the increasingly irrelevant central library was not an issue: public love for symbolism and nostalgia would have made this course unacceptable, no matter what the effect on maintenance of the community libraries. And community libraries, in these old cities, are where the remaining public use, such as it is, still exists.

Given time, we have some confidence that city libraries will be able to redefine themselves, or more logically, join with other libraries in the edge cities and communities for more equitable and efficient service to the public. But, in order to do so, the increasing tendency of many Americans to build gated communities, providing only those taxes to support these services that are important to them personally, whether libraries, schools, or sewers, will have to take an almost about turn. Certainly, there are public policy issues here, but they are not issues that librarians can solve or even exert effective influence upon, given our limited numbers, limited expertise and power, and our inability to deal, oftentimes, with the challenges and crises in our own profession.

Prisoners of the Past

We librarians are, perhaps more than other professionals in medicine, law, and formal education, prisoners of 1938, a past that looms more important than the present both in our own minds and that of the public. It's a past that really never existed in some areas of public library service, except in our minds, in our hopes, and in our good intentions.

Give 'Em What They Want means to most public librarians the provision of "trash," or at least an inexhaustible supply of current best-seller fiction, which, to the eyes of many librarians, nearly approaches "trash." Hence the description of the Baltimore County Public Library by *Library Journal* and others as "the bookstore library," filled with materials that appeal only to the "lowest" taste of the public. This, of course, contributes to the very high use of the library—circulation figures that almost "prove" that BCPL isn't really a viable public library at all, compared (I would assume) with other libraries with lower circulations, higher costs, and more responsible management.

We are always somewhat bemused by librarians who underestimate, or at least misjudge, the tastes of the public they serve. Our users are very often quite different from the kind of people who become librarians, and placing value judgments on other people's interests and reading is certainly a violation of the intellectual freedom which librarians profess to hold so dear. As self-appointed arbiters of taste, librarians have continued to strive to

A 1992 neon-lighted
community library

"elevate" the reading of library users, either by techniques such
as booktalking *their* approved books, or, much more seriously,
by structuring and limiting materials collections to their tastes.

Interestingly, this tendency seems to be less prevalent in
smaller libraries, where the administrator, or the book selector,
is also the librarian who has direct, day-to-day contact with the
library user. Only in the larger libraries do the policymakers remove themselves far enough from the public to comfortably
spend money on, say, *The Lancet,* a British medical journal with
predictably few, very few, readers in even the largest public library. Money spent on *The Lancet* is money *not* spent on books
for preschool children, who are served by no other library, or
money *not* spent on the current *Mobil Guide,* or Danielle Steel, to
put it bluntly.

A Fervent Hope   Certainly value judgments have to be made, even if a library
strives to *Give 'Em What They Want.* The best-sellers cannot be
bought in quantities to satisfy the entire demand except in those
libraries where money is never an issue. (Yes, Virginia, there *are*
some libraries out there like that, there really are!) But it's amazing
to see that libraries insist on buying materials for which there is *no*
demand from the people they are supposed to serve. Apparently,
a fervent hope on the part of a starry-eyed book selector with
impeccable "taste," a moral agenda, or a sociopolitical bent, is
enough to justify the purchase of material of a type with absolutely
no track record of use. It happens all the time, all over the country,
in all sizes of public libraries. It wastes millions of dollars, deprives

millions of children and adults of library materials they need, want, and have paid taxes for. This waste is often ignored by the leadership in the profession, by library education, and by citizens who suffer the result of this mismanagement.

Look in any public library that follows this policy—a policy that can only be described as *Give 'Em What They **Don't** Want*. Since actual use is not a criterion for retention of books, weeding hardly exists, and there will be an enormous number of items, whether books, periodicals, or reference works, that show no record of use at all, or very little use in any reasonable length of time.

Let's name this policy the *Fervent Hope* policy—representing the fervent hope of some librarians that the very presence of the material will cause its use, change a life, right a wrong, and thereby justify the expense. Fervent hope is seldom checked up on, seldom evaluated, and, most irresponsibly, the material is never discarded or deselected. That would be admission of failure, and none of us likes to do that. The result is building additions, more shelving, more heat and light, and eventually less and less money for giving the public what they want, need, and will *use*, which of course is the key.

We just can't rid ourselves of the custodial ethic. There may, in fact, be some justification for this in the academic library, but never, never in the public library. And we get away with it because we're more comfortable with materials-centered philosophies than with service-centered philosophies. Denial of this fact abounds throughout the profession, despite adequate evidence to the contrary, and of course the practice is gleefully fed by publishers who are only too glad to get rid of their "dogs" to public library selectors.

The Library's Public in 1992

Assessing and predicting demand is not easy. Maybe that's why more of us don't do it very well. The techniques and methods of client-centered materials selection and management, based on actual use, are not taught in library schools and are not discussed widely in the public library profession.

While the lack of client-centered service is most prevalent, most unnoticed, and most uncriticized by the profession itself and in the professional literature. There are a number of other areas of current public library management that contribute to limiting our impact and influence as an educational and informational resource. Some of them are mentioned here, but this book tries to cover some details of one library's dogged, decades-long, experiment-laden, and continuing attempt to *Give 'Em What They Want*.

Buildings

Most library buildings are community libraries, whether they be a single library in a town or a branch of a library system in a

A 20,000-square-foot community library—just the size for real people.

county or a city. This situation is just as it should be, to serve the people well—and just what has long been, the point-of-service policy of retailing (and public libraries are retailers of materials and information). Retail chains like Wal-Mart, or Macy's, or Walden's or Safeway, all of which distribute needed goods and services, have community-based facilities. No longer do they have large central stores in core cities. Regional superstores, community stores, and outlets are where they make their sales, make their profits. This is a rational, logical concept, transferable easily to any retail organization like libraries, where continued viability and existence depend on meeting current needs.

But we continue to build massive, expensive central libraries in the downtown of core cities, like the recently erected, highly expensive, glowering Bastille-like Harold Washington Library in Chicago. Just before the opening of this library—which received glowing accolades from the library press—it was announced by the City of Chicago that over 100 staff members would be cut from the library's budget. Doubtless Harold Washington, the former mayor, needed a monument. Doubtless the Chicago Public Library needed new libraries, community-based libraries, to serve its population. But any modern retailer, any thinking librarian interested in the client-centered service, would and can recognize this building as a financial service and administrative disaster.

The folly is being duplicated in large cities across the country—Phoenix, San Francisco, Memphis, and other cities. Few leaders in the library profession have spoken out, on the record, about this massive waste of library resources, resources which, if spent on materials and services that the people we serve want and need, might increase the actual use and relevancy of public libraries in these cities.

Sadly, not only in large cities: Tempe, Arizona, a wealthy suburban community of the middle class with an enormous university library within its limits, recently erected a public library that replicates a miniuniversity library in almost every detail, from plan to furniture to book collection. Where is a public library user to go? Evidently, the public library field supports not a few closet academic library directors.

Money

The public library system in Phoenix, Arizona, is supported by $13 per capita. Dallas gets $15 per capita. Baltimore County gets $33. Schaumburg, Illinois gets $34, and Arlington Heights $58. Boston spends $47. Middle Country, New York $85. They are all good libraries. They all are client-centered. They are all underfunded. They are all guided by responsible appropriating authorities, concerned trustees or advisory boards, and highly competent directors.

How's that again? Have I missed something? Doesn't the amount of money a library spends have something to do with how good it is? Are all libraries always better with more money? How much better than good since all libraries are good?

No matter what the per capita support, no matter what the policies, practices, and procedures used to administer the public library, all annual budget *decreases* are seen by the American Library Association, the professional periodicals, and fellow librarians as near disasters. Most budget *increases* are seen as insufficient to maintain services. Not surprising: Drucker, the writer on management, including management of nonprofit institutions, notes that budget increases and decreases are the most prevalent indicator of success or failure to governmental administrators.

This doesn't auger too well for the future: almost all economic predictions say that governmental revenues in the next 10 to 20 years will have very slow growth, while at the same time the public will resist any attempts to limit popular social programs such as Social Security, Medicare and Medicaid, and public education. It's doubtful if libraries fall into the category of essential public services to the extent that public safety and public health do, and it's likely that *they* will get the real budget increases, not libraries. We'll have to find ways to make the available money go further.

There is clearly room for massive improvement in management of financial resources by many public libraries, rather than concentration of effort in the kind of public relations campaigns indulged in by the American Library Association to prove that libraries are well-managed, effective, important bargains for library users. While there may be examples of good management, there are too many other examples of waste, mismanagement, or worse, lack of any attempt at all to manage any aspect of public library service, out there in libraryland.

Public libraries will never die completely. The same sentimentality and nostalgia that keeps libraries underused and undermanaged, along with the real value and use, albeit limited, which they supply, will keep some semblance of library service going in most American communities for some time—until a better, or cheaper, or more useful substitute comes along. And that, given today's technology, looms ever more likely.

Technology

Technology created libraries, and productivity made possible by technology created the middle class, which created public libraries. How so? Well, libraries weren't much when all books were incunabula. Printing on paper, which appeared about 1500, increased the supply of books enough so that libraries, collections of books, could be gathered. But still, you had to have readers, produced by education and leisure time. The increase in productivity per capita over 500 years that provided the resources for mass education and leisure time also provided the willingness to spend tax resources for the public good. Hence, the public library was given a shove by Andrew Carnegie, a product of steel-making productivity.

Technology has infiltrated public library operations, first by typewriters, then by copiers, then by computers, which enabled the adoption of circulation control, inventory control, financial control. Some technology that promised revolution in libraries never caught on very effectively—microfilm, for example. Nobody much likes microfilm. But revolutions, whether political or technological, are never avoided completely—they are only delayed. And often, like economic recessions or depressions, they are inaccurately predicted.

Indications in 1991 are that a revolution in reading materials is close. How close? We would say 10 to 20 years, with a 50 percent chance in 10 years, closing to a 100 percent chance in 20 years. But don't hold us to either the low or the high estimate.

The electronic book is nearly here. In November 1991, the Sony Data Discman, previously sold only in Japan, was made available in the United States. The September 20, 1991 issue of *Publishers Weekly* has a short article on a prototype of a commercially viable electronic book being shown to publishers.

Sony's electronic book: a prototype for the future?

The Baltimore County Public Library's Sony Data Discman unit, together with the seven "books," or 2-inch CD caddies, is a portent of things to come, a sort of 1948, five-inch black-and-white television set. One of the discs, a book, contains the entire Bible, the complete works of Shakespeare and Conan Doyle, the Book of Mormon, and dozens of other documents, from the Constitution and Federalist Papers to the entire text of *War and Peace*. The $39.95 volume is called, interestingly, *The Library of the Future*.

And it has word search.

At $500, the Data Discman will hardly substitute for the printed word. Yet. But, it's a window on the future. The future of libraries.

Change is coming. Change is here. But then, it always has been, in one form of human endeavor or another. For public libraries, change in the format from print on paper to print on a screen will certainly eliminate our custodial role, our storage role, probably even our "place," library buildings. But it will bring other opportunities, other responsibilities. Who will navigate the huge amount of information thus made available? Who will assure access to free information, even if this information is limited in amount (as it is now)?

The public library will change, and soon. Our responsibility as librarians—or as information consultants, (perhaps a more appropriate term) will depend on our clarity of mission, our best traditions of public service, and our ability to adapt to change. The next 10 to 20 years will tell whether we are up to the challenge, and the following chapters will give some pointers on the BCPL's Blue Ribbon Committee's ideas of good management of the public's library. This management can assure that provision of the public's access to education, education in its broadest sense, encompassing all the resources available presently in the printed word, and in the future in electronic form, can be preserved.

2 GIVE 'EM THE MATERIALS THEY WANT

What do you mean you don't have another copy and I can't renew this one because it's a new book? I'm a taxpayer.

I don't care if it's a best seller and I can't reserve it—my neighbor got a copy here yesterday—what's the matter with you all?

But my kid needs to get his report written tonight, and I can't Xerox the whole book—don't you have a copy I can take home?

Miss, this book covers the 1983 Toyota Corolla but I need one for the 1982 model. I just took apart my engine and it's lying in the middle of my driveway.

I just went through all those cassettes you have over there in that room but all I see is how to stop smoking and how to thin your thighs. I'm driving down to Atlanta for a big sales conference and I need something on selling and customer service. Don't any of your branches carry some serious things to listen to?

Meeting Patron Demand

How would you define DEMAND? Webster's ninth says AN URGENT NEED. At Baltimore County Public Library we can define demand with one word: PATRON. The reading and listening public, with their urgent needs set the demand.

As you are reading this chapter, library patrons all over the United States are leaning over information desks in their local libraries, with frustrated looks on their faces, as they are told that the book they just heard about on Donahue, or the local radio station, or the book they saw in the bookstore in the local town center, is not in or not even owned. Students who thought they could waltz right into their local library and magically find five periodical sources they needed to cite for a paper on the destruction of the ozone layer are stricken to learn they will have to spend some time looking through the periodical indexes to get the needed information. They may have to wait for the sources to be faxed to them, sent from another branch, or even another library system. Here's the woman who comes in every week like

A future taxpayer
gets what he wants

clockwork and takes about 20 to 25 paperback romances and today she complains she can't locate about six in the latest bodice ripper series. What ever happened to the regular folk who wanted *Gone with the Wind* or even *The Odyssey*? What happened to the good ole days when you decided what patrons should read? When Sally Jesse Raphael and Geraldo didn't probe people's minds. Then the patrons didn't come and tell "*you*" about a new book due out in six months that they had read about in *Publishers Weekly* (*PW*).

How can we possibly meet these demands put upon us?

Centralized Selection

Before technical services can catalog and process a book quickly or before a librarian can walk a student to the newest CD-ROM index, the materials need to be selected expediently, in the right quantities, and for the right reasons. In 1975 Baltimore County moved into centralized selection of materials.

At that time we were purchasing most new and replacement books in hardback. We had recordings and eight mm film collections. All branches had periodicals in paper and microfilm format and large reference collections to support the information needs. We had monthly book selection where all the librarians drove from their branches to look at the titles displayed for selection. All librarians read all the reviews, fondling the books as they made decisions which they then passed on to the department head, who made final selections for each branch. A selection process of at least six weeks took place before the books were actually ordered. Some of the hot adult fiction and nonfiction titles were ordered prepublication, but everything else waited for this expensive process to be completed each month. *So we centralized.*

The newly formed Materials Selection Department, with two librarians, both with MLS, and 3 clerks, was set up to handle all new purchasing and to supervise replacement buying. The conversion to centralized selection was done over an 18-month period for adult and a two-year period for children's selection. *The transition was not easy.*

Initially there was a great uproar. It was difficult for librarians to relinquish one of the jobs they felt made them a librarian—book selection. It was also one of the jobs they enjoyed the most. Proponents of the new system had to convince the opponents to "wait and see; give it a chance." Opponents didn't trust the selectors. "Why are they doing the selection instead of me?" The informal lines of communication that existed for department heads and branch managers, who visited the administrative offices monthly, were now dissolved. Peer support was less accessible when you didn't see colleagues once a month. At most branches, book selection had been part of staff development. Staff would discuss ways to use a title. Comparing new titles with existing titles in the collection helped with weeding and collection maintenance.

When moving toward buying centrally for a multiple branch system, we found a lot of communication and trust-building were necessary. In the early days of centralized selection, many buying errors were made. Some branch staff assured us that their branch was unique and questioned how we could possibly know what they needed for their collections. Getting them to cooperate took time. Regular branch visits to discuss problems were necessary. But the opposition did not keep the administration from proceeding with this reorganization. *The bottom line was it cost too much to do it the old way.*

When initial planning began to launch centralized selection, committees spent hours working on formulas for buying books. Branches were asked to respond to questionnaires about how many copies they would buy of a specific author or on a specific subject. Adult fiction formulas covered authors from Richard Adams to Phyllis Whitney, for example, with a grid showing each branch's symbol and the number of copies they needed of any new title by that established author. It was a similar setup for adult nonfiction, which was done by subject. All the children's buying areas, easies (picture books), children's fiction and nonfiction, and young adult (YA), were selected the same way. *It was cumbersome!* Flipping through pages and pages of formulas (buying grids) by author or subject to order one book proved to be inefficient, but it helped to make central selection tolerable to branch staff. They had major input into the formulas and were reasonably assured that most new titles would fit into a formula.

After six months of centralized selection of adult materials being handled solely by the Head of Materials Selection, it was apparent that branches didn't have a formal method of commenting on selection errors. A Central Purchase Advisory committee began meeting every Tuesday to assist in the selection. Four branch staff members, representing various size branches and librarians with multibranch experience, were given a year's appointment to this committee. We began with an adult central purchase advisory committee, and once children's centralized selection was underway, a children's advisory committee was appointed.

Around 1978 we merged the two advisory committees, kept it at four staff members and alternated the selection to cover adult materials one week and children's materials the next. This change coincided with system conversion to generalism. (Generalism meant for us that there we're no longer children's, young adult, or adult specialists. Every librarian was trained to serve all age groups. See chapter 4 "Where They Want It" for a fuller explanation of generalism.)

Centralized selection worked because we couldn't afford to do it the old way; and it was too labor intensive. Massaging books rather than buying books could be eliminated and save the system a lot of money. And as a fairly homogeneous county, we could easily identify the needs by the requests we received.

Fifteen years later we have a larger Materials Selection Department with four full-time selectors and one part-time (two of the four full-time selectors have an MLS); three full-time and three part-time clerks; and three volunteers. Although the staff is larger, we have a greater workload and have been forced to streamline many procedures.

Fifteen years later we still have a print advisory committee made up of four branch staff which meets once a month, but they see only about 15 percent of the print materials ordered, acting more in a real advisory capacity than a selection one. We also have a nonprint advisory committee made up of four branch staff and one selector. This committee meets once a month and makes buying decisions on approximately 60 percent of the new nonprint purchased, excluding videos. This means that in the realm of print selection 85 percent of the buying of new titles is done by the four full-time and one part-time selectors, and 40 percent of nonprint (cassettes and CDs) and 100 percent of video selection is done by one full-time and one part-time selector.

The assistant coordinator of the department does all new adult fiction selection including science fiction, mysteries, and westerns. She is also responsible for buying the new children's and YA fiction and deciding which titles need to be reviewed by a staff member. Over the last fifteen years we have moved from having all children's and YA books reviewed by staff, originally by only children's librarians, to the present time where about only 10 percent of all the children's and YA books we buy are reviewed by a staff member.

The coordinator of the department selects all the new trade nonfiction and has selection responsibilities in such major areas of collection building as art, black interest, pop psychology, self-help, and religion. The remaining adult nonfiction subject areas are shared by one full-time and one part-time selector. The one full-time assistant who does subject selection, such as test books, tax books, college books, antiques and collectibles, travel etc., is also responsible for all the reference and standing orders buying. She also handles children's nonfiction and periodicals. The part-time selector who does nonfiction handles the remaining adult subject areas and also buys talking books.

The fourth full-time selector buys the children's picture books, adult paperbooks, (most of which are on a subscription basis), adult large type, (also mostly subscription) all of the non-print, including videos but excluding talking books.

At the beginning of each new fiscal year, we may do some job shifting such as reassigning who buys large type or YA but generally the selectors have had these same assignments for the last few years.

Formulas

In fifteen years we have streamlined the formulas to grids which have been reduced to one or a few pages per buying area. For example, adult new fiction formulas are featured and only include 21 formulas (see figure 2-1). There are three pages of formulas for new adult nonfiction and the formulas for the other buying areas fall somewhere in this range. The method used in producing the formulas will be discussed later in this chapter.

Formulas are based on circulation and budget numbers factoring in demographic or specific branch needs. They are used as guidelines in selection. We can add or subtract copies from any formula for any branch based on input from them, knowledge of how items circulate in their agency, or simply if we've overspent their budget.

When a title has been underbought, the branch staff has an opportunity to respond to the purchase by asking for a BEEFUP. For example if a nonfiction title is originally purchased for only four agencies and then it appears on the best-sellers list and nonowning branches have received requests, Materials Selection will send the title out on the CLSI (automated circulation system), asking branches how many more copies they think they need to meet the requests. This is followed up by a phone call to our jobber and verbal confirmation of the order, and the beefup is on the shelves within 10 days or less.

What about overbuying of a title? We don't do this frequently but when it happens branches do all they can to move the copies,

FIGURE 2-1

ADULT FICTION BUYING GRIDS

FORMULA	AR	CA	CY	DU	EDG	ES	HE	JAC	LN	LR	MR	NP	OW	PA	PH	PI	RA	RN	ROS	TO	TS	WEL	WM	WO	INS	CC
SPECIAL	()	x	x							()					()	()	x	x	x	x			()	()		2
SCI FIC	x	x/2	x/2	x/4	()	x/2	()	x	x/4	x		x	()	x	()	x	x/2	x	x	x/2		x	()	()		4
MYS 1	x	5	6	x		2	x	x	x	3	x	2	x	2	x	2	4	2	2	5		x	2	2	x	5
MYS 2	2	6	8	x	x	2	x	x	x	4	x	2	x	3	x	3	5	2	3	7	()	2	2	2	x	6
25 A		2	3							x		()		()		x	x	()	()	2						4
25 B		3	3							2		x		x		2	3	x	x	3			x	x		4
45 A	()	3	5			()				2		()		()	()	x	3	()	()	4		()	(x)	()		6
45 B	x	4	5			x				2		x		x	()	3	4	x	x	4		x	x	x		6
55	2	5	7			2	x	x	x/4	3		2	x/4	2	2	4	5	2	2	6		2	2	2	2	6
70 A	2	8	11			2	()	()		4		3	()	4	2	6	8	3	4	9		2	3	3		10
70 B	2	9	11	()		2	2	2	()	5	()	3	x	5	2	6	9	4	5	9		3	3	3	x	10
125	4	13	15	x	x	4	3	3	x	8	x	6	2	7	3	9	13	6	7	13		5	6	5	2	12
175	7	19	23	x	x	5	4	4	x	12	x	8	2	10	4	13	19	9	10	19		7	8	8	2	15
250	8	23	30	2	2	7	6	6	2	15	2	10	5	13	6	22	25	11	12	25	x	9	10	10	2	20
350	11	23	43	2	2	10	7	7	2	22	2	16	7	19	8	26	34	18	19	36	x	18	13	14	2	23
400	13	37	47	2	2	12	8	7	2	25	2	17	7	20	8	31	39	19	20	38	x	24	16	17	2	25
500	17	43	56	3	2	16	9	10	3	26	2	22	8	25	11	34	45	24	25	46	x	28	20	21	2	35
600	19	51	66	4	2	19	11	13	4	38	3	25	10	29	13	42	53	27	29	54	x	34	23	24	3	45
700	21	62	78	5	3	20	13	15	5	44	4	28	12	33	15	48	60	30	33	66	x	40	26	26	4	50
800	28	67	85	6	3	27	13	15	6	67	5	35	12	42	18	67	67	35	40	76	x	46	31	32	5	55
1000	32	88	100	8	5	32	18	27	8	79	6	49	18	59	28	81	87	49	59	94	x	50	37	49	5	60

BRANCHES: AR-Arbutus CA-Catonsville CY-Cockeysville DU-Dundalk EDG-Edgemere ES-Essex HE-Hereford JAC-Jacksonville LN-Lansdowne LR-Loch Raven MR-Middle River NP-North Point OW-Owings Mills
PA-Parkville PH-Perry Hall PI-Pikesville RA-Randallstown RN-Reisterstown ROS-Rosedale TO-Towson TS-Turner's Station WEL-Wellwood WM-White Marsh WO-Woodlawn INS-Institutional Services CC-Carroll County

using special displays of DID YOU MISS THIS and others, until it appears nothing more will work, and then the books are withdrawn. When central purchase was in its youth, overbuying happened frequently.

An area that continues to plague us in over/underbuying is biographies. Although it is one of the most interesting nonfiction areas to order, it is the most challenging and risky. Biographies are often heavily promoted, but some celebrities fail dismally to appeal to our patrons, while other dark horses just take off. We believe we should not judge the public on their taste—we just need to be able to react.

How do we find out about demand? We listen to what the public requests, what the publishers promote, and react to what has circulated well in the past. When we buy books or nonprint, we base a high percentage of the selection on proven demand of similar titles or subjects. We use our automated circulation system (CLSI) in decision making. For example, CLSI will tell us how well Anne Tyler's, Jack Higgins's, or Julie Ellis's previous books circulated, and we base the purchase of the next title on this information. For an unknown author or a brand new subject we make a judgment based on the publishing market.

- Is this the first of many books on a hot topic?
- How heavily is the title being promoted by the publisher?
- Will the book be a talk show candidate?
- Is it likely to be a best-seller?
- How many patrons have already asked for it even though it is not due to be published for three to six months?

We use the same judgment any librarian would use only we must decide how much to duplicate it as well.

Our Deputy Director described demand this way:

> We are . . . engaged in making choices on the selection of titles for our collection. We must determine, for example, whether to buy more books on psychology, less in travel, or more mysteries and less general fiction. Within these broad choices, we must also decide on the basis of what the user will find most valuable. For we must remember, that it is the user who is paying for this service, these collections, through his or her taxes. We believe that our collection development can be based on actual demand for two reasons. First, we set no value judgment on the choices among classes of books. Reading psychology is no more uplifting than, say, reading general fiction. Secondly, the nonuse argument is particularly important. We are all aware that many readers want either a specific book, or a book in a specific class, that is, fiction, picture book, travel book. If so, books in another class which librarians purchased from their best interests for their patrons, will have no impact on the reader's choice—he or she will simply ignore them.

In other words "you gotta give 'em what they want."

Essential tools for
materials selection

*The Five-Percent
High Interest
Buying*

Baltimore County Public Library's selection of high interest fiction and nonfiction is the most controversial area of its service. Baltimore County is always pointed to as only buying best-sellers. The library press and the local press often use this point to debate library service. To shed some light on this situation, I shall discuss the steps we use to select the books that receive the greatest number of requests, to which we respond by purchasing in heavy duplication.

The following outlines the steps the selectors go through to make decisions on most hot new trade adult fiction and nonfiction:

1. We start with available reviews, usually *Kirkus Reviews* because it reviews approximately 3300 new books a year before publication. We like the reviews because they are descriptive, critical, and include all bibliographic information necessary for ordering. Plus they are in alphabetical

order and indexed for immediate access and in the majority of reviews *Kirkus* cites another book by that author or on the subject, which is very helpful. We buy approximately 72 percent of the titles reviewed in *Kirkus*. We have found that *PW* alone does not work when ordering new books.

2. Then we look for publicity, advertising, promos, book club announcements, searching through *Booklist* "Upfront," Baker and Taylor "Booking Ahead," Ingram "Advance," "The Get Ready Sheet."

3. Next we peruse publishers' catalogs, checking out cover art (fiction primarily), length of book, catalog description, advertising and promotional notes by publisher. The old adage "don't judge a book by its cover" doesn't affect most people. A glamorous cover will sell a book and for our heavy reserving communities, the women demand lots of these glamorous "glitter novels."
   We also pore over *PW*'s big seasonal forecasts in the spring and fall announcement issues.

4. The fiction buyer refers constantly to the *Library Journal* "Prepub Alert" because we submit many of the very popular fiction orders four months in advance of publication.

After putting these steps into the selection hopper, we make final determination about whether to add the title or not based on circulation information when available. We also consider direct patron requests that we receive from the branch staff via a card—the Materials Information Card or MIC. The MIC is filled out at the information desk when a request is made for a title we don't own or own too few copies, or a subject for which we need to consider new material.

Ads, promos, author talks, *PW* forecasts, all the methods publishers use to promote the books to us as the selectors and buyers, are also used with the public. Bookstores cram windows with recent arrivals, our patrons read the trade journals, and the grapevine makes people aware of titles they've heard about and want to read immediately, so they too can discuss it at a party. Some patrons don't note that the book they request has not yet been released.

We allow reserves on titles on order (but not after titles have hit the *New York Times Book Review* best-seller lists) and as a result reserves are a major measure of demand for several of our larger branches. Two of our largest branches are not at all surprised by 200 to 300 reserves each on a hot fiction title.

Perhaps we have an unusual public with people reading prepublication announcements and demanding titles before we have them. But we also have the communities where people don't reserve heavily and would not know Danielle Steel has a new title until the day it arrives in the local bookstore. But by then the library better have it, too! The minute they are aware of its existence, the less savvy patrons are as anxious to read it as those in their neighboring communities. In one of our branches the staff decided to advertise the imminent arrival of the newest Danielle Steel title. Not usually a heavy reserving branch, there were 60 reserves on the title before the copies arrived at the library.

How long will the people who didn't reserve Steel's title have to wait to get a copy to read? Is their demand any less valid than that of the student doing a paper on the ozone layer, or the patron who asks for George Eliot's *Mill on the Floss*, or the gentleman who wants to take the post office exam and needs the latest Arco test, *today*?

In 1990 we instituted "systemwide hold" to help with the tremendous numbers of holds a few branches would get on a popular fiction title. Branches were already doing agency holds with lists running as high as the aforementioned amounts. With systemwide hold whoever is next in the systemwide queue gets the copy. Systemwide hold has been instrumental in reducing hold queues of 300 plus reserves per branch that could take as long as nine to twelve months to fill. Fortunately only a small percentage of our patron requests generate demand for a title that sends reserve lists into the hundreds. Despite the press to the contrary, demand buying at Baltimore County Public Library is not an exclusive interest in best-sellers.

A quick and dirty study of our buying of first novelists shows us at approximately 50 percent owned. When we had a graduate student do a thesis on the *New York Times* selection of the year's most notable fiction titles, it showed we owned 82 out of 95 titles or 86 percent. Only about five percent of the new fiction and nonfiction titles that we buy for Baltimore County falls into what could be termed best-seller category. And because these titles are top priority, they are ordered Rush ITC (which stands for via inter-telecommunication). We call the order in to the jobber for immediate confirmation of shipment and, as stated earlier in this chapter, the books are on the shelves within 10 days.

The Other 95 Percent

The other 95 percent of our requests are probably typical of what is requested in public libraries all over the country, titles students were assigned in school, titles heard about on TV or from magazines, or from some friend, from classics like the *Odyssey* to the latest diet or children's fad. Subjects for self-improvement to home improvement are requested elbow to elbow with information on tax laws, business ventures, and the latest singing group.

Over the last fifteen years demographic changes in the county have extended the breadth of requests for materials. One of our largest branches, with a history of heavy reserving interest in hot fiction, continues to experience this demand along with extensive demand for materials supporting the African-American experience. This same neighborhood is the home to many Jews

"The other 95 percent"—well-used nonbest-sellers

from the former Soviet Union who need materials they can read in their native language.

In two opposite ends of the county the Chapter II schools, serving the disadvantaged child, are receiving service via our READ ROVER mobile, which houses picture books and some adult materials. The increase in adult basic education students, adults learning to read, led us to produce small collections of adult basic education materials. The increasing numbers of small businesses begun in the mid to late 1980s forced us to respond to the requests for materials on entrepreneurship and starting a small business. We set up small business centers in three of our full-service libraries. (You will read more about these special interest groups in later chapters.) The tremendous increase in the senior population in the county has forced us to increase the information available on retirement, wills, death, health issues, as well as increased numbers of titles and copies in our large-type collection.

The demand buying of Baltimore County takes into account the changing demographics, and the way in which we develop and apply the buying formulas allows us the flexibility to address these differences in communities.

Now one might say the patrons want everything. This is true, so what do we do first? One of the first things we did when we began to select our books centrally was to set up some title limitations.

Title Goals

We looked at the number of new titles we were adding each year and made some cuts. What if we were adding 14,000 new titles each year, could we cut it to 10,000 or 8,000? This would allow us to order duplicates of titles that were asked for constantly but were never found on the shelves. By reducing the number of new titles we added each year we cut down on the little used materials. We stopped buying with "their best interests in mind" and bought "what they were interested in."

Today we choose to buy copies in a ratio to the projected demand. We choose to buy fewer titles so we can buy more copies of requested titles. We currently have a goal of adding 8200 new cataloged titles a year. The following chart does not include uncataloged original paperback titles, or titles bought in series, or on subscription, nor open-entry standing orders.

New Title Goal	*8200 Titles–FY92*
(CAH) Adult Fiction	1100
(CNF) Adult Nonfiction	5100
(CJF) Juvenile Fiction	350
(CJN) Juvenile Nonfiction	900
(CJN) (Easy Nonfiction)*	120
(CYA) Young Adult Fiction	110
(CEA) Easy (Picture Books)	500
(YANF) Young Adult Nonfiction	20

*We started a separate collection of easy nonfiction in 1986.

When we have the amount of available information that we feel is sufficient to buy a book, we determine the number of copies by applying formulas that are based on budget and circulation. For instance, our largest circulating agency, Cockeysville, with a circulation of over 1,398,000 items a year captures 13 percent of the system's circulation, which is now over 12 million. So Cockeysville gets 13 percent of the book budget. Therefore Cockeysville will have the highest formula for copy duplication. Cockeysville will likely get a copy of almost every title we buy, with some exceptions.

Circulation statistics are produced monthly, broken down by major areas such as general fiction, mysteries, science fiction, etc., and are used by Resource Managers (RMs) (see chapter 5 "Where the Rubber Meets the Road" for further definition of Resource Manager's role) in branches to monitor areas of use and disuse (see figure 2-2). Any patterns the RMs can track in circulation are communicated to Materials Selection to help us in the ordering of new materials. (Further discussion of the uses made by the circulation statistics in branch can be found in "Where the Rubber Meets the Road.")

The crux of centralized selection for Baltimore County is the formula buying. The principle of formula buying is based on the foremost principle of marketing: ACCESS YOUR USER.

Formulas are based on need and on input from the users as evidenced by circulation; they are the GUIDELINES used for the purchase of every new print or nonprint title ordered for the Baltimore County collections. They are a shorthand way of allotting the number of copies to be ordered per branch. To devise our formulas we use the following criteria:

budget
circulation-systemwide; branch (figure 2-2)
new title count
special user group/or areas of growth in population
branch input

We begin by breaking the materials budget into accounts. There is a set of formulas (the formulas are synonymous with buying grids) for each of the following accounts:

CNF—Adult nonfiction
CAH—Adult hardback fiction
CAP—Adult paperback fiction
CEA—Easies (picture books)
CJF—Juvenile fiction
CJN—Juvenile nonfiction
CYA—Young adult
CLT—Large type
ACASS—Adult cassettes
TCASS—Talking books

FIGURE 2-2

Baltimore County Public Library
MATERIAL CIRCULATION STATISTICS FOR 12/91
Reported by group

CATEGORY	YTD 12/90	YTD 12/91	CHANGE	CHANGE
General Fiction	818,487	888,020	69,533	8.50
Mysteries	203,210	229,650	26,440	13.01
Westerns	3,779	5,156	1,377	36.44
Science Fiction	26,146	29,280	3,134	11.99
Short Stories	12,541	17,253	4,712	37.57
Foreign Language	1,865	2,171	306	16.41
Large Type	36,625	45,621	8,996	24.56
Total Adult Catalogued Fiction	1,102,653	1,217,151	114,498	10.38
AGF	104,190	117,026	12,836	12.32
M	27,533	34,343	6,810	24.73
R	249,015	258,046	9,031	3.63
SF	16,674	18,147	1,473	8.83
W	18,886	17,907	-979	-5.18
Total Adult PB Fiction	416,298	445,469	29,171	7.01
Total Adult Fiction	1,518,951	1,662,620	143,669	9.46
ADULT NONFICTION REF	1,030	1,312	282	27.38
000's	32,153	39,196	7,043	21.90
100's	59,328	63,854	4,526	7.63
200's	23,200	25,553	2,353	10.14
300's	175,669	206,431	30,762	17.51
400's	10,947	11,097	150	1.37
500's	34,610	41,553	6,943	20.06
600's	352,926	412,296	59,370	16.82
700's	192,894	211,918	19,024	9.86
800's	42,796	51,638	8,842	20.66
900's	132,121	150,846	18,725	14.17
Biography	83,562	90,358	6,796	8.13
Maryland	8,355	10,244	1,889	22.61
Total Adult Catalogued Nonfiction	1,149,591	1,316,296	166,705	14.50
ADULT PB NONFICTION	33,719	32,618	-1,101	-3.27
Total Adult PB Nonficiton	33,719	32,618	-1,101	-3.27
Total Adult Nonficiton	1,183,310	1,348,914	165,604	13.99

JCASS—Juvenile cassettes
CD—Compact discs
VID—Adult and children's videos

We have several other accounts for which we have no formulas but which get a budget for new materials bought under the formulaic process:

CNR—Adult reference
CSO—Standing orders
PRRE—the budget used for beefup titles and some replacement titles
PRRL—the budget used for replacement lists

We arrive at the amount in each of these accounts by looking at systemwide circulation figures (see figure 2-3 which is a sample page from a systemwide circulation report ranked by highest to lowest).

We see from these figures that adult fiction is the highest circulating area of the collection. Easies (picture book) circulation is close to the top too. We will appropriate money for the general accounts based on circulation, after we have set aside money for miscellaneous areas. Because we want to protect some of the smaller areas of the collections, such as large type (CLT) and YA(CYA), where we'd like to see growth in circulation, we appropriate sufficiently to buy new materials throughout the year. By sufficiently, I mean we use information on the success of the previous year's selection and circulation for these specific areas. So there are variables that impinge on the money that rightfully could be spent on adult fiction or easies. Once we've budgeted the major accounts based on rank in circulation, we subdivide each account by branch using the branch's circulation stats.

For example, Arbutus, our smallest full service agency, gets 60,813 circulation in adult fiction (CAH). This circulation is then divided by the total system circulation for adult fiction giving Arbutus 2.85 percent of the total fiction circulation, or $24,795 to spend on adult fiction. (These amounts are based on FY91 budget figures.) (See figure 2-4 for sample page branch circulation report broken down by budget accounts.)

As noted earlier in this chapter we have goals for new titles added. These goals are most crucial for devising adult fiction formulas. We plan to buy 1100 new adult fiction titles a year, five percent of which are bought in quantities of 125 copies or more. The fiction selector uses the variables of new book cost, new titles goal, circulation per branch and is able to come up with a ceiling of duplication we can afford for about two to three super hot titles a year. We end up with a formula that says if we order 900 copies, Cockeysville, the branch with the highest circulation of adult fiction at 13 percent of the total,

FIGURE 2-3

Baltimore County Public Library

MATERIAL CIRCULATION STATISTICS FOR 12/91

Reported in reverse statistical count order

CATEGORY		YTD 12/90	YTD 12/91	CHANGE	CHANGE
1	Adult Fiction	818,487	888,020	69,533	8.50
159	Easy	739,712	833,767	94,055	12.72
154	A videos-784.5, 791.4, & 792.2	468,898	331,588	-137,310	-29.28
128	R-Romance/Gothic	249,015	258,046	9,031	3.63
2	Adult Mystery-M	203,210	229,650	26,440	13.01
160	J Fiction	212,141	223,635	11,494	5.42
148	A AudioCAS 000-699/800/900/Bio	166,679	221,111	54,432	32.66
248	Juvenile Videocassettes	232,385	167,824	-64,561	-27.78
149	A AudioCAS 700	148,394	159,860	11,466	7.73
231	J-General Fiction	104,857	141,933	37,076	35.36
158	Easy-E-I can read	96,757	133,257	36,500	37.72
155	Pam/Mag/Comics-A and J	118,319	121,888	3,569	3.02
126	General Fiction	104,190	117,026	12,836	12.32
42	610	81,003	93,503	12,500	15.43
230	C-Children's Picture Bks.	69,874	90,927	21,053	30.13
99	Biographies	83,562	90,358	6,796	8.13
146	A CD's-000-783, 785-999, Bio	57,322	71,639	14,317	24.98
49	641	57,013	65,787	8,774	15.39
25	360	50,669	61,265	10,596	20.91
147	A CD's 784	44,333	56,935	12,602	28.43
245	J AudioCAS E/0-699/800/900/Bio	47,901	54,934	7,033	14.68
153	Adult videos-except code 154	63,913	54,260	-9,653	-15.10
176	J398	39,944	49,295	9,351	23.41
0	Undefined	50,347	49,254	-1,093	-2.17
48	640, 642-645, 647-649	41,179	48,361	7,182	17.44
63	744-746, 749	40,909	47,681	6,772	16.55
131	LT-Fiction & NonFiction	36,625	45,621	8,996	24.56
88	917	37,129	43,372	6,243	16.81
132	Young Adult	36,752	41,809	5,057	13.76
134	Young Adult PB's	34,811	39,710	4,899	14.07
10	000	32,153	39,196	7,043	21.90
22	330	31,702	37,005	5,303	16.73
127	M-Mystery	27,533	34,343	6,810	24.73
51	650-651, 654-657, 659	26,154	32,419	6,265	23.95
73	796-799	29,645	32,376	2,731	9.21
246	J AudioCAS 700	20,308	30,880	10,572	52.06
4	Adult Science Fiction-SF	26,146	29,280	3,134	11.99
53	658	23,694	27,123	3,429	14.47
26	370	23,143	26,816	3,673	15.87
92	940	21,743	26,161	4,418	20.32
16	200	23,200	25,553	2,353	10.14
14	150-154, 156-159	23,077	25,099	2,022	8.76
71	790-791, 793-795	22,409	24,519	2,110	9.42
17	300-all except codes 18-19	20,019	24,379	4,360	21.78

FIGURE 2-4

Baltimore County Public Library

MATERIAL CIRCULATION ANALYSIS
BY SUPPORTING BUDGET FUND-HARD CIRC FIGURES

(This is a sample; not all branches are shown)

FISCAL YEAR 1992
FROM: JULY, 1991 through DECEMBER, 1991

	AR	CA	CY	DU	HE	LR	BCPL
CAH (A Cat Fic-No LT)	34,616	119,726	170,819	4,600	17,595	79,241	1,171,530
CLT (A LT)	2,118	4,672	5,495	304	368	3,695	45,621
CAP (A PB Fic & NF)	18,833	42,686	47,857	4,986	6,066	31,603	478,087
CNF (A Cat NF)	38,866	138,468	180,690	2,546	17,891	71,934	1,316,296
CEA (ICR, E, C)	33,022	112,859	136,659	2,554	29,943	64,632	1,057,951
CJF (JCat, PbFic, PbNF)	10,710	38,812	54,462	1,059	11,422	20,495	400,584
CJN (JCat NF)	12,293	41,592	50,306	900	8,789	23,928	417,450
CYA (YA Cat & Uncat)	2,185	6,329	9,505	166	1,605	4,324	81,519
Total Print	152,643	505,144	655,793	17,115	93,679	299,852	4,969,038
A Cas	12,176	37,385	56,015	468	6,481	20,964	380,971
J Cas	2,666	7,304	12,062	142	2,098	4,664	85,814
Total Cass	14,842	44,689	68,077	610	8,579	25,628	466,785
A CD	4,944	14,594	14,735	6	32	9,304	128,574
J CD	52	135	149	0	6	115	1,531
Total CD	4,996	14,729	14,884	6	38	9,419	130,105
Total Audio	19,838	59,418	82,961	616	8,617	35,047	596,890
A Video	15,479	39,732	45,754	0	10,383	17,134	385,848
J Video	8,339	17,653	19,644	0	5,867	7,625	167,824
Total Video	23,818	57,385	65,398	0	16,250	24,759	553,672
TOTAL	196,299	621,947	804,152	17,731	118,546	359,658	6,119,600

AR - Arbutus (Small full service branch)
CA - Catonsville (Large full service branch)
CY - Cockeysville (Large full service branch)

DU - Dundalk (Satellite-not full service)
HE - Hereford (Large satellite-full service-parent branch is CY)
LR - Loch Raven (Medium sized full service branch)

would receive 13 percent of the 900 copies, or 117 copies. This may leave a tiny agency with only one or two copies for one of the biggest titles published in the year. We would make adjustments and shave from the top branch's amount and create a formula with heavy duplication but with a more equitable spread. Our fiction formulas range from copy duplication of 900 down to copy duplication of four with an average duplication rate around 70. This is for 24 agencies. The fiction formulas are adjusted to reflect black interest fiction, Jewish interest fiction, SF, westerns, and mystery usage.

The other buying formulas use smaller average duplication rates, such as adult nonfiction, where we select about 5100 new titles a year averaging 17 copies per title. This means the range in nonfiction falls somewhere between 2 and 150 copies, from special to super, covering titles of editorial choice in the *New York Times* to potboilers (see adult nonfiction formulas figure 2-5).

We duplicate as demand warrants and still have branches with bottomless pits where no amount of duplication could fill the frequency of requests.

*Children's
Materials*

Some of the same pressures exist in selection of the new materials for children's collections, but generally preschoolers don't approach the information desk requesting the latest picture book best-seller. The highest area of use in the children's collection is from the least vocal segment of the community, the preschoolers. Therefore it is an area of our collections that receives heavy buying emphasis. The substantial use of the picture book collections makes a strong statement about demand so we put more money into children's picture books. In FY89 and FY90 they were a top priority for replacements. Heads of collections in branches were given a mandate to spend a certain percentage of their replacement budget on picture books and the central selector substantially increased the number of copies ordered of new titles. The Berenstain Bears and Spot can vie with any adult best-seller for popularity.

The major difference between the selection process of adult and children's books is not in the application of the formulas but in the fact that we see about 85 to 90 percent of the children's books before we select them. We are on a first copy plan with Book Wholesalers in Kentucky. We receive the books as published and order over 60 percent of the books as soon as they are received, matching them with any available reviews. The other half of the books are seen by the central purchase advisory committee with, as previously mentioned, 10 percent of the titles reviewed by staff. Although children's books aren't regularly featured on Donahue and Geraldo, we recognize the need to select and order them quickly. Circulation demonstrates demand. Empty *I Can Read* shelves in summer led us to do heavy *I Can Read* replacements in time to meet the summer reading push.

The core of a public library collection—children's books

We order about 10 percent of our children's materials prepublication and plan to increase this percentage. We look at the same information as when making a decision about an adult title: print run, promotional potential, catalog writeup, and the track record of the author exhibited through circulation statistics.

Demand is crucial to buying of children's materials. When we received requests for more up-to-date materials on countries for middle elementary assignments, we combed the literature for new titles. We found that several publishers had introduced new series on countries, each a little different, but none of them top notch. Yet we couldn't buy a book that hadn't been published. So we compared and evaluated the available series and bought the ones that would be the most useful for the children's assignment needs. Would it have been easier to say to the fourth grader: "We don't have anything on that country because we didn't like any of the books published?"

Low use of the hardback YA titles, even after heavy concentration on merchandizing, indicated the need to cut back hardback duplication and raise the number of paperback copies. If young adults aren't going to read hardbacks we are going to dramatically reduce our new hardback buying and we will replace in paper.

Special Interest Buying

Earlier in the chapter there was a reference to black interest and Jewish interest fiction. In Baltimore County the demographics

FIGURE 2-5

ADULT NONFICTION BUYING GRIDS

FORMULA	AR	CA	CY	DU	EDG	ES	HE	JAC	LN	LR	MR	NP	OW	PA	PH	PI	RA	RN	ROS	TO	TS	WEL	WM	WO	TOT	CC
1 Special																				X					2	0/X
2 N.Y. Times		X	X																	X					3	0/3
3		X	X														X			X					4	0/3
4		X	X/2			(X)				(X)						(X)	X		(X)	X/2					4/9	3
5	(X)	X/2	X/2			(X)				X		X		X	(X)	X	X	(X)	X	X/2			(X)	(X)	9/16	4
6	(X)	X/2	X/2			X	(X)			X		X		X	(X)	X	X	X	X	X/2			X	X	13/18	5
7	(X)	2	2			X	(X)			X		X		X	(X)	X	X/2	X	X	2			X	X	16/19	5
8 Sch Assign	X	x	x			X	(X)			X		X		X	X	X	X	X	X	X			X	X	15/16	5
9	X	2	3			X	X			X/2		X/2		X/2	X	X/2	2	X	X/2	3			X	X	21/26	5
10	X	2	3			X	X			2		2		2	X	2	2	X	2	3			X/2	X	25/28	5
11	X	2/3	3/4			X/2	(X)	(X)		2		X/2		2	X	2	2	X/2	2	3/4			2	X/2	27/35	5
12	X/2	3	4			2	X			2		2		2	X/2	2	2	2	2	4			2	2	34/36	6
13	X/2	4	5			2	X			3		2/3		2/3	X/2	3	3/4	2	3	5			2	2	44/50	6
14	X/2	4	5			2/3	X			3		3		3	X/2	3	3/4	2/3	3	5			3	2/3	50	6
15	2	4	5			3	X			3		3		3	2	3	4	3	3	5			3	3	52/60	6
16	2	4/5	6/7			3	X	(X)		3/4		3		3/4	2	3/4	4	3	3/4	6/7		(X)	3	3	52/61	6
17	2	5	7			3	X	(X)		4	( )	3/4		3/4	2	4	4/5	3	4	7		(X)	4	3	59/64	8
18	2	6	7			3	X	X	( )	4/5	X	4/5	( )	4/5	2	4/5	5	3	4/5	7		(X)	4	3/4	64/74	8
19	2	7	8	( )	( )	3	X	X	(X)	5	(X)	5	(X)	5	2	5	6	3	5	8		X	5	3/4	73/79	8
20	2	8	9	(X)	(X)	3/4	2	X	(X)	5/6	(X)	5/6	(X)	5/6	2	6	7	3/4	6	9		X	5	3/4	82/93	8
21	2	9	10	(X)	(X)	3/4	2	X	(X)	6	(X)	6	(X)	6	2	7	8	3/4	7	10	(X)	X	6	4	93/101	8
22 BIOG		(X)	X																	X					2/3	0/X
23		X	(X)																	X					2/3	0/X
24		X	X													(X)	(X)			X					3/4	0/X
25		X	X													(X)	X			X					4/5	X
26		X	X							(X)						X	X	(X)	(X)	X					5/7	X
27		X	X							X		(X)		(x)		x	X	(x)	X	X/2			(X)	(X)	7/13	2
28		X/2	X/2							X		X		X		X	X	X	X	X/2		X	X	X	12/15	4

BRANCHES: AR-Arbutus CA-Catonsville CY-Cockeysville DU-Dundalk EDG-Edgemere ES-Essex HE-Hereford JAC-Jacksonville LN-Lansdowne LR-Loch Raven MR-Middle River NP-North Point OW-Owings Mills
PA-Parkville PH-Perry Hall PI-Pikesville RA-Randallstown RN-Reisterstown ROS-Rosedale TO-Towson TS-Turner's Station WEL-Wellwood WM-White Marsh WO-Woodlawn INS-Institutional Services CC-Carroll County

ADULT NONFICTION BUYING GRIDS cont'd

FORMULA	AR	CA	CY	DU	EDG	ES	HE	JAC	LN	LR	MR	NP	OW	PA	PH	PI	RA	RN	ROS	TO	TS	WEL	WM	WO	TOT	CC
29	(X)	X/2	X/2			X	(X)			X		X		X	(X)	X	X	X	X	X/2			X	X	13/19	5
30	X	X/2	X/2			X	(X)			X		X		X	X	X	X	X	X	X/2			X	X	15/20	5
31	X	2	2/3			X	(X)	(X)		X/2		X		X	X	X/2	X/2	X	X/2	2/3			X	X	18/26	5
32	X	3	4			X	(X)	(X)		2		X/2		2	X	2	2/3	X	2	4			X/2	X	28/33	6
33	X	4	5			X	(X)	(X)		3		2		2/3	X	3/4	3/4	X/2	3	5		(X)	2	2	38/45	6
34	X/2	6	8			2	X	X	(X)	4	(X)	3		3	X/2	6	6	2	4	8		(X)	3	2/3	61/65	8
35	2	8	10			3	X/2	X	(X)	6	(X)	4	(X)	4	2	8	8	3/4	6	10		X/2	4	3/4	84/91	8
36 HOT BIO	2/3	10	14			4	X/2	X	(X)	8	(X)	6	(X)	6	2/3	10	10	4	8	14		2	6	4	112/118	9
37 HOT NF	3/4	12	16			6	2	X/2	x	10	(X)	8	x	8	3/4	12	12	6	10	16		2	8	6	143/147	9
38	4/5	14	18			8	2	X/2	X/2	11	X	9	X/2	9	4/5	14	14	8	11	18		2	9	8	157/162	9
39	5/6	16	20	(X)	(X)	8	2/3	2	X/2	12	X	10	X/2	10	5/6	16	16	8	12	20		2	10	8	185/191	9
40	6	18	22	X	X	8	3	2	2	13	2	11	2	11	6	18	18	8	13	22	(X)	3	11	8	209/210	10
41	6	20	24	X	X	10	3	2/3	2	14	2	12	2	12	6	20	20	10	14	24	(X)	5	12	10	232/234	10
42 Black Int										(X)							X							X	2/3	0
43										X							X							X	3	0
44		(X)								X/2						(X)	X/2			(X)				X/2	3/9	0
45		X								X/2						X	2	X		X				2	8/9	0
46		X								2						X	2/3	x		X				2/3	9/11	0
47		X/2	(X)							2						X	2/3			X/2	(X)			2/3	9/15	0
48		2	X							2/3		(X)				X	2/3	(X)	(X)	X/2	(X)			2/3	11/18	0
49	(X)	X	(X)			(X)				X/2		(X)		(X)	(X)	X	X/2	(X)	(X)	X	(X)		(X)	X/2	6/19	X
50 Jewish																X/2	X/2	(X)		X					2/4	0
51		(X)	(X)													X/2	X/2	(X)		X					3/9	0
52		X	X													2	2	X		X					8/9	0
53		X	X			(X)				(X)		X				2	2	x	(x)	X				(X)	8/12	0
54		X	X			X				X		X		X		2	2	X	X	X		X	(X)	X	12	X
55 Sm. Bus.																							X		3	3
56		(X)	(X)											(X)		X	X/2			2			X		4/7	3
57		X	X											X		X/2	X		(X)	2			X		7/12	3
58		X/2	2			(X)				X		X		X		2	x/2	(x)	x	2			x	X	14/18	3
59	(X)	2	2			X	(X)			X		X		X	(X)	2/3	2	X	X	3		X	2	X	20/23	3

BRANCHES: AR-Arbutus CA-Catonsville CY-Cockeysville DU-Dundalk EDG-Edgemere ES-Essex HE-Hereford JAC-Jacksonville LN-Lansdowne LR-Loch Raven MR-Middle River NP-North Point OW-Owings Mills
PA-Parkville PH-Perry Hall PI-Pikesville RA-Randallstown RN-Reisterstown ROS-Rosedale TO-Towson TS-Turner's Station WEL-Wellwood WM-White Marsh WO-Woodlawn INS-Institutional Services CC-Carroll County

BLACK EXPERIENCE

Special interest
buying well
merchandised

have changed since the early days of centralized selection. The neighborhoods that were predominately "noveau riche," or in the present day referred to as "yuppies," have become mixed with "buppies" as well. Six of our full service agencies serve a growing African-American population and presently two of these agencies have permanent African-American collections. When we central purchase we use the "black interest formulas" that we've set up for each buying area: adult fiction, adult nonfiction, easies, juvenile nonfiction, and juvenile fiction.

A Soviet Jewish influx into two neighborhoods has led to relegating a very small amount of budget to support a collection of titles in Russian, predominately fiction. A recent request for more gay interest materials led to an evaluation of the collections, and using some standard bibliographies we added some titles we didn't own and purchased some additional copies of titles sparsely owned. We are using the same approach to consider the increasing requests we get for "Christian fiction." In both of these cases we have ordered materials centrally but have not had a specific formula to use. We will use circulation as a measure of how to buy for all special interest groups, coupled with the demographic information about branch service areas.

The common denominator with all special buying areas is the fact that the buying is generated by multiple requests from our users. We are reacting to demand.

Nonprint

After we were two years into the process of centralized selection we added the selection of nonprint. At that time we were buying recordings and cassettes using a committee of branch staff to make the selection suggestions. Then each branch, using budgets allotted to them, would mark a list compiled by the committee, making their own choices for new materials.

Today, as mentioned earlier, we have a central purchase nonprint advisory committee that makes the selection suggestions. Formula buying has replaced individual branch selection and the same methods of devising nonprint formulas are used as print. In 1986 we added compact discs to our collections and to our formula grids. In February 1988, we stopped buying recordings and within three years had phased out all record collections in our library system. Both of these decisions were based on use by patrons, coupled with requests for a new format. CDs were growing in popularity and the trend of the recordings industry was toward producing fewer and fewer RLPs.

Historically the nonprint area of our materials budget has always come under scrutiny by the local government. For many years it was a struggle to get any increases in money for recordings and cassettes despite the tremendous increases in circulation that indicated the taxpayers wanted the collections to exist.

When in 1988, videos took over the spotlight and it became imperative that we introduce them as a library material, the man-

The new formats for libraries—compact discs

date was that they would be a self-supporting collection, which they are to this day.

Cassettes and CDs continue to be very popular, but they have a lower priority than other materials when budgets are appropriated. A history of difficulty with fill rates and locating reliable distributors has been coupled with always having inadequate nonprint budgets to meet the demand.

Even more frustrating than the "bottomless pit" of print demand is the attempt to get *Billboard's* top-charted titles in modest duplication of one to five copies, small to large branch, and still be able to order in areas such as children's picture books on cassette or holiday music.

Then the explosion in audio books added further to the frustration of making choices. The intensity and variety of requests we receive for nonprint materials are challenges. We meet them head on by purchasing very hot popular interest music cassettes and CDs for adults and children and doing the same for the talking books. We respond to the 70 systemwide holds we have for a multicassette packet on motivational study skills by ordering a few copies at the cost of $150.00 each. Then, for example, we need to choose among the classical versions of Beethoven's 5th and Mahler's 3d, the seven new notable children's lullaby cassettes, and the myriad of self-help titles available in the talking book version. Not easy choices, but we make them using whatever information we can get from the producers' publicity and circulation history. We all face the same challenge in nonprint, which stems from a rapidly changing industry that produces costly items out of the realm of the consumer's pocketbook and soon to be out of reach to libraries.

Communication

Now it has been established that budget, circulation, new title count, and special interest groups all affect the method used to develop and apply formulas. The final major step is branch input.

We have already mentioned the print and nonprint advisory committees both of which assist the selectors in making final decisions on purchasing of materials. Crucial to centralized selection is the direct input gathered at quarterly collection development meetings attended by the collection heads of each branch.

At these quarterly meetings, the collection managers come prepared with statements of specific need for both old and new titles and subjects (almost exclusively nonfiction, adult and children's). The end product of these four meetings will be a schedule for ordering from replacement lists, and a list of subject gaps for which Materials Selection is expected to look for new material.

The final means of formal branch input is through a yearly visit the Materials Selection staff makes to each full service branch. A questionnaire sent out prior to the visit allows the branch staff time to prepare answers about collection use and disuse.

Replacements

Replacements is the one area of collection development and maintenance that changes almost yearly at Baltimore County Public Library. To find the perfect way is the search for the Holy Grail, but we always arrive at a more streamlined method.

Presently we do replacement lists yearly for adult fiction, easies (picture books), *I Can Reads*, and, in alternate years, children's fiction, YA, folk and fairy tales. We divide the Dewey collection in half and compile replacement lists for one-half one year and the other half the second year. We don't aim for comprehensive lists but rather include titles that need to be replaced because they are perennially requested. (Figure 2–6 is a sample of a page from a Dewey Replacement List.)

The Resource Managers at our 15 full service branches are given a budget to use solely for ordering titles from the replacements lists we issue. Over the last few years, as we experienced no increase in budget and in some cases a decrease, the money allotted to branches to order from replacement lists as well as the number of lists issued has decreased.

Another major factor affecting the method used in replacements has been the discontinuation of branch-initiated orders. Prior to 1989 each branch had a budget allotted to them for ordering from replacement lists as well as ordering titles they individ-

FIGURE 2-6

Baltimore County Public Library
REPLACEMENT LIST SAMPLE, BIOGRAPHY
March 1992

J796,0922 S Sullivan, George SULGLSP99	Great Lives: sports Macmillan - 1988	22.95		_____
J796.323 D Deegan, Paul J. DEEMJOR99	Michael Jordan Lerner Pub. - 1988	3.95	pb	_____
J796.323 L Levin, Rich LEVMJCM99	Magic Johnson: court magician Children's Press - 1981	3.95	pb	_____
J796.357 B Buck, Ray BUCSSCR99	Sports Stars: Cal Ripken, Jr. Children's Press - 1985	13.27	plb	_____
901.941 T Tuchman, Barbara TUCPTOW99	Proud Tower Bantam - 1986	6.95	pb	_____
909 B Boorstin, Daniel J. BOODISC99	Discoverers Random - 1985	12.95	pb	_____
909 B Burne, Jerome(ED) BURCOTW99	Chronicle of the World Ecam Pub - 1989	49.95		_____
909 C Cantor, Norman CANMHIS98	Medieval History Macmillan - 2nd.Ed. - 1975	51.00	pb	_____
J 909.07 C Caselli, Giovanni CASMAGE99	Middle Ages Pub Group West - 1988	16.95		_____
(REF)909.82 C Clifton, Daniel (Ed.) *COTTCE99	Chronicle of the 20th Century Simon & Schuster - 1987	49.95		_____

The new formats for libraries—videos

ually submitted as necessary for their agency (branch-initiated orders). The process peaked when technical services, charting the numbers of branch orders for individual titles, the "oneses and twoses" as we'll call it, found the number to be around 35,000. This was costly, both in staff time and technical costs.

Presently the branches have no money for branch-initiated orders. The MIC card, referred to earlier, is one of the major methods for branches to indicate replacement needs. The card presently says: "Why can't this wait a year?" This statement is to remind branches of the tight budgets and the need to prioritize replacement requests.

In this chapter's *Title Goals* section, there is a reference to the various budgetary accounts. The PRRE budget is noted as the one "used for beefups and some replacements." This budget, controlled by the Materials Selection staff, is used for "why can't this wait a year?" titles. It is also used to support more widespread requests, for example: The black fiction list, which was a short replacement list (made up, sent to branches for input, and ordered all within six weeks) to address a high priority need in the six black interest branches for African-American fiction.

Periodicals and Standing Orders

When considering new periodical titles to add, about 8–10 new titles a year, we use branch staff to do the reviewing. For a very long time we have existed on a drop one, add one status for periodical collections. Branches continue to make the drop and add decisions for these collections which total 4084 subscriptions, or 557 titles, for the whole system.

The rising costs of standing orders and reference materials made it imperative to do some major cutting of collections this past year. We used an ad hoc committee of branch staff to recommend the cuts. We will continue to fine tune the application of formulaic buying to the purchasing of reference materials, incorporating the faxing capability and the "hub branch concept" into the decision making. You will read more about the fax and hub setup in the chapter "Does This Completely Answer Your Question."

Summary/
Conclusion

The variety of patrons' interests never cease to amaze us. We have to admit that every reading expectation we as librarians have could be filled by some patron, but we have to be aware of what the cost would be. We could never afford to meet each and every patron's expectation, all of the time.

Are we working to buy for the nonlibrary user in the FERVENT HOPE that he or she will soon darken the door, and not concentrating on the frequent user who requests that his or her needs be met?

We think not. We give 'em what they want. And 'EM = USERS.

3

WHEN THEY WANT IT

The underlying and motivating philosophy and practice of technical processing of materials at BCPL are speed: it does little good to give 'em what they want if libraries don't also pay equal attention to when they want it. Many of the users of public libraries are, like all of us, affected not only by current events, tastes, and fashions, but also by reviews of the latest books, both fiction and nonfiction, appearing in the press and on television. Public library users have a right to expect, by their financial support of the library, that those who manage the library, presumably for their benefit and in their interest, will have the right book at the *right time*.

At least most of the time. Let's just say, 90 percent of the time for 90 percent of the users. This formula, while difficult in the extreme to fulfill practically, seems to run counter to the desire of public library administrators and many librarians who work directly with the public. Many apparently believe that they should supply *all* demands at *all* times. Except, perhaps, in the case of children's books or best-sellers, both of which types of material are not really needs that deserve serious attention or serious expense, in their opinion.

This whole idea "most of the time" did not come quickly or easily at BCPL, any more than it would in any library with traditional values and traditional paradigms. In the early 60s, BCPL was expanding its physical facilities and its book collections rapidly—at the rate of about one to two new branch libraries annually—in order to meet the demands for library service in the county. In a typical suburban area (albeit with an industrial base that includes a steel plant), the new residents first demanded an adequate elementary educational system. When their children progressed to junior high and needed better and larger book collections than their school libraries could provide, they discovered an inadequate library system. Their demands were heard by elected officials and an expansion program recommended by

that eminent library consultant, educator, and sage of the period, Lowell Martin, was put into effect. Dr. Martin's recommendations were supposed to have been implemented in about five
years. They were not fulfilled for 13, but even that stretched-out
schedule was not easy for the young and largely inexperienced
staff of BCPL to handle.

*The Road Less
Travelled*

Ignorance of the conventional wisdom and the exigencies of
the period combined to encourage carefully calculated risk-tak-
ing and the adoption of unconventional solution to problems—
especially problems associated with not only materials selection, but the processing of the hundreds of thousand of items
needed each year for new libraries. This was in addition to new
books for the existing branches, which of course grew more
numerous as time went on. In other words, desperate situations demanded desperate solutions and in the early sixties
this meant computers.

*The Fiscally
Responsible
Catalog*

When a local resident walked into the administrative offices of
the library system in 1962 and offered to completely computerize
the system's catalog of 55,000 titles for $18,000, it didn't take long
for his offer to be accepted. It was only too evident that the
challenge of producing the thousands upon thousands of catalog
cards needed for each new agency was a task that was numbing
in its time-consumption, and expensive when each dollar
counted toward a larger collection—preferable even then to
spending dollars on a catalog. The solution decided upon was to
put all the catalog information on the then new magnetic tape,
sort it into author, title, and subject files, and print the resulting
information into book form. The result, a *book* catalog, was old in
concept and had been supplanted by the *card* catalog, easier to
update than the book catalog of the 19th century. Then the computer came along, with its ability to sort at comparative lightning
speed. BCPL's computer-produced book catalog was updated
quarterly, with resulting massive savings in comparison to the
production and maintenance, including filing, of a score of card
catalogs.

This computerization of catalog data was one of the earliest
examples of its kind in the nation (1963), and was originally produced by Documentation, Inc. of Bethesda, Maryland. That firm
was bought out a short time later by Leasco, a computer-equip-
ment leasing firm, and in 1971 their contract with BCPL was
transferred to Auto-Graphics, Inc. of Pomona, California. Thus
was started a relationship between BCPL and a vendor that has
greatly benefited both since 1971. As a result of technological
change, Auto-Graphics has moved the catalog production over
the years from paper to computer-output microfilm to roll fiche
and finally to CD-ROM. Along the way, massive savings in unit

The impact of mass storage: the book catalog of 1963 and the CD-ROM catalog of 1992

costs have been achieved, along with comparable improvements in utility and user satisfaction. The business relationship has been a model of cooperation through very rapid technological improvement, marked by a willingness by both vendor and library to take the kind of risk that is necessary to attain the early benefits of change. And, our catalog has, in relationship to catalogs chosen by similar libraries, especially online catalogs, been a proper balance between utility and cost, at least in our opinion.

Relatively cheap or not, production of the original book catalog, even with only 55,000 titles (and, of course, four times as many entries, at an average of four per title), was still costly—mostly, it turned out in terms of the cost of paper on which to print the information. Very quickly it became apparent that there were two ways to keep the cost of printing and paper down: 1) keep the entry short—that is use only the information about the book that would satisfy 90 percent of the users 90 percent of the time, and 2) limit the number of titles going into the catalog by limiting the number actually purchased, titles that would satisfy the demand 90 percent of the time for 90 percent of the users.

Short Entries

Our estimate in 1963, based on anecdotal evidence, was that only 15 percent of library users consulted the catalog during their visit to a BCPL branch. We found later that a study of catalog use in a university library revealed a use rate of 14 percent, so it appeared that our estimate had some validity. In any event, that low use rate, while in no way eliminating the necessity for a catalog, led us to carefully consider the cost factors associated with catalog entries that were as detailed as those produced by the Library of Congress.

The result, of course, was short-entry cataloging. Even with the growth of use in the library system to 24 libraries with a combined circulation of nearly 13 million, the purchase of only 8,000 book titles and 2,000 titles in other formats, chiefly audio-visual, the catalog was not only economical but satisfactory to both staff and public. Short-entry cataloging at BCPL reveals to the user only those elements that may be of use, even if only occasional use, to 90 percent (or probably more) of the 15 percent of the public that actually uses a catalog at all: call number, main author, title, subject or subjects, illustrators for picture books, and date of publication. Sometimes series.

Limited Titles

The limitation of new titles purchased annually to 8,000 results, of course, with a book budget of 20 percent of the entire budget (or even with 15 percent or less) in the forced purchase of more *copies* of a title. Unfortunately, it does not guarantee the selection of the *right* 8,000 titles, but that's a question for materials selection rather than technical processing. The choice of the number 8,000 (in 1961, with only 11 libraries and a circulation total of under 2 million, over 14,000 new titles were purchased) was arbitrary, since no professional or experiential advice was available from any source consulted. Arbitrary or not, it has worked for 30 years of continuously growing use, and the limitation of new titles has saved millions of dollars in both selection and technical processing costs over the period.

Both short-entry cataloging and limitation of titles in libraries the size of BCPL have been almost universally rejected by the profession, as far as we can tell, but it has worked for us.

More Is Too Much

Cataloging, or the description of a book, in sometimes excruciating detail, revealing and "printing" on tape or disk almost everything everyone could possibly want to know about the book, excepting only such things as the color of the binding and the smell, has proliferated wildly in public libraries. It is now almost all electronic in medium and large libraries and many small ones. Bibliographic utilities like OCLC, originally started to *save* cataloging costs in academic libraries, and the advent of the Library of Congress MARC service in 1968, have ballooned costs in description of books beyond anyone's imagination of thirty years ago. At the same time it has created a whole new industry serving libraries in such areas as resource sharing (an activity only serving two percent of ordinary library users at best), retrospective conversion, online catalogs, and electronic networks. State libraries and the federal government have poured hundreds upon hundreds of millions of dollars into the support of these new industries and into libraries taking "advantage" of the technical advances, all of which are based on the detailed description of books, descriptions that are used hardly at all by any public library users but paid for by all on a continuous basis, year after year.

The process, of course, gets cheaper and cheaper *per title,* as storage costs keep going down. Printing cataloging information on paper no longer is a cost factor, even at BCPL. But costs of buying information from bibliographic utilities are rising every year, and the cost of communication, the network of transmission lines that tie together the information and "resource-sharing" databases, grows dramatically. And, "it doesn't matter how much it costs, we *have* to do it!" To give adequate public service, presumably.

But the public hardly looks at cataloging information in public libraries, except to determine shelf location. And having determined once where the needlework books, or the cookbooks, or the gardening books are, shelf location then becomes part of the amazing memory powers of the library user. Any library worker who has weathered the storm of indignation resulting from shifting the collection is aware of *that* phenomenon!

The Sooner the Better

The use of bibliographic utilities, besides being very costly and furnishing generally unneeded and unwanted information, creates *delay* in getting the book on the shelf. Generally, no one in the library profession cares about this, despite the fact that library *users,* time after time, and on a continuing if despairing note, place heavy emphasis on speed in getting a book on the shelf in enough copies to give them a fighting chance to read the book when it's still useful, still wanted, or still fashionable, if you will.

In the daily world of BCPL technical processing, speed in getting the book from the wholesaler, through the cataloging and processing ritual, to the shelf of the community library, is paramount. Everything else is subject to this overriding concern. As a result, many of the professional shibboleths become obstacles to the process and are rejected. Eighty percent of titles purchased are cataloged by using Cataloging in Publication, a free service provided by the Library of Congress and the book publisher. Professionals say that at least 15 percent of the time CIP information is later revised and corrected by LC, so waiting for the "correct" information by a bibliographic utility is much the better choice, even if it results in delay. BCPL rejects this notion, and uses CIP whenever available, only rarely correcting the catalog information. The public, the users, have never complained. Never. The remainder of non-CIP titles are cataloged by *one* professional and *one* paraprofessional cataloger—not a slow process when short-entry cataloging is used. This technique is

Short entries in the book catalog: *very* short!

also applied to the approximately 2,000 audiovisual (audiocassettes, compact discs, and videocassettes) items cataloged annually.

We find it interesting that visitors from other libraries to BCPL very often are curious about the speed in which the materials reach the shelves, the almost complete lack of any backlog, except temporarily at the peak of publishing seasons, and the lack of expenditure for any bibliographic utility services. In every case, however, as far as we are able to determine from feedback from visitors, the techniques used at BCPL, are universally rejected as unwise, unworkable, and unacceptable to the professional and/or administrative staff in these other libraries or library systems. Almost always, of course, they cite the necessity of "service to the public."

When Some Is Good Enough

"Service to the public" is also applied to that new product of technology, a new product seldom, if ever, demanded by the public and universally expensive: the online catalog, or OPAC (online public access catalog). This product combines the ability to store vast amounts of cataloging information about each title (sometimes even two screens full, for *one* title), provides all sorts of search capability (difficult and time-consuming even when relatively user-friendly), shows the status and location of the item (some, even most of the time), and does this sometimes, if you can afford it, in color. The public, almost all of them, just want to know where the books on that subject are in their library. The user is then prepared to go to the shelf to look for those books or perhaps another book that may be just as useful, or more so. That's pretty much it, for 90 percent of the relatively few people who use the catalog are almost never used, (online or not), 90 percent of the time. All the other features of an online catalog, while costing thousands and thousands of dollars, are better spent on more copies of the books people want so that there is a likelihood of the books being *there* when people want them.

The BCPL solution to a catalog is not cheap, but it's the cheapest thing we can find: a compact-disc catalog, updated four times a year, with none of the communication costs of a sophisticated OPAC, and only basic search capabilities and no location or status information. The difference in original cost, downtime, maintenance, and upgrade costs are remarkable and enable more money to be spent on books. We might have color terminals one of these days, if they are cheap enough, on the same principle that we spend money on attractive furnishings or merchandising.

Technical Services

Acquisitions

An important part of technical processing is Acquisitions, which in BCPL used to be called the Ordering Department. In truth, this title was more descriptive in comparison to other "acquisitions" departments in some other libraries, where selection of material may be part of the process. Acquisitions has, like the cataloging function, one overriding priority: speed. Accuracy, or getting the title actually specified by materials selection, is of course important, and sometimes takes some skill and experience, but speed is paramount. Price is a factor, too, but variations in price between suppliers is so small that in most cases it becomes relatively unimportant. Whether a supplier actually has the title desired and can ship it immediately are very important.

Vendors

Seventy percent of all titles purchased by BCPL are ordered pre-publication, again in the interest of getting the books to the community libraries while they *are* still of interest. Therefore, doing business with a wholesaler who not only can order the titles we want but *does* order in sufficient quantity to supply our needs quickly becomes of great interest to the Acquisitions Department. Other factors in relationships with vendors are important. These include clear and accurate invoicing, the existence of an effective and efficient customer service department to assist in solving the problems so often created by publishers (whose predicted publication dates resemble fond hopes rather than dependable estimates), and the vagaries of the computerized ordering system both of the wholesalers and of the publishers.

The problems that crop up in the acquisition of thousands of titles (even if fewer thousands by far than comparable libraries) are legion. For example, the automatic cancellation of titles three months after the order without any indication of *why*, recently gave BCPL and its wholesaler an interesting challenge. Investigation revealed that a weekly review of titles on back order for more than one month would find all sorts of interesting practices by publishers. These affected other customers of the wholesaler as well as BCPL. The initiation of a new procedure helped fulfillment rates for both of us.

Both the performance of individual wholesalers and the appearance of new formats purchased by public libraries, such as compact discs or videocassettes, demand constant attention by those staff members ordering materials. Staff members should also know and understand the problems and policies of suppliers. It is vital to have close relationships with vendors and, most important, to recognize that they and we are part of the same team and share the objective of getting the book to the user. Treatment of a vendor as an adversary, or treatment by the vendor of a library as a cash cow, always results in poor service to the end consumer, the taxpayer and supporter of the library.

Fund Accounting

Another very important function of any acquisitions or ordering department is, of course, the accounting function. In BCPL, the accounting for purchases of materials is largely done by the Acquisitions Department, with the final handling of invoices and payment done by the Accounting and Fiscal Services Department of the library. In other words, acquisitions is responsible not only for making sure that the right price was paid for the book, the proper number of copies was received, and, probably of most interest to those on the staff interested in controlling the materials budget, that the money was spent in the right place—where it was intended to be spent, in a multiple-agency system with multiple materials funds.

Fund accounting has always been a challenge in BCPL, as it is in most libraries. It is of little interest to accountants, who are most concerned with price and receipt of the merchandise, but balancing the amount of money spent per agency, whether for materials for adults or children, fiction or nonfiction, new or replacement, is vital to the successful implementation of *Give 'Em What They Want*. While vendors of control systems, whether in circulation, bookkeeping, or catalog authority files, have developed generally acceptable systems that can be used in most libraries, this does not seem to have been effectively or acceptably applied to fund accounting of materials budgets for internal control. Not for lack of effort, perhaps—CLSI, the leader in library automation, actually came out with such a system as its first product in about 1972. They found, as did others, that fiscal controls varied so much in the library field, especially in public

Ordering and fund
accounting made
relatively simple:
Baker and Taylor's
Libris online system

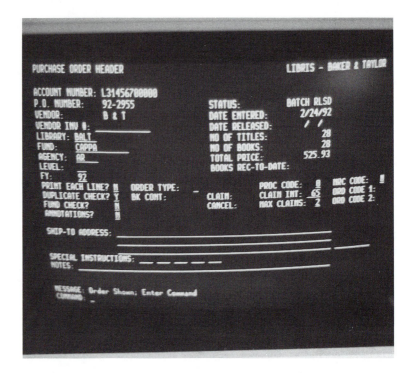

libraries, that every system had to be customized to such an
extent that economies were difficult. Also, many libraries deal
through their governing bodies for purchasing and must fit with
the larger system.

BCPL used the first CLSI system, and it was satisfactory—
only, however, because as we grew almost anything would have
been preferable to the handwritten, calculator-driven reports
necessary for management of the materials budget. Worse, these
reports took so long to produce that they were only available two
or three times a year. This lack of current management information, while perhaps acceptable in a more traditional library
where response to materials use was not as important as in
BCPL, was totally unacceptable here. While the CLSI system was
an improvement, it was a business that CLSI abandoned very
early in its existence, although our system was maintained for
some years, until the staff at CLSI changed to the extent that no
one there was familiar with the software, and the hardware
could not be maintained any longer.

On a temporary basis, the first PC (an Apple) was bought and
VisiCalc was used to produce a report, until our major wholesaler, Baker and Taylor, came out with the LIBRIS system, which
had the extremely valuable asset of mainaining its own database
of titles, a feature the CLSI system did not have. Baker and Taylor, of course, maintained such a database of available titles primarily for its own use, but tied together with a fund accounting
system for individual users of the system, it has become invalu-

able to us. This, perhaps, can be viewed as an early example of the kind of privatization that is so popular a term in governmental circles today.

While fund accounting may not be a problem in smaller libraries, or in libraries where staff and funds provide expertise for homegrown fund accounting systems, LIBRIS was, and is, a major contributor to the control of materials funds in BCPL. The cost of the system is not inconsiderable, but it is insignificant when compared to a homegrown system, at least in our view. There may be commercially viable software available for fund accounting, just as there is for general accounting, but the kicker is the availability of the wholesaler's title database, the availability of which is invaluable when tied to a fund accounting system. Because so few libraries across the country take advantage of this LIBRIS system, there may be cost or service problems. Doubtless better systems will be developed, but as far as we know none has appeared yet. We wait with everlasting hope for better or less expensive systems, but we are truly thankful for what we have, remembering the "old" days.

Processing

Forty years ago, the most revolutionary concept in the processing of individual books in a public library setting was the advent of the plastic see-through jacket, a development that may have been the most important merchandising event to affect public libraries in their history. The resulting preservation of bookjackets through the handling of multiple borrowers not only increased circulation, and the use of books, but also took full advantage for the first time of the art and design expense of the publisher—an expense that not only served to sell books in bookstores but also to "sell" books to users in libraries. The only jackets removed by BCPL are those on picture books *if* the jackets are replicated on the bindings.

Every library uses plastic jackets now—but many in the profession remember that universal adoption was a very slow process, because librarians thought, it seemed, that retention of the jacket somehow cheapened the material inside the book. The whole process is somehow analogous, perhaps, to the reluctance of librarians to adopt display shelving in public libraries, except in very limited use. They are in the "collection" mode, rather than, it seems, in the "distribution" mode. Other than plastic jackets, of course, the major impact on technical processing in most libraries has been the adoption of automated circulation and the resulting "zebra labels," or bar-encoded labels. In most libraries, however, advantage has *not* been taken of the very considerable savings, not only in book-processing expense, but also in clerical time (perhaps the biggest expense of all), in one area—the placement of item identification and due-date information on the book.

Labels on the back
speed checkout in
busy libraries

True to the tradition that nothing revolutionary has ever been originated at BCPL, the president of CLSI suggested that not only the bar-encoded item label be placed on the *outside* of the book (on the back), but also a sticky label which could hold the due-date stamps. While we were initially unenthusiastic because the due-date label often obscured the blurb on the back of the book, especially on paperbacks, we accepted the suggestion. We did so because in a high-circulation environment, opening each book to charge it out, or to find identification of the library it was borrowed from upon its return, would be time consuming and therefore labor intensive.

Even in the salad days of governmental revenue, 1975 (we didn't recognize them as such then, but we certainly do now, in 1992), it was obvious that the willingness to add staff, even desperately needed staff, was not a priority of the appropriating authority. In a low circulation environment, the adoption of such a technique may not be as advantageous as allowing the reader to view the blurb without the interference of a due-date label. Unfortunately the stated mission of ensuring customer satisfaction is often impeded by insufficient resources, even with a very successful service, in a governmental environment. In exchange for this, however, we must remember that we don't have all the headaches of taxes and other governmental regulation that drive small businessmen to distraction.

Another direction BCPL has taken in its technical services, especially in book processing, has been the extensive use of part-time staff, especially students. This is not unique, but we have always been fortunate that this use of part-time employees has been possible. It is not in all libraries.

Contractual Services

Almost unique in any public library in the United States, BCPL and a neighboring county library, the Carroll County Public Library, have been for many years participants in a contract that supplies materials selection, processing, cataloging, and automation services from BCPL to CCPL. Originally conceived when CCPL, now serving more than 100,000 residents, was growing rapidly, the contract has been repeatedly extended. This arrangement has been termed a "mutual rip-off society" because advantages of scale extended these services at low cost to Carroll County while providing income to Baltimore County. This cooperative effort has proved, at least to observers from BCPL, that these activities, so jealously guarded by almost every library in the nation as vital local concerns that must be held in-house, are a viable and a remarkably effective way to lower costs, unlike the only other major cooperative effort between libraries, interlibrary loan, which all evidence proves raises costs enormously, even if these costs are paid by others, like the state or federal governments. The key to success in such a venture, by and large, is unacceptable: you must allow the *other* library to select your books. This is discussed in the chapter on materials selection.

The processing of these books for CCPL has provided few problems, and the cataloging of them few more. Where there have been problems they are solved, or ameliorated by open discussion rather than confrontation, and the result has been generally acceptable. It is interesting to note that the Carroll County Public Library has a circulation per capita almost as high, 18.5 annually, as BCPL. Their per capita expenditure is about 80 percent of BCPL's.

The point of view expressed here about the success of the cooperation is not necessarily shared by the administration of CCPL. While they have been growing, they also feel that their growth has been such that they can do their own selection, processing and automation at lower costs than they are now paying Baltimore County. They then would have more "flexibility" at the same costs or lower. Whether and when they leave the cooperative arrangement are unclear at this time of fiscal constraints, but BCPL has serious doubts that CCPL can attain anything near the fiscal savings that they expect and we would guess that they underestimate the administrative and management challenges they would encounter. Nevertheless, it has been the experience of cooperative endeavors in libraries that substantial innovation and the resultant shift in paradigms have almost always lost to the interests of local control and the retention of maximum autonomy, even if costs associated with such a course are high.

While this is true in many areas of local government, it is particularly true of public libraries, where community orientation is rightly strong, and where the institutions concerned are of a size that goes almost unnoticed in the general range of governmental services. For these and other reasons, CCPL may be correct to set up their own support services. Under any circumstances, it's a tough call.

4

WHERE THEY WANT IT

The choice of Popular Library as the paramount role for BCPL came as no surprise to the Long Range Planning Committee in 1988. Many beliefs and practices in this library system contributed to that outcome. One contributory factor was the branch library organizational structure.

Department Stores and Libraries

Some interesting comparisons can be made between the retail industry with its department store components and the public library systems in the United States.

The erosion of the general downtown department store as the single major entity in the retail service market has been pronounced for almost twenty years. The resurgence of the central downtown library has been just as pronounced over the same time period. Why are the differences occurring?

Both department stores and public libraries began as examples of "tall" organizational models. There was a flagship department store in the central downtown area of cities in the same way that there was a flagship central library building downtown. Both organizations also developed systems of branches. The public libraries created these very early in their history, department stores much later as suburbia began to emerge after World War II.

Today there is a significant divergence in the two organizational models. Who can recall when a full-scaled downtown department store was last erected? In contrast, the library profession has seen in recent years the erection of large downtown central public library buildings to replace or expand existing facilities. Denver, Chicago, San Francisco, Atlanta, Albuquerque, and Phoenix come to mind easily.

In the department store model the "tall" organizational structure has become a "flat" one. To this observer who is not engaged in the retail business world, the flagship central store appears to have been relegated to a partnership role as first among equals, but not much more significant in the alignment with the branch department stores. Lord and Taylor's and Nordstrom's would be examples. There are exceptions: Macy's survives in a flagship-style building in New York, but Macy's has also opened strong regional branch stores.

Location, Location, Location

The point to be made here is that in one business, at least, a large number of retailers made the decision to cater to the shopping public where they lived or where they were willing to congregate. The "community" of downtown no longer supported the flagship store as in earlier times. Hence, the plethora of convenient locations for shopping, primarily in malls situated at reasonable distances from the homes of the shoppers and with adequate parking. The branch concept was strengthened at the cost of the single downtown location, which appears to differ from the recent public library development.

There are even further refinements in the retail marketing business as some firms have established more than general branches. Specialty type stores are a subsection of the retailer's services. For example, a dress shoe store may have a companion sport shoe outlet, or a clothing store may have three separate outlets for men's, women's, and casual clothes. These outlets may be under the same corporate name or under varying names controlled by a single retailer. The multiplicity of stores presents some very practical considerations. Will the volume of business justify the operating expenses? Are the supply lines in place and adequate? At what level is personnel staffing needed, etc., etc.?

Obviously, the retail trade saw the potential for attracting customers in a decentralized setting. Serve the people where they live or where they are willing to congregate for shopping purposes. Shopping is a voluntary activity in which people will engage if given sufficient incentive. Convenience is a big factor, or as we hear in the real estate business, "Location, location, location."

Flagging Flagships

For the most part public library systems have two types of service outlets: a central library and a branch library system. The regularly reported statistics in annual reports show that the preponderance of circulation activities comes from the branch libraries. If one is willing to view circulation as a payoff in terms of satisfaction to library users in the same way that retail sales are a payoff to satisfied customers and store owners, what are the implications here?

Why are the central libraries being built, but are no central department stores being built? Why are the branch libraries not seen as the stronger partners in the central/branch relationship for meeting the *overall* service demands of the public? Why are branch libraries not considered in relation to a central library in

This community library had no handicapped ramp when opened in 1963 by Spiro Agnew

the same way as the retail trade has been treating the single department store versus the multiple outlets?

Branch libraries *can* have appropriate collections, information services, and programming services to meet their "shopping" public's needs. Public library use is an entirely voluntary use, so convenience in access is a highly desirable feature, bearing both on location and hours of service. "Time is of the essence" is a standard phrase in many contracts and the satisfactions in many of life's activities are related to the speed with which a service can be provided. Where central libraries exist, adequacy in collections has been denied to the branch library users in favor of the strengthening of the central library's collections. Collection strengths also bear on the degrees of adequacy of information services, so here again, branch library users may not be as well served as they might be if the resources did not go first to a central library.

The "Community's" Libraries

A community library is the bedrock point of service for residents and commuters within a certain contained geographic area. Somebody can determine the population to be served or the square miles to be included. Choices will vary for all kinds of reasons, probably the political condition as the foremost selector. Certainly conducting a study to tackle the determination of the communities to be served by branch libraries is an advisable farsighted decision, but really only practical for a newly created library system. For the rest, opportunities to change locations or to open or close agencies occur on a random basis, not infrequently in connection with some political or fiscal crisis. Boards of Library Trustees and library administrators have varying degrees of clarity on the organizational setup of the branch libraries, but there is generally agreement on a structure that bears on the physical size, the collection size, and the staffing pattern.

BCPL Branch Structure

In BCPL there are four distinct types of libraries: area, community, satellite, and mini (which is also a satellite). If thought of in a retail sense, their services can be directly compared to the general branch and specialty stores mentioned earlier in this chapter. The full-service libraries, area and community, are general branch stores, and the mini and satellite libraries are specialty shops. Outside of their services allied to libraries, their absolute necessities are well-functioning HVAC systems, dry interiors, and available parking spaces.

The most obvious but not entirely consistent distinction in the hierarchy of branch libraries in Baltimore County is in the physical size of the buildings. Area branches range in size from 20,000 to 30,000 square feet, community are between 10,000 and 20,000 sq. ft., and satellites and minis range from 2,000 to 5,000 sq. ft. There are aberrations, primarily in the designation of two community-size libraries as area ones. Figures 4-1 and 4-2 give some details on the types of libraries.

The staffing in the branches provides for librarians only in the full-service branches, that is area and community, and clerks in all agencies. Full-service libraries (the general branch retail stores) offer the full range of information and programming services. Volunteers are also in full-service branches (and in central office departments).

Mini libraries were established in the early 1970s when communities continued to seek libraries that could not be justified in the library's physical facilities plan for the county. A county executive promoted the idea of volunteer-run libraries for which the county would provide leased quarters and collections. The idea worked to the extent that four minis were provided and are still in operation with volunteers and one full-time clerk in each. They are stocked for quick pickup selection of popular adult and children's materials (a specialty type retail store) and are based in small neighborhood shopping centers. They are administered from a nearby full-service library. Labor costs are the single most expensive part of the operating budget, so the opportunity to serve a community through volunteers has a very favorable aura in both a political and economic sense. Here is the affordable way to match a specialty store direction at a significantly reduced cost to taxpayers.

Satellites are also attached administratively to full-service branches. For the most part they are the older, established branch libraries superseded in services by newer, larger branches in their general areas. They remain open for service

FIGURE 4-1

Baltimore County Public Library

ORGANIZATION OF BRANCHES, FISCAL YEAR 1991

Area Branches: 8
(Catonsville, Cockeysville, Loch Raven, North Point, Pikesville, Randallstown, Rosedale, Towson)

Square feet:	13,000 - 30,000
Population served:	24,000 - 55,000
Hours open:	2,900 - 3,537
Circulation:	580,000 - 1,600,000
Librarian FTEs:	8.7 - 18
Clerical FTEs:	13 - 31.5
Total collection:	80,000 - 197,000

Community Branches: 7
(Arbutus, Essex, Parkville, Perry Hall, Reisterstown, White Marsh, Woodlawn)

Square feet:	8,000 - 20,000
Population served:	19,000 - 66,500
Hours open:	3,148
Circulation:	400,000 - 735,000
Librarian FTE's:	6.6 - 8.2
Clerical FTE's:	7.7 - 12.4
Total collection:	51,000 - 92,500

Satellites: 5
(Dundalk, Hereford, Lansdowne, Middle River, Turner's Station)

Square feet:	2,000 - 6,000
Population served:	3,700 - 22,000
Hours open:	935 - 2,525
Circulation:	11,500 - 235,000
Librarian FTE's:	0 - 2
Clerical FTE's:	1 - 2.4
Total collection:	2,300 - 32,000

Minilibraries: 4
(Edgemere, Jacksonville, Owings Mills, Wellwood)

Square feet:	2,000 - 4,000
Population served:	9,200 - 22,000
Hours open:	1,300 - 2,500
Circulation:	18,000 - 193,000
Librarian FTE's:	0
Clerical FTE's:	1
Total collection:	2,300 - 32,000

FIGURE 4-2

Baltimore County Public Library

COMPARISON OF BRANCHES, FISCAL YEAR 1991

BRANCHES	Percent of COLLECTION	Percent of TOTAL SERVICE UNITS[a]	Percent of TOTAL STAFF	Percent of REGISTERED BORROWERS
Arbutus	2.9	3.4	3.5	3.6
Lansdowne	1.2	0.6	0.5	1.3
Catonsville	10.9	9.9	9.4	8.4
Cockeysville	10.1	12.7	11.3	10.4
Hereford	1.8	1.9	0.8	0.9
Jacksonville	1.3	1.2	0.2	1.0
Essex	4.7	4.6	5.0	6.7
Middle River	0.6	0.4	0.4	0.7
Loch Raven	5.9	5.3	6.1	5.4
North Point	4.0	4.7	4.9	6.9
Dundalk	0.5	0.3	0.5	0.6
Edgemere	0.4	0.1	0.1	0.2
Turner's Station	0.2	0.1	0.2	0.1
Parkville	5.2	5.8	5.1	4.9
Perry Hall	3.5	3.3	3.6	3.2
Pikesville	4.9	5.8	6.2	5.2
Wellwood	1.8	1.5	0.4	1.2
Randallstown	9.0	8.7	9.2	8.5
Reisterstown	4.6	5.2	5.2	3.8
Owings Mills	0.9	0.7	0.2	0.6
Rosedale	6.0	5.7	6.1	5.5
Towson	10.0	8.4	11.6	12.3
White Marsh	4.6	5.2	4.7	3.0
Woodlawn	4.8	4.8	4.7	5.7
TOTAL	**100.0**	**100.0**	**100.0**	**100.0**

[a]Service units equal the total transactions for the FY'91 annual circulation, readers' services and program attendees.

A typical shopping center minilibrary

limited to circulation only, and constitute another variation in the specialty store analogy.

Bookmobile Services

Bookmobiles were and are a part of BCPL services in different ways. In the 1950s when branch library facilities were meagerly scattered throughout the county, three bookmobiles gave services to the communities. Each was attached to an area branch library for at least three reasons: 1) convenience in meeting a schedule of stops in a geographic area of the county (east, central, and west), 2) utilization of the branch collection to stock the bookmobile, a far more economical choice than the creation of a centralized collection reserved exclusively for bookmobile stock, and 3) availability of branch staff as immediate backup for staffing on the bookmobile.

A frequent role for a bookmobile was identification of a potential branch site, not very hard to do in the 1950s and 1960s in Baltimore County. In a role of almost the same importance, the bookmobile served as a justification for not building a branch library because of the adequacy of service through the vehicle.

As branches were built, bookmobile circulation fell, and, predictably, the vehicles became more of drop-off sites for returns to branch libraries than lending agencies. By 1979 all of the general service bookmobiles were gone from the system. Their disappearance has been planned for and slowly implemented for over two years and the abandonment led to no public outcry for their retention.

In 1970 a small used bookmobile was bought off the roof of Cobo Hall in Detroit at an ALA Conference to serve as a summer book van for children in camps and recreation centers. During the winter the vehicle stopped at institutions such as nursing homes and retirement communities. That service has continued to this day through the third replacement vehicle.

With LSCA grant funds in FY91, another vehicle has been put in place to serve children in registered day-care family settings and in day-care centers. Materials may be borrowed and programs for the children are offered on board the vehicle.

Staffing   Librarians are retained in the full-service branches, but if there is a satellite or mini assigned, librarians visit those agencies for collection maintenance and occasionally programming for children. In both satellites and minis, staffed by clerks and/or volunteers, direct line phones are available for reaching librarians at the administrative branches so information services may be handled from there.

Master's degree librarians hold the positions of branch managers. In addition, the two librarian department head positions in branches are filled by master's degree librarians. They are the Materials Resources and the Information and Programming managers. A decision made some years ago led to the recruitment and hiring of master's degree librarians only at a supervisory level; but there are a few who remain at the entry level position.

The majority of the service librarians in the branches are library associates, a group of paraprofessionals whose training began in Baltimore County Public Library in the early 1960s. These are the paraprofessionals who are trained for service in formal classes run by the public library systems in central Maryland. The library associates are hired by the individual systems for a combined work-study program of a year's duration. Successful completion of the program leads to certification in the state of Maryland. The position of library associate is a career choice and in BCPL has three levels of advancement. The strengths of the library associate program in BCPL led in part to the generalism concept which is recounted elsewhere in this chapter.

For many years the staffing for the branches has been reassigned annually. The librarian FTEs are assigned using a formula that includes a branch's share of the system circulation and information transactions. Clerical FTEs are assigned solely on the basis of the branch's share of the system's circulation totals. Formula staffing is not unknown, but the simplicity of the BCPL model may be unusual. After a study some years ago, the determination was made that the inclusion of many more factors, e.g., telephone calls handled by clerks and librarians, reserves taken, etc., did not appreciably change the staffing and only required more record keeping and handling than necessary. More recently, the branch managers decided to drop the programming statistics as insignificant in the staffing formula. The level of busyness for circulation and information services, not the physical size of the building, determines collection and staffing allocations so that a community library may exceed an area branch in one or both.

In the light of the formula pattern used in BCPL there is no minimum guarantee to any branch for staffing. In reality, however, a few caveats have been built in to assure coverage in a building by at least two persons at all times, as an example.

Collections

Twenty years ago area branches had collections of specialized subjects for system use, for example art in one, business services in another, but this concept was dropped when community use became the sole criteria for collection building. An area branch forced to hold specialized collections for intralibrary loan or an occasional visitor to the area was being penalized when the staff were trying to encourage high usage of their collections by their own users. Community branch librarians without this assigned responsibility were more unrestricted in their collection building. In fact, they were trying to acquire some so-called specialized books because of the use they predicted.

Use was determined by turnover figures for each of the Dewey classes. If these could be raised, circulation increases followed. In the beginning of the use of the turnover figure as an analytic tool, an increase in the withdrawal rate for materials wrought the benefit desired. This seemed puzzling and inexplicable at first, but branch managers provided some reasons: 1) when shelves were not so crowded, it was just physically easier to browse among books; 2) there were more opportunities for "old fashioned" merchandising with a book displayed at the end of a shelf; and 3) a user did not need to pull off older unused materials in fields where up-to-date information was most wanted, eliminating discouragement in the search. Hence, use rose from a smaller collection than had been provided formerly.

A mix of materials is important

The policy then became clear: the number of volumes was not as important as the mix of materials and the provision of duplicates for the most used and wanted. This policy does not mean that best-selling novels are the mainstay of the collections to the exclusion of other materials. Duplication is just as important in children's picture books, for example. Also, the so-called "specialized" collections gained a systemwide status. If art books and business services were needed in branches they were bought as demand required, not limited to an area branch location.

The numbers of books and other materials in a branch library are determined by the shelving capacity and the turnover. BCPL branches are built with the most minimum storage areas for anything and certainly it is almost fair to say with no storage areas for collections. If materials are to be used they must be on display, not secreted in storage.

The book count in an area branch should hover between 100,000 and 150,000, with the remainder of items, up to a maximum of 200,000, reserved for nonprint and periodicals. Because the system limits new title coverage to 8,000 annually, an area branch with over a 1,000,000 annual circulation could expect to have the full range of titles. Varying business levels of branches will determine their title and stock counts.

Funds for these collections are requested in the amount of 20 percent of the total annual budget request. This policy has been a standing tradition of the Board from its inception in 1948. No branch manager needs to file a request form, nor does any supervisor need to review requests and decide on their priority order. When the appropriated funds are known, then the allocation of monies for branches is made based on a branches prior years percent of the system circulation. If Branch A had 14 percent of the system circulation in the last fiscal year, then 14 percent of the materials budget will be spent for that agency.

The Materials Selection Department, located at headquarters, is responsible for all new title purchases in BCPL in every format carried, but is still responsible for apportioning purchases as the individual branch materials budgets allow. The ways in which this is done are reported in chapter 2.

The main points to be made in this discussion of allocations by formula are their flexibility to existing situations and the built-in equity throughout the system no matter what the tenor of the times. Regardless of the size of the appropriation for personnel and materials there is a way to allocate based on the relative busyness of the agencies in the past year. When appropriations are reduced then the staffing and materials expenditures are proportionately reduced in each agency and vice versa.

Services

Regardless of size, the full-service libraries (the area and community branches) are expected to provide information and programming services. The expectations for information services, the highest priority in the branches, are discussed in chapter 6. (Readers should note that collection building is the highest priority for the system. The provision of the materials to meet the role of a popular library is the overarching concern in BCPL. In the branches, however, branch managers have designated information services as the highest priority in terms of their responsibilities. To clarify further, one shorthand way to express this is: collections are built centrally; information services are first given locally.)

At the branch level, the managers have the most influence on the service levels of librarian staff to the public through the information services. Here is the one-on-one exchange that sets a tone for a user's positive or negative recognition of staff effectiveness. To many users the materials' collection must exist as a monolith, an impersonally rendered service provided to attract catch-as-catch-can browsers. Not so are the personalized information services.

As a support to the highest priority service in the branches, the Information Department at headquarters, through its Clearinghouse, handles the centralized refrence backup function for all questions referred from branches. Also the Information Services Coordinator at headquarters takes the lead in the training in information services and in the new technology experiments handled by various branches for recommendation or rejection for the system.

The collection maintenance work, the second priority at the branch level, is, for the most part, a scheduled activity for librarians constituting about three hours weekly. Direction is given by the Resources Management Department head on growth, decline, or stability of the collection parts based on analyses of reports on use. More detailed explanations of the work are in the section "Day to Day Operations" in chapter 5.

Programming activities are the third priority in branch library work in BCPL, behind information services and collection maintenance. Recently coordination of programming was transferred to the Marketing and Programming Department at headquarters. This transfer took programming from the headquarters' Information and Programming Department where it had been placed as a group information function. The newer concept had programming as an activity directed to a targeted segment of the population, hence applicable to a marketing department.

The prime audience for programs is children and they are attracted through traditional story hours for three- to five-year-olds; two-year-old craft programs where an adult joins the child; two- to six-year-old programs with adults; and family events, e.g., turtle races. The central support office coordinates a number of events that the branches may opt to present, such as magician or puppet troupe. Staff also have formed three theater groups which present original shows twice a year in every branch. Every branch is a participant in the annual summer reading program for school-age children.

Numbers of programs are not mandated, and there are variations in the types and numbers by branch, but each branch offers some programs for children. There is no requirement for programming for adults and there is some variation in the system, from nothing to modest numbers (maybe two a year).

Staff Policy Changes

Services from the staff in BCPL are identical to those of librarians in other public systems insofar as the general descriptions of duties: collection building and maintenance, information services, and programming. Where differences occur and have been looked at askance by many librarians, generalism is frequently the most susceptible to disapproval, even vehemence in

Full service now demands lots of state-of-the-art equipment

rejection. Some background on the development of generalism is included here to clarify the thinking behind this innovation.

First, return to the comparison between retail stores and libraries. In the established old department stores there were long-term sales staff who had built up a working knowledge of products that bordered on an expert classification. In the same way the so-called department specialists staffed the central libraries. Most did not have degrees in the subject matter of their departments, but their long experience in the same departments enhanced their knowledge of the fields.

The branch stores and branch libraries do not have the so-called experts or specialists in subject knowledge. With branch stores spread throughout a wide geographic area, with long hours of opening over a seven-day week, the economics of the retail trade argue for the hiring of the most competent people at the most economical costs. This is not to say that customers would not like to have more skilled staff in stores (indeed even more staff, in many cases), but the customers have shown enough satisfaction with the merchandise, the locations of the stores, and the shopping hours to allow the retailers to forego the expert knowledge as an added cost of staffing. In other words, people are willing to use the stores under the circumstances that they will be assisted by a minimally knowledgable staff about the products sold. That staff can be hired at less cost than any specialist staff.

The same line of thought can be introduced into the staffing of libraries. If staff can be trained to give the broadest level of service, i.e. through all age levels, economies in operation will follow compared to the costs of hiring specialists for each age level of service. Where the level of questions, inquiries, etc. can be handled by staff competently trained for the job but with an education below that of a graduate level, savings can be made in salaries. Is this a justifiable decision? If the savings can be turned into the materials budget thereby giving the library users greater resources than they otherwise would have, the answer is "Yes," in Baltimore County.

Economics have always played a large role in decision making in Baltimore County, and the decision above may be seen in that light. Actually, the dearth of master's degree librarians in the 1950s led to the use of the paraprofessional, a kind of back-handed result of an economic situation with the master's degree librarians. The paraprofessionals have proven their value many times over, both for their service record and for the reduction in personnel costs, which have allowed a higher percentage of the budgets to go into materials than would have been the case with more master's degree librarians.

A comparison may be made here, too, with the retail trade. Well-stocked stores and libraries are busy centers even in the absence of specialist staff. Shopping and library use have a browser attraction in common.

Generalism in the Making

The professional services staff in branches are responsible for all areas of service to the public without regard to any age-level distinctions in those services. Their job assignments will be organized from among the functions of service offered by BCPL, i.e., (1) information, (2) collection development and maintenance, and (3) programming.

Each librarian should expect to have a responsibility in each category and to meet a satisfactory performance standard in both quality and quantity of work performed.

Generalism is intended to offer in all branches the most stable level of service to the users of BCPL, consistent with the personnel available. Staff concerns with all aspects of service foster this stability by giving each staff member a perspective on total branch service, involvement in a team approach to carry out the services, and the flexibility to assume a partnership in that effort.

That quotation is from a policy statement on generalism issued in BCPL by the Associate Director in September 1980. The directive came after 18 months were spent on the conversion process from age-level specialists to generalists in public service in BCPL.

Anyone who has observed activities in a branch library is aware of the unevenness of the public service demands. For at least two service desks, children's and adults', demands will peak and wane at different times in the workday. Preschool children, not in day-care facilities, may accompany a parent or babysitter in the early morning hours; senior citizens may arrive in the mornings; elementary school-age children will arrive in the early afternoons; teens and older students will arrive in early evening hours, as will the large majority of working adults. The consequence is drought or glut at a service desk.

To even out this discrepancy requires a relatively simple solution. Establish a single service desk and assign all librarian staff there with the responsibility to assist the next person in line for service. Implementation of that idea required the year-and-a-half conversion. The process was helped by the background of training previously given to librarians for staffing public service desks in BCPL.

Evolution of the Generalist Concept

When BCPL was founded (1948) the expectation was that this new system would offer strong, traditional library services in branches and without a central library. The expectation was hampered by two immediate problems: 1) Baltimore County Public Library was largely unknown, and 2) the nation's libraries were faced with a severe shortage of MLS graduates. Inability to recruit competitively for the pool of MLSs led BCPL's director to introduce the library aide (now library associate or LA) in 1962, a career position in public service.

The library aides were trained in both adult and children's work before being assigned in one of the two areas. As a result, they had an *overall* on-the-desk competency exceeding the MLSs who joined BCPL. The MLSs had, for the most part, decided on an age-level specialty before choosing their course work, hence their service was weighted in one area over the other. (Consideration of young adult as a separate age-level specialty has been omitted here because in BCPL that service was never at the level of adult and children's services.)

As the "new" MLSs and LAs moved out and up in BCPL their numbers did not keep apace with the demands from the public for services, especially in a system where a new or remodeled branch was opened every year for over a decade.

Branch managers asked that some systemwide training be given to bring up skill levels in adult and children's services, hence Crossover Training was instituted about 1975. The coordinator and librarians of adult services prepared the content for the children's librarians and vice versa. For several years these training sessions helped to improve communications at the branch level, prepared staff for crossover desk assignments to meet increased workloads, cover for vacations, and to instill a sense of mission shared by the entire staff of a branch.

Impact of Interfiling Nonfiction

Along the way, as the system grew and some branches became satellites of other newer larger ones, the interfiling of nonfiction in small agencies began. These experiments were deemed successful and, coincidentally, found to be in use in King County

(Wash.) Library System for branches with 100,000 plus volumes. The newly located Towson Library of about that size, opened in 1974, began with a single service desk and interfiled nonfiction. Because of sight lines that made a one-desk operation difficult, Towson reverted to a two-desk arrangement but continued with the interfiled nonfiction. Where interfiling existed in BCPL and where it was instituted as quickly as possible in remodeling projects, the collection development and maintenance work brought adult and children's staff into a closer relationship, both at the branch and central office levels.

Interfiled nonfiction has the obvious assets of one location for all circulating books on the same subject; the opportunity to adjust buying materials from a two-location to a single-location shelving place (very apparent in reducing duplication rates for titles in both adult and children's collections); and a location without prejudice for "new" adult readers whether as a result of literacy training or learning English as a second language. Referral of adults to children's wings has been a very sensitive issue in many library situations, and interfiled nonfiction obviates the problem.

The less than completely satisfactory aspects of interfiled non-fiction are the overwhelming collection size for a small child and the physical problems of reaching top shelves of adult-height shelving. The first concern can be minimized by putting books for children up through the third grade in special shelving locations, and the latter is handled by a multiplicity of stepstools in the stacks.

A much later development in interfiling came in late 1980s when reference and circulating books in community libraries were interfiled, except for a small ready reference collection at or near the Information Desks. Again, the idea of fostering a one-stop location for materials was in the forefront of the decision. The opportunity for more self-help by the users was a related factor and has proved helpful based on the reported in-library use of the reference titles. This interfiling presents the opportunity in community branches to expand the subject coverage of the circulating collections since the community libraries have less materials than the larger libraries.

Significant Shifts

By the mid-1970s the interaction of four significant factors became apparent in BCPL.

First, was a slowdown in building growth. After opening an average of one library a year for some eleven years (1963–1974), the new branch growth ceased as the 1956 survey goals for physical facilities were met.

Second, staff immobility was experienced for the first time. The librarian staff had a very low turnover because their salaries were competitive nationwide, there was a glut of MLSs on the market, and the BCPLers were relatively young with no retirements to create vacancies. How could staff prepare for limited promotional opportunities? Did an adult or children's librarian classification offer a better preparation?

Third, the organization in the central offices of the Public Services Support Departments along function lines, eliminating the former departments of age levels of service, had been followed up in three branches in experimental reorganizations.

Fourth, and not least, were the previous and anticipated erosions in funding support. The Board, administrative staff, and branch managers had all agreed to reductions in personnel by attrition in preference to any reduction in the materials budget.

Increased productivity of the staff had to be achieved and generalism was the logical answer in 1979. In the ensuing year and a half the branch organizational structure was changed to the function, not age-level distinction; intensive staff training was conducted; committees were reconstituted; branch/central office relationships restructured; and staff performance expectations revised.

In the branches, two librarian department heads were designated: Resources Management and Information and Programming. Librarians below this level were in the pool of staff to fulfill all assignments connected to both of these functions, i.e., be responsible for a section of the collection for adds and discards, work at the information desk, and give programs for preschoolers through senior citizens. The two librarian branch department heads rotated in their jobs every year or second year, hence keeping both on an even developmental program for their job skills. Both reported directly to the branch manager, and with the manager of clerical operations they constituted the senior management staff in the branches.

Generalism Results   Ten years after generalism was introduced into BCPL the concept is just as viable as at its inception. Funding support has fallen below inflation rates, business levels are still climbing, and staff attrition is still preferred to materials' reduction. A powerful byproduct of generalism has been the cohesiveness of branch staff in formulating and meeting annually set branch-initiated service goals. With all staff engaged in identical services, there is no friction because of a we/they mentality about what the goals should be and their priority order. The latter was a frequent occurrence in the organizational structure that had age-level coordinators "in charge of" services, or so they perceived their roles, even when they had no stated supervisory control in a branch library.

One modification has recently been introduced into generalism. Instead of two MLS librarian department heads in a branch, a single one to cover both functions has been introduced experimentally in one community branch. This change appears advantageous in reducing the multiplicity of meetings for communication, aiding in clarity of assignments, and strengthening of the roles of the supervisory level of the Library Associate position. Further experiments can occur as attrition diminishes the number of librarians at the department head level.

Generalism is really in effect in branch libraries throughout the country. People can get help in libraries: by volunteers if there are no clerks, by clerks if there are no librarians, and by librarians if they are assigned. Certainly no administrator would admit that service is denied to a child or adult because a librarian classified for the relevant age-level service was not available. In BCPL generalism for librarians has just been institutionalized instead of accepted "under the counter."

A Central Library for BCPL?

The organization of branch libraries in BCPL is an ongoing project. The original plan, developed by Lowell Martin and the BCPL staff in 1957, took some 20 years to implement. Locations and designations of libraries were fairly closely followed. The neighborhood book centers called for in the plan became the volunteer-run minilibraries. The area branches were spread about to satisfy the political issues of coverage in a county of 610 square miles; the community libraries were built in the interstices between area libraries. No need for a central library was expressed in the original study and no need is expressed currently. To many people the absence of a central library in Baltimore County flows directly from the location of the Enoch Pratt Free Library in Baltimore City. Their central library has been thought of as a central library for the Baltimore County Public Library system. This is not the case nor has it been since the building of the BCPL libraries from the early 1960s.

The impact of the new technology has been studied in relation to the organization of branch libraries in BCPL. Since the subscriptions to CD-ROM products and online services, the development of LANs, and the advent of FAX transmissions, the opportunities to move information from one library to another have been greatly enhanced. There is now a new type of regionalization being planned whereby certain of the technology products are placed in a limited number of branches with a system of intratransmission of materials throughout the system. This pattern could prefigure an organizational model of a central library with branch libraries; but there is no need to establish a central library. Any one or several branches can be the access point(s) serving the system, or a centralized information support department attached to the administrative offices may be strengthened for a new role. At this time, a combination of branch regionalization and strengthening of the Clearinghouse, the centralized information support department, is being phased in. No one believes now that a central library will be required, and, in fact, the technology appears to reduce the need for a central library.

Most library efforts
come down to this

Any branch library can serve as a distribution point to any other agency in the system, or to agencies/individuals outside the library system.

Summary

The four roles for the Baltimore County Public Library: popular materials library, reference library, preschoolers' door to learning, and formal education support center are handled through an all-branch library system. The reasoning has been that the library users should have the most effective library centers that can be afforded from the funds for libraries in the most convenient locations for their use:

- Put the libraries and the resources where the people will go easily and willingly.
- Have a staff trained in as broad a coverage of users' needs as possible and spend monies for collection resources with any savings in the personnel costs due to using para-professionals.
- Concentrate on serving each community with the most appropriate mix of staff, materials, public service schedules, and functional buildings.
- Engage in materials selection, not collection for the sake of collection.
- Do not provide branches with storage space for lesser used materials; discard them.
- Keep the collections current and with a high turnover.
- Forego the temptation to build central libraries as a monument to the civic pride when the alternative is a decentralized system more satisfying for actual use to the majority of the taxpaying owners.

5 *WHERE THE RUBBER MEETS THE ROAD*

A careful analysis of organizational development of BCPL over the years would probably show that just as most problems connected with service to the public exist at the point of service, the community libraries, the solutions to the problems have their genesis there as well. Operational theory in libraries with the traditional branch/central library organization is often collection-based rather than user-based, and the priorities of users are very often subsumed in the "needs" of building a materials collection which, at least in the central library, has few users.

At BCPL the users, through their actual use of the community libraries, drive the practices, the philosophy, and the planning of the library system as a whole. The interpreters of that use are the branch managers and the managers of clerical operations in each library, with input from all staff, including part-time and volunteers. Just as in the retail sector, pragmatism is paramount in planning and practice, and results are measured by the number of people who come in our doors and use our products: materials and information.

One of the popular current concepts in management training at the present time is that of the upside-down organization chart, where the administrative and management staff at the bottom of the chart is supportive of the top of the chart, the community libraries in this case. BCPL branch managers know that above all else they can rely on the support offered by the staff at the central offices. The Board of Trustees provides policy direction; the Director provides the financial and political link with the county government; and the Deputy Director provides day-to-day support, interpreting policy, and coordinating the other departments. The Personnel Department runs the staff development office in addition to providing librarians and clerks for each agency; Materials Selection orders all the new material and coordinates the ordering of replacements; Information Services provides a special clearinghouse to help with lengthy and more difficult questions and coordinates the provision of the newer technology to branches. The newest department, Marketing and Programming, has the dual yet compatible function of providing Public Relations for the system and any flyers and signage needed for publicity, and of coordinating the programs branches' schedule, sometimes providing complete, centrally planned programs ready for performance. Branch managers count on each of these departments without a second thought to provide support so they can go about the business of *Giving 'Em What They Want.*

Just as a great deal of study has gone into discovering *what they want* in the way of materials, information services, and programs (see relevant chapters), much effort has also been put into discovering who "they" are. As retail outlets study their clientele and know their target shoppers, the library also wants to know its users and potential users. BCPL has recently completed its third edition of a report called *Statistical Community Analysis*, known as SCAN. It uses statistics, census data, and other observed and gathered information to detail characteristics about the county and its communities. From SCAN the system has learned that although the branches' populations have many similarities throughout the county, there are observable differences that can be addressed. BCPL knows, for example that one area of the county has a segment of Russian immigrants, that 6 of the 24 branches can be targeted for somewhat larger black interest collections, and that a couple of the branches have a predominantly Jewish population. This information is used both centrally and at the branch level when decisions are being made about materials and services.

Branch Managers

Branch managers at BCPL are actively involved as a group in the operation of the library system. Known as MOB (Managers of Branches), they meet twice a month to address common concerns and especially to coordinate the setting of priorities for the next fiscal year. Guests from the administration or other leadership groups attend their meetings when invited, but MOB generally sets its own agenda. Throughout the year MOB considers problems that arise at the branch level, recommends new policies and procedures or changes to existing ones, and generally reacts to current events in the library system. The branch managers also spend several months gathering information from the other management groups (the Resource Management Department heads, the Information and Programming Department heads, and the Clerical managers) and using that information and its own ideas to prepare recommended priorities for BCPL for the coming fiscal year. MOB presents the priorities document to the administration which reviews it and presents it to the Board of Library Trustees.

A branch
management team

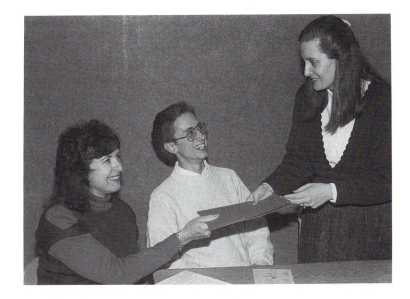

Far from simply being supervisors, BCPL branch managers are true working managers. They spend daily time (15 percent – 20 percent) working at the information desk and carry other duties at the branch, sometimes maintaining a section of the collection and doing an occasional program. However, there is much involved in overseeing branch operations, including maintaining the physical plant, solving staff problems, handling complaints from the public, representing the library to the community, and generally seeing that in each operation, system and branch priorities are followed.

Branch Organization

Most branches have three department heads under the branch manager: the Resources Manager, the Manager of Information and Programming, and the Manager of Clerical Operations. The department heads generally meet weekly to discuss how things are going and to share ideas about projects and plans for the branch that might involve interdepartmental cooperation. This is a very valuable time for communication because with the heavy business level in the branches and the involvement of these supervisors in so many other committees, meetings, and activities, they work independently most of the time.

Branches' clerical staffs include both full-time and part-time people. In addition to the clerical manager there is an assistant manager, usually the supervisor of the part-time clerks, and a number of clerks who work at the circulation desk and take care of the "back room" work. The part-time clerks do the shelving in addition to helping at the circulation desk in busy times.

The librarian staff also includes both full- and part-time staff members. The branch manager and two department heads have master's degrees in Library Science; the rest of the full-timers fall into three grade levels of library associates who have bachelor's degrees and have completed the yearlong training program described in chapter 4. The full-time staff are true generalists, performing a variety of services for all age groups. Each day librarians are assigned to work at the information desk for up to 50 percent of the time. They also put on programs, maintain their sections of the collection, do committee work and other tasks such as scheduling. Their part-time counterparts spend most of their hours at the information desk, providing scheduling flexibility and allowing the full-time librarians more time to get their other work done.

Day-to-Day
Operation

Let's look more closely at the kind of work that goes on in a BCPL branch on a daily basis. The information desk is staffed at all times by enough librarians to handle the business level with minimal waiting for the public. At that desk librarians help patrons of all ages find answers to reference questions and use reader's advisory skills to help them choose reading material. Librarians not working at the information desk may be assigned to merchandise the collection, because BCPL is committed to having materials displayed attractively so that patrons who want to browse and help themselves can easily find what they are looking for. Displays are refilled during the day to maintain their appearance and to provide materials quickly and conveniently.

Collection maintenance is also part of a librarian's daily routine. New materials are ordered centrally, but replacement copies are ordered at the branch level from short lists of books identified by staff as titles or topics in need of attention. Only about 10 percent of a branch's materials budget is spent on replacements. The bulk of collection maintenance time at the branch is spent on weeding copies of titles that are too worn to keep or have outlived their usefulness. Date-due stickers on the backs of books let librarians see just how much use a title has been getting. One method of deciding that copies to weed is to look at the sticker and notice how many times the book has circulated in the past year or so. A librarian may notice that interest has dropped off for a particular title, that the subject matter is no longer in vogue, or that perhaps one less copy would now be adequate.

The average turnover for each item in BCPL's collection for FY91 was 6.85, meaning that most things went out almost seven times last year. Using that as a guideline, decisions can be made about weeding a copy, although there is a great deal of leeway to allow for differing use of individual sections of the collection. Picture books tend to go out twice as many times as the average turnover rate and are usually weeded simply because of wear and tear. Other sections may be used seasonally because of

Collection maintenance is essential to assure an up-to-date collection

school assignments or connection to a holiday, so acknowledgment of that is made and materials are kept with fewer than the average number of circulations. Staff are aware of the statement in the library's mission about providing materials proportionate to levels of demand and use, and they weed accordingly.

A second option used for weeding is the Slote method. Here the librarian notes the amount of time between the last two circulations for each book (or a sample if the section is too large) and charts the number of months. As a pattern emerges the librarian decides to weed the books with greater than the designated amount of time between those last two circulations; these are the books now getting the least use in the section.

All librarians also program and may need to spend part of their day planning or carrying out a story time or school visit. Effort has been made so that some programs are planned centrally and don't involve so much work at the branch, and there is a revolving troupe of storyteller/puppeteers who tour the system a couple of times a year. However, individual story times are still planned and carried out at the branch level and tours of the library with an explanation of available resources are done for all sixth graders, again by librarians at the branch.

While the librarians are busy providing information service and carrying out their behind the scenes duties, the clerical staff is also busy doing a variety of tasks important to the provision of

A smiling shelver
and her daily
challenge

excellent public service. Their first priority is to staff the circulation desk, checking out items with as little waiting time as possible for the public. Almost equally as important is the sorting and shelving of returned materials. As with most tasks in BCPL, this one carries with it its own priorities, and there are procedures for knowing which materials should be shelved first (new books and videotapes) so that the public has the most access to the materials most in demand.

Shelving Materials

Like it or not, once you buy the books and put them on the shelves you can run a library only as long as those books get back on the shelves and can be found again. This is a job done mostly by part-time staff in every library.

Last year Baltimore County Public Library had an annual circulation of more than 12,000,000 items. Keeping track of all these items is a major undertaking. In the late seventies, with circulation rising every year, we found that we were losing control over the shelving process. We didn't really know who was doing what. So we took a hard look at who, how, what, and when this job gets done and then looked for ways to improve productivity. Four major changes resulted:

The generalism concept was applied to part-time clerical staff. We dispensed with the separate job titles of "desk assistant" and "page" and called all part-time staff members "circulation assistants" (CA). We also ended the practice of assigning each CA to his/her own area of the collection. We started to train each CA to shelve materials in all areas: adult, children's, and nonprint. Only after meeting all shelving standards was the CA trained to work on the circulation desk. This improved the sense of team-work among the CAs, and gained the system the flexibility to use staff where they were needed most.

We stopped using sorting rooms. Book trucks labeled in broad categories, such as easies, fiction, nonfiction, and new, were placed behind the circulation desk. All returned material was immediately sorted onto the appropriate truck. Filled trucks were then taken to the workroom where they were numbered and dated. The first material in would be the first shelved. CAs could put a book truck in exact order within 10 minutes by working from the truck instead of shelving units. Reducing unnecessary handling of books by using presorted book trucks and dating incoming material greatly reduced both backlogs and turnaround time. Ninety percent of all material is now shelved within 24 hours and ninety-six percent within 48 hours.

We established standard or "required times" for shelving. Appearances can be deceiving. Staff that look busy are not necessarily the most productive and vice versa. In order to establish accountability for circulation assistants, required shelving times were established for each type of cart, e.g. 15 to 20 minutes with no mistakes for a fiction cart. Now CAs must shelve within the required times. Each CA must meet the required times in every area within the first two months of employment. Shelf reading is scheduled 30 minutes out of each four hours worked. Four sections/units should be read within 30 minutes with fewer than three errors. Required times for shelf reading checks are done on every CA at least six times per year (more for a newer CA or one whose performance needs improvement). Leave guidelines were also established that allow no more than four unexcused absences within 12 months. By establishing fair and consistent measurements, we are able to objectively evaluate the performance of every CA.

We hired part-time supervisors. As our circulation increased, we hired more and more part-time staff (often turning full-time positions into part-time hours) because we needed greater scheduling flexibility and more shelvers. The ratio of full-time to part-time staff reached the point that we could no longer adequately supervise the part-time staff. The result was that we had a large workforce with little or no supervision, especially on nights and weekends when we had less full-time staff. To solve the problem, we turned some of our shelving hours into part-time supervisory hours, and created a new position, CA II. Although some branches were initially hesitant, this has proven to be one of our most effective management tools. There is one CA II for every 15 CAs. CA IIs spend 75 percent of their time on supervisory tasks and 25 percent on typical CA duties. They work an average of 25 hours per week. CA IIs range from high school students to senior adults. They are responsible for hiring, training, scheduling, taking required times, and evaluating part-time staff.

Without this position, we would not be able to closely monitor the shelving operation.

Most users come to the library to find the books they want. Getting the books back on the shelves is the most important thing we do. As a result, the thought and effort we have put into improving shelving productivity has been well spent because it has greatly added to our ability to *give 'em what they want, when they want it.*

Full-time clerks spend 50 percent of their time at the circulation desk. Their remaining hours are spent on sorting mail, processing delivery, checking in periodicals, handling reserve material, overdues, catalog changes, and all money operations. Each job has written requirements and clerks are rotated every two to three months to allow for flexibility and variety.

Clerical Managers and Assistants spend 30 percent of their time on the circulation desk. In addition, they are responsible for performance evaluations, budget allocations, staff development, training, monthly reports and CLSI equipment.

Statistics

Now that you know exactly what gets done by the staff in a BCPL branch, let's look more carefully at why they do what they do. Priorities are constantly being examined and adjusted, projects dreamed up, and experiments begun. This is because attention is paid to a variety of statistics gathered by computers and by using sampling techniques. Circulation statistics are used in a number of ways: total system and branch-by-branch circulation help make up the formulas used to staff the branches; full- and part-time clerks are distributed based on the workload indicated by the circulation studies done by the branches during the previous fiscal year, and the same numbers are part of the formula used to assign the librarian staff. Circulation statistics also determine the percent of the total materials budget allotted to each branch.

Statistics are collected at the information desk through sampling 50 days each year to determine the number of questions answered annually. These totals are used as another part of the formula to distribute the librarian staff. To help us know how to staff the information desk the questions are also broken down into several different kinds: reader's advisory, subject requests, simple title checks or reserves, etc. and can be broken down by time of day, day of the week, or season of the year. Branches also keep track of subjects and questions that were difficult to answer so that they know what materials to target for purchase (and what training might be needed—more on that later).

The use of circulation data on books to help decide what to weed has already been mentioned. Many more statistics are collected and are available to help the materials selection department know what to buy, to help branch resource managers know what to target for special attention, and to help individual librarians know what to weed or purchase. Through BCPL's automated circulation system each item is assigned to a statistical category (SCAT). Each SCAT represents a very small segment of the Dewey Decimal classification system, so that when branches get monthly circulation figures broken down by SCAT, branch staff can make comparisons and use real data to make decisions about collection maintenance. For example, librarians can observe the downward trend in videotape circulation over the past year and know that it is paralleling the retail trade. Staff can also look at the circulation of the mysteries over the last few months and see that the change in shelving location that was made has improved it by several percent. Use of these figures is very similar to what retailers do in controlling their inventory by computer; deciding which stock is most beneficial, will produce the most sales, and will turn the most profit.

Statistics on programming are generally kept by hand. Attendance by age, by time of day, and by type of program are all useful for future planning efforts. One branch might observe that late morning story times are better attended than early morning, or that most five year olds in the community go to afternoon kindergarten and can only come to the library in the morning.

In addition to the general community information available from the SCAN reports, the data supplied by patrons registering for borrower's cards is analyzed by the computer to provide detailed information about the library users. Priorities can be set and long-range plans can be made knowing, for example, what percent of the patrons in our main zip codes are school-age children, or seniors with college degrees. Plentiful preschoolers mean extra picture books; more city residents mean fewer agricultural materials.

All of this specific, practical information can be studied and used in the reactive way suggested in the examples, but it can also be used proactively as planners look for ways to change, ways to improve, ways to branch out, ways to do more with less. Discussion about sluggish sections of the collection can lead to the creation of a branch committee, including both clerks and librarians, to look at ways to rearrange collections and displays so that access to the materials is improved and perhaps shelving is more efficient as well. Discussion of increasing information statistics at a systemwide department heads meeting led to the development of a formal procedure for handling especially busy times at the information desk. As library programs were being planned the realization that younger school-age children were missing out led to the scheduling of elementary school nights where a whole school was invited to come for a visit, involving older students as volunteer helpers. BCPL makes changes as a result of analyzing data about past patterns of use and through anticipating future needs and fads so that BCPL is always ready to *Give 'Em What They Want*.

Staff Development

Training is particularly important in a system where the staff are generalists because there are so many skills to be maintained. BCPL has an extensive program of staff development that works on a number of levels. At the branch, regular meetings are held in both the clerical and librarian departments to provide a chance to focus on particular, timely needs of staff. This is when training needs in specific subject areas of the collection can be addressed somewhat informally, e.g. car repair manuals, legal or business questions, and when new reference books can be highlighted. Some of these topics can be addressed using packets of training materials prepared by individuals and small committees for just such a purpose. Packets, available for booking through the central offices, might include sets of practice questions that can be answered using the books in an area of the collection, a bibliography, a chart highlighting the features of each reference book, and, depending on the topic, perhaps even a videotape to help spark discussion.

Six times a year on two successive days, to allow as many as possible to attend, systemwide workshops are held on a variety of topics determined by a biennial needs assessment survey. Recent examples are "Dealing with Difficult Patrons" (for clerks and librarians at all grade levels), "Handling Homeless Patrons" (for supervisors), and an annual "Newbery/Caldecott Workshop" where librarians hear a keynote speaker and discuss new children's titles. Various people might present these workshops. In some cases it is a BCPL staff member who has expertise in a certain area, e.g. a librarian who has been on ALA's Caldecott Committee. A number of BCPL staff members, again clerks and librarians, have been to a workshop offered statewide called "Train the Trainer" where they have learned skills in how to lead workshops effectively. Frequently an outside expert is hired to present the training session. This was the case with the "Dealing with Difficult Patrons" workshop where a psychologist, briefed ahead of time on the staff's needs and questions, was brought in to address the topic.

Additional training tools are available on an as-needed basis. Procedure manuals written by staff committees help allow people at all levels to make and defend decisions. One particularly helpful manual is called STEPS—*Staff Training for Emergency Procedures*. It addresses ways to handle a number of problems that may come up when a less experienced person is in charge. Other manuals help with programming, computer operation, and clerical procedures to help staff at all levels be more independent.

New ideas from all staff are encouraged and a great deal of effort is made to keep everyone fresh and creative. There is support available to send people to outside workshops and to conferences put on by the state library association. Participation in system, state association, and ALA committees adds to the opportunities staff have for staying interested, up-to-date, and vital. One reason generalism has been accepted is the variety of opportunities it provides and the flexibility librarians gain in scheduling and job descriptions. Further, the systemwide policy of transfers means that every few years staff members may find themselves in a different location, working under a different supervisor, and probably in a different size agency. This changing of the mix of staff members contributes to the creativity BCPL relies on from all of its employees.

The Bottom Line

So, what makes it all work? What is the glue that keeps everyone working together toward the same goal? Communication. BCPL concentrates on communicating every detail to every person. Clerks are as aware of system and branch priorities as librarians. Attention is paid so that part-time as well as full-time staff get "the message." There are many avenues of communication, all of which work together to keep every staff member not only up to date, but interested to see what's happening next and where they fit into the big picture.

BCPL has a numbered memo system for communicating with the staff in general or with particular groups, and memos arrive each morning from the central offices so that all staff have information available simultaneously. After board meetings the director meets with the branch managers to share board actions that have been taken. After those meetings, branch managers meet with their staffs as a group to pass on the news and open up time for discussion. The management groups meet monthly to address issues particular to their job assignments. Branch supervisory staff meet with the deputy director quarterly to keep her up to date about how things have been going and what projects are being planned for the future. And there are less frequent occasions for communication as well. The director makes an annual video message which is distributed to every branch just after the final budget is announced. He explains how the budget will affect daily life in the branches and at central offices, commenting on salaries, the anticipated materials allotment, and the capital as well as the operating budget.

Finally, there is the annual staff day program. Instead of taking a Columbus Day holiday, BCPL closes on the second Friday in October so all staff can attend this meeting. The day always includes an address from the County Executive, a few words from the president of the Board of Library Trustees, and, of course, a message from the director. Service awards are given out, and each year three $500 merit awards are given, chosen by a committee representing the staff, to recognize overall exem-

Staff communication in action—a committee meeting

plary service. There is also a keynote speaker, chosen to present a program of interest to the entire group, and there is a lengthy segment set aside for brunch and socializing. Each part of this staff day meeting is an important communication tool and is recognized as valuable and an integral part of the staff training package.

And here you see the overlap. Training is communication. Statistics communicate the direction to go and the changes that must be made. All of this communication, the training and meetings and committee work, the formal and informal, contributes to staff members continually seeing the direct relationship between their duties and Baltimore County Public Library's effort to *Give 'Em What They Want*.

6 DOES THIS COMPLETELY ANSWER YOUR QUESTION?

An Overview of Information Services in BCPL

The nature of information service in the Baltimore County Public Library is reflected in the library's mission statement: "To make readily available to Baltimore County residents library materials and information services in a cost-effective manner, proportionate to the levels of demand and use, and to provide access to resources outside the library system." The library's information service insures the maximum use of BCPL's resources via the librarian's interaction with the users.

It is the library's objective to provide information services to meet the expressed demands of the community, and where possible, to anticipate demand. In doing so the library considers the needs and interests of all its users including children, young adults, and adults. Meeting the information needs of the community involves not merely acquiring information, but making it available and accessible.

Information service in the Baltimore County Public Library System is a function of convenience, access, collection, and staff. The location of branch libraries and hours of operation are convenient for our users. Access to information within the physical facility is encouraged and made easy by the use of signage, prominent placement of information desks and public catalogs, well-stocked and attractively displayed materials that have been carefully selected to reflect the interests of the community, and the visibility of staff.

Access to information within the Baltimore County Public Library system is made possible first within the branch itself. For materials available in other branches' collections, there is a well-established and effective system of reserves and intralibrary loan that is handled by a systemwide van delivery service that delivers the materials to the branch where the patron requests pickup. Recently we have instituted intralibrary faxing of periodical articles and other information found in print materials, if the patron's need is immediate. Access to materials owned outside our system is facilitated by cooperative agreements with local colleges and universities and the State of Maryland Interlibrary Loan (MILO) system.

BCPL branches are designed to be as self-service as possible. Each library features highly visible displays on topics of interest to the general public. All branches have signs that assist patrons in locating popular subject areas within the stacks. Current periodicals and back issues are out on open shelves. The reference collections are fully accessible to the public. Microfilm collections in some of our branches have been placed on the open floor for self-service. Nevertheless, we have also strategically placed our information desks to be in prominent view of the person walking in the door.

As information service is our first public service priority, our information desks are placed front and center readily identifiable by patrons as the place to go for assistance. Whether in person or by phone we accept and respond to all requests for information. The librarians staffing these information desks are the critical link between the patron needing assistance and the resources and services available to them.

Defining Information Service

What constitutes information service in Baltimore County? The following activities are performed by librarians at information desks in all full-service branches.

- Answering requests for specific/factual information
- Responding to subject requests
- Providing reader's advisory both for fiction and nonfiction materials to patrons of all ages
- Checking shelves for the availability of specific titles
- Checking the automated circulation system for systemwide ownership of titles
- Reserving materials for patrons
- Instructing patrons in the use of library resources, print and nonprint
- Referring patrons to outside agencies and/or organizations that can best respond to their need
- Providing information about library programs
- Distributing tickets and registering patrons for library programs
- Directing patrons within the building
- Distributing a variety of national, state, and local forms and applications

All of these activities take place either in person or over the telephone. Most of our libraries have one information desk from which we serve all patrons, adults and children alike. Each branch staffs its information desk according to the usage patterns of its community and the systemwide guidelines established as priority recommendations by the Managers of

Branches. Currently, all nonsupervisory librarians spend an average of at least 50 percent of their workweek on the desk. Supervisory staff are to average at least 35 percent of their time on the desk and Branch Managers 25 percent.

The information desk staff of the 16 full-service branches of the Baltimore County Public Library answer approximately 2 million requests for information annually. Of this total more than 800,000 are requests that are defined as true reference transactions according to the *PLA Output Measures for Public Libraries,* 2d edition. The highest proportion of these requests are for subject-related information.

The Management of Information Services in BCPL

The management of information service in the Baltimore County Public Library system reflects the team concept. The system Coordinator of Information Services works closely with the Administration, the Managers of Branches, and the Information and Programming Managers in developing and implementing information services.

The Coordinator keeps abreast of developing trends in the delivery of information service and recommends testing of new products for possible systemwide purchase. Vendor products and services are studied for their ability to increase the availability of information and make it more accessible to our staff and patrons. The identification and selection of new products require frequent communication with the Materials Management staff as they will ultimately need to fund new resources that are to be purchased. As new products and services are made available in the branches, the Marketing and Programming department works with the Coordinator of Information Services to create a means of promoting their use to the public.

Each month the Coordinator of Information Services meets with the Managers of Branches to keep them informed of current information issues and projects affecting branch operations. In addition, the Managers of Branches have an opportunity to ask questions and make suggestions. The need to provide fax machines in all full-service branches for improving patron access to information was a request made by the Managers of Branches. Building on the experience of six branches already connected by fax, each branch manager wanted this method of delivery expanded to be available in all full-service branches. Not only from an accessibility point of view but also from a materials point of view, this type of information delivery system would increase the return made on the library's investment in five subscriptions to Magazine Collection by making full-text periodical articles immediately available to patrons in all 16 full-service branches. In response to the strong case made for systemwide fax, the Coordinator of Information wrote an LSCA Title II grant requesting funds for technology enhancement that included a provision for money to buy the remaining 10 fax machines. The grant request was awarded.

The Information and Programming (I&P) Managers of branches meet bimonthly. The Coordinator of Information Services attends each meeting to learn of service issues of concern to all levels of branch staff and to introduce new ideas for the improvement of service. Information discussed in these meetings often leads to creating new or modifying existing approaches to public service. Discussions may focus on the analysis of the fluctuation of information statistics; training staff in the use of new resources both print and nonprint; clarification of policies such as fees, ILL procedures, etc.; and the best way to handle high demand for service during a time of decreased public service staff. Subcommittees may be formed to work on such issues. They are given a specific charge and a time frame in which to respond with recommendations. The concern about decreases in staff with a continuing public demand for service resulted in the creation of a subcommittee, comprised of two Branch I&P Managers and the Coordinator, charged with drafting information desk guidelines to be put in place during busy times. This document provided for limiting the quantity of selected services during extremely busy desk times. It was approved by the I&P Managers group as a whole, the Managers of Branches, and the Deputy Director.

The Information and Programming Managers are responsible for overseeing the delivery of information and programming services in the branches. They assess the information needs of the community and establish goals and objectives for meeting these needs within the framework of BCPL's Long Range Plan. They are responsible for supervising the training of staff in reference interview and communication behaviors, knowledge and use of tools, and branch and system policies and procedures relating to information services. I&P Managers oversee the organization of the information desk, scheduling of staff desk time, and they are directly responsible for monitoring and analyzing branch information statistics.

Information statistics are gathered using a sampling method. Each branch records statistics on 51 randomly selected sample days during the year. These days are determined annually by the Coordinator's office. Statistics are gathered on the same days in every branch for the total number of hours open. The statistics are sent in monthly to the Coordinator and the secretary inputs them into a systemwide template that manipulates the sampling data to reflect annual statistics. There are systemwide totals as well as totals for each branch. Reports are issued twice a year at six months and at the end of the fiscal year. Information statistics have been used in the past as a component to determine librarian staffing patterns by the personnel office.

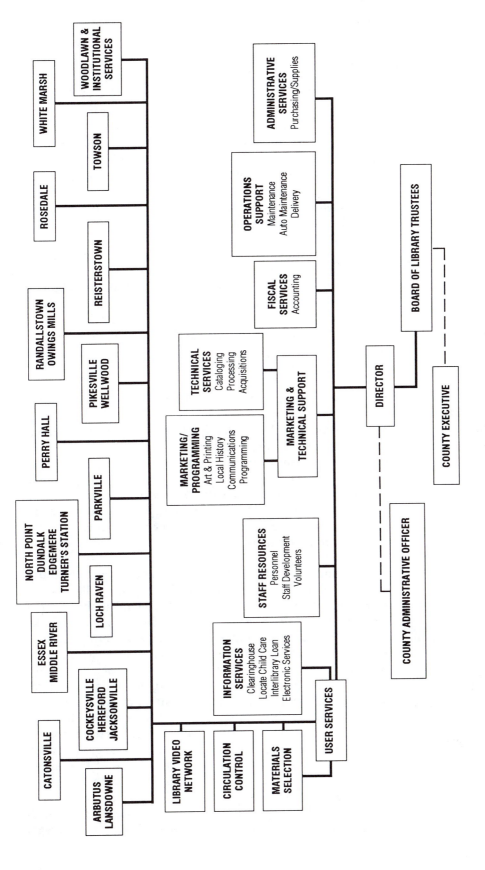

Baltimore County Public Library
Organization Chart

The Coordinator of Information Services and the I&P Managers use the statistics to determine what changes have occurred in type of service used by the public and why. Increases and decreases may indicate a change in community needs, a need for additional staff training, or a need for better promotion of services within the community. Using these statistics, for example, the Coordinator is able to see, on a systemwide basis, the effect introducing new technologies has on the amount of instruction required of the branch staff and the public in the use of tools and resources. These statistics always fluctuate. Once the public has learned to use a new resource and another has not been introduced in the next year, the "instruction" statistic usually will decline.

The above description of the management of information services within the organization of the Baltimore County Public Library system is a brief illustration of staff participation in decision making and teamwork. It serves to provide a sense of how all the parts of the system work together to deliver quality information service proportionate to the levels of public demand and use in Baltimore County.

Training Staff to Provide Quality Information Service

In order to provide quality information service that meets the identified need of the patron, the staff must be knowledgeable about collections and consistently utilize interpersonal communication skills that insure an effective reference interview. Every new BCPL librarian, with or without a master's degree, receives on-the-job training. In the case of paraprofessionals, formal classroom training is given in basic skills and resources, covering reference work and reader's advisory. Beyond the formal training, branch staff meet regularly for purpose of branch and systemwide communication about resources as well as system policy issues.

A standing agenda item at these branch meetings is the introduction of new reference materials added to the collection. In addition to reference materials, each staff member shares what they have read in keeping with a branch-developed personal reading plan that incorporates both fiction and nonfiction titles for all ages. This assists staff in broadening their reader's advisory skills.

In addition to branch-initiated collection discussions, the Staff Development specialist conducts a biennial training needs assessment and develops in-service training activities that also serve to expand staff knowledge of collections. The needs assessment process has resulted in several training packages designed as refreshers for staff who have the knowledge of specialized subject areas, but do not use the materials frequently enough to become expert with them. These self-administered packages cover such subjects as business/company information, small business information, census, Consumer Price Index, and legal

Quality information service takes constant training

materials. In-service training workshops are also offered. They might focus on reader's advisory and communication techniques to use with target population groups in helping them select materials.

There is a symbiotic relationship between the knowledge of collections and the direct provision of information service in libraries. Librarians cannot provide accurate information without having broad-based knowledge of the resources available to them. However, all the knowledge of resources in the world is useless if the librarian has not identified each patron's specific information need. That need is often not the one stated by the patron in his initial attempt to ask the librarian for assistance. Therefore, librarians working the information desk must utilize reference interview skills that will allow them to draw out the patron's real question.

In 1988 the Baltimore County Public Library embarked upon an extensive reference interview training program for all information desk staff, full-time and part-time. Using an adaption of the Maryland model developed by the staff of the Division of Library Development and Services (DLDS) of the Maryland State Department of Education, four BCPL trainers introduced the staff to the key model reference behaviors that directly affect their ability to accurately respond to patron requests for information. The trainers were the Coordinator of Information Services, the Staff Development Specialist, a Branch Manager with expertise in training and the then Chairperson of the Branch Information and Programming Managers group.

The full-day training session was extensive. It provided staff with the rationale for the system's decision to invest time in this training effort. We had documented system performance in reference accuracy from the previous two unobtrusive reference surveys of Maryland public libraries conducted by DLDS. The trainers had experienced, first hand, the training program developed by DLDS to improve the 55 percent rate of accuracy in the state. Using BCPL's survey data the trainers pinpointed specific areas for improvement in the staff's reference interview techniques. The findings were presented to the administration of the library system and they bought into the program as a means of improving the effectiveness and efficiency of the information service we provide to our patrons. The staff bought into it as well.

Our program outlined the stages of the reference interview and identified those behaviors that significantly affected each stage. Our staff was taught to always:

- *probe* the patron for more information by asking a series of open questions,
- *verify* the patron's specific question before beginning to search for the information by paraphrasing what they un-

derstood the patron to want and then asking the patron to confirm this understanding,

- *follow-up* with the patron after providing the information to make sure that it met the patron's need.

The training experience provided opportunities for staff to practice each of the behaviors within the workshop environment. Staff were introduced to the concepts of "technical feedback" and peer coaching. This form of feedback enables peers to observe one another in the real life performance of the behaviors and provide objective and specific reporting on the appropriateness of their use. At the conclusion of the full-day training session, staff were sent back to the branch with an assignment to team up and coach one another in the use of the behaviors as learned and practiced in the workshop. Each staff member provided technical feedback to his peer on the use of the behaviors during actual reference interviews with patrons who approached the information desk. Using technical feedback in combination with peer coaching placed the emphasis on staff's learning new or modifying existing behaviors rather than making them feel they were being judged or evaluated during observations.

Peer coaching continues in a variety of forms in BCPL. We have incorporated the key behaviors into the annual performance review for all information desk staff. Each staff member is observed by a supervisor twelve times over the course of a year to determine his appropriate use of the behaviors. To receive a "meets expectations" in this particular category of evaluation for information desk performance, the staff member must use the behaviors appropriately 80 percent of the time. After three years of coaching and system emphasis on reference communication skills, the majority of our staff are performing according to expectations.

Moreover, in the latest unobtrusive reference survey conducted by DLDS, BCPL improved its rate of accuracy by 6 percent. We continue to emphasize those behaviors that significantly affect the successful outcome of the reference interview. Currently we are planning a much less intensive refresher program that will focus on the need to *always verify* the patron's question before beginning to search for information. The results of the 1990 statewide unobtrusive reference survey indicated that *verifying* is the most powerful behavior a librarian can use to assure understanding the patron's specific need and, therefore, being able to respond accurately to it.

Accessing Information Service within the System

A staff knowledgeable in resources and trained in reference communication skills is one that provides quality reference service. However, several other components must be in place to insure a consistent level of service to our patrons. BCPL has clearly defined information services guidelines for the staff to follow. These guidelines are designed to be flexible and to encourage staff to use professional judgment in a variety of situations. Our guidelines do not set time limits for information transactions. We give the same attention to questions that come in by phone as we do to the individual who approaches the desk in person. Children are given the same degree of service as adults. Students' homework questions are given the same degree of consideration as those of the small business person. Our staff does not make recommendations of any kind nor do they offer interpretation of information given in response to an inquiry. They are encouraged to share their expertise and rely on each other's subject area strengths when responding to patron information requests. All information service is to be delivered in a manner that conveys the commitment of a staff dedicated to serve the public.

Using judgment based on such things as the availability of resources, immediacy of need, current demand for service at the desk, a staff member may go to great lengths to respond to a patron's request for information. It may involve making a long distance phone call to a nonlibrary organization. It may involve calling a local community college or university, with which we have an agreement, to check the availability of material and request its being sent to a branch for the patron to borrow.

Centralized Information Support Services

If the question is beyond the scope of that branch's collection and/or there is not enough time available for the librarian to devote to the patron's information need, the librarian is encouraged to refer the question to BCPL's Information Clearinghouse. The Clearinghouse is an office in the administration staffed by two and one-half paraprofessionals. Their role is to respond to those questions that cannot be answered in the branches for whatever reason. It is a service that is only accessible to librarians. Patrons may not call to institute a search for information. However, Clearinghouse staff respond directly to patrons with information requested. They also provide the staff member who initiated the request with the answer and the process they used to locate it.

The Clearinghouse makes use of a small ready reference collection, the resources of the area branch located in the same building, online database searching of DIALOG, and the Maryland Interlibrary Loan Organization (MILO) to answer the incoming requests. In addition they will call any organization anywhere in the world to get the information the patron needs. This office also serves as the information service for county government.

Clearinghouse also supports the branches by maintaining a large database of community information. The Community Information File (CIF) for Baltimore County contains detailed information on approximately 2600 agencies that represent local, state, and national services including government. Each record in the file is updated annually except for local government which

The public catalog also has a community information file

is updated semiannually. New agencies are added as we learn of them and those that cease operation or do not respond to our requests for updating are deleted. The Community Information File is made available to the public on our public access CD-ROM catalog that is updated quarterly. The patron searches for information either by agency name or subject heading. Hence, any patron can use the CIF feature of the catalog to locate information about an educational service, a self-help group, a department of county government, a health service, or a local club.

BCPL offers another form of Information and Referral (I&R) service to our public that is unique in public libraries. We operate LOCATE: Child Care, a centralized telephone I&R service that provides parents with information on the location of registered and licensed day care available in private homes and centers throughout Baltimore County. The service was established in response to a county task force report that indicated the need for a service that would assist parents in locating regulated child care in Baltimore County. The library was selected as the agency to best provide the service because of its well-established information role in the community and its neutral position in the mind of the community. In cooperation with the county's Office for Children and the Maryland Committee for Children, the library maintains an up-to-date database of registered home day-care providers and licensed day-care centers. Parents call the LOCATE number to obtain customized lists that match their needs with the services of available providers listed in the database. Limited lists of providers are given by counselors over the phone and more detailed lists are sent to the branch library most conveniently located to the patron's home or place of business for the information pickup.

The LOCATE staff also counsels parents on how to be informed consumers of child care. They network with provider associations, the state licensing authority, and the County Office of Children to insure the accuracy and quality of the service they provide. One highly trained paraprofessional and two well-trained part-time clerks handle an average of 400 calls per month.

The Role of Technology in Accessing Information

Approximately six years ago, the librarians of BCPL relied almost exclusively on print materials for responding to patron information needs. In 1985, the Coordinator of Information Services introduced online database access via EasyNet in seven branches. In 1986 BCPL's first CD-ROM database was made available to the public with the introduction of Information Access Company's *Magazine Index Plus* in one branch. The Clearinghouse has been searching DIALOG since the early 1980s.

Currently every full-service branch has a CD-ROM periodicals index with abstracts available to the public. Eleven branches have Grolier's *Electronic Encyclopedia* on CD available for public use. One full-service facility has a four station CD-ROM network for public use that makes EBSCO's *Magazine Article Summaries, the Electronic Encyclopedia, McGraw Hill's Science and Technical Reference Set, Facts on File*, and our own public catalog available to patrons. All online database searching has been centralized in the Clearinghouse, except for one area branch whose staff has been trained to use DIALOG to respond to its community's demand and need for current business information.

Technology is a means of improving and increasing access to available information. Just as the printing press revolutionized the availability of information to the masses, existing and emerging technologies are revolutionizing the library's ability to respond to patron information needs. Access to online and CD-ROM databases provides patrons with more comprehensive and relevant data that is more current and more readily accessible than anything found in print resources.

BCPL recognizes the efficiency and effectiveness of using technology to better meet the information needs of our users. That is why we have invested standing order materials money in subscriptions to these resources and have sought grants to fund the initial investment in hardware needed to run the software. However, there are other significant considerations that administrators need to recognize before jumping into the fast-moving technology bandwagon. These considerations also have an impact on staffing.

Training for Technology

Staff must be taught to use the technology. There is no product out there that is so simple to use that you just plug it in and walk away. Each product has its own search protocols. If you have mastered an IAC product, that knowledge does not translate to a UMI product or Grolier or EBSCO. General conceptual knowledge of Boolean operators, key word searching, and the importance of creating well-defined search strategies are not natural to most staff's approach to delivering information services. As an aside it should be noted that a strong foundation in effective reference interview skills as described earlier makes searching electronic resources easier as you have a clear idea of the patron's requirements. In our experience there is very little assistance offered from the vendors in training staff. We have depended upon or designated power users to learn the products and create training tools which are then shared with staff in the other branches. The staff must master each product made available for public use because someone needs to instruct the public in how to use it. Once taught the public usually does not require repeat assistance.

In addition to mastering the navigation of the information product itself, the staff must also develop knowledge and skills for trouble-shooting in case of hardware failure. If the equipment

Technology comes easily to the young

is leased from the product vendor, then there should be an effective vendor support service available to assist the staff with correcting hardware and software problems. Replacement equipment should be available and speedily delivered to minimize the downtime during the service. If equipment is owned and not leased, then there must be someone on staff, either in each branch or employed by the system, to quickly respond to and trouble-shoot hardware problems. They need to know operating systems and have access to spare parts or services for the repair of hard drive, CD-ROM drives, keyboards, cards, and so forth.

BCPL has the advantage of having staff in branches who are truly interested and challenged by technology. They are the power users who will experiment and take risks with equipment. It is the responsibility of the Information and Programming Manager in each branch to oversee the maintenance of electronic information products as well as the training of staff in their use. They may undertake this role themselves or delegate it to one of the power users. In addition, we employ a full-time staff member who trouble-shoots and does repair on all PC equipment owned by the system.

Selection of Products and Their Use by the Staff and Public

The electronic products that we have selected were chosen for their general interest focus that meets the needs of our users. We have identified products that are overtly intuitive in their search protocols so as to minimize the amount of time spent training staff and public. They either provide more information with greater frequency than their print equivalents or they provide the ability to quickly get at the greatest amount of information in the shortest time frame. For example, a CD-ROM version of an encyclopedia quickly gives the user all specific and related information on a subject by using one search strategy. A print search for the information would result in the patron consulting more than one volume to get the same information. This is also true of the periodicals indexes when compared to the multivolume print version of a *Reader's Guide*. We recognize that with nonnetworked CD-ROM products only one user can search the database at a time. That is why we have not dropped any of the corresponding print products. In all instances the cost of the print products is considerably less than the electronic version. Except for the network, we have devoted each workstation to a single product and do not have a variety of products available for patrons to switch and load.

Once trained in using the products, both the staff and public come to rely heavily upon them. Our most heavily used and popular products are the periodical indexes with abstracts and the general encyclopedias. Printers attached to these products make it easier for both staff and patrons to list the information they have identified as best meeting their needs. The periodical index products allow us to indicate which periodical titles are owned in that particular branch so patrons are aware of what to attempt to ask for first. The speed and ease with which patrons locate relevant periodical titles have resulted in their expecting the same speed and ease of retrieving the corresponding full-text articles. How do we respond to this new expectation of service?

Currently the systemwide response to quickly meeting the full-text periodical needs of our patrons involves a mix of "old" technology and "new" technology. Five area branches own IAC's microfilm based *Magazine Collection* and have reader/printer equipment from which to print the articles from the film cartridges. All branches have fax machines. We have established a network for the request and delivery of copies of articles found in Magazine Collection. The five area branches owning Magazine Collection have been designated as fax "hubs." Each of the community branches has been assigned to a hub for the purpose of requesting full-text articles found in electronic periodical index but not available in hard copy in the branch. They forward to the hub, by fax, the request with the corresponding Magazine Collection reel number. Circulation assistants at the hub take the request and process it returning the full-text copy via fax within thirty minutes of having received the request. We are also using fax transmission to fill subject requests received in community branches with smaller collections. The librarian faxes the subject request to a hub library. The request is given to a librarian who finds the information in an appropriate resource and faxes it back to the requesting branch, again within thirty minutes.

This is an appropriate place to mention fees. With the additional expense of using technology to provide improved access to information, we have imposed fees to help us offset the costs involved in the mechanics of provision. We are providing enhanced access services for the convenience of our public. Our patrons pay twenty-five cents per page for faxed information. We equate these fax fees with those of photocopying. Every branch has at least one pay copy machine (at twenty-five cents per page) that is regularly and heavily used by patrons.

Long-Range Planning for Technology

BCPL looks to increase the accessibility and availability of information for our users through a variety of existing and emerging technologies. We have tested and continue to explore full-text periodical CD-ROM products currently available in the market. We have not yet found one whose scope of coverage meets the nonscholarly information requested by the majority of our patrons. Also the hardware provided by the vendors of the products often does not withstand the heavy demand that our patrons place upon it. We are in the process of setting up another CD-ROM network in one of the area branches with products that will respond to the strong business and medical interests as well as the general needs of that community.

Unfortunately, microfilm has not yet been displaced by full text

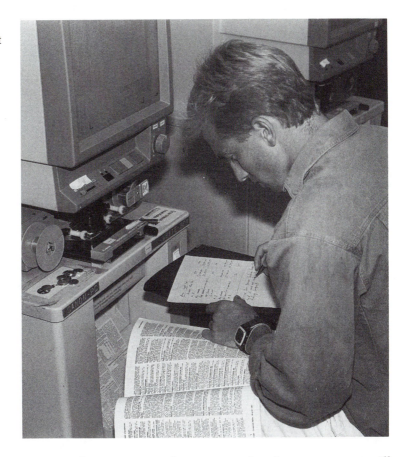

As we begin our next long-range planning process we will address technology as it relates to the future information role of public libraries. The information age will require public libraries to function as intermediaries for the public's access to information that will only be available in electronic formats over high speed local, regional, and national networks. We will have to address broader use of telecommunications for locating and delivering information to users in a physical location that will probably not be the library branch. Once the information is retrieved librarians will have to format it to make it useful to the patron.

How will BCPL make the resources found in our libraries more readily available to our users using technology? Are there advantages to having an online public access catalog with dial-up access by patrons? Will we maximize our investments in CD-ROM or tape databases by making them available via home computer access? What about the public that cannot afford the technology that will make delivery of information directly to one's home a standard mode of service? What plans do our neighboring library systems, public and academic, have to use technology as a means of increasing access to and availability of information? What plans does the State Library Network have for electronically connecting libraries throughout the state? Are there economies of scale to be realized if we join together in some technology ventures? Where do we get the funding to support the expensive costs of technology? Obviously, at this point in time, we have lots of questions. Our long-range planning process will provide us an opportunity to come up with the answers.

Accessing Information Outside the System

Our information service mission provides for access to information owned outside of BCPL collections. This access is made possible in two ways. First, BCPL participates in the Interlibrary Loan Network of Baltimore County (INBC). INBC is a product of informal agreements between colleges and universities, both public and private, located in Baltimore County to share their respective resources. Using the statewide union catalog of holdings of most libraries in Maryland, our patrons or staff locate materials, books, and periodicals, owned by the cooperating INBC libraries. Our librarians call these institutions directly and ask if the material is available for loan. If it is, it is sent directly to BCPL via our van delivery service and sent on to the requesting branch for patron pickup.

For materials not owned by these Baltimore County institutions or not currently available from them, we use the Maryland Interlibrary Loan network operated by the State Library Resource Center (SLRC). Our patrons can request any material found in Microcat, the statewide union catalog, or any material not found in the catalog for which there is bibliographic information. These requests are sent to our central interlibrary loan department (ILL). They use an online hookup to the statewide database to place requests complete with last date needed. Once placed on the network requests are searched in sequence of ownership by the owning libraries. The first library to fill the request sends it back to SLRC who sends it on to BCPL for delivery to the requesting branch for patron pickup. The patron is notified of its arrival by postcard. If instructed by our ILL department, SLRC will go outside the network using OCLC and ALA request forms for materials not owned by Maryland libraries.

In FY91 BCPL made 11,300 requests of the network. Total network requests made by public libraries numbered 75,000. We were number eight among requesting public libraries. BCPL filled a total of 7,300 requests made of public libraries on the network. The total number of requests filled by public libraries was 39,000. We ranked first among public libraries filling requests. Our materials management staff are identifying and purchasing materials that not only meet the needs of our patrons but also meet the information needs of people around the state.

Considering BCPL's limited Interlibrary Loan activity, the provision of resource sharing via a statewide ILL network is an expensive operation for BCPL to provide. Our total annual ILL activity represents less than .001 percent of our total annual circulation. Yet, we spend expensive personnel dollars for two full-time clerks and two part-time clerks to handle this workload. Much has been written about the failure of resource sharing in public libraries, but the decision to continue to provide Interlibrary Loan services in BCPL is based in the reality of politics and a strong foundation of supporting statewide cooperation among libraries in Maryland.

Summary

The provision of information services to the residents of Baltimore County is given a high priority by the Baltimore County Public Library system. Access to information is a crucial factor in fulfilling all of the library's identified roles: *Popular Materials Library, Reference Library, Preschoolers Door to Learning,* and *Formal Education Support Center.* Thus BCPL is committed to delivering information services of the highest quality. The administration has invested in materials, staff, training, special services, technology, and resource sharing to insure that, to the best of our ability, we completely answer our patrons' questions.

7

WHO WILL GIVE THEM WHAT THEY WANT?

From a personnel standpoint, BCPL lives in "the best of all possible worlds." Because we have an administrative Board of Library Trustees, we have been able to build and maintain our own independent personnel system. We can decide when to fill vacancies, and have the flexibility to move positions among programs. We can also create positions, however the county does not automatically fund them. We do not have a union. Although we try to parallel county personnel rules, we are free to implement our own policies and procedures. The impact this has had on our ability to provide service cannot be overstated.

Although we do not have a union, Baltimore County coattails the library on all union-negotiated health care contracts. Because we have a relatively small work force, it is cheaper to include us in county health care contracts than to negotiate separate library contracts. We are also included in the county's worker's compensation plan, and we can use the its legal counsel for any suits filed against us. We send our staff to the County's Health Clinic and Employee Assistance Program, and we have access to other services. We are very fortunate indeed to have all these services provided and to maintain our position of control.

BCPL has had the same Director and Deputy Director for twenty-eight years. Together they have nurtured a corporate philosophy that stresses communication, teamwork, trust, flexibility, and the importance of each staff member in moving the organization forward.

Robert Heinlein wrote:

A human being should be able to change a diaper, plan an invasion, butcher a hog, conn a ship, design a building, write a sonnet, balance accounts, build a wall, set a bone, comfort the dying, take orders, give orders, cooperate, act alone, solve equations, analyze a new problem, pitch manure, program a computer, cook a tasty meal, fight efficiently, die gallantly. Specialization is for insects.

BCPL operates on this principle and on the assumption that staff can successfully meet any challenge. Time and time again this has been affirmed. However, in order for staff to deal effectively with new challenges, the administration has had to provide goal clarity, protect the values of the organization, build trust, and empower staff. We strive to empower staff through training and staff development, ensuring that staff members share in the achievements of the library and have a sense of pride about what they do. We believe it is important to celebrate our accomplishments and to recognize staff for their individual efforts. We also believe that fun is a very necessary part of a successful workplace.

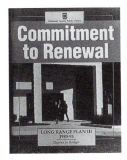

Long-range planning is essential for development of a common vision

Every year staff from libraries in the United States and abroad visit us. We also receive lots of requests for information about the way we run our library. These people generally perceive us as having initiated changes that improved both productivity and public service, and they want to know how we did it. We do it by involving staff at all levels in the decision-making process, encouraging their creative thinking, following through on their ideas, letting them know what we are doing and why, and making them accountable for their actions. Making this happen requires the need for constant communication among staff. While communication can be costly and time consuming, it is the key to innovation and good staff morale.

In preparation for our current long-range plan, *Commitment to Renewal*, the entire staff participated in a "Quality of Work Life" survey. We were very pleased with the results. Ninety-two percent of the staff rated work group cooperation favorably, 72 percent said that we had high productivity, 88 percent said the quality of our product was excellent, and 95 percent not only rated "impact on the community" favorably, but also were able to state our mission. The survey results throughout told us that the staff thought we were doing many things right. This is not to say that there weren't some areas that needed improvement, but it did affirm that we were heading in the right direction.

The Library Associate Training Program

In the early sixties, Baltimore County, then a small county in terms of population and wealth, began to experience tremendous growth. Beginning in 1962, we opened one new branch a year for the next eleven years. Rapid growth meant a need for additional librarians. In an effort to meet this need, we initiated an ambitious nationwide recruiting program. Recruiting was difficult because BCPL had no central library and sat next to the renowned and perceived as more desirable Pratt Library. The

Board of Library Trustees instituted a scholarship program that funded library school education for students who agreed to return to work at BCPL. However, we still were not able to find enough librarians to staff our branches.

Then we adopted a program that, while out of use in libraries at the time, had been tried by a number of libraries before the general adoption of the MLS qualification. We decided that if trained librarians weren't available, we would hire people who were eager to work in a library and train them ourselves. So, in 1962, the Library Associate Training Program (LATP) was started. Many of the students in the first class were already working for us in clerical positions. We used experienced librarians on our staff as the faculty. Both the students and the faculty approached this experiment with energy and enthusiasm, and it proved to be very successful. By the time the trainees completed the class they were well prepared to function as librarians. (Most stayed with us until they retired. Some of the 1962 graduates are still on the staff today.)

Since 1962, the program has expanded to include all library systems in the Central Maryland area. Currently it is administered by the Cooperating Libraries of Central Maryland (CLCM), under the auspices of the Maryland State Department of Education, Division of Library Development and Services, who pays for the program. A paid part-time coordinator, working in coop-

A graduating class of Library Associates

eration with an advisory board of representatives from each participating county, is responsible for setting up the schedule, assembling the faculty, and writing student evaluations.

The classes begin each fall and run for ten months (for a total of 75 hours of instruction). Students successfully completing the class get a certificate from the Maryland State Department of Education, which is recognized in every library system in the state. Classes are held in one of the branch meeting rooms of a participating system. Location rotates from year to year. The program has become so popular that CLCM often runs two classes per year, with approximately 30 students per class. The curriculum includes introduction to information and reference tools, reader's advisory for both children and adults, introduction to various fiction genres, programming skills, collection maintenance skills, and, in general, introduction to public library philosophy and theory. The classes are demanding. Students are given regular homework assignments, and they have to prepare programs and other presentations for the class.

The faculty consists of librarians from the participating systems. This approach provides the trainees with knowledgeable instructors who know exactly what is needed to give good public library service and provides the librarians on the faculty an opportunity to share and be recognized for their expertise. Being asked to teach an LA class is considered quite an honor. Because the faculty is already on the payroll, there are no additional costs involved in hiring instructors.

Who are the students? Most applicants are either long-standing, savvy library patrons, who are eager for the opportunity to work as librarians, or students who have worked as pages and have some familiarity with the library. All applicants must hold a bachelor's degree. Because these jobs are highly sought-after, library experience is to the applicant's advantage, but not required.

Trainees in Baltimore County are hired for full-time positions. They attend classes two days per week and receive on-the-job training the rest of the week. Each trainee is assigned a senior staff member who plans and oversees the in-branch training, supplements class training needs, helps solve problems, and prepares the trainee's six month and annual evaluation.

From its inception, the Library Associate Training Program ended all of our recruiting problems. We always have more highly motivated, qualified applicants than we can hire. We receive at least 100 applications per year and usually interview thirty to forty people for no more than ten positions. (Our annual hiring ranges from ten to zero depending on turnover and availability of funds.) Currently of our 152 full-time librarians, 93 are library associates. They have the same responsibilities as MLS librarians, that is they work on the information desk providing information and reader's advisory to patrons of all ages, maintain assigned areas of the collection, and plan and present programs for all age groups. They may even have some supervisory responsibilities such as coordinating volunteers. They also serve on branch and systemwide committees, and in that capacity, are involved in decision making throughout the system. Many are also active in the Maryland Library Association. The one job responsibility that differentiates library associate positions from those requiring an MLS is management. All MLS positions include management and/or administrative responsibilities.

Currently we have four library associate grades, including trainee. The pay ranges from $20,074 for a trainee (a one-year assignment) to $39,054 for a Library Associate III who has been on the staff for 25 years. By comparison, the entry level pay rate for an MLS position is $29,151 (all incumbents come with some library experience because all MLS positions include management responsibility) to $60,590 for an area branch manager with 25 years of service. (Many of our library associates eventually go to library school, then apply for management positions here or in neighboring counties.)

Involving more than one library system in the program not only allows all systems to share resources, but also gives the students an awareness of library operations beyond their own system, and an opportunity to begin networking with fellow librarians, adding to the already strong spirit of cooperation throughout the state.

Transfers

An important element in our ability to implement new approaches to work has been our policy of systemwide transfers. Since the early sixties, when staff were moved constantly to open new branches throughout the county, all librarians (including library associates) have been hired with the understanding that they are eligible for systemwide transfer at any time. We do not move librarians from day to day to work as substitutes; rather, we may assign them to one branch this year and another the next. We have found transfers to be immeasurably valuable in:

- Moving ideas around the system
- Maintaining good communication
- Fostering a sense of teamwork throughout the staff
- Helping staff to keep a systemwide perspective, thereby avoiding the development of territorial rights
- Capitalizing on individual strengths and minimizing weaknesses in putting branch teams together
- Developing management potential of staff members by moving them to branches of varying size and with different problems

Unfortunately, we did not initially require clerical staff to accept transfers. As a result the clerical departments became much more entrenched, more likely to do things the way they had always been done, and less likely to share in a systemwide common vision. Even though clerical managers met monthly to share problems and new ideas, they were not necessarily implementing these ideas. This lack of flexibility and resistance to change became very obvious as we put the branches online.

In 1977 we contracted with CLSI, then a fledgling company, to put our branches online over a 10-year period. We shake our heads today at some of our planning. First, we started with our busiest branch. Then, rather than train our own staff who knew about libraries, if not about computers, we brought in a staff funded by CETA (The Comprehensive Employment and Training Act, a federally funded jobs program). These were 13 people who knew nothing about libraries or computers, many of whom had very little work experience. In addition we had one manual with which to train these people. That was not the best way to put a branch online, and we learned our lesson. By the time the last branches went online, we had a highly developed training checklist, and we sent a very knowledgeable, organized, and highly respected clerical manager to each branch to oversee the training and ensure a successful conversion. Her visits revealed the territorial mind-set of many of our clerical departments. We decided that it was time to implement clerical transfers.

We began by dividing the system into four zones. All clerical staff hired or promoted after July 1, 1983, had to accept a transfer to any branch in the zone where they were hired. Then in July 1, 1986, we eliminated the zones and anyone hired or promoted thereafter had to accept a transfer to any branch in the system. Currently half of our clerical staff members are eligible for transfer, including most of our supervisory staff. Since we implemented transfers, the difference in the clerical operations has been remarkable. The clerical staff now think of themselves as part of a system and ideas are eagerly shared.

In the early days of BCPL's development, communication was fairly easy because the staff was relatively small, and people were moving from branch to branch frequently as new branches were being opened. However, as building slowed and the staff grew, we needed to develop other methods for staff and the administration to communicate.

Committees

Committees have proven to be an effective way to keep ideas flowing and staff communicating. In fact, they are critical to problem solving, and often provide an impetus for action. Even though it adds to everyone's workload, committee work is important because it gives staff the opportunity to:

- Get involved in decision making at a systemwide level
- Contribute ideas and solutions
- Develop and utilize new skills
- Meet and work with other staff members
- Get an occasional change of scenery

Over the years we have formed many committees to deal with specific concerns, and they have managed to find solutions to seemingly insurmountable problems. There is no question that without the committee system, we would never have been able to implement *central selection* or *generalism*. In both cases, the staff was told by the administration to figure out a way to put these programs into place.

Central Selection   In the early seventies, all librarians were responsible for selecting books, which meant traveling to the administrative offices every other week to buy books for their area of the collection—a very time-consuming and expensive process. The Director and Deputy Director thought the materials selection process could be done more efficiently. Bookstores with outlets throughout the country were doing central selection successfully, so they began to look at retail models.

At first the librarians were outraged at the thought of losing selection control. Book selection is, after all, one of the sacred

Visitors from Philadelphia help BCPL maintain an information network

cows of librarianship. They believed that only branch staff had the expertise and knowledge of the community necessary to correctly choose materials for the branch. A committee was formed to test out this long-held maxim. At the committee's suggestion, the branch staff began putting a hash mark in the back of each book as it went out, to see what really did circulate. After six months, librarians began to review the results of the hash mark experiment. They discovered that, in many cases, what they were sure the public was reading was, in fact, not what they were checking out. The librarians began to allow that perhaps selection could be done just as effectively, and more economically, by the central selection staff.

Next, the committee, which included the deputy director, members of the materials selection staff, some branch managers, and librarians from all other grades (including library associates) began to develop the formula buying system (see chapter 2 on "Materials Selection"). They also recommended the formation of an advisory committee to meet regularly with the materials selectors to discuss problems and suggest solutions, thereby keeping the branch staff somewhat involved in the buying process. The implementation of central selection meant that branch staff had more time to devote to the other side of collection maintenance, i.e., weeding and turnover. Librarians at the branch level were now concentrating on making the collection work harder.

Although central selection was initially criticized severely, it is now viewed as an efficient and effective way to buy materials. We are constantly responding to requests for information and hosting visitors who want to see how it works. Our staff is also frequently asked to speak to groups about the process. This positive feedback encourages the staff to continue creative thinking.

Generalism

Generalism is another example of a work method that we could never have implemented without the committee system. The staff was very distressed when they were told by the director (often referred to as a "benevolent dictator") and deputy director to begin planning the move toward generalism, which was an idea generated out of the need to distribute the librarian's workload more equitably and to make better use of staff. (Chapter 4 outlines our reasons for developing generalism and discusses its pros and cons.) Up to this time, the staff had been working as either children's or adult librarians. How could we get a staff member who had been working on the information desk for 25 years to agree to plan and present two-year-old story hours as part of his regular assignment? The task seemed insurmountable. In fact, the only way we could have broached the subject at all was because the staff trusted the administration, believed that someone would listen to their ideas and concerns, knew we had a record of successful innovation (central selection), and knew

TRAINING CHECKLIST
FOR
LIBRARIANS

Baltimore County Public Library
1986

Training manuals for
almost all activities
need constant
updating

that change was inevitable at BCPL. Still, the staff was not happy!

After it was announced that generalism *would* happen, the responsibility of figuring out how it would happen was turned over to the staff with the intelligent and caring guidance of the deputy director. Committees were formed to work out the details. They developed timetables and excellent training tools. One of the best results was a crossover training manual, *A Training Checklist for Librarians*, which is still in use today. It has been updated and is viewed as a valuable training tool for trainees and part-time librarians.

After the training tools and timetable were established, each librarian was given two years to complete the crossover training. Progress was included on all performance evaluations. Side benefits to crossover training were:

- It gave experienced staff an opportunity to share and be recognized for their knowledge, which boosted their morale and helped them get through their own training. (The fact that we had the library associate program in place also helped, because those folks, at least in their training year, had worked in both areas.)
- Excellent crossover tools, in addition to the crossover training notebook, were developed.
- It created a more even development of staff e.g., no longer was it perceived that the route to the top was through information or adult services.

Generalism has more equitably distributed the workload, allowed us to work with fewer librarians, and ended the need to look for the elusive children's specialist. It has been accused of diminishing our service to children; however, this is not the case. "Preschooler's door to learning" is one of our service roles as stated in our current long-range plan, *Commitment to Renewal*. We put a large amount of our book budget into easy books. Our summer reading program is tremendously successful—more than 21,000 children registered in 1991, and we continue to prepare quality story hours and family programming.

We know about the benefits of generalism now. It wasn't an easy transition, and we lost a few staff members over it, but we would never have been able to try it had our committee system not been in place. Staff involvement in the development of generalism was crucial to its success.

Other Committees

Committee work is just a part of doing business at BCPL. Some committees are ongoing such as MOB, a twice monthly meeting of our Branch Managers; MACO, a monthly meeting of Managers of Clerical Operations; and Administrative Council, a weekly meeting of administrative department heads. We also have ongoing advisory committees, i.e., Central Purchase–Print and CP–Nonprint.

We form committees to create products, such as Tale Spinners, charged with planning and presenting to each branch two major children's program productions a year; Summer Programming Committee, responsible for selecting a theme and developing support material for the annual children's summer reading program; and Annual Staff Day, charged with planning events for the day in October when we close the library and bring the entire staff together (Staff Day is discussed further in this chapter). We form ad hoc committees to deal with current needs; for example, the African-American Collection Interest Committee is charged with developing collections to meet the needs of the growing black population of Baltimore County. The Clerical Managers Sub-Committee met for two years to standardize branch and materials processing procedures. We also form committees to write grants. Every five years we form a Long-Range Plan Committee to write a new long-range plan. The plan itself calls for the formation of task forces to deal with specific goals or strategies. For example, *Commitment to Renewal* called for a visitor impact committee to meet with members of the community for ideas that would improve both the look of our branches and ease of access to library materials and services. The committee produced a list of ideas for every branch. One major result of this study was that we purchased completely new sign-making equipment and changed all branch signage.

Each year staff are given the opportunity to sign up for committee work. One of the most popular and most demanding committee assignments is the Newbery/Caldecott Roundtable. Modeled on ALA's Newbery and Caldecott award process, the committee members, using ALA guidelines, read and review a tremendous number of children's books in the course of a year. They compile annotated reading lists for BCPL librarians and then they choose the "best" book. This is done at a very exciting meeting just before ALA Midwinter so that our "picks" can be compared with ALA's. (This year we both chose the same Caldecott winner!) Finally they prepare and present a four-hour book discussion workshop. This extremely popular workshop is held twice to accommodate librarians not only from BCPL, but also from neighboring public and school libraries. A children's illustrator or author always gives the keynote address and stays to give a public presentation. Authors who have participated include Trina Shart Hyman, Jack Prelutsky, Ashley Bryan, and Tommie DePaola. The public program has grown so large that we now have to use a school auditorium to seat the crowd. We have also enlisted the help of a local bookstore, Greetings and Readings, which covers most of the cost of bringing in the speaker, handles all book sales, and manages the autograph sessions, a popular feature at these presentations.

In summary, there is no question that committees are time consuming and expensive, but their value as a tool to convey ideas, boost morale, empower staff, and effect change is immeasurable. The importance of committee work to the staff was reinforced to us in FY90 when we interviewed nearly all of our library associates for some promotional opportunities. Having some sense of the economic cutbacks we were going to face, we asked these staff members what cuts they would recommend to save money. With only one exception, the things they asked us *not* to cut were staff development and committee work. They said they would spend more time on the information desk, take more work home, or do whatever else was necessary to keep their committee assignments.

Staff Development

BCPL puts a great deal of emphasis on staff development. Committees are just one aspect of our staff development program. In FY81 we formed a task force to review our staff development needs. Out of that came a staff development process statement and our first needs assessment. Shortly thereafter, we reorganized the administrative offices (something we usually do every five years just to get a new perspective and to keep things interesting), which resulted in the creation of a staff development specialist position assigned to the department of human resources (a.k.a. personnel) whose job it was to oversee the needs assessments and, in conjunction with the staff development committee, provide opportunities to meet those needs. In FY83 we added the clerical staff to the needs assessment and our second long-range plan, *Growth without Expansion*, specifically mentioned staff development for staff at all levels as a goal.

Since 1983, we have spent one percent of our annual personnel budget on staff development, which includes the cost of planning and presenting in-house workshops, the staff development specialist's salary, and expenses for sending staff to workshops, conferences, and other staff development opportunities outside of BCPL.

The staff development committee meets quarterly to identify needs and plan up to six in-house activities per year. Training needs are identified via a needs assessment survey given to the entire staff every two years. The process involves meeting with representative groups from each grade level and area of responsibility to create a list of possible needs. This list is then sent to all full-time and part-time staff who rate each item on the list from "need immediately" to "don't need at all." With this information, the staff development committee determines priorities and begins to plan activities. The staff development specialist looks for individual opportunities that may not be a priority across the board, but may be extremely important to one staff member or a small group of staff members. The staff development committee, also helps prepare and update training tools, and drawing on staff expertise, develops self-help training packages. These "Beyond the Basics" packages are geared to help staff improve their reference skills in specific areas, such as business services.

In order to reach as many staff members as possible, in-service workshops are usually offered twice at two different locations, although some programs, such as the Myers-Briggs Workshop, had to be repeated many times over a few years to reach all staff who wanted to participate. Staff are required to evaluate staff development activities in which they participate. Some of the most successful activities, not only in terms of the presentation and enthusiasm of the participants, but also in terms of overall improvements to our operation have been: *The One Minute Manager*, presented by members of the staff using the Blanchard videos and workbook, which improved the communication between supervisors and staff; *Myers-Briggs*, presented by a consultant, which greatly improved our understanding of, and ability to work with coworkers; *Put It In Writing*, an eight-week video/workbook program presented by the staff development specialist and another member of the staff development committee, which improved the writing skills of all participating staff members; and the *Excellent Librarian Program*, presented by June Garcia, Deputy Director, Phoenix Public Library, which resulted in our librarians adopting an annual personal reading plan that has broadened their reader's advisory skills and added to a personal sense of achievement.

Some staff development workshops are optional, others are required. For example, the STAR behaviors program, designed by the coordinator of information services, the staff development specialist, and two other staff members and based on a model designed by the Division of Library Development and Services of the Maryland State Department of Education to improve reference service, is mandatory for all full-time and part-time librarians (see chapter 6 for additional information). A two-part performance evaluation preparation workshop is also required of all staff involved in writing performance evaluations. Recently, members of the staff development committee, as part of a statewide committee, developed a customer service training program that all new staff will be required to attend. A record is kept in Personnel for each staff member of all activities attended.

Part of the staff development budget is used to pay ALA and MLA (Maryland Library Association) membership dues for all MLS librarians, and MLA dues for library associates. Involvement in library associations deepens staff's commitment to BCPL and to excellent library service. It offers many of the same benefits as committee work, introduces staff to different perspectives, and broadens their knowledge of librarianship.

In addition to committees and workshops, another way in which we empowered our clerical staff was to reclassify the clerical supervisors to higher grades and change their job title to Clerical Services Manager. This not only gave them recognition for doing an important job, but also let them know that we expected them to play an active role in the management of the branch, and to get involved in systemwide decision making.

Staff Recognition

Staff Day

Each year we close one day in the fall to bring the staff together for a half-day program devoted to activities that recognize and celebrate accomplishments of the staff and the library over the past year, and give the staff a chance to see old and new friends.

The day's activities begin with the director summarizing the highlights of the year, thanking staff for their achievements and giving them his assessment, good news and bad, of what we will face in the new year. That is followed by a short address from the County Executive and the Board President.

The names of all staff receiving service awards are read. This is followed by the highlight of Staff Day, the Staff Merit Awards. Each year the Board of Library Trustees approves the giving of three $500 awards to staff who have been judged by their peers as having made an exceptional contribution to BCPL. The specific criteria are:

- Personal involvement and dedication as demonstrated by helpfulness, loyalty, and concern for the best interest of the library and its users
- Demonstrated consistent superior achievement and performance

A Staff Merit Award Committee is formed each year to call for nominations, select award winners, write commendations on each, and submit them to the administration for final approval. The award recipients are not notified in advance. In fact, except for the committee and the administration, no one knows who the winners are until Staff Day. The staff eagerly await this emotion-packed event of the day, and quite often as the winners walk to the stage, there isn't a dry eye in the house! In addition to the $500 check, the merit award winners get an engraved desk set and their names are engraved on a perpetual plaque in the board room.

The merit award presentation is followed by a skit produced by the staff, spoofing events of the past year and the administration. The tremendous creative talent of the staff always combines for a very funny, stress-relieving skit. Over the years the staff has spoofed everything from central selection to no smoking policies—very cathartic! The director has, for the last several years, been played with great hilarity by one of our delivery drivers. The skit is followed by a brunch, allowing staff to meet and greet one another, and congratulate the Merit Award winners.

The Staff Association then recaps the activities of the past year, announces the results of the United Way Campaign, and conducts the United Way drawing, a lottery for all staff who participated in the campaign by giving $26 or more. The Staff Association generously supports this activity. Last year they gave the winner a limousine ride to a five-star restaurant and a $100 gift certificate towards the cost of the meal. A measure of the generosity of our staff is shown in this campaign. Last year, even though staff were on a ten-day furlough, and we had less staff than the year before, the staff increased its United Way contribution by nine percent for a total of $25,000.

The Staff Association presentation is followed by a zany video presentation, a product of the mega-talented Library Video Network staff. Last on the agenda is a guest speaker. Most recently Michael Blake talked to us about his experiences that led to writing *Dances with Wolves*.

People question us, especially in times of funding cutbacks, is Staff Day worth the time and the money? We have asked ourselves and the staff this question many times, and the answer is always yes. Yes, because it gives the administration the chance to address the staff and to thank them for doing an excellent job. It brings the staff together (quite an impressive sight!), gives us an opportunity to celebrate our achievements, and reminds us that we're working together for a public good. Especially in these tough economic times, we need to make opportunities to affirm the good work we do.

A monthly newsletter focuses on accomplishments of the staff

Service Awards

Service awards are given in five-year increments, and range from an engraved key chain for five years of part-time service to a $300 gift of the staff member's choice for thirty years of service. Each year we invite staff to a Service Awards brunch. A board member always attends to thank the staff and present the awards. The staff seem very appreciative of this recognition.

"Branching Out"

"Branching Out" is an upbeat, photo-filled monthly staff newsletter, published by the marketing and programming department with help from a staff committee, which focuses on the accomplishments of the staff. It highlights individual staff members, gives Staff Association news, reports on board meetings, and includes a classified section and other features that keep the communication among staff flowing.

Other Opportunities for Staff Recognition

At each monthly meeting of the Board of Library Trustees we invite a staff member to give a "staff report." The report could be on any facet of our operation, from vehicle maintenance to introduction of the annual summer reading program theme. The board members are very appreciative of these reports. It keeps them informed about staff activities, and gives them an opportunity to meet members of the staff and experience their dedication and enthusiasm. And, although staff get nervous at the thought of addressing the board, they would generally agree that it is worth the preparation and anxiety. They get to meet the board members, talk about what they do well, and be recognized for a job well done. It is always a pleasure to listen to these staff reports.

Members of our staff have been asked to speak to other groups and we encourage them to do so, because it provides them with another opportunity to share and be recognized for their expertise. The Hawaii Library Association recently invited our coordinator of materials management to speak at their annual conference with all expenses paid. We are very pleased to see our staff get opportunities like that!

Hosting Visitors

Each year we get a number of visitors from libraries in the U.S. and abroad. Although spending time with visitors is time consuming, we always welcome them, because it has been our experience that the visitors are impressed with what they see and convey their enthusiasm to the staff. This boosts the staff's morale. It gives them another opportunity to talk about and be recognized for what they do well.

Visiting Other Libraries

Visiting other libraries can also boost the morale of the staff. There is a sense of pride in being asked by the administration to visit another library. It gives staff an opportunity to pick up new ideas and share experiences with staff from other systems. They come back willing to try new ideas and approaches. For example, when June Garcia came to BCPL to present the Excellent Librarian workshops, our staff was amazed to discover how few staff members Phoenix Public Library had in relation to BCPL. They wanted to find out how Phoenix was able to provide service, so we sent six staff members to Phoenix for a week, and they came back convinced that we could run a library with less staff. Of course it would mean a diminution of service, but it could be done. They presented their report to several management groups and the Board of Library Trustees. (Their visit could not have been more perfectly timed, occurring immediately before the economic downturn that has resulted in a job freeze and a loss of positions.) Also, fortunately, staff come home feeling pretty good about working at BCPL.

Hiring Staff

For the most part, full-time vacancies are advertised and filled as they become available. The two exceptions are the library associates and entry-level branch clerical staff. As discussed earlier in this chapter, library associates have to go through a ten-month training period that begins in the fall. This means that we sometimes have to hire trainees in anticipation of future vacancies, so they will be trained where vacancies occur.

These staff members learned much from their visit to Phoenix, Arizona

The classification in which we have the most staff is entry level branch clerical staff. Rather than repeat the interviewing process every time there is a vacancy, we interview for these positions at the beginning of the fiscal year and establish an eligibility list from which vacancies are filled throughout the year.

Each branch does its own part-time hiring. To help them in this effort, and to ensure that established personnel procedures are being followed, we developed a step-by-step *Circulation Assistant Supervisor's Manual* that includes: what to look for on an application, how to set up an interview, sample interview questions, procedures for notifying applicants, sample completed personnel forms necessary to get the new staff member on the payroll, an orientation checklist, and a training checklist, which covers shelving through check-in procedures. The *Circulation Assistant Supervisor's Manual* assists part-time supervisors in hiring and training staff. We have similar manuals for hiring part-time librarians and volunteers.

Training Manuals

We try to develop training manuals for as many procedures as possible. In addition to the training checklist for new librarians, and the manuals for hiring part-time staff, a committee regularly updates a CLSI procedures manual, and the information desk manual. We have an orientation video and manual and, a customer service video and manual, and an emergency procedures manual. We also have a permits and licenses manual developed by one of our staff members at the time that we agreed to handle simple permits and licenses at the circulation desk, in cooperation with the county department of permits and licenses.

Part-time Supervisors

Our part-time work force is considerably larger than our full-time work force, and the turnover rate for part-time staff is just less than 50 percent (which we expect in a work force of primarily students). We found that we did not have the full-time work force necessary to effectively train, supervise, plan work assignments, and evaluate this important work-force; therefore we made some of our part-time staff supervisors. A part-time supervisor, Circulation Assistant II, is paid at a higher rate than a Circulation Assistant I. Currently the CA II pay ranges from $6.45 to $7.83 per hour. All branches have at least one CA II, and usually keep a ratio of one CA II for every 15 part-time staff members. In addition to hiring and training part-time staff members, the CA II also plans and assigns work, does required time studies, and motivates and evaluates staff. All of the CA IIs meet twice a year to share ideas, of which they have many. Several are computer whiz kids who have come up with scheduling templates and other work simplification measures. Others have started very creative branch newsletters for their CAs.

Monitoring Productivity and Staff Performance

We have talked in general about the ways in which we encourage staff, but how do we specifically develop and monitor staff performance? One of the key workload measures used in our branches is required times. Each branch has established required times for shelving based on their floor plan, shelving procedures, etc. All CAs are hired with the understanding that once they are trained, they must shelve within the required times. Shelvers are timed at least six times per year, in addition to filling in a daily log of work completed. Staff members who cannot shelve accurately within the required times are counseled and given a certain amount of time to improve. Failure to improve within a specified period of time will result in termination of employment.

Required times are an indispensable tool in helping us plan our workload and staffing needs, and in helping us to fairly evaluate the work of each CA. The required times method of monitoring shelving is one of a number of workload measures in place throughout the system. It is more difficult to establish workload measures for librarians; however, the STAR behaviors discussed in chapter 4 require specific behaviors of information desk staff that have resulted in improved information service.

Sick leave use of all full-time staff is also monitored. In the early eighties we compared our sick leave use to the national average and found that our use was high, so we developed an awareness campaign that was presented to the entire staff. We produced a video that dramatized the impact sick leave use has on the staff that do come to work, and emphasized the fact that sick leave should be viewed as an insurance policy, rather than something to be used to get an occasional rainy Monday off. In addition we required that a comment about the nature of the use be included in the performance evaluation of any staff member who used more than 56 hours—then the national average. The awareness campaign worked. The sick leave use at one of our busiest branches dropped to an average of 24 hours per staff member. Overall, the usage, with maternity leave included, dropped well below the national average. Now supervisors add a comment on the performance evaluation to commend a staff member for using very little sick leave.

Performance Evaluations

Each staff member gets a performance evaluation at the six-month period of employment and annually thereafter. We use a long form for the first six evaluations and a short form for subsequent evaluations. Performance evaluation forms are on a computer template and are generated at each branch based on a list sent from the Personnel Office. As stated earlier, all staff involved in writing performance evaluations, including CA IIs, are required to attend a performance evaluation workshop. In instructing staff to write performance evaluations we stress the importance of:

- Developing of a list of behaviors expected from staff members, and basing all performance evaluations on these behaviors
- Training staff so that they can do the job
- Monitoring performance early to make sure the staff member is not learning the wrong way to do the job
- Using verbal counseling forms as a first step to identifying behaviors that need to be improved
- Using commendation forms to recognize staff effort for a job especially well done
- Backing with specific examples all areas listed as "needs improvement" or "exceeds expectations"
- Writing all counseling forms and performance evaluations, clearly, concisely, and without spelling or grammatical errors
- Including areas for future development

By stressing these points and emphasizing to staff the importance of performance evaluations as documentation for personnel action ranging from granting of increments and promotions to terminations, we have put into place a very reliable performance evaluation system. Because our performance evaluations are well documented, we have been able to successfully defend our personnel actions both to the Board of Library Trustees and to outside agencies such as EEOC.

Staffing Patterns   Branch staffing allotment is determined each year by applying the available number of FTEs to a formula, based primarily on circulation for clerical staff, and information workload for librarians. The formulas have some drawbacks in that they cannot recognize maximum or minimum staffing needs. Also, as our personnel funding continues to get slashed and all branches reach a minimum staffing level, the formulas' usefulness diminishes. Still, they do give us a workload comparison among branches. Currently we have a productivity committee which is studying staffing patterns and looking at workload and productivity measures to determine how best to use our shrinking personnel dollars. The productivity committee is also experimenting with the "teamwork" concept of management in two branches. This could result in a restructuring of our organization chart and a change in our staffing pattern. We are also investigating new information technology and its potential impact on staffing patterns and service provision.

Volunteers   In addition to our 800 paid staff members, BCPL has 560 volunteers—325 work year-round and an additional 235 students help with our Summer Reading Program. Our volunteers work approximately 45,000 hours per year, giving us an additional 21.5 FTEs a year. We also place community arbitration volunteers in each branch.

Volunteers are involved in many aspects of the work we do, from shelving materials to sorting paychecks, and from working on the circulation desk to maintaining local history collections. Currently we have four minilibraries that are run primarily with volunteers (one paid staff member coordinates the schedule and trains the staff at each mini). These volunteers are trained on our computer checkout system, and can offer registration and circulation services, provide reader's advisory, direct patrons to specific areas in the collection, and shelve materials. One of the minis staffed by volunteers does an annual circulation of more than 200,000.

Volunteers work not only at minilibraries but also with paid staff in the other branches. Our busiest branch, circulating a million and a half items per year, has 30 volunteers who work on the circulation desk, shelve, shelfread, and mend. With their current staffing, it would be nearly impossible for Cockeysville to handle its current level of business without the help of volunteers. (Even so, it is not unusual for patrons to be lined up twenty deep at checkout at peak circulation periods!)

Volunteers become experts at all kinds of tasks

Each branch has a staff member in charge of volunteer activities who recruits, interviews, and hires volunteers, plans work assignments, and ensures that they are treated as members of the staff. The staff member makes sure the volunteers are doing work that is meaningful to them and is a help, not a hindrance to the rest of the staff. Volunteer recognition activities at the branch are planned by this staff member.

All volunteer record keeping is done centrally by the volunteer coordinator in the Personnel Office. At the end of the year she sends a letter to each volunteer giving total number of hours worked and number of trips made to the library. The trips are tax deductible.

The volunteer coordinator also coordinates systemwide volunteer recognition activities, and is a member of a statewide committee of volunteer coordinators who, in addition to sharing problems and ideas, plans a statewide recognition day for library volunteers.

Volunteer Recognition

We spend, by some libraries' standards, a lot of money on volunteer recognition, but it is a miniscule amount when compared to the value of our volunteers. Even at our lowest per hour pay rate, the cost of the hours the volunteers give us would be more than $200,000. To express our appreciation, every year we give each branch $10 per volunteer to use toward a volunteer celebration. (Previously we held one large reception for all of our volunteers; however, they seem to prefer having individual celebrations at their home branch.)

In addition, we give volunteers a silver bowl when they reach 1,000 hours of service, a letter opener and their name engraved on the "full-time club" plaque when they reach 2,000 hours, and pewter bookends when they reach 3,000 hours. Many of our volunteers have been with us more than 10 years and 38 have worked more than two thousand hours.

Staff Association

As stated earlier, BCPL does not have a union, but we do have a Staff Association. All staff members are eligible to join the Staff Association except the director, deputy director, and assistant director. Dues are $2.00 per year. The Staff Association Board of Governors consists of an elected representative from each branch, two elected representatives from the administrative offices, and four elected officers. The president of the Staff Association attends the monthly Board of Library Trustees meetings and reports back to the Staff Association representatives who also meet monthly. The Staff Association representatives are given time and mileage to attend meetings.

The Staff Association handles staff grievances through its Staff Relations Coordinating Committee, whose members are also elected by the general membership. SRCC provides staff with a vehicle for submitting grievances without having to identify themselves to the administration. When a grievance is received, SRCC reviews it and decides whether or not to take it to the administration. If so, the name of the staff member(s) submitting the grievance is never known to the administration. The administration responds only to SRCC, who, in turn, reports to the Board of Governors of the Staff Association. This system has been in place for more than 20 years and works very well, both from the members' and the administration's point of view. The Staff Association also has a sick leave bank, offers emergency and a scholarship funds, runs the annual United Way campaign and other events for charity, participates in the Red Cross Blood Program, and plans social activities for the staff.

In Summary

The key to BCPL's success rests with its staff and the energy and ideas they generate. It is our job to give staff the opportunity for skills development through training; to create vehicles for understanding and idea sharing such as committee work, teamwork and transfers; to provide direction; to provide recognition programs; and to make staff accountable through a performance measurement system. By tapping into the staff's energy, encouraging them in their efforts, and listening to their concerns, we have been able to weather some very difficult times (a ten-day furlough in FY92), to put creative projects into place, and to continue to offer progressive library service.

Staff Statistics

Baltimore County Public Library has 511.5 FTE in staffing which include 361 full-time staff and approximately 450 part-time staff working the remaining 150.5 FTEs. (The number of part-time staff fluctuates depending on the number of hours assigned to each staff member.) The following organization chart shows position distribution.

In FY92, BCPL's personnel budget was $12,432,897, or 58% of the total budget. Figures 7-1 and 7-2 show how the personnel budget is used.

Benefits

Benefits for full-time staff are:

- Four weeks of vacation from the first year of employment with the addition of two and one half days after eight years and an additional two and one half days after 12 years of service
- Three weeks of sick leave per year which can be accumulated and converted into retirement credit. (However, sick

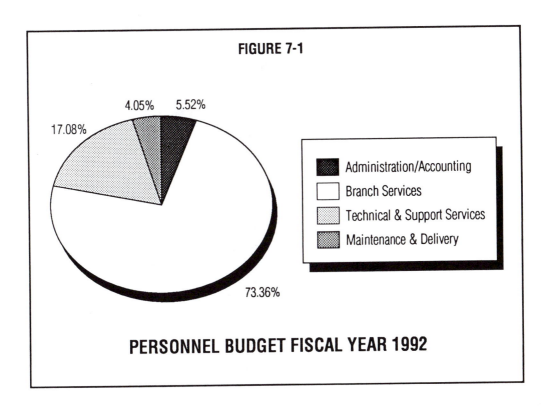

FIGURE 7-1

4.05%   5.52%

17.08%

- Administration/Accounting
- Branch Services
- Technical & Support Services
- Maintenance & Delivery

73.36%

PERSONNEL BUDGET FISCAL YEAR 1992

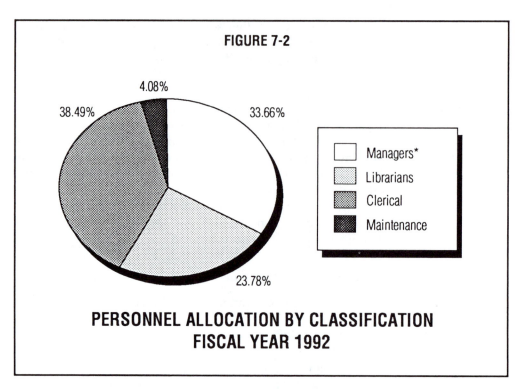

FIGURE 7-2

38.49%   4.08%   33.66%

Managers*
Librarians
Clerical
Maintenance

23.78%

**PERSONNEL ALLOCATION BY CLASSIFICATION
FISCAL YEAR 1992**

* Includes staff with both management and other responsibilities.

leave use is carefully monitored as discussed earlier in this chapter.)

- Maternity/Adoptive/Paternity leave plan which allows staff to use up to six weeks of sick leave after the arrival of the child, and up to six months of total leave
- An open-ended family leave plan that allows staff to use sick leave to care for family members
- Seven personal leave days (some of these days are in lieu of holidays when the county/state is closed and the library is open)
- Up to nine paid holidays (in response to midyear budget cuts, three of these paid holidays were converted into leave without pay in FY92)
- Membership in either the state or county retirement system
- Opportunity to enroll in the Staff Association's sick leave bank
- Opportunity to enroll in one of eight health care plans as well as vision, dental, and prescription plans, with at least 80 percent of the premium paid by the library. Family members are included in all plans. (We, like the rest of the nation, are struggling with rising health care costs. In FY92 our health care costs will be $2,000,000.)

- Opportunity to enroll in a group term life insurance plan with 80 percent of the premium paid by the library
- Worker's Compensation coverage
- Deferred Compensation Plan
- Credit Union
- Dependent Care/Health Care pretax accounts
- Red Cross Blood Assurance Plan

Part-time staff members get no paid benefits (except for a few salaried part-time staff members who get prorated vacation and sick leave and can join the retirement system.)

8 *THE BUILDINGS THEY WANT*

BCPL's *Give 'Em What They Want* philosophy could be subtitled "in as small a space to heat and cool as is practical." We have always been careful to maximize every square foot of space partially because our operating funds are actually a grant in aid from the appropriating authorities and we pay all of our own bills including utility bills. An analysis of FY91 circulation showed that BCPL branches circulated 41 items for every square foot of branch space, the total branch square feet being 302,900.

Still a relatively young library system, BCPL has no Carnegie-style buildings. Our branches come in a range of sizes as described in chapter 4. Of the thirteen buildings constructed before 1977, only two are one-level buildings. Most were designed to fit the site and public elevators were not included in the design. The interiors were designed with wings for adult and children's services separated by the circulation services desk. Even during the early years spaces within the building's interior were designed as open areas. This type of arrangement made it relatively easy to convert the interior layouts to coincide with the system's gradual shift from age-level service wings to a picture book/fiction wing and an integrated nonfiction wing.

The Setting

While there have been clusters of people living in Baltimore County since the 1800s, Baltimore County as a large urban/suburban metropolitan jurisdiction is only 25 years old. The county surrounds the city geographically, and the citizens rely on and contribute financially to city-based cultural institutions and recreational centers. Perhaps this is why Baltimore County citizens have not felt compelled to create architectural edifices to house their public services. The citizens as a whole are very practical people who want their public buildings to be accessible with good parking. With today's fast-paced lifestyle, they expect to come to the library, browse or find a specific item quickly, and then leave to do something else. BCPL's service philosophy accommodates this lifestyle, and our buildings, most of which look more like retail stores or warehouses than libraries, are arranged to support this service philosophy.

All library facilities are either owned by or leased by Baltimore County government. They are under the care of the Board of Library Trustees. Whether a full-service branch is owned or leased is due largely to the local economic conditions at the time the building is in the planning stage. If the county is willing to support building construction and furnishing through the sale of bonds, then the land and building are paid for using capital funds. If, however, the county is trying to reduce its indebtedness, the building is built to library specifications and then leased by the library. Funds for leased facilities are appropriated in the library's operating budget. This works well until operating funds are reduced because of an economic downturn. Then the library is constrained in its ability to reallocate appropriated funds to materials and service because of the lease money that must be paid. The best long-term solution, other than up-front purchase, is proving to be a lease purchase agreement at the time the contract is being negotiated.

Leasing a facility is a surefire strategy for testing the true versus the perceived need for library service in a community. Three of our minilibraries are rented storefronts in small strip malls. The anchor store in each of these is a large grocery store. The average lease for each minilibrary is 10 years with five-year renewable options. Minilibraries average 2,000 square feet, making a lease much more cost effective than constructing, maintaining, and staffing a larger and possibly unwarranted facility. While the minilibrary will draw shoppers to the strip mall, the level of traffic in and out of the shopping center is a clear indicator of how successful the minilibrary will be. If shops in the shopping center are not well patronized the minilibrary will be underused. In 1989 we moved a minilibrary into a shopping center 1.3 miles south of its previous location. The circulation increased 20 percent from 39,761 to 47,888 in the first six months after the move as compared with the same six months the year before.

BCPL's branch location plan was developed originally by Lowell Martin in 1957. Most of the branches ring the beltway that loops through the lower half of the county. Branch locations correspond to the population centers. In an effort to contain the governmental costs associated with provision of services in new locations, the county has designated two areas of the county as growth areas that will be supported with governmental services. These areas are called town centers. BCPL's newest branch, White Marsh, is located in one of the town centers. In 1991, the Board of Library Trustees removed plans for a library in the second town center from the capital budget request, pending assur-

Lowell Martin's 1958 report—the first BCPL plan

ance from county government that sufficient operating funds would be appropriated annually to maintain an adequate level of service without draining resources away from existing facilities.

Criteria

Ease of access and "elephant tracks", i.e. personal habits, are two of the criteria we have identified as key to a successful facility. Some users are drawn to our larger facilities because they perceive a larger collection as being better able to serve them. Other users are motivated by convenience and will use the branch closest to the stores where they shop. As an example of the convenience factor: the Loch Raven Branch is a 13,000 square-foot building with ample parking (see chapter 4 for specific statistics). The collection and the service desks are housed in 6,000 square feet. The branch circulated 653,797 items in FY91, resulting in a circulation per square foot of public service space of 109 a year. This is not to say that the square feet at Loch Raven is adequate. It simply indicates that size is not an indication of success. Parking (preferably free) is a key ingredient, but users will pay to park if they perceive the cost of the parking to be worth the ability to find the materials for which they are looking.

Since the late 1970s BCPL has studied retail store design, particularly store layout and merchandising strategies. Our expectation is that users will come to and leave each facility in a relatively short period of time. Public service areas are crowded with shelving, book displays, and users. It is not unusual on a busy morning in a community branch for the picture book/fiction wing to be filled with an equal number of users over 65 years old, and preschoolers under age five with their mothers. The challenge is to design a layout that gives each group a sense of their own space so that neither intrudes upon the other.

Branches are furnished with standard commercial grade furniture, usually purchased at "metro contract" prices. Metro contract is a term used to refer to prices agreed upon in a contract between a local jurisdiction in the metropolitan area and a vendor. If chairs are upholstered they are purchased in a vinyl upholstery. We look for furniture that is durable, easy to clean, and comfortable enough to sit in for an hour or less. The furnishings, walls and carpets, are generally neutral and are considered to be background for the colorfully displayed library materials. The picture book areas are the exception to the rule. (As we renovate our older branches, rejuvenating the picture book areas with colorful laminated shelving, creative graphics, and special furniture is a priority.)

When planning a new facility or remodeling an existing building, we place the return/circulation services desk close to the most used entrance so users can free themselves of returned items as quickly as possible. Each full-service branch has one

In new BCPL branches, all shelving can house books face-out or spine-out

information services desk located within easy sight from the entrance.

Layout

All branch layouts encourage users to browse through the collections. Branches have experimented with a variety of collection layouts looking for the perfect traffic pattern that will take users through the general collection as they head for their special area of interest such as new books, videos, or magazines. Special subject and seasonal displays are deliberately placed near checkout stations to encourage users to borrow a few more items.

Collections are allocated space in a branch based on the amount of circulation or level of reference use each collection contributes to the overall circulation and use of the materials. In order to tighten collection security, audiocassettes, compact discs, videotapes, and books on cassette are housed together in one location. This section, labeled AUDIO-VIDEO, is also a high noise area because of the number of users who congregate there.

Generally fiction collections for all ages are placed in one wing or public service section. The fiction collections are separated into picture books, juvenile fiction, young adult, and adult fiction. There are also subcategories within collections such as *I Can*

Reads or "Science Fiction." Each picture book area is easily identified by the large wall-mounted graphic of picture book characters created by the art department. If the fiction collection is in an actual wing, a small service desk is included in the layout. This desk, called the Reader's Advisory Desk, may simply be a single or double pedestal office desk.

Shelving

In the last ten years we have moved almost exclusively to "book store" display shelving of our collections. The first installations of display shelving were shelving actually manufactured for bookstores. The pressed wood shelves proved to be too flimsy to hold up under the weight of hardback nonfiction titles. In 1987 we contracted with Maryland State Use Industries (goods produced in the Maryland state penal system workshops) to build all of our display shelving. State Use Industries now has available a full line of display shelving with special shelf depths for videotapes and audiocassettes as well as books. In our last installation, we specified that the shelving units be constructed with a slatwall finish at each end.

Prior to this innovation, the library's maintenance staff added the slat wall after the units were installed. Since the slatwall comes in a variety of wood grains and colored laminates, colorful slatwall end panels can be used to designate specific areas of the collection such as children's fiction or beginner readers.

In most of our installations, the shelving is in widths of 36 inches. Lighted displays are 82" high. Shorter units are 60" high and are frequently topped with a 26" × 4" sign. The basic layout strategy is for the library user to be able to look over an entire public service area while standing at the entrance to that area. A typical layout would show the 60" shelving units toward the front and middle of the room, followed by rows of the 82" units. Plexiglas holders installed on the slatwall ends serve as additional points to display titles. In a small facility, the 82" shelving would line the walls and the shorter shelving would be placed in the center of the space, frequently at an angle. Each of the lighted displays has a sign indicating the kinds of materials shelved on the unit. The space required for this type of shelving is greater than traditional library shelving. But the ability to display materials face out increases their turnover rate so that more items are in circulation at a given time. The lighting on the taller units makes it much easier for users to see the books. Visiting colleagues automatically assume that BCPL's collections have no depth because they are housed on display shelving, and not on serious "library" shelving.

The White Marsh Success

BCPL has always encouraged staff participation in planning services and setting priorities for the system. In 1988 BCPL took a radical departure from the previous practiced policy regarding facilities planning by instituting a staff committee to plan and furnish the White Marsh Library. Out of this committee grew the design for our picture book shelving, subject collection reference kiosks, and our service desks. These designs are a very positive example of the results that can be achieved when staff are given the opportunity to create truly useable work spaces and shelving for public service areas.

Because White Marsh was a completely new facility, the staff committee was drawn from around the system. Their charge was to create an exciting, interesting, efficient, effective layout with comfortable seating that made maximum use of the space. The branch was designed to enable library users to be as self-sufficient as possible. This concept, adapted from the retail environment, reflects the beginnings of an administrative shift toward

Shelving is designed for merchandising

downsizing; i.e. a need to work with fewer staff per facility in an effort to reduce personnel costs and maintain the materials budget. The assumption being that if the collections were well signed, and the shelving layout was arranged so that a user could be self directed, fewer librarians would be needed. Those librarians available would have more time to answer reader's advisory, and factual and subject requests.

Particular attention was paid to the design of the information and circulation services desks. As is probably the case with many libraries, automation had resulted in service desks that were too small to accommodate librarians or clerks and terminals. Electrical wires hung like tentacles over the fronts of desks, or down the backs. It was relatively easy for the committee to design the desk tops to accommodate needed technology because terminals are allocated based on an output formula. In this case, White Marsh was expected to circulate 500,000 items a year and was allocated four terminals at the circulation services desk and one at the information desk. Because of the volume of check-outs and returns anticipated, particular care was given to the length of the returns portion of the circulation services desk, and to the open space in front of the desk where users would be queued for check-out. With the help of an interior design consultant the desks were designed with electrical raceways. The raceways allowed the staff to relocate terminals on the desks, and hid the electrical wiring and computer cables. The committee also designed the desk interiors. The branch is four years old. The White Marsh staff have found all the designs to be very practical with the exception of the built-in shelving at the information desk. The committee assumed they would be adjustable but this was not specified on the millwork drawings.

The committee developed the idea of housing frequently used reference materials on square reference kiosks that measure 54" wide and 44" high. The kiosk has three shelves per side. Each 36" shelf holds an average of 25 items. The kiosks are well signed with a Plexiglass sign holder on the top of each. The tops serve as an additional writing surface for users. At White Marsh the five kiosks are: Encyclopedia and Quick Reference, General Reference (2), Literary Criticism (2), and Biography and History. The subject groups follow Dewey order. The kiosks have been constructed for other branches as well. They work best in a branch with a community branch-size collection. They can be used successfully in large area branches but only to highlight small special reference collections.

The picture book shelving grew out of a need to display titles at a height appropriate for young children and to house the picture book collection at the same time. The result is a unit 48" high × 42" long × 25" deep with traditional bin shelving at the top and four display shelves at the bottom. In a community size branch with a picture book collection of 12,000 volumes, you

Special picture book
shelving has worked
well

would need 16 units. This assumes that two thirds of the collection is in circulation at any given time. These units do take up more square feet than traditional shelving but young children and their parents love them. They display children's picture books wonderfully and they encourage circulation.

Proportionate to the cost of a construction project, BCPL puts relatively little money into furnishing a branch. Service desks and shelving are custom made, but chiefly because the features required cannot be purchased on the open market. Typical service desks have been constructed of laminated plywood and laminated pressed wood with laminated sides and tops in a contrasting laminate. Specifying a laminated material for a service desk top has turned out to be a poor long-term investment. The sheer volume of business wears off the laminated surface in less than five years. Service desk tops are now typically constructed from a polymer material such as Avonite or Fountainhead. The interior furnishings at White Marsh cost $242,000, 16 percent of the construction cost.

Visitor Impact Study

In each of the three consecutive BCPL five-year plans, there has been a facilities component. Each of the plans reflects the BCPL philosophy that public libraries are service points, not archival depositories. As the system and the facilities have aged, the emphasis has shifted for developing standards for new facilities to developing objectives relating to adequate repair and renovation.

In our 1989–93 long-range plan *Commitment to Renewal*, we reemphasized the principle that library facilities be easy to use, comfortable, and attractive. In order to evaluate how well we were adhering to that belief, we decided to undertake a facilities audit for each BCPL facility. A staff task force with a branch manager as project coordinator was appointed to initiate and then implement this project. The resulting study, *To See Ourselves as Others See Us,* Visitor Impact Study, 1989 gave a much needed focus and sense of direction to our building maintenance efforts. It also gave us a document that could communicate library system as well as individual branch recommendations for action and that could support our requests for both operating and capital improvement funds.

The task force developed a survey tool that would enable the system to document the public perception of each of the libraries facilities. The survey began with questions about building exterior, parking, easy identification, and general condition. Once inside, each surveyor was asked to comment on his or her first impression. Other questions dealt with condition, upkeep, cleanliness, signage, layout, and lines at the service desks. Surveyors were asked to respond as a new user to three pages of questions regarding ease of locating specific collections and service points.

To collect the information to be compiled in the study, the task force recruited six teams to survey our facilities. Team members represented a cross section of library users as well as design professionals. All team members served in a voluntary capacity. Use of the teams instead of library staff was crucial to the credibility of the results. When the teams completed their surveys and their debriefing sessions, task force members compiled the final report. The short version of the report includes an executive summary, systemwide recommendations for action, followed by a summary and listing of recommendations for each facility. The full report filled large loose-leaf notebooks and includes copies of the completed surveys. Each branch manager received a full report on his or her branch.

Renovation Plan

Largely because of this study, we undertook a major renovation plan to update and revitalize the exteriors and interiors of our older buildings. Between 1989 and 1990 we renovated five full-service branches and one minilibrary. Because none of the renovations required structural modifications, we were able to limit branch closings to four to six weeks with the exception of one branch, Loch Raven, which required nine weeks to renovate. At Loch Raven the staff turned the meeting room into a minilibrary open during daytime hours. We have experimented with keeping a branch open during renovation based on our observation of how department stores and hotels renovate space. This has not proved to be successful for us unless the branch is sufficiently large enough to close off an entire wing and the open section has a separate entrance that can be used as a public entrance. The branches were closed as long as they were because we insist that shelving sit on top of the carpet. This allows us to shift the layout of the public service area as needed. The buildings renovated had no storage areas for boxed books and furniture. We rented storage trailers and had them moved from site to site. Because our funds were limited, we were limited as to the amount of new shelving and furniture we could buy for each facility.

The Visitor Impact surveyors had commented that one of the branches looked like a stepchild because of the variety of shelving styles and colors that was in the branch. Since our budget did not allow for new shelving for that branch, we saved the old shelving from another renovated branch and built the new color scheme around that shelving, which happened to be olive green. The branch got new carpet and a new coat of paint. The aging, sagging draperies were replaced with miniblinds, which the staff can adjust to increase or reduce light levels, and the interior took on a whole new look.

Signage   One of the most consistent criticisms made by Visitor Impact team members was the inconsistency in the quality of the interior signs in each of the branches. Most of the branches were

Library users and design professional from Visitor Impact teams

Good signage is important!

oversigned. Branch-generated dot matrix printer signs added to the clutter and confusion. The marketing and programming department, working with branch staff from across the system and the art department, used the Wayfinding approach, a sign system from the users' point of view, to create the BCPL Sign Specification document. The Wayfinding approach is very ably described in *Sign Systems for Libraries*, compiled and edited by Dorothy Pollet and Peter C. Haskell, Bowker, 1979. The document specifies the signs to be posted in all branches. Signs for all branches now fall into one of these categories:

Major Identification signs name large or important areas and services.

Major Directional signs point the way to large or important areas and services at places of possible confusion.

Permanent Book Display signs name segments of the collection that are cataloged as a special collection or are shelved in a separate area for ease of access.

Temporary Book Display signs are used with display shelving to highlight titles and to encourage their use. The signs can be used to meet a seasonal demand, as in holiday or gardening displays, or to draw attention to subjects or titles that might otherwise be overlooked. An objective of these displays is impulse pick-up by the patron.

A modern
signmaking machine
eases the task

Subject Heading signs translate the Dewey decimal system into everyday language. They are the signposts of the nonfiction collection.

Informational signs describe special conditions and regulations about such things as library hours, smoking, eating and drinking, how to use catalogs and other equipment, copy machine fees, etc.

Marketing and programming and the art department again working with branch staff created a sign color specification chart for each branch. The chart enables the system to maintain consistent colored signage for each branch regardless of staff turnover. The color specification chart is also taken into consideration when a branch is to be renovated. Because all BCPL facilities were or would be in need of a signage overhaul, the administration chose to purchase the necessary equipment to produce all interior signs in-house. Signs are created using the Gerber Supersprint vinyl lettering system, and a Macintosh computer.

Planning Teams The staff design committee for White Marsh was such an outstanding success that BCPL has continued to use a staff planning team for each facility project. Subsequent committees have been branch based rather than systemwide because of the nature of the projects.

When we are planning a relocation or a renovation the planning team consists of the branch manager working with a team of branch staff, the Administrative Services staff and the Operations Support staff. The team approach is used from the beginning of each project until the move is completed. One month

Planning teams of branch staff members participate in renovation or relocation of facilities

prior to the move, a daily work schedule is developed and distributed to all staff even remotely involved in the project. The schedule helps us to track how well we are working within the deadlines we've set for ourselves, where we are ahead or falling behind. It also defines priorities so that the maintenance crew and the contractors are not sidetracked with unapproved requests. Planned expenditures and layouts are submitted in draft stage to the Deputy Director and the Director for approval. The amount of money spent on furnishing the facility is limited to funds available at the time. We have learned from experience that durability is a mandatory requirement for long-term use items such as service desks and carpet. Premature replacement of carpet due to the inappropriateness of the original selection is costly not only in dollars, but also in public service hours lost.

Frugal Focus   In the spring of 1992 we will be relocating the Arbutus library into a small office/industrial park directly across from its present location. The current location is a facility the library has leased for 30 years. The facility is two stories and inaccessible to the disabled. The public service area is inadequate. We will be moving into a space currently occupied by a large retail furniture chain. Creating a public service area and staff quarters out of a rabbit warren of individual furniture displays has been an interesting challenge for both support and branch staff.

Due to budget constraints, we will be reusing all of the existing branch furnishing in the new location with the exception of the picture book shelving. The new location will have 10,030 square feet of public service area, and a 980-square-foot meeting room. The branch circulates 428,000 items a year with a collection of 52,000 items. To house those items we will be using the following shelving units:

16	picture book display units
7	60″ high single-sided display units—fairy tales and *I Can Reads*
12	60″ high double-sided units—children's fiction
1	60″ high double-sided unit—special display for children
5	60″ double-sided units—impulse pick-up displays
4	60″ double-sided units—new fiction
4	60″ double-sided units—new nonfiction
2	60″ double-sided units—adult audiocassette
1	60″ double-sided—children's audiocassettes
14	82″ high single-sided units—videocassettes
2	tier circular rack—picture book tape sets
3	CD bins
6	towers—books on cassette
7	single-sided display units—periodicals
3	82″ single-sided units—young adult
6	82″ single-sided units—paperback
8	82″ single-sided units—mysteries
4	82″ single-sided units—large type
2	82″ single-sided units—westerns
3	82″ single-sided units—science fiction
29	82″ single-sided units—nonfiction
46	82″ double-sided units—nonfiction
18	82″ double-sided units—fiction

We will provide meeting room seating for 80. Because the cost of the carpet and the paint have been worked into the lease agreement, we have allocated $65,000 to buy additional shelving and furniture, wire the service desks and the lighted shelving units, and refurbish the service desks and replace public seating. The layout below provides a good illustration of how a typical public service area is laid out, as well as an idea of how space is apportioned for each kind of material.

Maintenance Services

We work under the rationale that library facilities should be easy to use, comfortable, clean, and as attractive as funding will allow. Adequate air-conditioning is considered essential. Users stay away if the air-conditioning is not working properly. As staff costs have increased, most building maintenance services

Figure 8-1

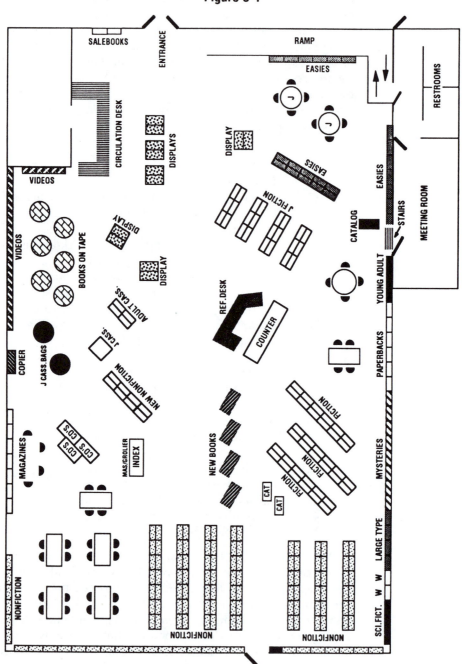

Planned public service layout, Arbutus Branch 1992

including janitorial services have been contracted out. The number of hours of cleaning each facility receives depends upon the size of the facility and its business level. Janitorial performance is monitored by the staff in each facility. Generally speaking, the more carefully the work is monitored, the cleaner the branch. Branches that circulate one million or more items are more difficult to maintain because of the sheer volume of the foot traffic. Public restrooms can be a chronic problem in any public building regardless of the size. In newer facilities where we have been able to design restroom entrances without doors, similar to the design used in high traffic airports, we have fewer problems.

The library staff includes a small core group of building maintenance personnel known as the maintenance crew. Maintenance performs minor repairs, changes bulbs and ballasts, moves tables and chairs around the system, and moves furniture in the branch. They also assemble all of the State Use Industry display shelving. Electrical and plumbing repairs are contracted out. When it is in the library's best interest we ride the county maintenance contracts with other county departments. Maintenance staff also fill in for delivery drivers and rotate on and off the delivery route schedule. There are seven delivery routes. Daily delivery takes priority over maintenance requests. Each weekday morning the Coordinator of Facilities assigns the maintenance tasks for the day. He then faxes a message to those branches scheduled for maintenance, giving the names of the maintenance crew members and the list of branches scheduled.

We are able to accomplish quite a bit with a few people because of the team effort that exists among branch and support staff. Over the last several years, branch managers have become more actively involved in building maintenance responsibilities. We prepare a weekly memo to all staff with the imaginative name of "The Weekly Report." It is two or three pages long, depending on the level of activity for the week. Typical topics covered are buildings and grounds, HVAC, roofs, telephones, and shelving. Much to our surprise and delight, the memo is consistently read by a majority of staff members. The memo is also distributed to the Board of Library Trustees and the county budget analyst who reviews our annual budget request.

Clean, attractive, and adequately maintained facilities are an important aspect of the total service philosophy. Poorly maintained facilities create a negative perception with the public that eventually translates into reduced use of the facility. Staff may also develop a feeling of being undervalued when necessary repairs or renovations are not made in their work areas in a timely fashion. As governmental resources continue to shrink because of reduced revenues and increased mandated expenses it is going to become even more difficult to balance the cost of facilities maintenance against higher organizational priorities such as money for materials.

9 WHO IS "THEY" AND "WHAT" DO THEY WANT?

Consumer Driven Library Service

The fundamental reason why BCPL is referred to by us as the public's library is that finding the answer to who our "public" is and what it is that they want from their library undergoes constant searching and attention, not just by one individual, one department, or one committee, but *by every staff member, all the time*. While there is a department in BCPL entitled "Marketing and Programming," strictly speaking marketing is not a department at all; it is a planning and management philosophy, perhaps even a "corporate culture" or professional lifestyle, shared by staff throughout the organization. There are a number of reasons why marketing, or more simply put, the development of a library service that is consciously and determinably customer driven, exists at BCPL: long-range planning, user orientation, cost/benefit analysis, staff involvement in decisions and planning, and a common vision. These five factors are elaborated below.

Long-Range Planning

Probably the most obvious reason has been the exercise of long-range planning, which includes mission identification and the difficult task of setting priorities. This is now a long-standing process and, in 1992, might elicit such comments as "what else is new?" But fifteen years ago, when the concept of planning was originally urged and encouraged by Maryland's Division of Library Development and Services, this process and activity, leading to a product (the plan), was new to the public library field.

User Orientation

BCPL's mission statements through its three long-range plan cycles reveal a marketing orientation. Each of the three plans have emphasized the user of the library, not the product or service:

> To make readily available to the greatest number of county residents the most wanted library materials of all kinds, and to serve as a point of access for any needed information.

To Satisfy Demand: A Study Plan for Public Library Service in
Baltimore County
Vernon E. Palmour and Marcia C. Bellassai
June 1977

To make readily available to Baltimore County residents library
materials and information services proportionate to levels of demand and use, and to provide access to materials and information outside the library system.

Growth Without Expansion
Long Range Plan II
Eleanor Jo Rodger and Vernon E. Palmour
November 1983

To make readily available to Baltimore County residents library
materials and information services in a cost-effective manner,
proportionate to levels of demand and use, and to provide access
to resources outside the library system.

Commitment to Renewal
Long Range Plan III
Eleanor Jo Rodger
December 1988

These three mission statements were obviously refined and
added to as the years went by, and have been implemented by
the board and staff of BCPL. They have been publicized and
commented on in the public library profession, and have caused
endless controversy outside BCPL. This controversy has been
largely based not on mistaken assumptions, such as frequent
characterizations as "the bookstore library," "all they buy are
bestsellers!" and "they couldn't do that if there wasn't a serious
library (Enoch Pratt) downtown!"

Cost/Benefit The management consultant, Peter Drucker, in his book *The
Practice of Entrepreneurship, says:

> The most important reason [that obstacles to innovation exist],
> however, is that public-service institutions exist after all to "do
> good." This means that they tend to see their mission as a moral
> absolute rather than as economic and subject to a cost/benefit
> calculus.

There lies the fundamental reason for the widespread discomfort
with BCPL's vision and practice among traditionalists in the
profession.
All of BCPL's long-range plans have relied heavily on cost/
benefit comparisons, and the definitions of "benefits" have been
used on statistics of demand and use by the people who support
the service, the residents of Baltimore County. At the same time,
recognition is made of the concept of the "public good" to support

such obviously expensive services, in terms of cost/benefit, as interlibrary loan or some outreach services to population groups who are ordinarily nonusers. Even these services, however, are looked on as political investments rather than defended as moral absolutes. There is a great deal of sentimentality, nostalgia, and desire to "do good" associated with much public library priority-setting, tendencies that are looked on by BCPL with suspicion.

Staff Involvement

The *process* of long-range planning at BCPL carefully includes large segments of the staff, rather than just a small group of administrative staff, with the intent not only to gain a common vision of the library's mission, but also to take advantage of the wide knowledge and varied skills of the staff. Emphasis is placed on the experience of branch staff who work "Where the Rubber Meets the Road." Both statistical and anecdotal evidence are necessary to gain a true perspective of "What They Want."

Common Vision

One of the results of the long-established process of planning in BCPL is the recognition and acceptance of the mutually agreed-upon mission. With individual conviction that we are engaged in the right mission at the right time comes enthusiastic cooperation between different departments and branches on varied projects. All business is everyone's business, from the Processing Department to Delivery and Maintenance to Personnel and Materials Selection. The process of communication and commitment is aided by many standing and ad hoc committees of all levels of staff and the creation of "turf" is actively discouraged. This book is a case in point: all members of the BCPL's Blue Ribbon Committee are equally responsible for each chapter.

Before staff can *Give 'Em What They Want!* they need to define "they" and then design the "what." Administrative office and branch staff work together to analyze the community and customers of a branch, select segments of this population, and design services and methods of communication for these target groups. This chapter will describe how the following questions are approached by BCPL staff:

1) Who Is "They"?: Defining the Community
2) What Do They "Want"?: Defining the Services
3) How Do They Find Out?: Telling the Public

Who Is "They"?: Defining a Community

BCPL is a branch system in the management as well as the delivery of services. Each branch has been assigned a block of census tracts as its primary service area. The tracts were assigned after an analysis of a branch's circulation reports. It is the responsibility of each branch to create a detailed description of the communities within its service area. This report is called SCAN (Statistical Community Analysis).

Defining Baltimore
County communities
is essential for user-
based services

The SCAN report has gone through three revisions (1979, 1984, 1991). The first two editions were very similar. Each branch team compiled the following information for its service area: brief history of the community, demographic data, topography and transportation, community activity (i.e., active associations, churches, service clubs, recreation centers, senior centers, scouts, etc), schools and day care, and finally a staff assessment of the state of the community based on the above information and observations.

The third edition of SCAN (SCAN Three) was enhanced by incorporating two major management tools adopted by BCPL staff since 1984: staff generated templates for the Macintosh and circulation statistical reports (BCPL uses the CLSI automated circulation system). These enhancements have not only allowed branch staff to describe their communities more quickly and efficiently but they also help staff develop a portrait of their customers. The specific improvements in SCAN Three include:

- Demographic data can be entered and tabulated on a Macintosh template.
- A Macintosh database of some community items was created for each branch.
- Circulation statistical reports allow staff to identify and analyze what materials are actually being checked out from the branch and in what zip codes the users live. These reports enable staff to have a more focused perspective on branch services, providing a picture of who is actually using the library and what they are using.

The SCAN Three report includes the following specific components:

- Suggestions for a branch planning process and specific discussion aids in order to help branch staff identify the most appropriate user services in response to changing demographics. All staff are urged to view the ALA/LVN video *Marketing: A Planned Approach for the Public Library*. It is strongly urged that the branch team responsible for creating the SCAN Three report be composed of managers, librarians, and clerks.
- The portrait of the communities in the branch service area is created through completing the census template, maintaining the community database, and writing a narrative description of the service area.
- The portrait of the customer of the branch is created by analyzing circulation reports, information statistics, programming statistics, and various output measures. Some of the circulation reports analyzed by staff include:
  - monthly circulation by group
  - item circulation by statistical category with percent of total circulation

- item circulation by statistical category with ratio of circulation to total number of items in each statistical category
- patron circulation statistics by group
- turnover rates by each group
- circulation by zip code. This information has allowed staff to make use of Donnelley Demographic reports and psychographic (lifestyles/attitudes) descriptions we were able to obtain for the county. Both of these reports analyze the population by zip code, not census tract. The Donnelley Demographic reports and the psychographic descriptions for each branch's highest circulating zip code are included in SCAN Three.

Communities never stop changing, so neither does a branch's SCAN Three report. When it is completed for the first time it provides the staff with a benchmark and a formal document to update and change as needed.

A completed SCAN report presents the staff with a detailed mosaic of the branch's many neighborhoods and individuals as well as its customers. All this information, however, is still not enough to answer "Who Is They?" BCPL staff does not try to be all things to all people; thus, when the SCAN report is completed, the community and customers have been broken down into segments with similar characteristics. Preschoolers in day-care settings, sixth grade students, readers of new titles, borrowers of nonprint, and small business owners are some of the many possible segments. The branch team then chooses the target groups that they feel should be emphasized for their community. Obviously, certain systemwide priorities must be taken into account when the branch makes this decision; for example, the priorities in the long-range plan and any that may have been established by the Managers of Branches (MOB) committee.

The community and customer have been defined, they have been broken into segments, and a decision has been made as to which of these segments will be targeted for special services. Now, what service should be offered?

What Do They "Want"?: Defining Services

Commitment to Renewal (Long Range Plan III, 1989–1993) prioritized four roles from *Planning and Role Setting for Public Libraries* to guide the staff's delivery of services: popular materials library, reference library, preschoolers' door to learning, and formal education support center. These roles were chosen and the strategic directions defined by the seventy-plus staff involved in the committees that created this long-range plan. The management decisions are the result of the observations and data collected from all levels of staff who worked in all areas of the system.

When the term "management" is used here, it is very difficult to define in BCPL. Over the years the team approach to decision making has developed to the extent that it is hard to identify where ideas have come from and exactly who made the decision to implement a new service or to terminate an old one.

The planning process, renewed every five years, involves, as has been noted in earlier chapters, major segments of the staff as well as a steering committee made up of all levels of staff, administration, county officials, and trustees. Roles are discussed and adopted here, as well as strategic directions and opportunities. Aside from those decision-bearing on internal operations, such as centralized selection and generalism, how is the need for services identified?

Standing staff committees, on a regular basis without involving the administration or trustees, generate ideas and solutions that staff, in daily contact with the public, determine are important to users. Input about state library agency priorities is communicated to staff preparing grant requests for LSCA. Local needs are determined from close cooperation with schools, other governmental agencies, and from the private sector through such groups as the Chamber of Commerce. The staff themselves are a very valuable community resource.

The planning process goes on all through the period between new long-range plans—actually, it's a constant updating process. When recommendations from the many and varied staff groups and individuals come out in both formal and informal discussions with the administrative team, decisions about services to the public are made. When these decisions involve policy, they are presented to the Board of Trustees; when they involve money, especially substantial money, the board includes recommendations in the budget request. At this point the County's Budget Office and often the elected officials are involved. Their network of information and opinion is often very different, but often just as valid as the library's. The resulting decision making, especially if coordinated with the Board of Trustees, is often a very accurate reflection of what the public "wants."

The best way to get a flavor of what special services have been developed in response to the priorities laid out in *Commitment to Renewal* is to describe a few.

Read Rover is a 24-foot bookmobile which takes materials and programs to preschoolers in day-care centers and registered day-care homes in economically disadvantaged communities. The management of this service is the responsibility of a branch in one of the communities visited by Read Rover. The Library Associate and clerk on the mobile visit over 90 locations and circulate over 1,000 adult and juvenile items per month. The impetus for this service was the decline in use of a special project that utilized

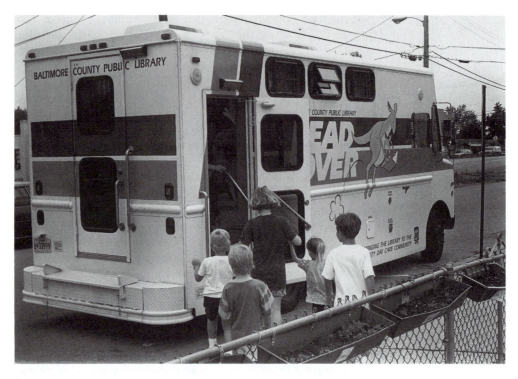

Read Rover visits day-care centers

volunteers to take materials into these homes and the attendance at story times and use of the picture book collections in branches serving these communities.

Basics Count! Books for New Adult Readers resulted from a *Commitment to Renewal* task force. Ways to improve service to adult basic education (ABE) and English for speakers of other languages (ESOL) students was explored by this task force. The staff appointed to this task force analyzed the county population to determine where this service was needed and designated six branches; special materials, signage, and display units were ordered for the designated branches. The staff then networked with community agencies and organizations to promote usage.

Merchandising/book displays are determined by each branch team to meet the interests of their users and to promote the areas of the collection that needs to be highlighted. In some branches the staff lobby to have a book display unit for their area of the collection in order to increase its turnover rate. The necessary signage is ordered by the branches from the Marketing & Programming (M&P) Department. M&P staff create signs using vinyl letters on board.

Service brochures in other languages provide library information for new users. An influx of Russians to certain areas of the county prompted the staff at one of the branches to ask a community volunteer to translate library procedures into Cyrillic.

This information was then reproduced by the library's M&P department for distribution by appropriate branches. This initiative by a branch staff member has grown into a larger systemwide project. A new service brochure has been designed for speakers of other languages. One brochure contains information for new library users in the following languages: English, Spanish, Korean, Cyrillic. The content and the languages were recommended by the ABE/ESOL task force.

African-American interest groups stimulate appropriate materials selection. Certain areas of the county experienced a large growth in the African-American population during the 80s. The staff at some of the branches in these neighborhoods felt that their materials and programs needed to better reflect the interests and needs of this ethnic group. As a result, staff members from six of BCPL's 16 full-service branches meet regularly and serve as advisers to the administrative staff in Materials Selection and Marketing & Programming. As a result of this group, more appropriate and popular materials have been purchased, African-American displays of materials have been created in some branches, funds for multi-cultural programming have been donated by the Board of Trustees, and a special booklist celebrating the Coretta Scott King Award has been produced.

Small Business Matters Centers are developed. The demand experienced for information about starting a small business at one branch prompted an LSCA grant request, which has resulted in three full-service branches designated as Small Business Matters Centers. Special materials purchased for these branches are displayed and housed separately within the branch, the staff at these branches network with business organizations to promote the services, and special publications (booklists, directories, flyers) are created by M&P to meet the information needs of operating a small business.

Branch Visits by Sixth Graders introduce students to full library services. To meet the role of formal education support center a strategy was developed by staff of BCPL, in collaboration with teachers and media specialists at the local public school system. The school system pays for the bus transportation of every sixth grade student to the school's local library branch for a tour and an introduction to the branch's electronic reference tools. Handouts were designed by BCPL staff and the school personnel with the production done by BCPL: "Homework Success Tips for Students/Teachers" and "Keys to Information Success" which give instructions on how to use the various CD products owned by BCPL.

Summer Reading Program in all 24 branches provides the summer activities for the children in their communities. During the summer of 1991 over 24,000 children registered. This service is given top priority by all departments: materials are ordered and delivered to the branches for the summer onslaught of children and families; librarians spend time at in-branch meetings sharing children's books to sharpen their reader advisory skills; a committee of branch staff plans the theme and activities for each summer; M&P staff coordinate promotional efforts with the elementary and middle schools; special programs are offered throughout the summer to attract children and their families; informational materials are designed and run through the printing presses for reading logs, booklists, activity sheets, etc.; stickers and plastic bags are designed and printed by commercial firms. Last, but not least, tee-shirts designed by an M&P artist and printed by a commercial firm are sold to the public to raise revenue for the next summer's extravaganza. In 1991, a $7,000 profit was made.

How Do "They" Find Out?: Telling the Public

Communicating with Customers

The Marketing & Programming Department is responsible for helping the branch staff promote their services. M&P's first priority is effective communication with the customer of the library branches. Some of the formalized channels used by M&P to meet their priority include: written requisitions submitted by the branches for flyers, signs, posters, and so forth; monthly meetings with the Managers of Branches (MOB); bimonthly meetings with the branch's I&P Managers; weekly meetings of the Administrative Council; monthly meetings of the Users Services Support (USS) Committee; management visits to each branch with the Deputy Director at least twice a year.

Communicating with the Community

The second priority of the M&P Department is effective communication with the community at large. Besides the obligatory press releases to the media, the M&P Department looks upon networking with outside groups and programming services as two very important ways of telling the county-at-large about their library:

- *Networking and Coalition Building.* The M&P Coordinator and the Programming Specialist spend a significant amount of time working with government agencies and community groups in order to maintain the long history of BCPL's goodwill and presence in the county. Some of these agencies and organizations include: a variety of different offices of the Baltimore County Public Schools and of the county government, Chamber of Commerce and business organizations, corporate and foundation funders, and literacy providers. The M&P Department also coordinates the collection and distribution of handouts from community groups and government agencies that are made available for public pick-up in branches.
- *Programming Services.* The system's goal for branch programming is twofold: to promote usage of the library and to provide free cultural and recreational entertainment for families.

Programs reflect the
county's diverse
population

Each branch is encouraged to offer programs that reflect the
interests of their communities, with an emphasis on programming for families with children. A glance at any issue of
the bimonthly *Calendar of Events* is an indication of the variety
in Baltimore County: German folk bands, Russian storytelling, native American dance troupe, African-American
storytelling, traditional two-year-old story times in the morning, an evening program for two- to six-year-olds with parents, hunter safety and water safety courses. Programming is
a third priority for the system (behind collection and information) and the funding for special programs reflects that priority—$3,800 annually. Meanwhile, the branch staff has asked
the M&P Department to provide more support for professional storytellers and centrally produced programs to reduce
branch staff time planning and conducting programs. Necessity being the mother of invention, the M&P Department has
come up with the following strategies to assist branch staff in
offering quality, low-cost programming services: a storytelling puppetry troupe of nine librarians from the branches
plans and performs two programs a year designed for children three to ten years old and their families; outside funding
from a variety of sources (Arts Commission, foundations, a
local bookstore); coordination of at least six central programs
a year (fire safety, children's theatre, Ronald McDonald); and
planning, packaging, and promoting the Summer Reading
Program.

BCPL's Tale Spinners, a storytelling puppetry group, visits all libraries

Publications

The M&P Department designs and produces all flyers, booklists, brochures, signs, etc. for the branches. Again, BCPL's priorities are best described by our actions. Some of the publications made available to customers of BCPL include:

For the General Public
- *Report to the Reader*, bimonthly; November/December is the annual report issue
- *Your Library: Hours and Services*
- *Fines and Fees*
- *New Directions*, map of the county with branch locations
- *Your Information Line:* a business card for each branch
- *Keys to Information Success:* instructions for the CD catalog and other CD reference tools
- Branch signage

For Selected Target Groups
- *Small Business Information:* booklists, service flyers, and a 50-page *Directory of Resources* funded by a local bank
- *Street Card:* a wallet-size listing of community resources for people who are in need of shelter, food, or clothing
- *Basics Count! New Adult Reader Collections:* promotes these special collections at the six library branches

- *Illiteracy Affects You and Your Business!:* designed and created for the local Literacy Coalition
- *Branching Out:* a monthly newsletter for the staff and volunteers
- *Relive the Past:* promotes the local historical publications created by M&P staff and the local historical photographs collected and maintained by M&P staff
- *Baltimore County Panorama:* a pictorial history of Baltimore County which sells for $29.95
- *Directory of Organizations in Baltimore County:* an annual publication which sells for $6.00

For Children and Their Parents/Caregivers
- *I Love My Library:* a twofold activity brochure and reading log designed for children two- through seven-years old
- List of the Coretta Scott King Award winners
- Four different graded booklists contain titles for children in grades K–1, 2–3, 4–5, 6–7. Updated every two years
- *Stories to Share:* with three- to five-year-olds. Seven different lists, each reflecting a different topic
- *Caldecott Award winners:* updated annually
- *Newbery Award winners:* updated annually
- Dial a Story: advertises the telephone story-line service
- *Homework Success Tips for Students and Teachers:* to alleviate the last minute homework demands put on the branches by students and teachers in grades 5 through 12.
- Summer Reading Club: 12-page reading log, a host of activity sheets for different age groups, and booklists for five different grade levels
- *Story Times Are Special Times:* preschool programs
- *Day by Day: News and Activities for Day-Care Providers:* a bimonthly newsletter which is mailed to over 2,000 day-care centers, nursery schools, and registered home-care providers.
- *School Loan Library Cards for Teachers:* policy and procedures
- Programming promotion: individual flyers, posters, and press releases for each branch program as well as a bimonthly *Calendar of Events* which lists all the programs for the branches in one publication

Informed Choices   Analysis of a community and customer by branch staff and the decision as to where to focus their energies is crucial to the effectiveness of BCPL. BCPL does not try to be all things to all people: it is during this process of looking at a community and defining priorities that this becomes real. When one path is chosen another must be closed off or must be postponed for a while. That can create dissatisfaction with some staff and some public. But at least the choice is being made based on information, experience, and staff consensus.

10 *HOW MUCH WILL THEY PAY FOR IT?*

It costs money to operate a public library. The assumption is made by library administrators, trustees, staff, editorial writers, and the American Library Association (ALA) that the more money per capita that is expended by a public library, the *better* that library is.

How Much Is Enough?

ALA has devoted hundreds of thousands of hours of the time of generations of public librarians trying to answer the question of what makes a "good" public library, with no success at all. In the minds of librarians, and in the public pronouncements of Association staff and leaders, all public libraries are good, and all public libraries are administered by highly competent professionals (if they have the MLS degree) whose dedication is limited in effectiveness only by lack of funds.

Even a not very careful study of the annual statistical reports of the *Public Library Data Service*, a Public Library Association publication, does little to connect "goodness" with expenditures, but rather raises all sorts of other questions. It is fairly clear that, on average, public libraries in the United States spend between $16 and $23 per capita annually, but how to explain the difference between the $12 spent (in 1990) in such cities as Los Angeles and Houston with the $60 spent in Cleveland? Does that mean that the library service in Cleveland is five times as good as that in Los Angeles? Or that cost-effective management is alive and well in the West and nonexistent in the Rust Belt?

Dallas and Phoenix spent about $15 per capita on public library service in 1992 and they are both supported enthusiastically by the press and public. Dallas built a very large new central library some years ago and Phoenix is about to, with the proceeds of a multimillion-dollar bond issue approved by the voters. Their local governments, however, are busily reducing the

This ALA/PLA
publication is
invaluable for
comparison purposes
with other libraries

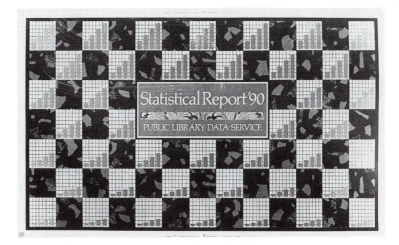

budgets of the libraries, necessitating drastic cuts in staff and in materials expenditures.

City and State magazine, in December 1991, in comparing the top 50 cities in terms of their fiscal strength, rated Phoenix number 1, Dallas number 5, and Cleveland number 41. Is it true that the weaker the fiscal condition, the more cities spend on public libraries? Or does spending on public libraries drain the coffers of the cities to the extent that their fiscal strength is adversely affected?

Confusing is not the word for it, and logical explanations are not forthcoming from any source, least of all from the professional association. It quite naturally is reluctant to offend any of its members, but in its strident public relations campaigns deplores the inability of the Federal, state, and local governments to find more money for public (and, of course, academic) libraries, in order to fight ignorance, illiteracy, economic stagnation, the effects of television and Nintendo, and racial, sexual, and ethnic discrimination.

To people, generally, across the nation, public libraries are a Good Thing. Unlike public education which is under attack from almost all quarters along with health care, the legal profession, higher education, and government in general. In survey after survey, the governmental services that rate the highest in people's minds are public libraries and fire departments. Apparently neither gives citizens any hassle and generally gratefulness is the dominant emotion.

*Influences
Affecting
BCPL's Search
for Mission*

The history of fiscal support at the Baltimore County Public Library is not distinctly different from other public libraries, at least in Maryland (known to some as "library heaven"), and it certainly illustrates many of the contending priorities of those guiding the policies and practices of the library system, whether these policies come from local government, the Board of Trustees, the library administration, or the staff. Like all libraries, we have had to contend with the following viewpoints of library services.

Political

The government in Baltimore County is really much more like a typical city government, since the county has no incorporated towns and there is an elected chief executive and an elected legislative body—a Mayor and a City Council—although called a County Executive and a County Council. The county is, interestingly, almost a cross-section of the nation economically, demographically, and politically. Politicians, always beset with more requests for spending than there are available fiscal resources, even in the best of times (the 80s), have never held the library system in the same high fiscal priority as public schools, the police, or the fire department. As such, the elected political structure is accurately reflecting the priorities of the voters. Citizens obviously feel that the education of their children and public safety are more important than the "quality of life" public services such as libraries or recreation and parks.

A nominally independent agency under both state and local law, the trustees and administration of BCPL have always recognized very clearly that this so-called independence is completely dependent on what one trustee has characterized as the three major tenets of library-government relations:

1. Keep your troubles in house
2. Get a prize
3. Be part of the team

Wise advice. Not always easily accomplished, but we have had some advantages in BCPL that other libraries have not enjoyed.

First of all, we have had the enormous advantage of a Board of Trustees who, while appointed by a series of county executives, have always had two overriding characteristics: they are truly representative of the people of Baltimore County rather than some elite social, political, or economic group and they think public libraries are a Good Thing. They also recognize where the money comes from, and they place confidence in and support the library staff—while still carefully guarding their right and duty to set policy. An excellent Board, over the entire life span (45 years) of the library, has been fundamental to the growth of library service.

Secondly, through eight county executives of differing political persuasions, perspectives, ability, honesty, and administrative and personal skills, the library has enjoyed support ranging from adequate to mildly enthusiastic. All have exactly reflected the mood of the voters at the time, as have the county's budget directors, perhaps a more important political fact.

Thirdly, the administrative team of Director and Deputy Director has been in place for 30 years, probably a record for public libraries in the nation, at least those serving over 100,000 people. While this kind of longevity is not necessarily to be recommended, it does ensure some consistency in outlook, even if modified by changes in governance and economic trends, and the staff generally knows what to expect of the administration.

Fourth, and perhaps most important, the nominal independence of the library from the larger bureaucracy of the County (with a $1 billion budget) has allowed authority and responsibility to go hand in hand. The fact that both purchasing and personnel are not subject to the much more complicated and slow-moving procedures of the County has enabled the Board and the library administration to move more quickly to meet changing conditions. The priorities of library service are kept from being subsumed in political or economic priorities which are sometimes more important to governmental concerns than they are to the library. In truth, this absence of the "back-seat driver" syndrome has been due in large part to those in charge of financial administration of the county as well as to other factors. The increasing tendency in government at all levels to avoid dictation of the smallest details of administration to operating units has been in place for decades in the relationship between BCPL and county government and, in large part, has greatly contributed to the library's abilities to meet its mission of service.

Economic

The most obvious characteristic of the economy, whether it be national, state, or local, is that it is cyclical. When the economy goes up and when everything looks good, you can be sure it will go down. Every librarian knows that every year at least one book is published that forecasts "the coming depression." In any one year, the forecast is generally wrong, but it seems to be inevitable that some year the book will be right, whether you call it a depression or a recession. What goes up must come down.

This is difficult for anyone to accept, but it is especially difficult for government administrators, and public library administrators are just that. Our institutions are based on a budget rather than results, and success is defined, as Drucker points out, by getting a larger budget rather than obtaining results. Budgets may depend on a multiplicity of factors locally, but over the years they depend mostly on the economy.

When the economy falters, our budgets either grow slowly, or, in some cases, even fall. Despair sets in, personal umbrage is taken, and prediction of skies falling abound. In fact, when percentage decreases in library budgets occur as the result of economic cycles—and they don't always decrease, by any means—these decreases are typically considerably smaller than the combined increases that have occurred during better times. It is true, also, that the inflation rate has its effects. In effect, the total per-

Each and every year brings forth doomsayers

The budget proposal—hope springs eternal!

BOARD OF
LIBRARY TRUSTEES
FOR
BALTIMORE COUNTY

Operating Budget
Fiscal 1993

"Hard times" are, of course, relative

centage of public revenues spent on libraries remains almost the same over decades.

At BCPL, library appropriations from county general funds here held almost steady over the years at 1.9–2.1 percent of the entire general fund budget, good years and bad. The likelihood of any major change in this allotment, in percentage terms, is unlikely, barring some catastrophic event or revolutionary technological change, like the commercial viability of the electronic book. It is possible that the kind of demographic changes which have occurred in some American cities, changes which require the expenditure of a larger and larger portion of the government's revenues on public welfare and public safety, could reduce drastically the portion available for activities involving quality of life, like library service, museums, or recreation. That eventuality is not controllable by libraries, but by general public policy, most likely at the Federal or state level.

Moral

Education, like religion, seeks to bring about a certain standard of behavior on the part of people, and in order to do that, education seeks change in human beings. Librarians, like teachers and ministers, have a very strong missionary streak—they are trying to make "better" people of us all. The library profession, like many other "do good" professions, is fond of expressions of mission in terms of moral absolutes, and nowhere is this tendency more evident than in the pronouncements and generally ineffective public relations campaigns of the American Library Association. In many ways, of course, this emotion is shared by the public, in whose minds libraries are close to churches in their imagined responsibility to "do good" especially to and for children. This is why the concept of intellectual freedom is so hard for library users to accept, and, in truth, hard for many library administrators and trustees to implement. But we are, in the broadest sense, an educational institution in our own eyes and that of the public, and that mission is often expressed in terms of moral absolutes. Much of our constituency is based upon this perception, as is much of our support from the press. It is also fed too often by our own desires as librarians to somehow effect a "growth" in reading tastes on the part of our users, and to show special partiality to the desires of people with similar tastes and educational background to our own. This "moral" viewpoint of library service probably is that which is the most damaging to user orientation and to the institution of truly cost-effective service. It's damaging to user orientation because it often assumes that the user doesn't truly recognize what is "good," because the user's wants, or motivations, or tastes are not the same as ours. It's damaging to cost-effective service because we are very apt to spend money on materials or services that few people (those like us) use, leaving fewer resources to supply the much larger number of users whose very legitimate demands are unfulfilled or only partially fulfilled.

This is also the viewpoint that has been given the least credence by BCPL over the years, to the discomfort of some, especially in the profession itself. It still crops up, of course, because morality means something to each of us in BCPL, but it is evident that the choice of minimizing the influence of the moral viewpoint of public librarianship has enabled us, we believe, to maximize public use.

Professional

Service professionals often assume, and often act as if, they understand the problems of their clients better than do the clients themselves. Most of us can cite difficulties with physicians, lawyers or teachers who seemed more interested in their own priorities than ours.

Librarians as service professionals are no different: we have our paradigms, our ways of doing things, our beliefs—all of which are rooted in experience at one time or another, or by what we've been taught, or what our colleagues tell us. BCPL also subscribes, in many areas, to the conventional wisdom, but it has developed a tradition over the past fifteen years of questioning the paradigm, the conventional wisdom, in many areas. Professional practice has met its greatest adversary in the emergence of emphasis on cost-effectiveness in the delineation of BCPL's mission. In earlier chapters this has been revealed in the process of cataloging, materials selection, and use of paraprofessional librarians. The reaction of professionals in libraries of comparable size to BCPL has been generally negative, and cost savings inherent in such policies have been generally ignored and condemned as either nonprofessional, immoral, or damaging to the readers' interests, at least in the critic's perception.

BCPL's fee-based videocassette circulation policies, for example, while both widely acceptable to users and certainly cost-effective from the point of view of appropriating authorities, were opposed by the entire profession in Maryland when the question came up in the Maryland legislature, and it has been excoriated by leaders in the profession. Recently, however, it has been evident that more libraries are adopting policies similar to BCPL's. It is interesting to observe those libraries most impacted by low revenues seem to be those least apt to adopt policies that have proven cost-effective in other libraries.

Romantic

This viewpoint of public libraries could also be called the sentimental or "nostalgic" viewpoint, and it is shared by much of the general public, nearly all newspaper editorial writers, and not a few elected officials—quite naturally in the latter case where they are representative of the general public. This viewpoint is one which is, at the same time, very supportive of public libraries as institutions, greatly discouraging of innovation and cost-effective management, and politically very powerful, especially in support of traditional professional management. The romantic point of view sees closing of library facilities as disastrous, even when such facilities have become obsolete, ill-used, or underused, and noncost-effective. Few library administrators can close any library for any reason, rational or not, without being pilloried by the public and by elected officials. Many other innovations or cost-saving techniques meet the same emotional opposition.

On the other hand, massive boondoggles on the part of library administrators are enthusiastically approved, such as the erection of central libraries as described in chapter 1. There always follows the reluctance of anyone, including appropriating authorities, to meet the increased cost of operation of these new white elephants. On a smaller scale, this same support may be given to building unneeded branch facilities which have little chance of being economically successful, or which promise to render other nearby facilities underused. And, of course, these older facilities must be maintained.

As in other towns and cities across America, the romantic view of public libraries has contributed greatly to the growth of BCPL: it only takes a handful of citizens in an area perceived to be underserved to gain a full-service library costing millions in construction and operating costs. This viewpoint was essential to BCPL improvement in its growth phase between 1948 and 1988, but it may become a detriment to the delivery of cost-effective library service in the future.

There is little doubt that a library Board or administration which, during the last 30 years, might have expressed a desire to build a multimillion-dollar central library in Baltimore County could have eventually accomplished their object. It is our view, however, that, given the limited amount of financial support available over the years, this course would have seriously lowered both the quality and quantity of service to the communities in the county. The lack of a central library, with its specialized and expensive services, has undoubtedly affected the institutional image of BCPL. It has, at the same time, enabled the system to maintain a very high quality of service in the communities. It is ironic to note that the exact opposite policy of the neighboring Enoch Pratt Library has resulted in very heavy use of BCPL libraries by city residents—to the extent that BCPL circulated more books to city readers in 1990 than did the Pratt library. There is no doubt in our minds that this is a result of management policy, not of relative support per capita. This last view is not shared by either the local or professional press and the profession at large. That fact is puzzling to some of us, but it is a graphic illustration of the romantic viewpoint.

All of these viewpoints of public libraries—the political, the economic, the moral, the professional, and the romantic—have had their influence in the formulation of the mission of BCPL and the management of the library to meet the requirements of that mission. It would be naive and inaccurate to say that the staff of BCPL and the members of the BCPL's Blue Ribbon Committee, at some point, did not share many of the feelings or convictions that make up these viewpoints of service. After all, almost all the members of the BCPL's Blue Ribbon Committee—which is another term for those who share in the management of BCPL—have worked in other libraries. Many of these libraries have radically differing philosophies or styles than does BCPL.

The Prevailing BCPL Viewpoint

While it is impossible for any of us to completely ignore our experience and the years of judgment formation which is the result of that experience, it is fair to say that the planning processes that most of us have undergone, together with many of the staff of BCPL, have brought us to a common approach to library service, an agreed-upon mission, even as that mission is subject to change. That mission seems to be built on a conviction that information, whether derived from one format or another, is important to people and also important to society. That's not unique in a committed professional—and we see ourselves as committed, enthusiastic professionals.

What may be more unusual is that we don't like spending the public's money on activities or services that, however much we may enjoy supplying those activities or services, are not widely used by the public. In plain words, we're looking for bang for the buck. This overriding practice results in lots and lots of books, plenty of videos, adequate but unimpressive buildings, few professionals and lots of paraprofessionals, no OPACs, barely clean buildings, ill-maintained grounds, vigorous staff development, and refusal to build new buildings without adequate operating funds. We feel we have the priorities straight for managing the public's library. When the long list of various library activities we *don't* engage in, such as saving books, adult programming, and highly specialized services, is examined, not everyone agrees.

Downsizing for Fun and Profit

In 1992, there's a lot of sackcloth and ashes in the public library field—but then again, there is in all other public services and in the educational community. Despite attempts by some to imply that libraries are unfairly treated in the current economic down cycle, there is little evidence to that effect.

What is interesting in the 1991–92 recession is that it is the first that has affected local government to the extent that it has since World War II—a period of 50 years, which encompasses the worklife of everyone involved in library service. We can leave the reasons for this to others.

Except in relatively isolated cases of local economic disaster, however, few libraries have heretofore experienced the, to them, drastic cuts in available funds which have occurred in 1992. BCPL is no exception: in 44 successive annual budgets, every single one has shown an increase, until in 1991 the total expenditures equaled about $34 per capita, not including about $4 per capita in state support of the retirement system. No Cleveland here, but certainly respectable support of a public library system, and support that has translated into a high level of service at the community library when the financial burden of maintenance of a little-used central library did not need to be funded.

In fiscal 1992, for the first time, midyear cuts in appropriation were made—to the tune of $850,000, or four percent of the planned expenditures. The cuts were no surprise, given the appearance of a diminishing rate of increase in government revenues of the past three years. In BCPL the ongoing planning process, involving large segments of the staff, clearly saw that priority choices would have to be made, and they made them, with the support of the trustees. There were no surprises, and as a result, no panic, no breastbeating, and no despondency.

One of the most valuable staff development projects we have done in recent years also helped: several years ago a number of our staff, including branch managers, exchanged visits with a similar group of staff members of the Phoenix (AR) Public Library. Phoenix is supported by a budget of $15 per capita, and has a central library; its population is larger, but they have fewer branches. As a result, their branches, like ours, are heavily used. We had an intimate view of the service that library gives with very limited resources and we learned lessons that were invaluable when our budget became tighter. Most interesting, we discovered that public expectations can be allied with their willingness or reluctance to pay for services.

In Phoenix and in other cities and in other libraries, library financial support has never been high enough. Relatively expensive service, such as highly responsive information service, has never been the norm. The expectations have never been raised, as it were, and high levels of personal service from clerical and professional staff are not missed, because they were never provided.

Public response normally to having a branch, a service, or a good supply of books taken away from them is outrage, and this outrage is frequently translated into more financial support. Often, however, this is "soft" money, because it is likely to be removed again when the outcry dies down. Another scenario appears when the economy generally declines, especially if this occurs for an extended period. Then even well-supported libraries who cut their hours, or raise their fines, or let their buildings deteriorate find little public reaction: the money just isn't there, and the public knows it.

A Cadillac and a Chevette can move to the same destination at just about the same speed. The difference is in how much you are willing to pay for comfort and convenience. That analogy is much too simplistic when you are comparing the quality of an educational and informational service, but it's another way of saying that the public gets the library service they are willing to pay for—given that management interpretation and implementation of their desires are equal. We can drive a Chevette, as they do in Phoenix, if that's what our citizens decide they can afford.

The *process* of downsizing is challenging and interesting because it stresses management, encourages innovation, and otherwise rearranges priorities. Except for the personal costs to staff, which can be minimized, the process can streamline and emphasize cost-effectiveness. Again following Drucker, we can optimize rather than maximize. The conventional wisdom that budgets must always increase, that services must always expand, that no service should be terminated, and that all libraries need more money will take a hit; but we are not sure that library service to the public will suffer irreparable harm.

Time will tell.

COLLECTION MANAGEMENT

Replacements

Replacements are ordered not only to replace worn or lost materials, but to fill the demand for specific titles or to build subject areas. Funds for replacements are limited. Care should be taken to be sure that titles suggested for replacement are essential.

System priorities determine what funds will be available for replacements. Resource Managers together with Materials Selection decide what schedule, if any, will be established for replacement lists.

There are two kinds of replacement lists: *Core Replacement Lists* and *Branch Generated Replacement Lists*. These will be defined below.

In addition to the replacement lists, branches may suggest titles for beefup. These are called *Replacement Beefups*.

Definitions

Core Replacement Lists. Core lists contain fiction titles which are so basic that most branches will need to own them. They are reissued or updated by branch staff yearly. Assignments are made by Materials Selection based on suggestions from the branches.

Branch Generated Replacement Lists. These lists are compiled by Materials Selection from subject and title suggestions submitted by Resource Managers and reviewed by Resource Managers at their collection development meetings. These are nonfiction lists. The titles vary considerably from year to year. In fact, the replacement list schedule may require that certain Dewey decimal collection segments be addressed only every other year.

Replacement Beefups. These beefups are for replacement titles that branches feel are essential to the system or to the branch. Unless there is sudden unforeseen demand, managers should avoid suggesting titles that have appeared on a replacement list in the last six months or that are likely to appear on replacement lists in the current fiscal year. Suggestions are sent to Materials

Selection on yellow Materials Information Cards (MICs) or on white Rush Beefup Forms as the need becomes apparent.

Beefup
Procedures

Replacement Lists.   The processes for creating, revising, and updating core and branch replacement lists will be explained in the *List Generation Section.*

Replacement Beefups.   The procedures for submitting replacement beefup suggestions are clearer when one knows how Materials Selection will use the information requested. The Materials Selection staff responds to replacement beefup suggestions under guidelines similar to those used for beefups of new materials.

1. If branch needs are obvious, the orders will be placed in one of the following ways:

   A. For the requesting branch only
   B. For those branches with obvious need due to missing copies, high circulation, etc.
   C. For the whole system

2. If a decision cannot be made based on CLSI printouts and information provided by the requestor, the title will be offered on a CLSI beefup list.
3. The beefup will be noted on CLSI as a point of information if it is a systemwide beefup request likely to be repeated before the replacement copies are received. (Example: Sue Grafton's mystery series)
4. If the purchase is unique to a branch, limited to a few branches, or unlikely to be repeated, a response will be sent to the suggesting branch only on the form submitted.
5. Materials Selection may need to limit spending. If suggestions can't be funded, branches will be informed.

A title qualifies as a replacement when it has a publication date no newer than the following:

Adult fiction	13 months
Audiocassettes	13 months
CDs	13 months
All others	19 months

Replacement beefups are either regular or rush.

Regular Replacement Beefups.   Submit requests on yellow Materials Information Cards (MICs). The following information is needed:

1. Author, title, current ISBN, and other publishing data
2. Explanation/Justification of need for the title; for example,

   A. Constant demand
   B. Best book on the subject

C. On reading lists
D. Author hot

3. A dated CLSI printout for the system (not just the requesting branch). These are essential if Materials Selection is to know how best to approach buying.

Rush Replacement Beefups. Submit requests on white Rush Forms when the need is urgent (i.e. so important that the order needs to be telephoned to the jobber and processing of new materials needs to be interrupted in order to process the replacements). Requests should be sent through delivery to Materials Selection. Materials Selection may be called in emergencies.

In addition to providing the publication information, the justification for the request, and a dated CLSI printout for the system, a justification for Rush status is also needed.

Responsibility of the Resource Manager (Head of Collections). The RM Head is responsible for reviewing all beefup requests, checking to see that information is complete, and eliminating questionable titles; for instance, those which are:

1. No longer current
2. Replaced by something better
3. Low circulators
4. On a previous or projected replacement list within the fiscal year on in the previous fiscal year but on order for six months or less and therefore unlikely to have been received in the branch.

Often it is more important to locate new materials on a subject than to replace older ones. If this is the case, a Subject MIC should be submitted.

List Generation Procedures

Core Replacement Lists

Core placement lists currently cover the following areas: Adult Fiction, YA Fiction, J Fiction, *I Can Reads*, and Easies. These lists will be revised on a regular basis to add new titles and delete older less popular and o.p. titles.

1. Each spring Materials Selection will issue a schedule of replacement lists for the coming fiscal year, giving dates cards are due to Materials Selection, dates lists are due to branches, and dates marked lists are due back in Materials Selection.
2. Replacement budgets will be given to branches with suggested amounts available for each list as soon as budget money is allotted in July.

Branch-Generated Replacement Lists

To prepare for the quarterly collection development meetings, Resource Managers send a specified number of titles and subjects to Materials Selection. These specifications are mandated in the "Current Replacement Schedule and Assignments" which is issued each fiscal year.

Branches use a combination of procedures to gain this information. Some suggested methods are as follows:

Ranking Method.   The librarian(s) assigned to the designated section(s) prepares a list of subject gaps. These subjects are voted upon at a librarians' meeting where librarians vote using a 5, 3, 1 method. The subjects are then prioritized according to the vote and submitted to Materials Selection. Titles are also suggested and are selected by librarians responsible for those specific sections.

Desk Sheet.   Some branches keep a sheet at the Information Desk where librarians note unfilled titles and subjects. The Resource Manager and his/her assistant review the information and submit specific titles and subjects to Materials Selection.

Computer Hold Forms/Scratch Cards Method.   Another method used is to review the Computer Hold Forms/scratch cards which have been filed, according to the Dewey classification, in a box kept at the Information Desk. The scratch cards contain unfilled title and subject requests. Throughout the year, while doing collection maintenance, librarians review titles and subjects for gaps in the collection. At a librarians' meeting they discuss these. The Resource Manager collates the information and sends it in to Materials Selection.

Once the final list and title selection have been compiled, these suggestions for new and older material should be sent to Materials Selection. Age level and focus (assignment use, popular, etc.) should be included with each subject. Titles may reflect subject areas or title requests.

Subject suggestions are compiled by Materials Selection into two lists: subjects requested by multiple branches and single branch requests. Subjects are starred when titles have recently been purchased or when unsuccessful searches have been made. These lists are discussed at collection development meetings and are used by Materials Selection staff when doing subject searches for new material.

Title cards from branches are used by Materials Selection as the basis for compiling nonfiction replacement lists. Circulations are checked to determine whether several branches might need to replace a title. If only one or two branches need a title, Materials Selection may order it for only a few branches. Titles are also weeded down to fit the approximate number of titles suggested for each list. Titles are checked in Baker & Taylor Link for availability. A list is then prepared and sent to branches.

Hardback vs. *Paperback*

If a book is available in paperback, it should be bought that way. Hardbacks may be purchased under certain circumstances:

1. Decisions are made under the direct supervision of the Resource Manager in each branch.

2. Such purchases are made to maintain the title in the collection and the remainder of multicopy purchases are made in paperback. Any decision made should be cost-effective.

3. Concentration of such purchases should be in the following areas:

   a. Titles whose paperback format won't support the sheer weight of the book or its heavy usage, e.g., *Chesapeake*;

   b. Easies, *I Can Reads*, Easy Nonfiction and single volume 398s and perennially popular J fiction titles, e.g., Curious George series, Cleary books;

   c. Juvenile books whose illustrations are as important as the text, but are omitted or truncated in the paperback editions, or lack color, e.g., *Wind in the Willows, Alice in Wonderland*;

   d. Perennially popular titles whose paperback format is so slim its title cannot be read from the spine, decreasing its chances of being circulated, e.g., *Stone Soup*;

   e. Perennially popular nonfiction titles whose spiral binding in paperback destroys the cover while the contents remain intact, e.g., *Typing for Everyone*;

   f. "Classics," where it is desirable to have a durable, dependable hardback copy in the collection at all times.

Weeding Guidelines

Supervising staff in weeding is one of the Branch Resource Managers' most important tasks. Weeding is important because it keeps collections current, attractive, and responsive to your community's needs. It ensures the most productive use of space. It is necessary to continually emphasize the importance of weeding and to monitor the process.

To maintain attractive, well-circulating collections, BCPL places emphasis on the importance of monitoring and weeding these collections. Such a process will maintain a high circulation and turnover of materials.

There are a number of methods of weeding that are described below. These are only suggestions that need to be adapted to individual branch collections, community needs, and staff abilities/knowledge. Staff members are expected to spend at least three hours a week on collection maintenance. If branch circumstances permit, scheduled time is recommended.

Each branch needs to have a way of determining growth of their collection. There are different methods for doing this; these include:

- Growth charts
- Book stock report (new CLSI packet)
- Shelf space
- Circulation

Resource Managers often utilize a ratio of adds to withdrawals (i.e., withdraw fewer in proportion to the number added). The add/drop ratios should be tailored to each collection, to the amount of space available, and to the level of branch circulation. The adds and drops per section may be individual to the needs of that particular section. Collection Managers should constantly review this ratio of adds to withdrawals. For example, a branch with a very high overall circulation may need to increase its collection size just to keep material on the shelves. A branch with a modest circulation may run into space problems if collections are not controlled more stringently. Fluctuations will often occur in specific collection areas. Growing collections (e.g. compact discs) should also be weeded minimally. Areas of high attrition (e.g., popular audiocassettes) should also be minimally weeded. Resource Managers should be aware of the total collection as well as the individual sections.

There is a *Collection Growth Chart template* which is a useful tool for monitoring weeding in the Macintosh. This spreadsheet will calculate adds and drops on a monthly basis for any division of collection areas deemed appropriate by the branch. It should be emphasized that the 1:1 ratio (one copy added, one copy withdrawn), with which the Growth Chart was originally programmed, was only a matter of convenience.

It is important to be aware of the amount of materials (adds) coming in to the branch. Methods of keeping apprised of new materials include:

- On order sheets
- New book shelf
- Growth charts

Weeding Criteria

Duplication

Heavily duplicated items such as adult fiction or true crime (364) may require weeding at the time of removal from the new book shelves. Certain areas, however, are purposely saturated with multiple copies which should not be withdrawn. These may be favorite booktalk titles or a subject of continuing interest such as resumes or GED examination books. Also consider weeding old editions when there is a new edition on the shelf.

Condition

A book showing obvious signs of wear or damage should be withdrawn unless it is mendable and the time and effort involved are warranted by its circulation.

Nature of Subject Matter

The subject matter of an item will determine if the contents are likely to become outdated. For example, a book on literature would probably not be withdrawn because of copyright date, but dates and editions are very important in the 600s and 300s.

Circulation

Various methods may be used to determine circulation. These include:

Turnover.   Periodic checking for turnover rate (number of circulations in one-year period) provides an index for comparison with system, branch, and other Dewey area averages. For example, an overall branch turnover goal may be established against which individual items will be measured. Or, turnover criteria may be established by Dewey section or within Dewey areas by SCAT.

Slote.   This method measures the length of time between circulations. It may be useful for establishing weeding criteria for areas with very high circulation such as feature films. Slote's Method is described in *Weeding Collections, 3d,* 025.16 S 1989, owned by all branches.

CLSI.   Items may be checked on the computer to determine the number of circulations. They may be useful, for example, in estimating the condition of items not on the shelf.

In-House Use.   While this is difficult to determine, it should be kept in mind that some materials that appear to be heavily used but have low circulation may be heavily used in-house.

Performance as "New."   When removing items from the new book shelves, remember that, in most cases, an item that has low circulation when new will die altogether when placed in the regular collection.

5 Percent Rule.   Some, but not more than 5% of a section, may be designated at "little used." These are usually school assignment-oriented or are the only source of a type of useful information.

Scenarios

1. You are weeding adult fiction off the new bookshelf. You have multiple copies on the shelf. Check the condition first, then you will want to weed down a number of copies, keeping those in the best condition. You may establish a rule of thumb that half the copies will be weeded at this time. However, you will want to consider:

   • the amount of shelf space available in fiction
   • the period of time between circulations (Is the material still going out regularly?)
   • the time of year (Is summer almost here—perhaps it should stay "New" a little longer. Do you want to store some copies in anticipation of high summer demand?)
   • the availability of replacement copies

2. You are weeding in 822.3. It is July and you notice most of the material has not circulated for 6 months. However, if you look back, you will see a concentrated period of heavy use in the fall and winter months. These are homework

titles and subject to seasonal demand. You will weed these titles by:

- comparing them to one another in terms of use
- considering subject and title requests and reserves which you accumulated during the high-demand period
- condition—this is an area in which you may consider sending a popular classic title that is in poor condition to the bindery if it is out-of-print.

3. You are weeding new nonfiction. You have multiple copies of a pop psychology title which has circulated well. All are in good condition. You will probably weed the one in poorest condition and keep the other two. If you have a space problem in your regular collection, you may need to weed some older material to make room for the new, since this is an area when currency is often important. This is an example of how important it is to distinguish the classic titles in your area (e.g. "Road Less Traveled") from the more ephemeral ones so that you can weed judiciously.

When removing a high duplication title with very good circulation from new nonfiction, you will probably want to hold on to as many copies as possible. These titles (frequently in 364) often have a sustained demand past their "new" period.

Children's Materials

While the criteria mentioned above will also be used in weeding children's materials, they should be modified to reflect the different circumstances surrounding these materials:

- Publishers produce high interest, browsable books that will sell, limiting the number of titles serviceable for school assignment needs.
- Titles go out-of-print more rapidly, limiting the availability of replacements.
- These materials serve a variety of public including children working independently, adults working with children, adults presenting materials to children, and adults with low reading levels.
- These materials should serve recreational and informational interests as well as supplement curriculum needs.
- Subject areas should be covered by a variety of reading levels.

Additional Criteria for Weeding Children's Materials

- In-house use may be heavy.
- There is increased likelihood of seasonal use.
- Materials that appear dated may still contain useful historical information.
- Children's fiction and easy titles should probably not be weeded when removed from the "new" shelves except in

cases of very low circulation or poor condition.
- The 5% rule stated earlier may be increased.

Scenarios

1. You are weeding the J 970s. You notice there is extensive duplication of material of Native Americans. While it does have heavy use during the fall, indicating assignment use, you wonder if you need so much duplication. However, after checking with other staff, you learn that the assignments on Native Americans cut across a number of grade levels, making it necessary to duplicate information at a variety of reading levels.

2. You are weeding *I Can Reads*. There are multiple copies of a number of Berenstain Bear titles on the shelf. There are very high circulations on this material, but do we need this many copies? Yes. You are weeding during December, one of the very few slow times in this area. In a few weeks all of these titles will be out. Weed for condition only. If there is high duplication in children's material, there is probably a good reason and it would be wise to investigate before weeding too vigorously.

Reference Collection

The reference collection also needs to be assessed regularly according to community need and use. Those branches that have integrated collections (reference and circulating titles shelved together) need to weigh whether they would weed more heavily according to availability of circulating material or other available resources (e.g. circulating materials, faxes, etc.). With the advent of fax machines and regionalization of reference collections, criteria for weeding reference materials will need to be reevaluated.

Nonprint

The same criteria apply to weeding this collection as the print, with a few exceptions. Turnover in videos should be examined differently because of the shorter loan period. Due to the high turnover rate of feature films, it is useful to use the Slote Method to gauge their popularity. The different nature and loan rate of instructional videos requires that they be judged by different standards than feature films, just as adult nonfiction books are judged differently from fiction.

Video

Videocassettes are difficult to assess for damage without viewing them. After three reports of damage a video should be viewed to verify the problem and noted by a code, such as a green dot, on the video. If a tape has more than 200 circulations and you have received at least two complaints, it may be more efficient to withdraw the copy than to spend time viewing it.

Scenarios

1. It is two days before Christmas and you are taking advantage of the business lull to weed videos. When you go to the shelf you find very few titles in. Consider them highly weedable. The period just prior to a holiday or three-day weekend will usually suggest likely candidates for weeding.

2. You are weeding J feature films and find multiple copies of "My Little Pony," "Strawberry Shortcake," and various "Ninja Turtles" titles. When you check circulation, you see that the "Turtles" are still moving fairly quickly but the other two have very low circulation. Fads in children's materials change rapidly and it is important to keep on top of them.

3. You are weeding videos in the 790s and you notice fairly good circulation for some sports titles but not others. On closer scrutiny, you realize that the ones going out are bloopers and star biographies while the shelf sitters are instructional. If you check circulation dates, you may find that the former are going out well because it's winter while the latter titles do better during the months when the sports in question are played.

Audio/CD

Audiocassettes. Audiocassettes (both music and books on tape) should also be judged by the same criteria applied to the remainder of the collection. Again, since turnover tends to be so high for these materials, the Slote Method may be helpful. For audio formats you can rely on patron complaint when determining condition.

Compact Disks. This area should be weeded with great restraint since it is a growing collection. If a CD has only one or two tracks damaged, it is not necessary to withdraw it.